MEL BAY PRESENTS

Flamenco Studies
Falsetas de mi Padre
by Juan Serrano

Cover photograph of Juan Serrano courtesy of **Benoit Provost.**

Guitar by **David Macias**

1 2 3 4 5 6 7 8 9 0

© 2009 BY MEL BAY PUBLICATIONS, INC., PACIFIC, MO 63069.
ALL RIGHTS RESERVED. INTERNATIONAL COPYRIGHT SECURED. B.M.I. MADE AND PRINTED IN U.S.A.
No part of this publication may be reproduced in whole or in part, or stored in a retrieval system, or transmitted in any form
or by any means, electronic, mechanical, photocopy, recording, or otherwise, without written permission of the publisher.

Visit us on the Web at www.melbay.com — E-mail us at email@melbay.com

CONTENTS

Author's preface 2
Introduction 3
Alegrias por Rosas 4
Bulerias 18
Bulerias en Am 40
Caracoles 62
Fandangos de Huelva 74
Farrucas 90
Granainas 104
Rumba 122
Sevillanas 146
Siguiriyas 176
Soleares 188
Taranto 204
Tientos 220
Verdiales 236
Zapateado 251

AUTHOR'S PREFACE

This book is composed of all of the falsetas that I learned from my father from 1943 until 1947.

My parents were professional flamenco artists. My father, Antonio Serrano, also known by the artistic name of Antonio el del Lunar was an extraordinary guitarist of his era from 1890 to 1964. My mother, Cecilia Rodriguez, known as La Niña de la Sierra was a great singer of her era from 1900 to 1984.

When I was very young I was fascinated just listening to my parents rehearse at home. I was mesmerized by the movements of the hands of my father. So strong was my love for flamenco that I was able to immediately memorize and sing the melody of any falseta that my father played.

At the age of nine years my father asked me the question that I had waited for so long; if I wanted to learn to play the guitar. I was so excited that I jumped from my seat screaming "Yes!" Thus began my first lessons in flamenco guitar. I studied with my father for 4 years. At the age of 13 I made my professional debut in the Grand Theater of Cordoba, Spain.

I hope that learning and interpreting these falsetas gives you as much satisfaction as they gave me during my apprenticeship and the beginning of my career.

Juan Serrano

I would like to thank my friend and former student, Fred Thrane for his encouragement, support and inspiration to begin and complete this project. It was very enjoyable for me to work on this book, because it brought back all the memories of my childhood.
Thank you Fred.

INTRODUCTION

Flamenco guitarist, Antonio el del Lunar, is one of the most influential figures in flamenco guitar in the last 100 years. His wife, Niña de la Sierra, and a very young Juanito Serrano toured for many years with the flamenco troupe of singers Pepe Pinto and Niña de los Pienes, whose given name was Pastora Pavon. This placed the family of Antonio el del Lunar in the daily influence of the most influential figures in the world of flamenco.

Antonio el del Lunar, in addition to being the primary teacher of his son Juanito Serrano was also the teacher of Rafael el Tomate, Alfonso Labrador, Antonio Verdu, Fernando Ortiz, Pepe Corralisa, Merengue de Córdoba and many others. They continue to influence flamenco guitarists around the world.

Backstage at many concerts was a young Juanito Serrano peering through the cracks between the curtains as his father's fingers cut the hearts of his audience with the "five daggers" of his right hand (his fingernails). Young Juanito could not always see exactly what the adults would be playing and invented many right-hand strumming *rasgueado* patterns. It was his patient father that showed him the first *falsetas* (variations) on the *cómpas* (rhythm) that influenced Juanito, who later become the guitarist for the troupes of Pepe Pinto, Niña de los Pienes, Conchita Piquer, Juanito Valderrama, and many other great flamenco artists. After several tours as a teenager, the 18-year old Juanito Serrano became a fixture as an accompanist in Madrid for the greatest singers in flamenco, including La Paquera de Jerez, Fernanda and Bernarda de Utrera, Fosforito, Manolo Caracol, Antonio Mairena and dancers La Chunga, El Farruco, Los Pelaos, Pastora Imperio and many others. Later he won the hearts of audiences in the U.S. and the world as a soloist.

The beauty of these compositions is only made more seductive by their simplicity and ergonomic synergy that is congruent with the hands and the instrument. Before these compositions have come to light via the heart, mind, and pen of the incomparable maestro Juan Serrano, some of the most simplistic and beautiful written studies in flamenco were those of Serrano's *Systematic Studies for Flamenco Guitar*, Mel Bay (96871BCD), 2001, and *Flamenco Guitar: Basic Techniques*, Mel Bay (93632BCD), 1979. The roots of this great tree that is so vital to the "flora" of the flamenco guitar are now visible. The inspiration for the greatness of so many flamenco guitarists that have followed him lies within these pages. These are exquisite complete compositions that are a natural progression from the study of music fundamentals, note-reading, and pedagogical exercise and repertoire found in *The Flamenco/Classical Guitar Tradition*, Mel Bay (21029), 2007 and are intended to be the flamenco repertoire studies for subsequent study.

For those guitarists who already read music and play classical guitar, these are excellent introductory studies in flamenco technique and repertoire that maintain a level of structural and superficial beauty that is worthy of performance in any concert hall. For those advanced flamenco guitarists, here is a glimpse inside of the historical world of flamenco that predates and influenced some of your greatest heroes in the flamenco guitar world. Let it ferment in your spirit and revolutionize your flamenco playing as the *duende* of Antonio el del Lunar has for so many before you.

Corey Whitehead, D.M.A.
Assistant Professor, Flamenco and Classical Guitar
Department of Music
The California State Univesity, at Fresno

ALEGRIAS POR ROSAS

Symbol G for the Spanish word "Golpe"--meaning to tap the top of the guitar only with the anular (a) finger

Strum every compas in the same manner

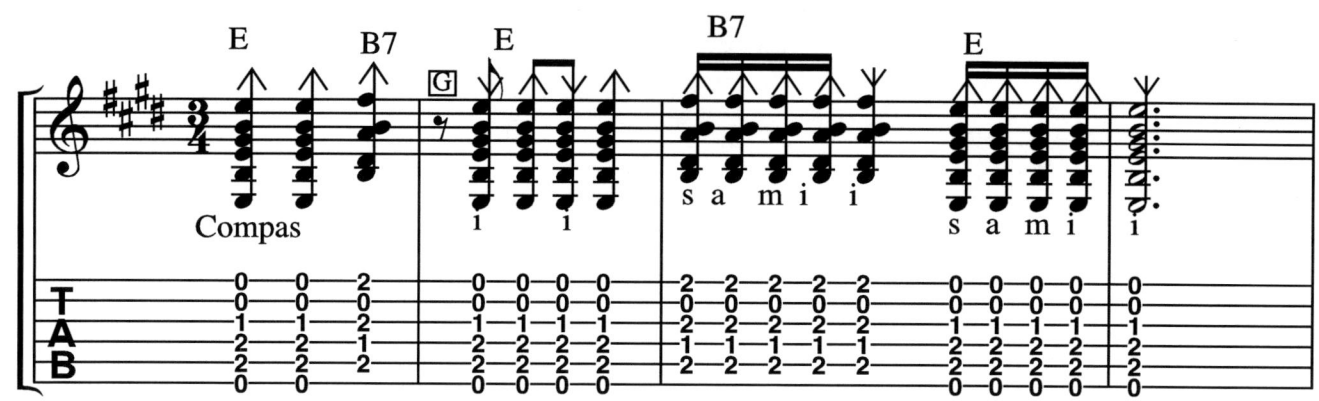

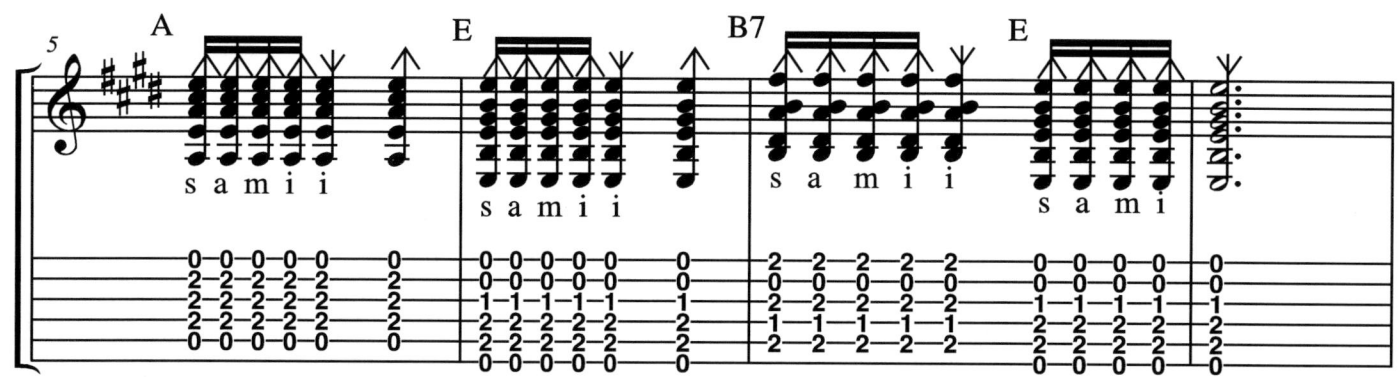

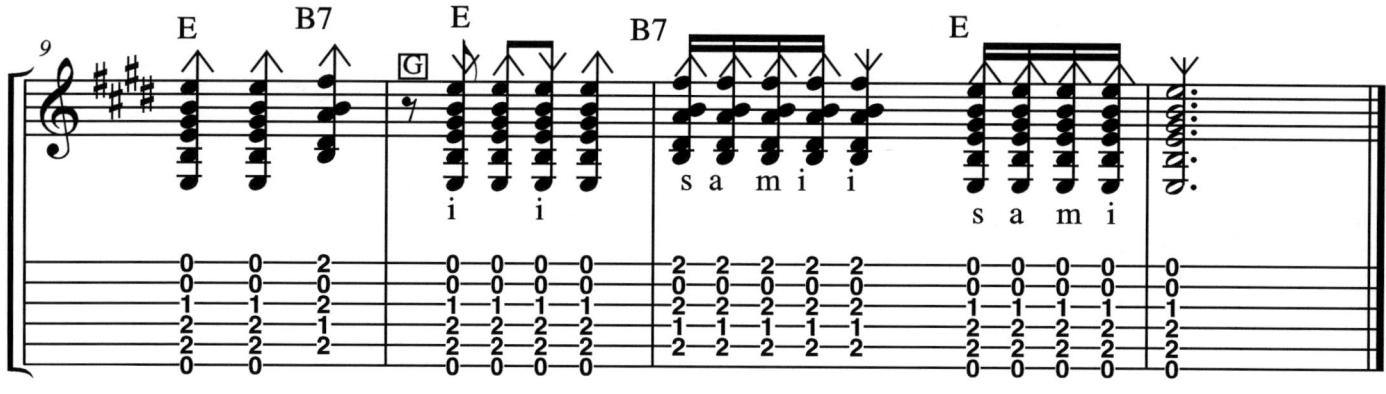

ALEGRIAS POR ROSAS

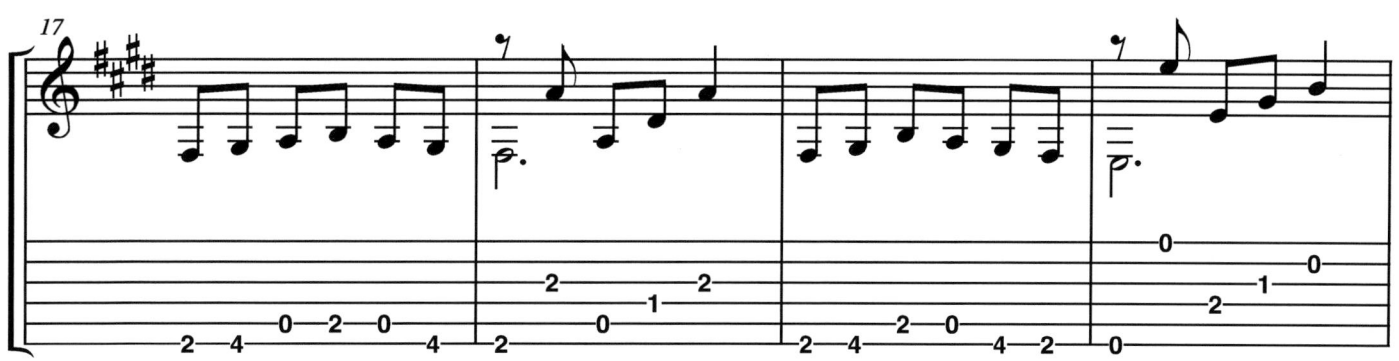
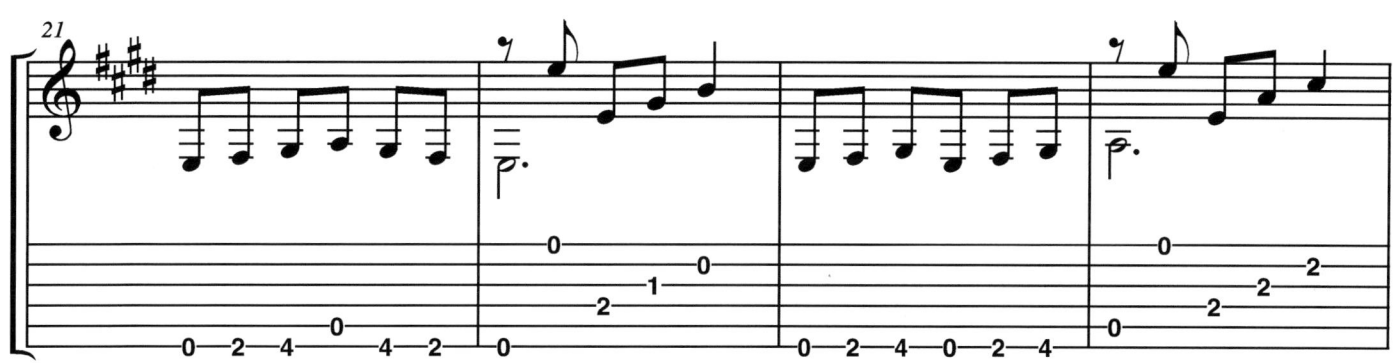
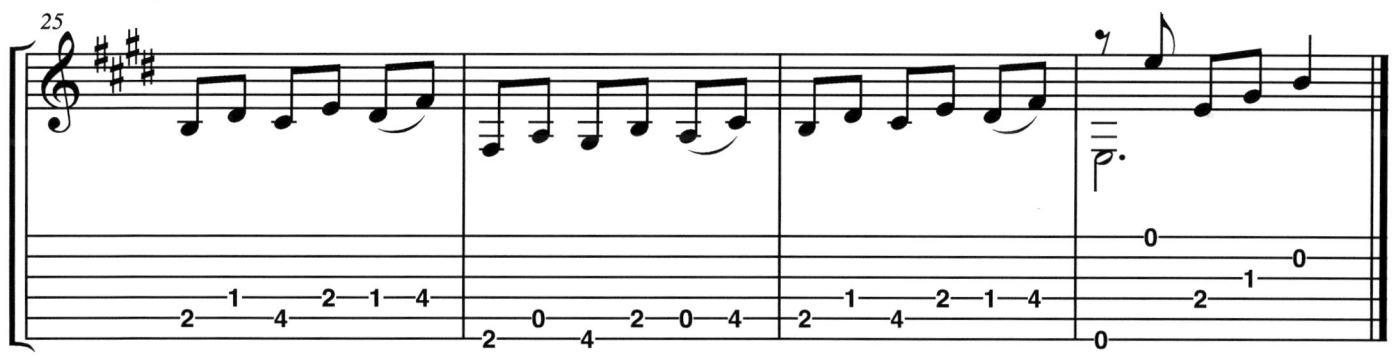
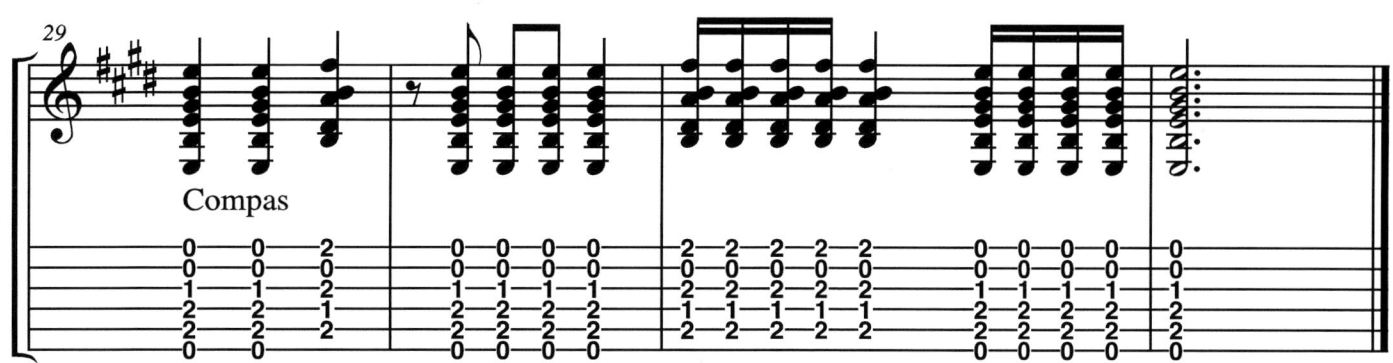

ALEGRIAS POR ROSAS

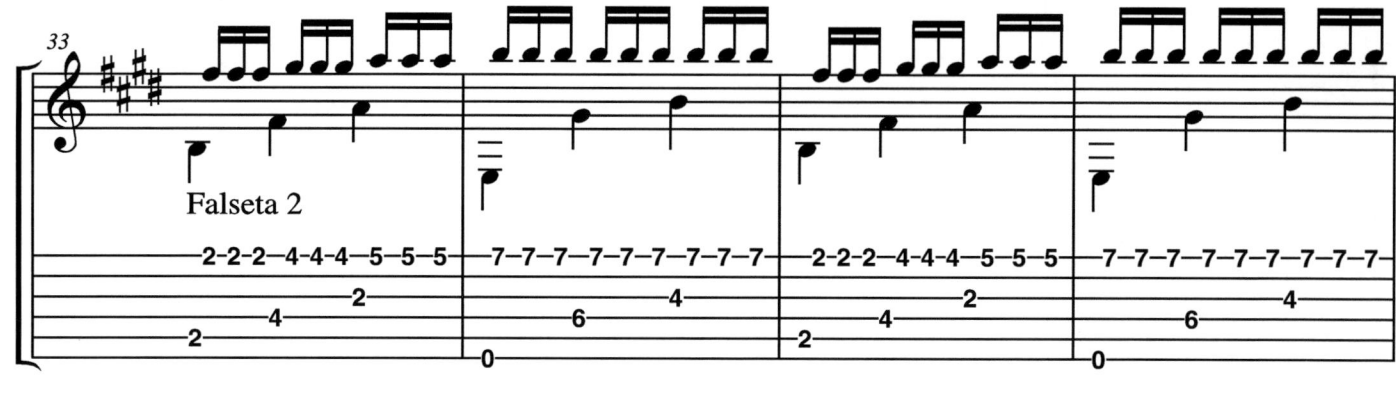
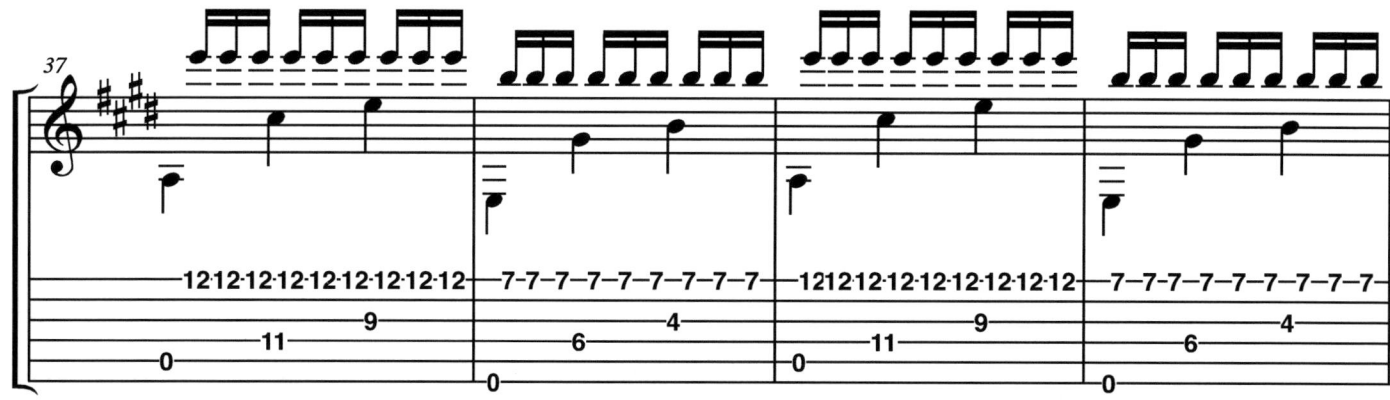
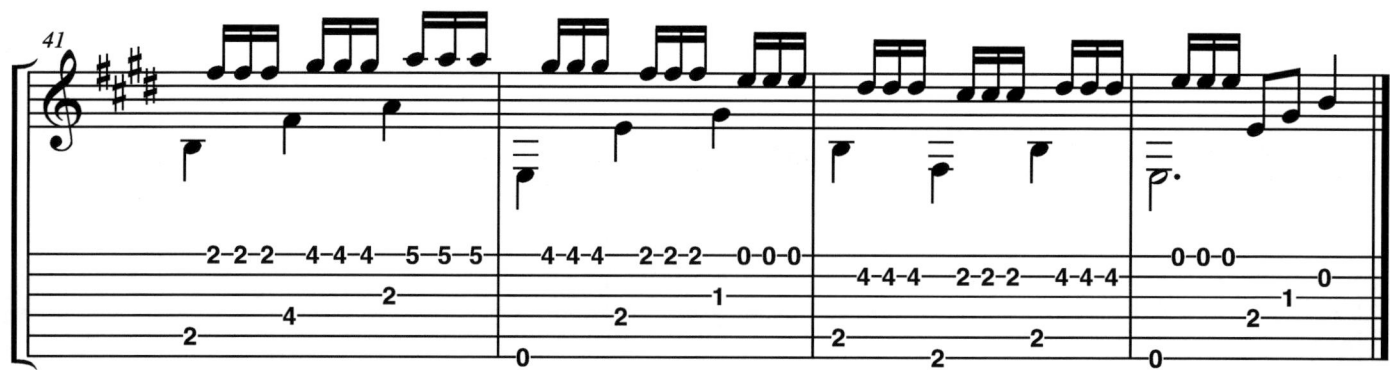
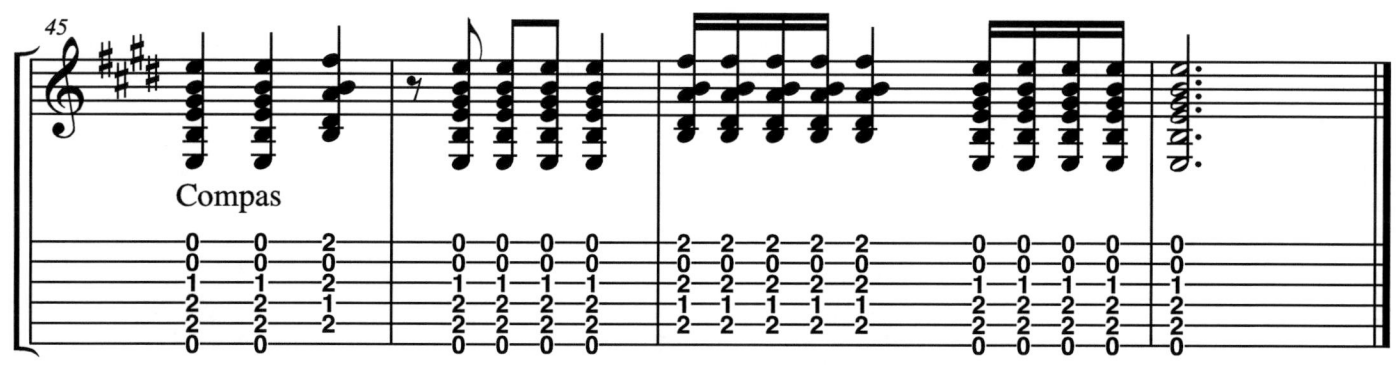

ALEGRIAS POR ROSAS

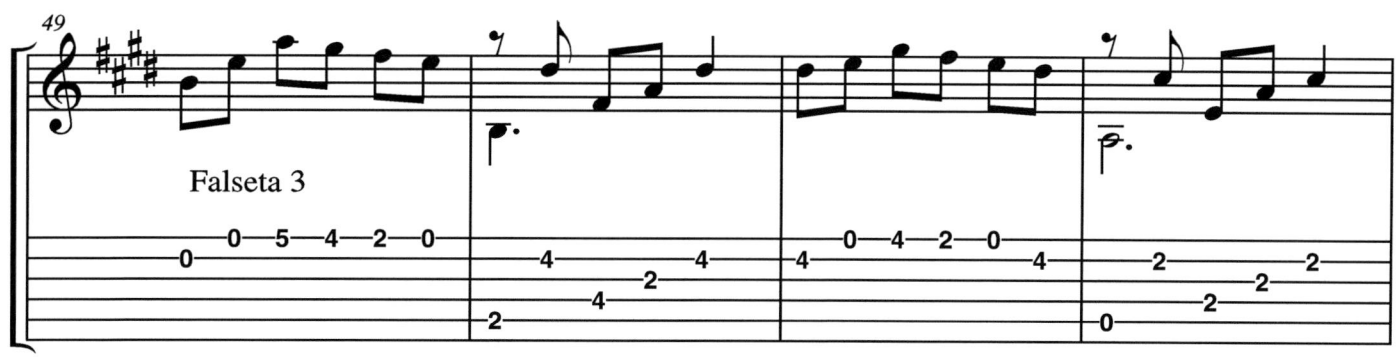

Falseta 3

ALEGRIAS POR ROSAS

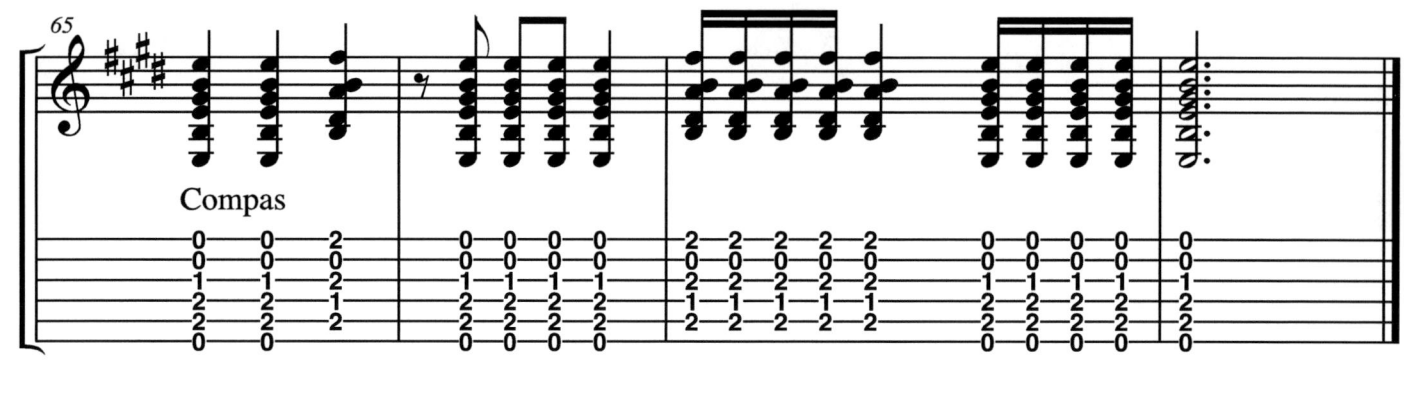

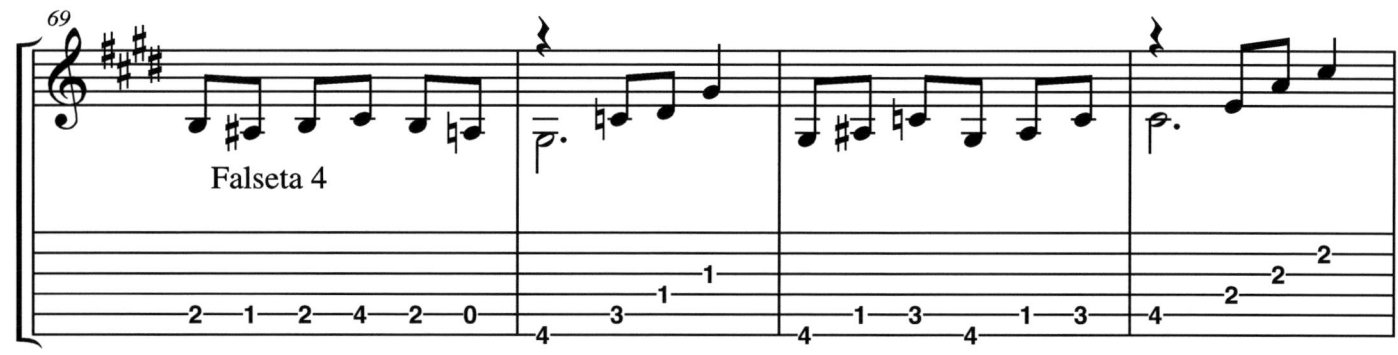

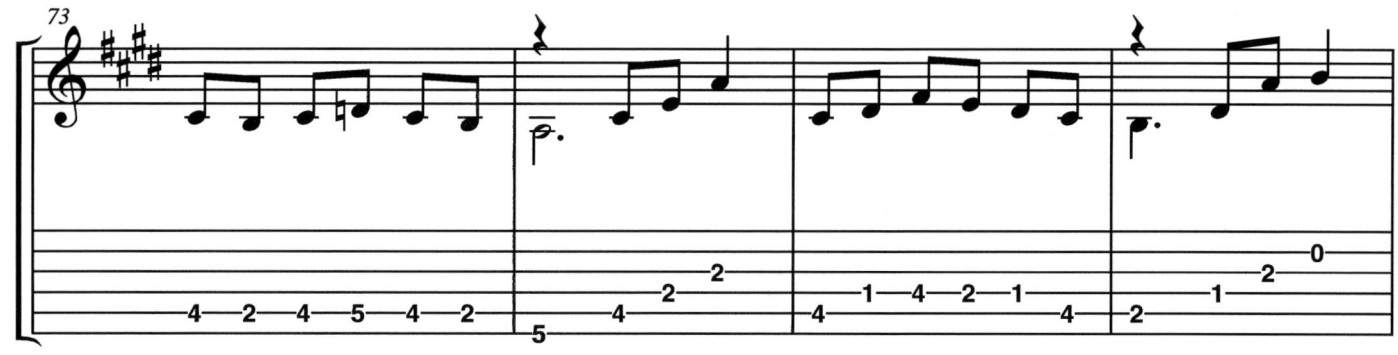

ALEGRIAS POR ROSAS

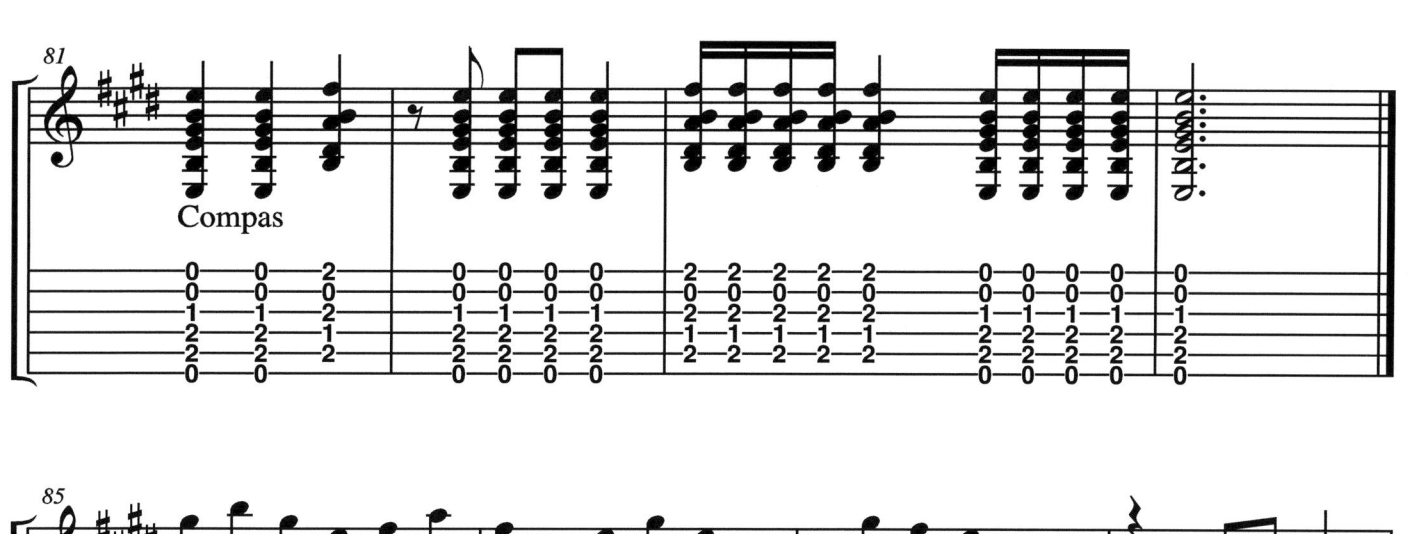

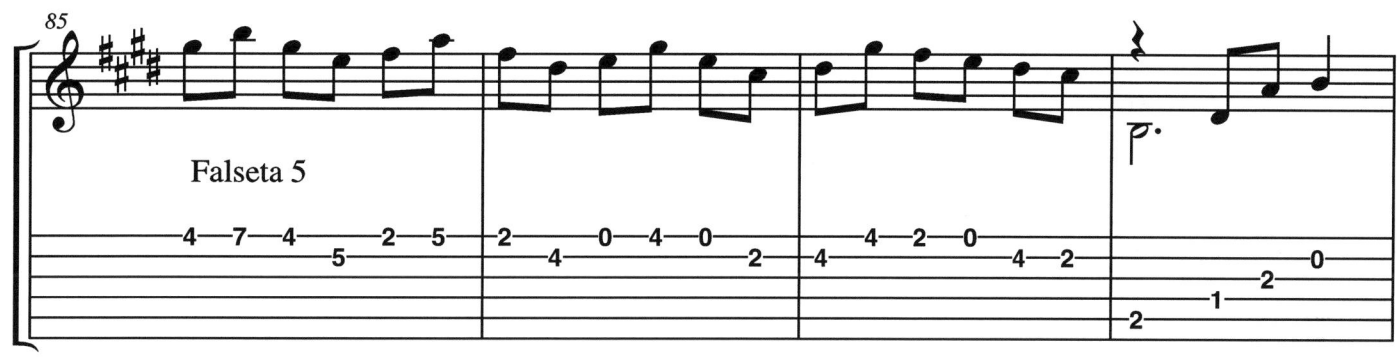

Falseta 5

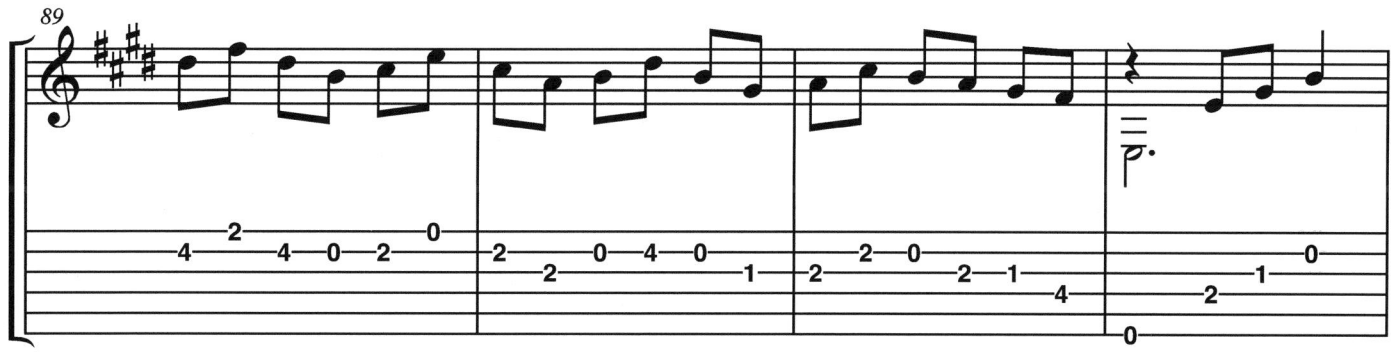

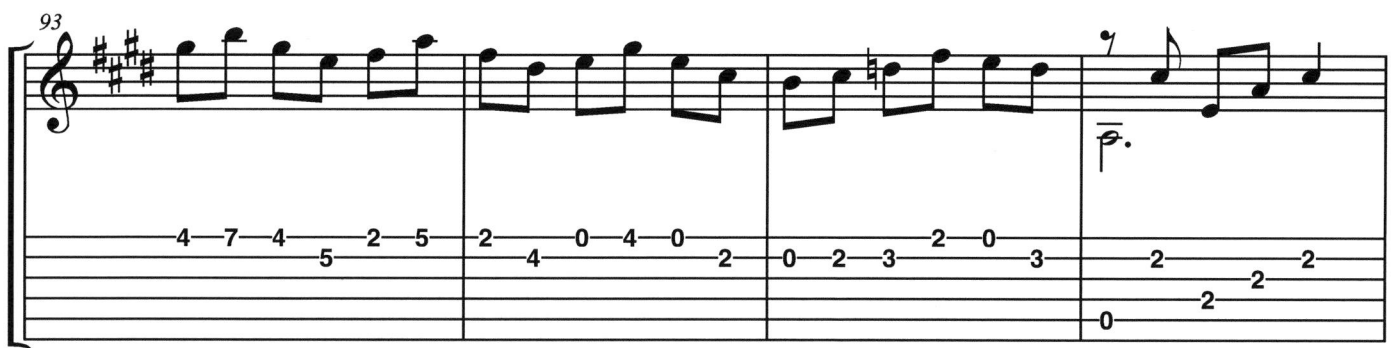

ALEGRIAS POR ROSAS

ALEGRIAS POR ROSAS

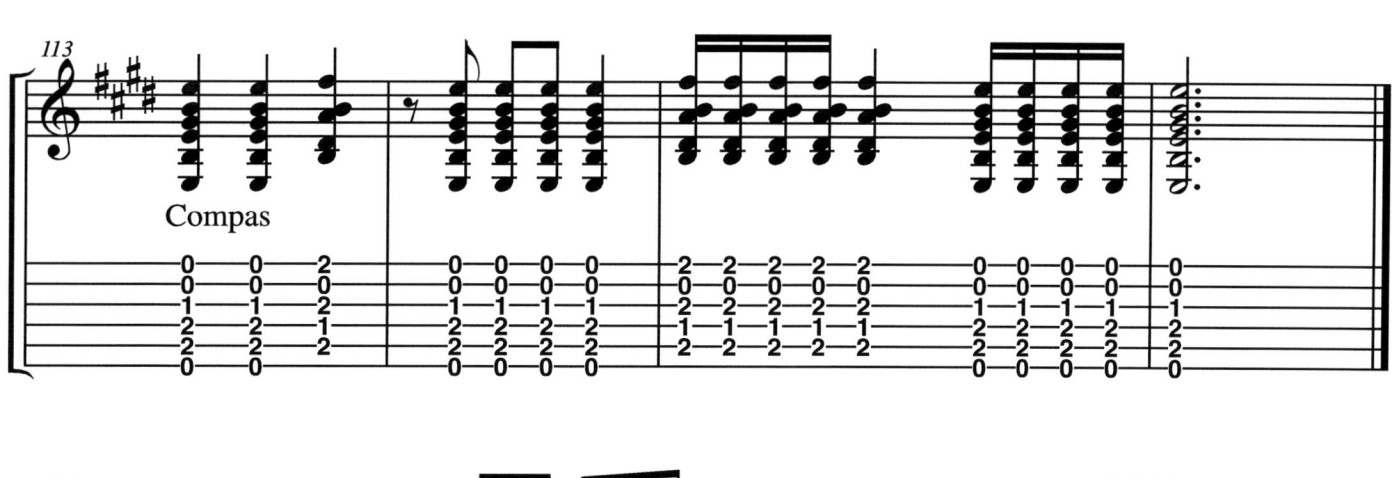
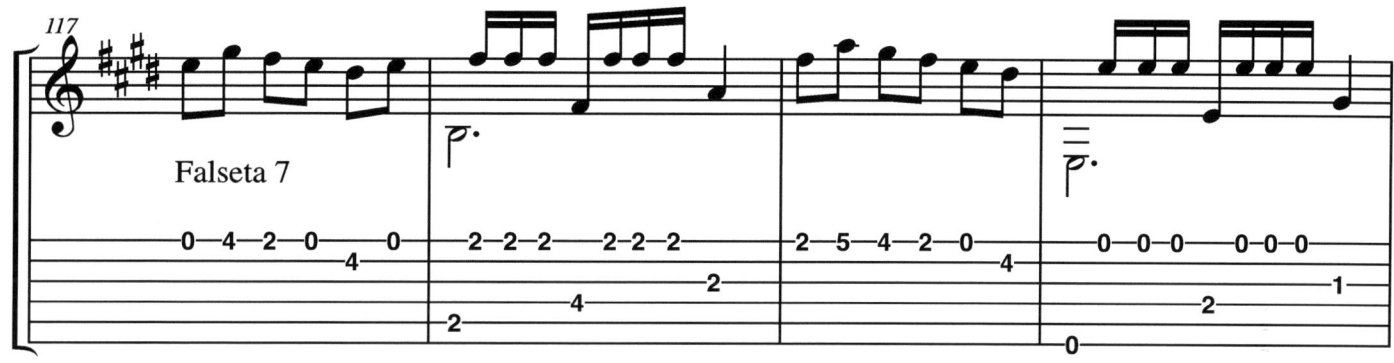
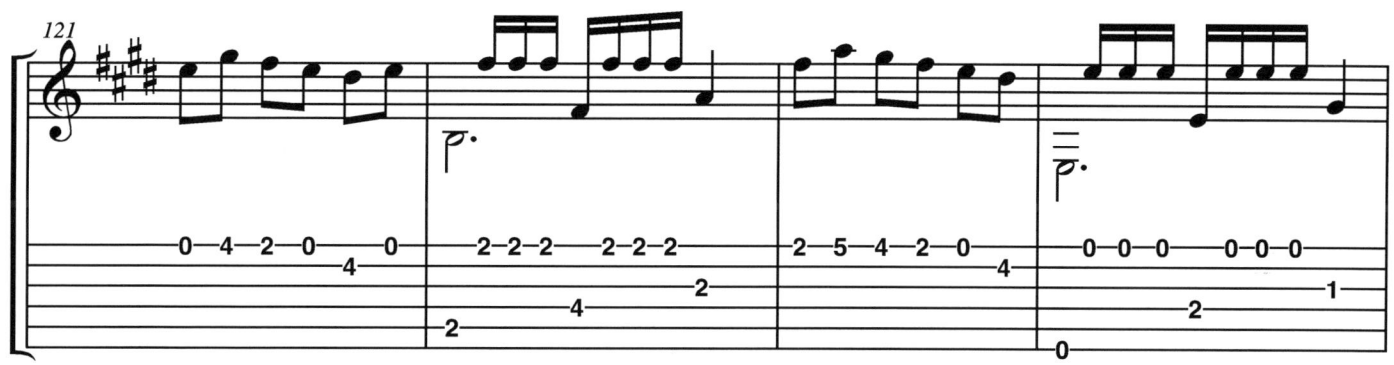

ALEGRIAS POR ROSAS

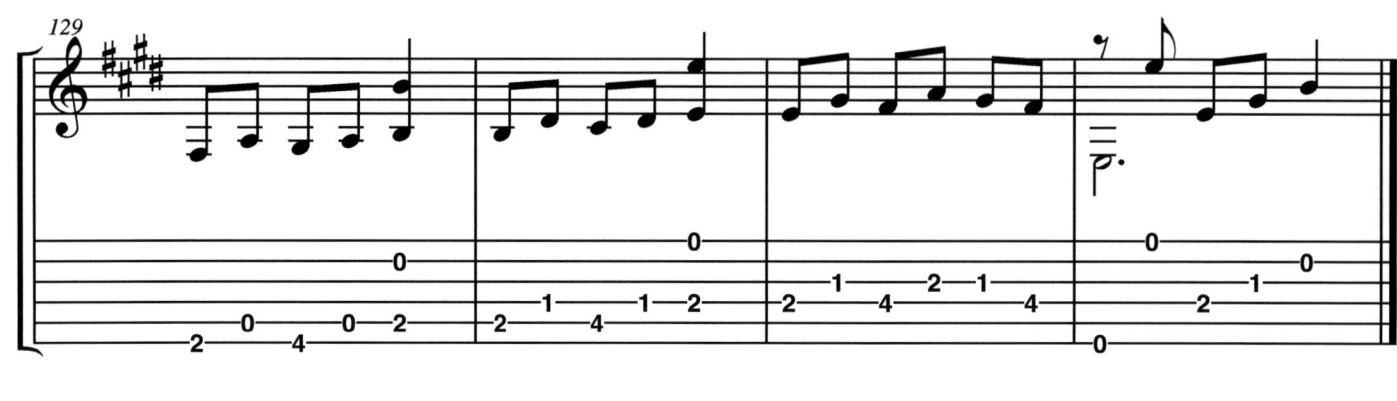

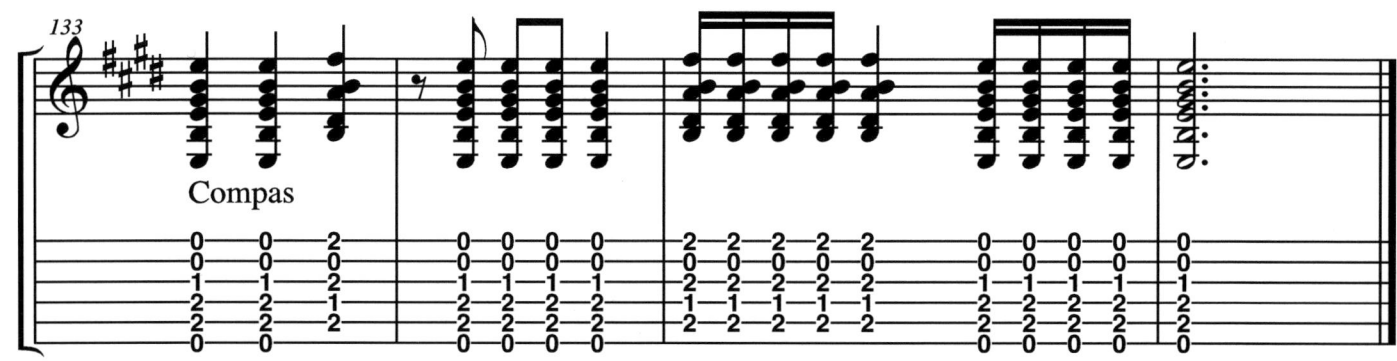

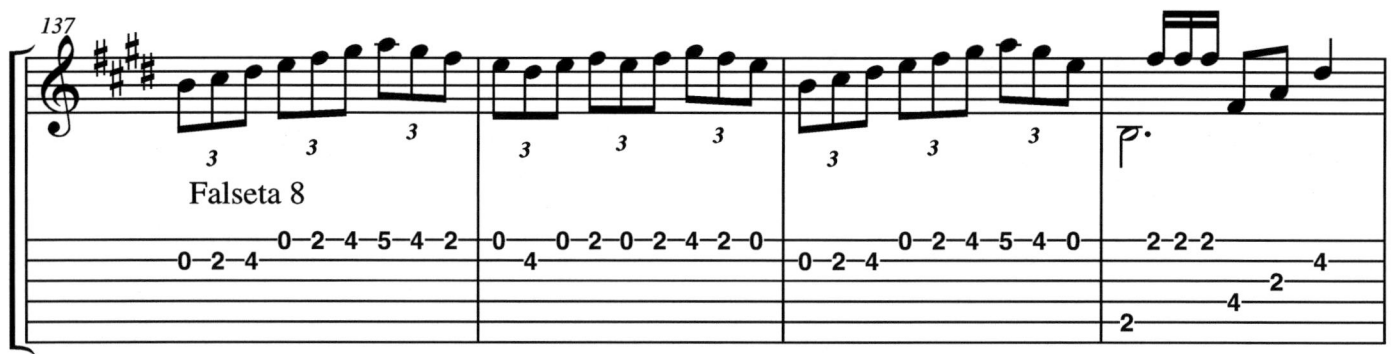

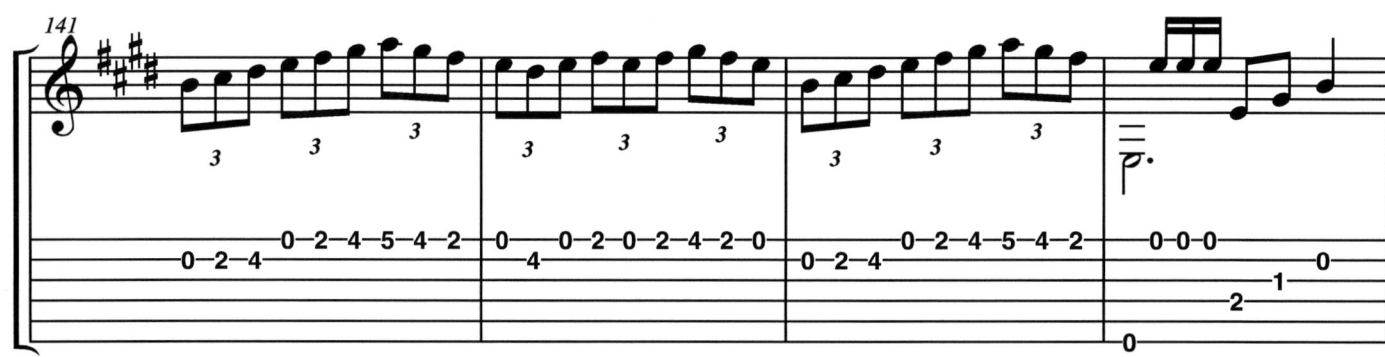

ALEGRIAS POR ROSAS

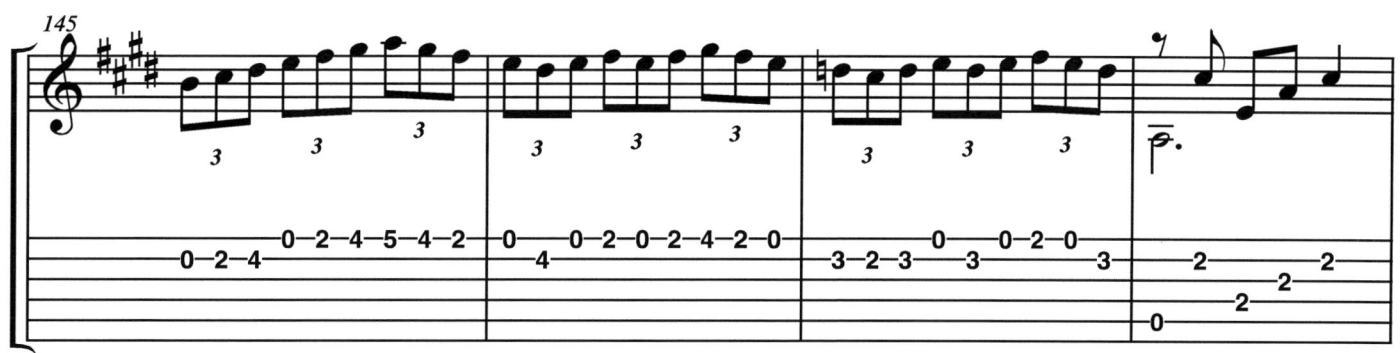
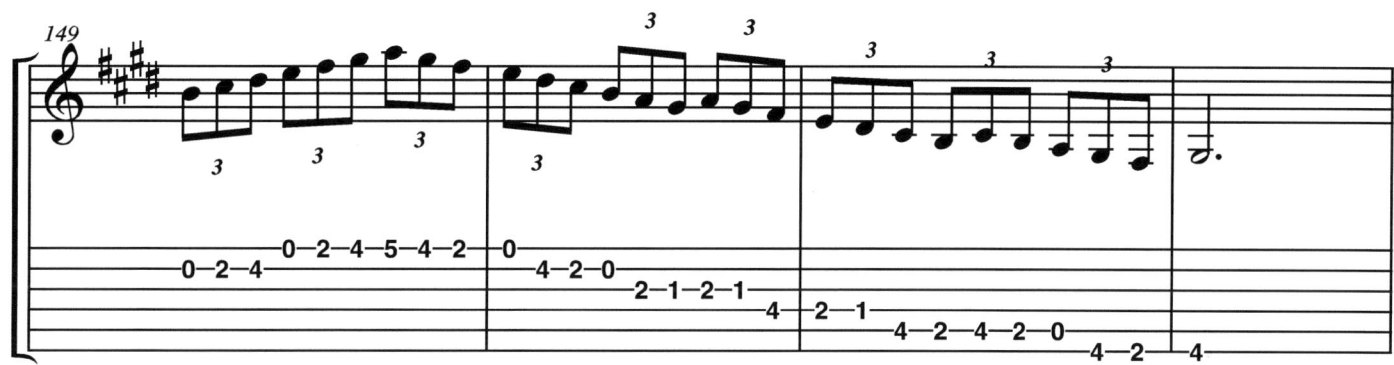
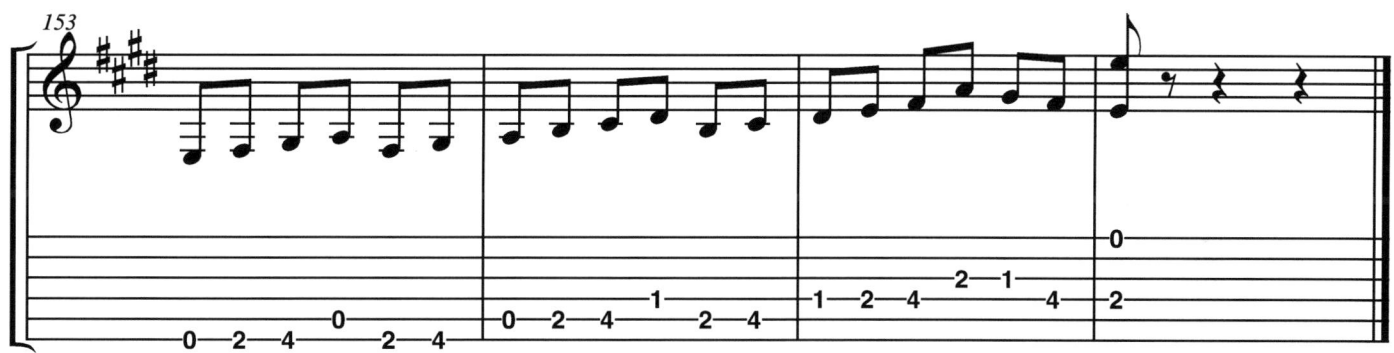
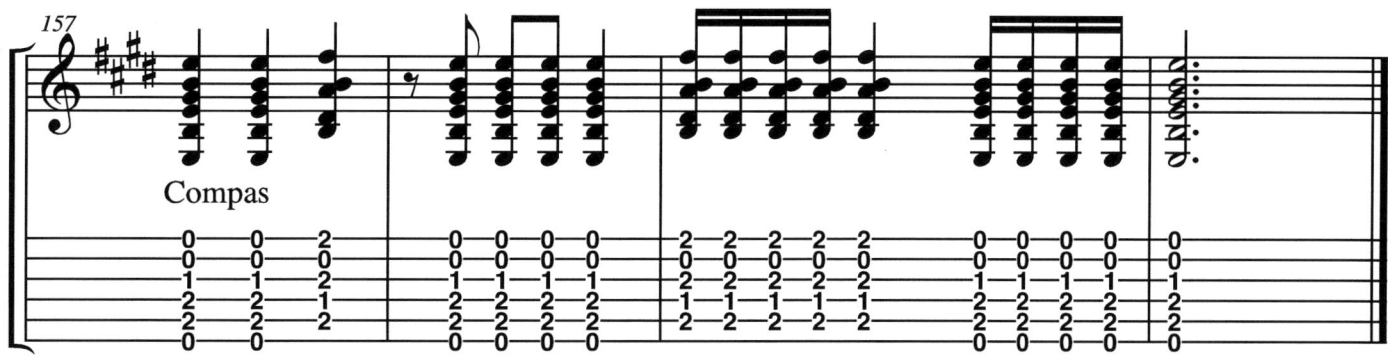

ALEGRIAS POR ROSAS

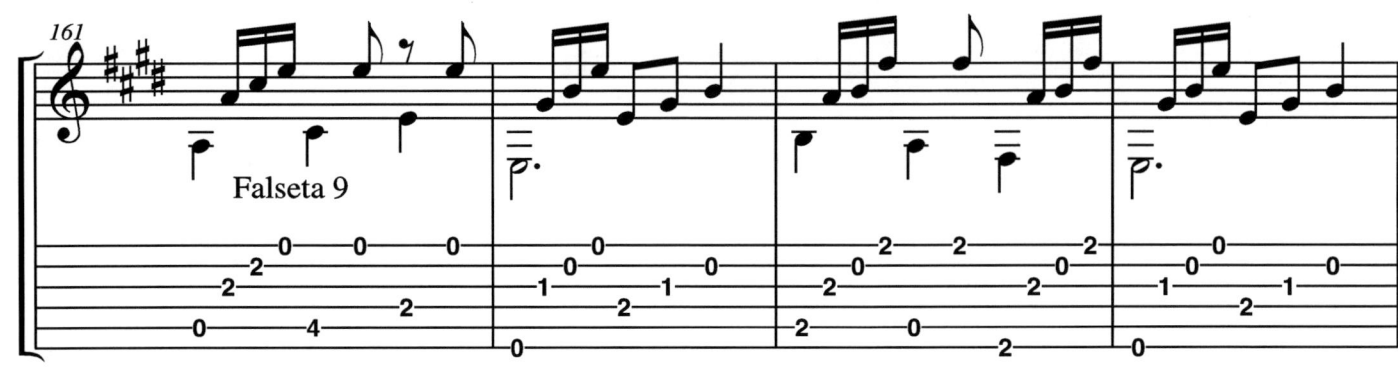

Falseta 9

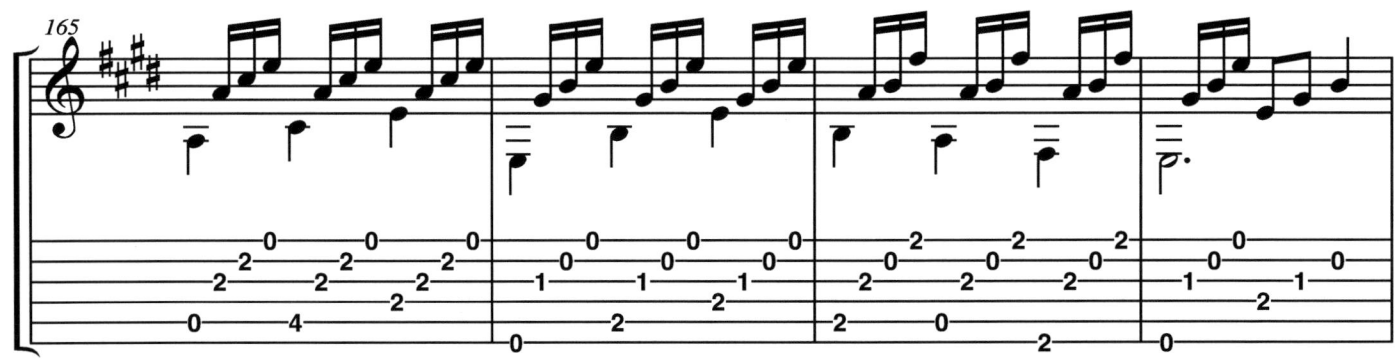

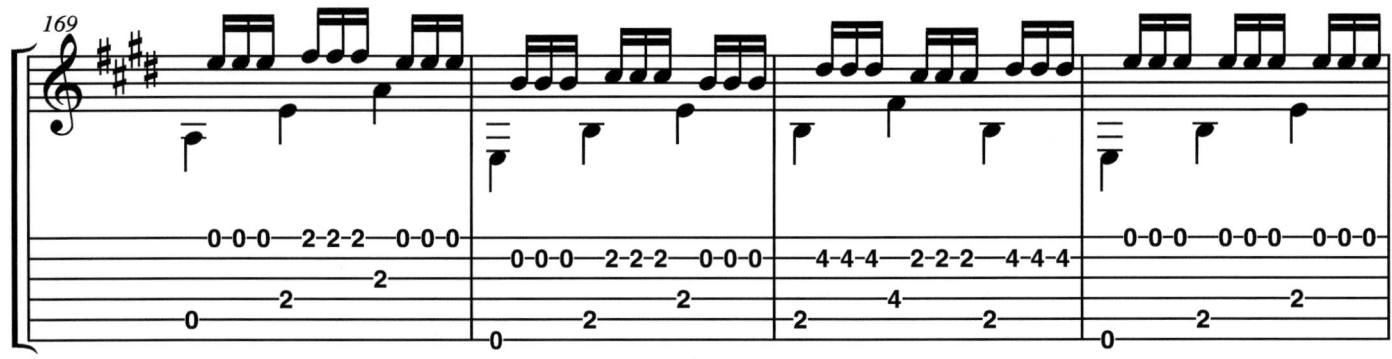

ALEGRIAS POR ROSAS

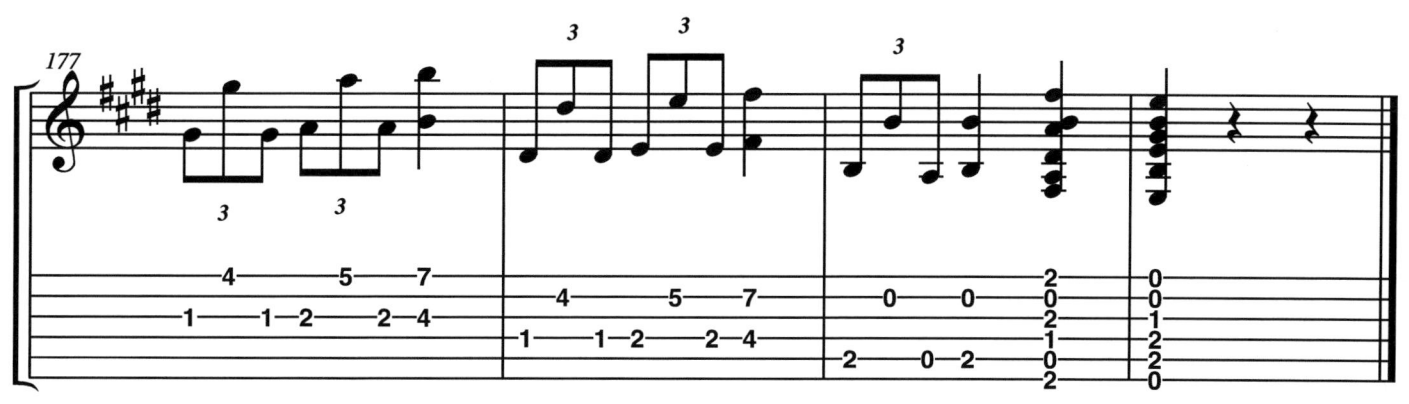

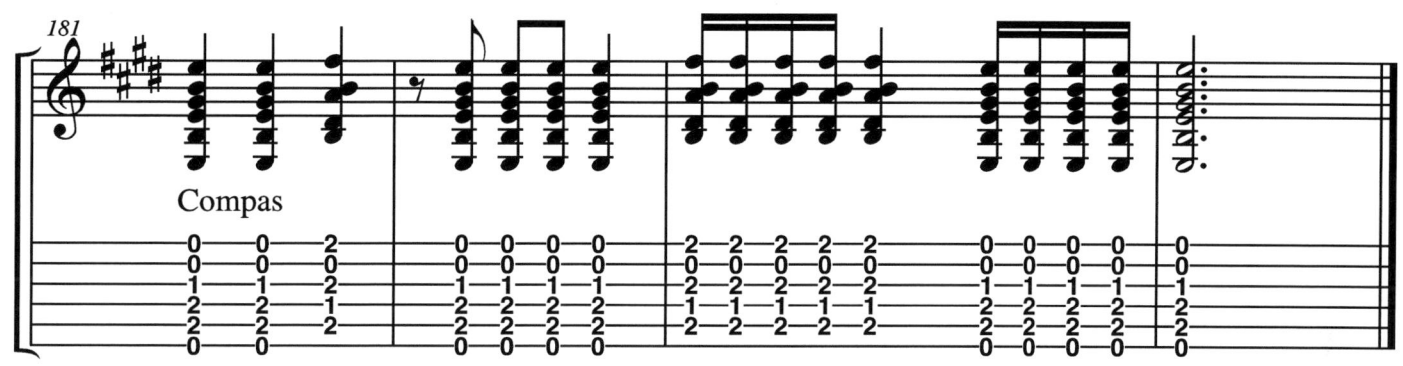

Compas

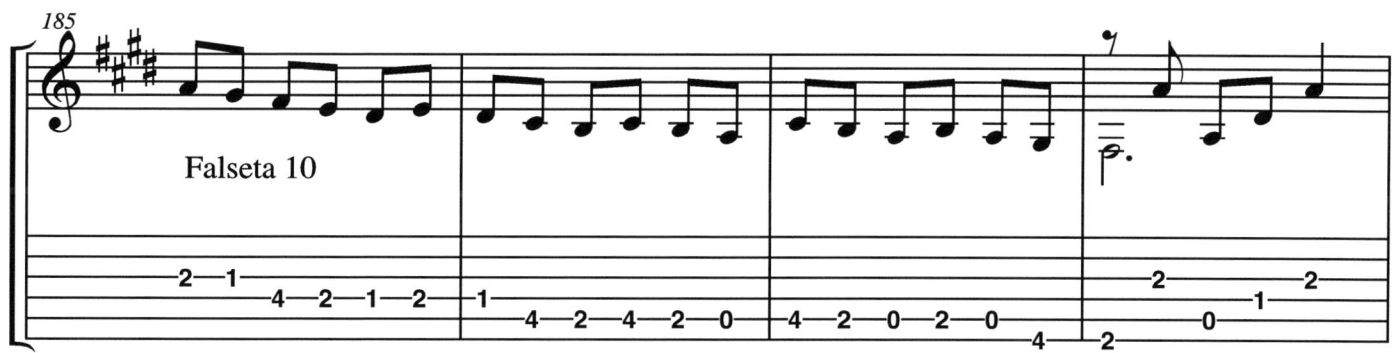

Falseta 10

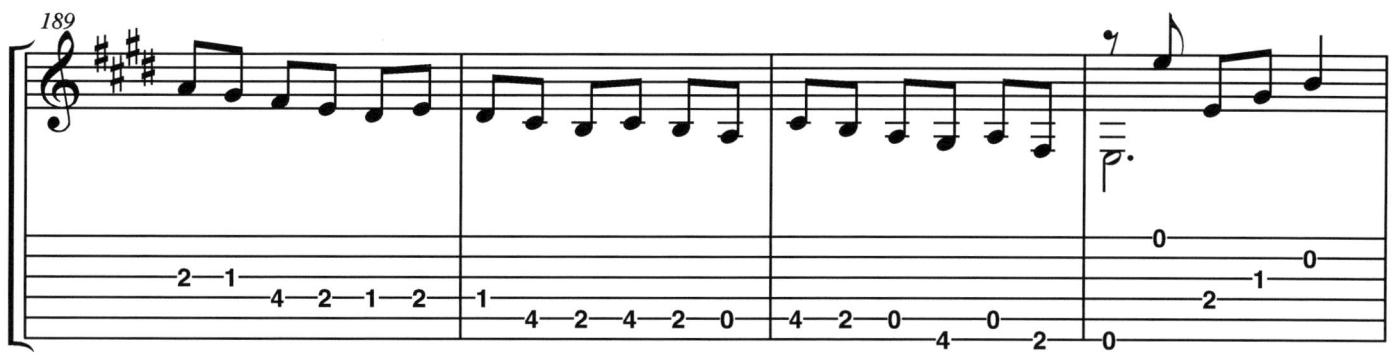

ALEGRIAS POR ROSAS

ALEGRIAS POR ROSAS

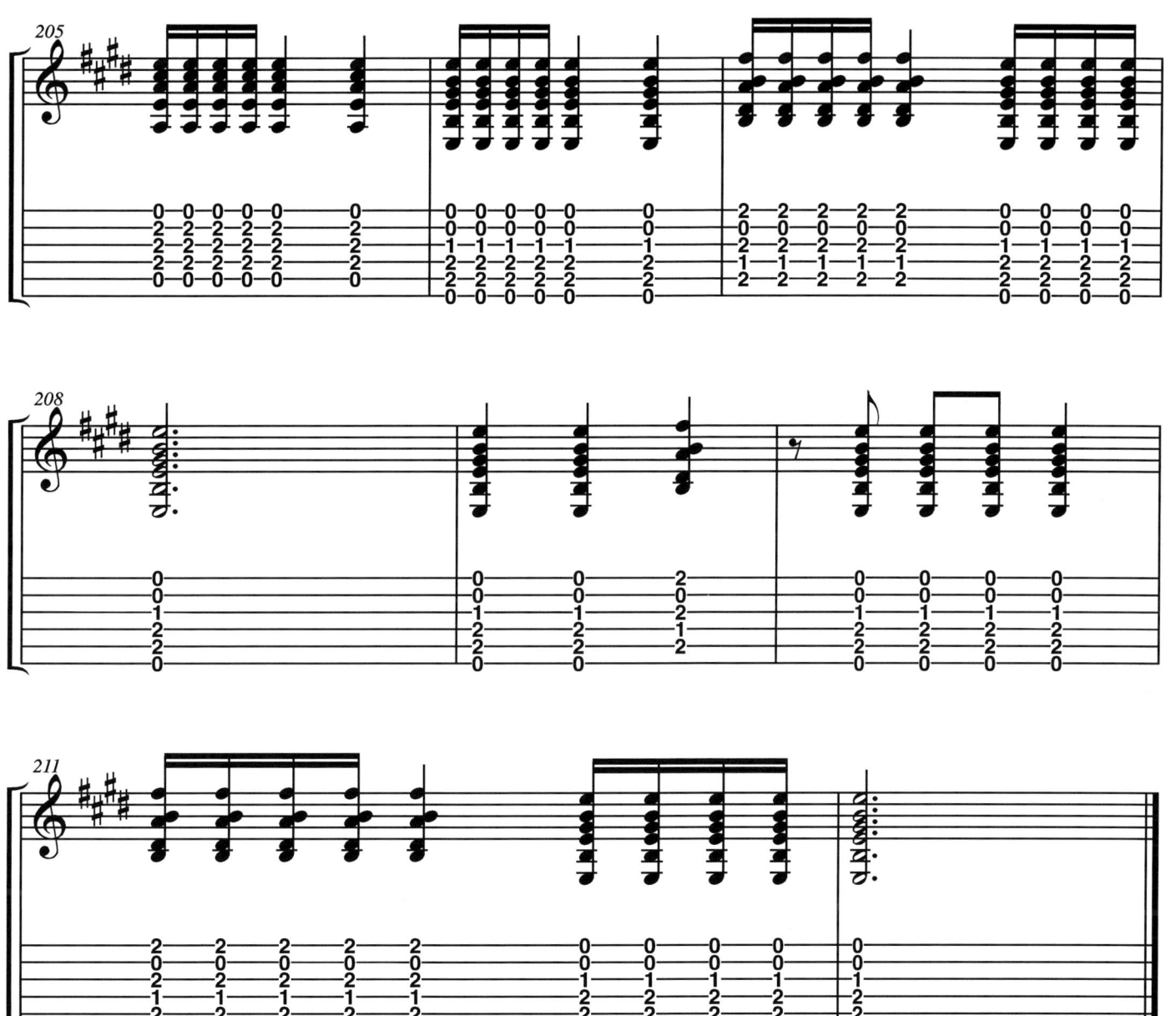

The numbers at the beginning of each falseta indicate on what beat the falseta begins

BULERIAS

Strum every compas in the same manner

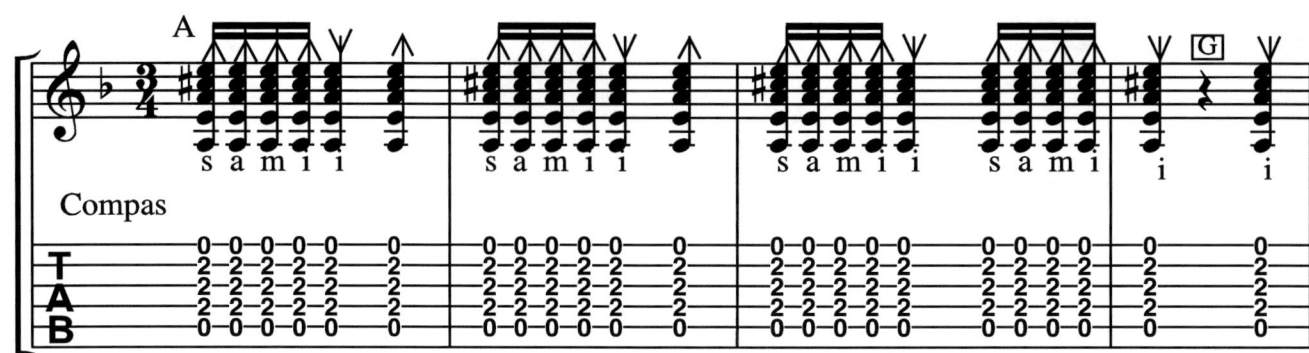

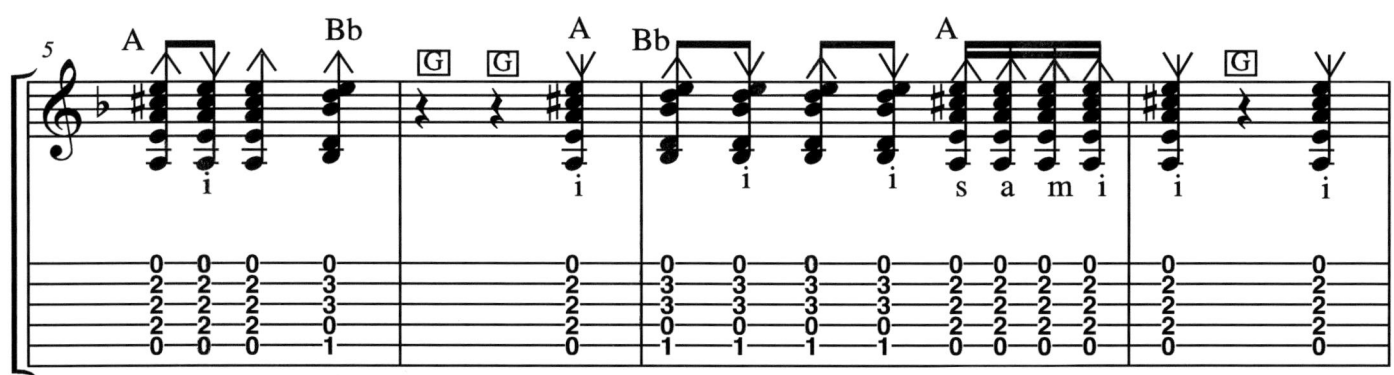

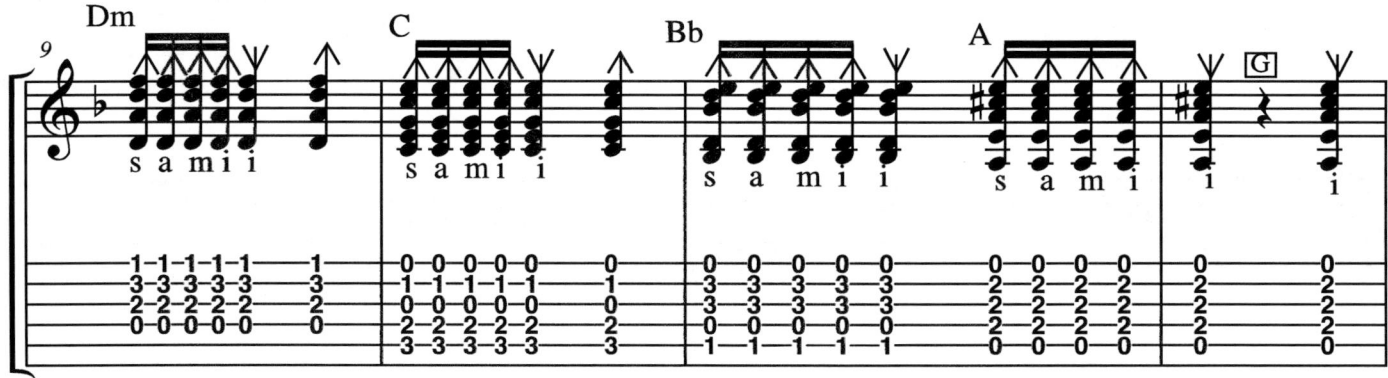

BULERIAS

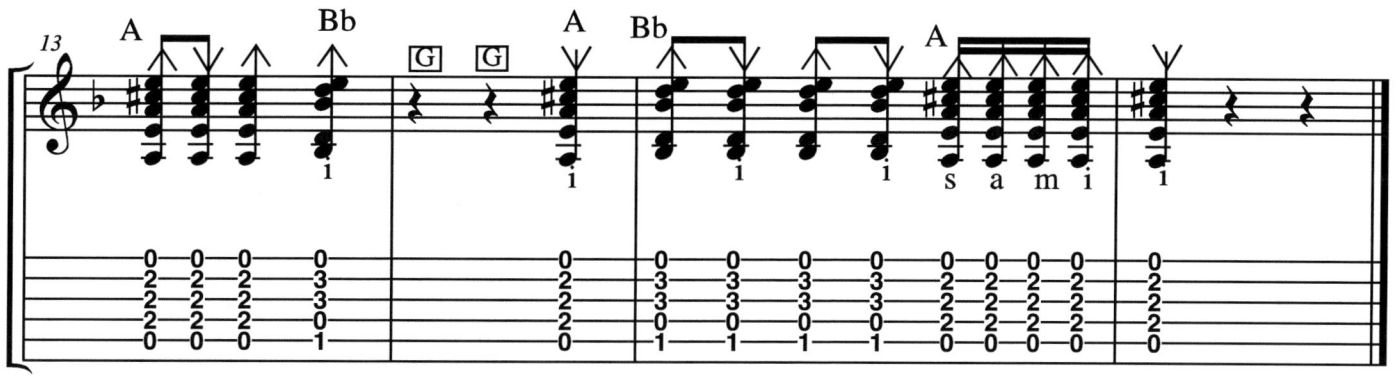
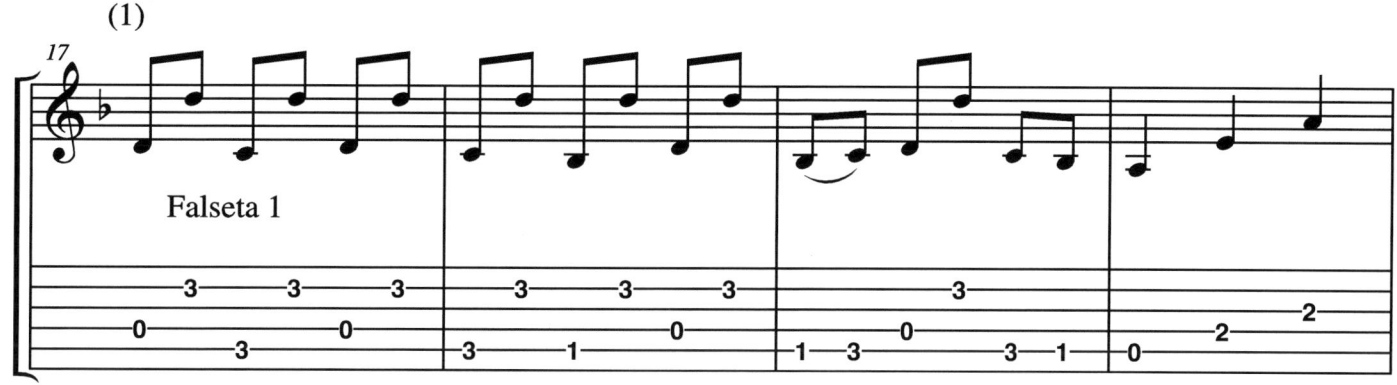
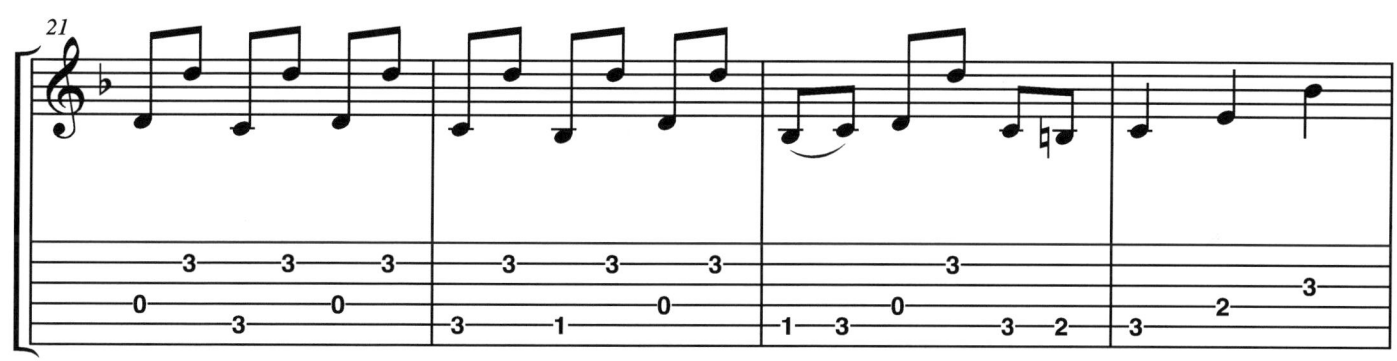
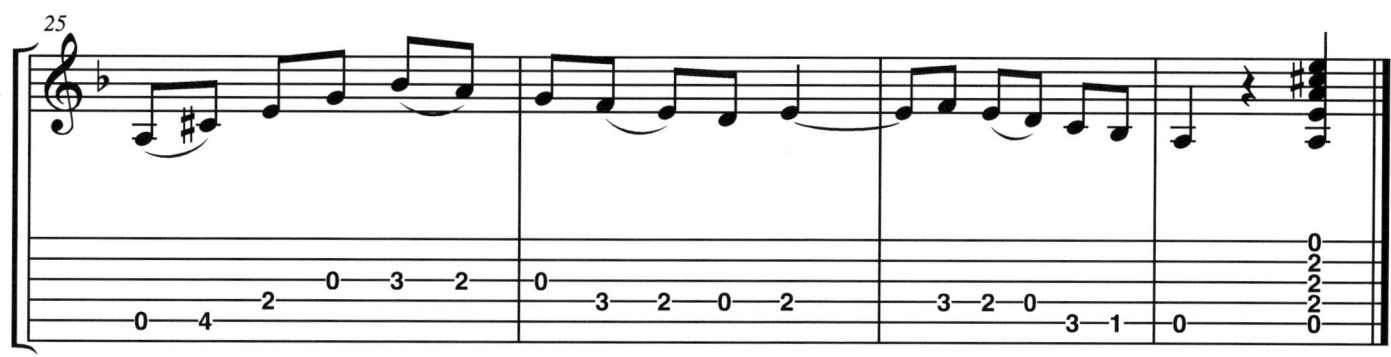

BULERIAS

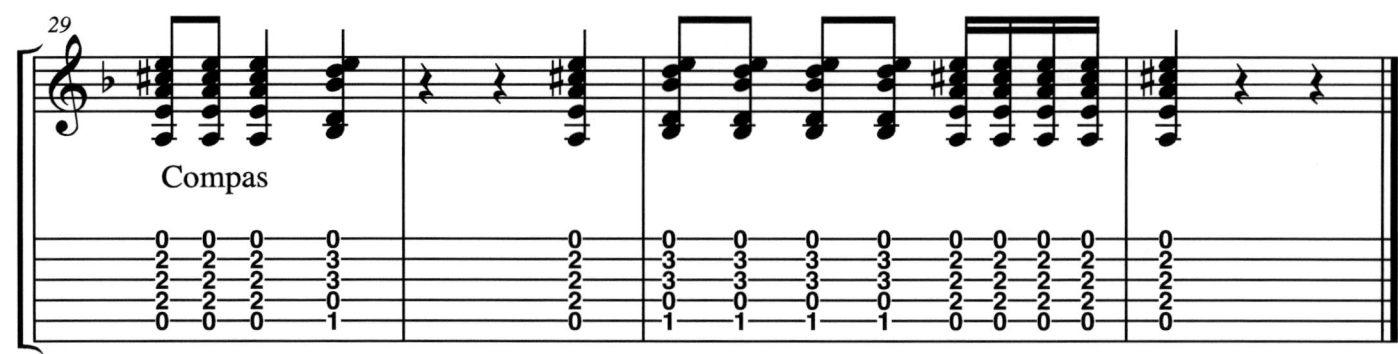

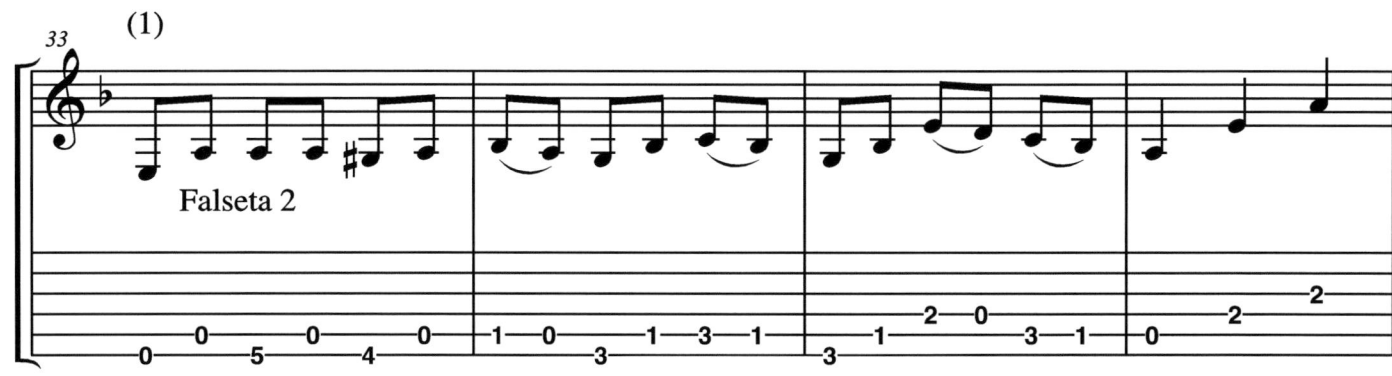

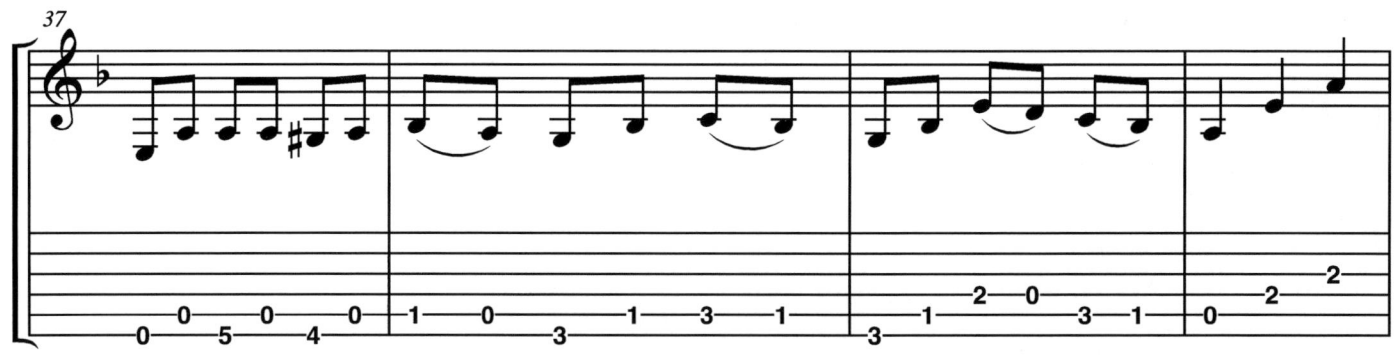

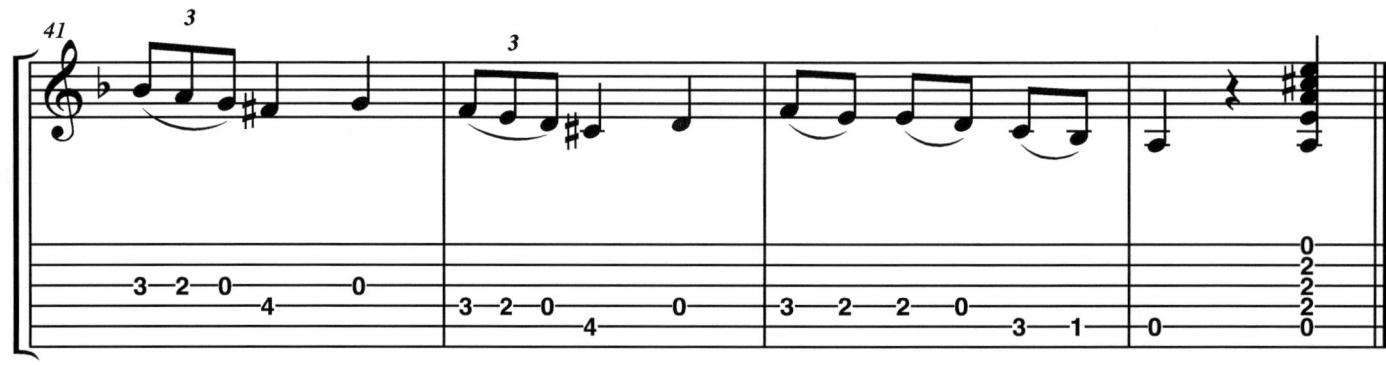

BULERIAS

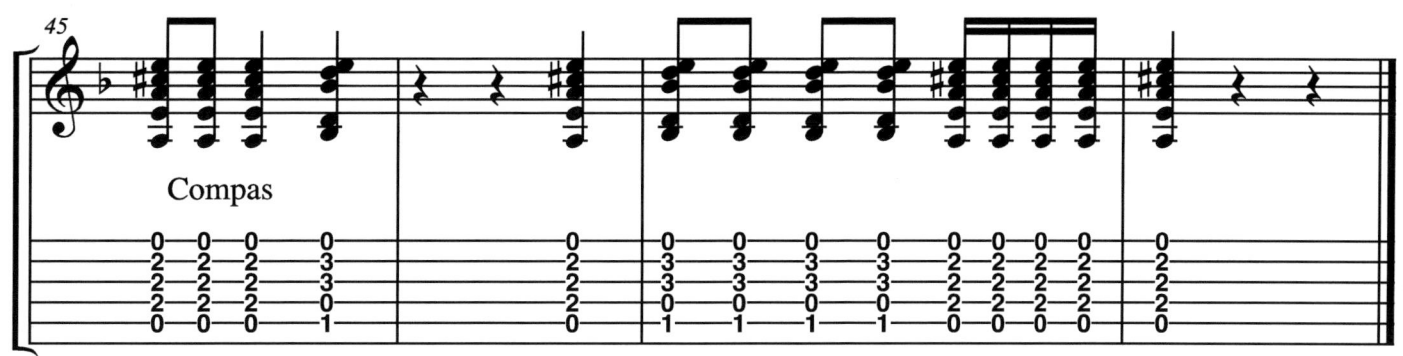

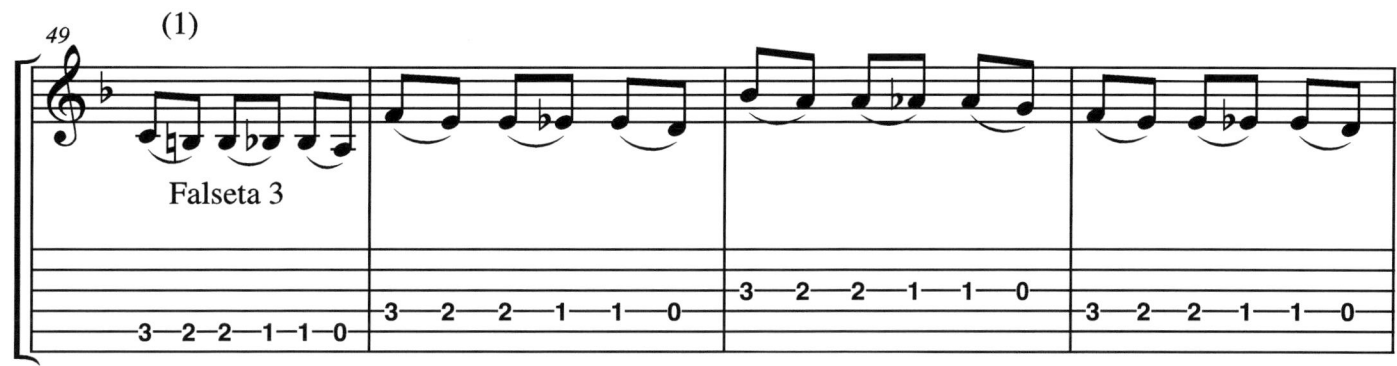

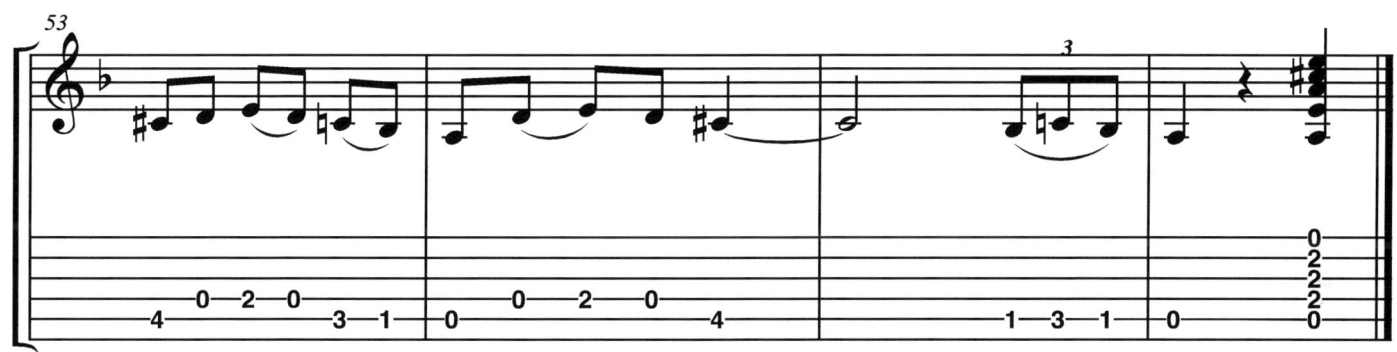

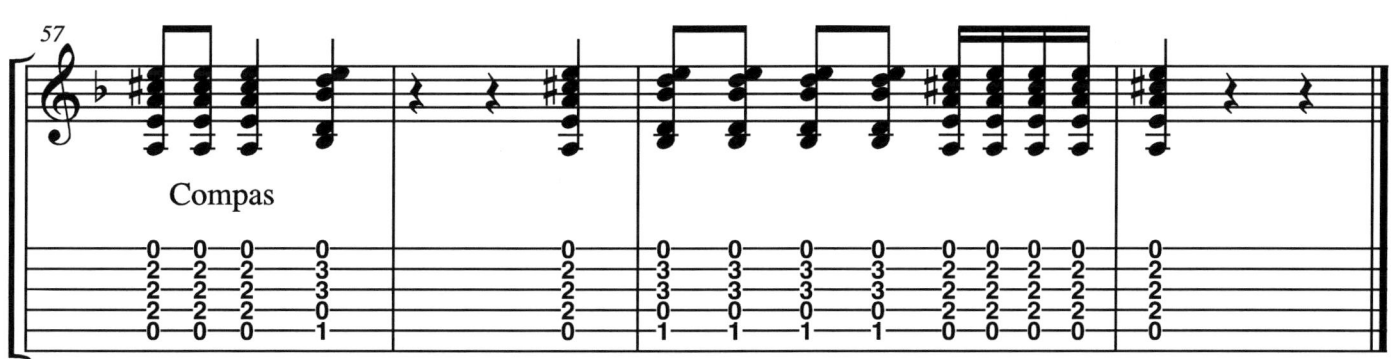

BULERIAS

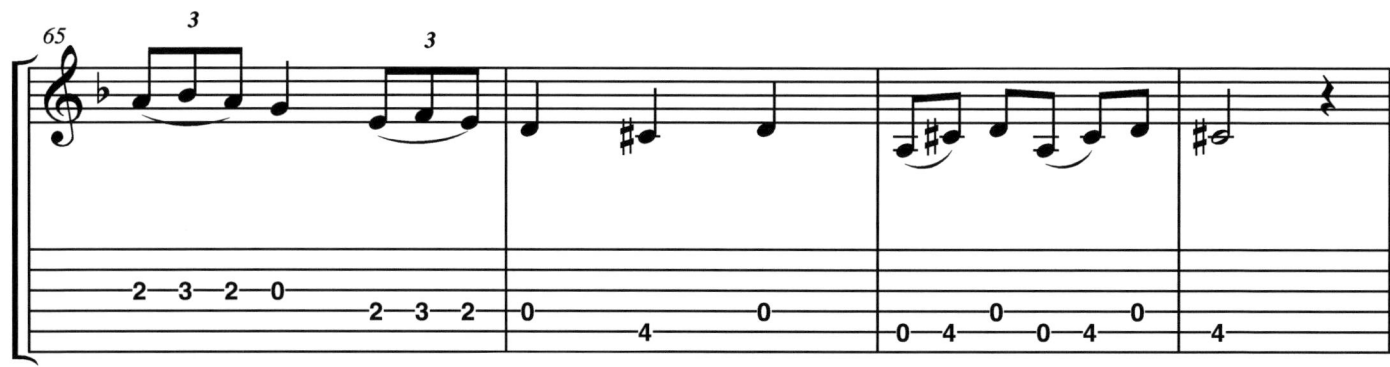

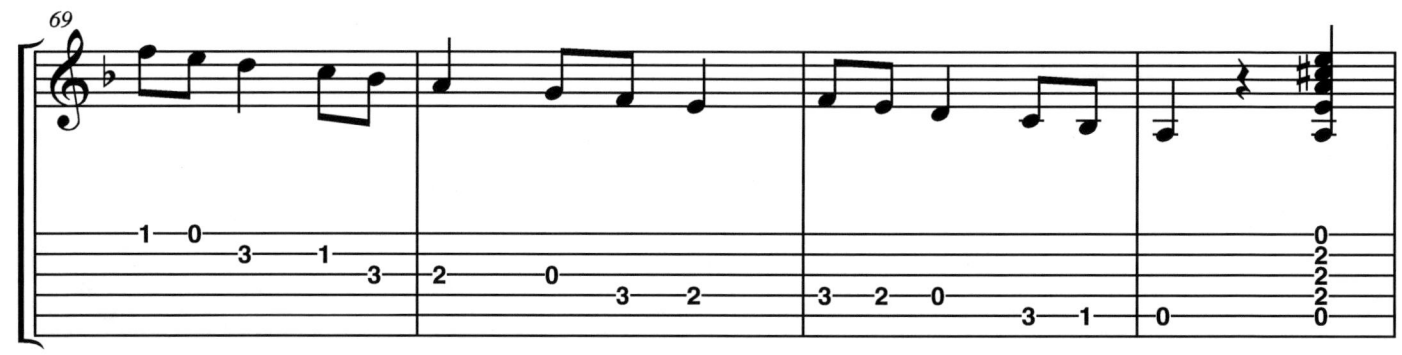

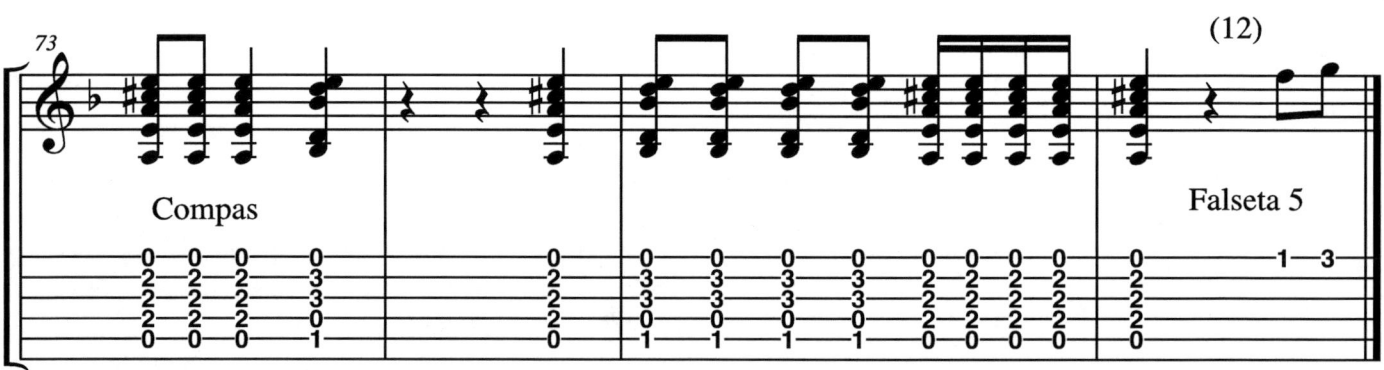

BULERIAS

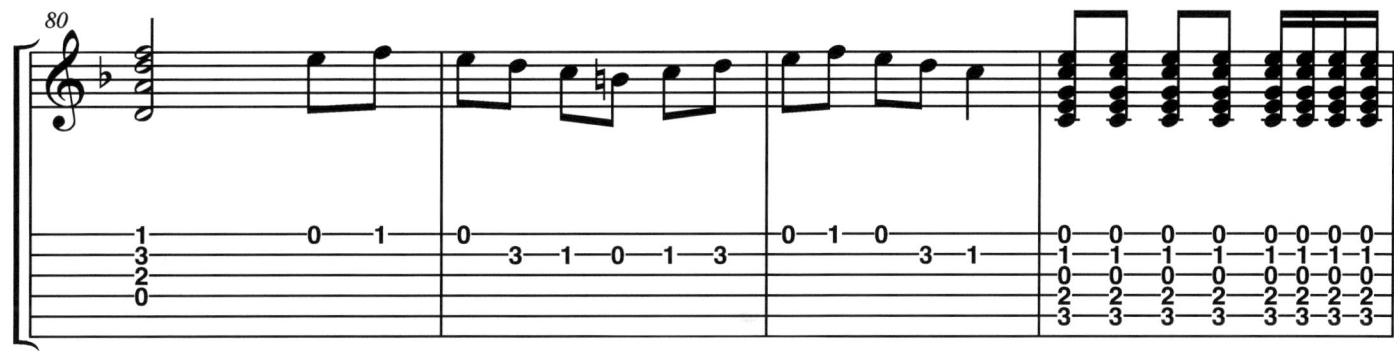

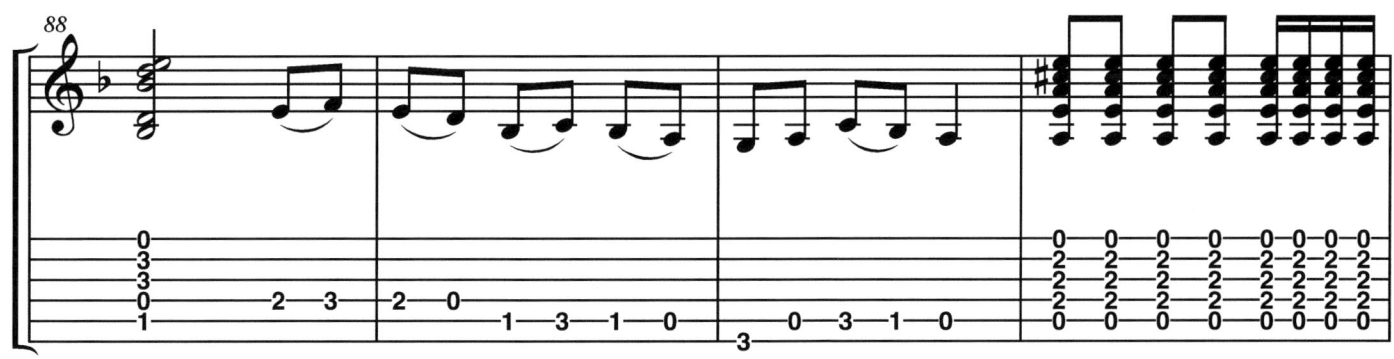

BULERIAS

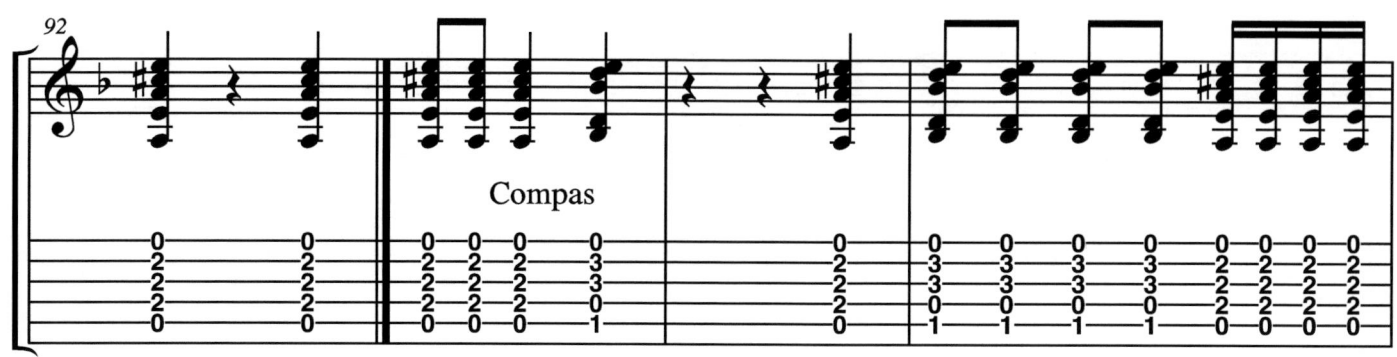

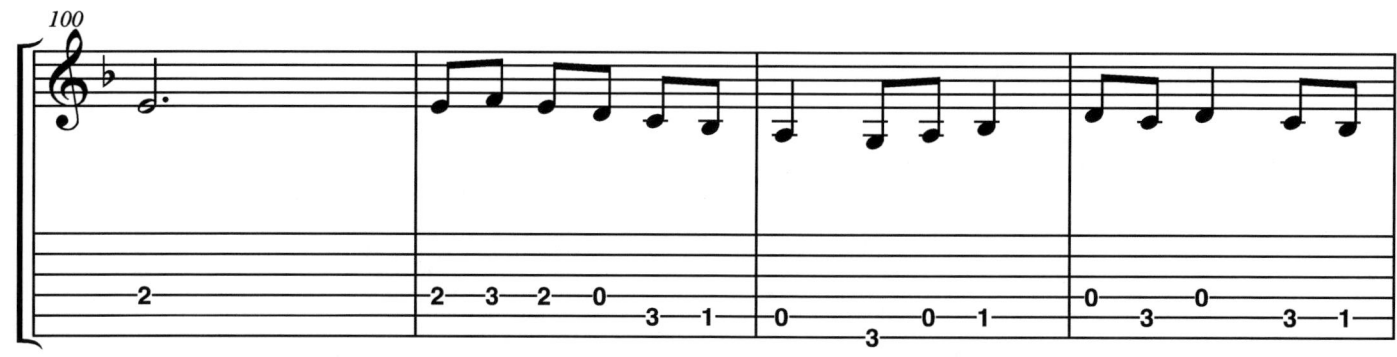

BULERIAS

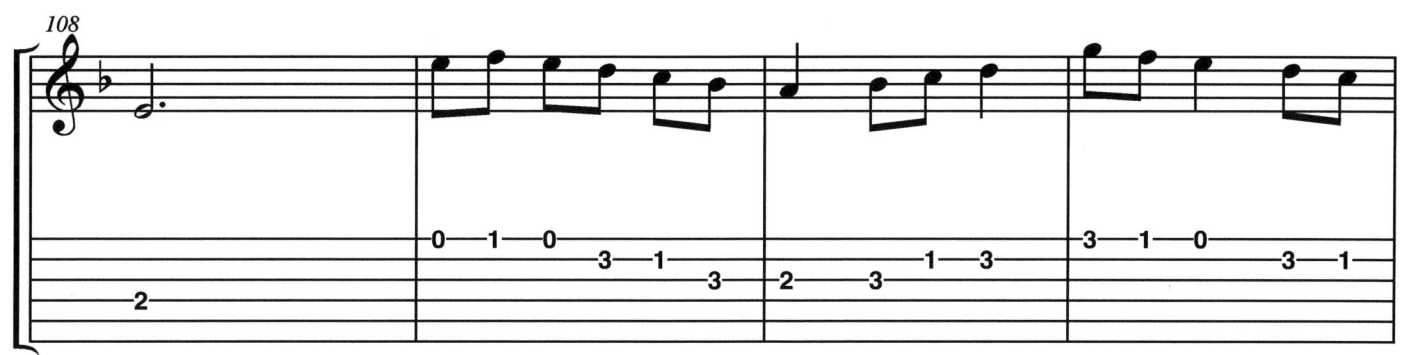

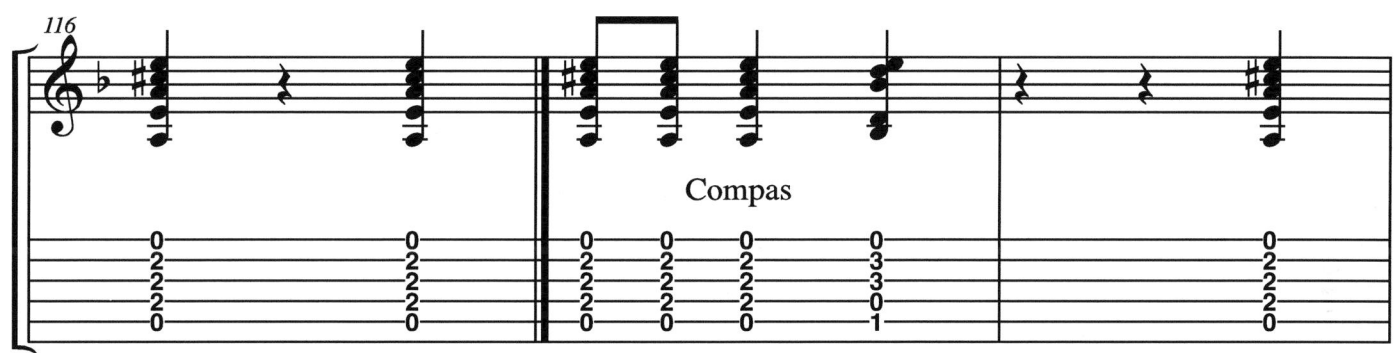

Compas

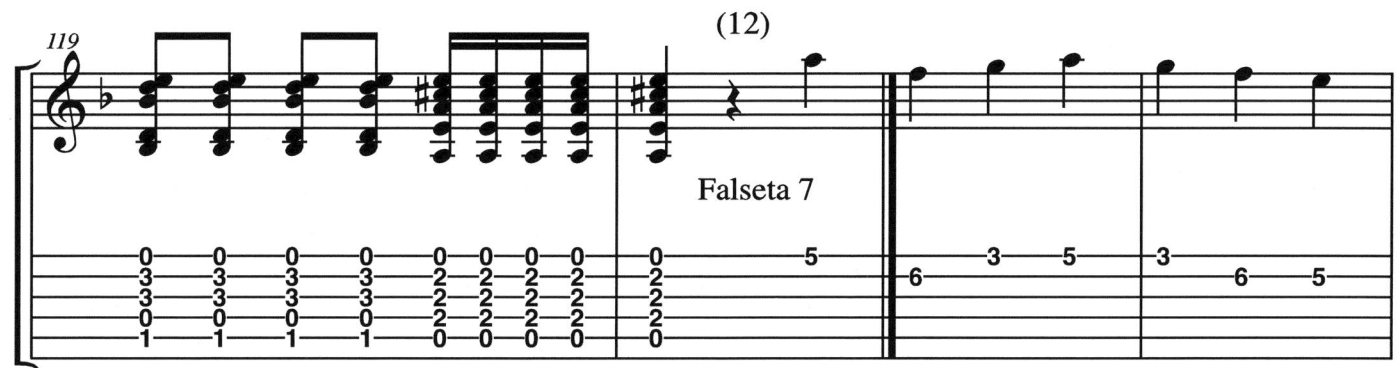

(12)

Falseta 7

BULERIAS

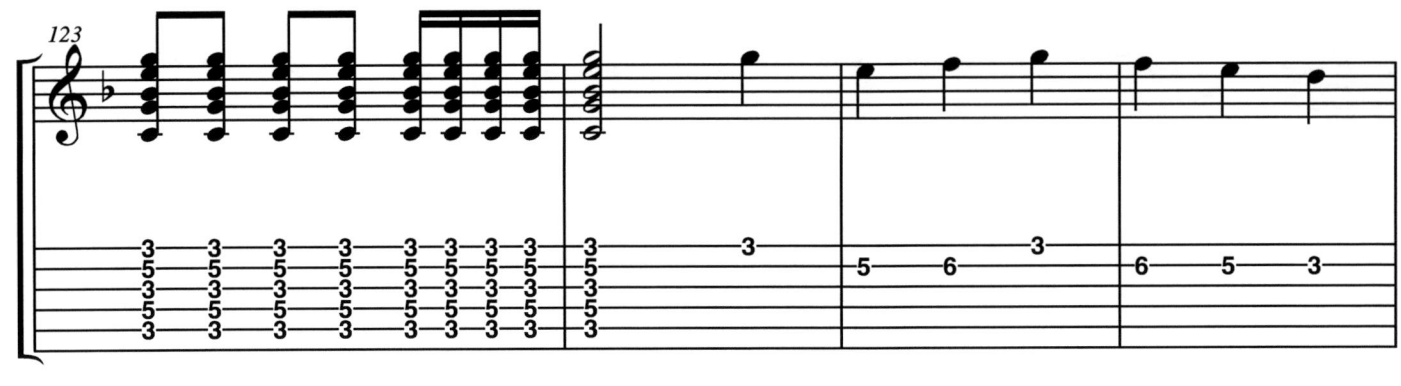
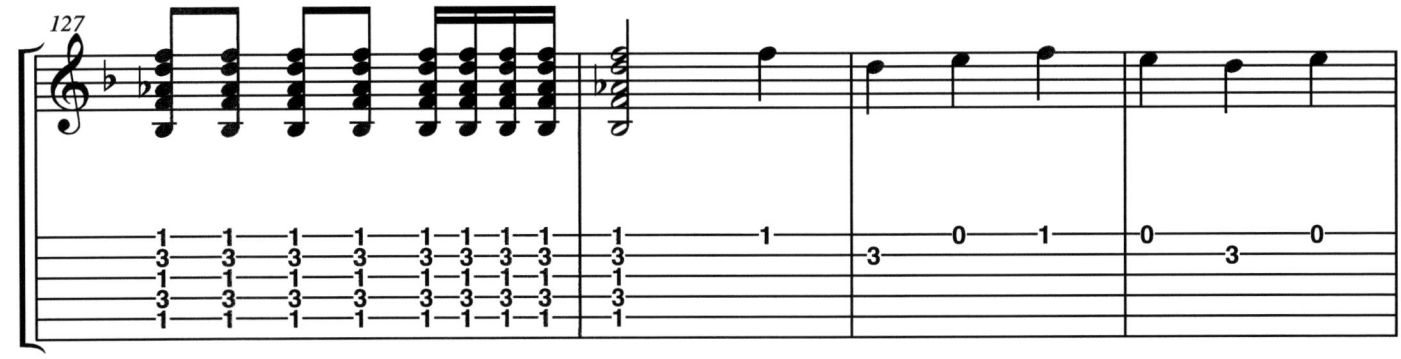

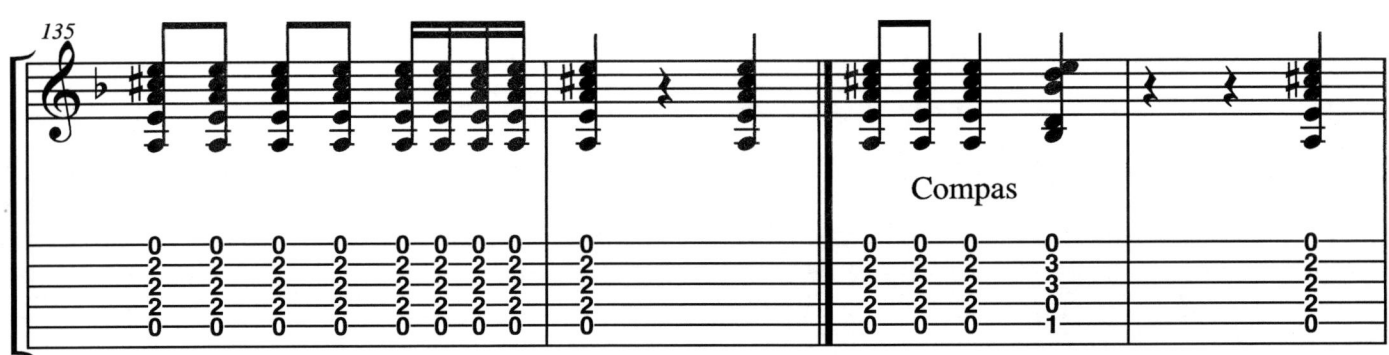

BULERIAS

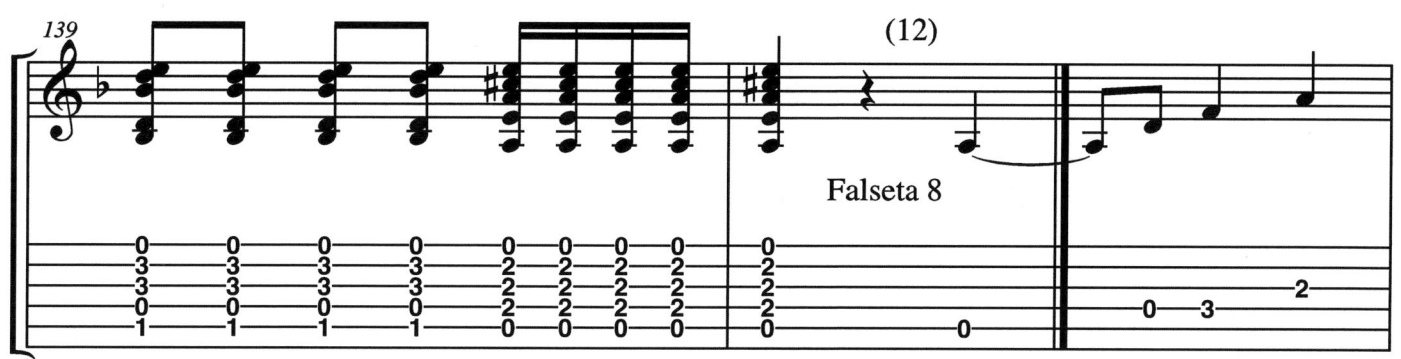

Falseta 8

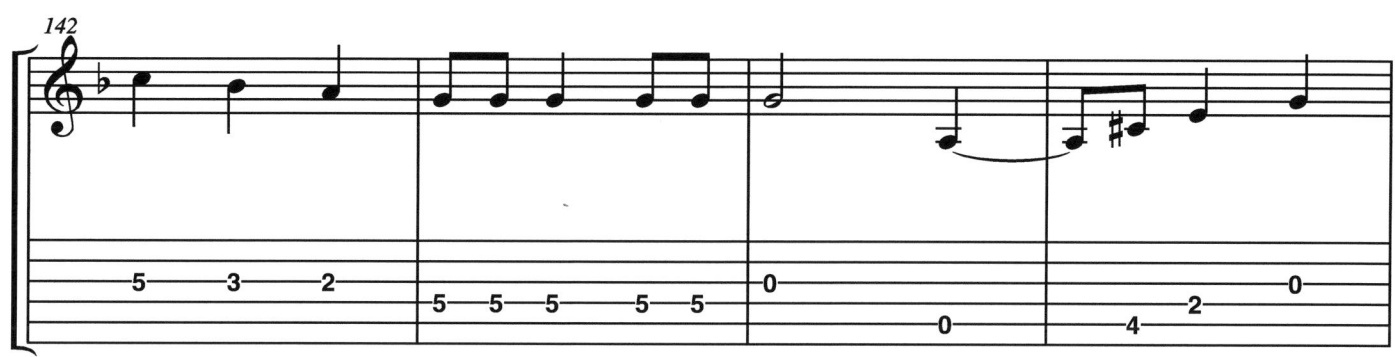

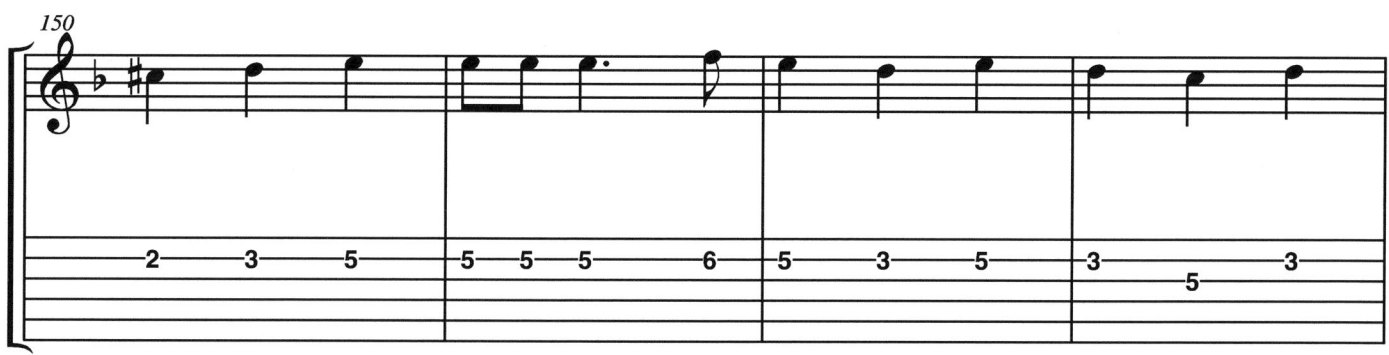

BULERIAS

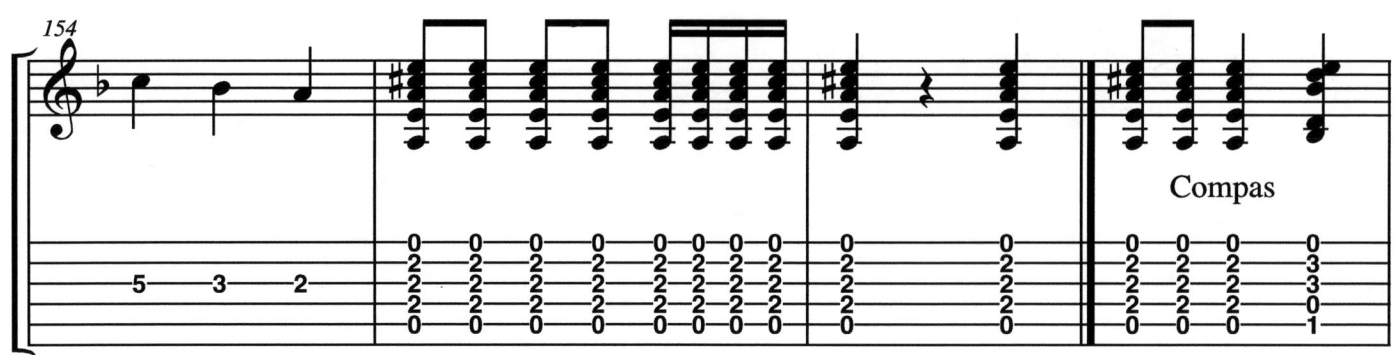

Compas

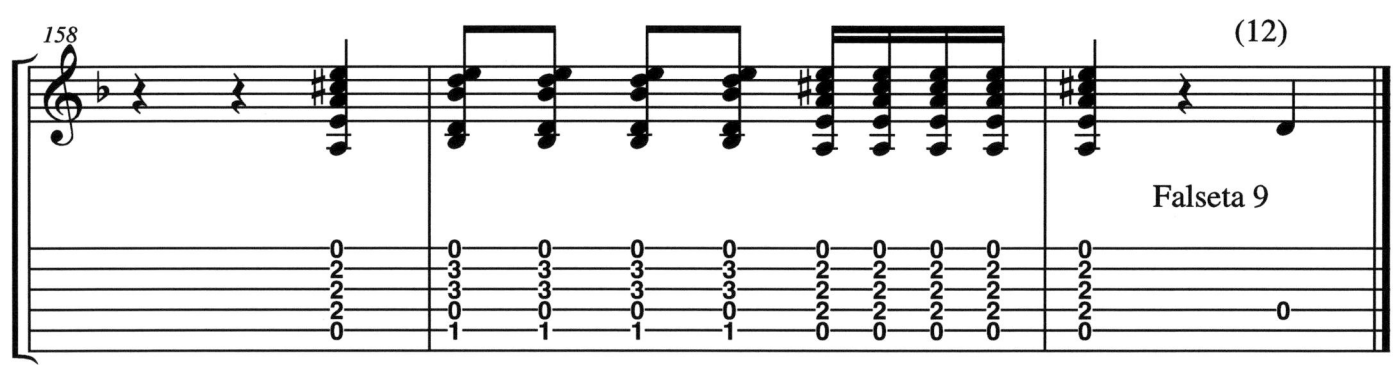

(12)

Falseta 9

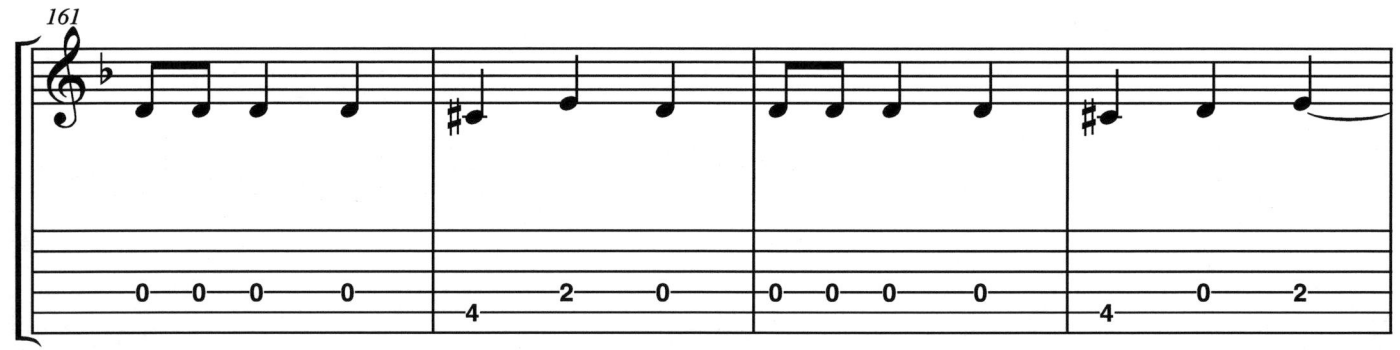

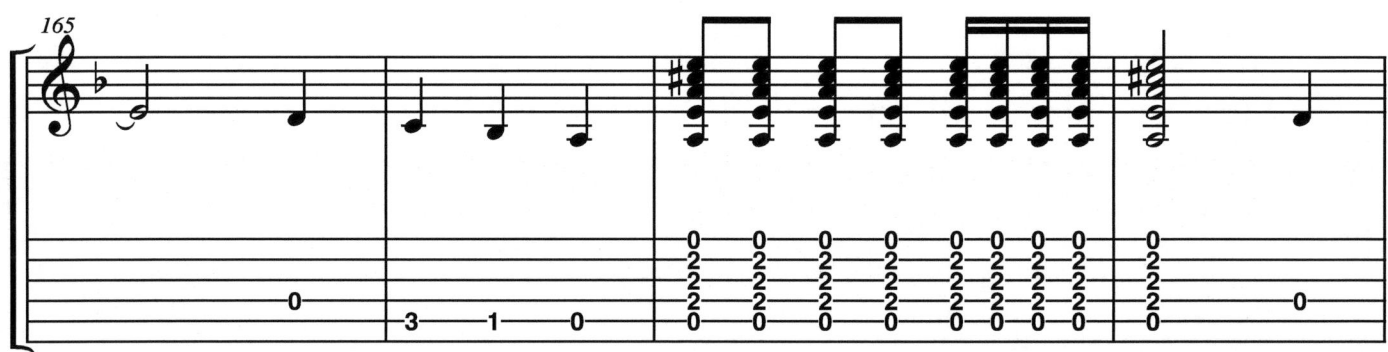

BULERIAS

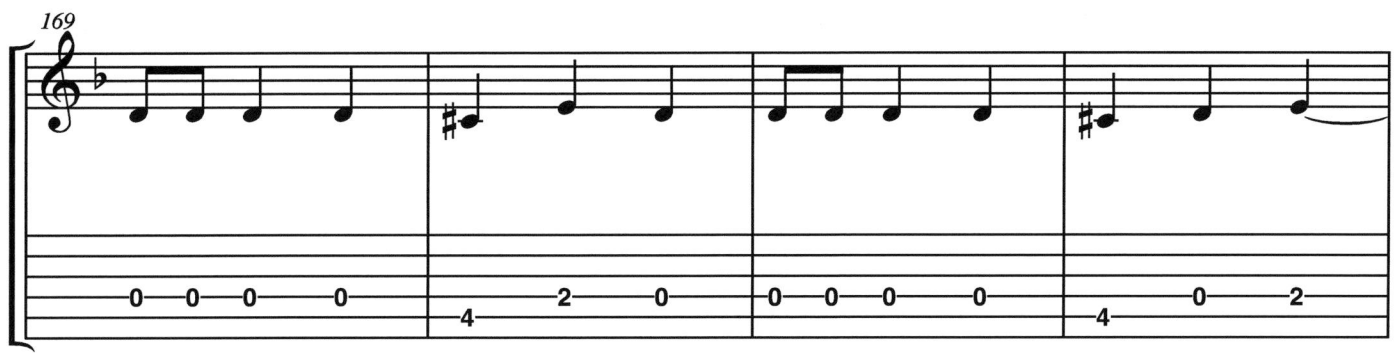
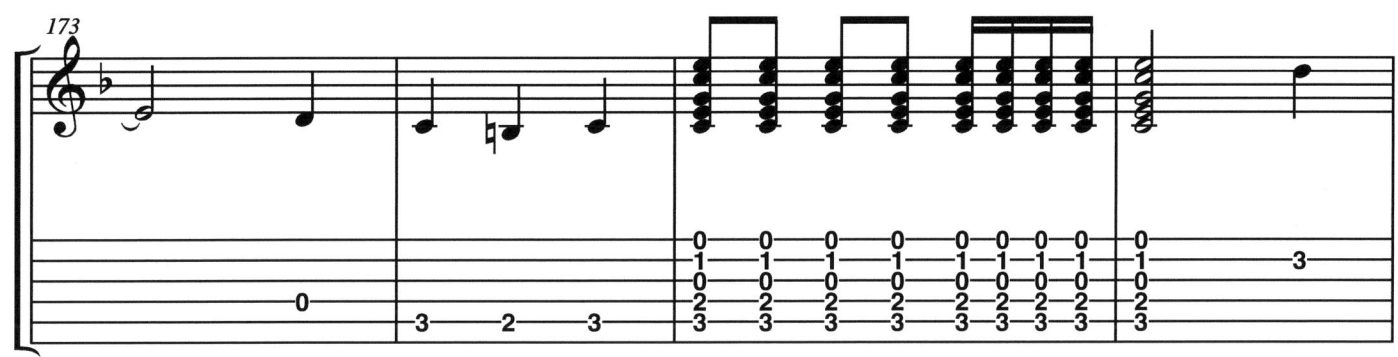
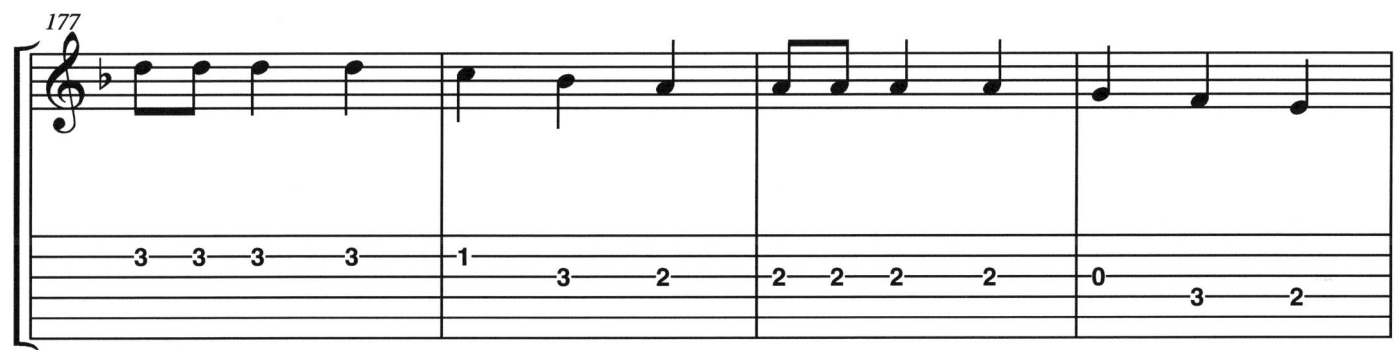
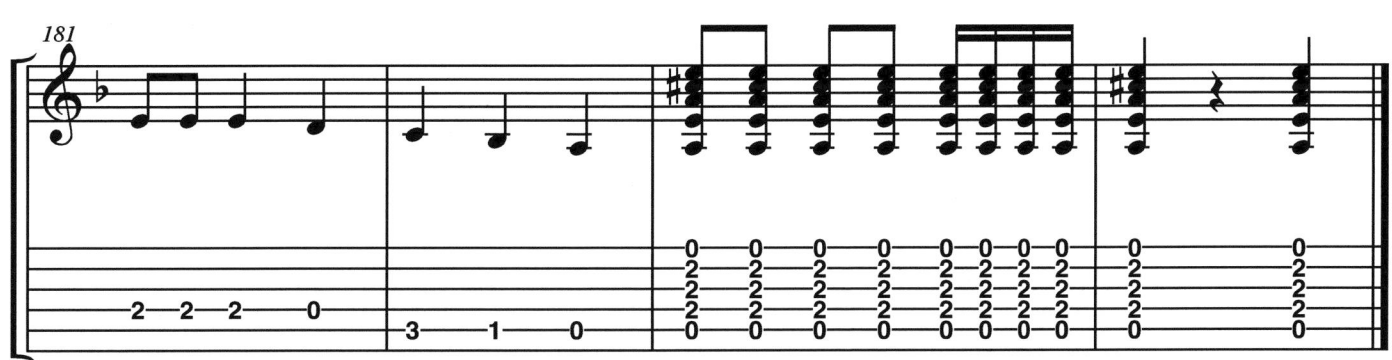

BULERIAS

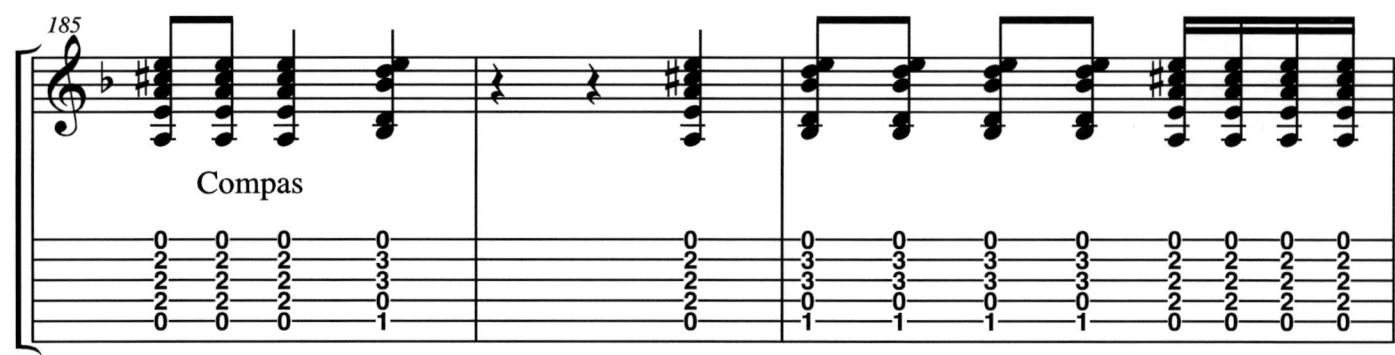

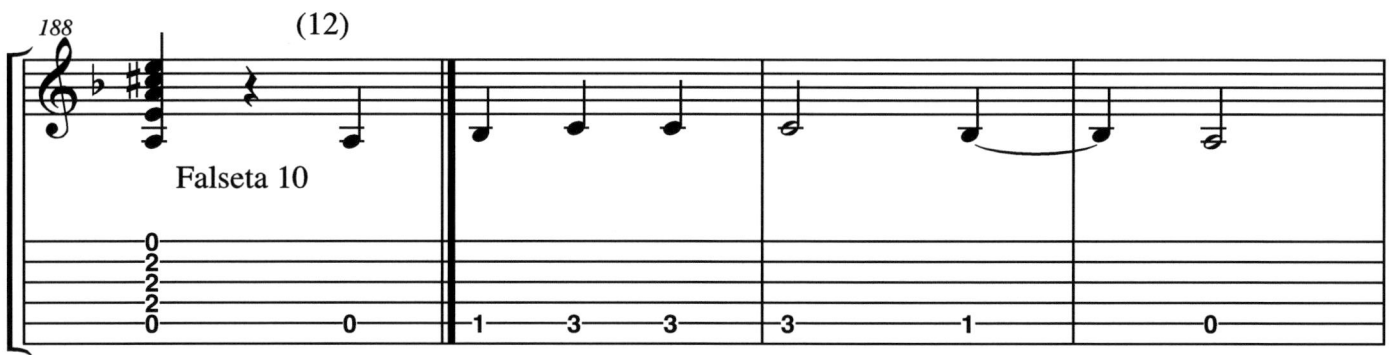

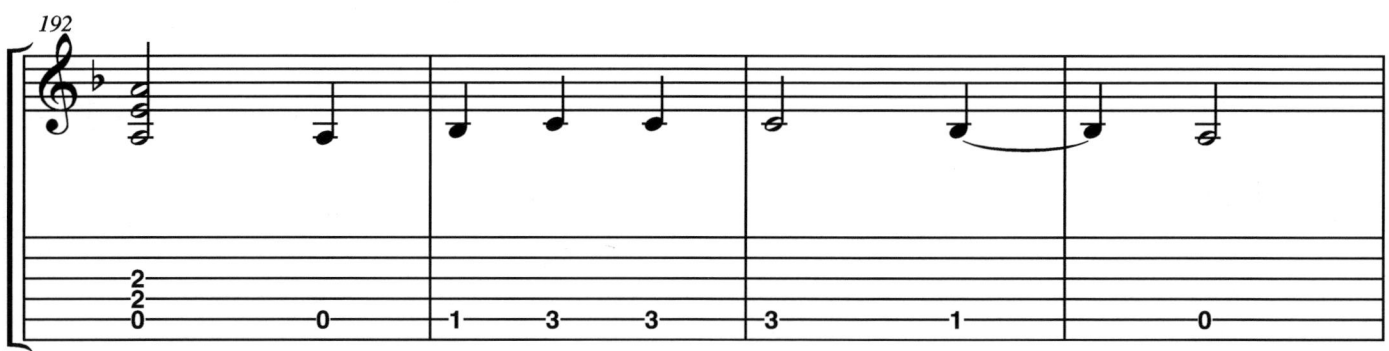

BULERIAS

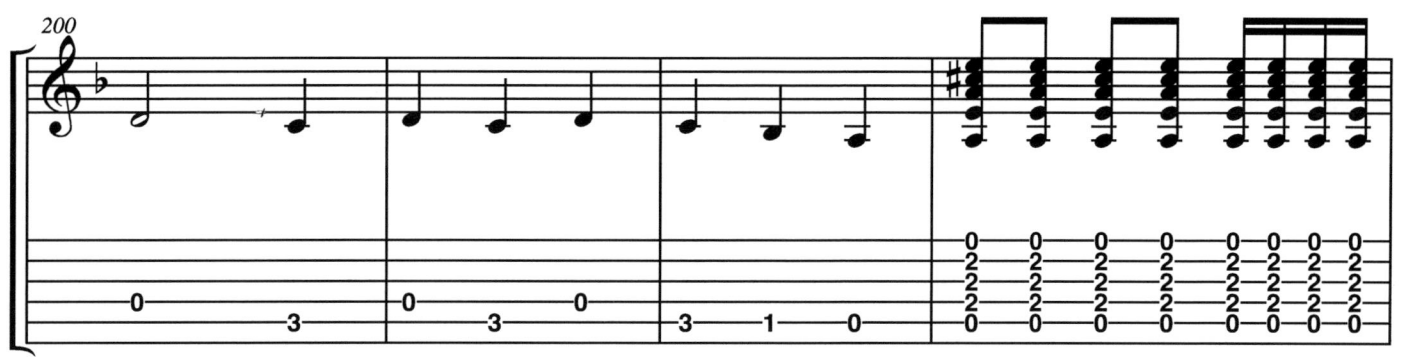
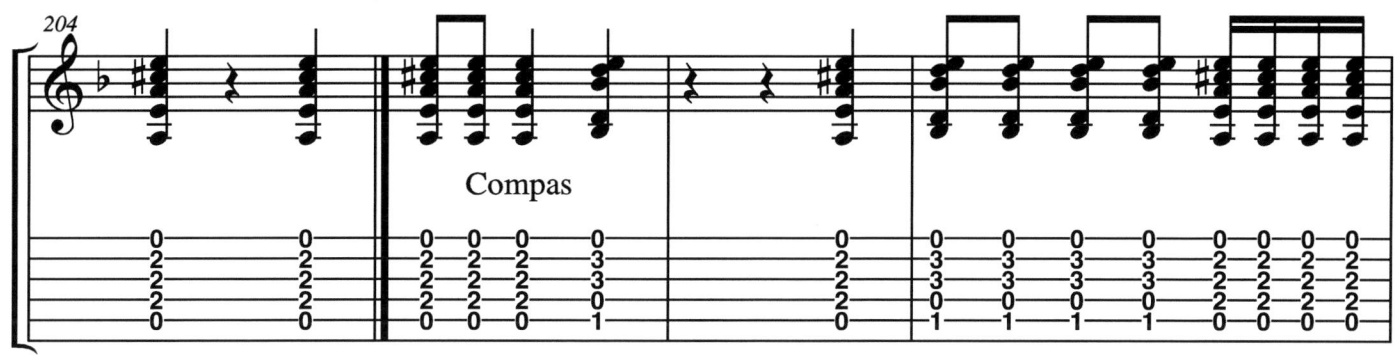

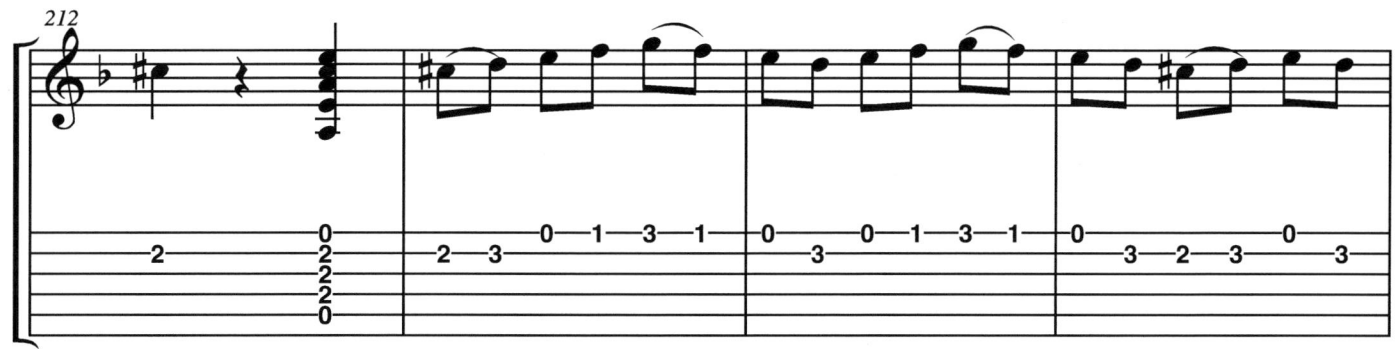

BULERIAS

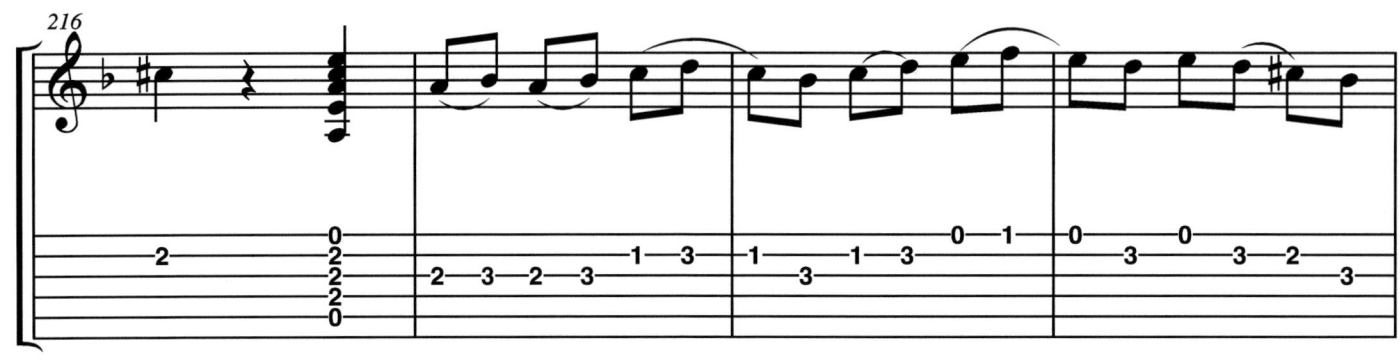
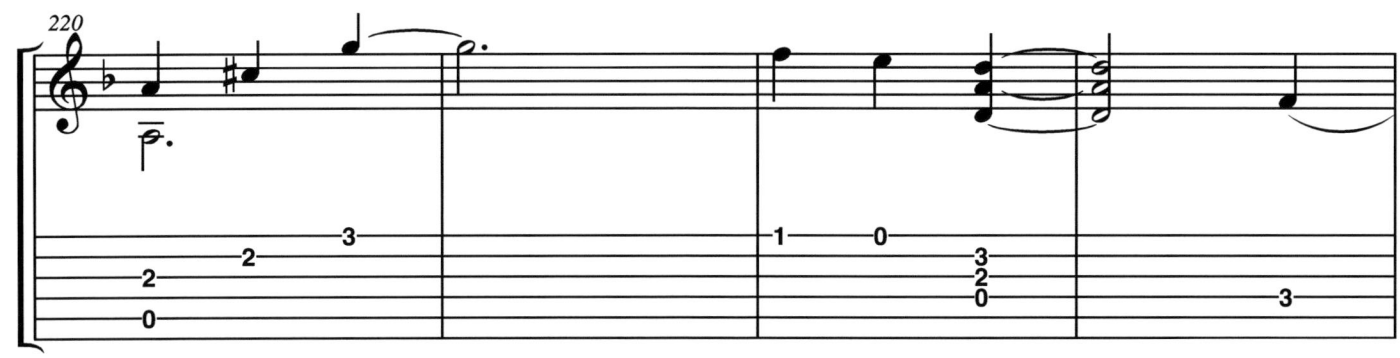
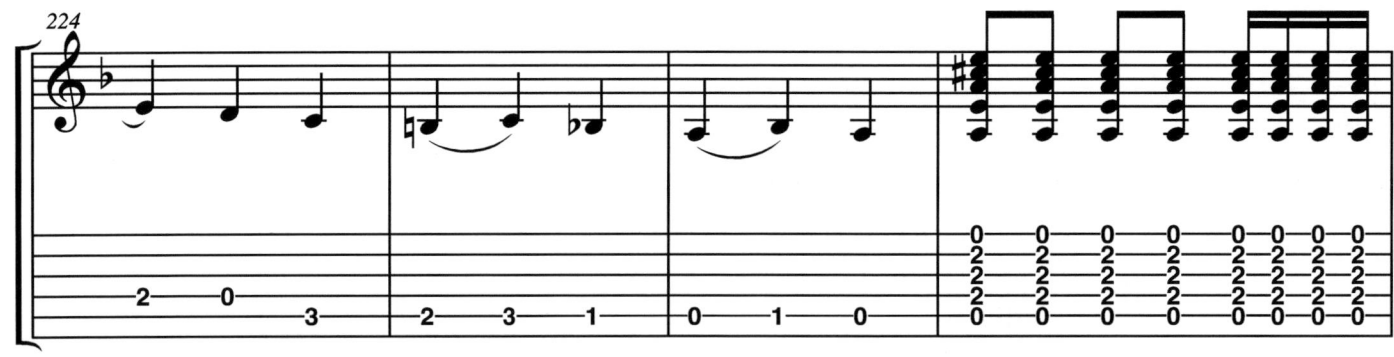
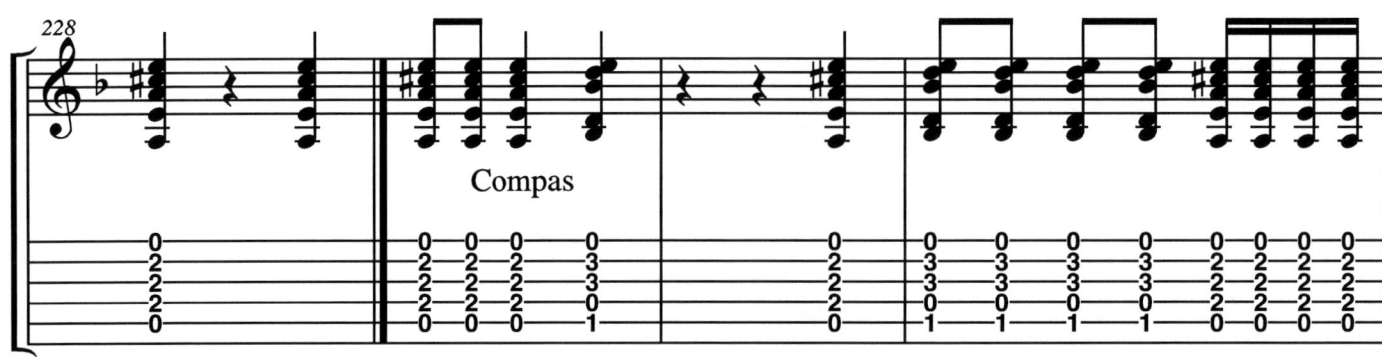

BULERIAS

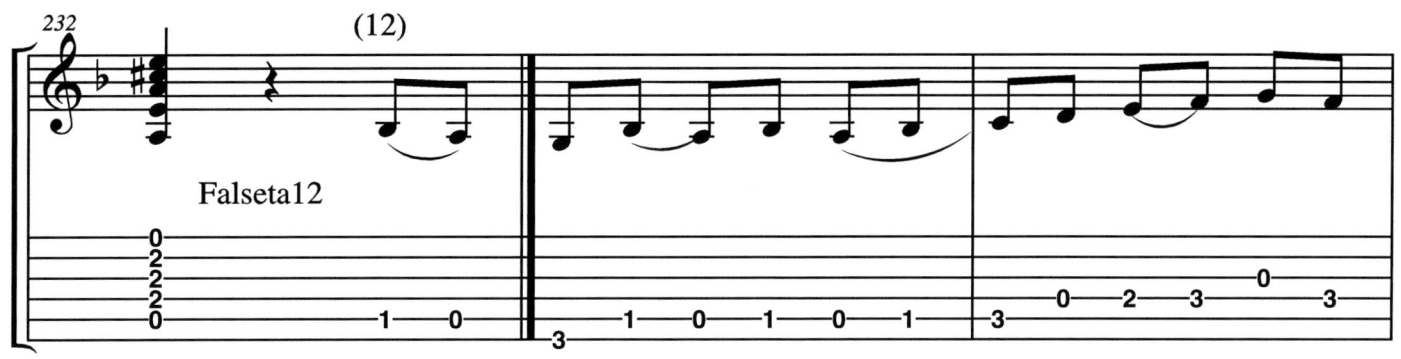
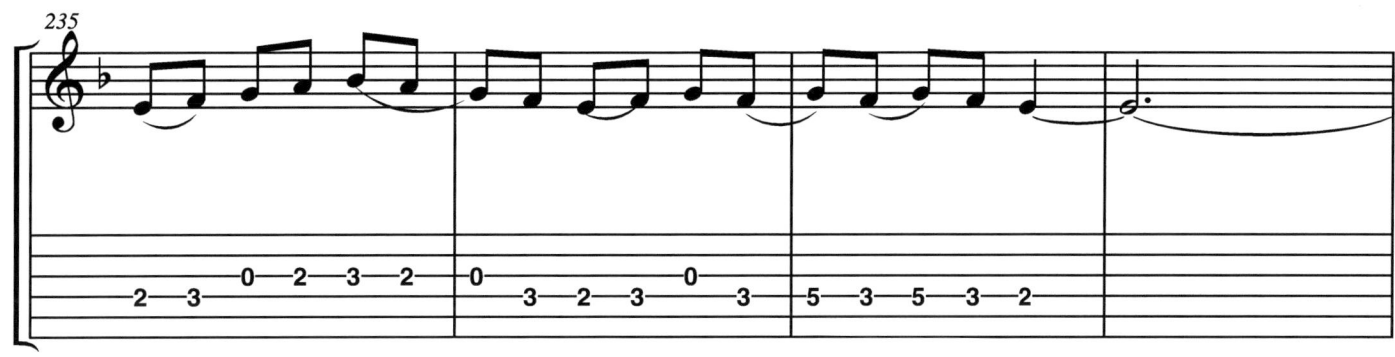
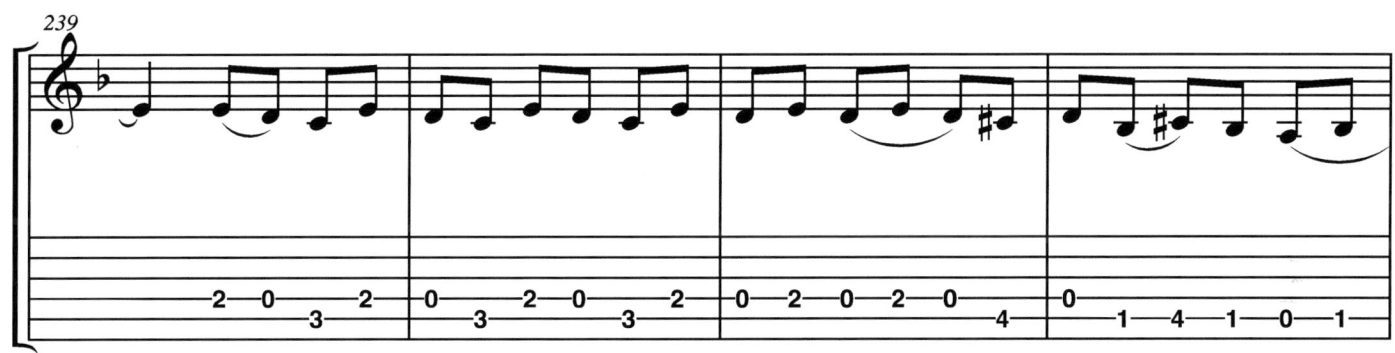

BULERIAS

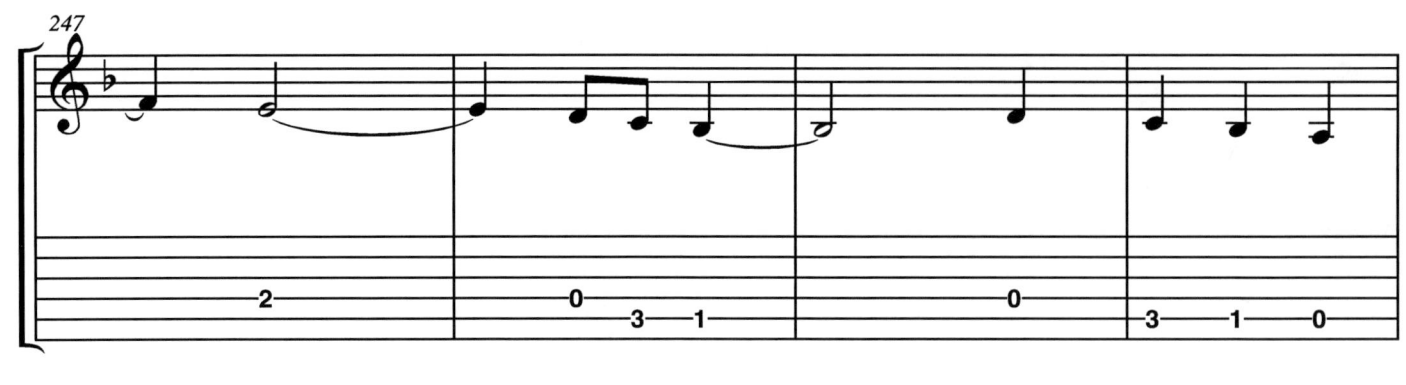

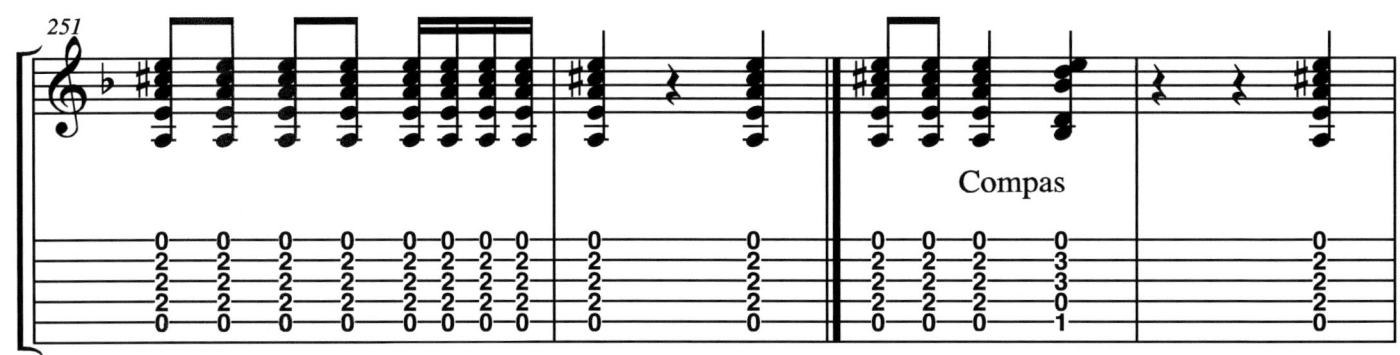

Compas

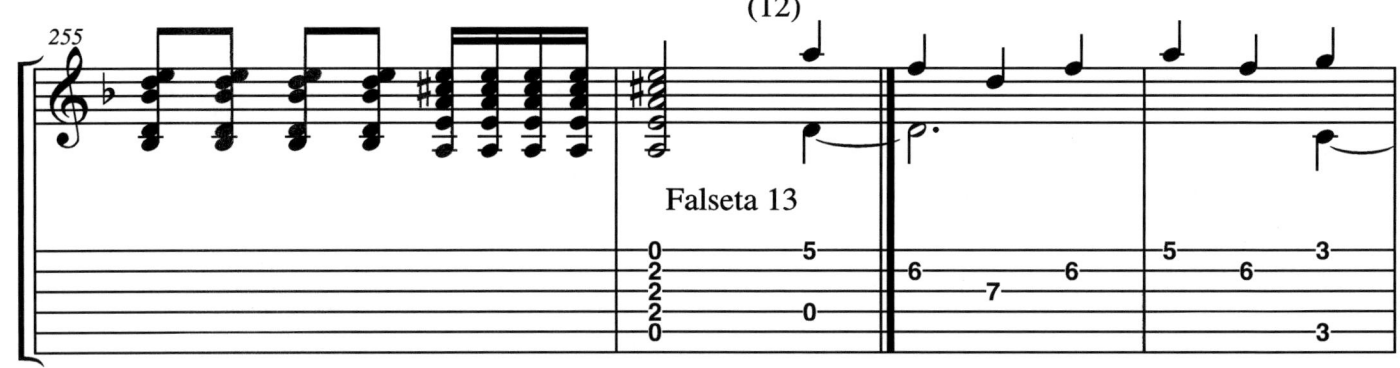

(12)

Falseta 13

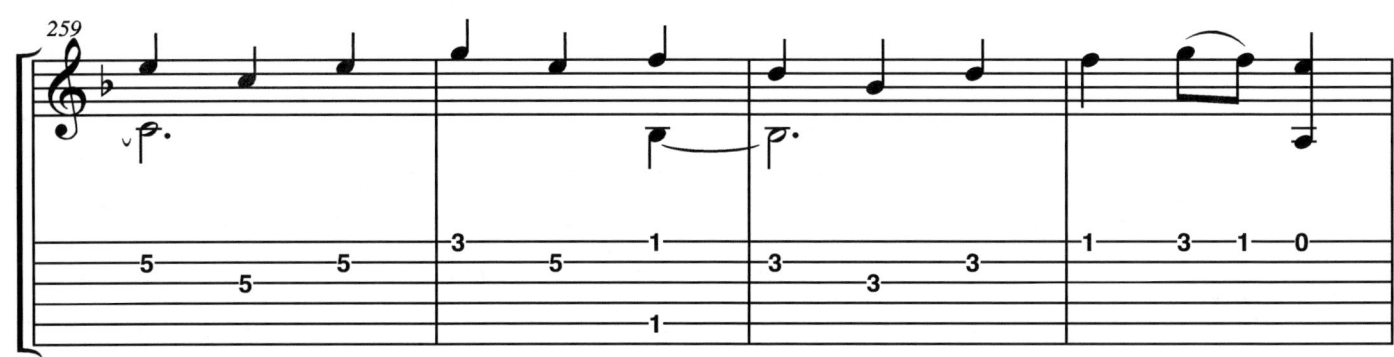

BULERIAS

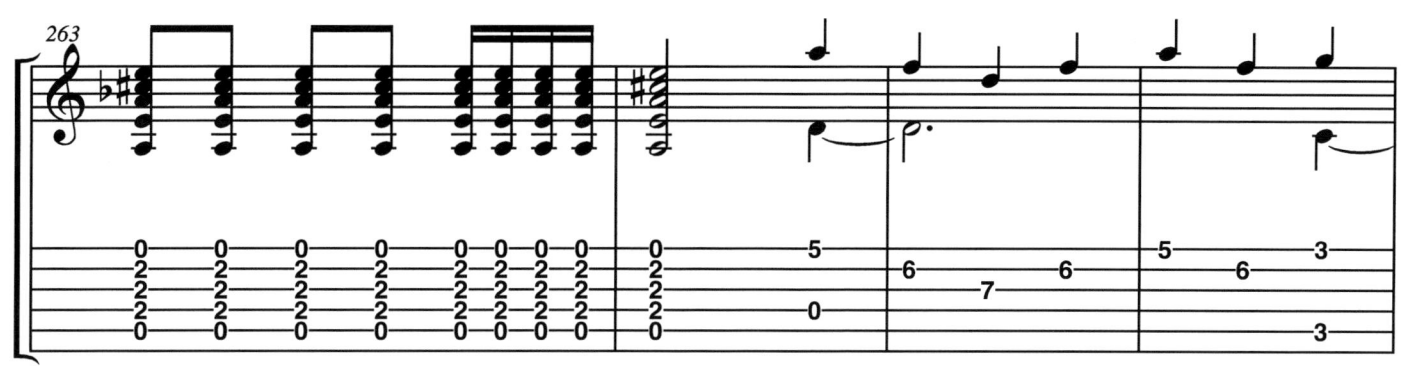
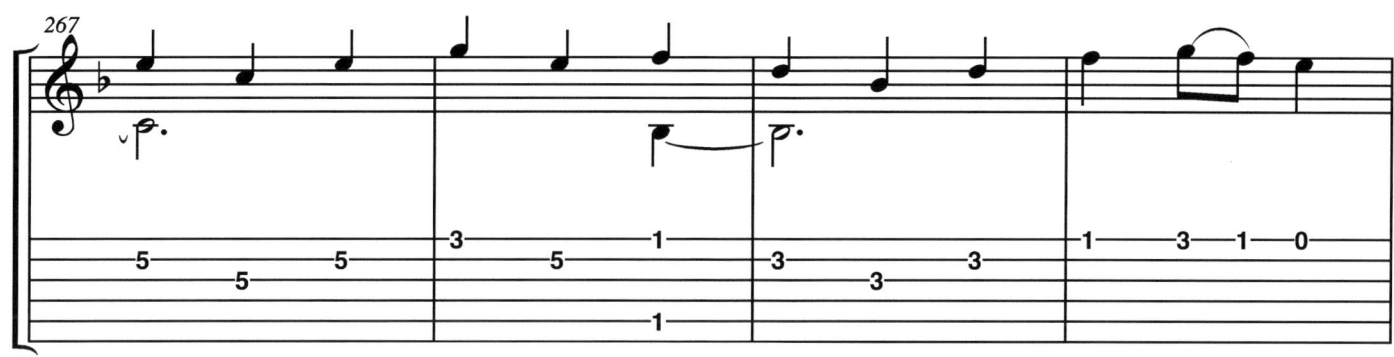
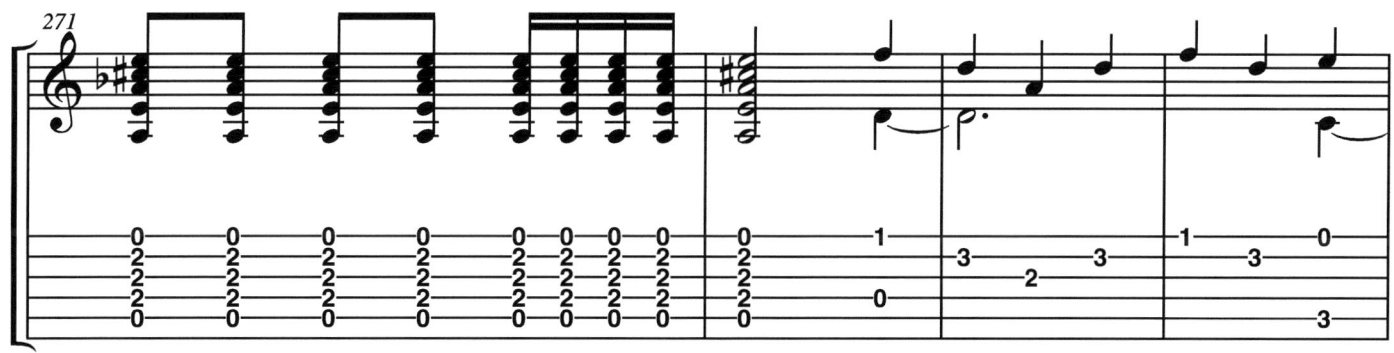
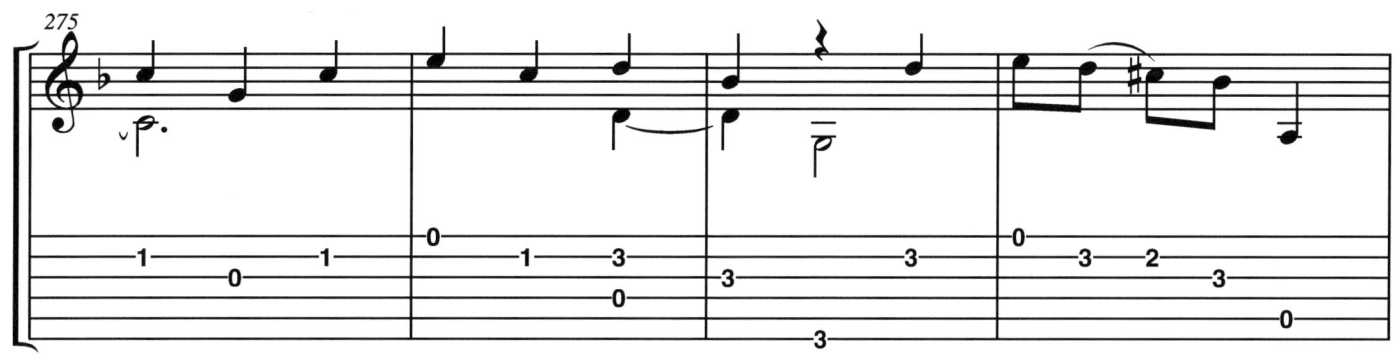

BULERIAS

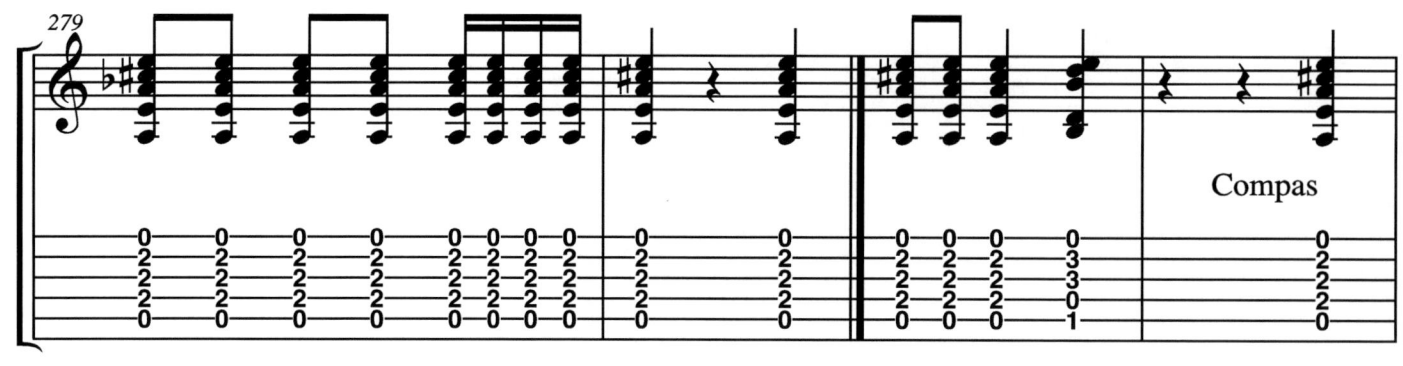

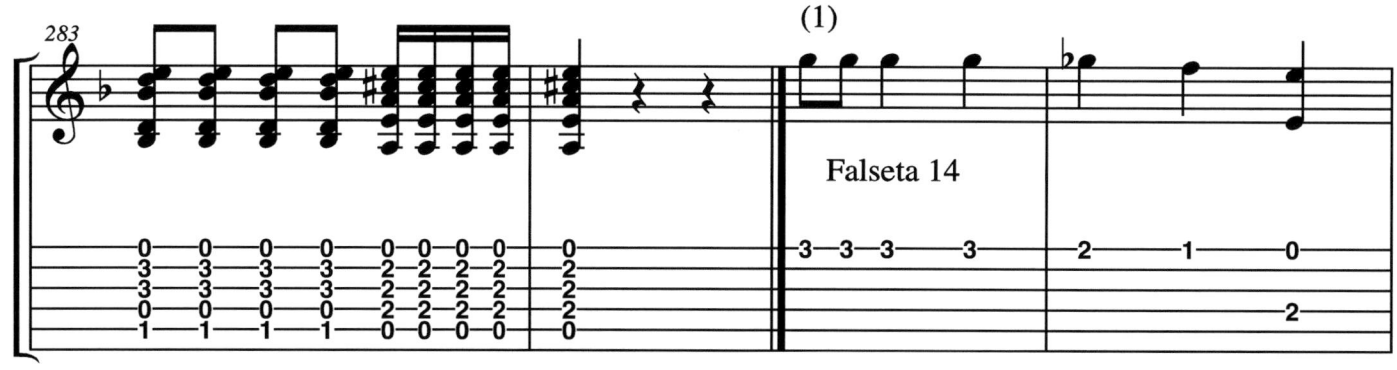

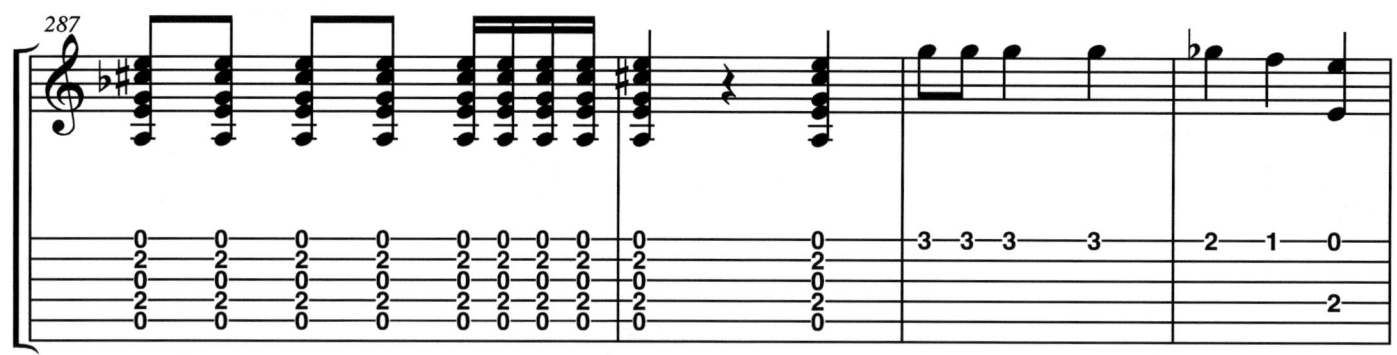

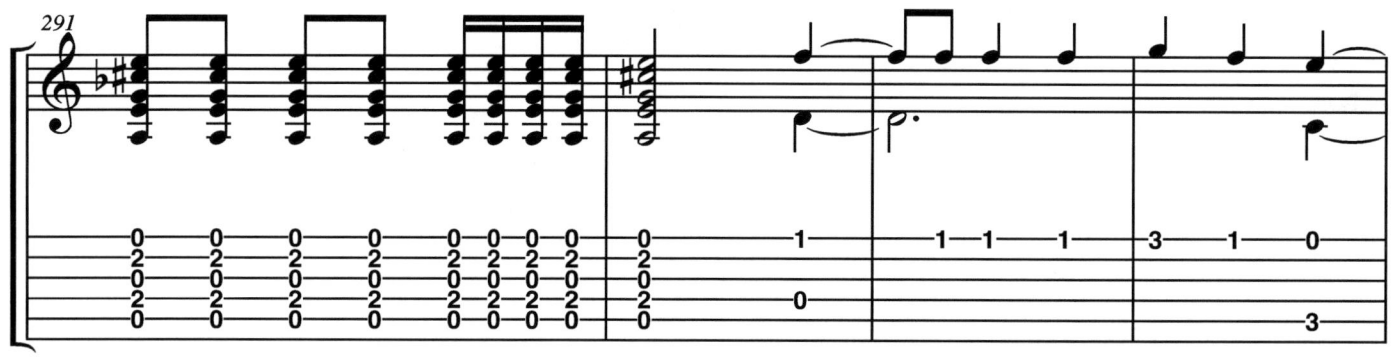

BULERIAS

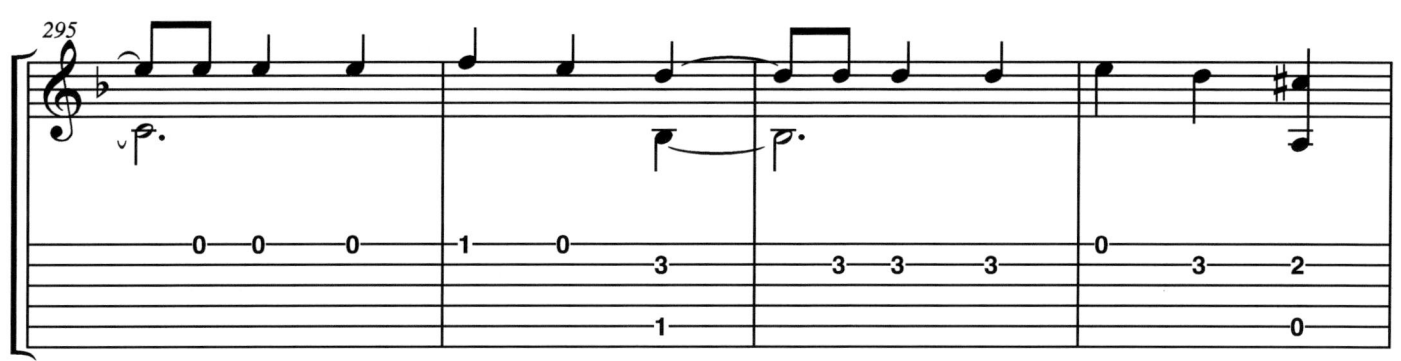
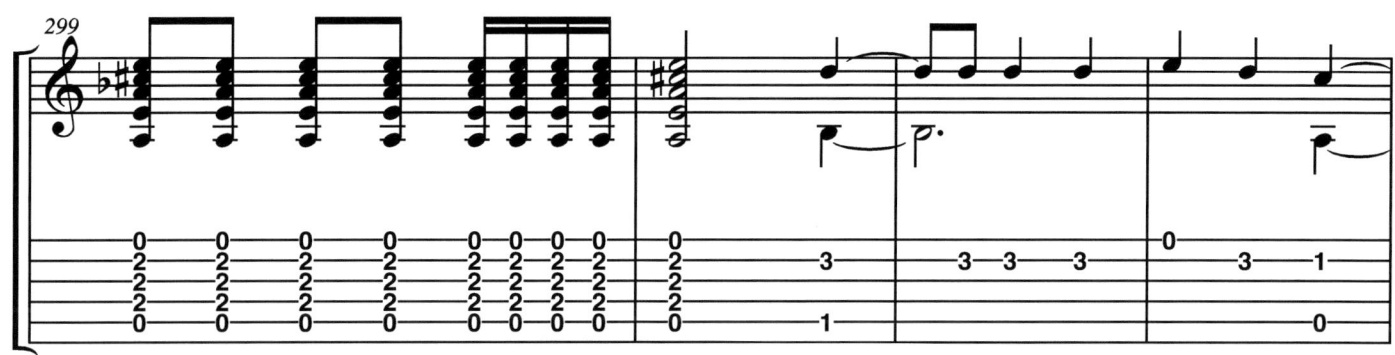
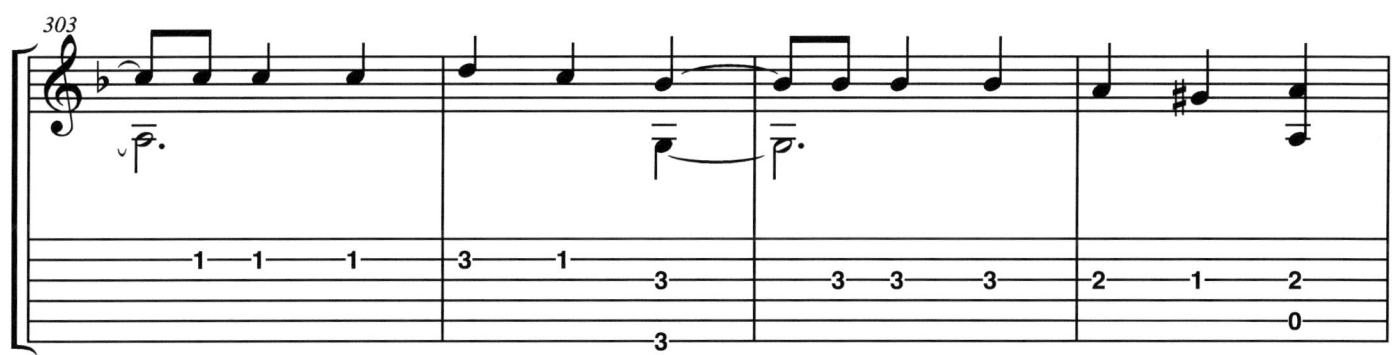
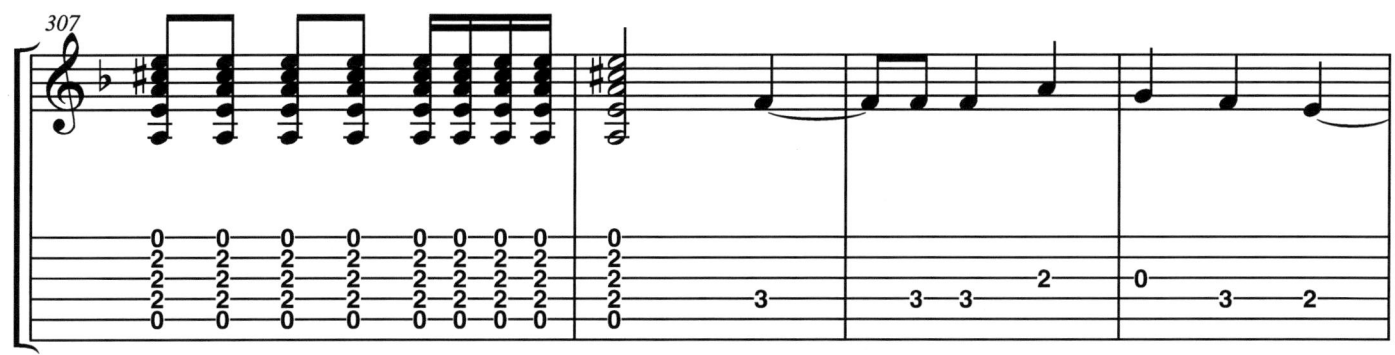

BULERIAS

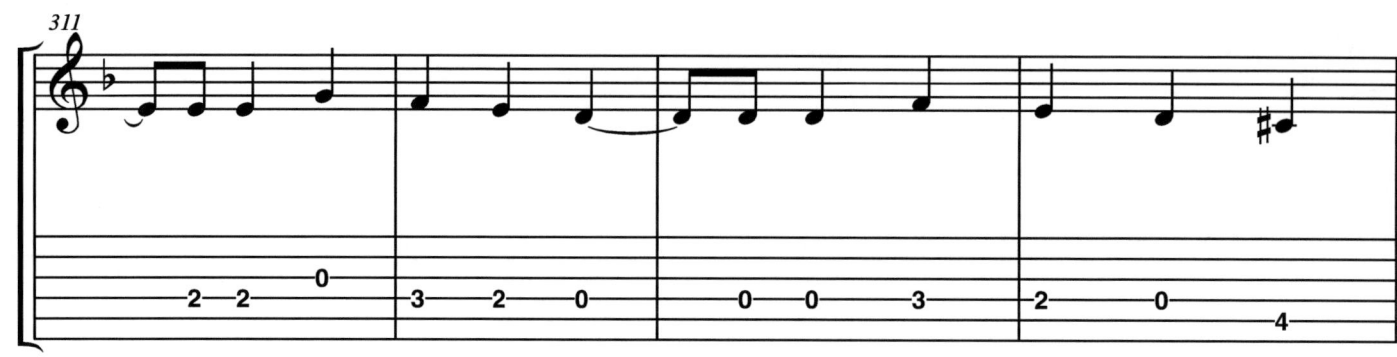
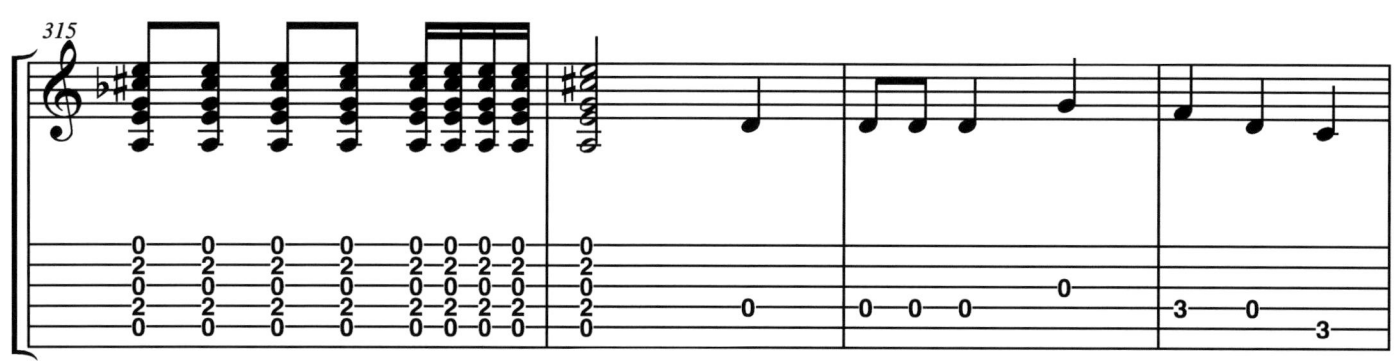

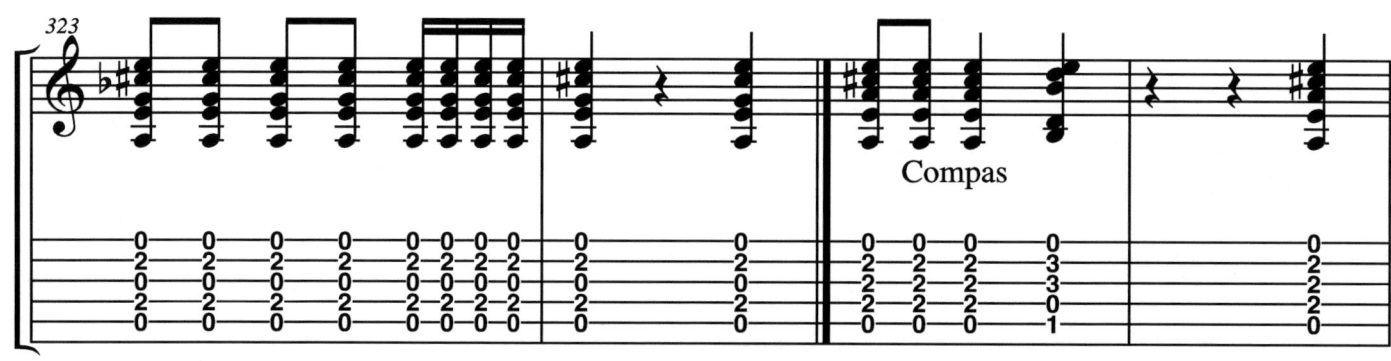

BULERIAS

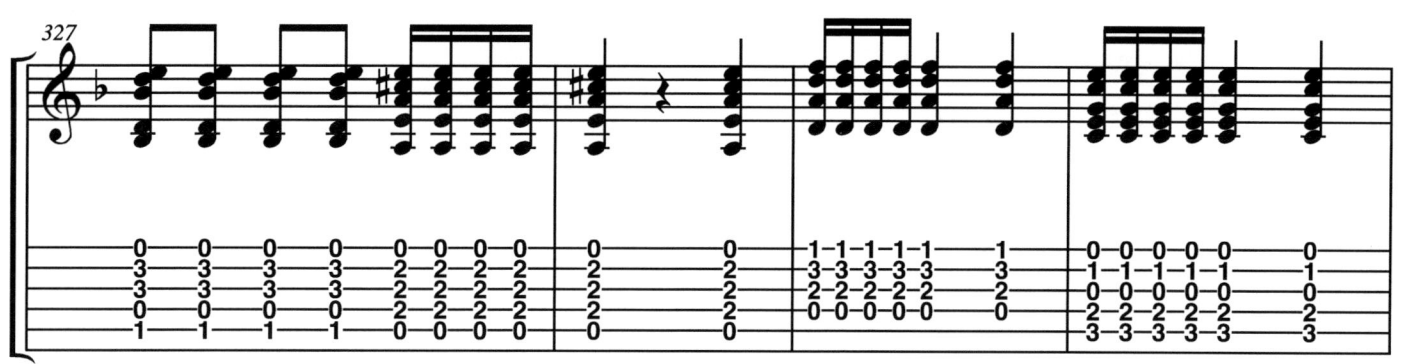
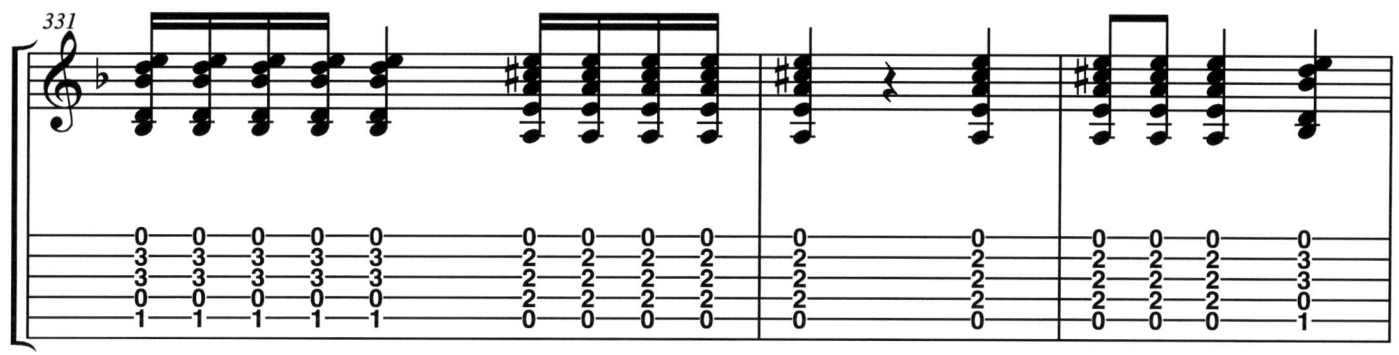
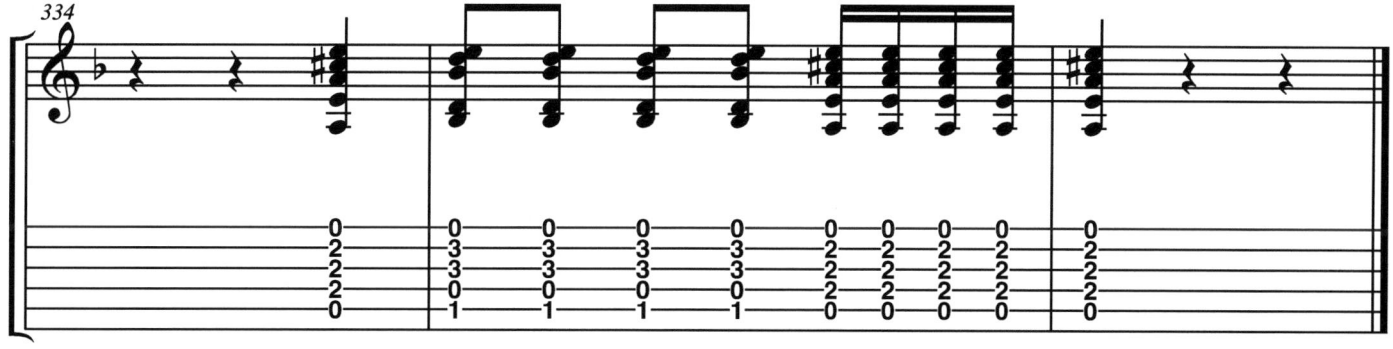

BULERIAS IN A MINOR

The numbers at the beginning of each falseta indicate on what beat the falseta begins

Strum every compas in the same manner

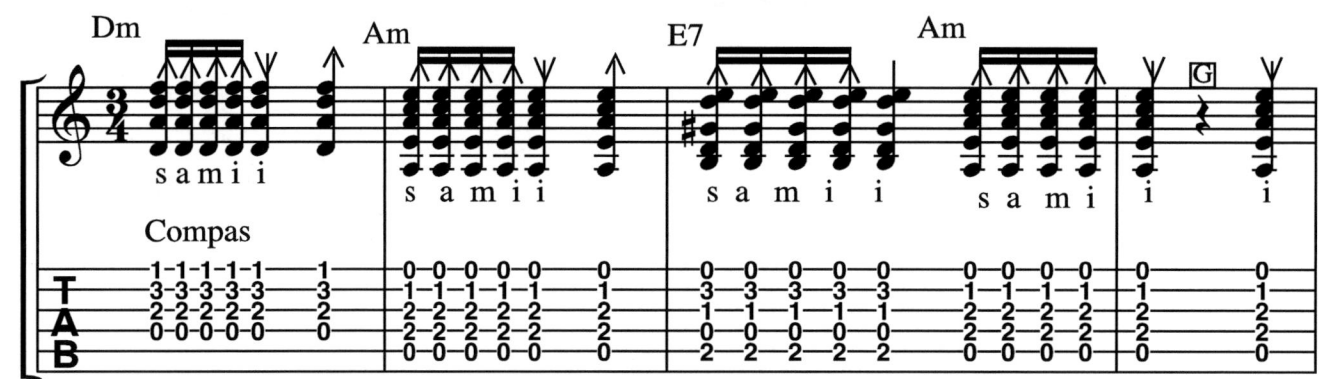

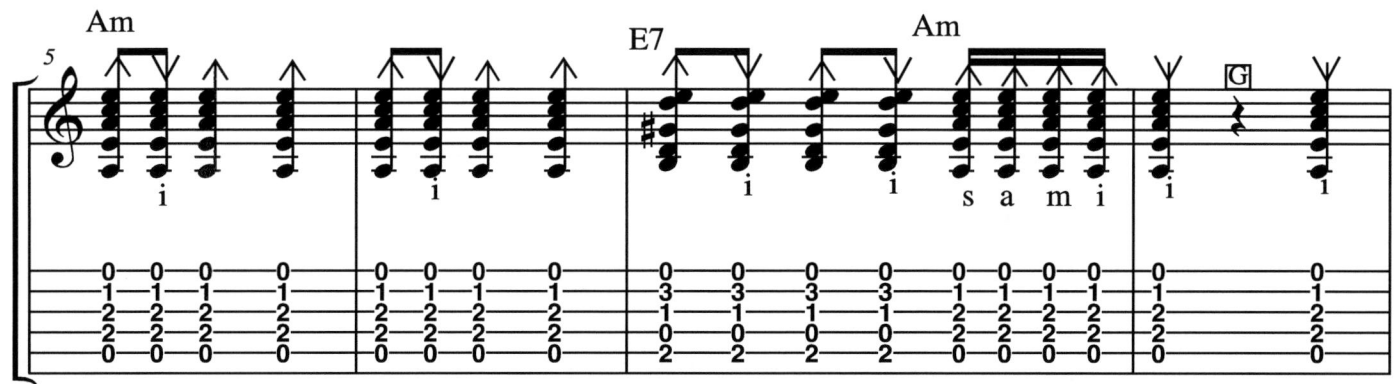

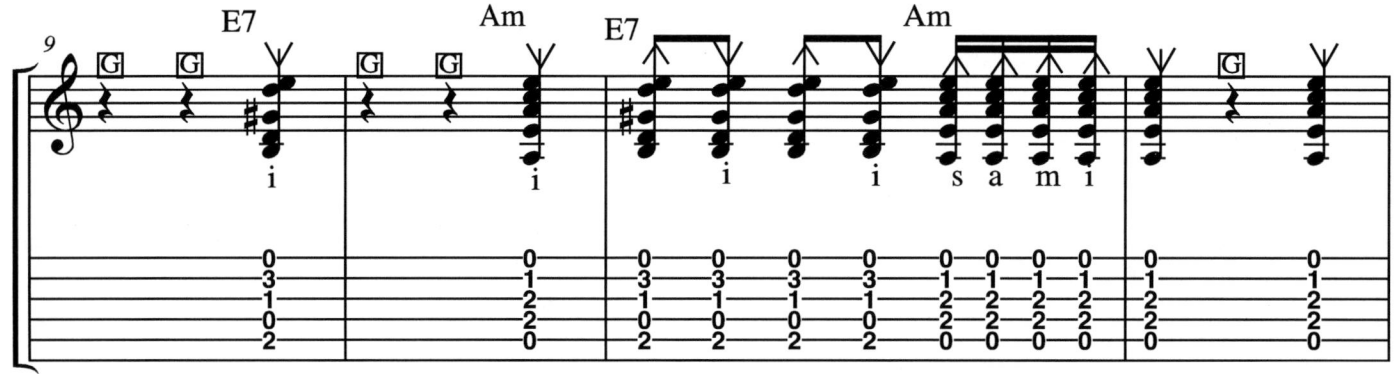

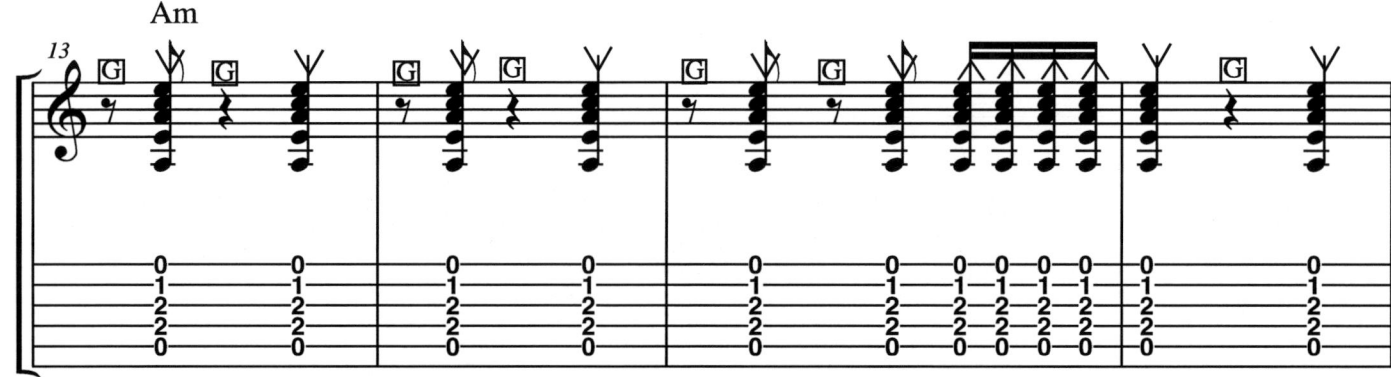

BULERIAS IN A MINOR

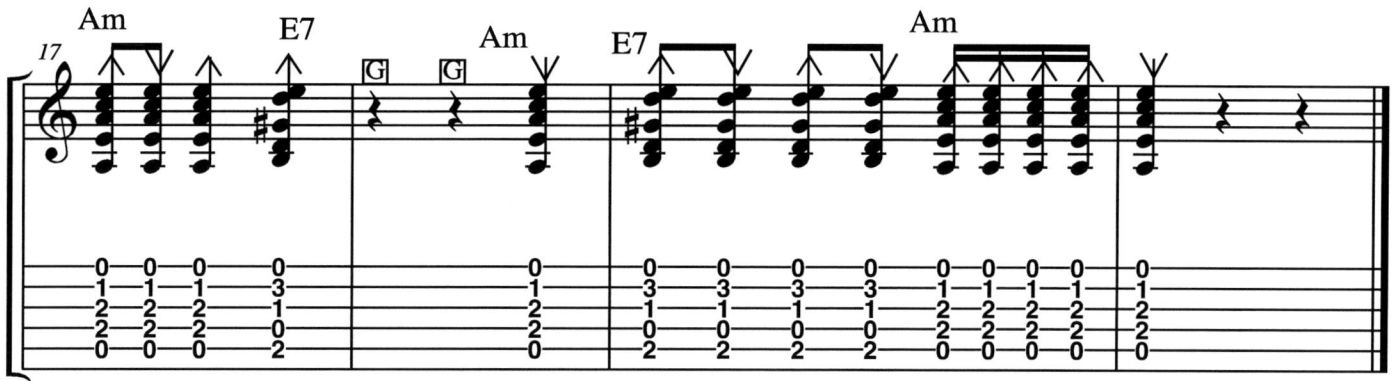
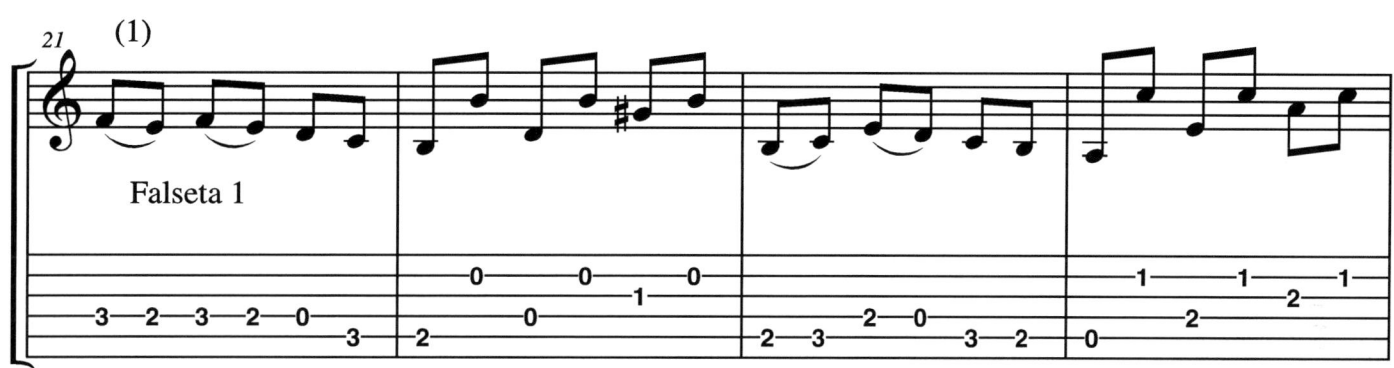
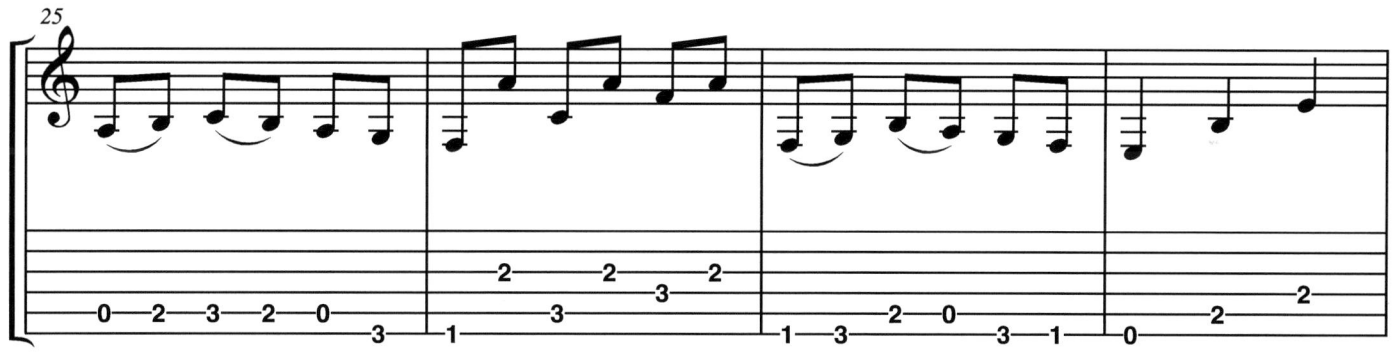
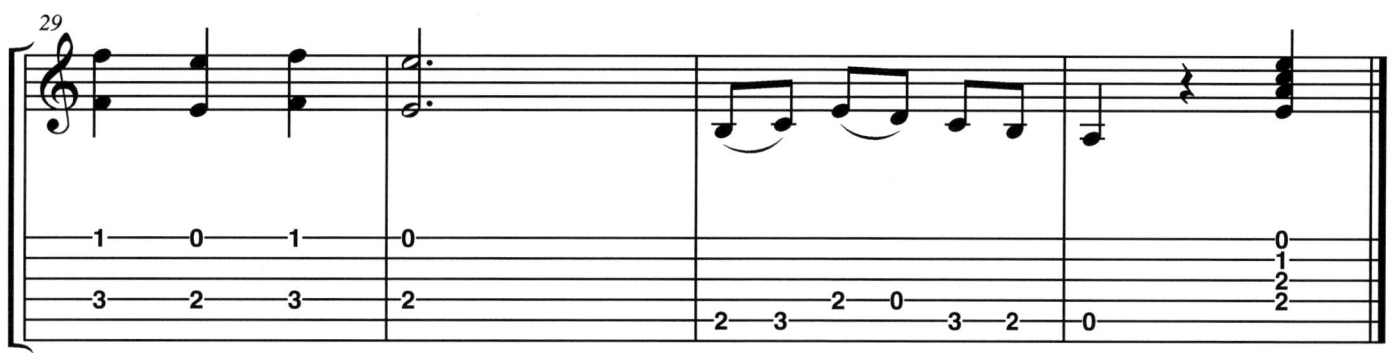

BULERIAS IN A MINOR

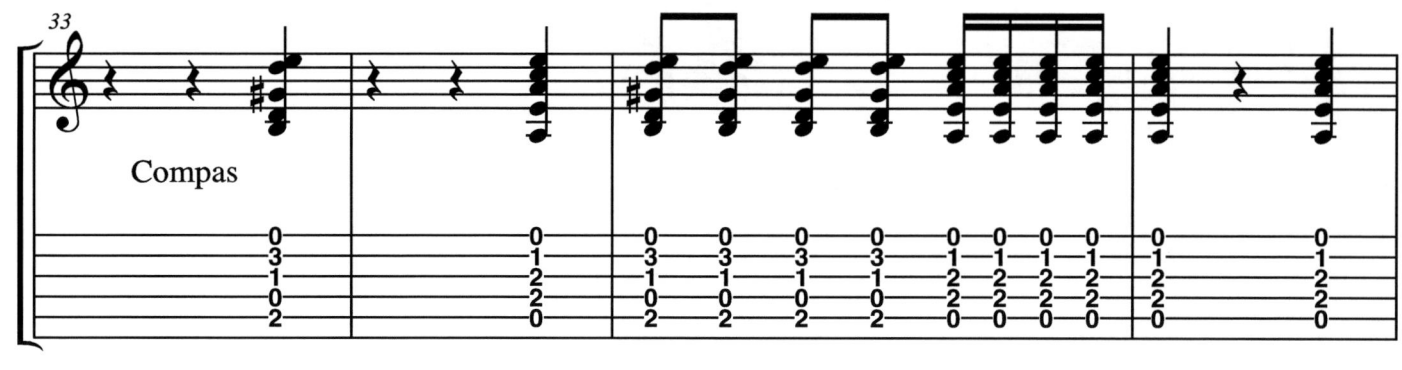

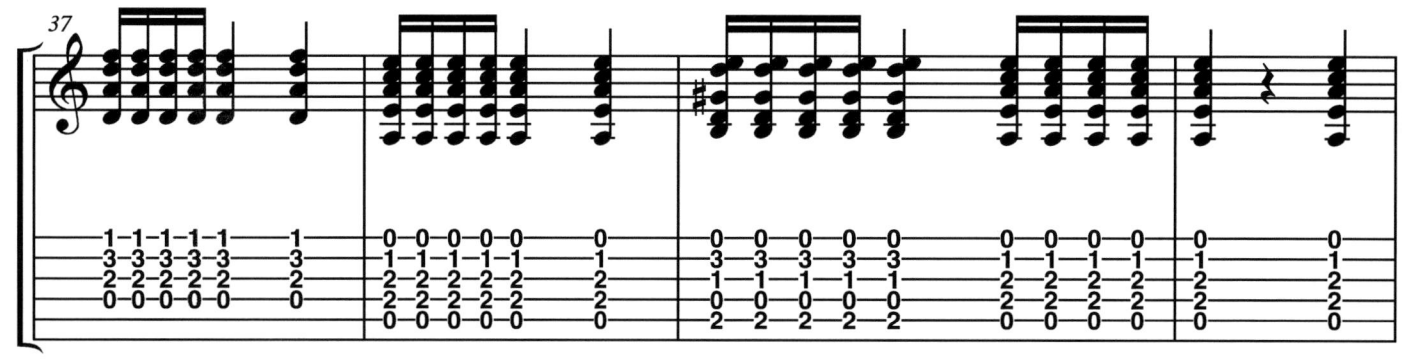

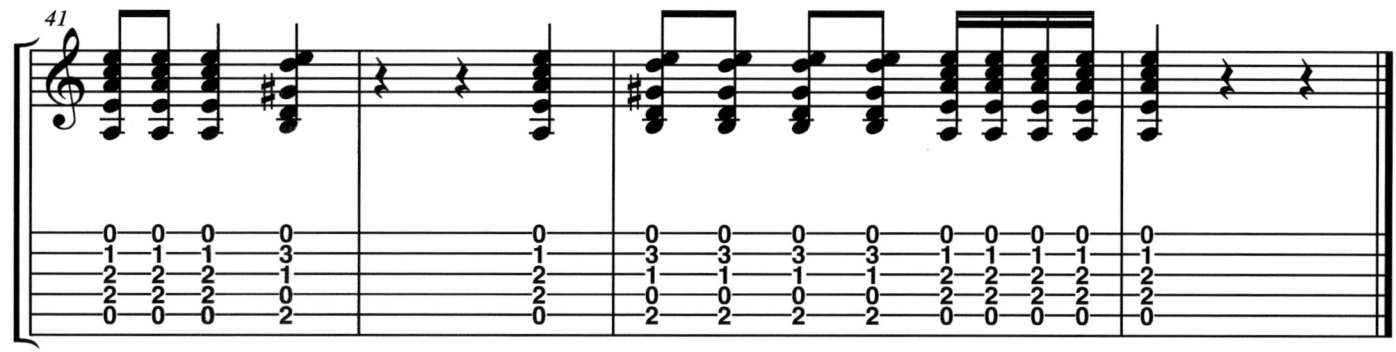

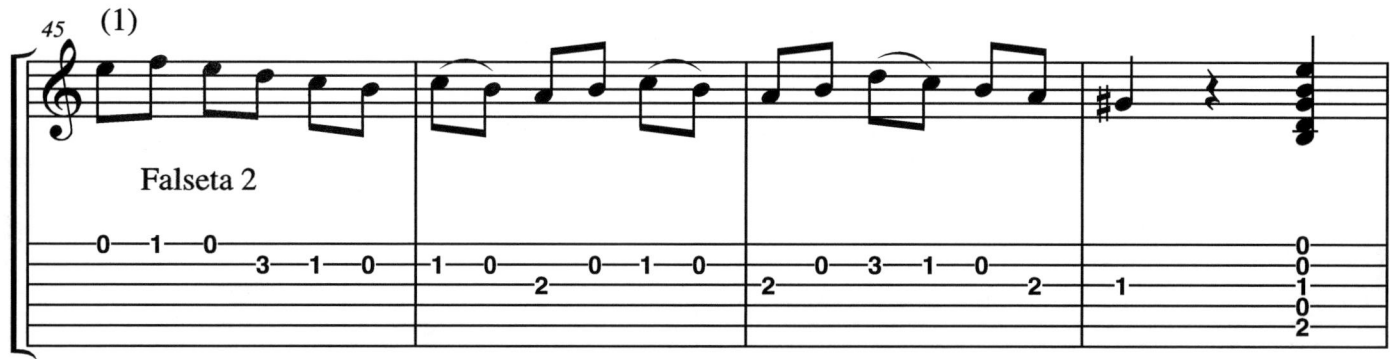

BULERIAS IN A MINOR

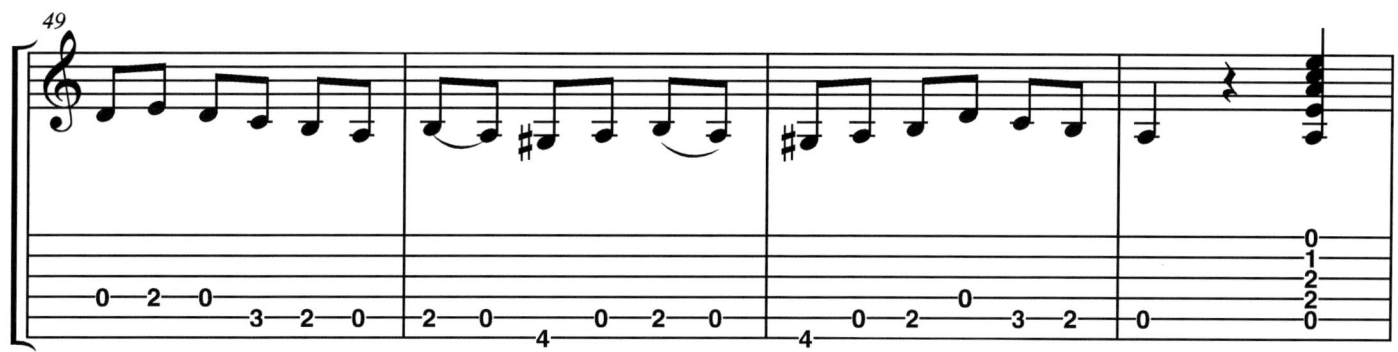

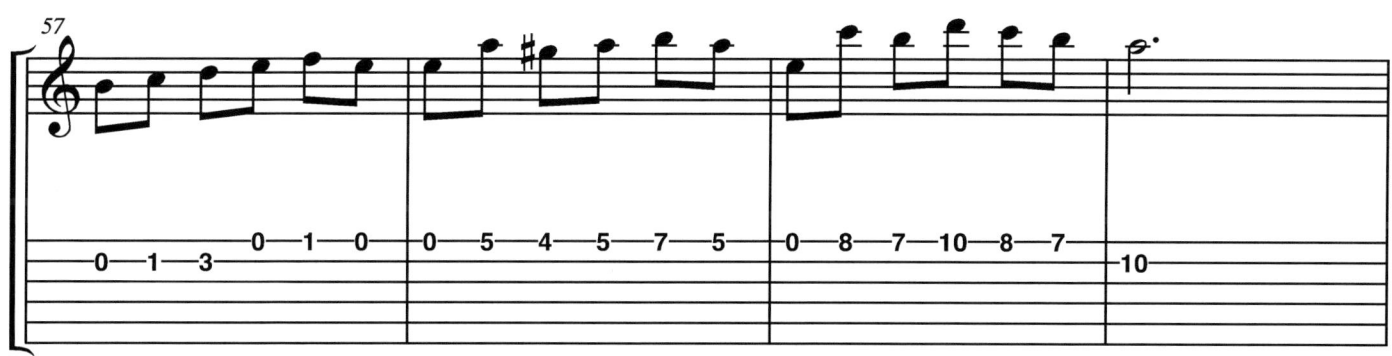

BULERIAS IN A MINOR

Compas

BULERIAS IN A MINOR

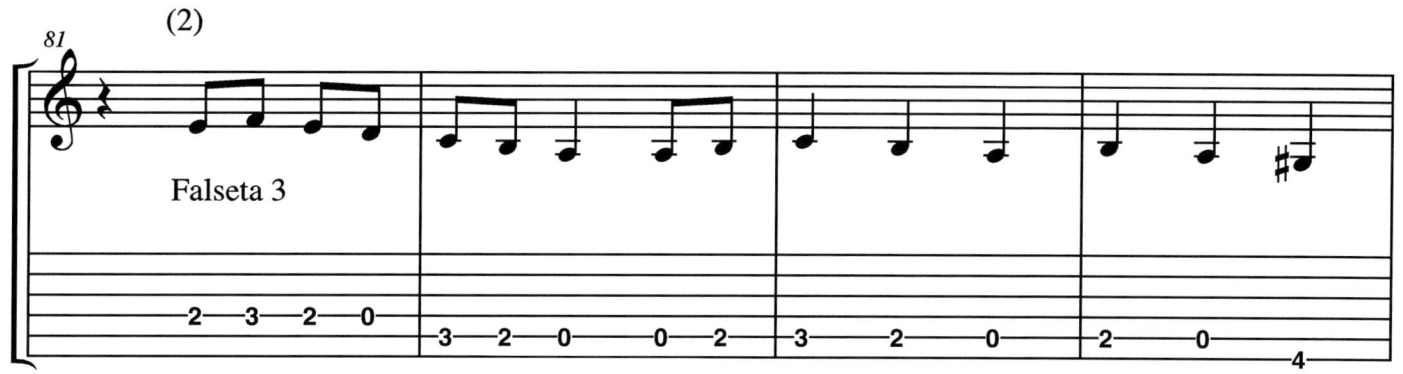

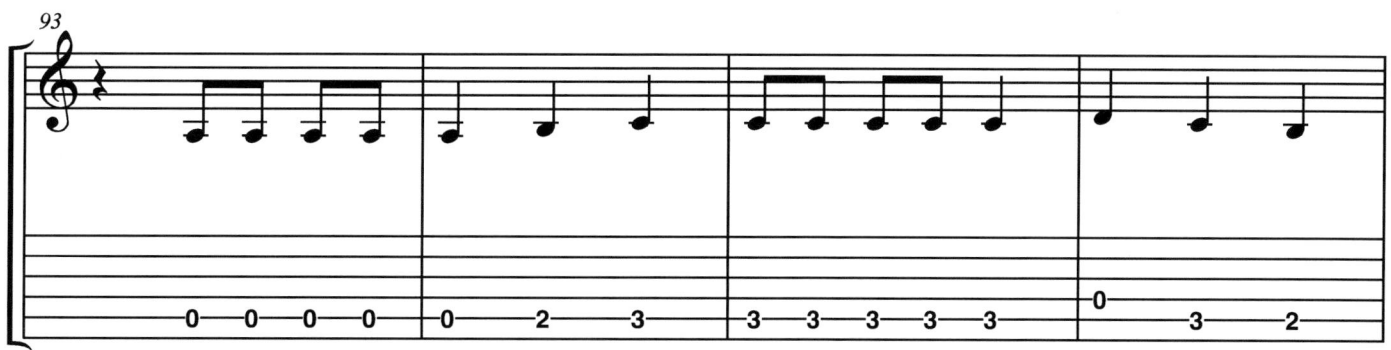

BULERIAS IN A MINOR

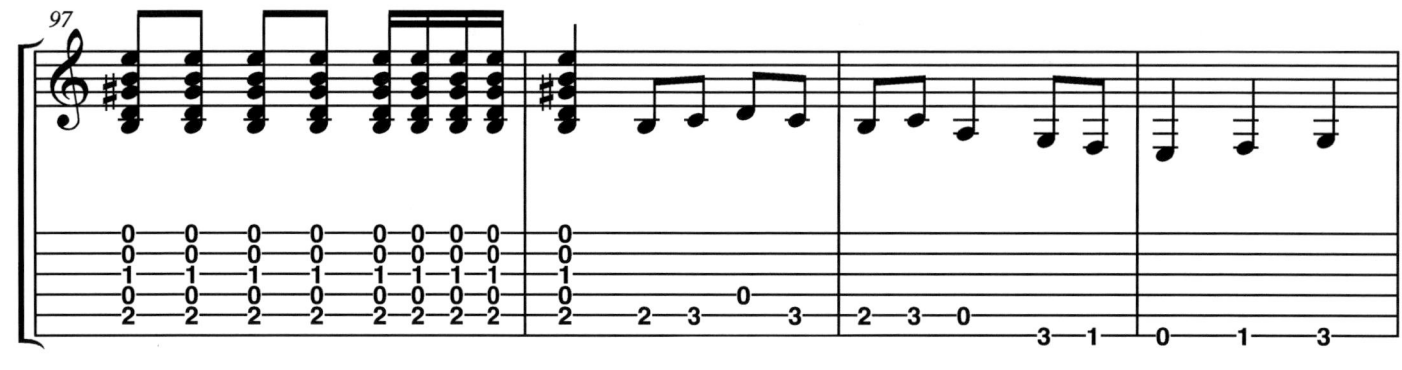
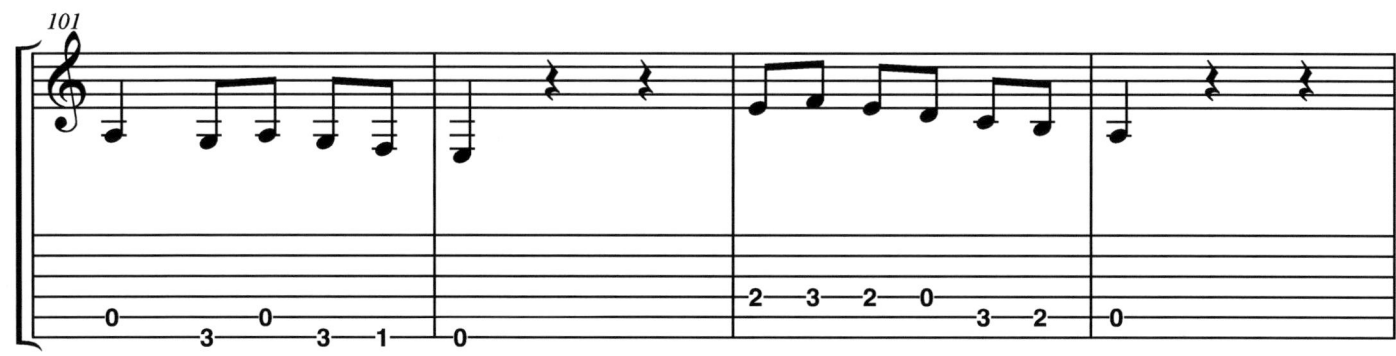
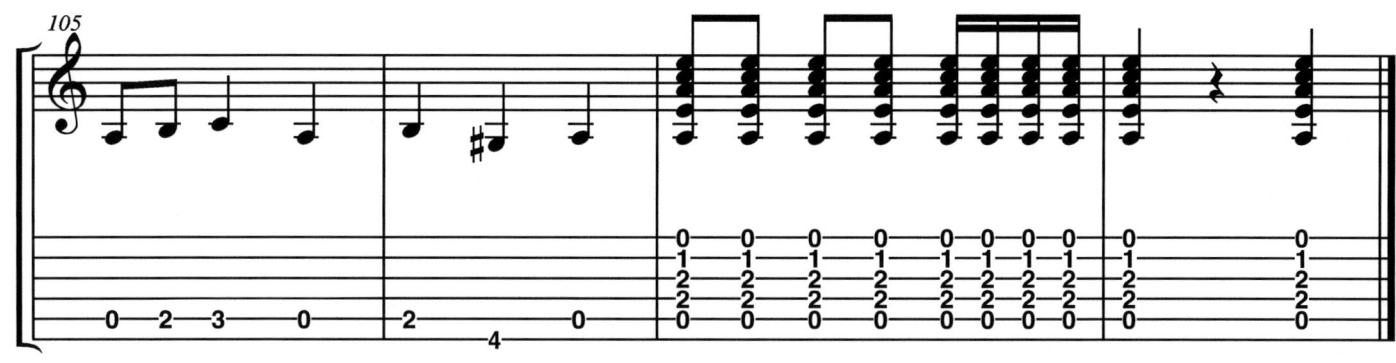
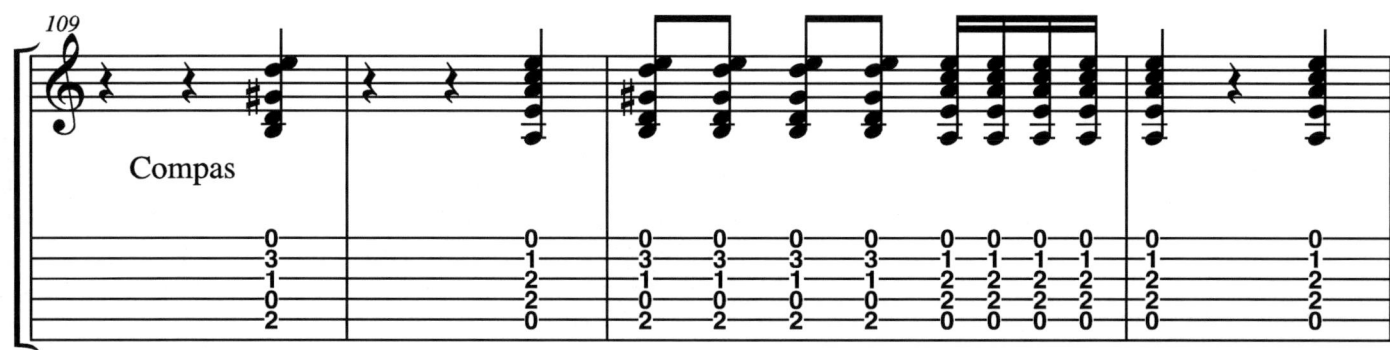

Compas

BULERIAS IN A MINOR

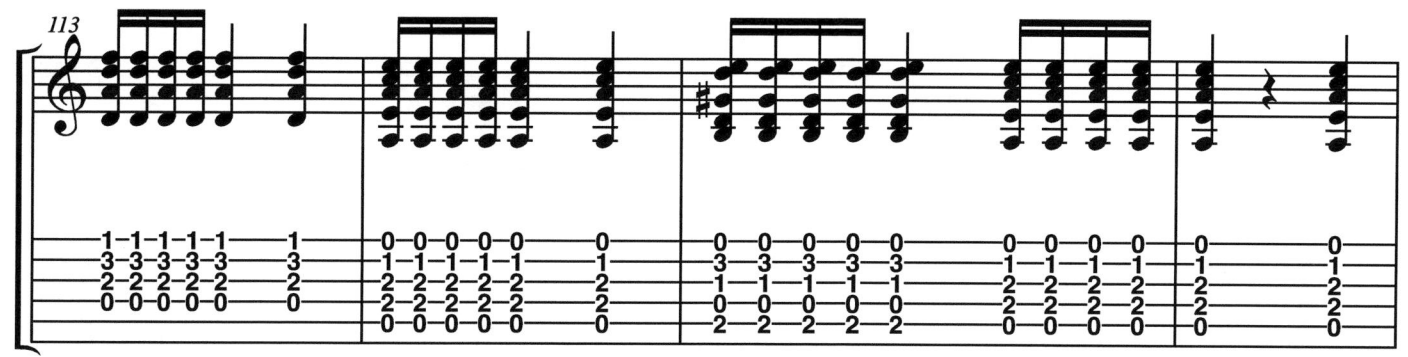
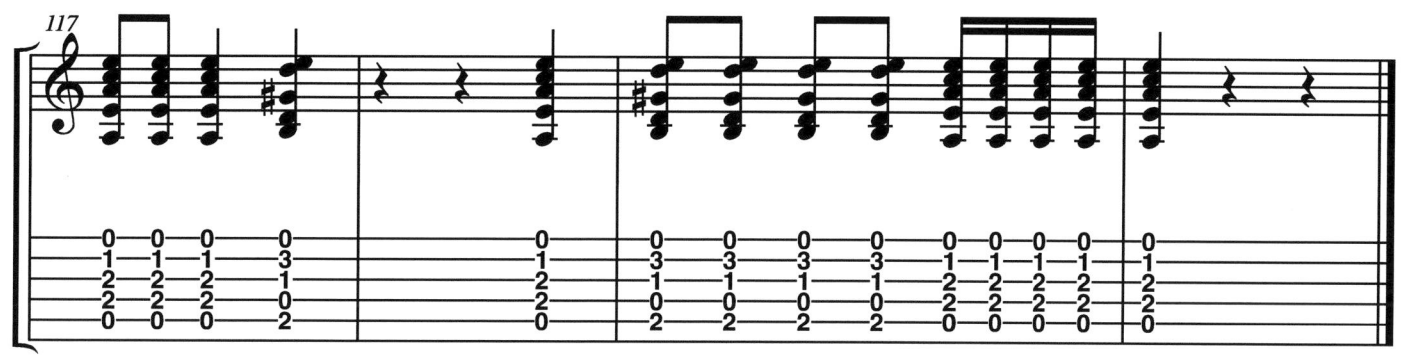

Falseta 4

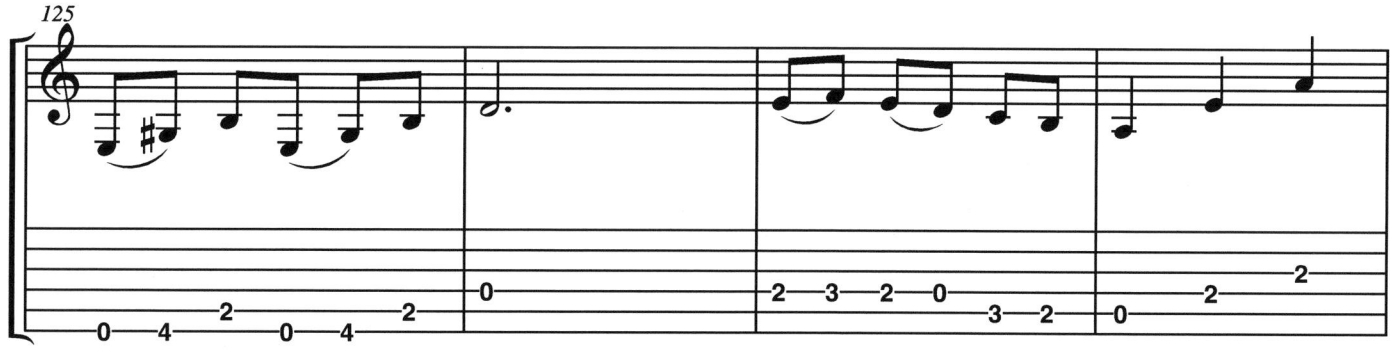

BULERIAS IN A MINOR

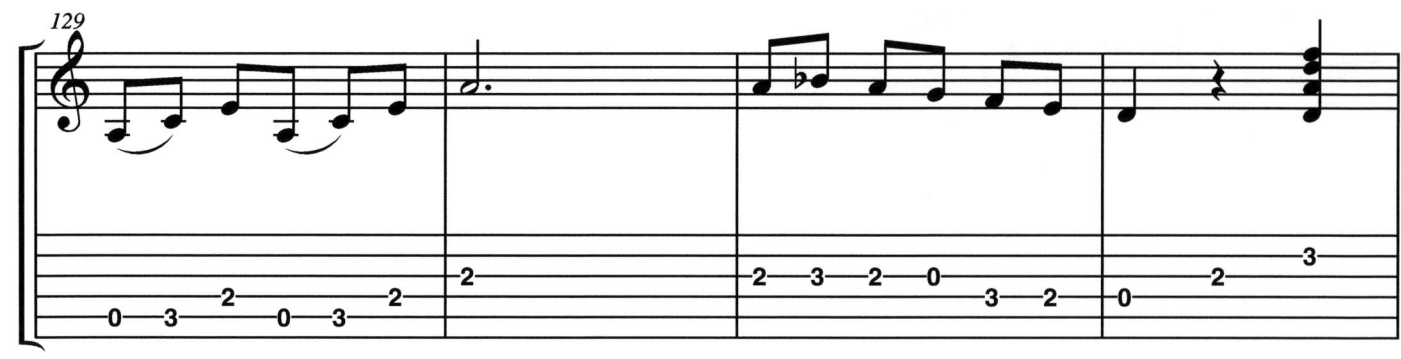

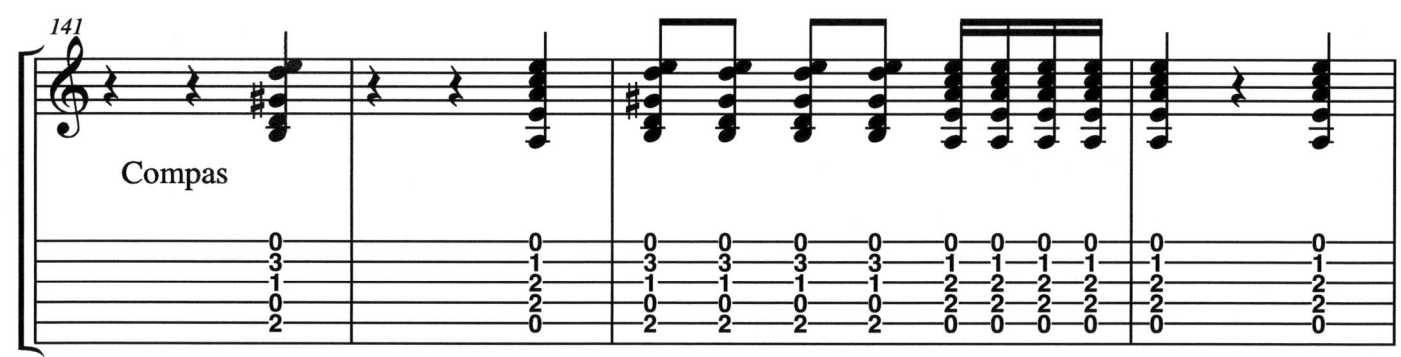

Compas

BULERIAS IN A MINOR

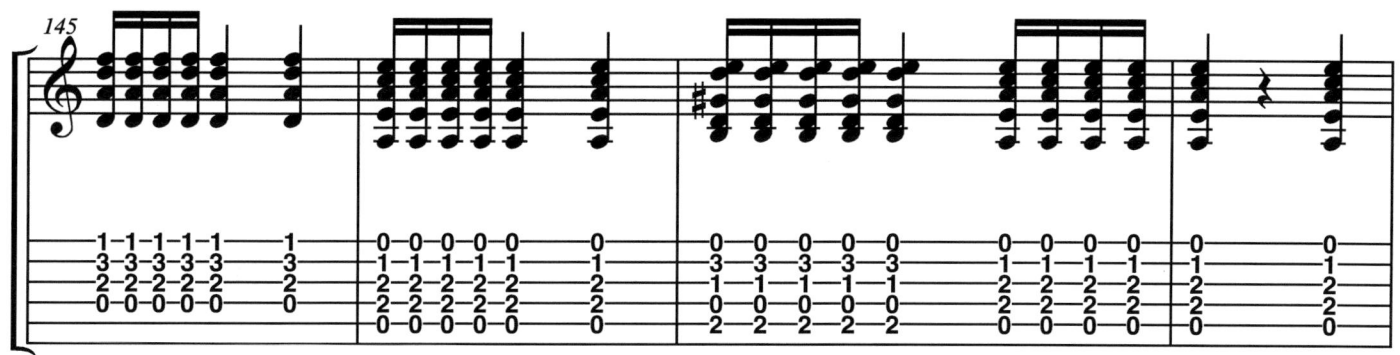

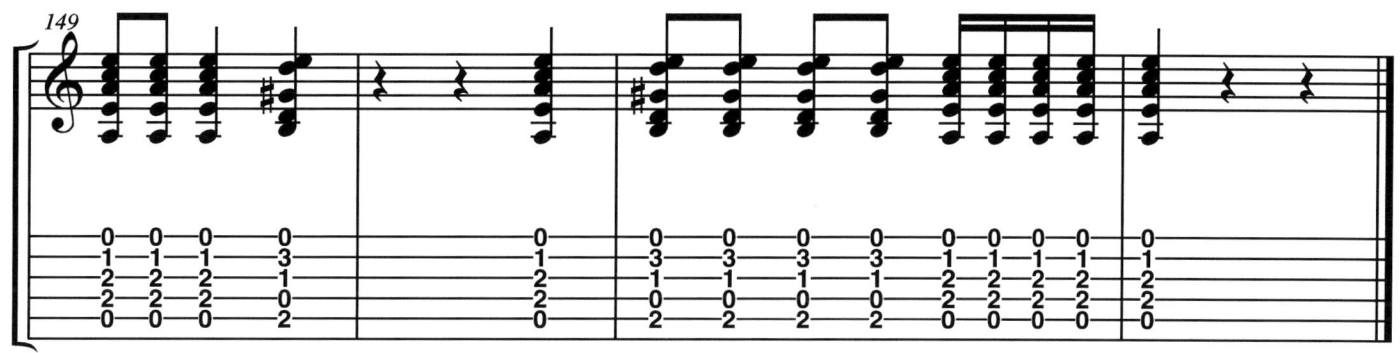

(1)

Falseta 5

BULERIAS IN A MINOR

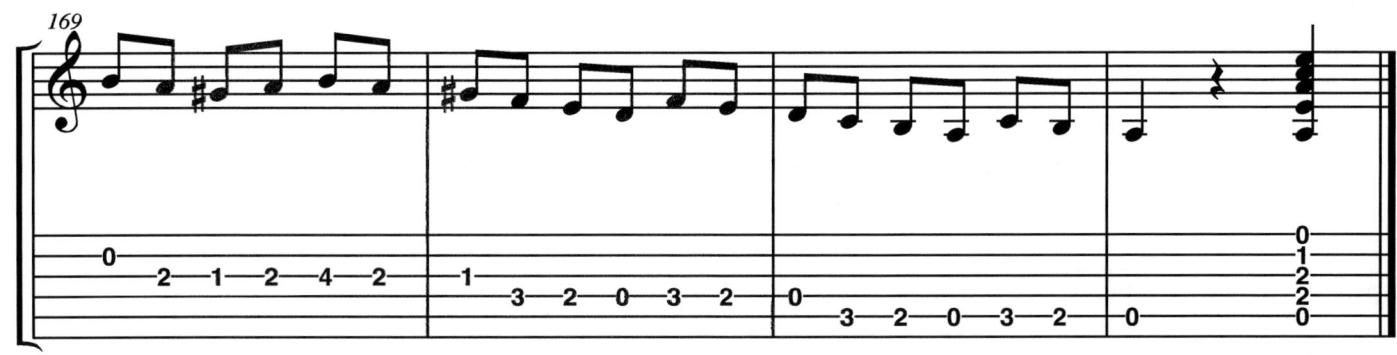
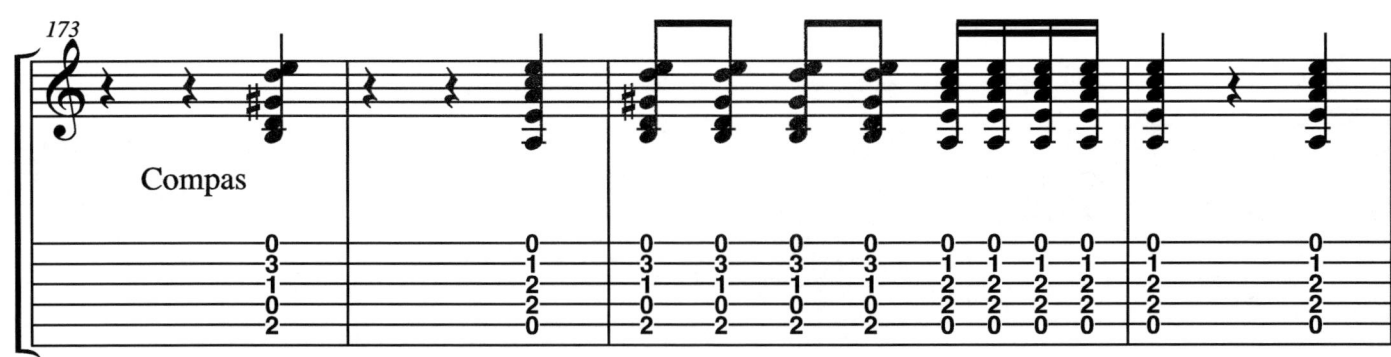

Compas

BULERIAS IN A MINOR

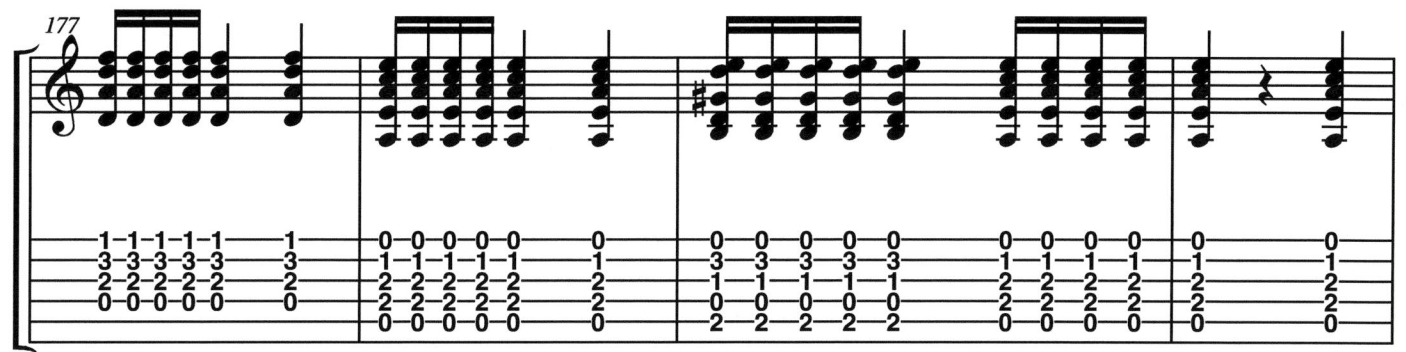
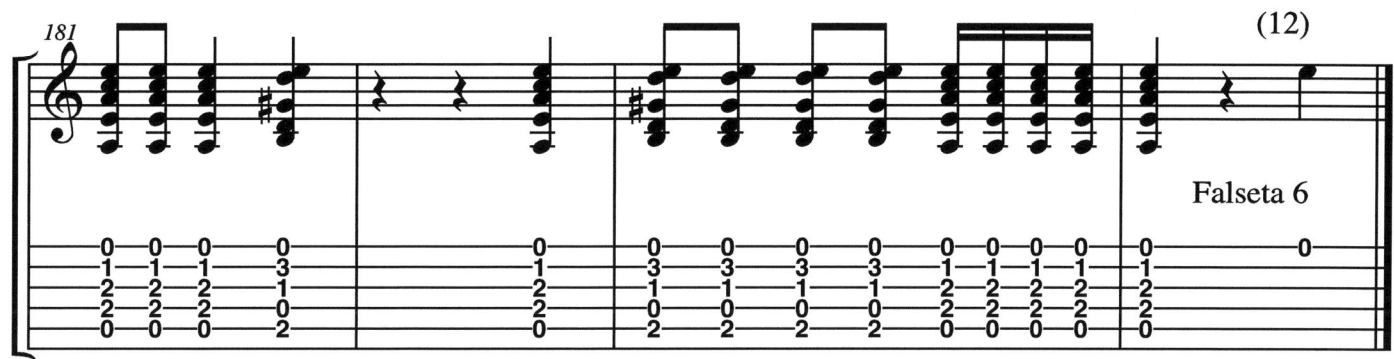

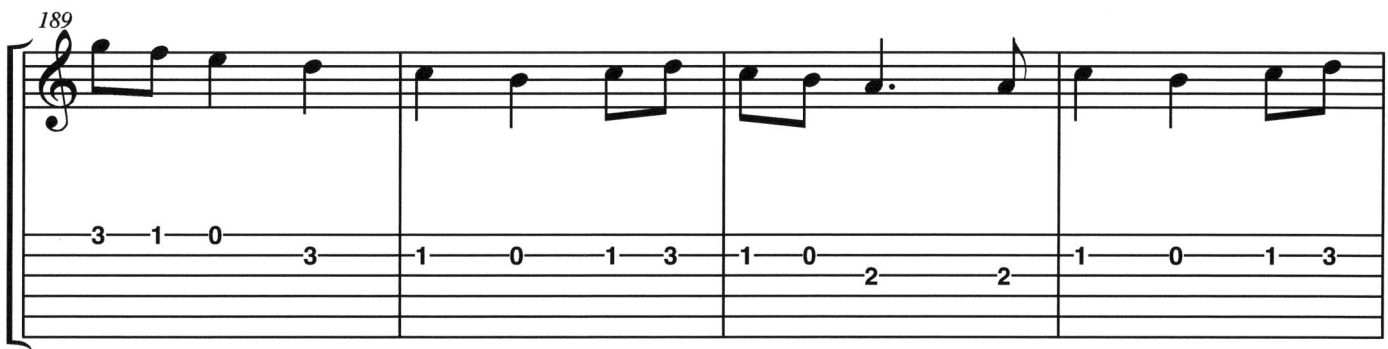

BULERIAS IN A MINOR

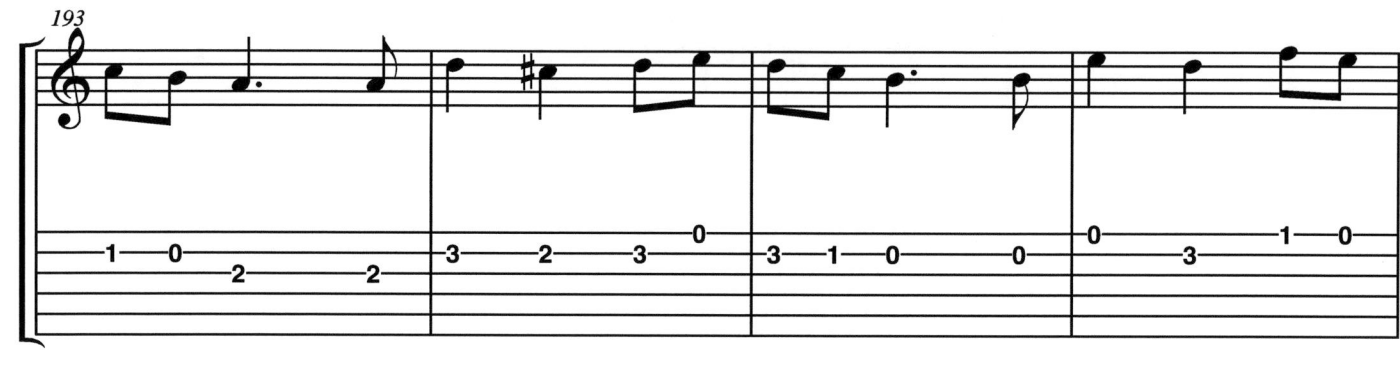
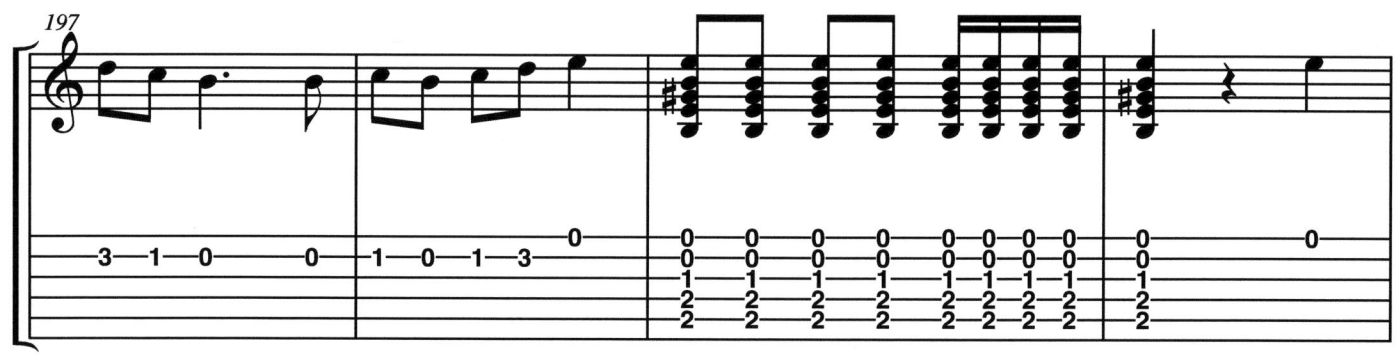

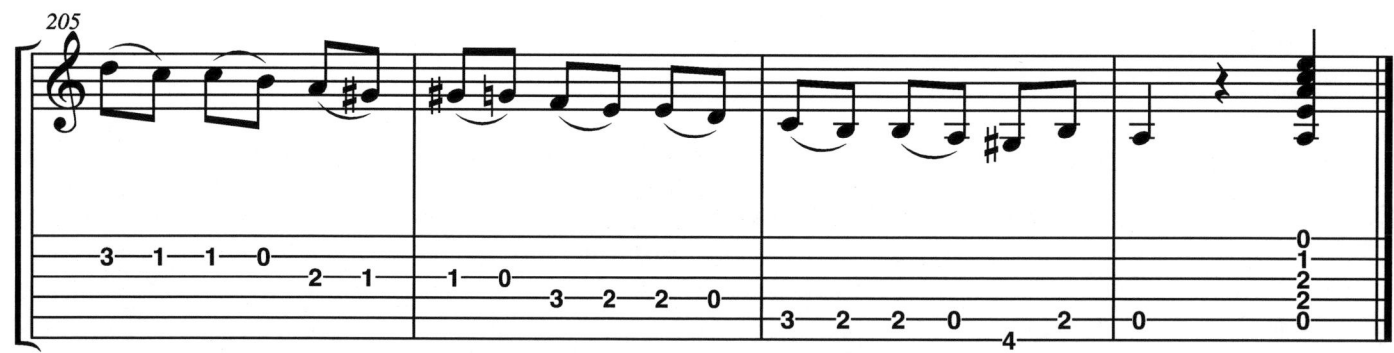

BULERIAS IN A MINOR

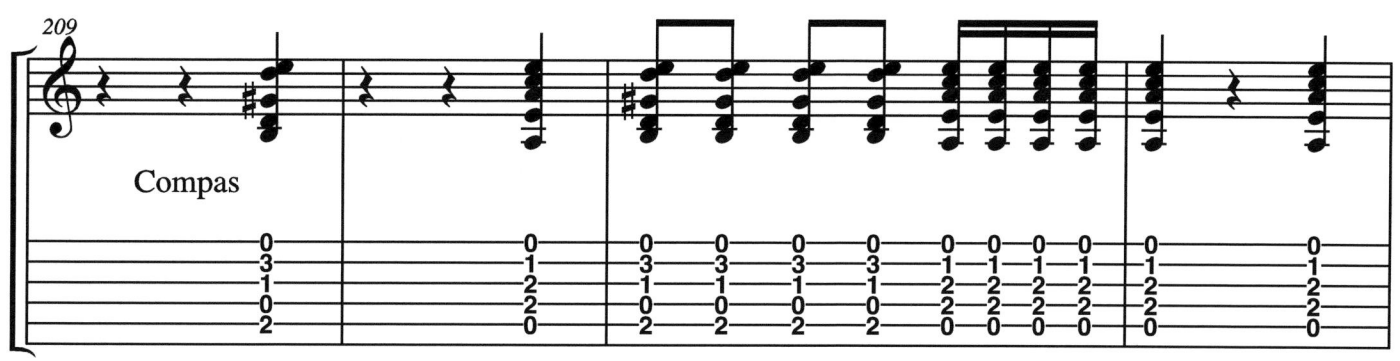

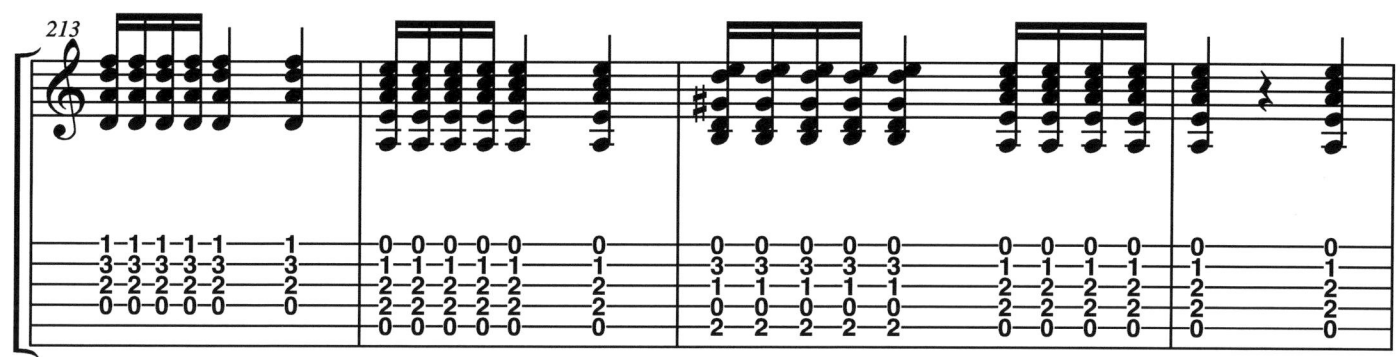

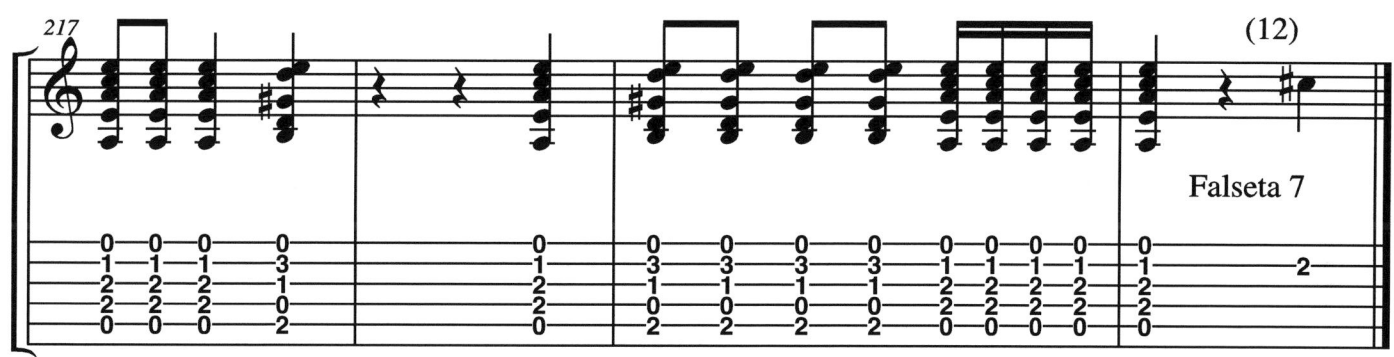

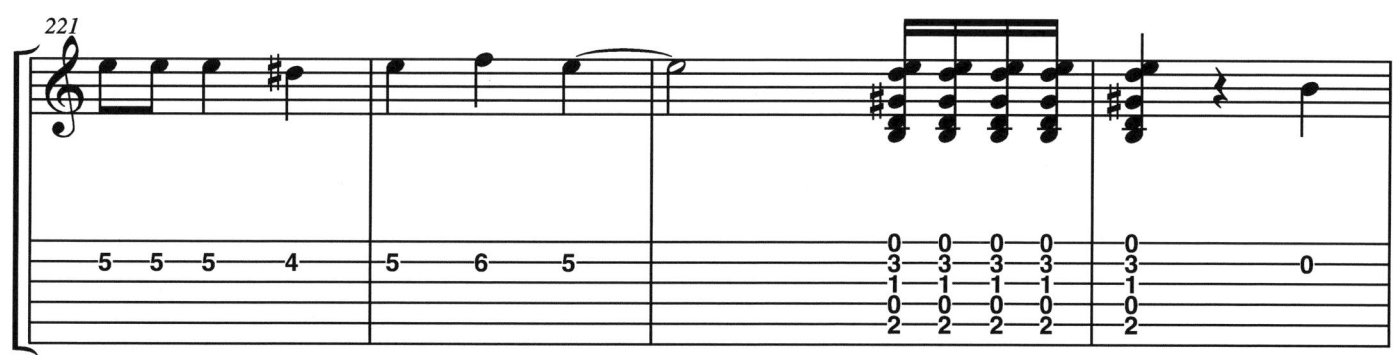

BULERIAS IN A MINOR

BULERIAS IN A MINOR

BULERIAS IN A MINOR

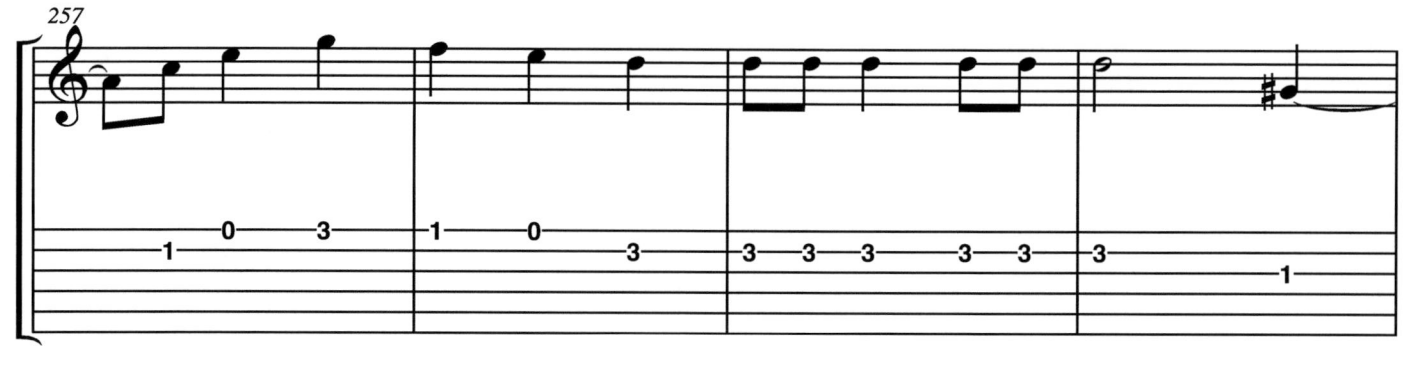

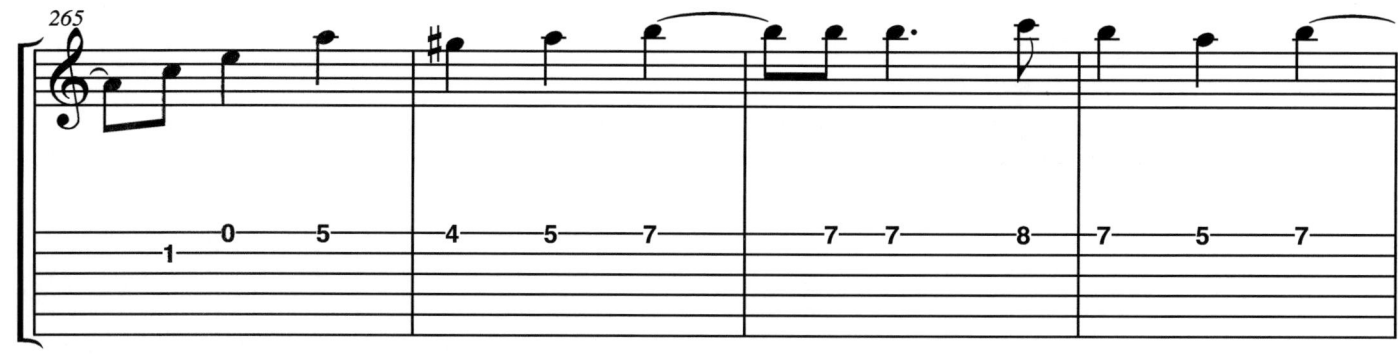
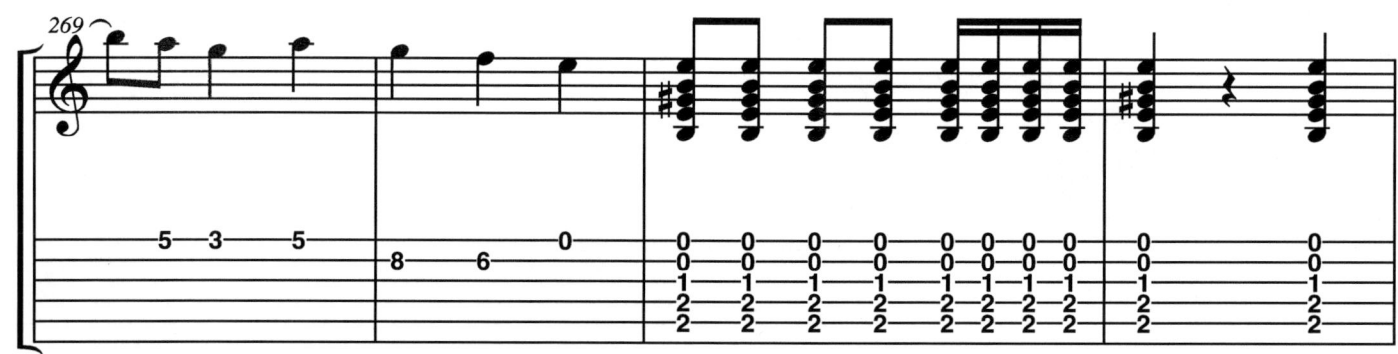

273
277
Compas
281
285
(12)
Falseta 9

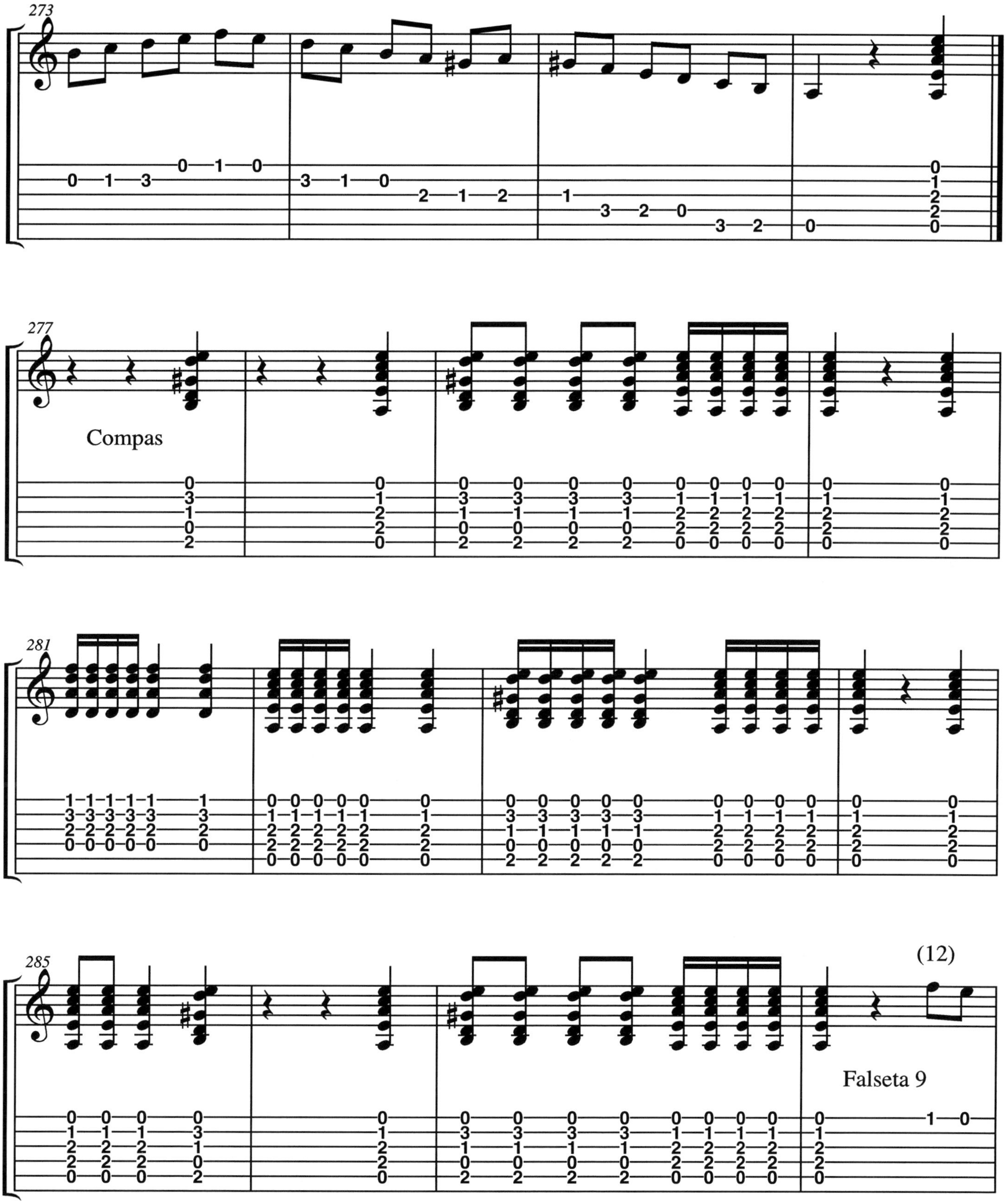

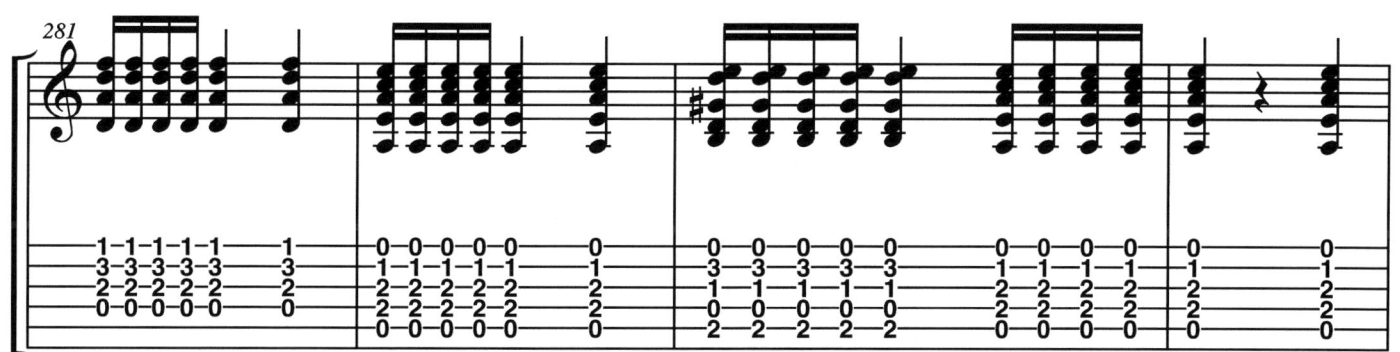

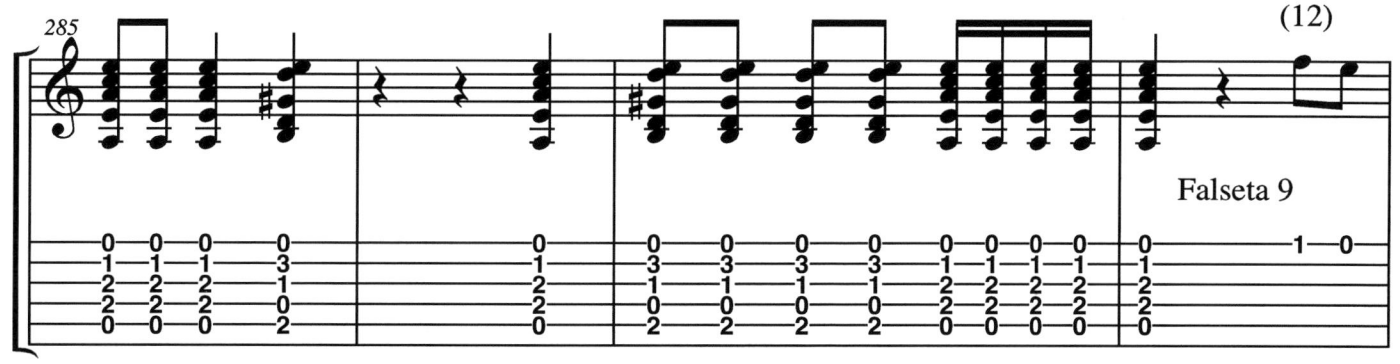

BULERIAS IN A MINOR

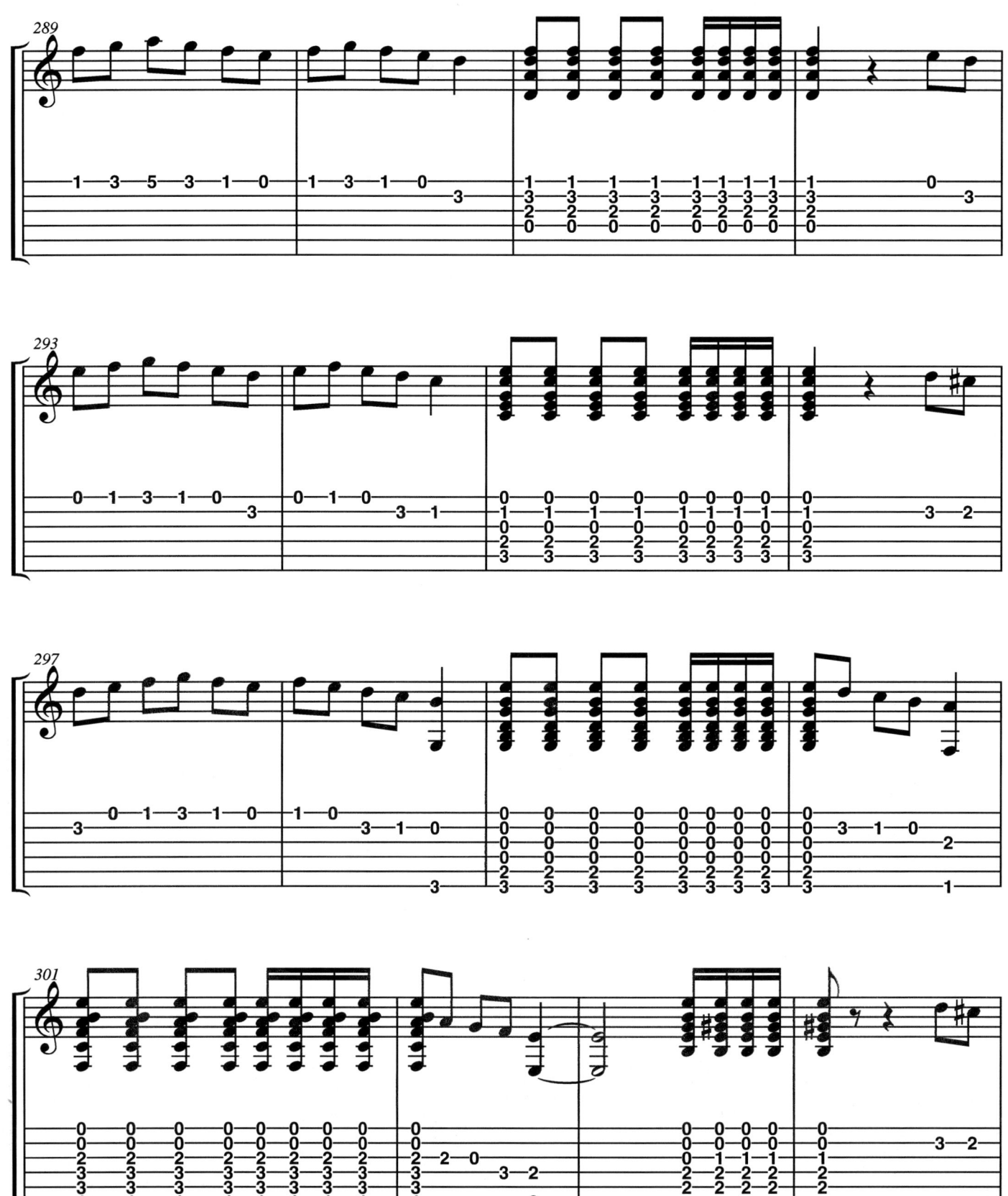

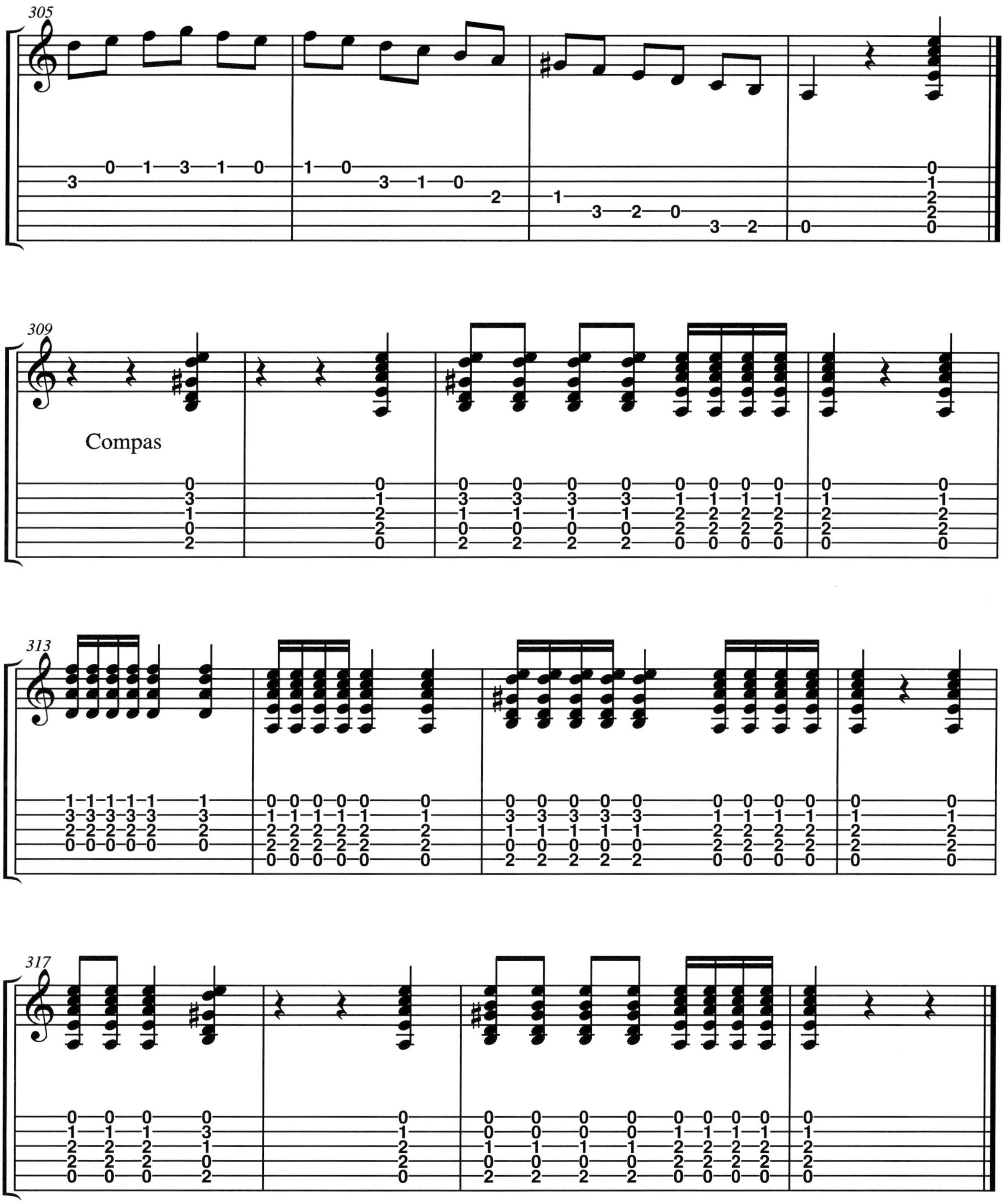

BULERIAS IN A MINOR

Compas

BULERIAS IN A MINOR

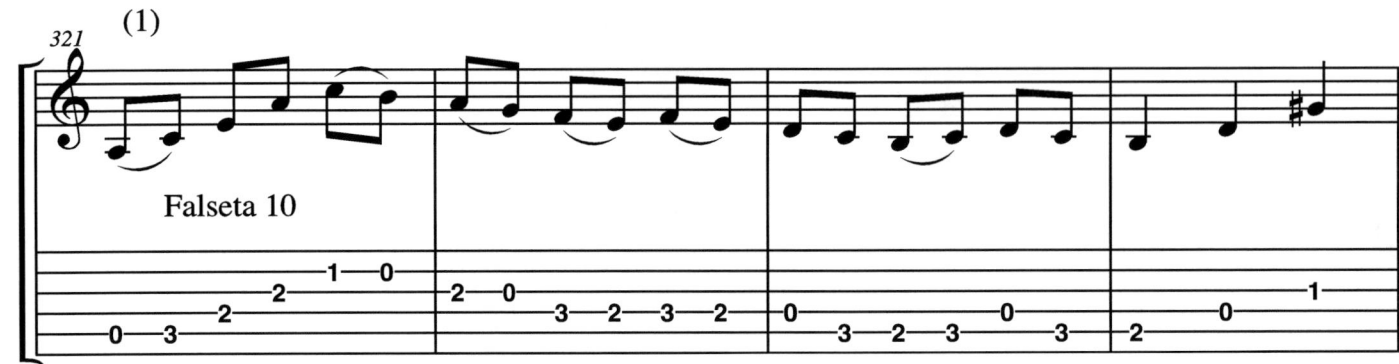

Falseta 10

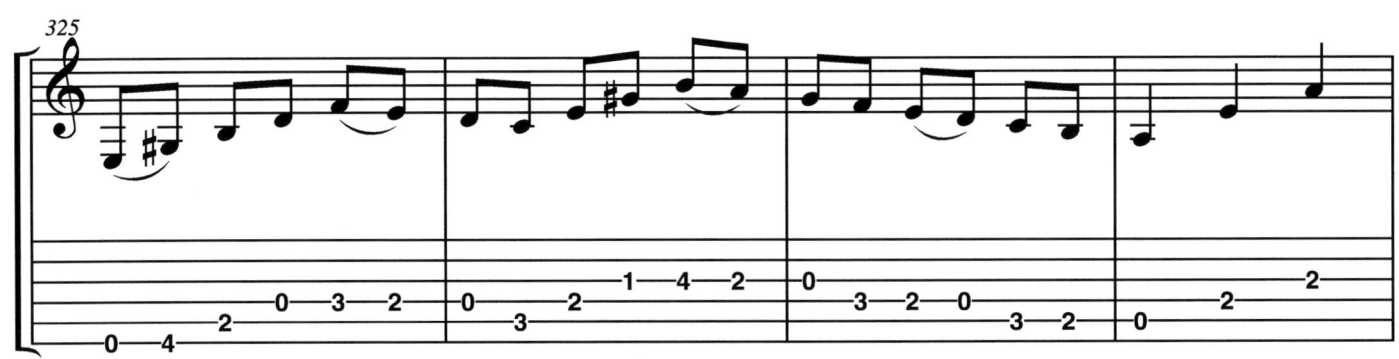

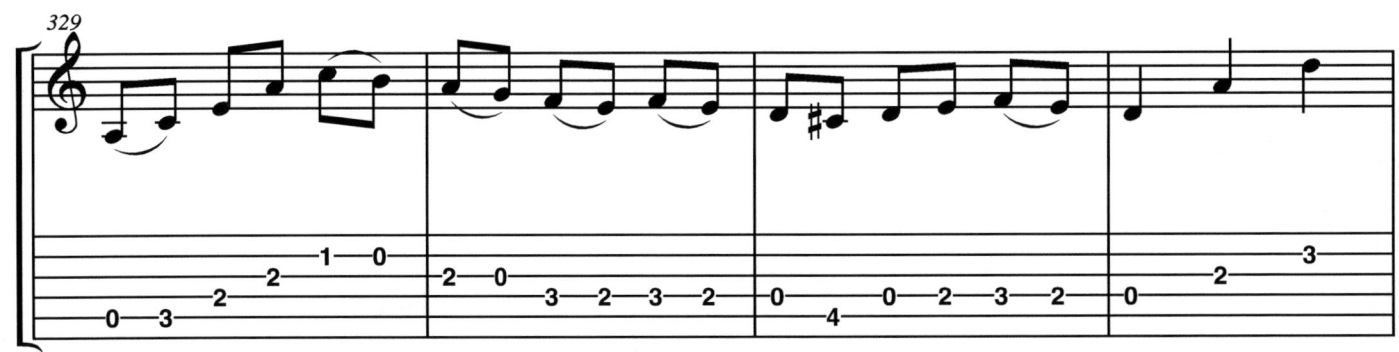

BULERIAS IN A MINOR

CARACOLES

Strum every compas in the same manner

CARACOLES

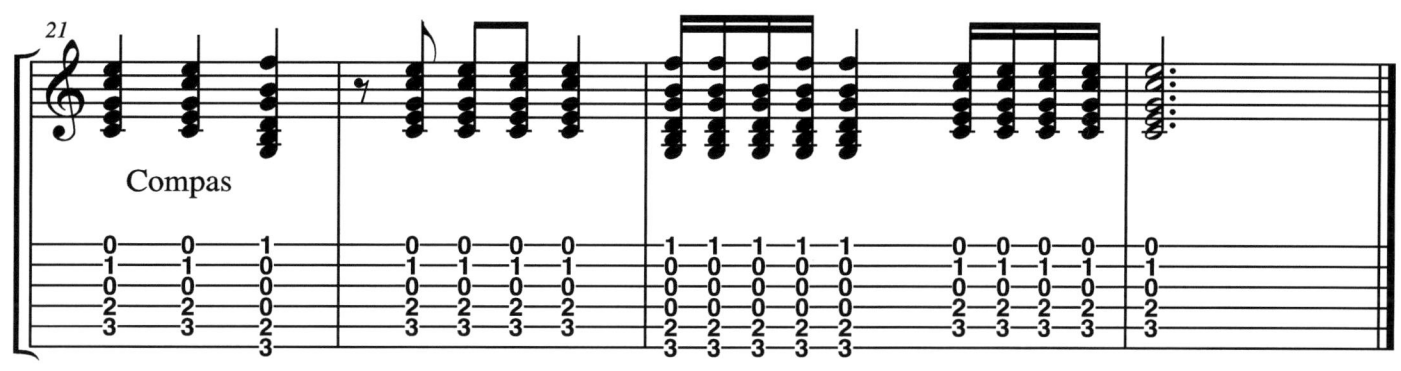

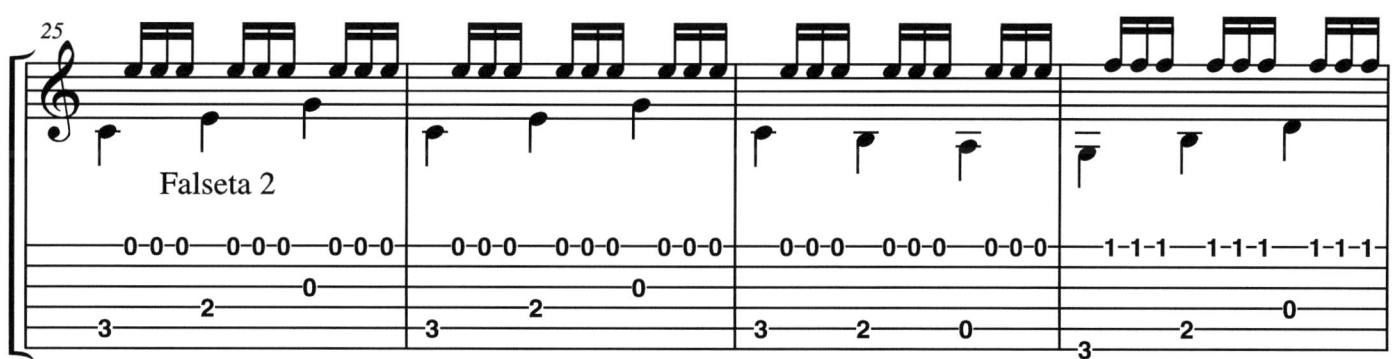

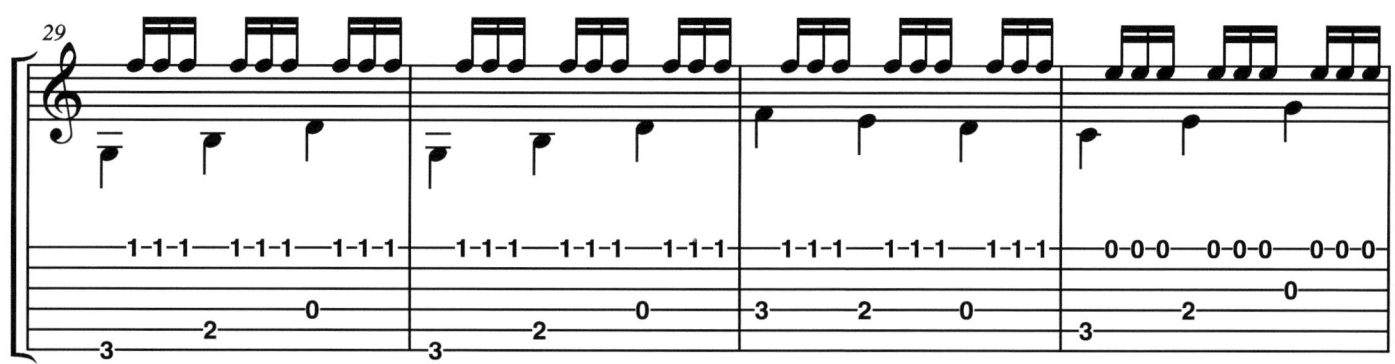

CARACOLES

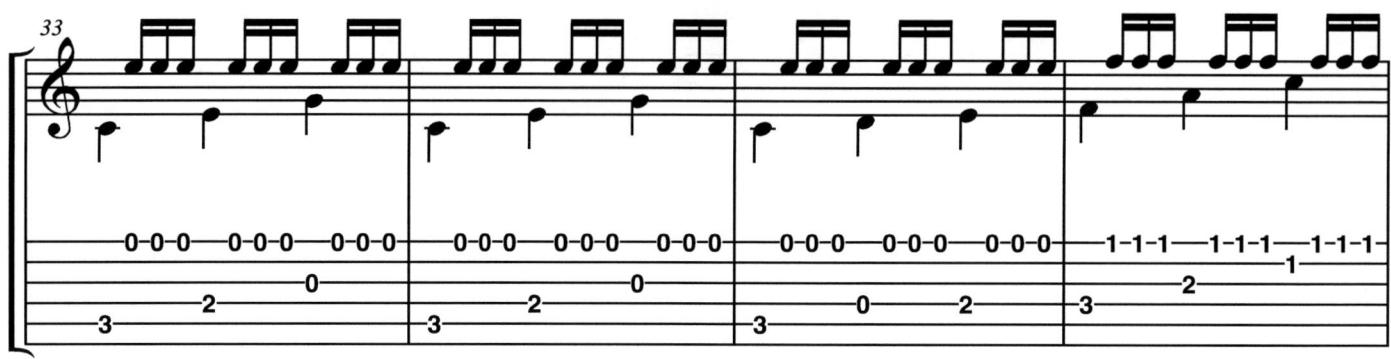

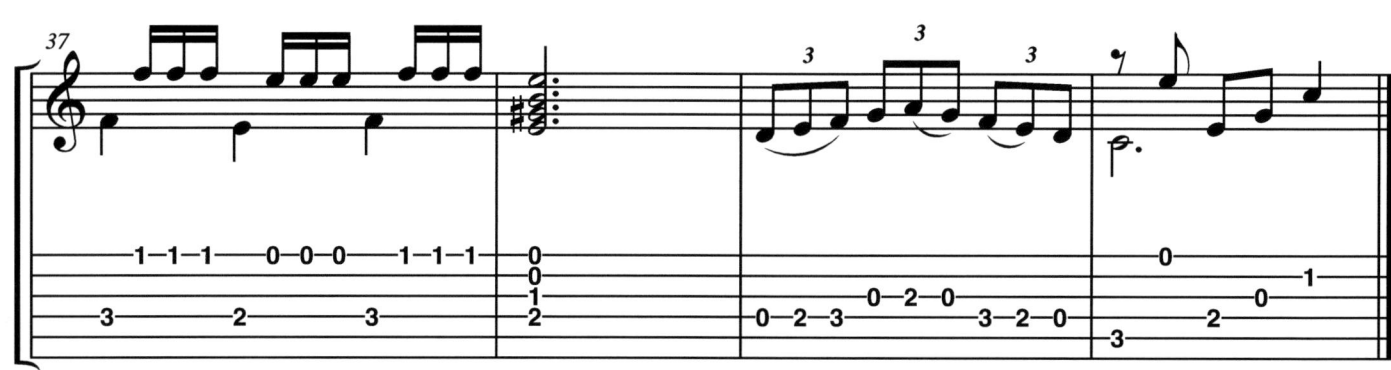

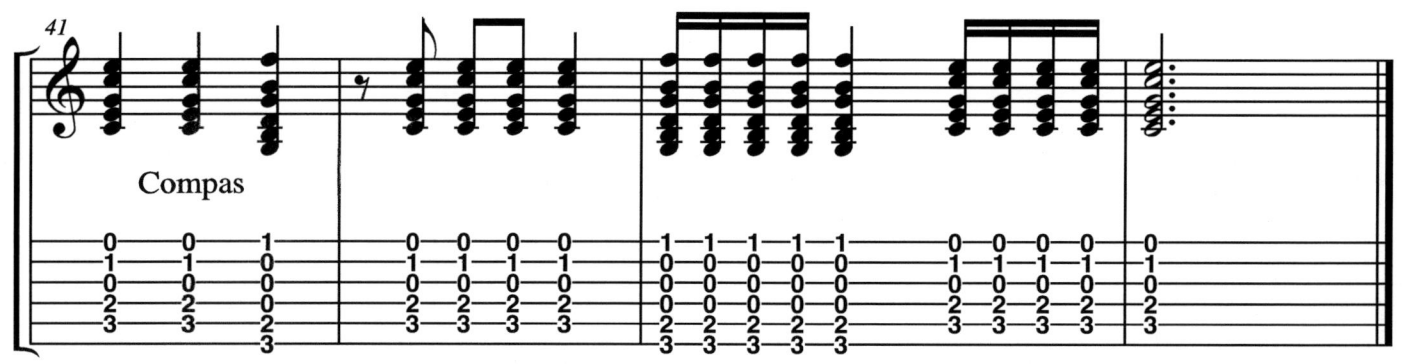

Compas

Falseta 3

CARACOLES

CARACOLES

CARACOLES

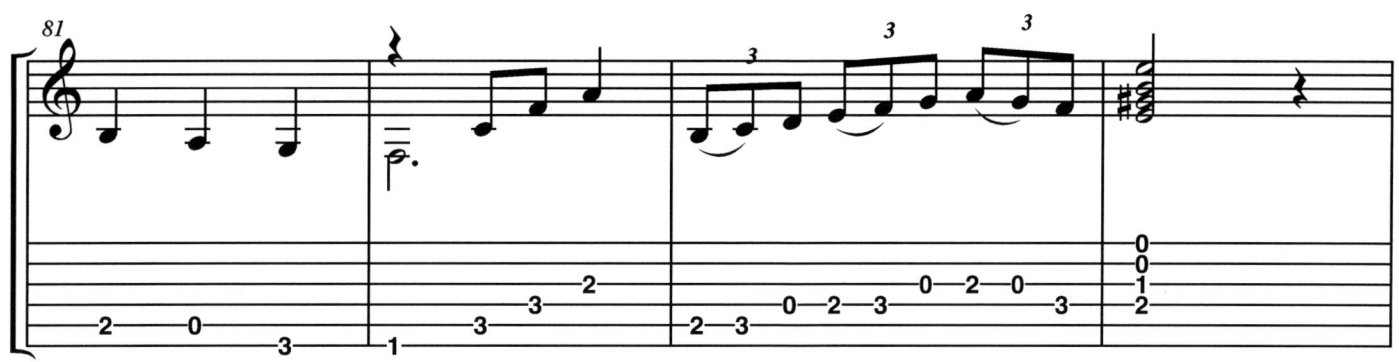
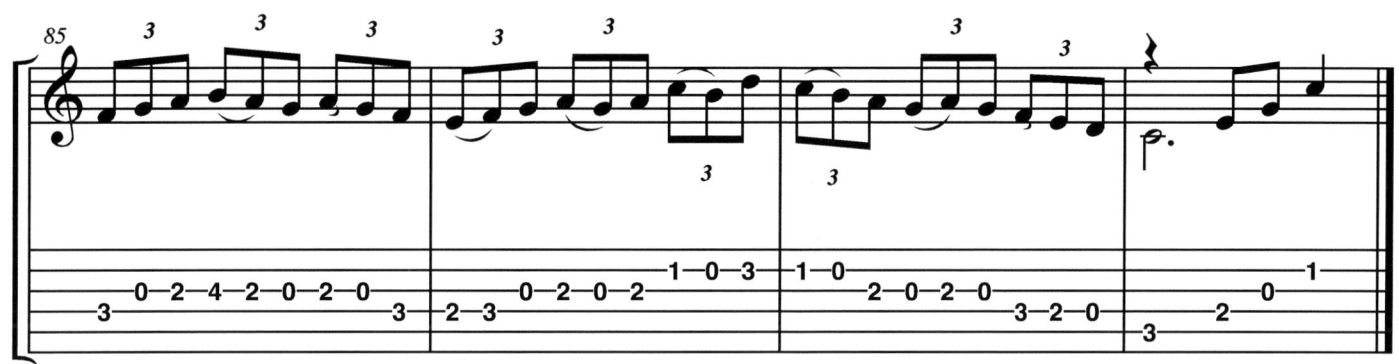
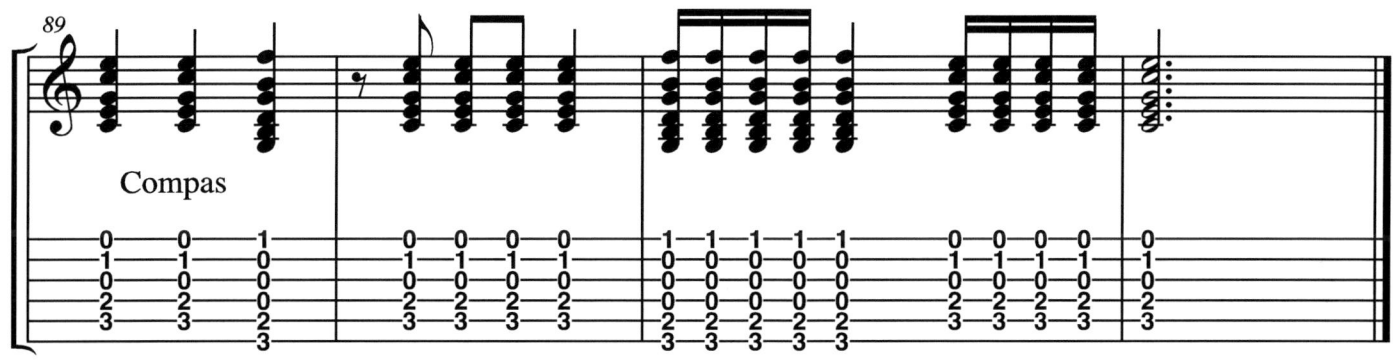

CARACOLES

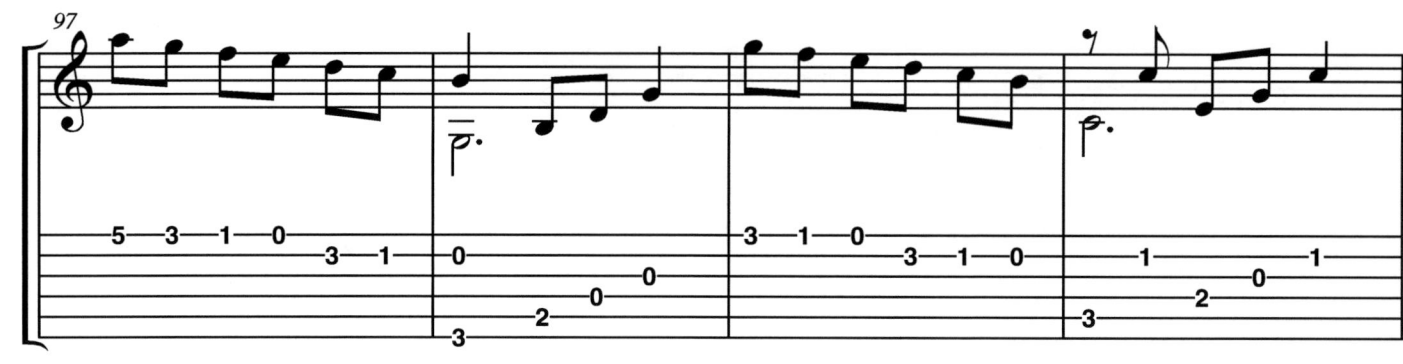

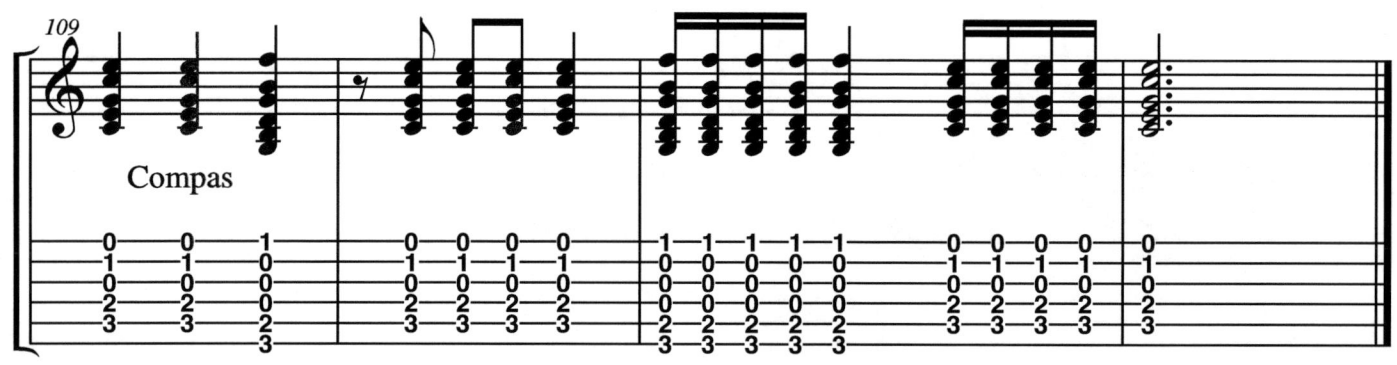

CARACOLES

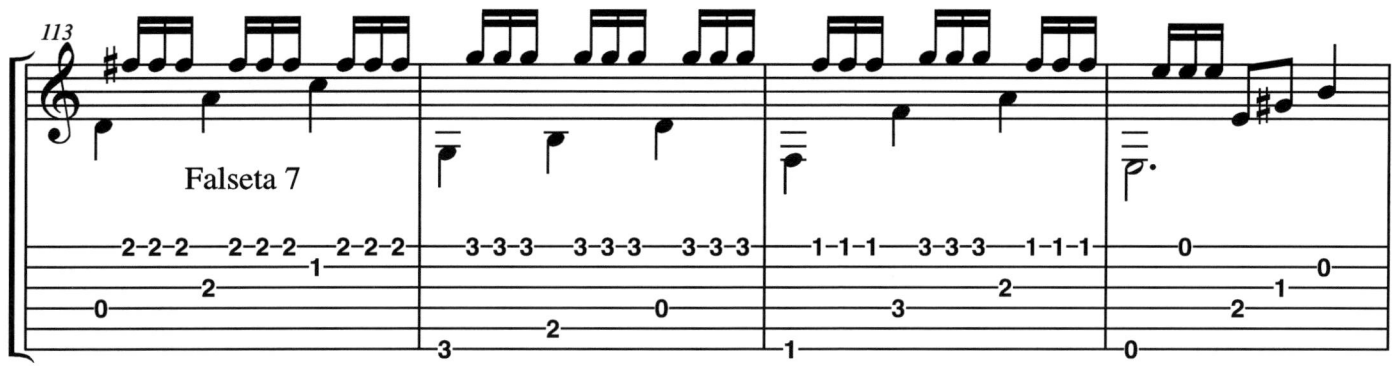
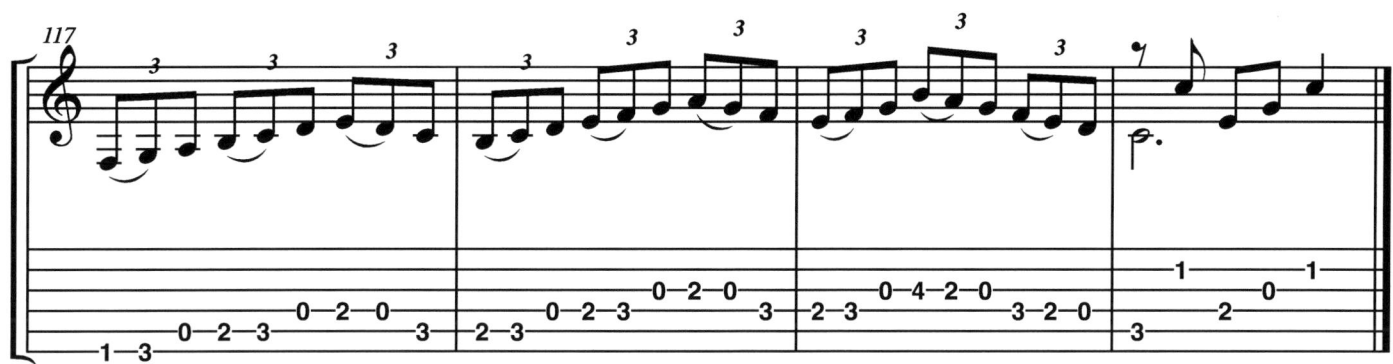
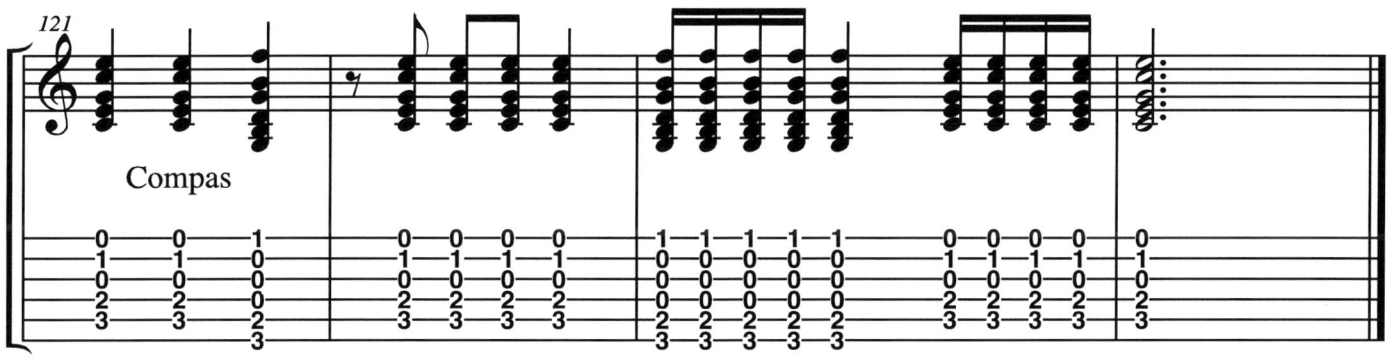
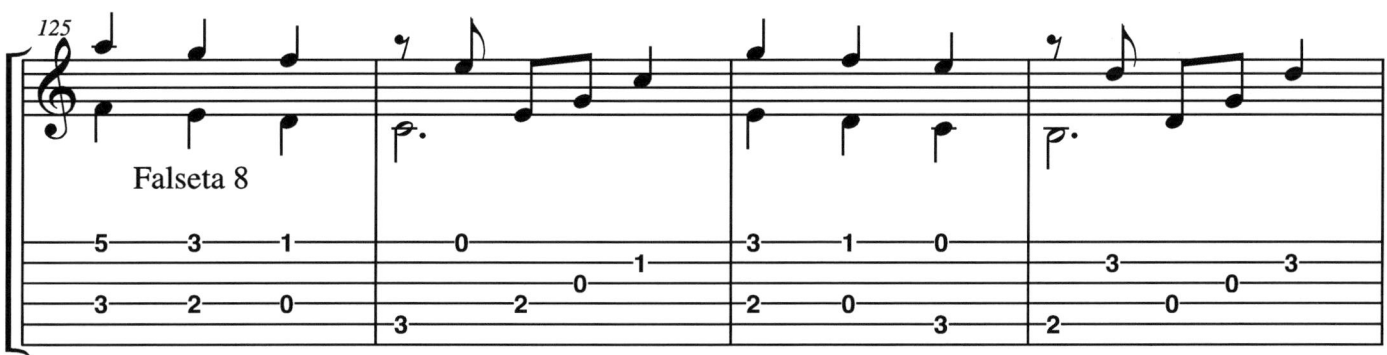

CARACOLES

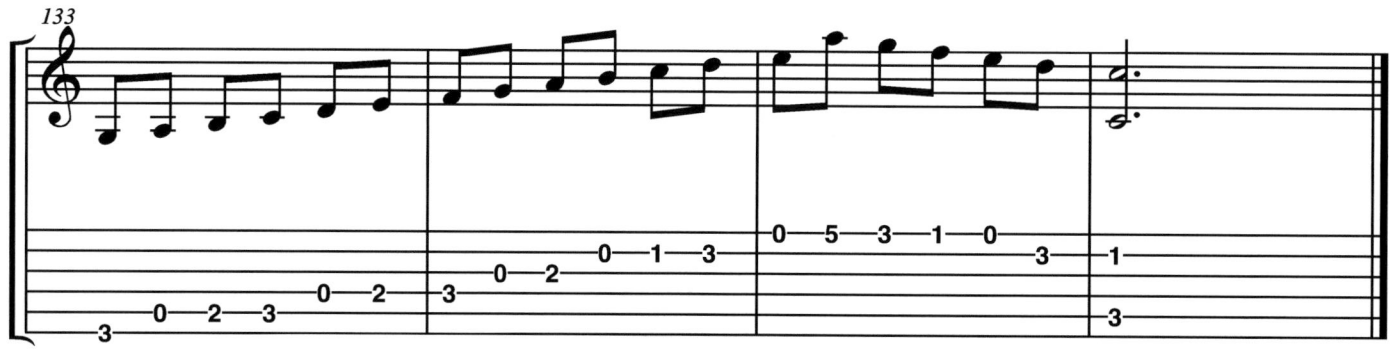
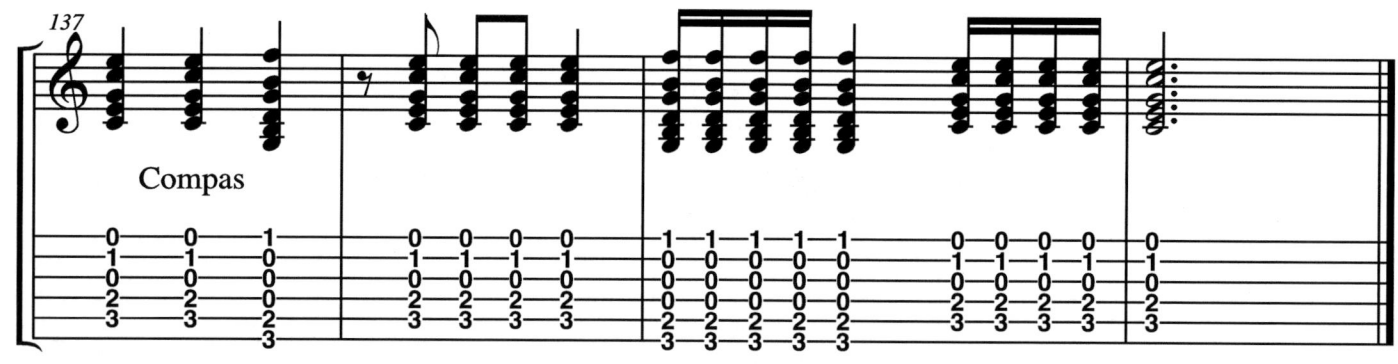

CARACOLES

CARACOLES

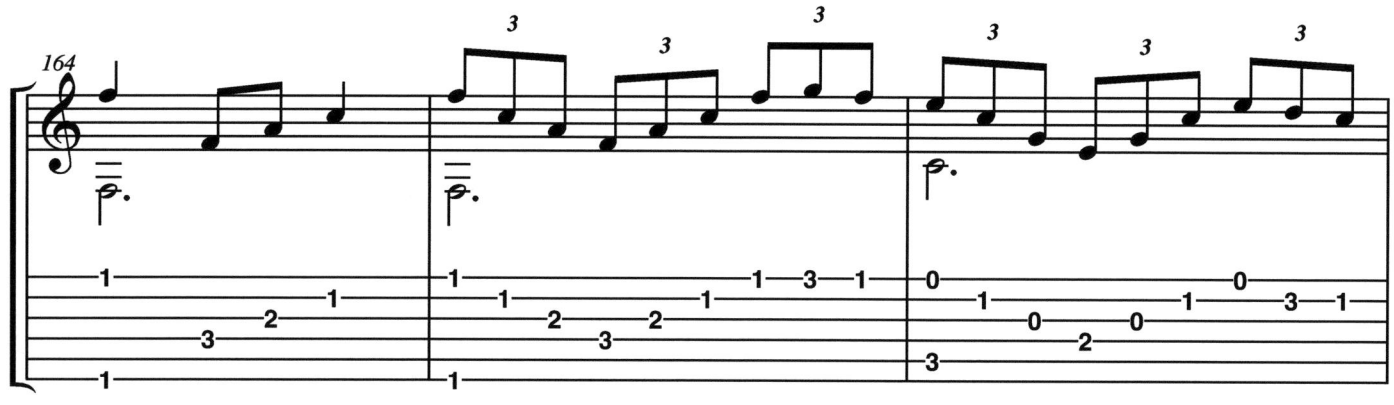

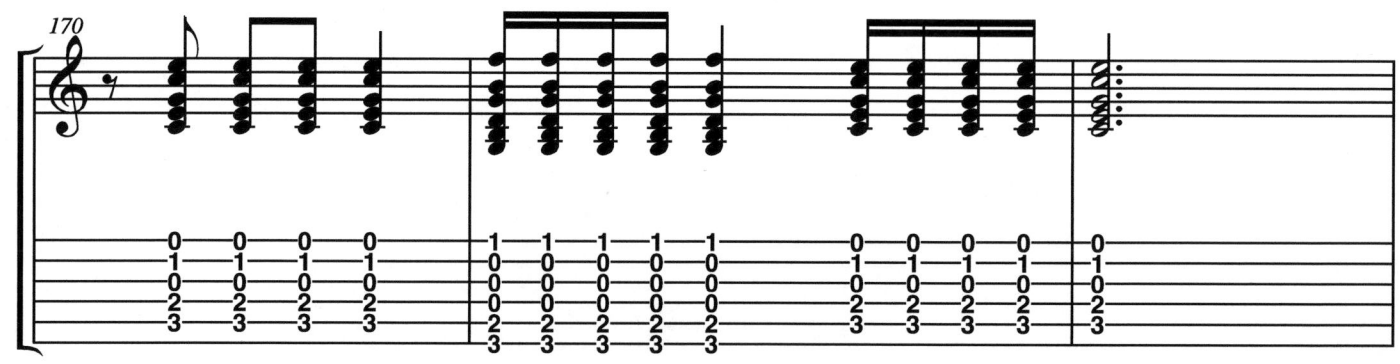

CARACOLES

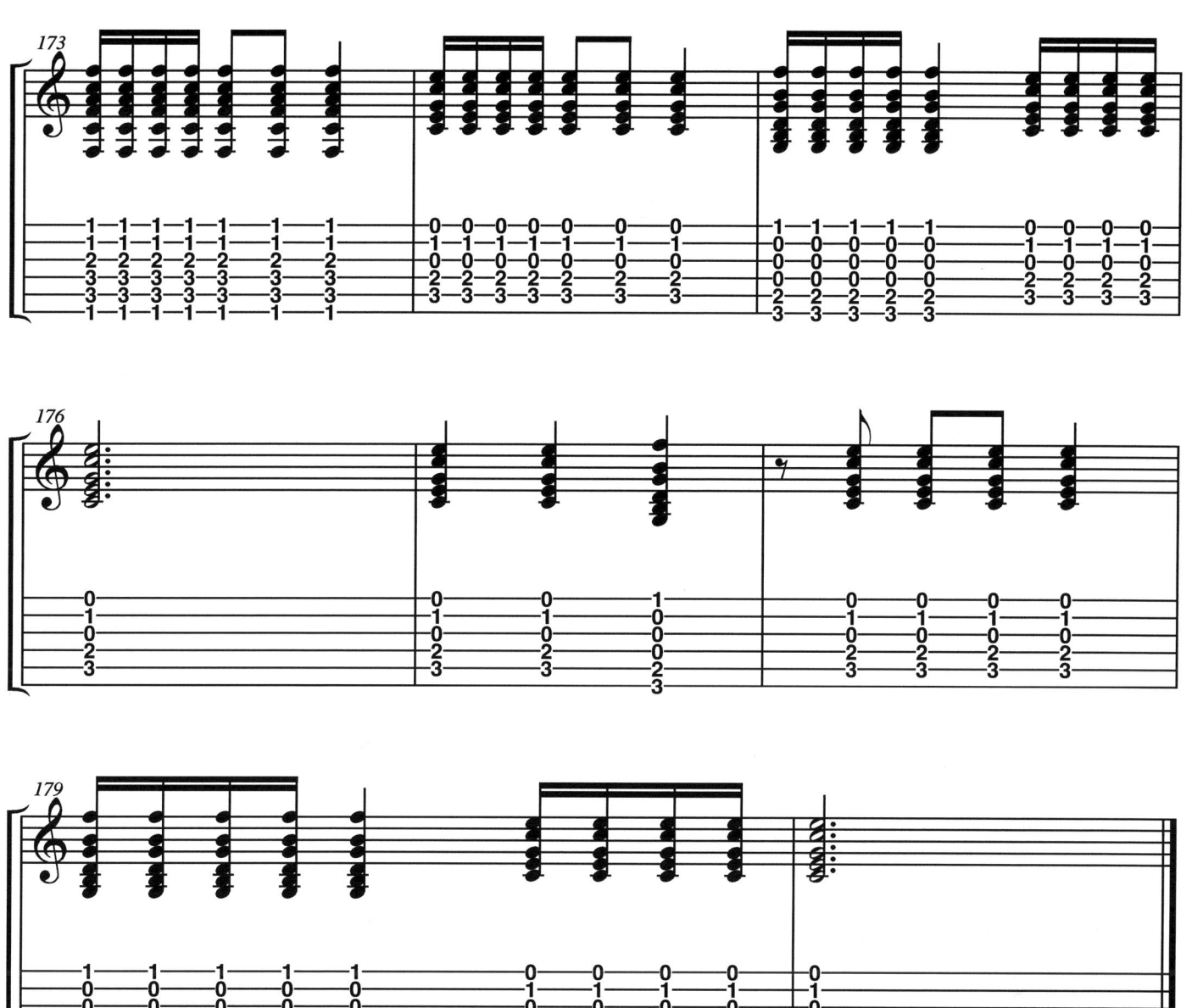

FANDANGOS DE HUELVA

Strum every compas in the same manner

FANDANGOS DE HUELVA

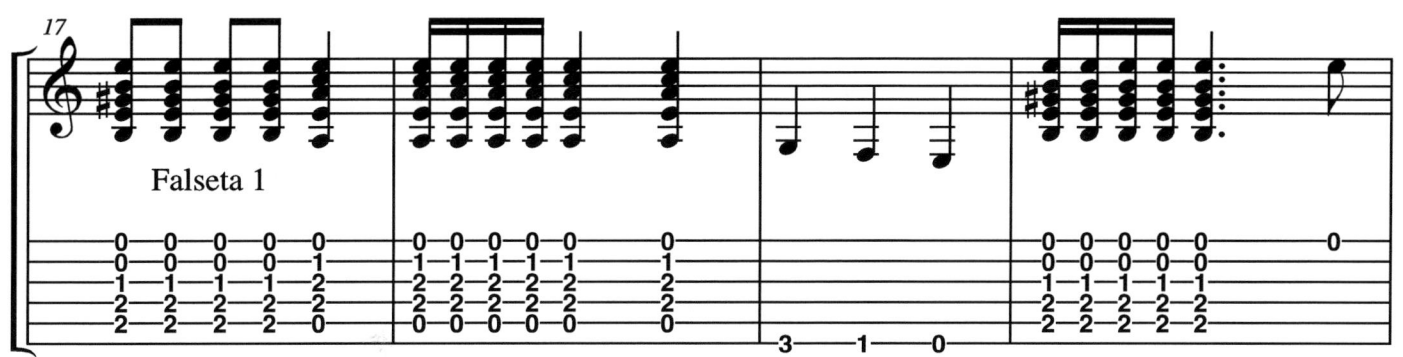

Falseta 1

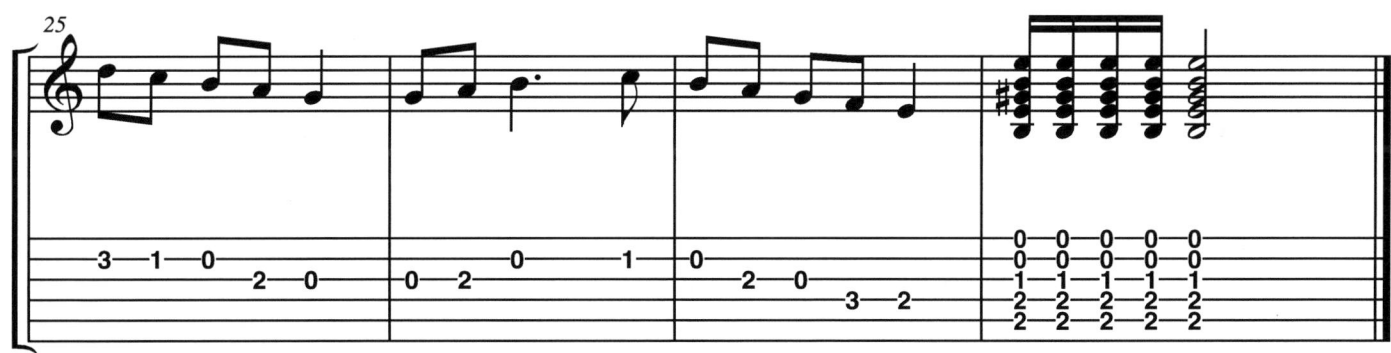

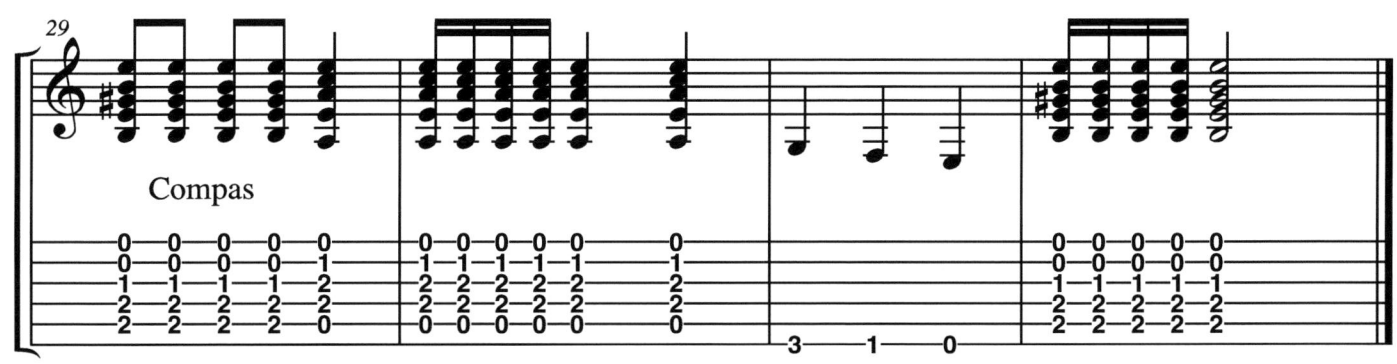

Compas

FANDANGOS DE HUELVA

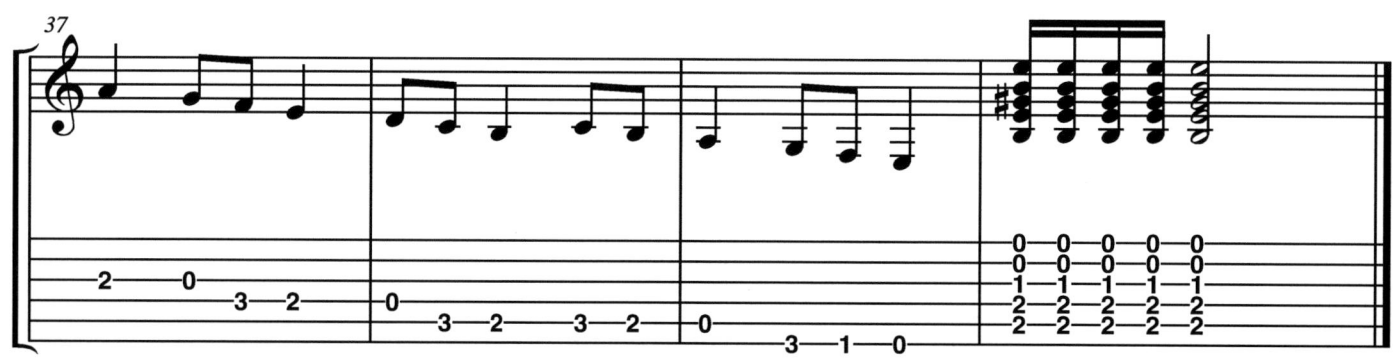

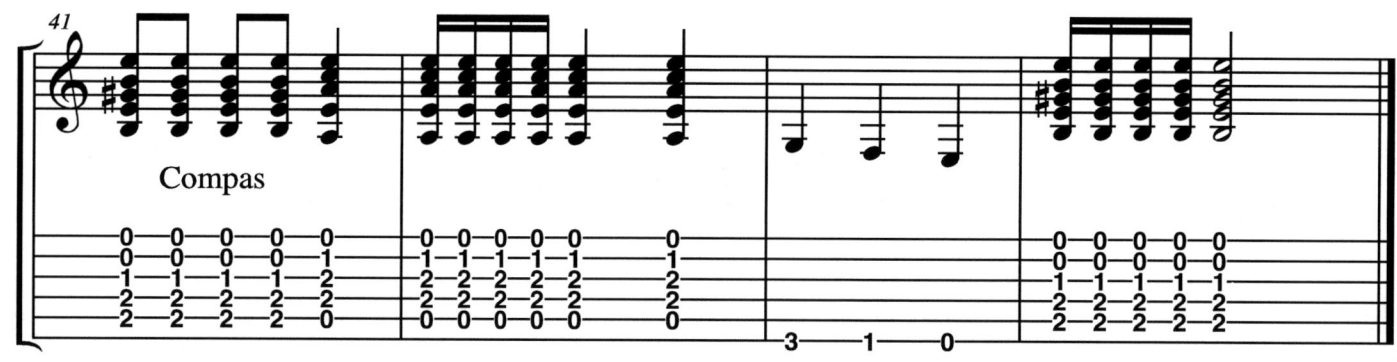

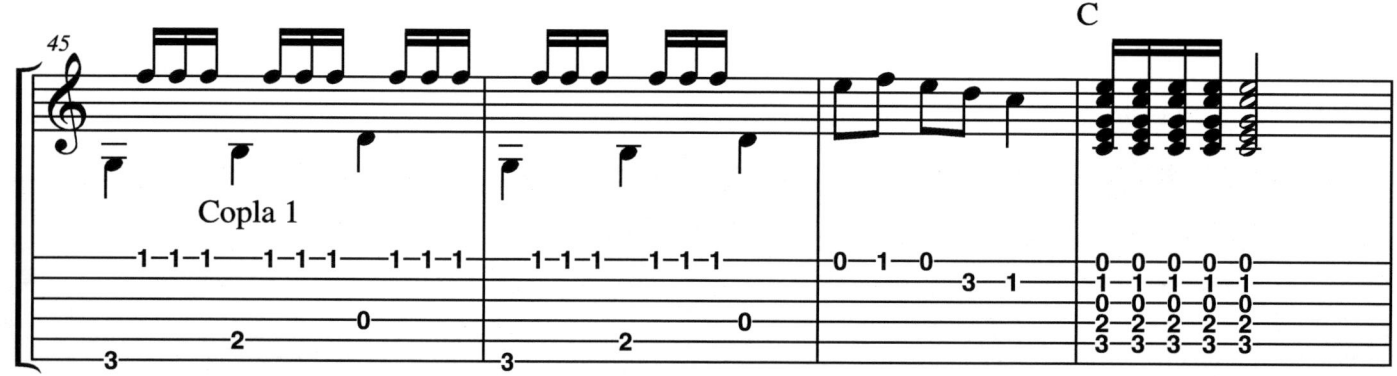

FANDANGOS DE HUELVA

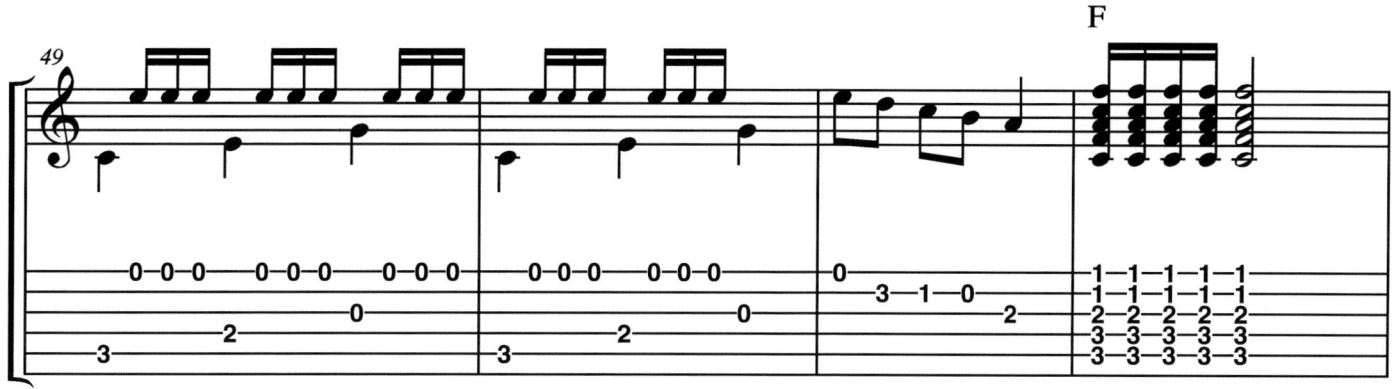
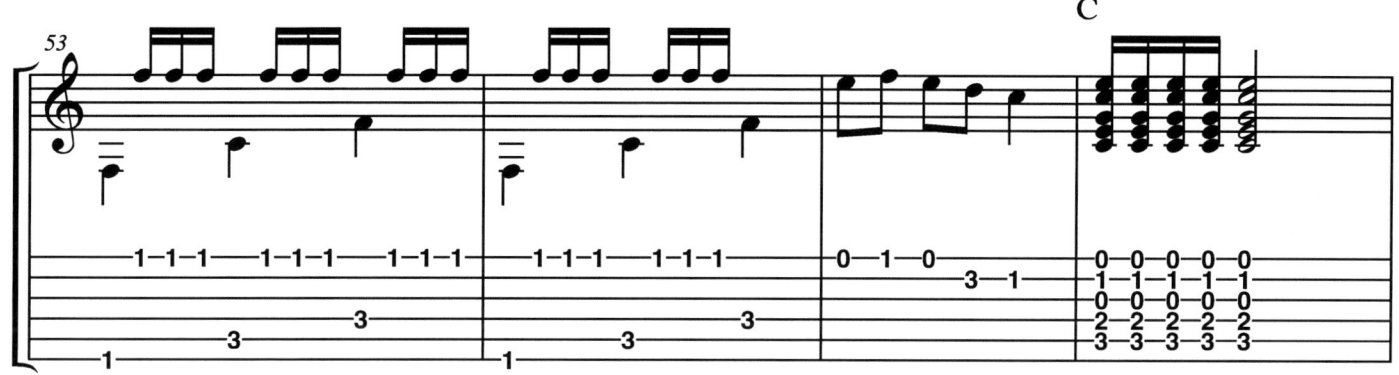
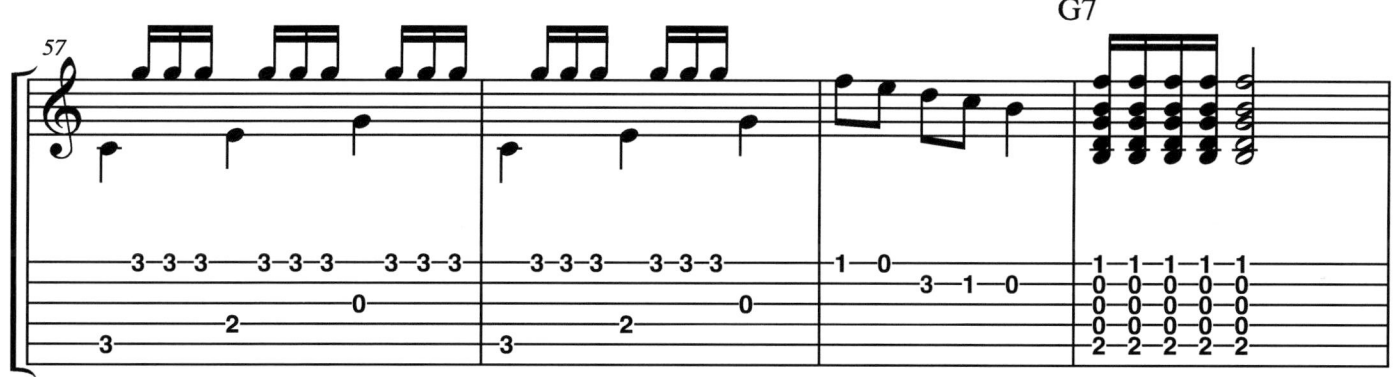
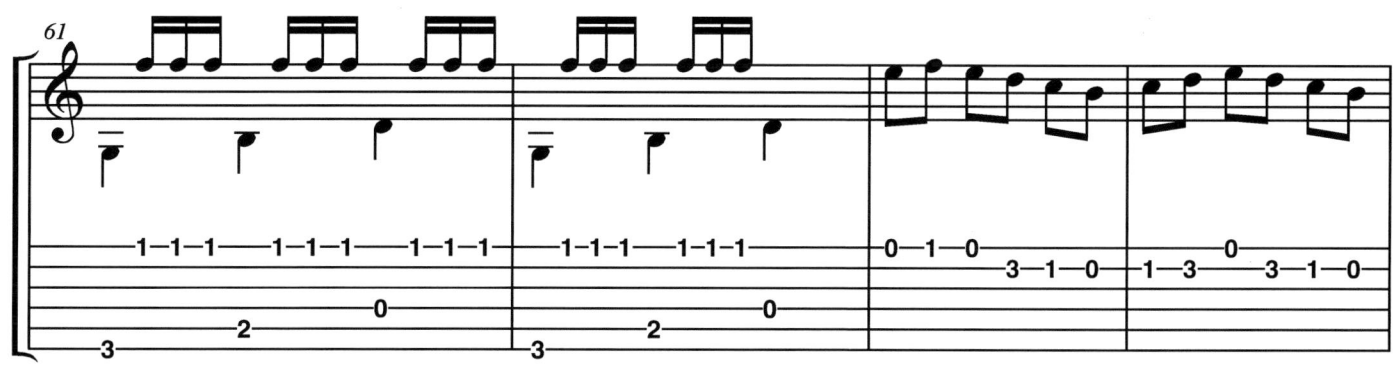

FANDANGOS DE HUELVA

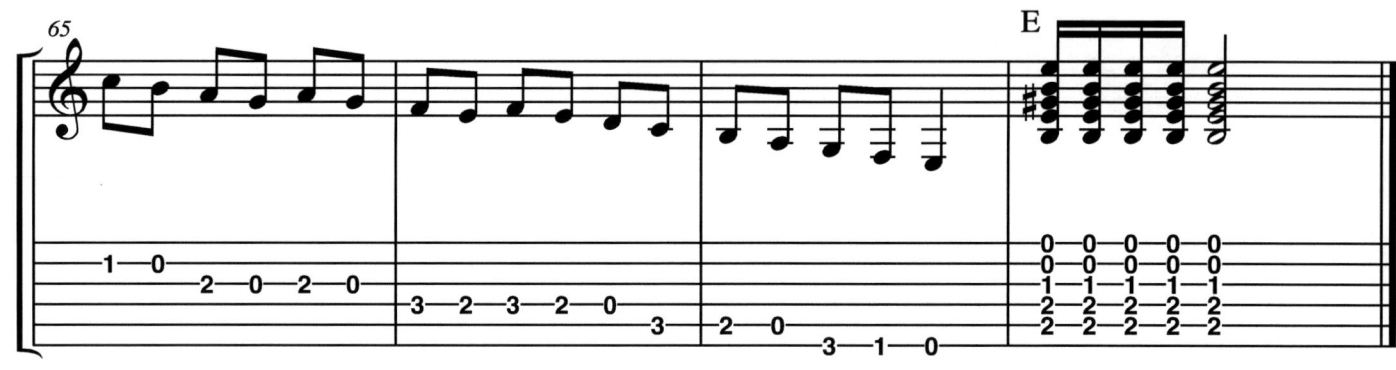

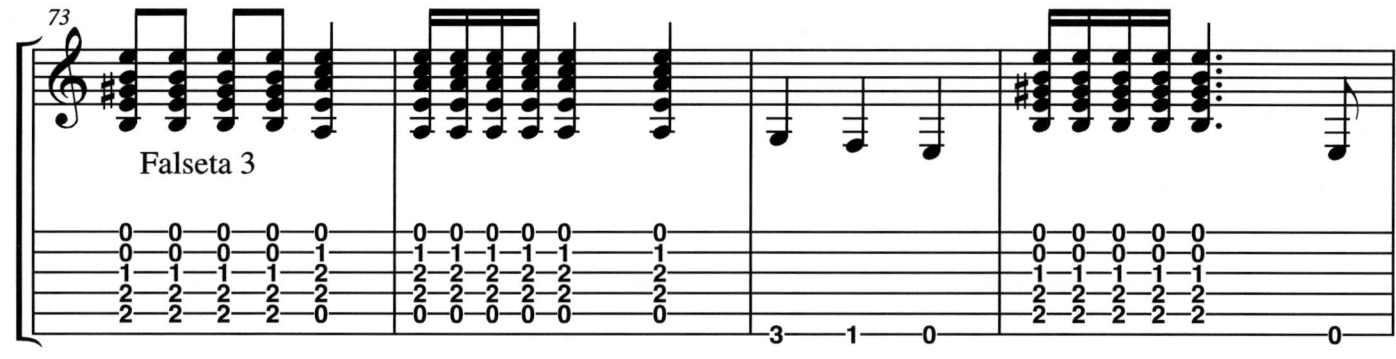

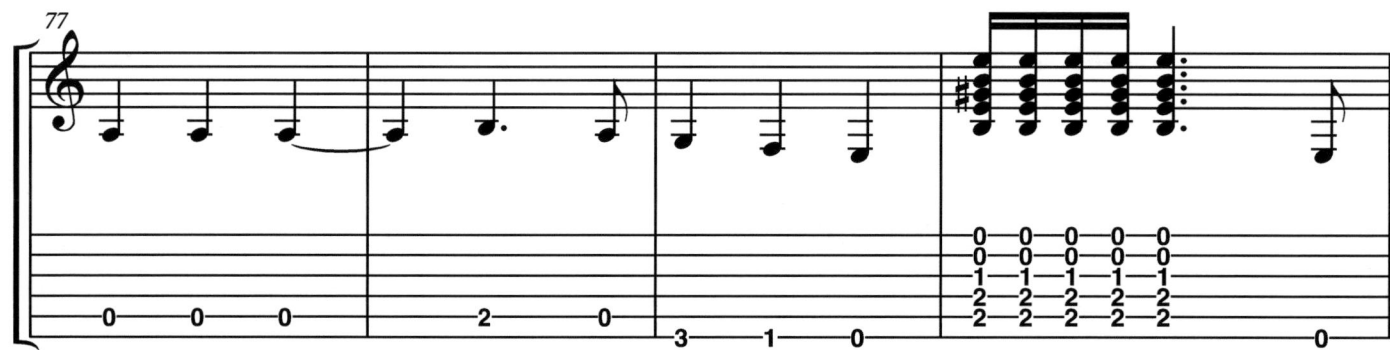

FANDANGOS DE HUELVA

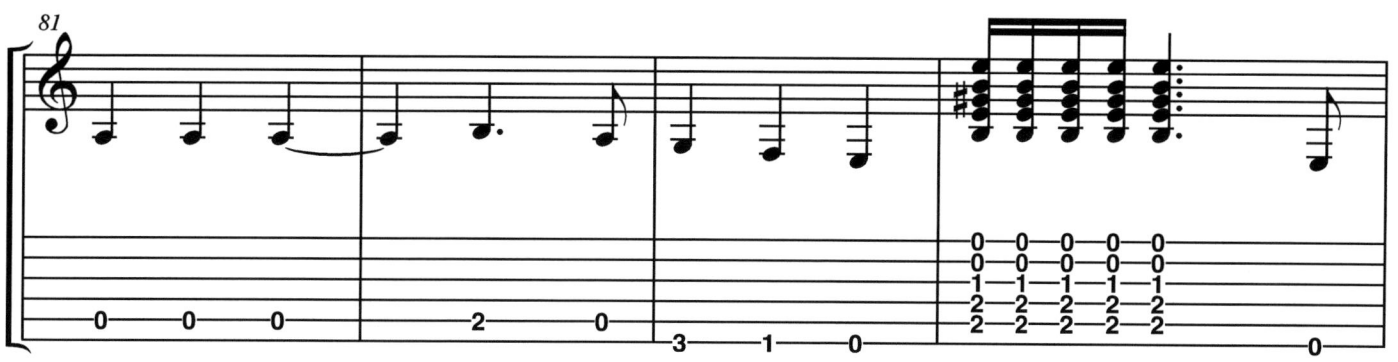

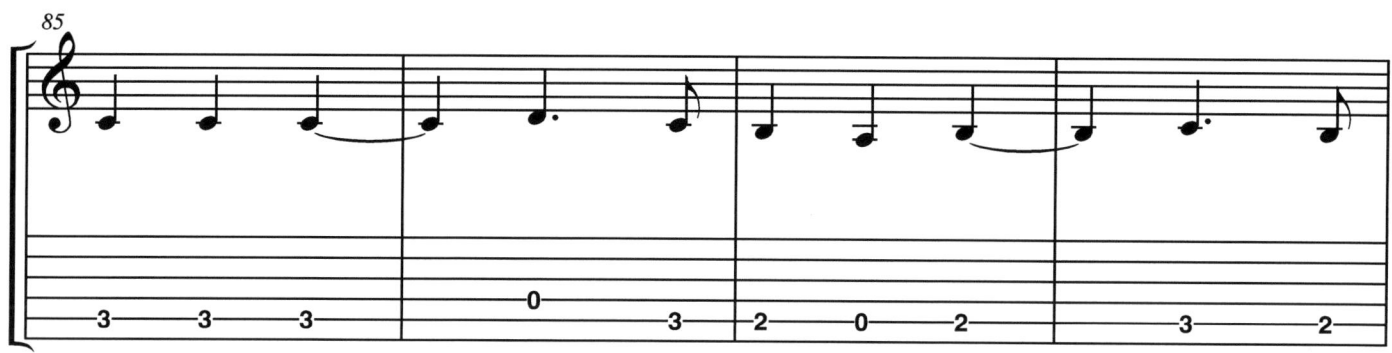

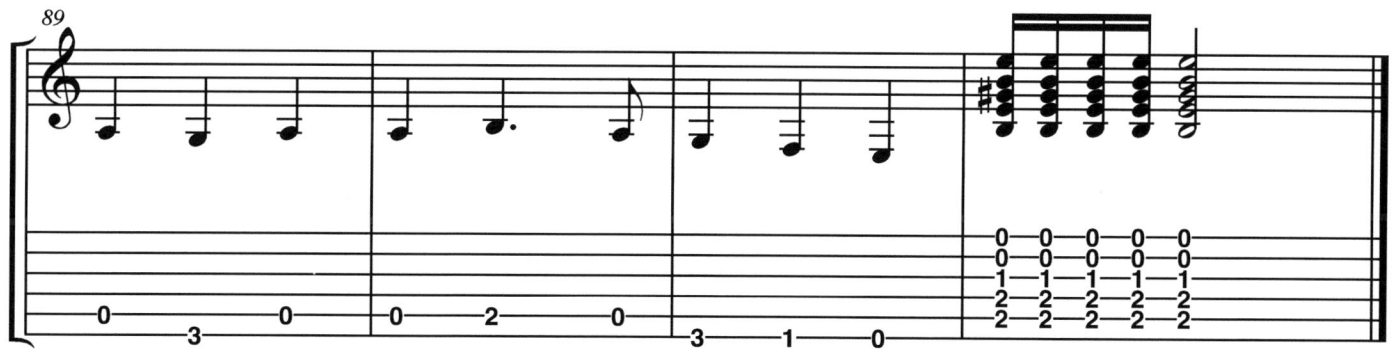

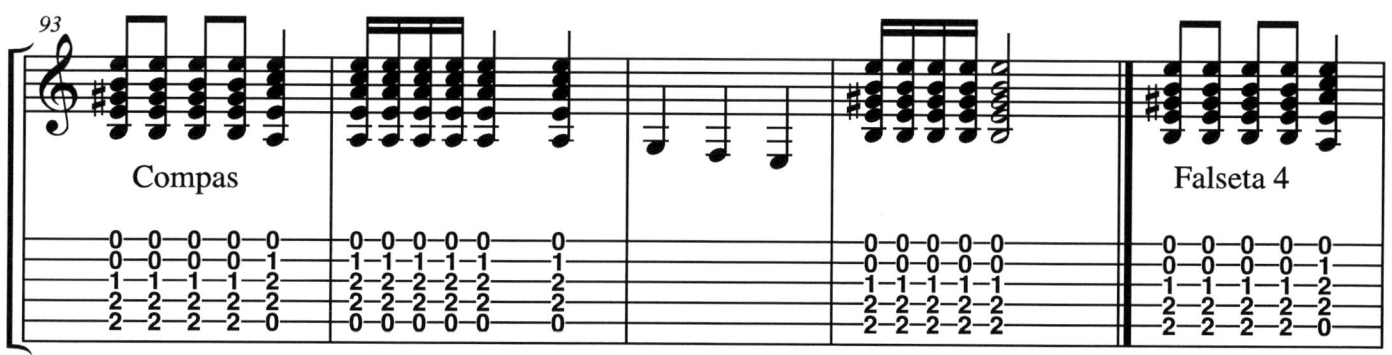

FANDANGOS DE HUELVA

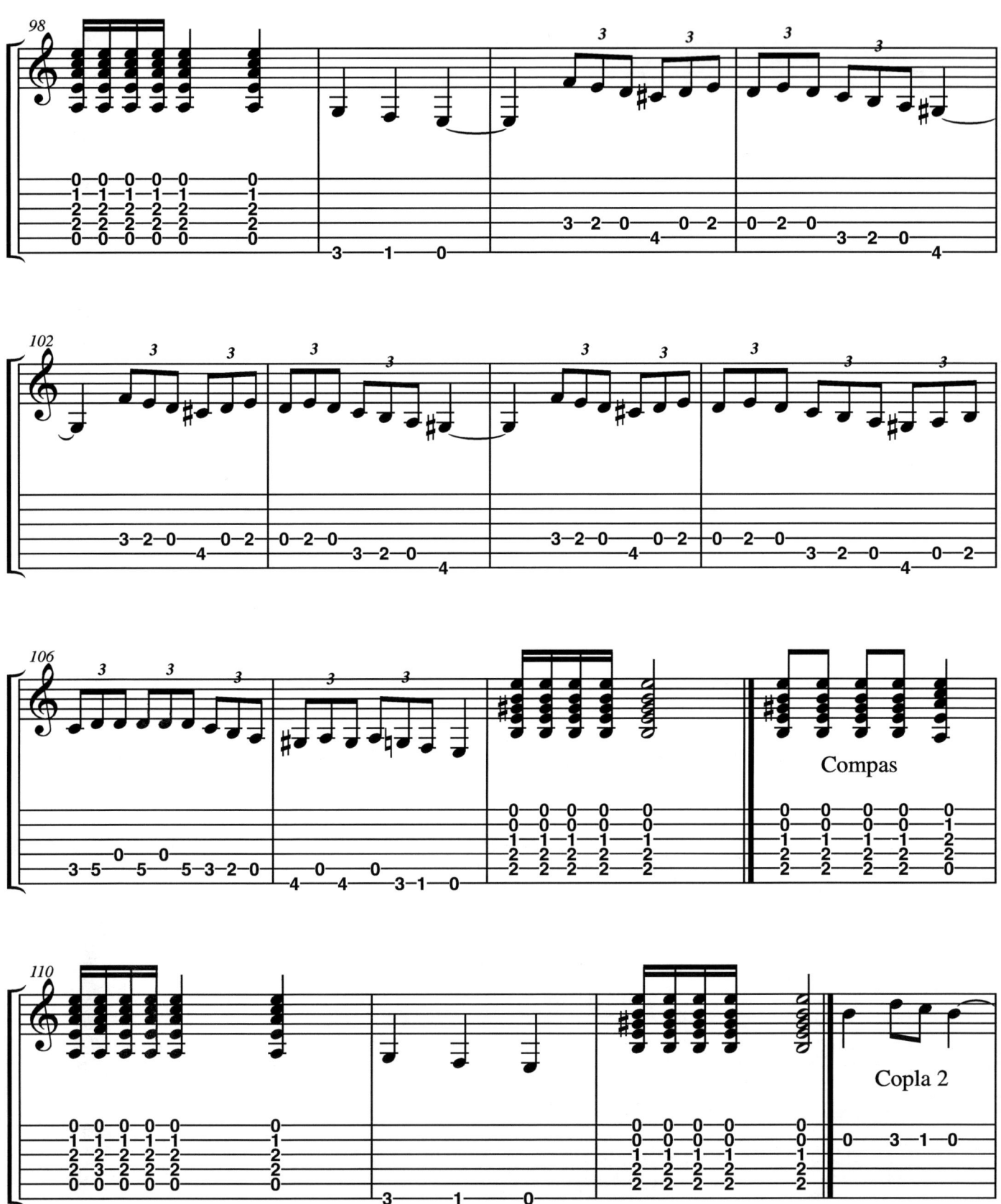

FANDANGOS DE HUELVA

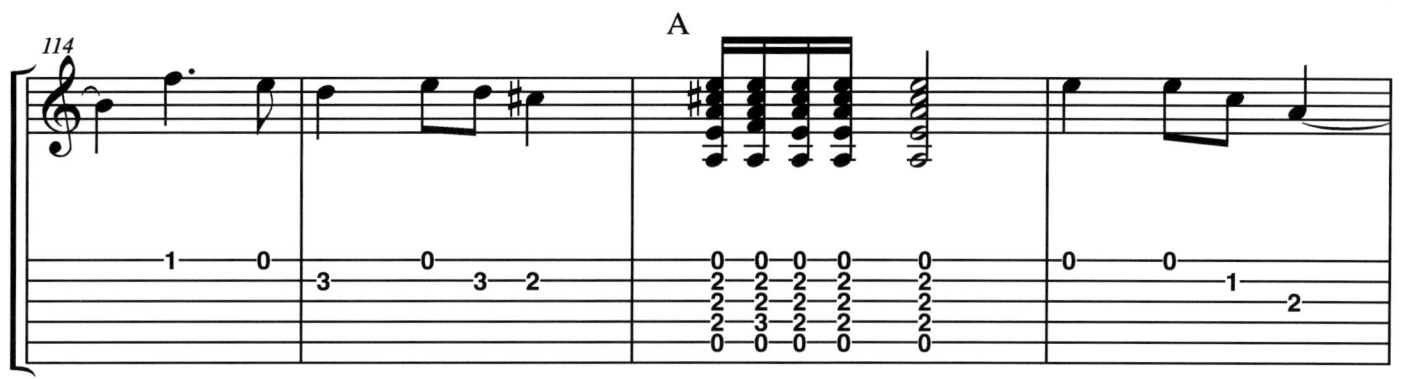
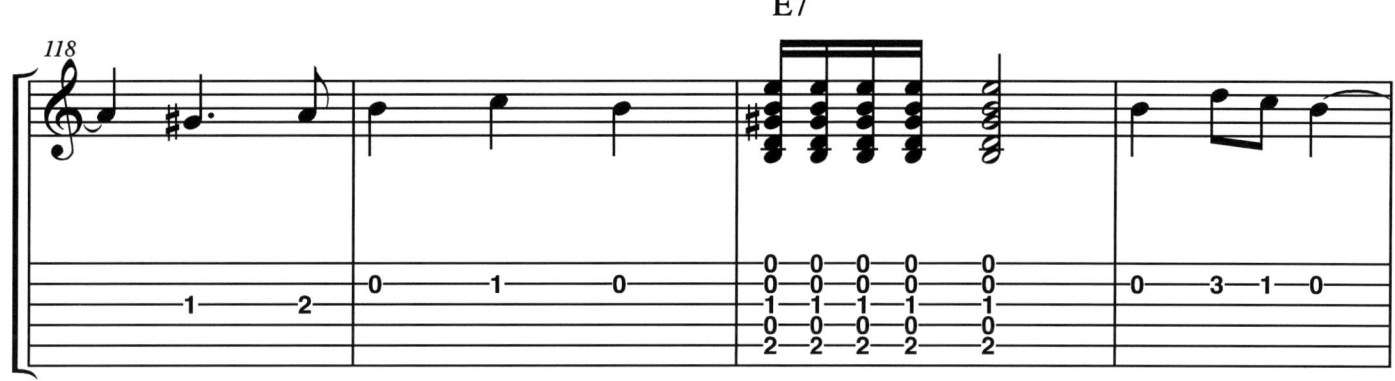
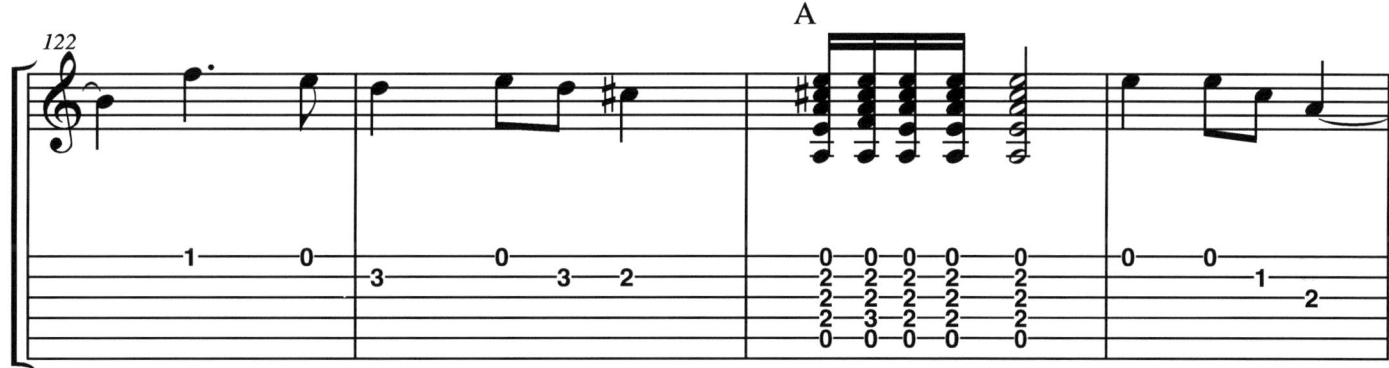
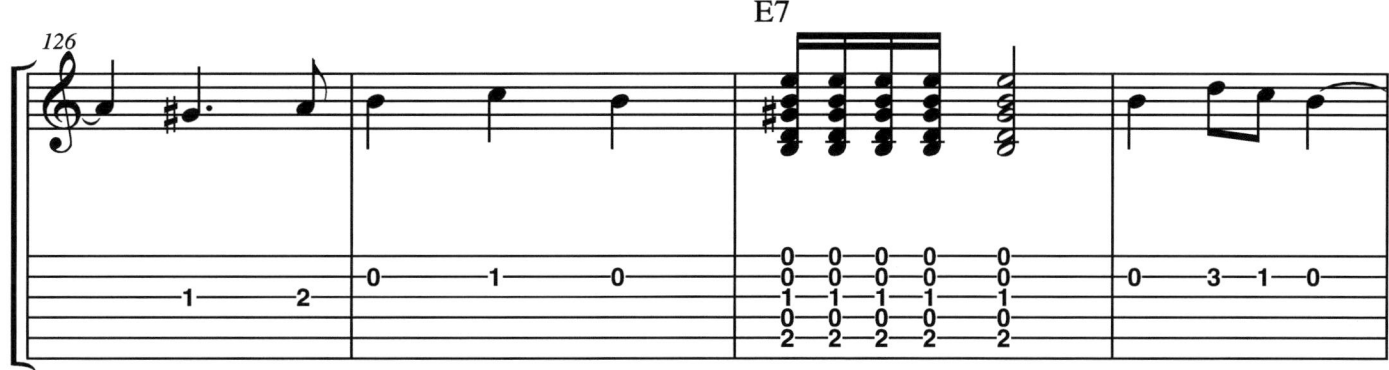

FANDANGOS DE HUELVA

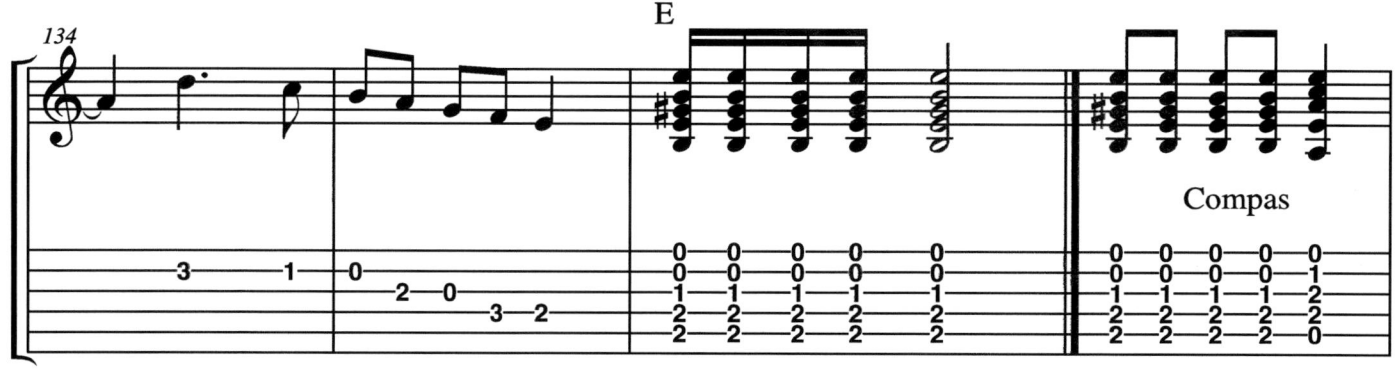

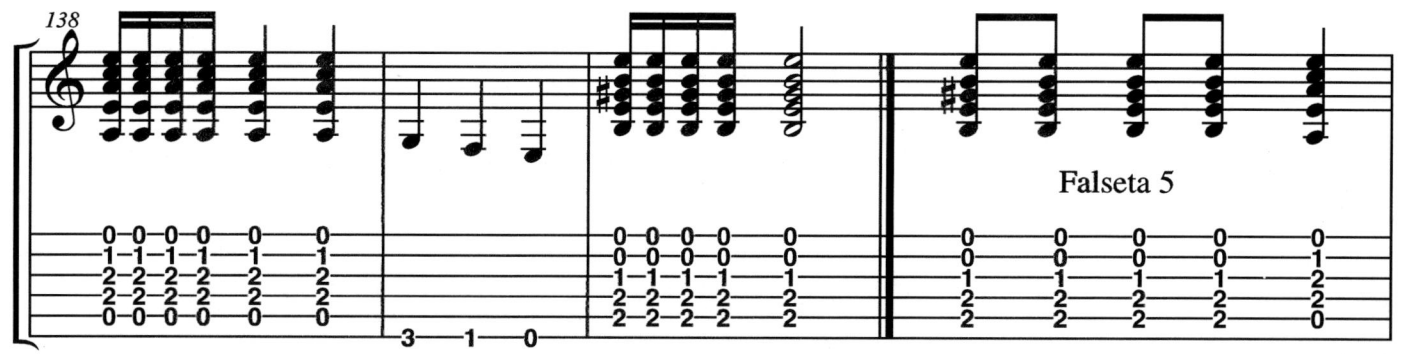

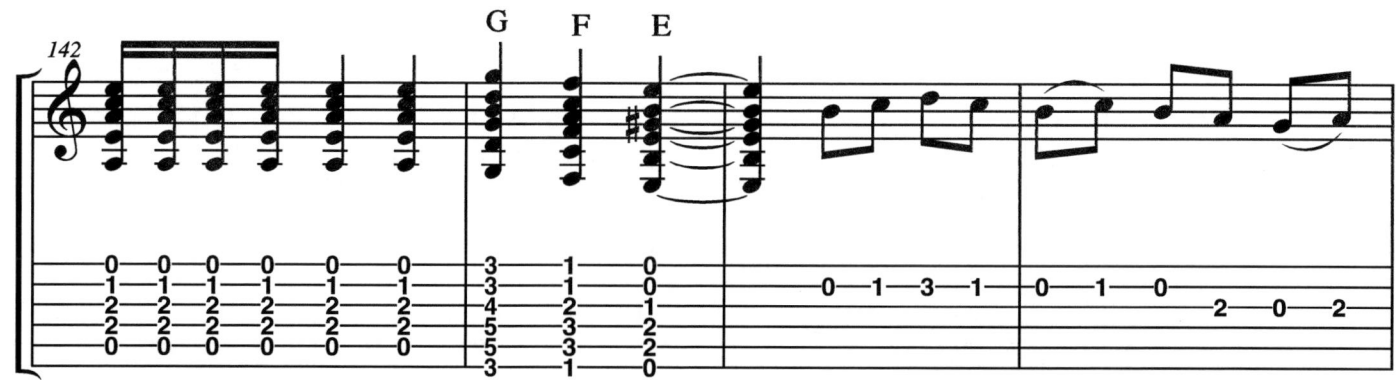

FANDANGOS DE HUELVA

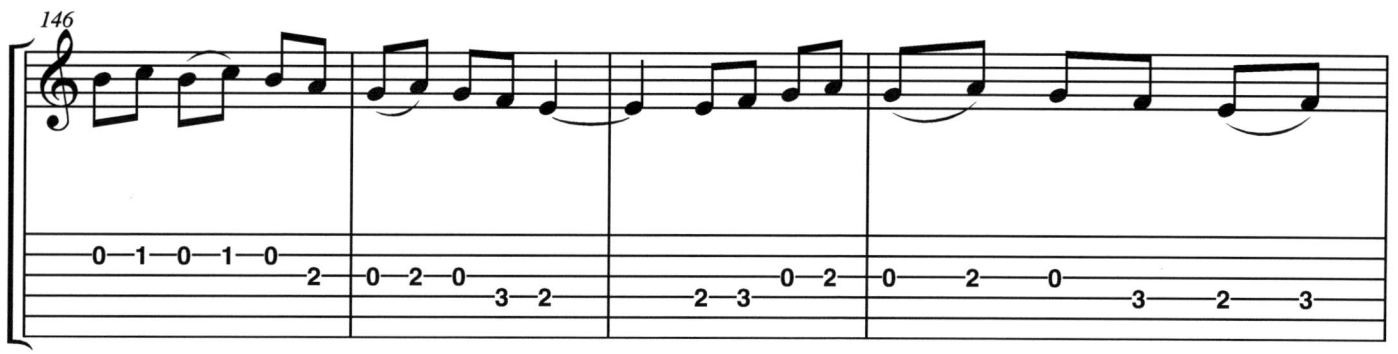
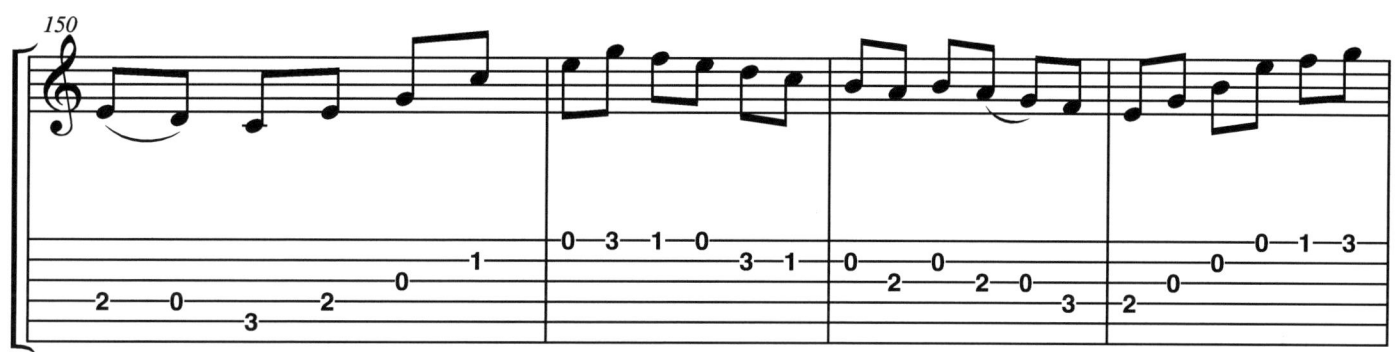
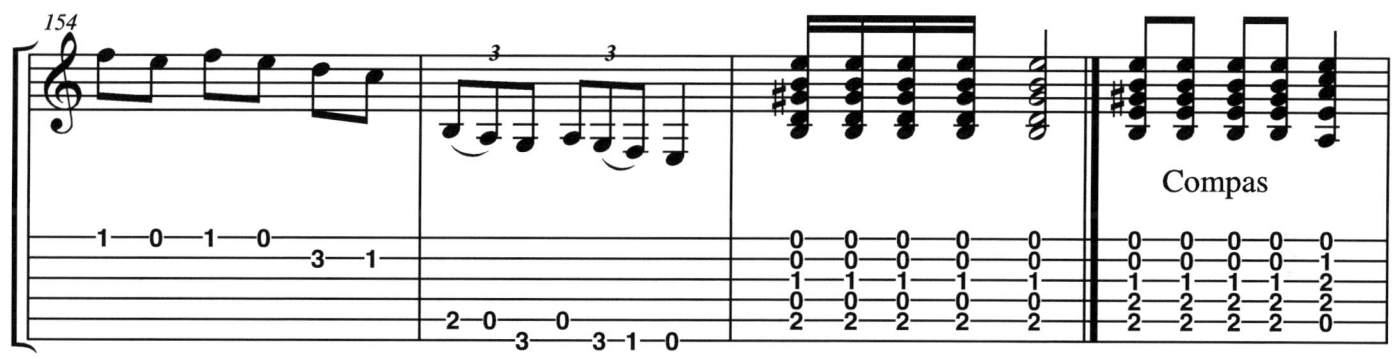
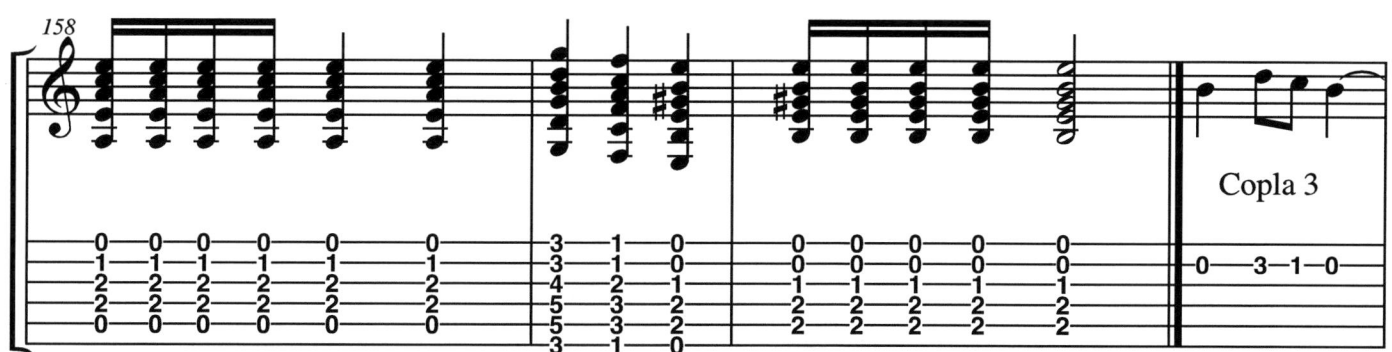

FANDANGOS DE HUELVA

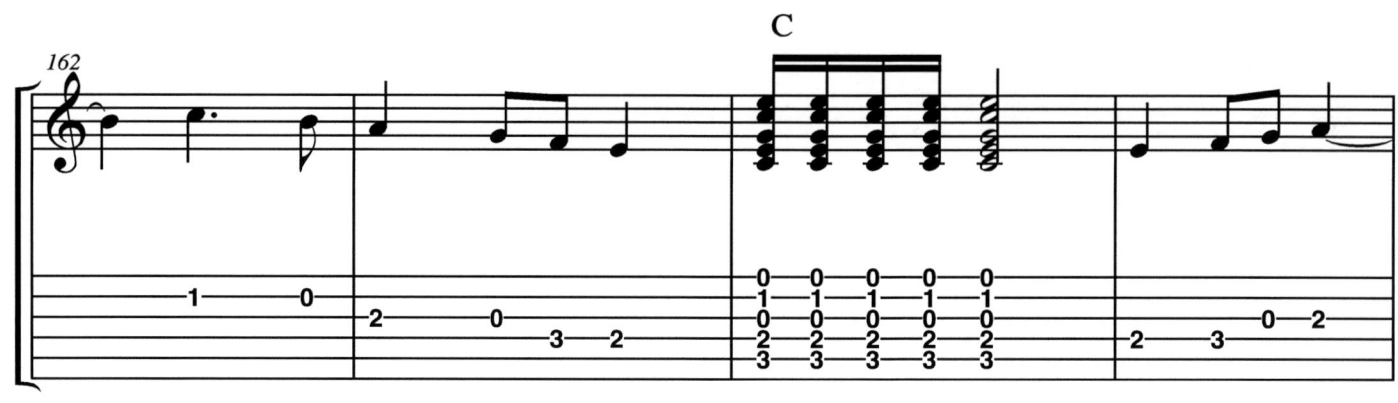
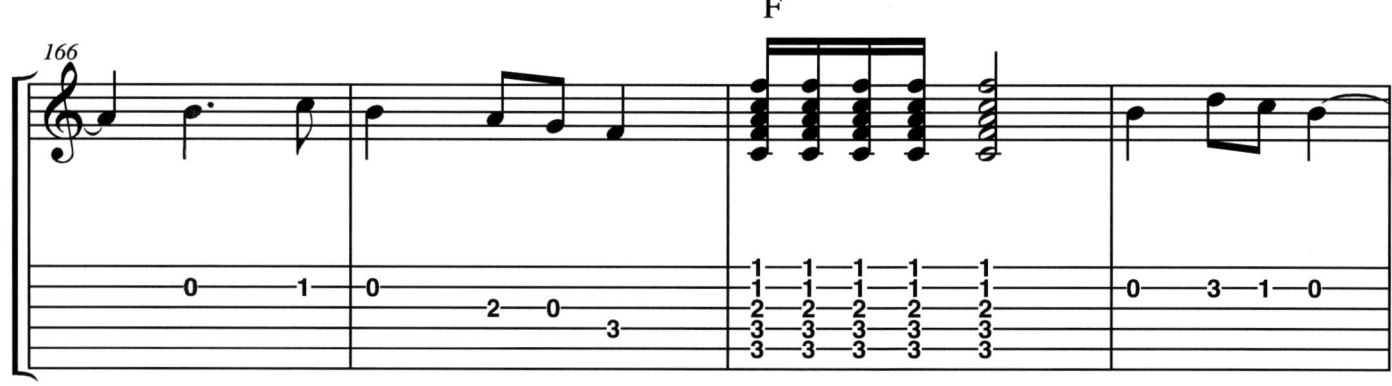
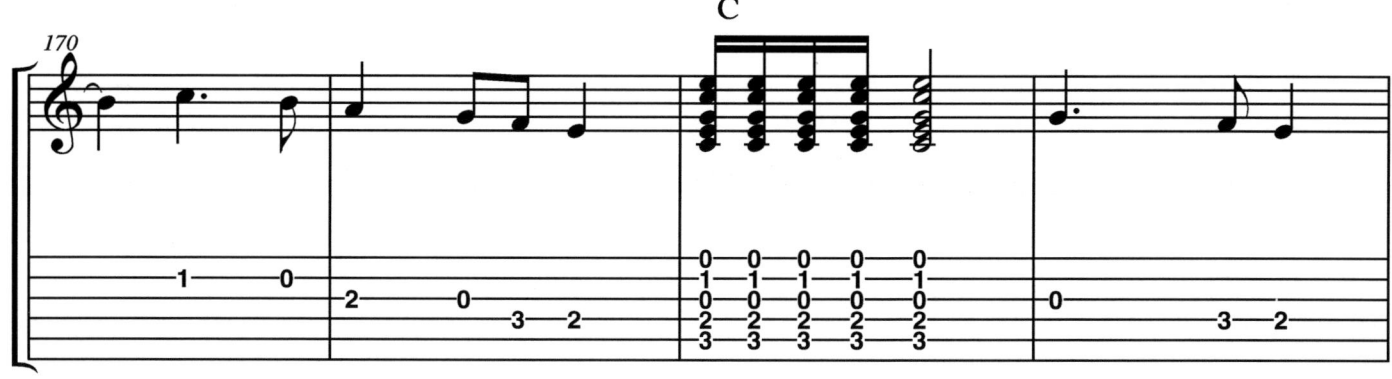
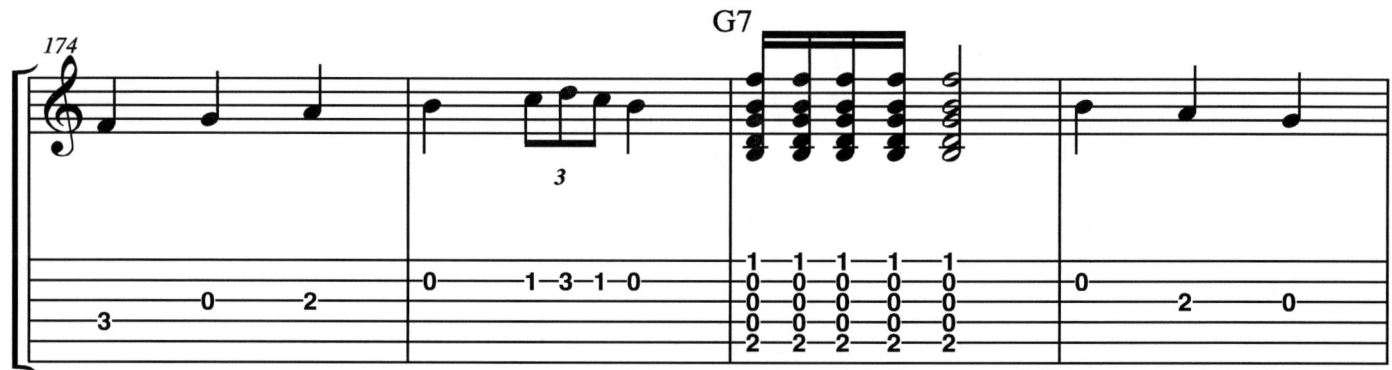

FANDANGOS DE HUELVA

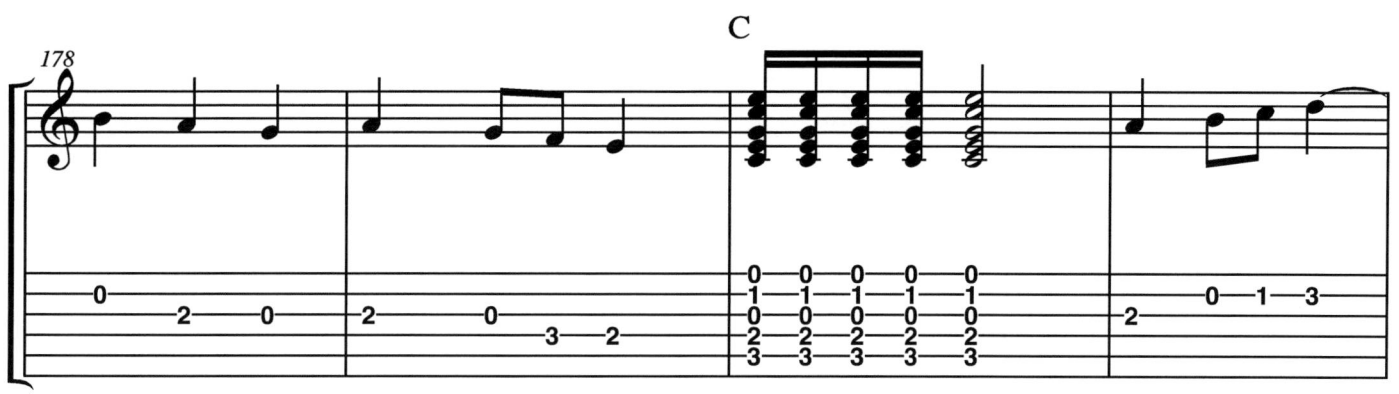
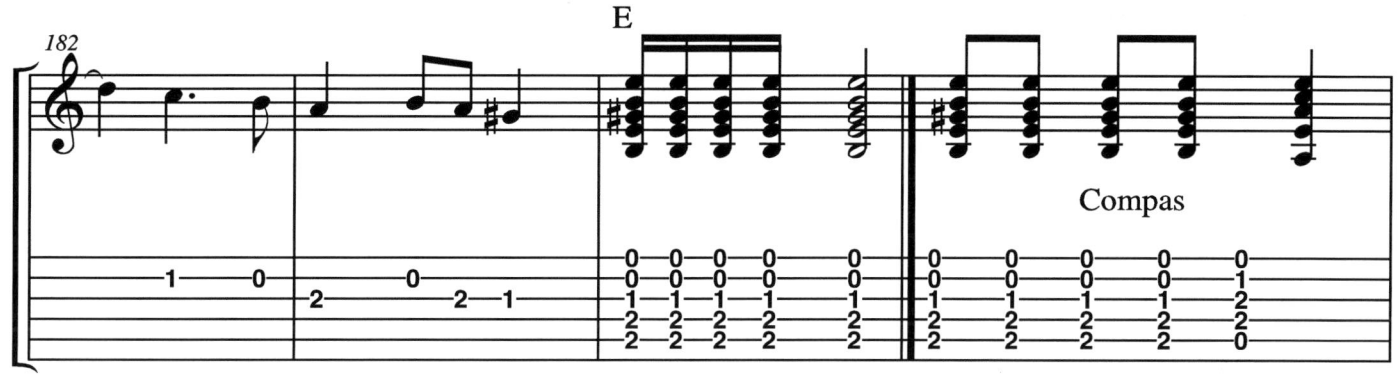
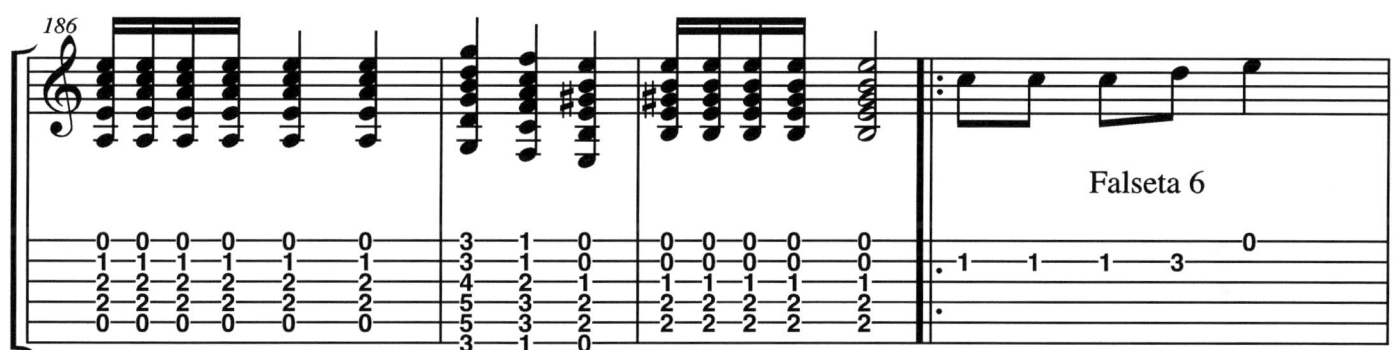
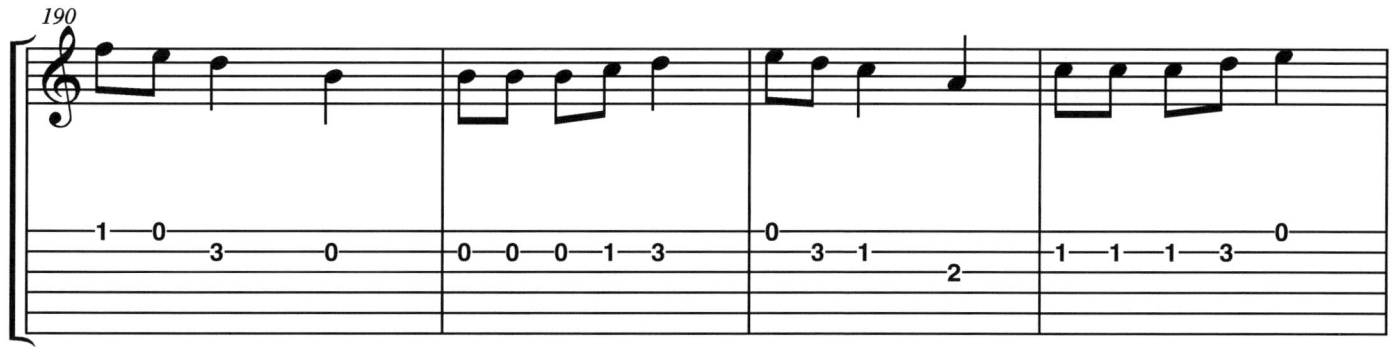

FANDANGOS DE HUELVA

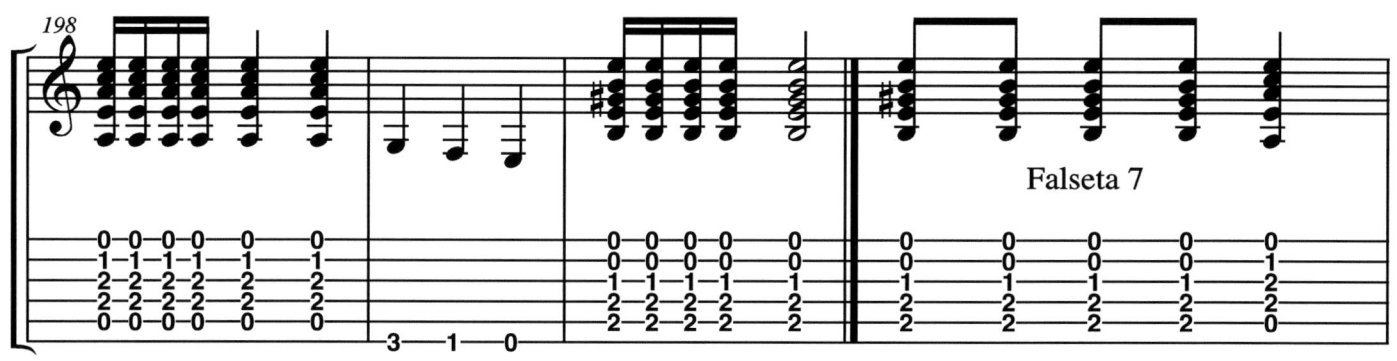
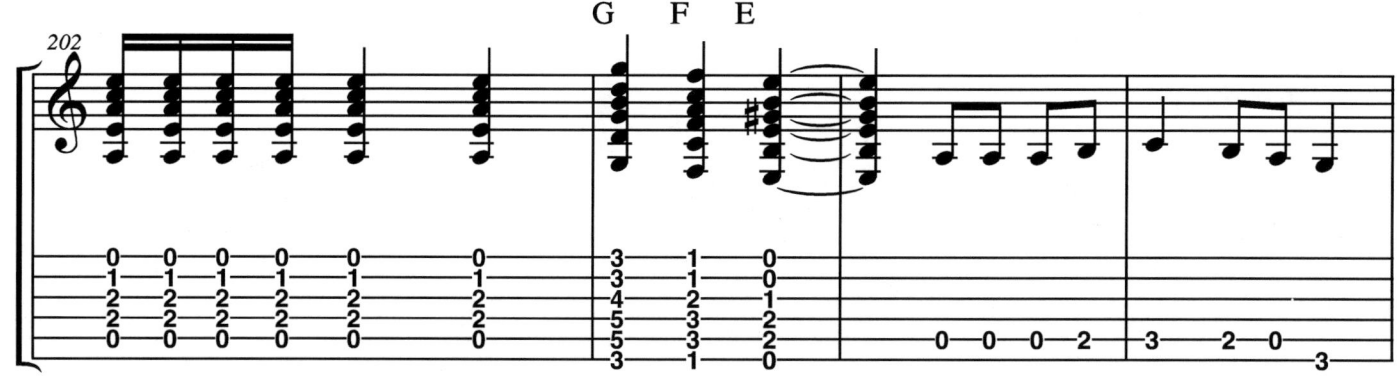
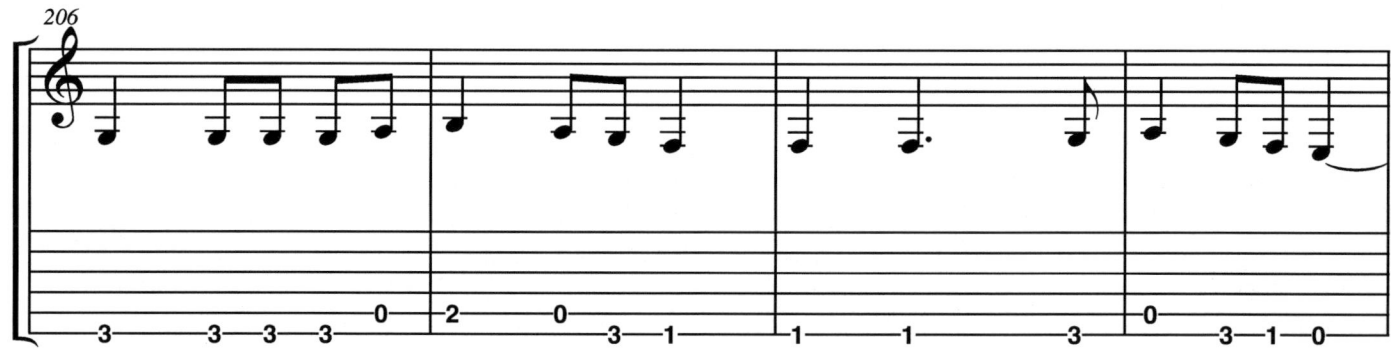

FANDANGOS DE HUELVA

FANDANGOS DE HUELVA

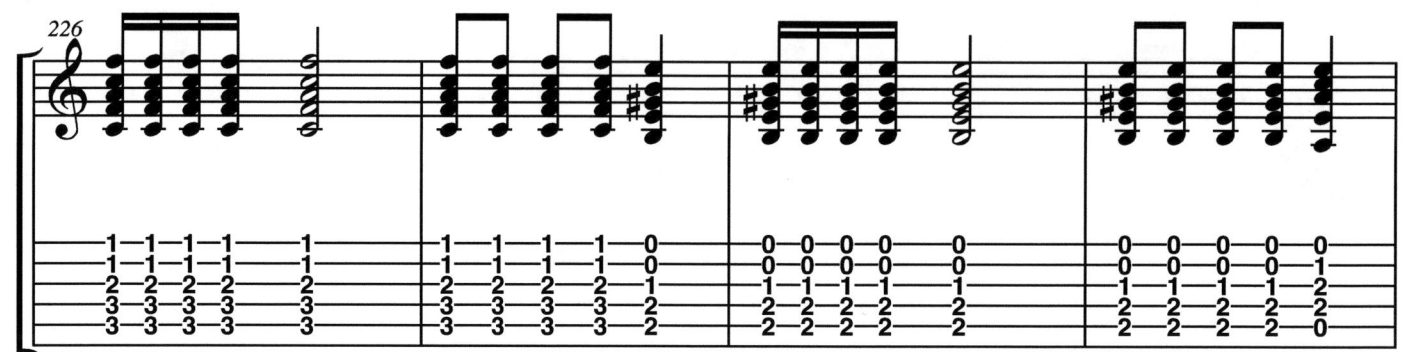
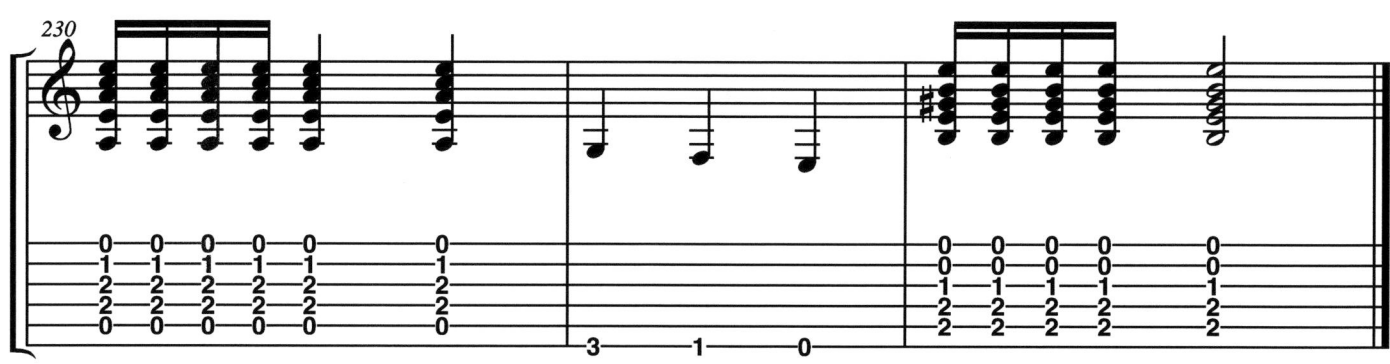

This page has been left black to avoid awkward page turns.

FARRUCAS

Strum every compas in the same manner

FARRUCAS

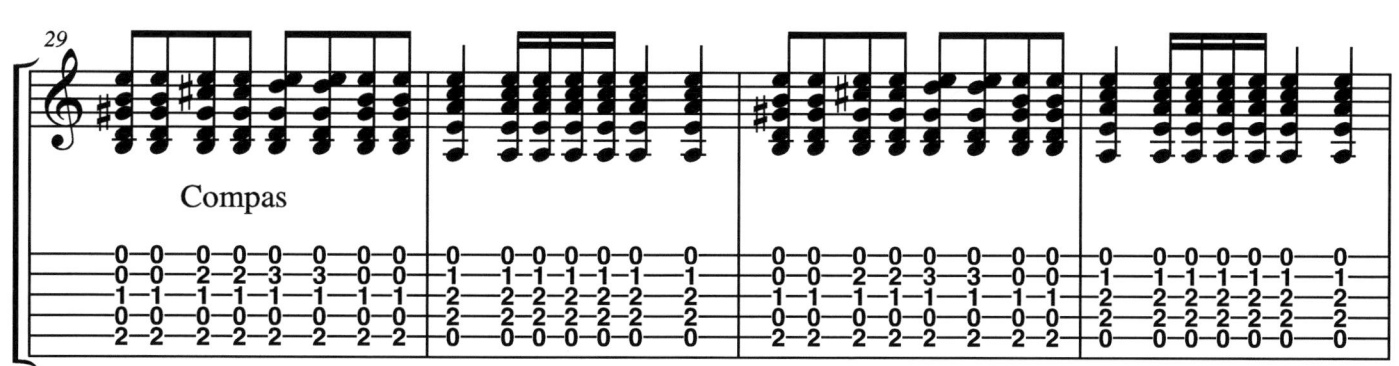

FARRUCAS

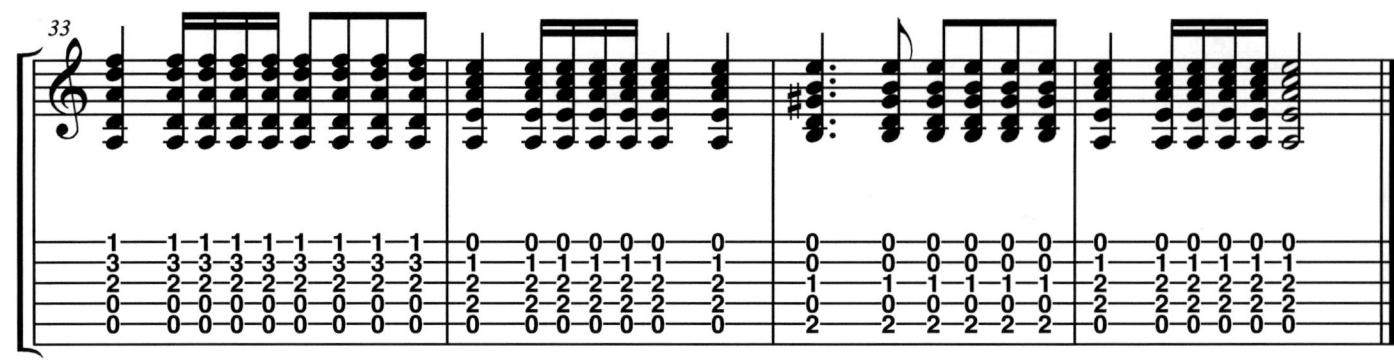

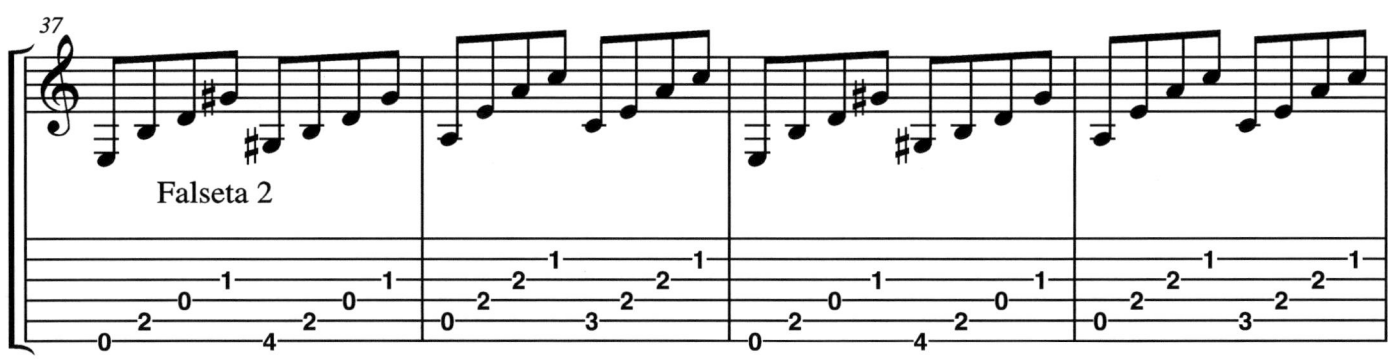

Falseta 2

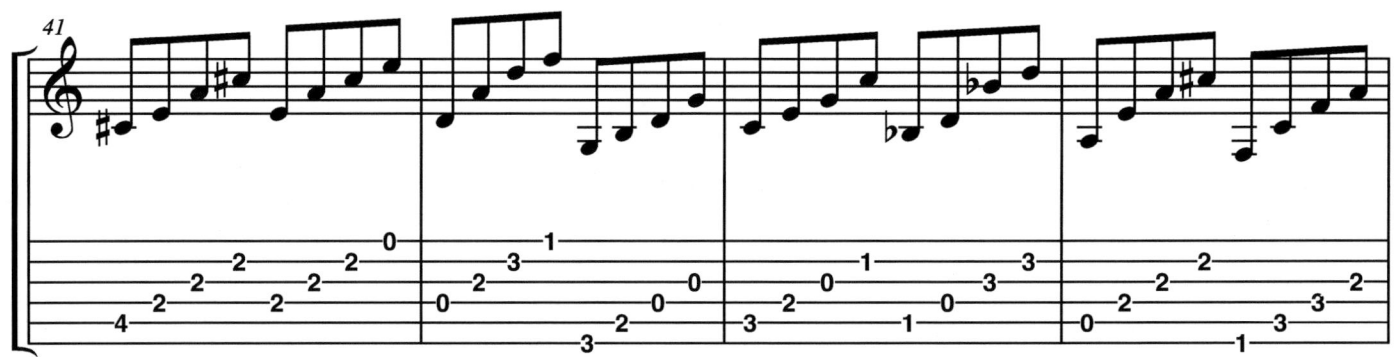

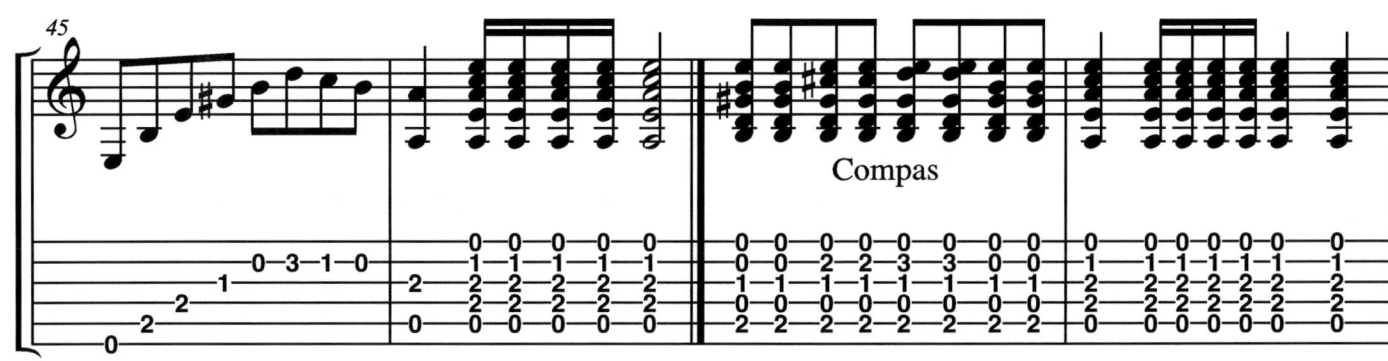

Compas

FARRUCAS

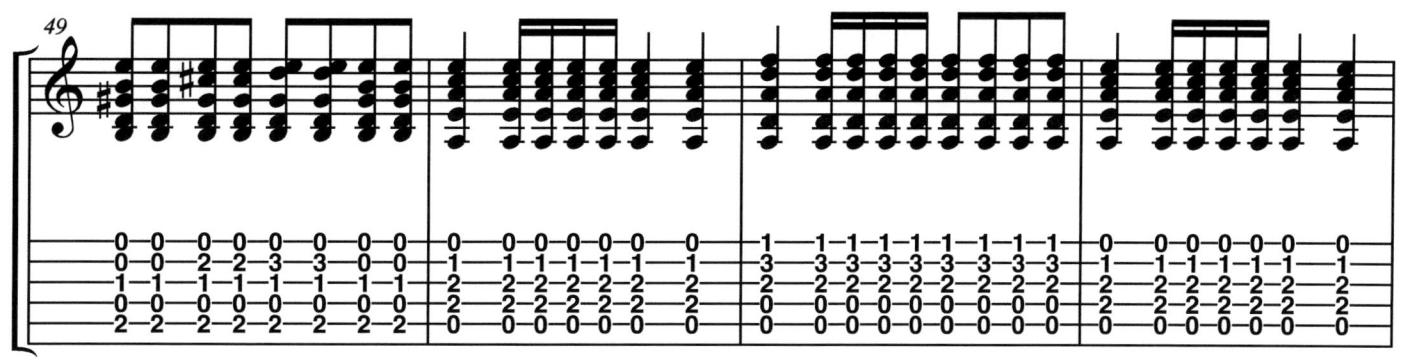
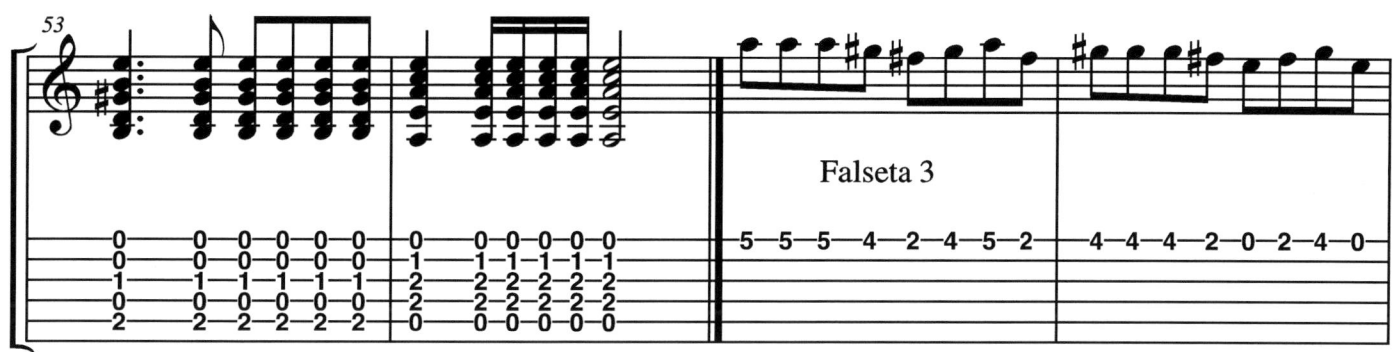

Falseta 3

FARRUCAS

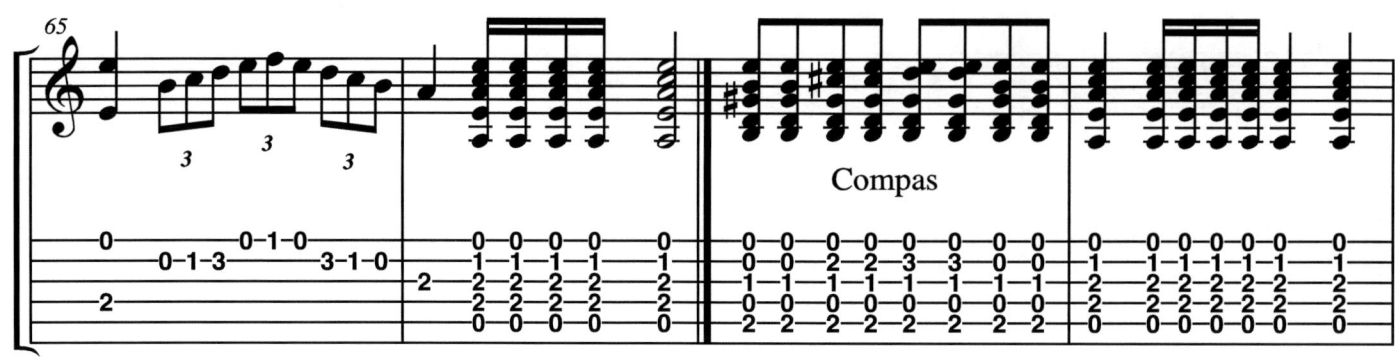
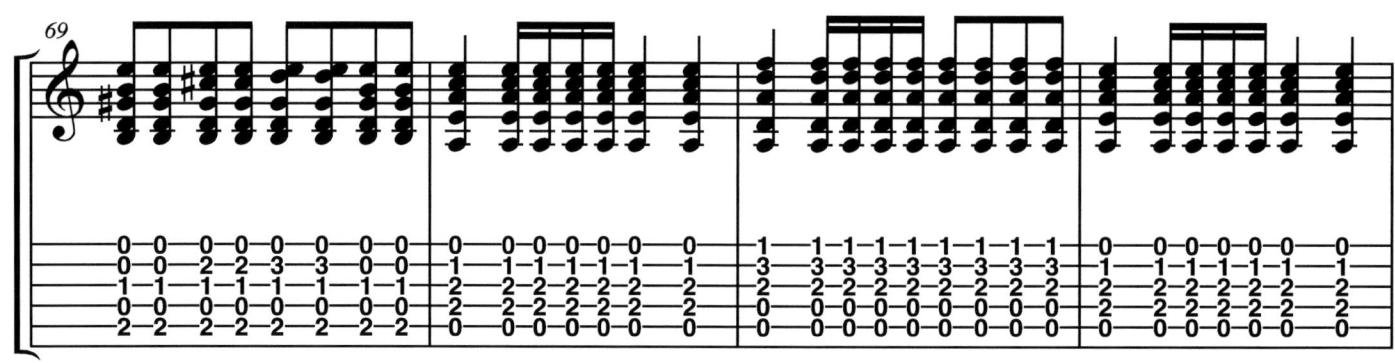
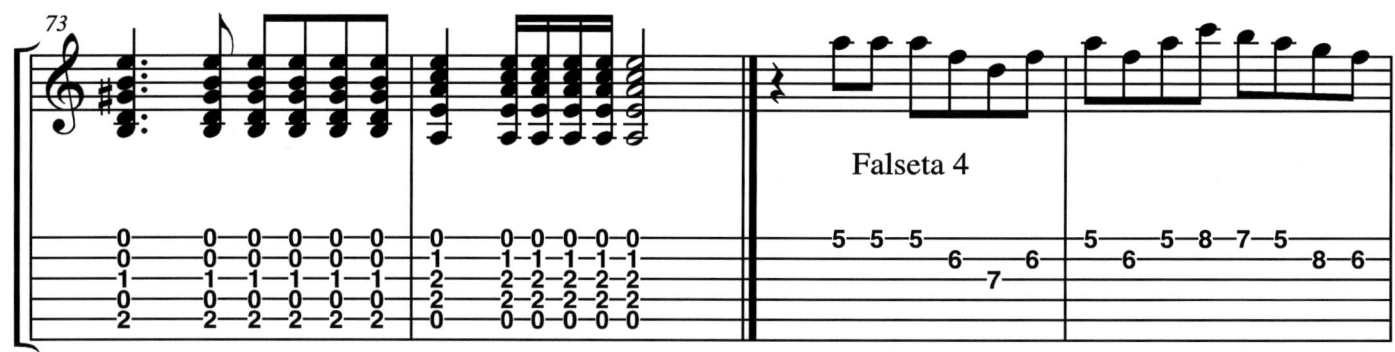
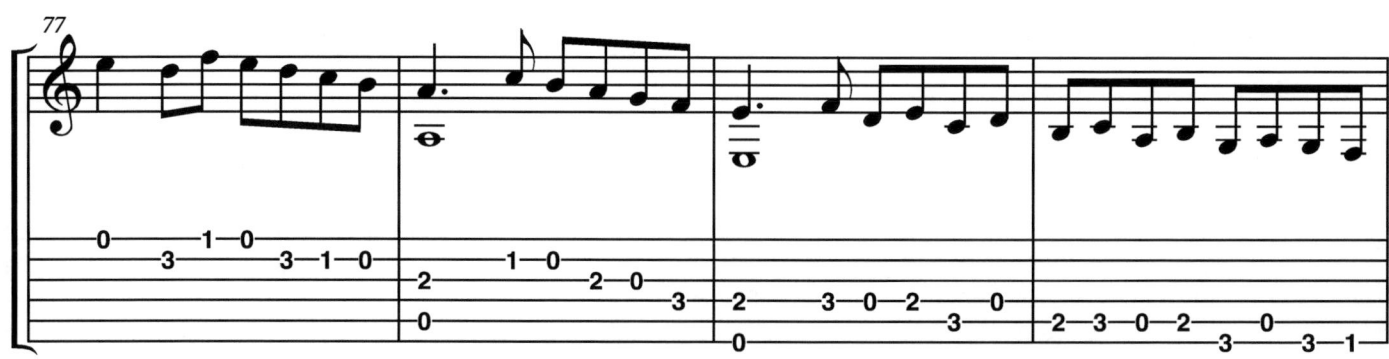

FARRUCAS

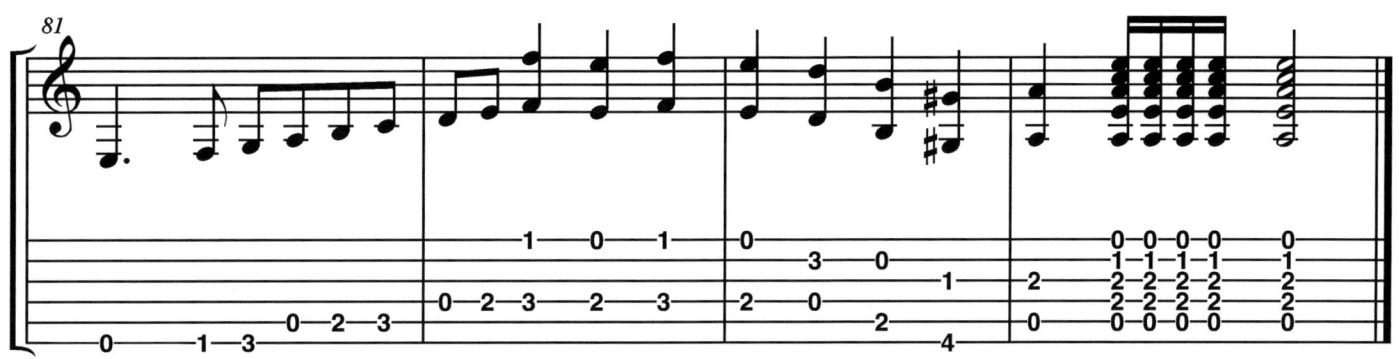
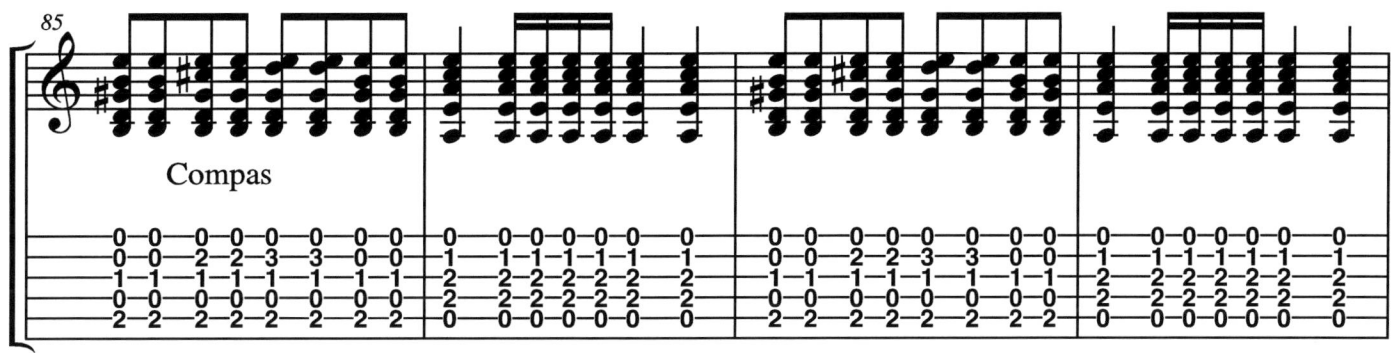
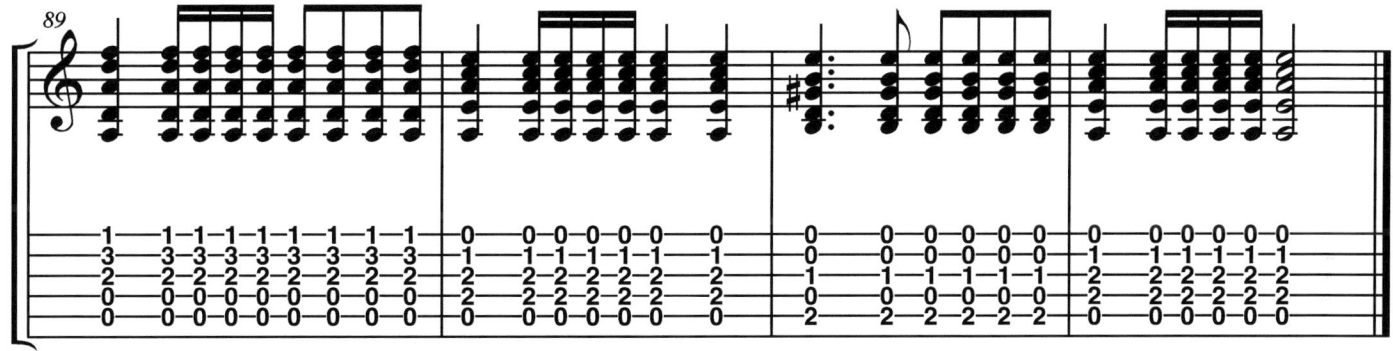
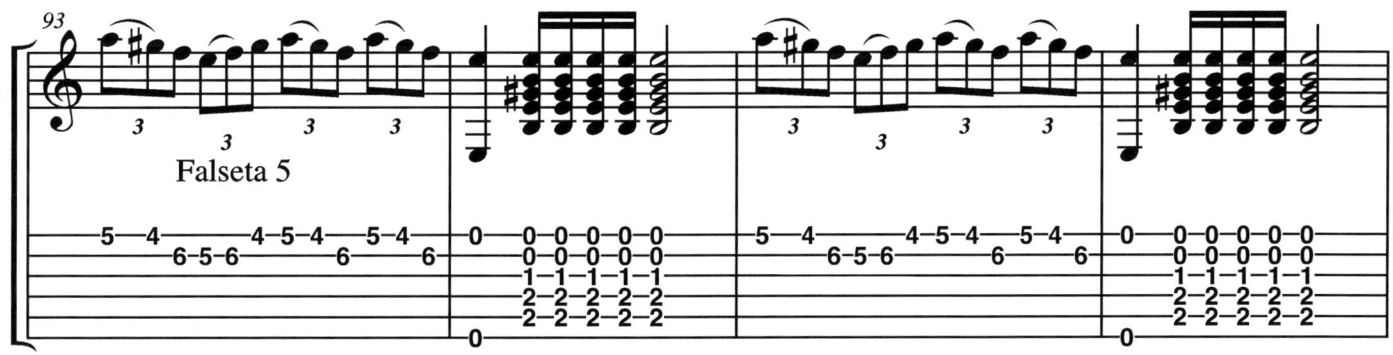

FARRUCAS

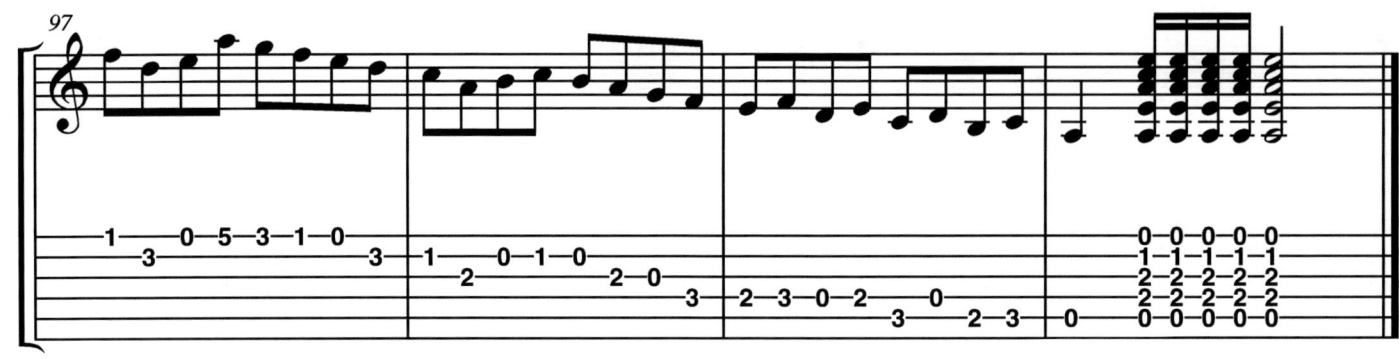
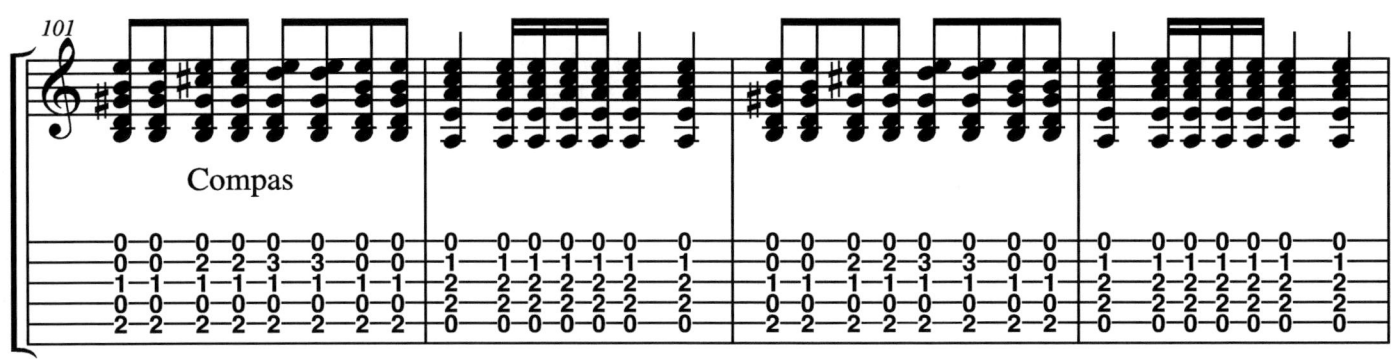
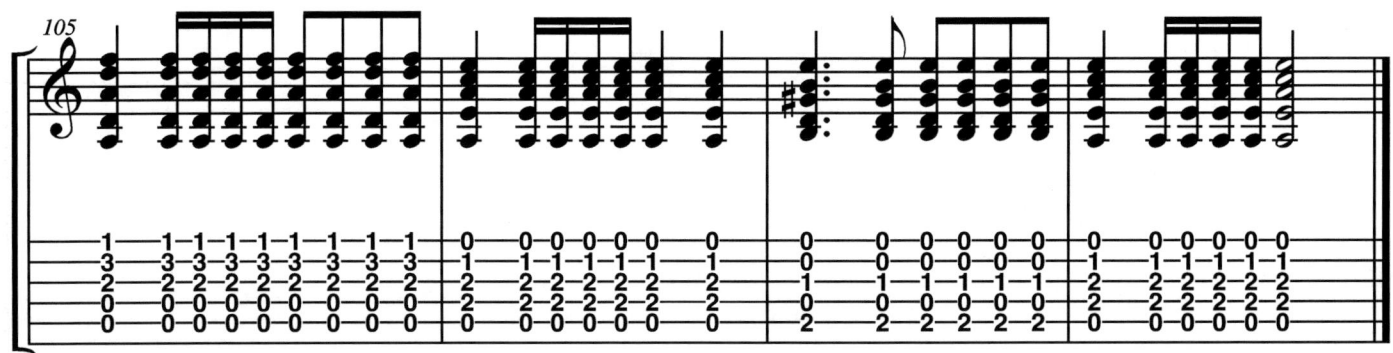
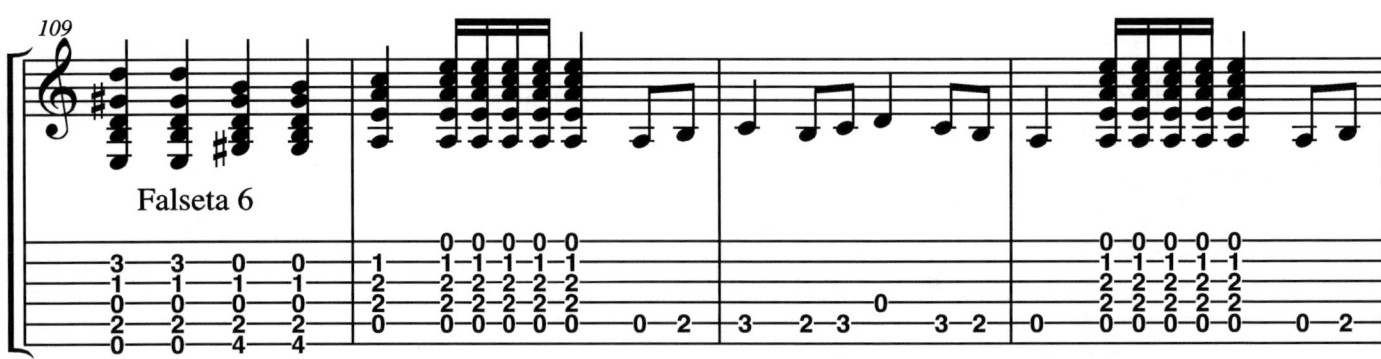

FARRUCAS

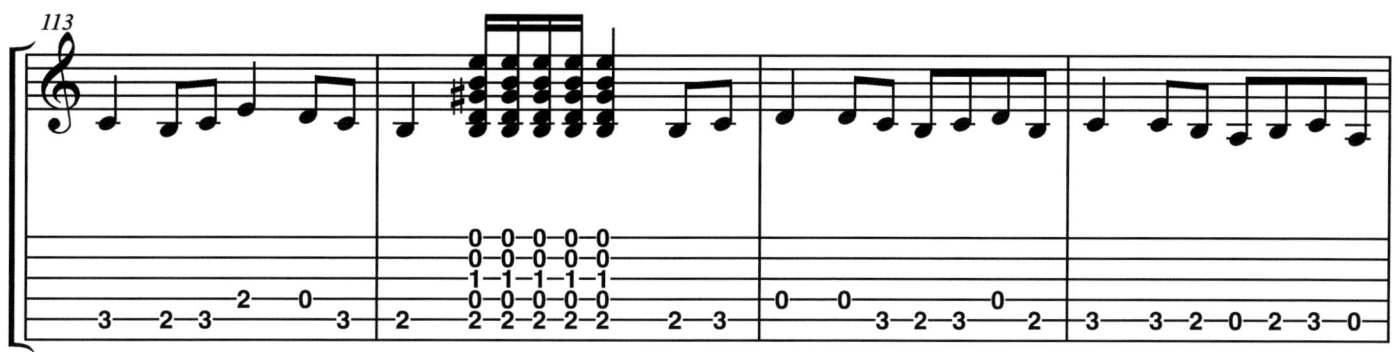
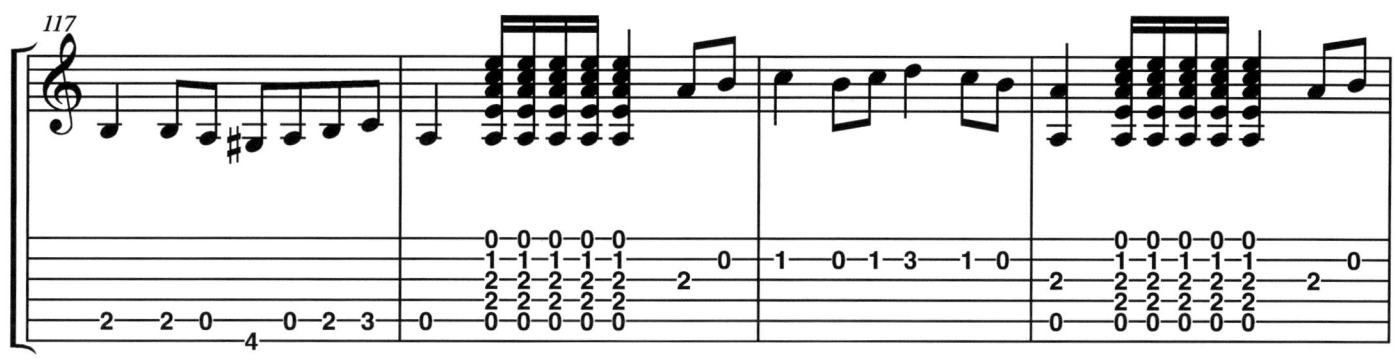
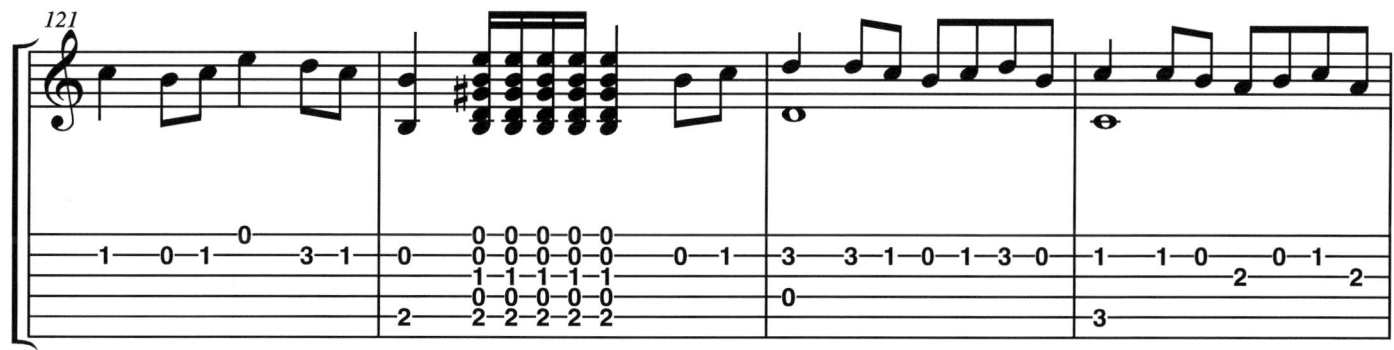
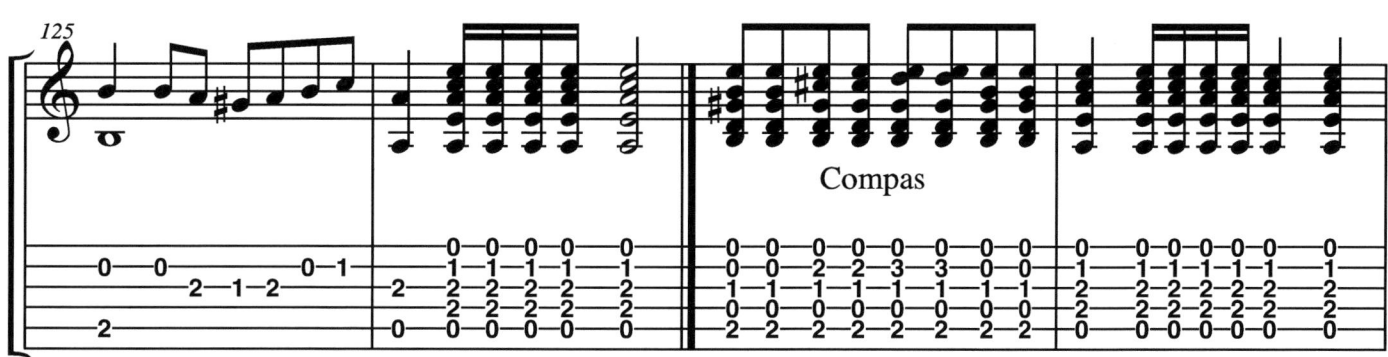

FARRUCAS

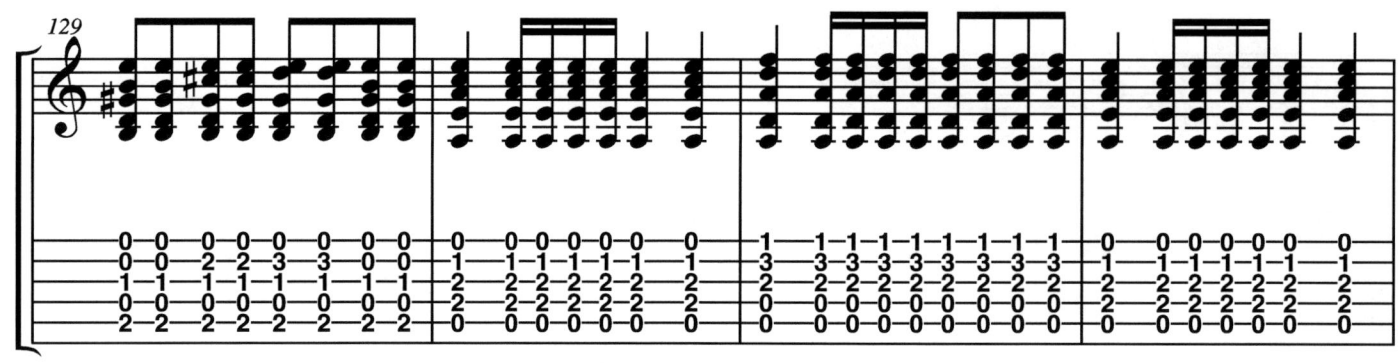
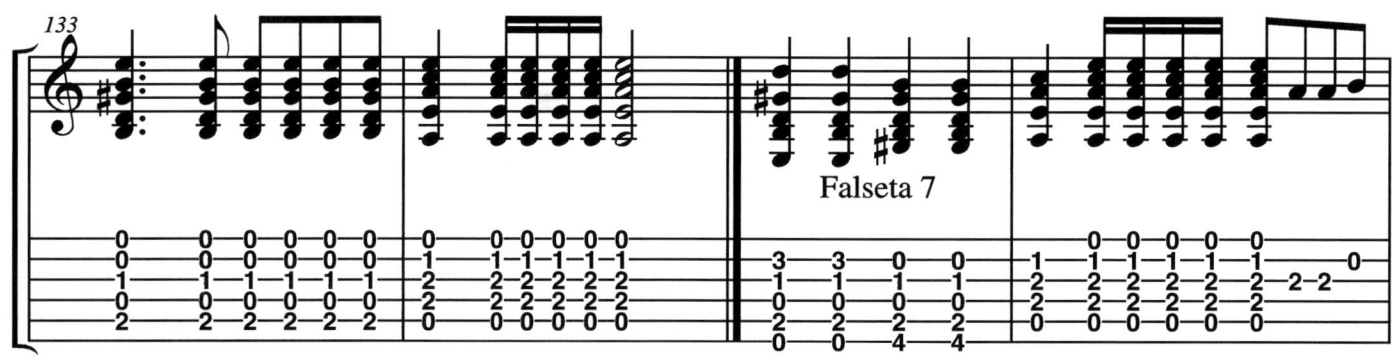

Falseta 7

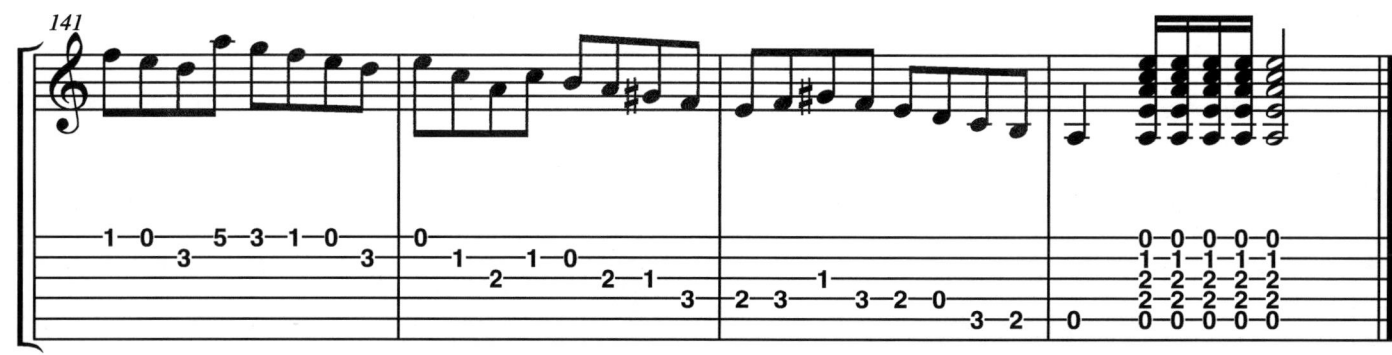

FARRUCAS

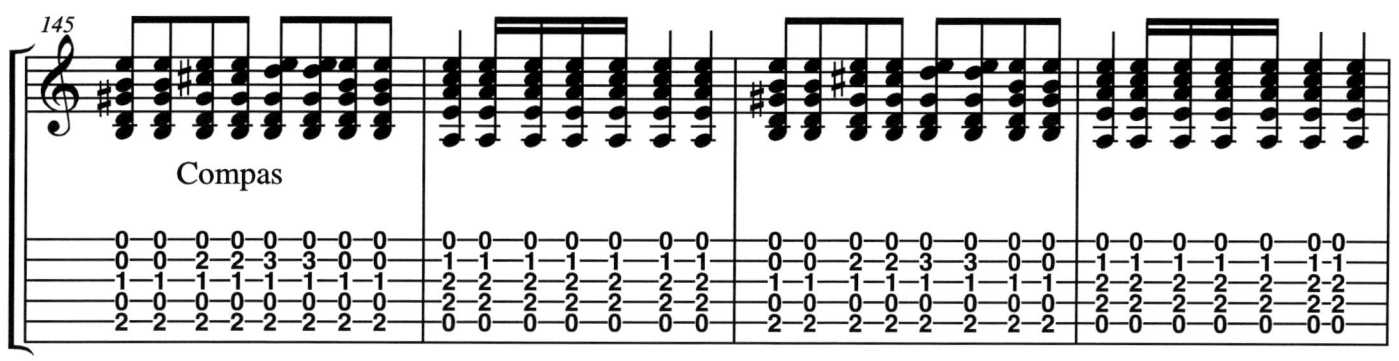

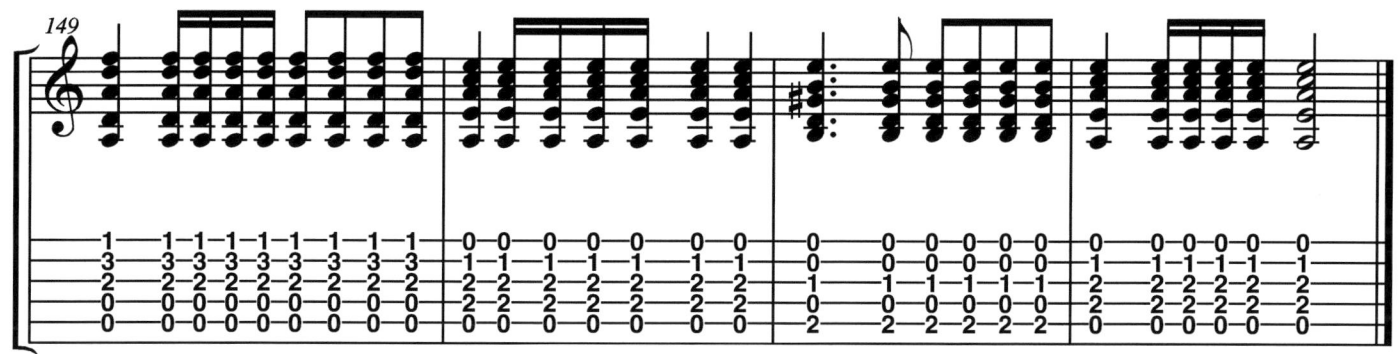

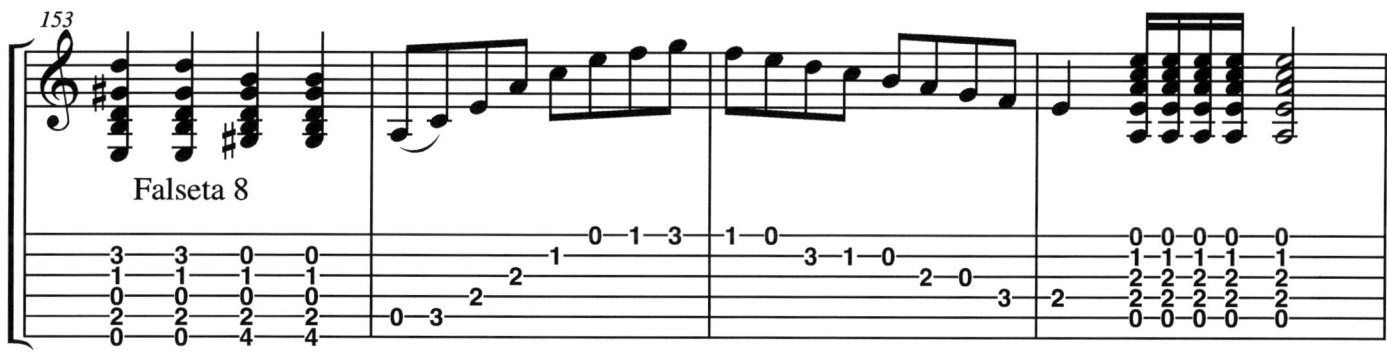

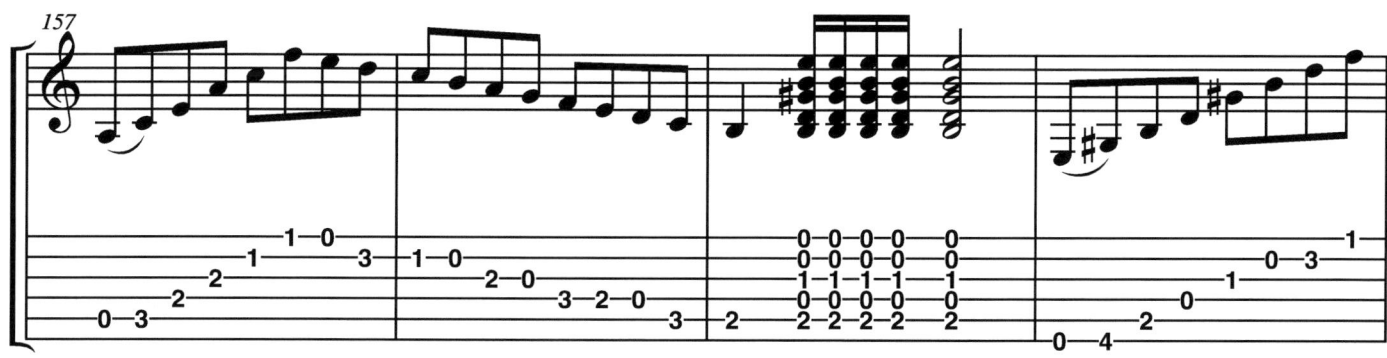

FARRUCAS

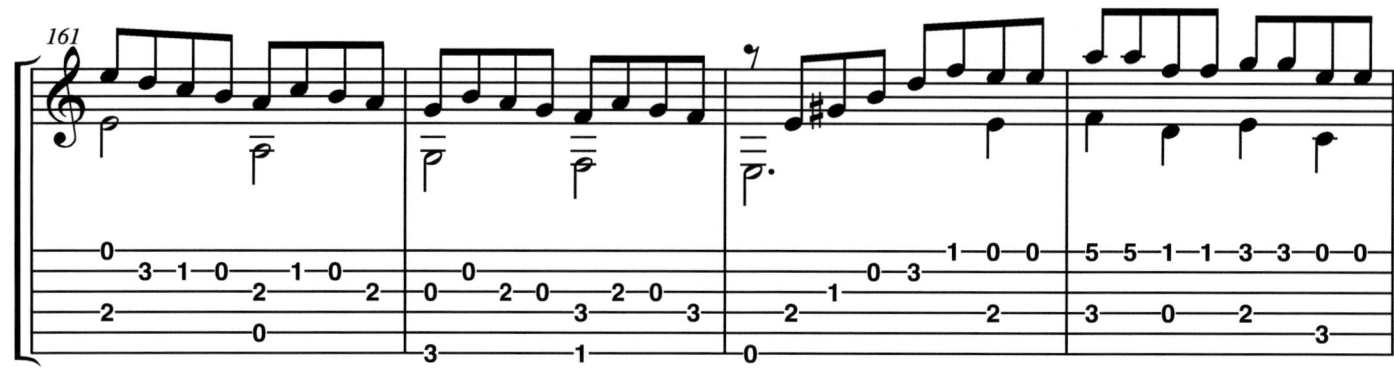
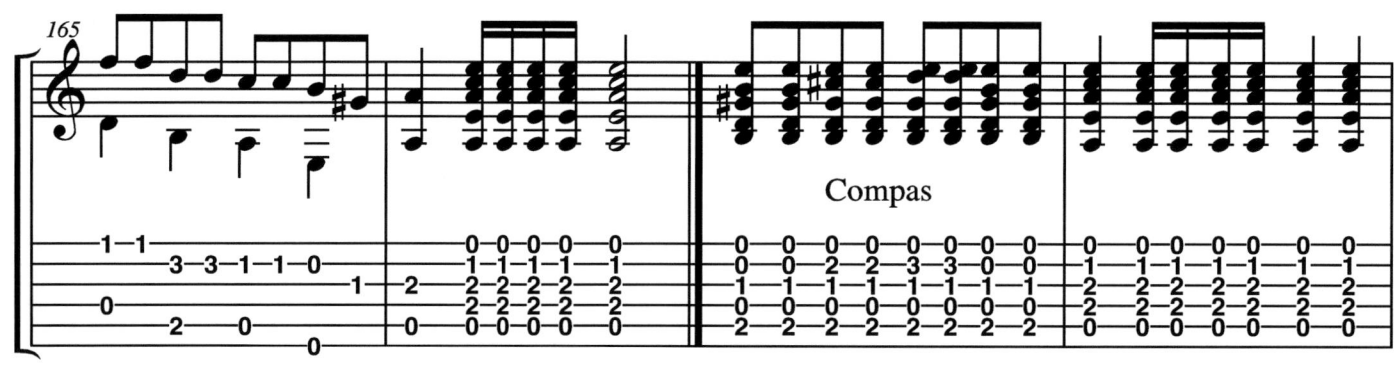
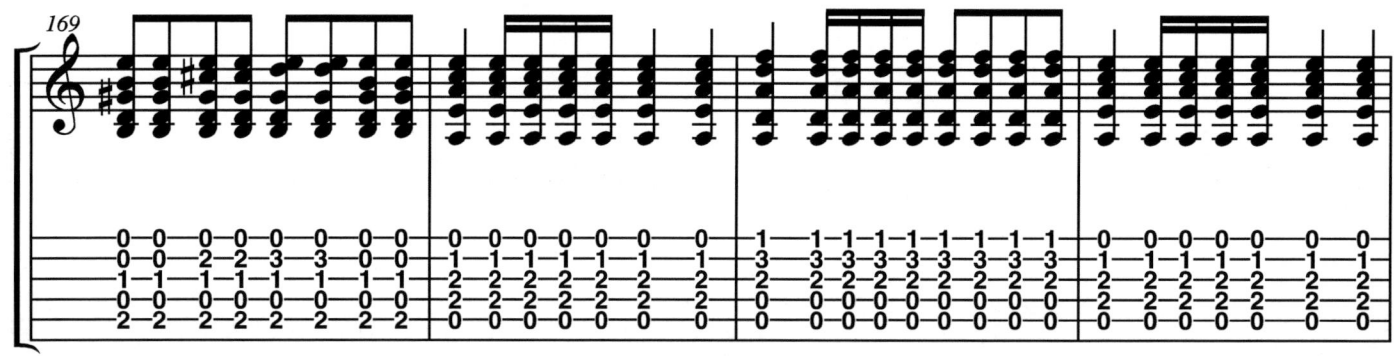
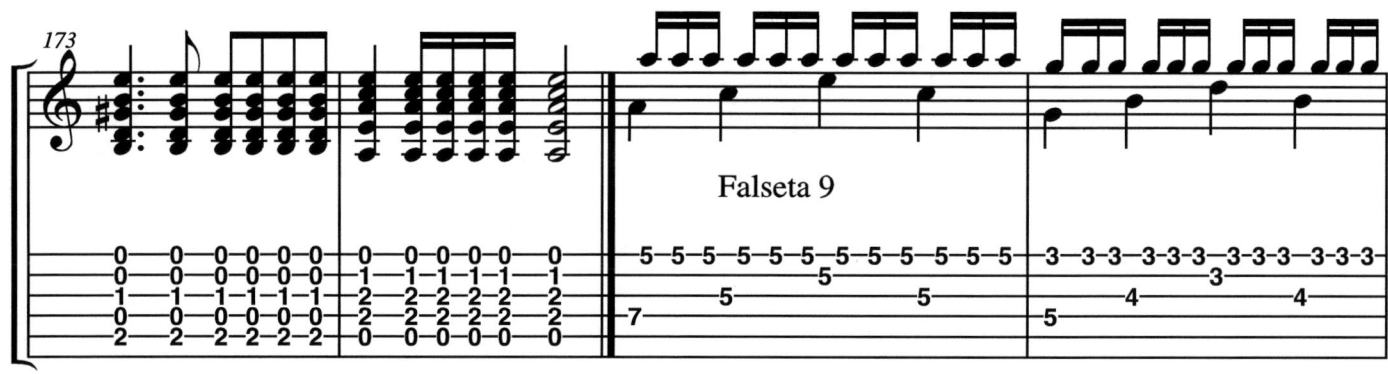

FARRUCAS

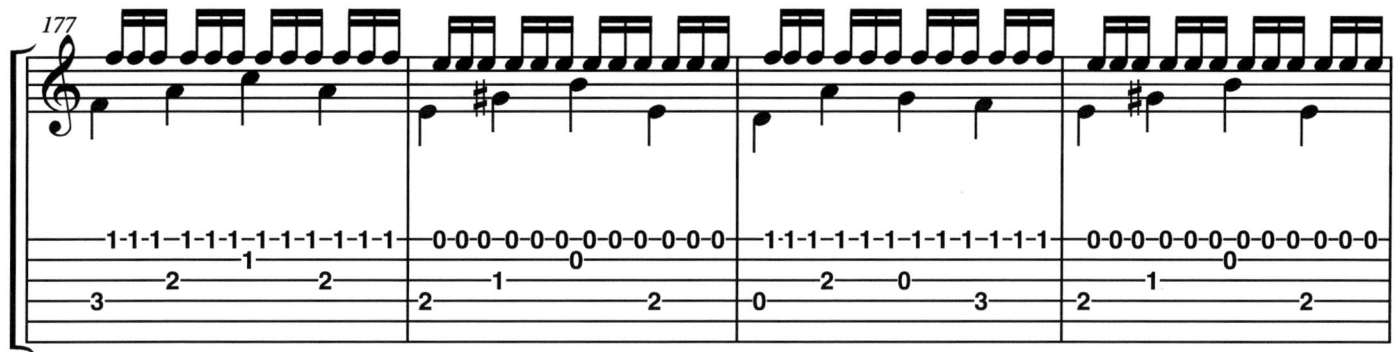
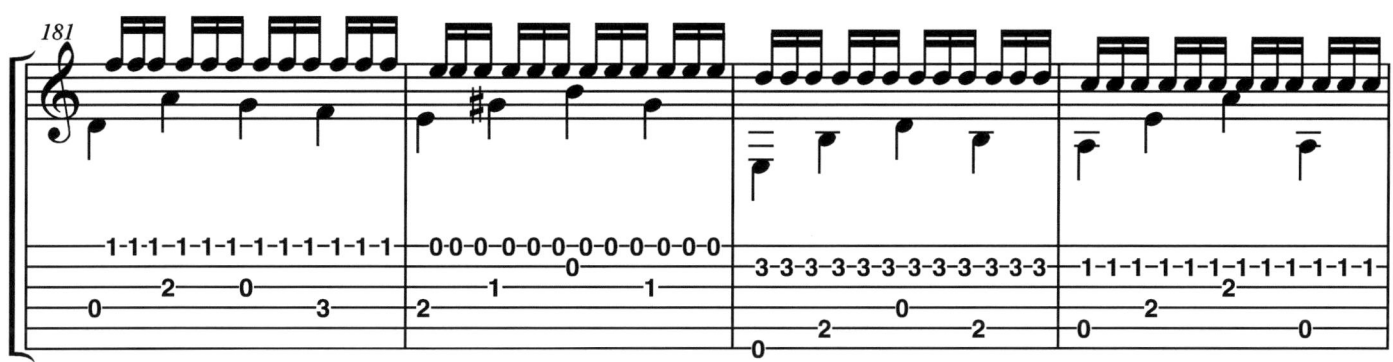
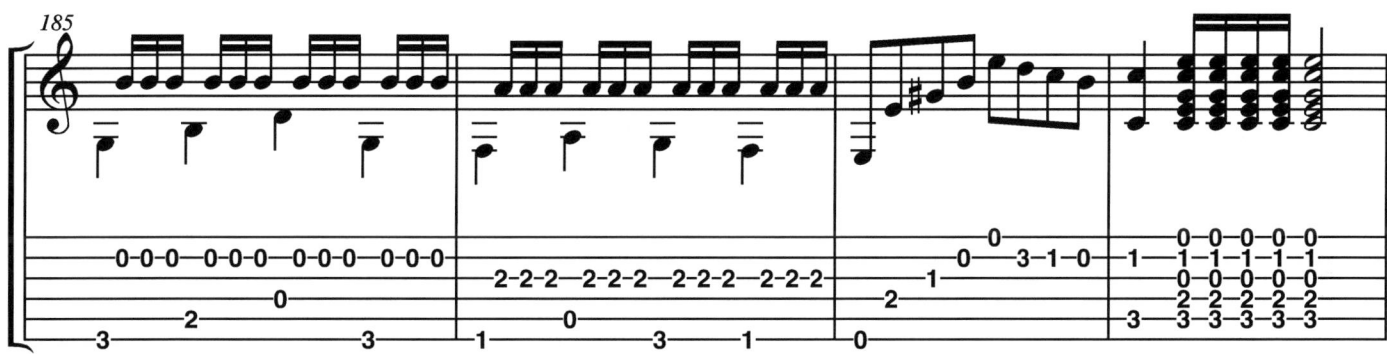
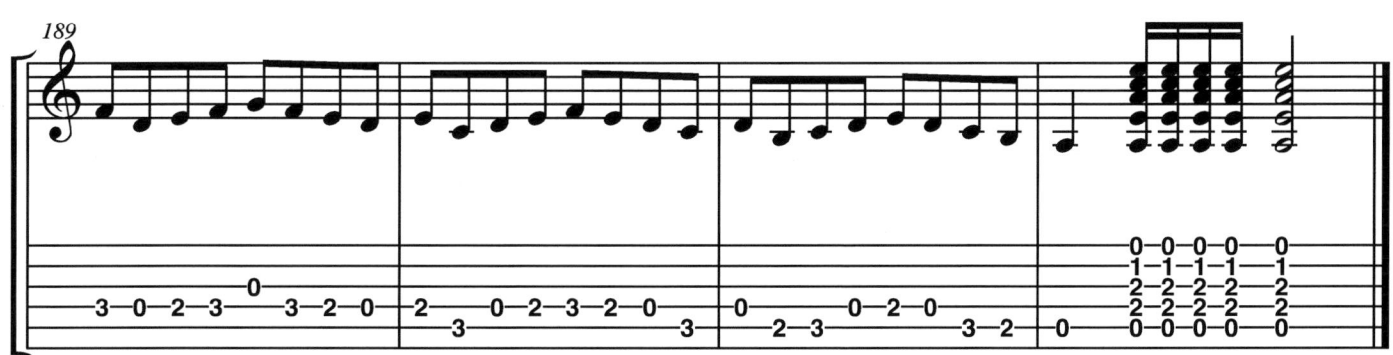

FARRUCAS

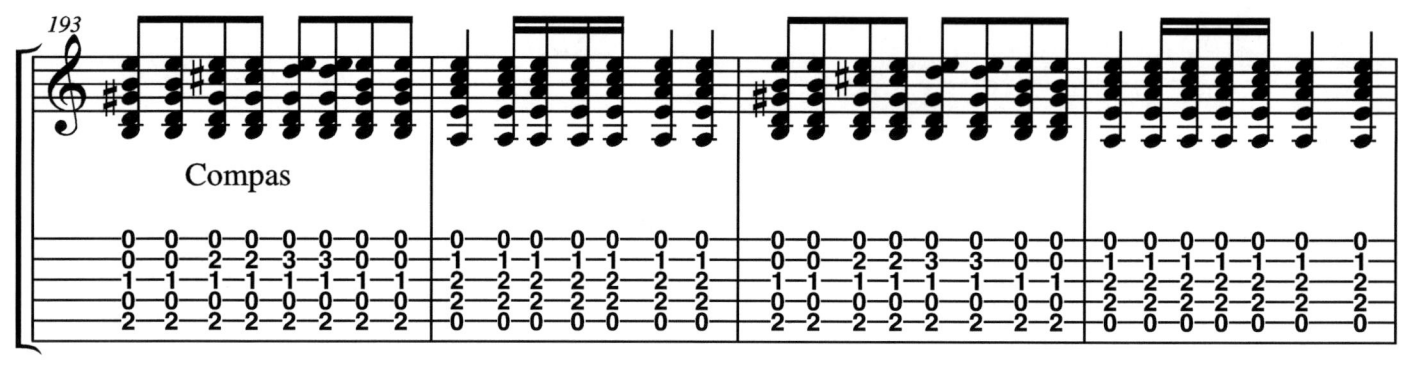

Compas

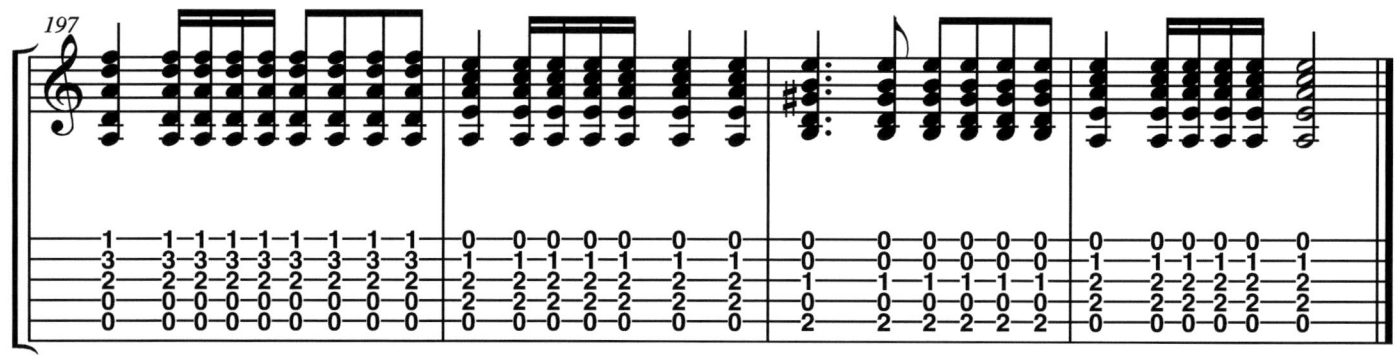

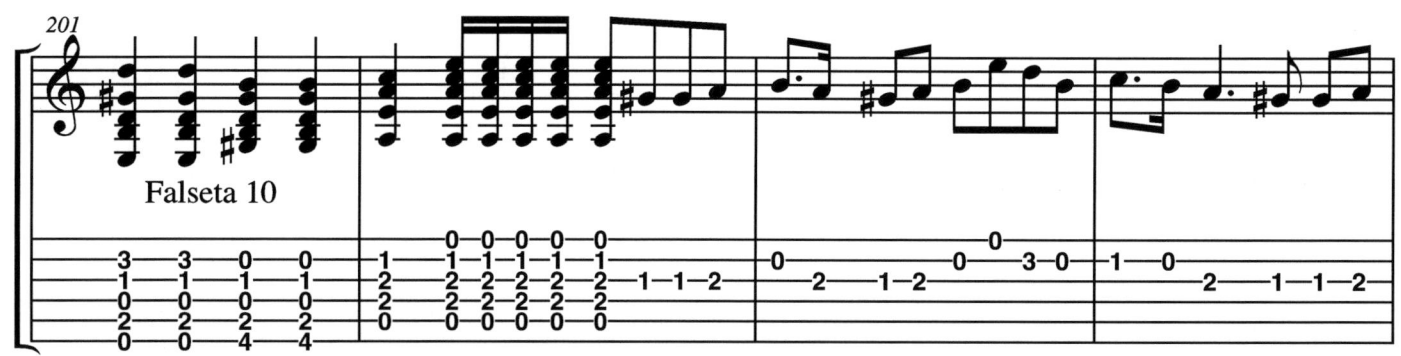

Falseta 10

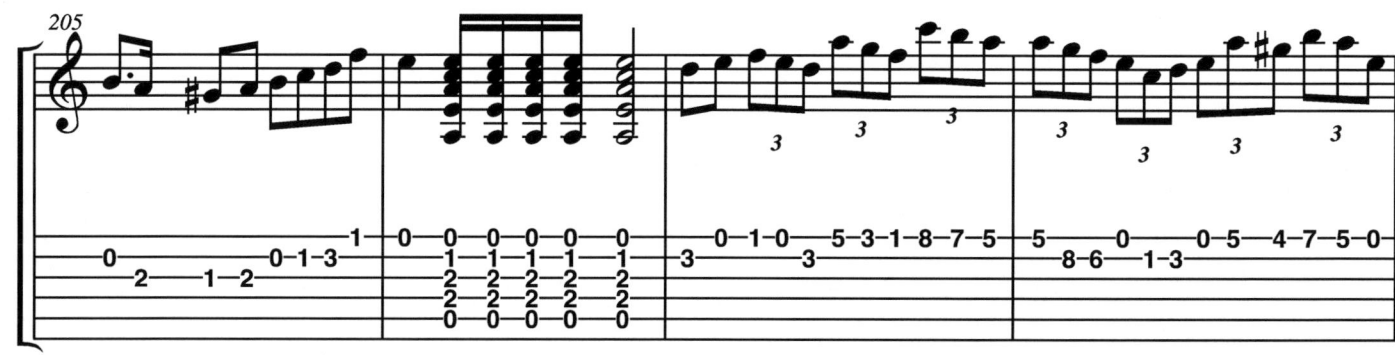

FARRUCAS

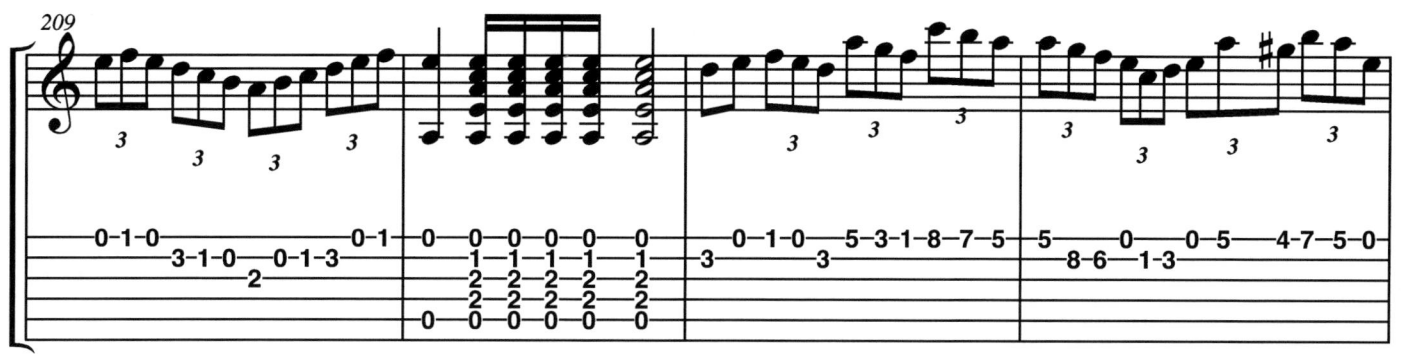
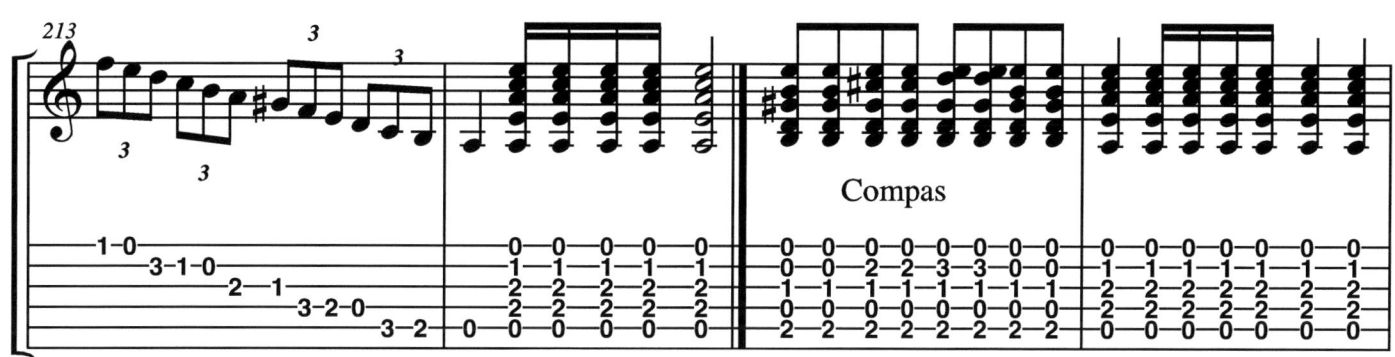
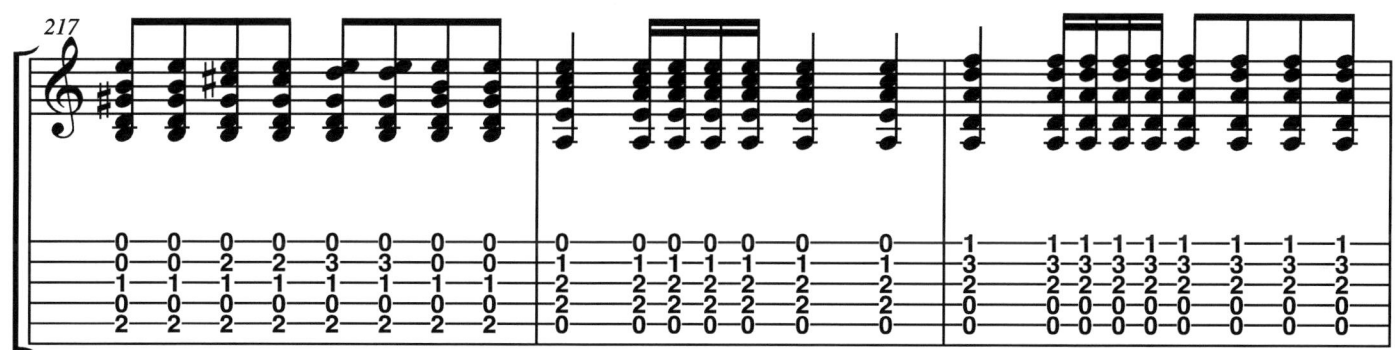
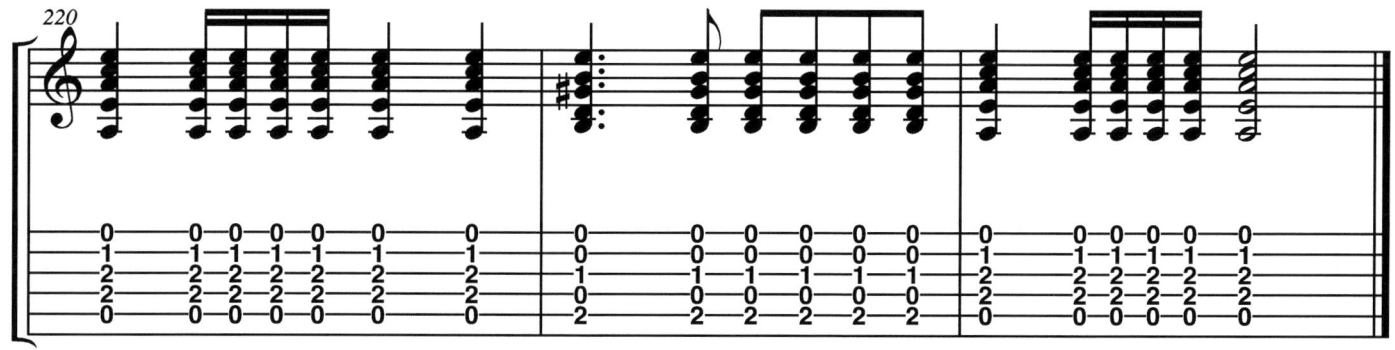

GRANAINAS

Strum every compas in the same manner

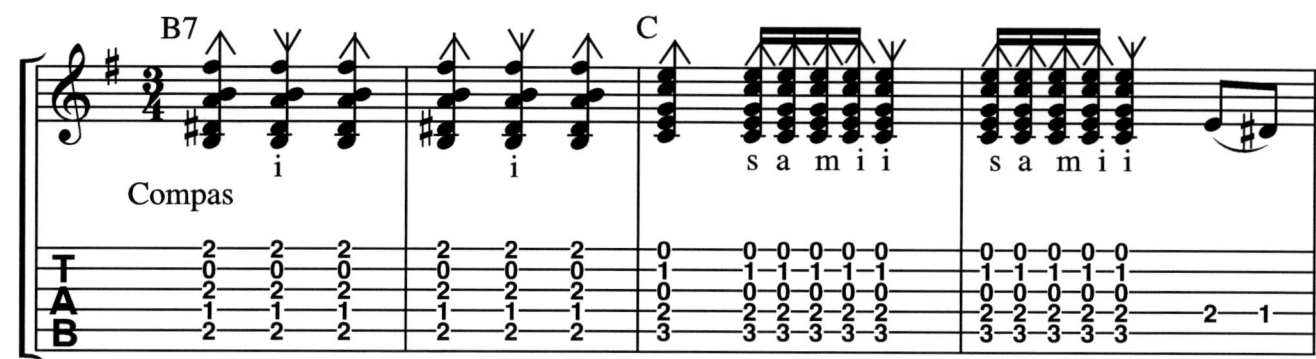

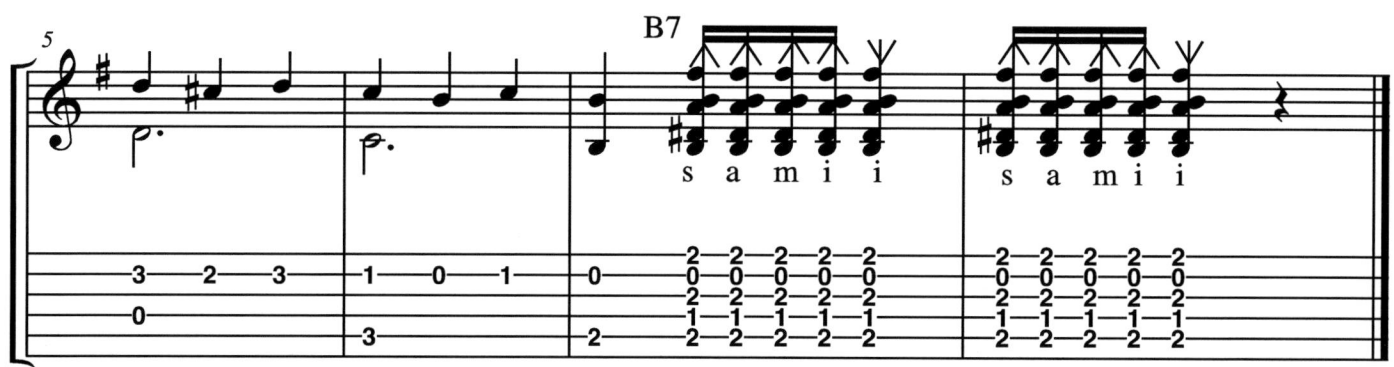

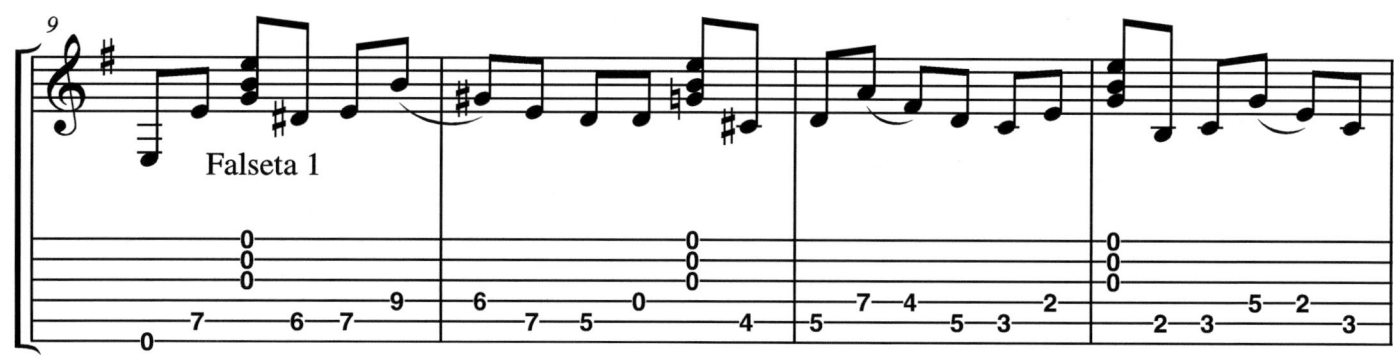

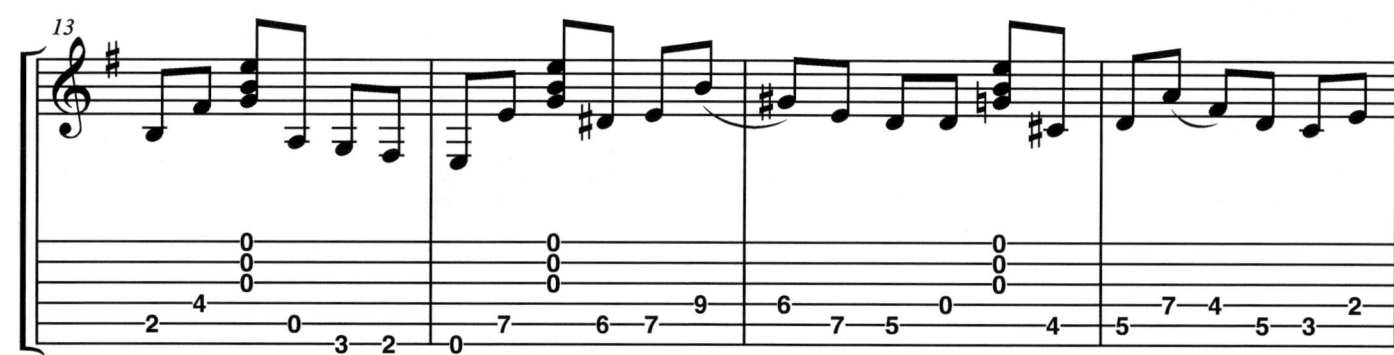

GRANAINAS

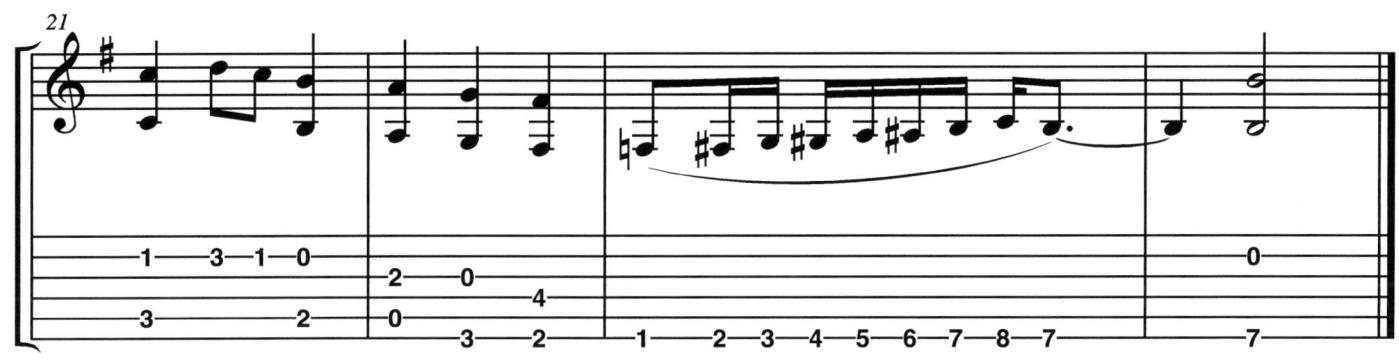
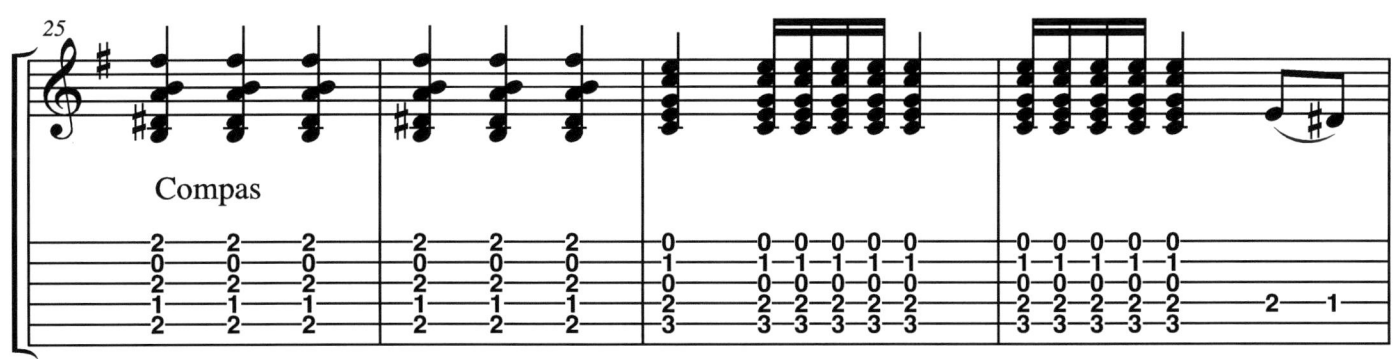

Compas

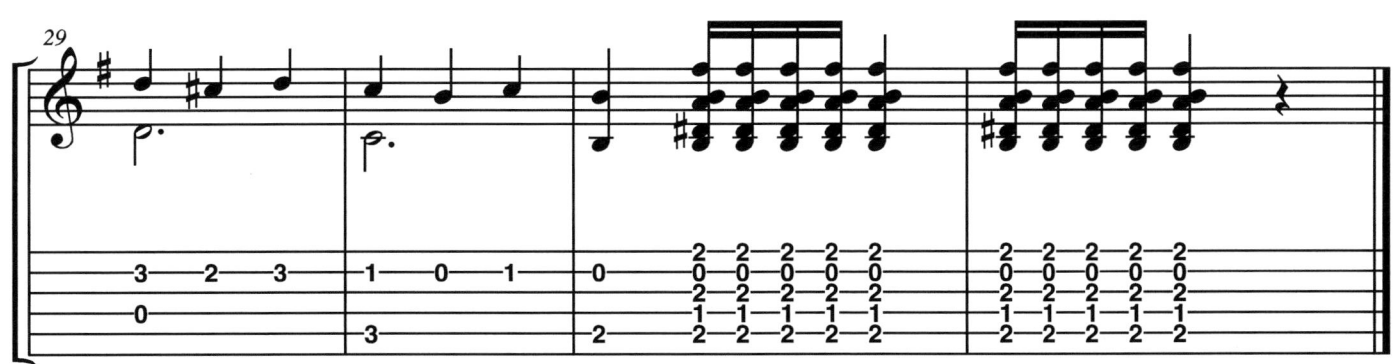

GRANAINAS

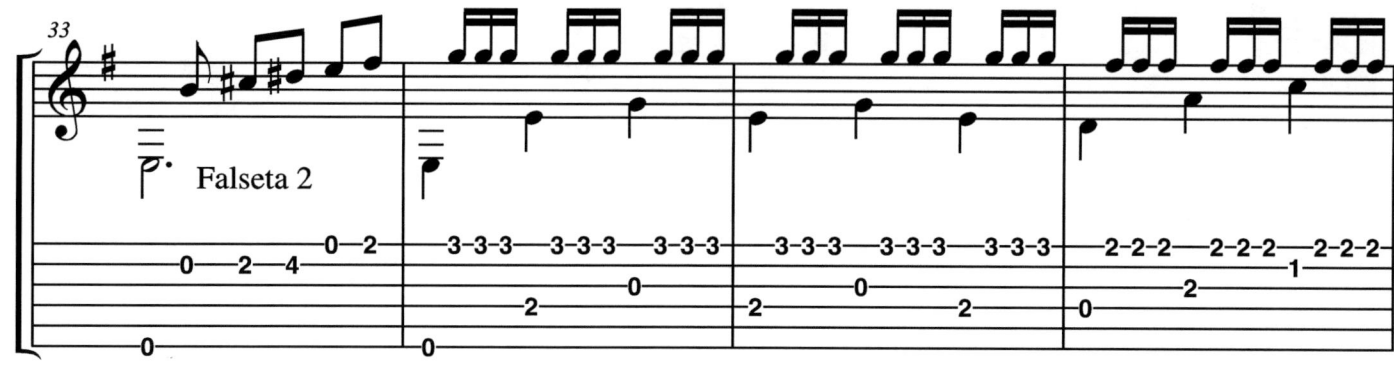
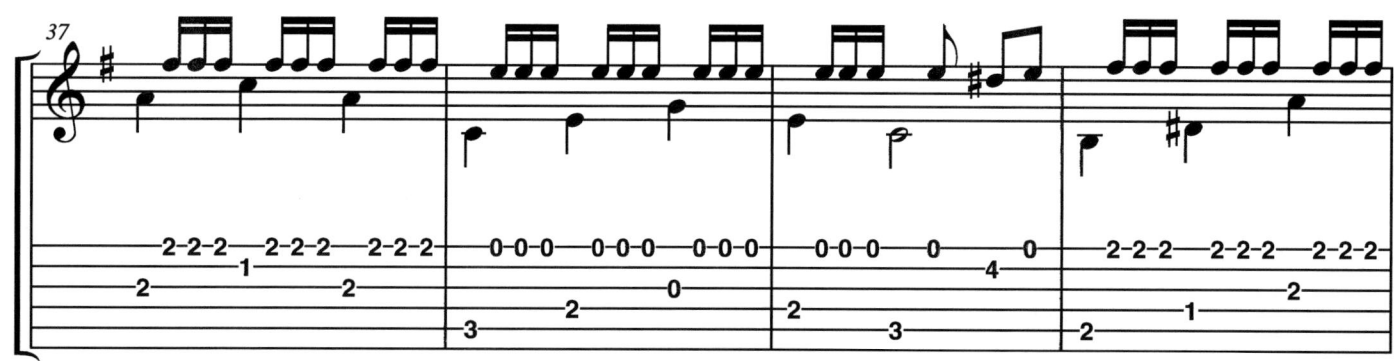
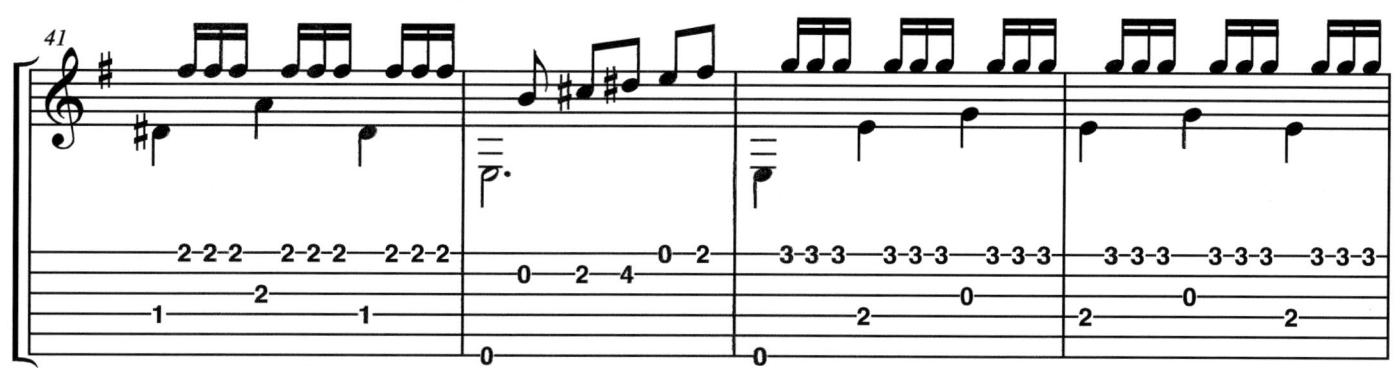

GRANAINAS

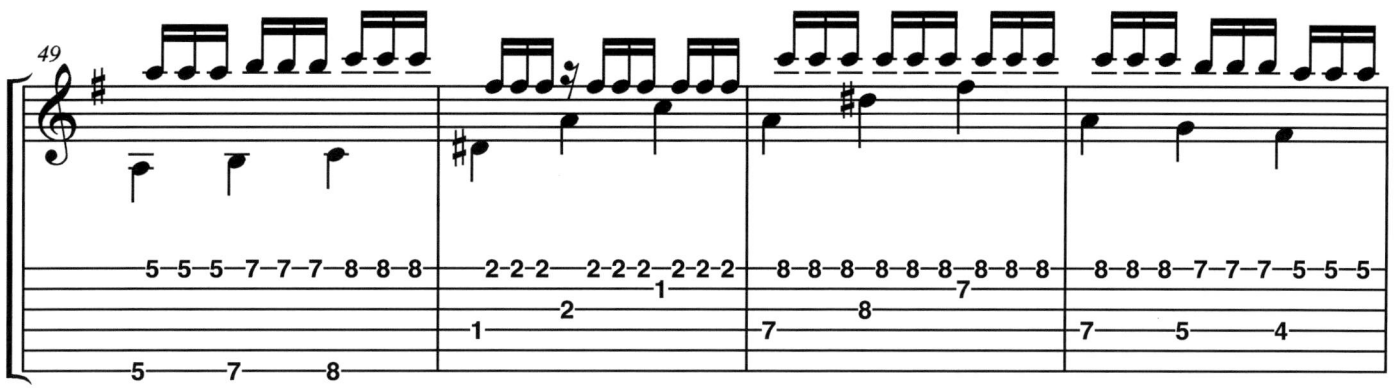
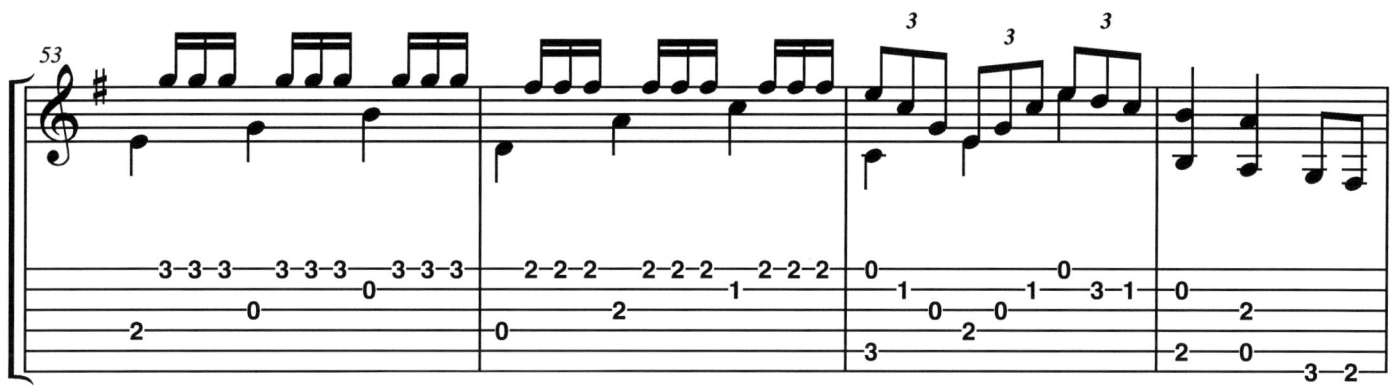

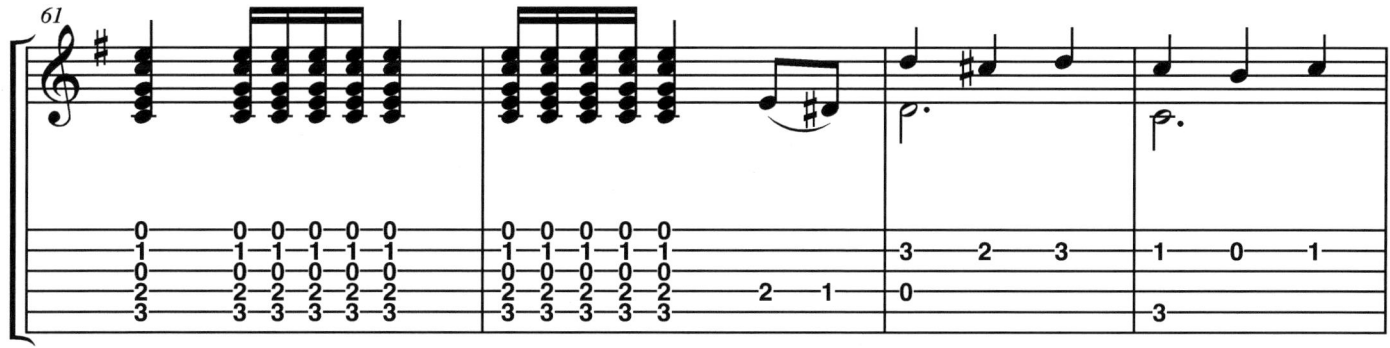

GRANAINAS

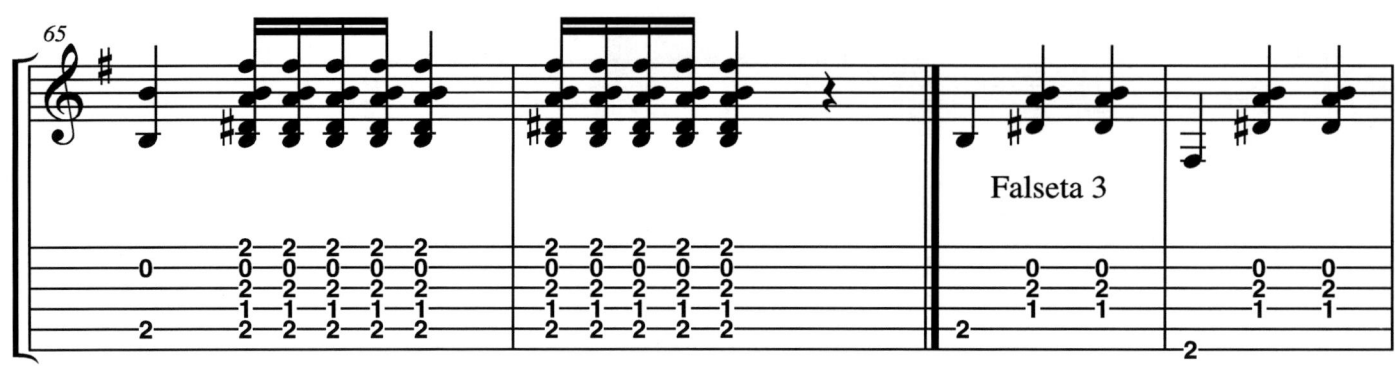

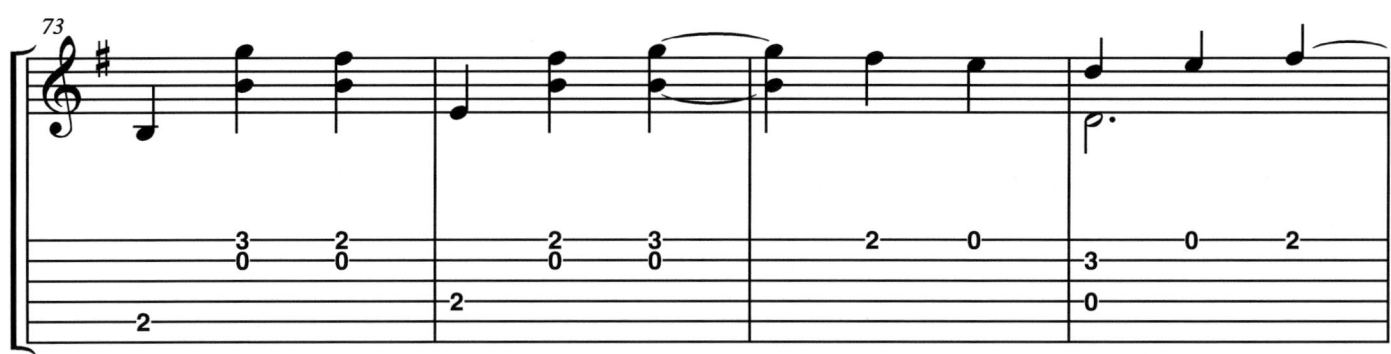

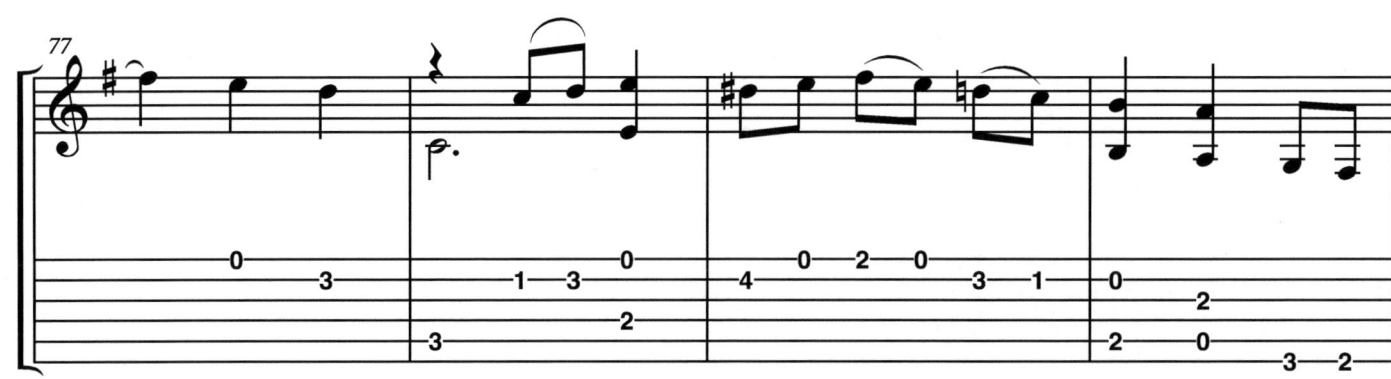

GRANAINAS

GRANAINAS

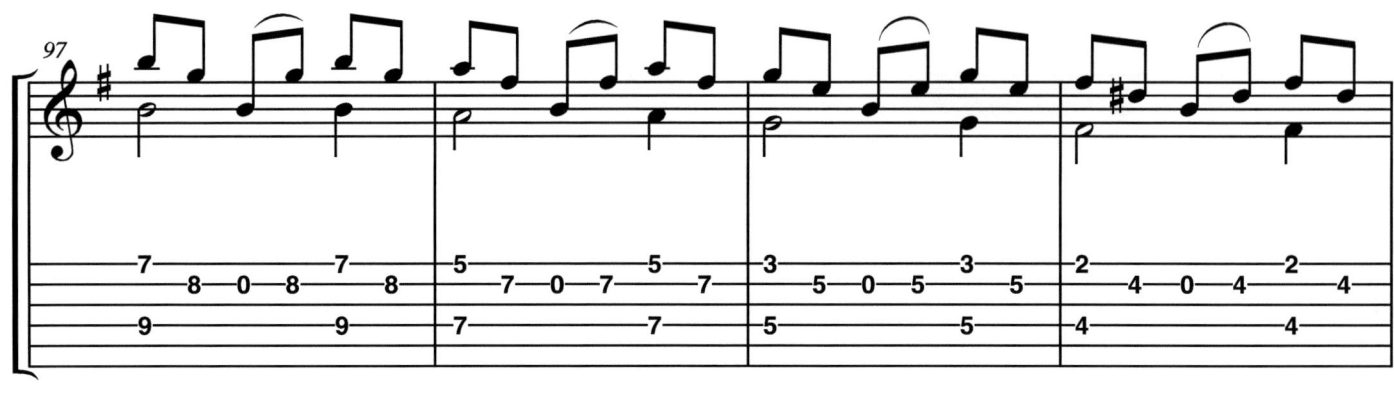
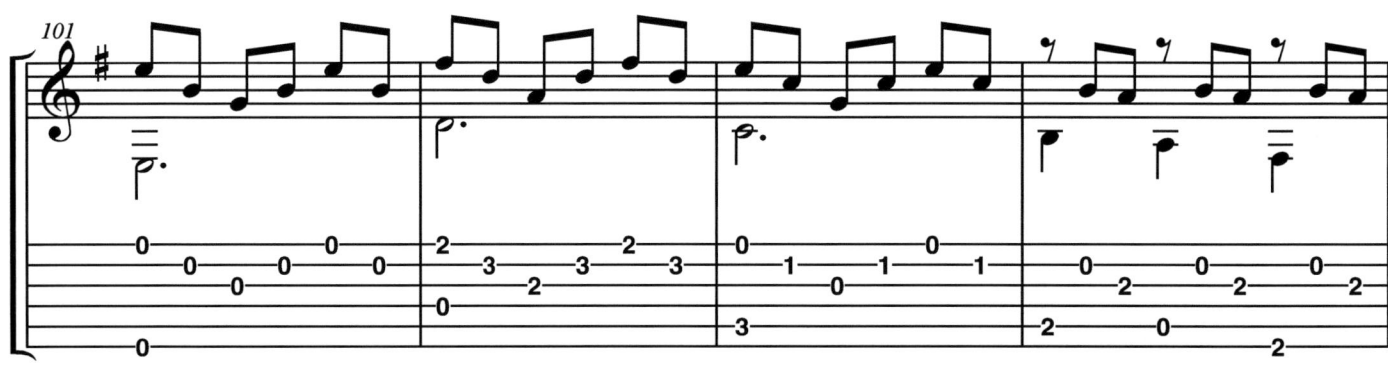

Compas

GRANAINAS

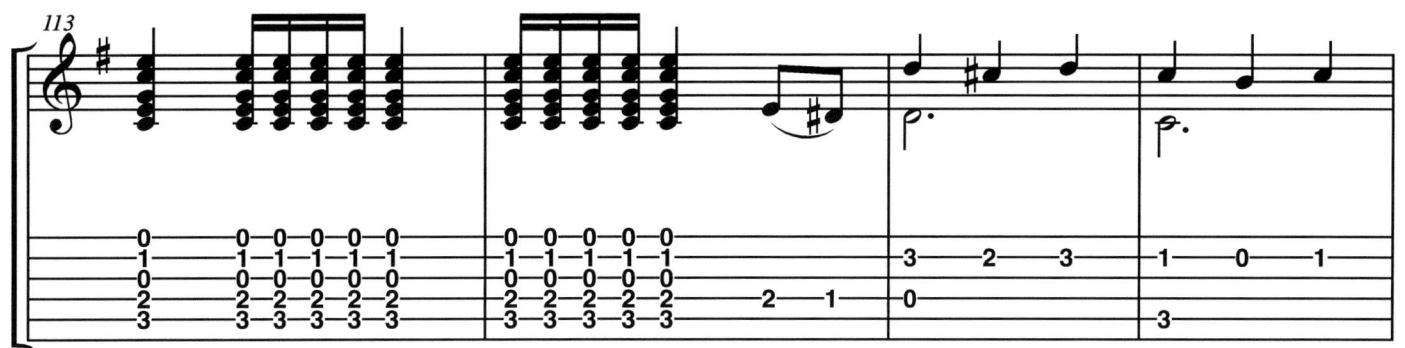

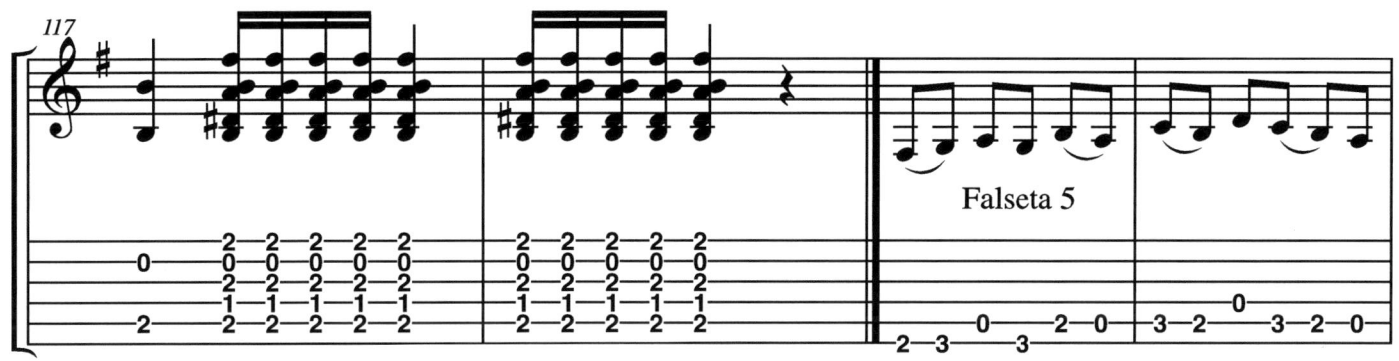

Falseta 5

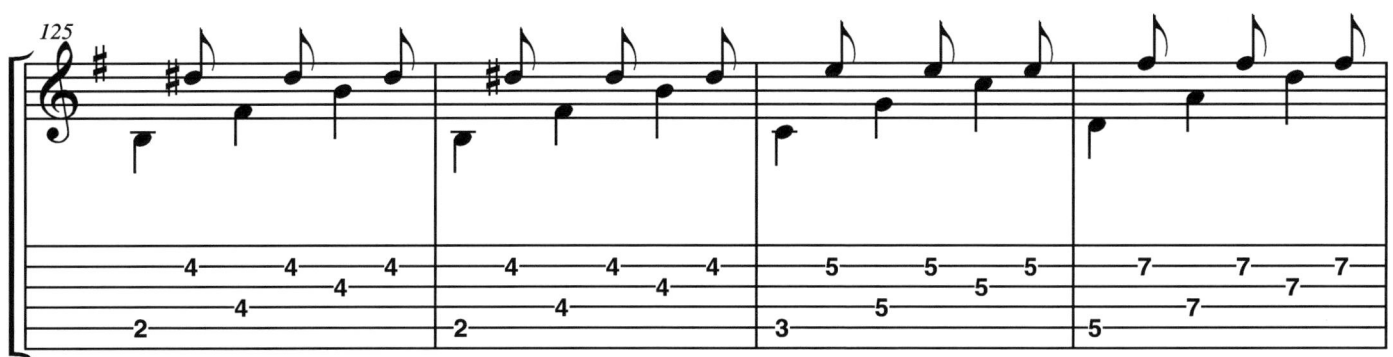

GRANAINAS

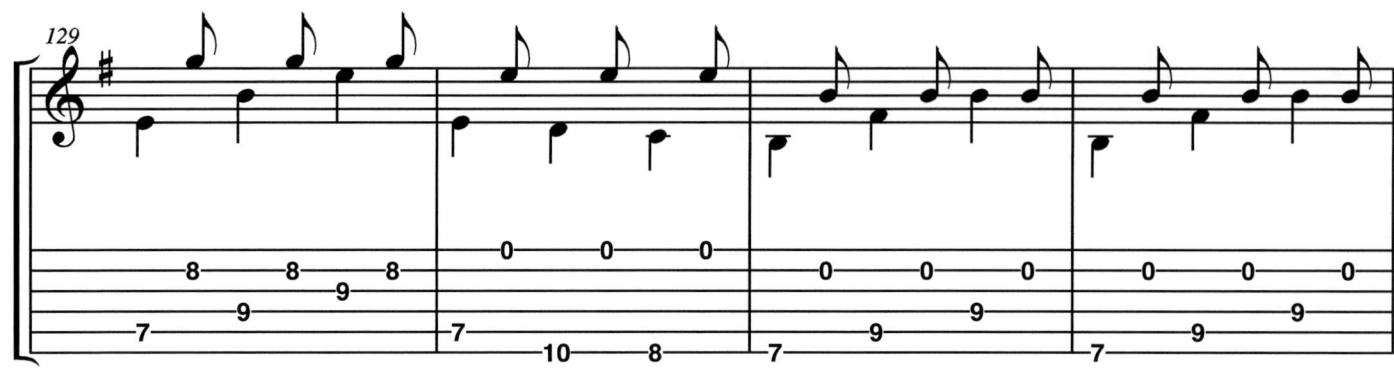
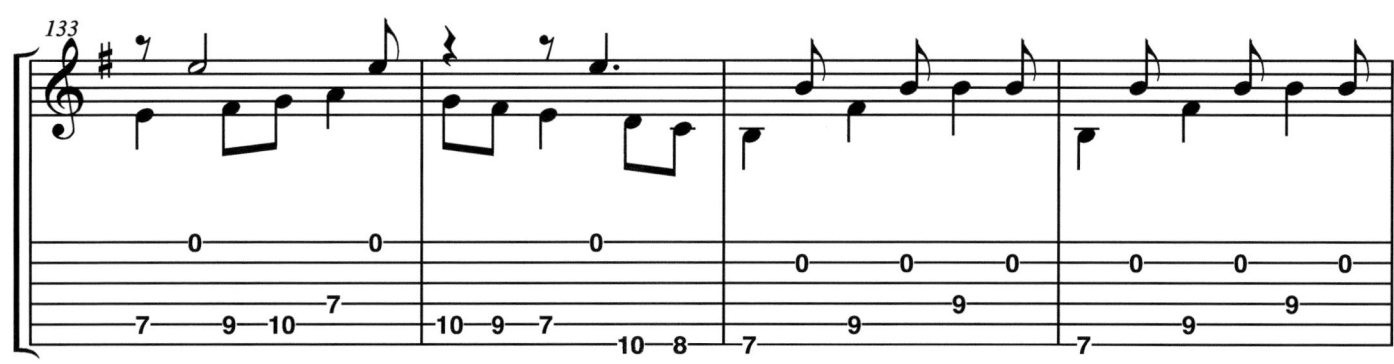
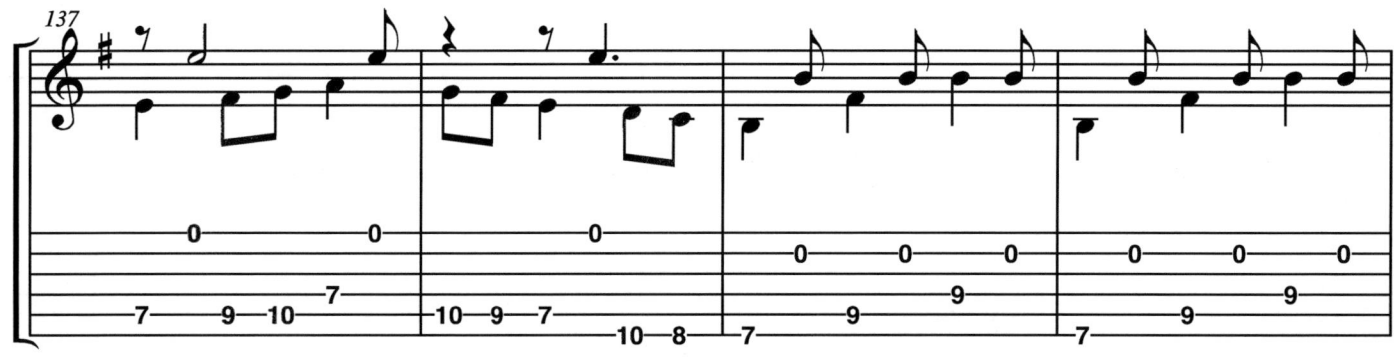
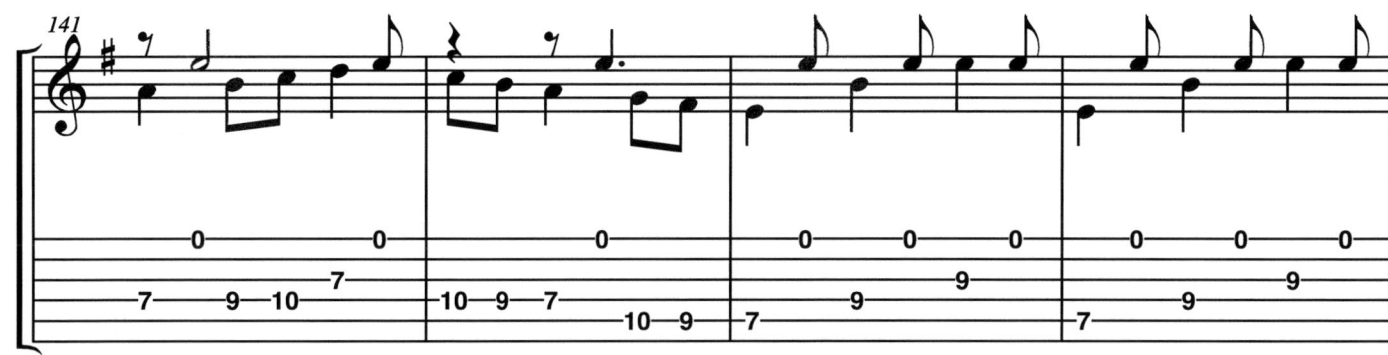

GRANAINAS

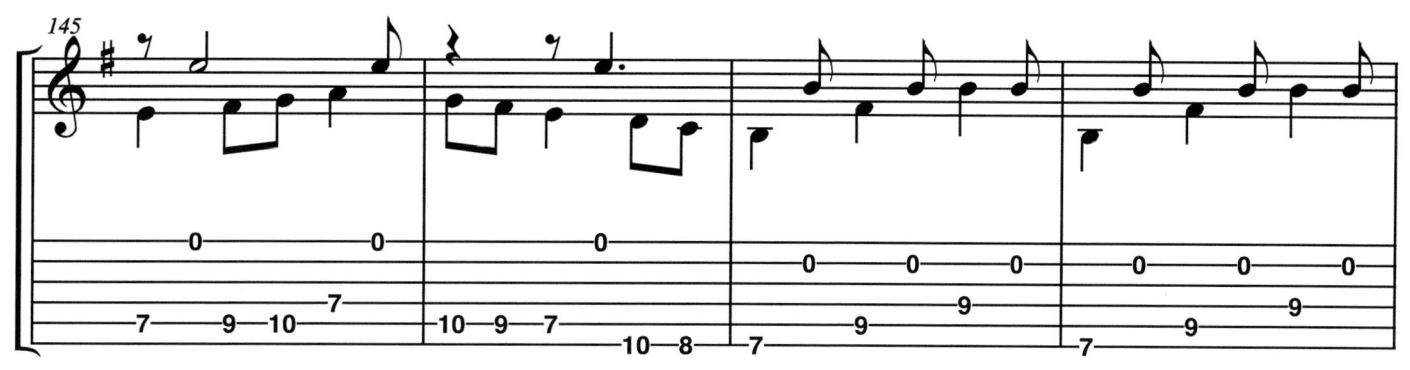
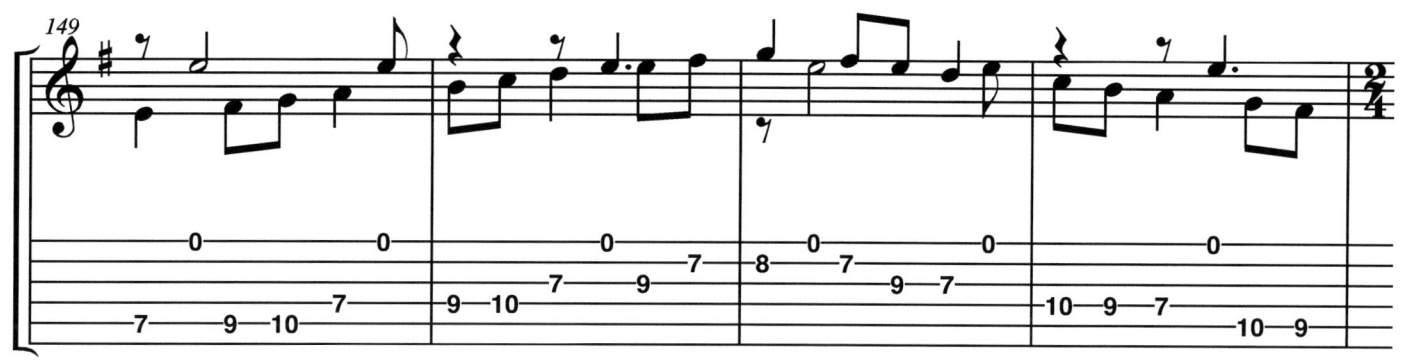
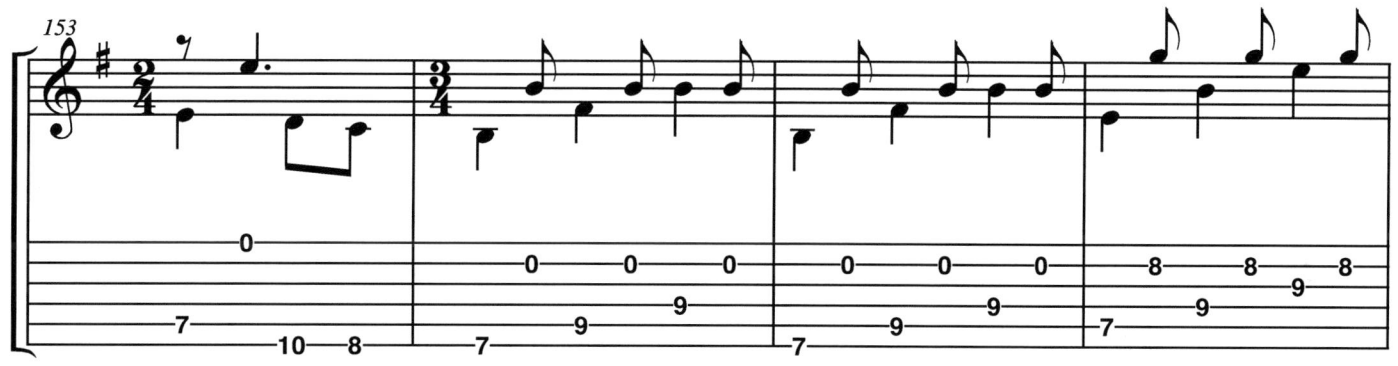

GRANAINAS

GRANAINAS

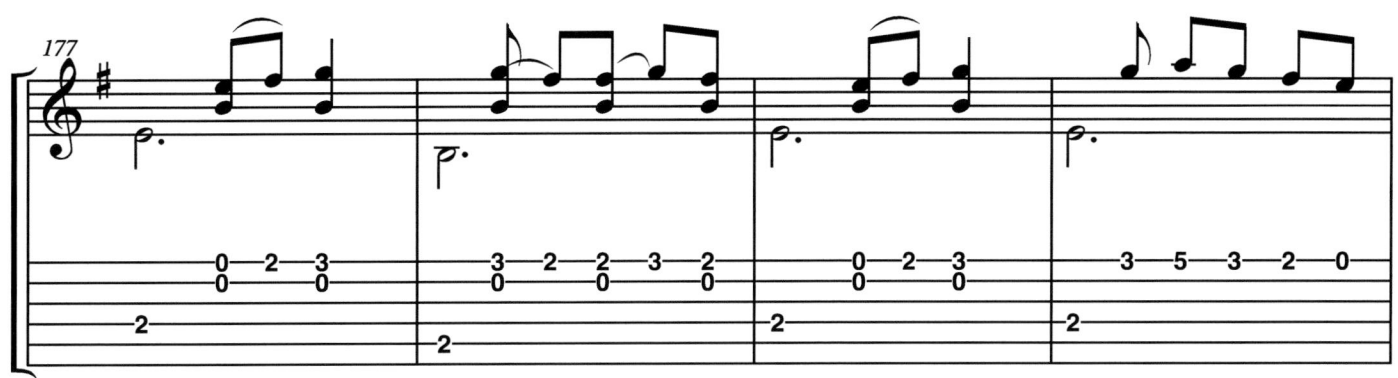
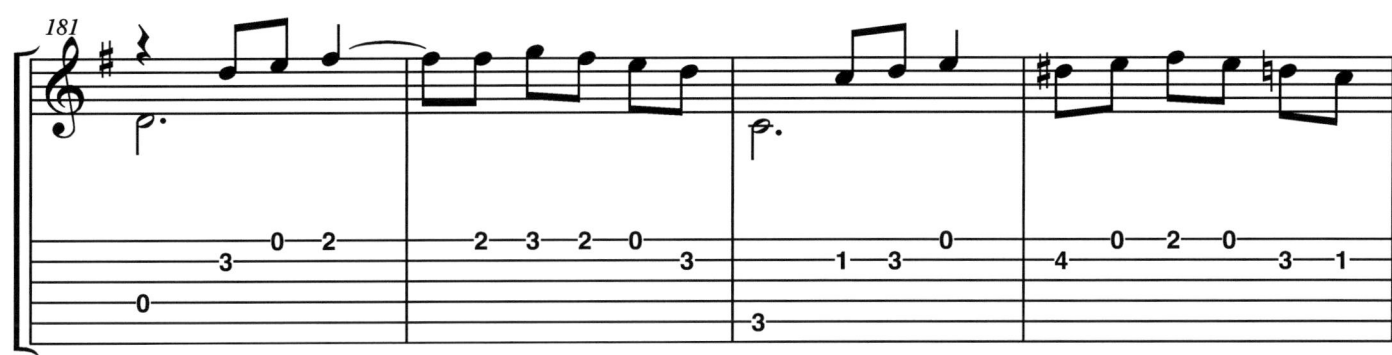
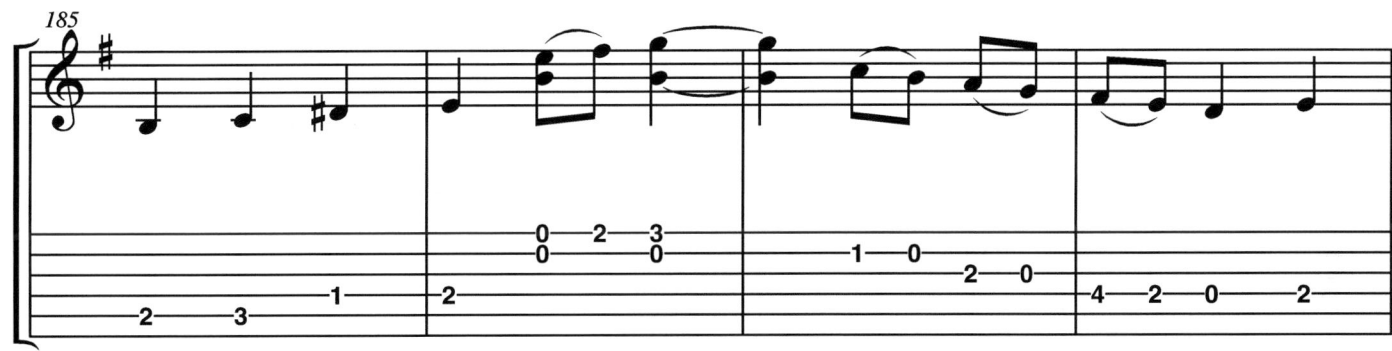
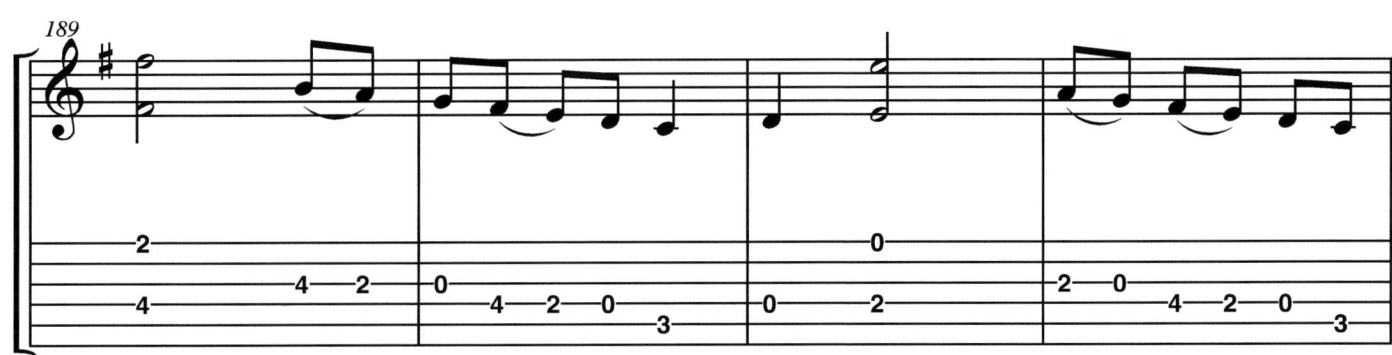

GRANAINAS

GRANAINAS

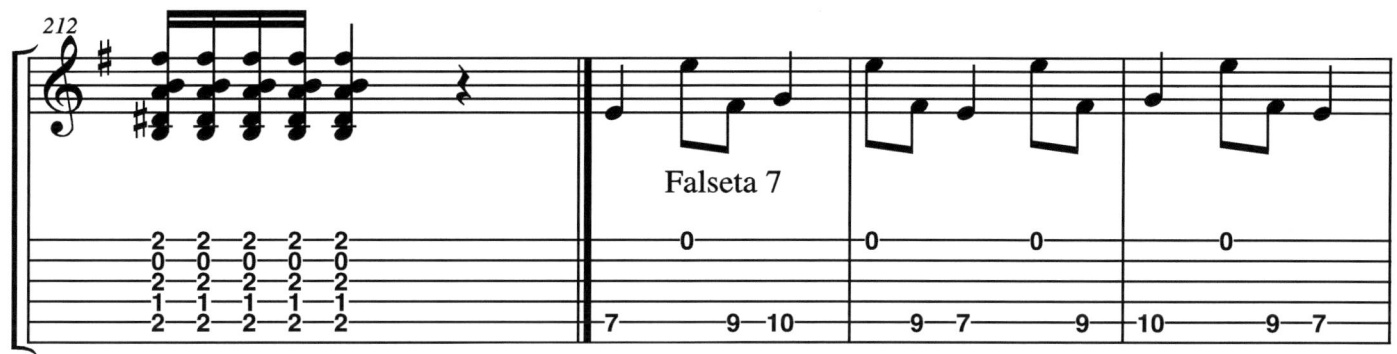

Falseta 7

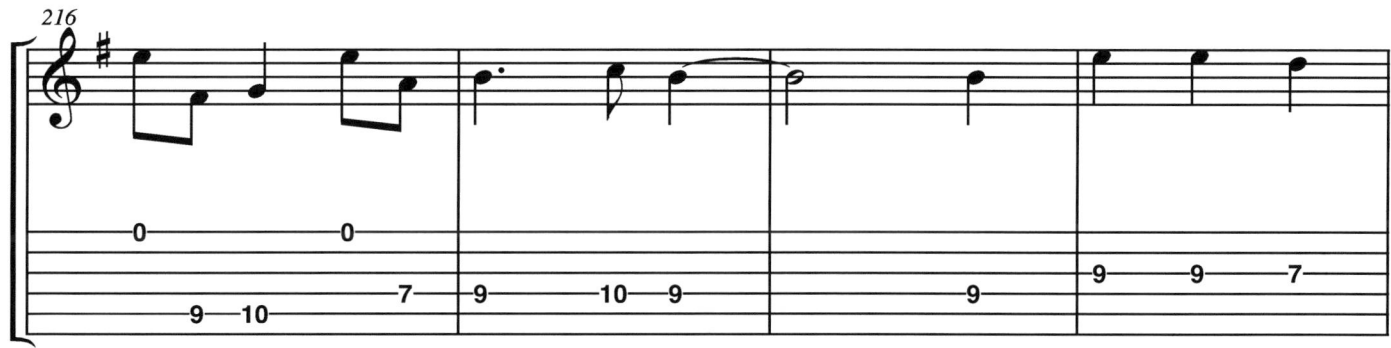
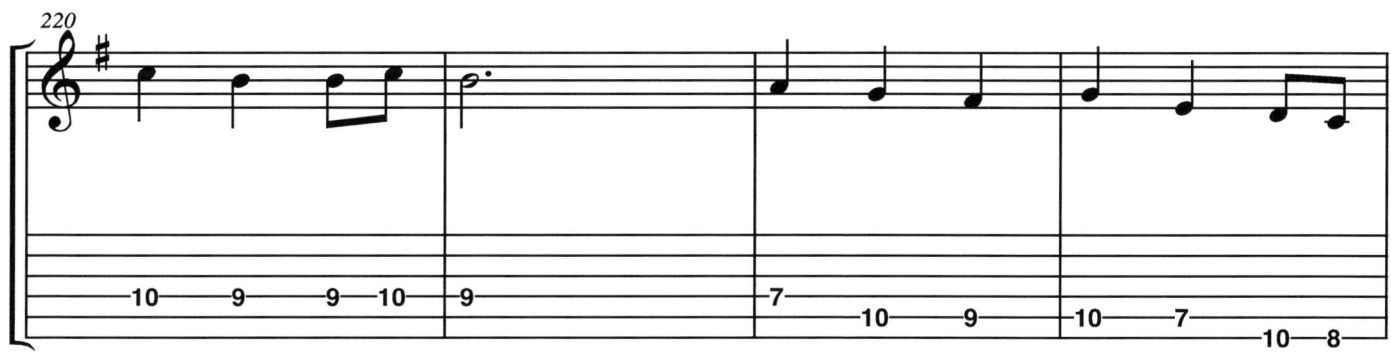

GRANAINAS

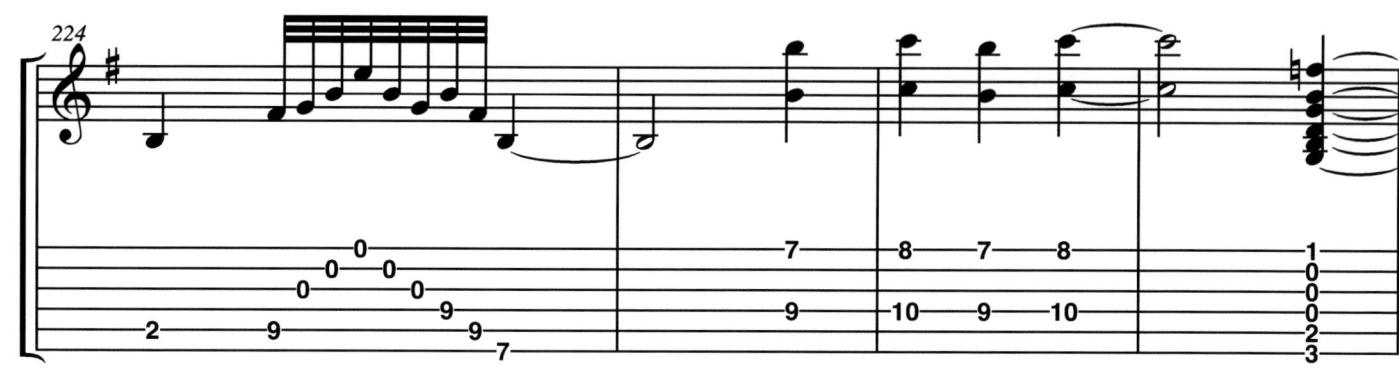
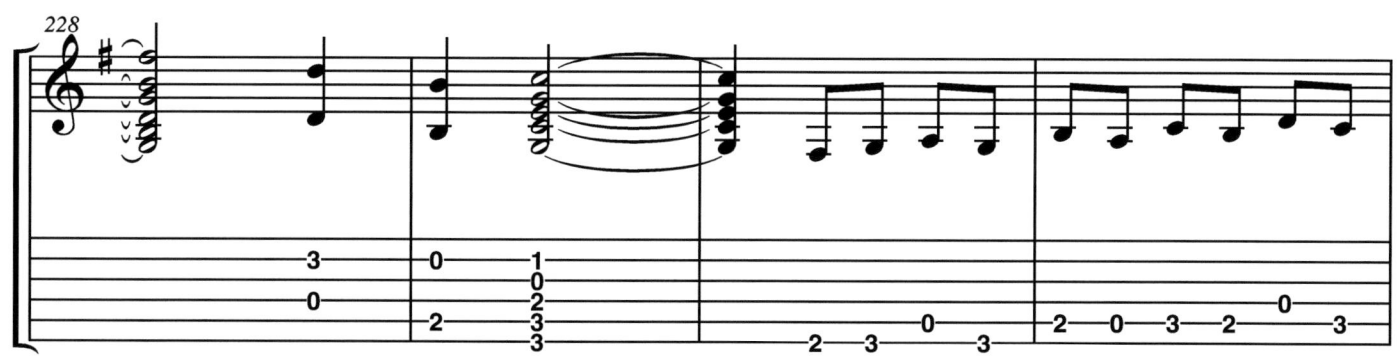
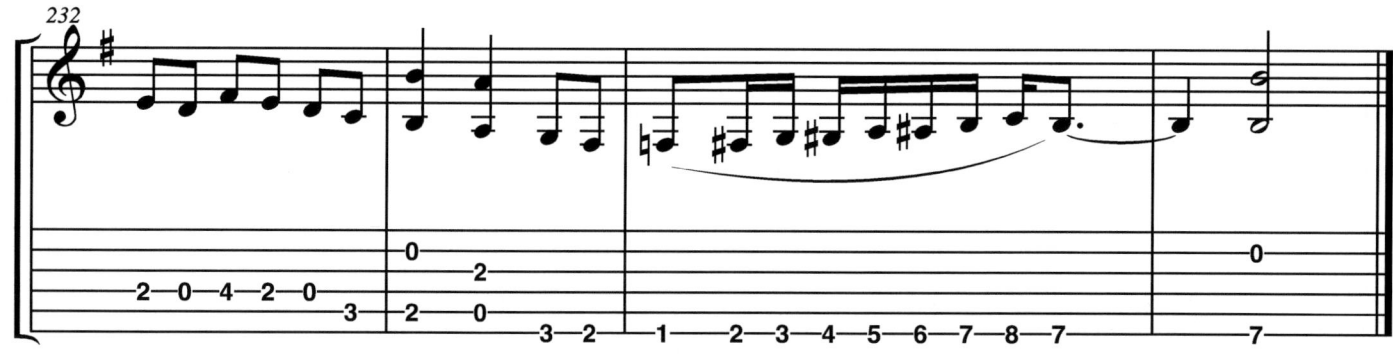
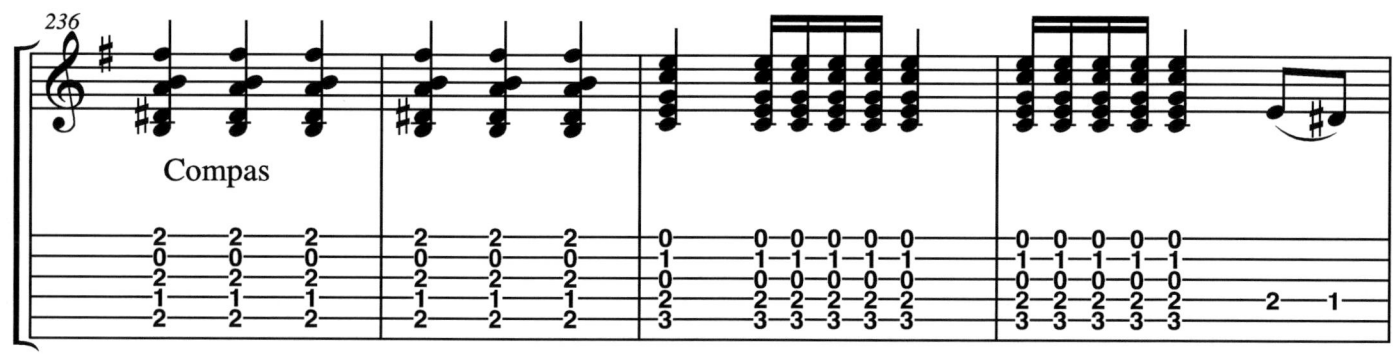

GRANAINAS

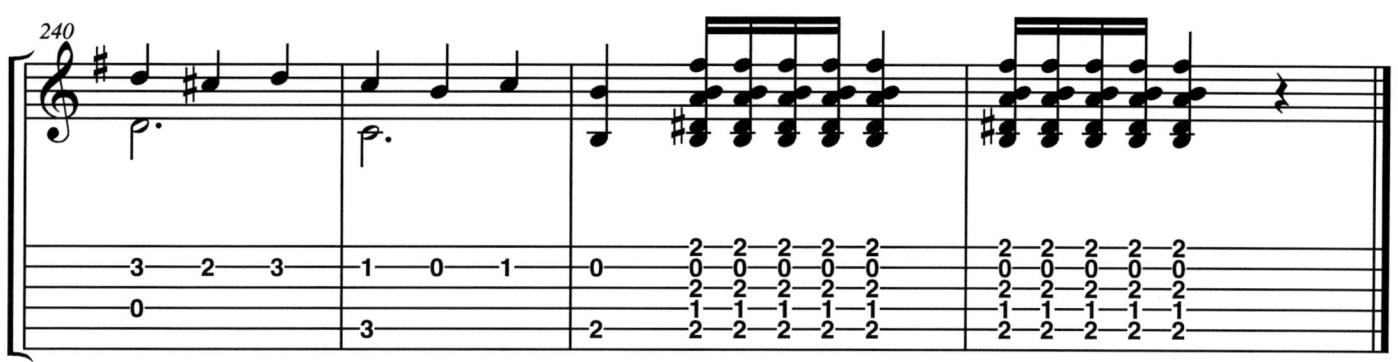
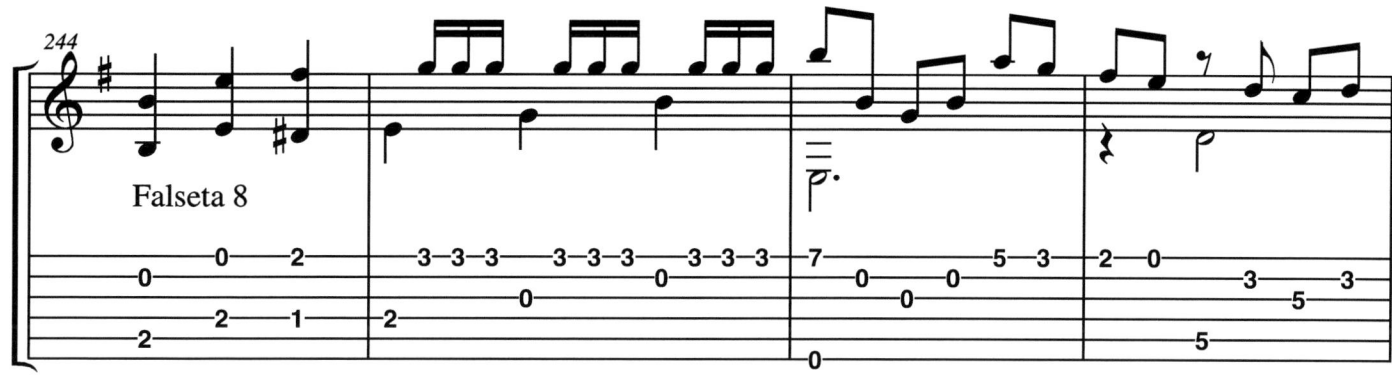

Falseta 8

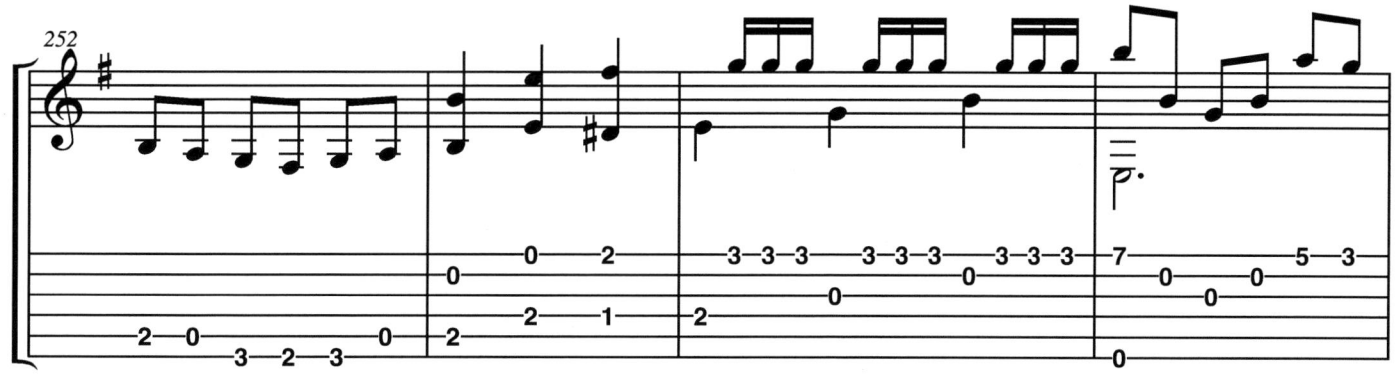

GRANAINAS

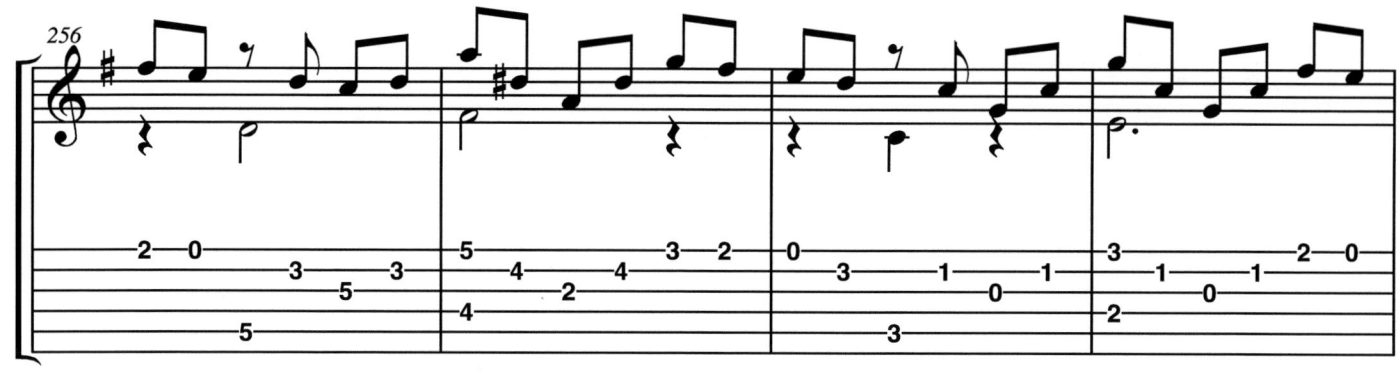
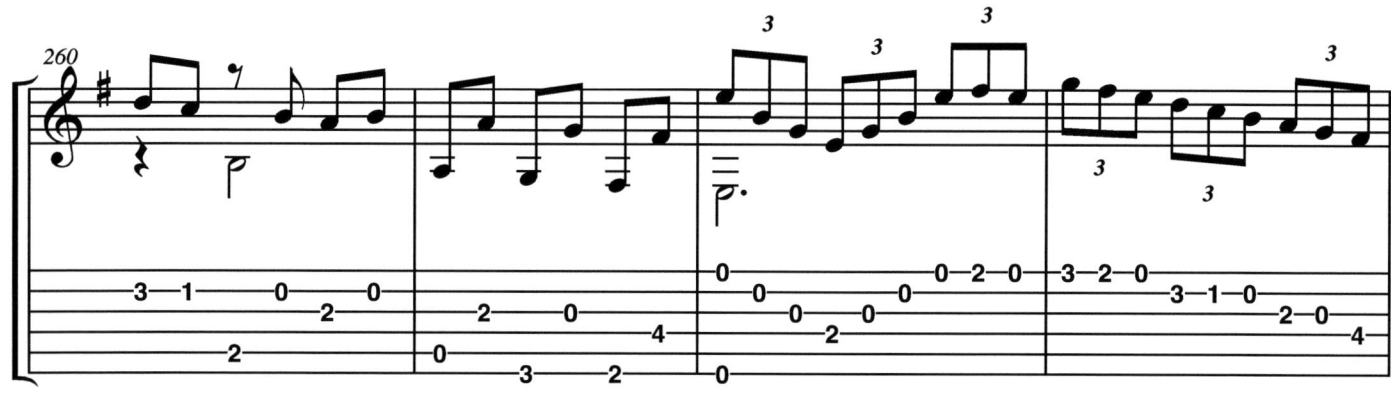
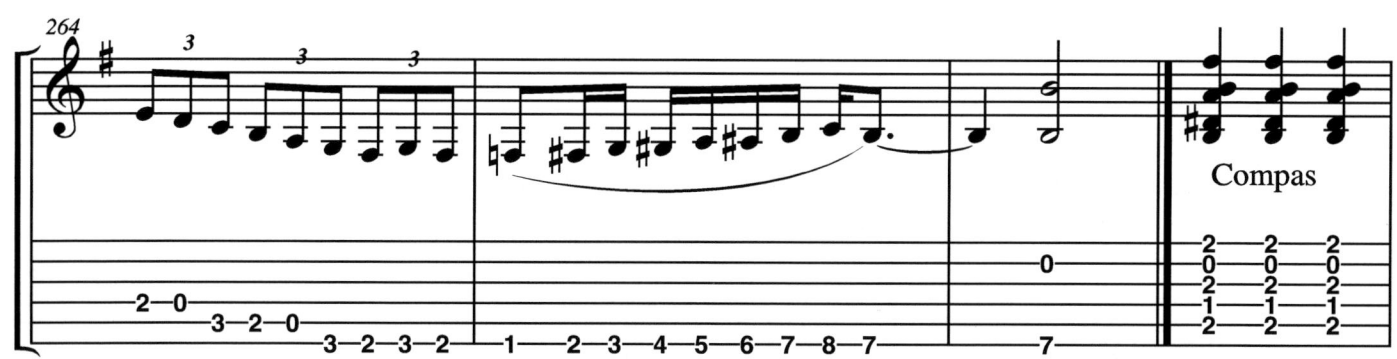
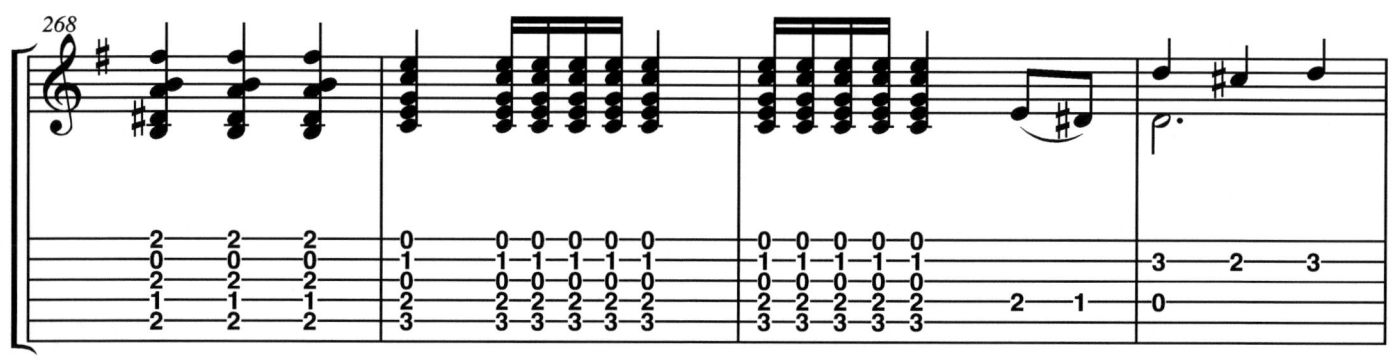

GRANAINAS

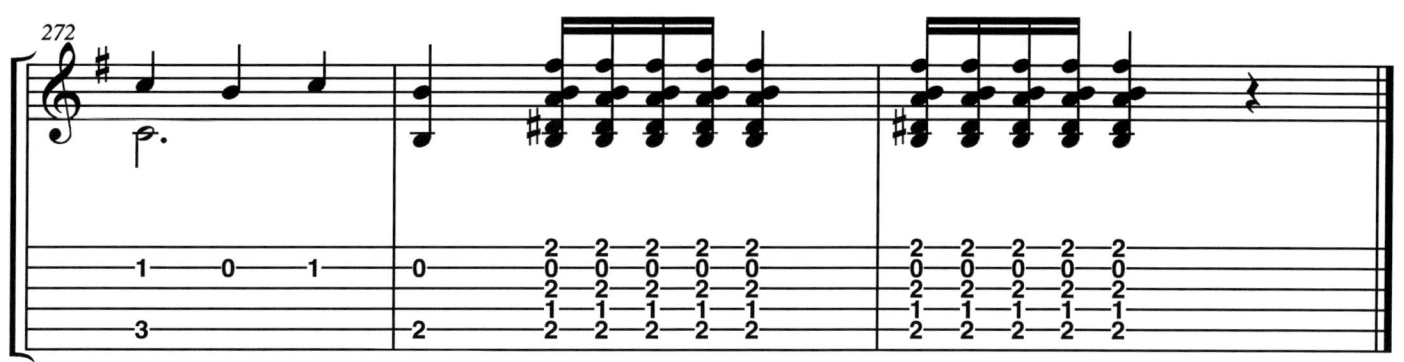

RUMBA

This symbol Ⓣ is played by crossing the right hand over the six strings at the lower end of the finger board and the tips of the fingers produce a soft stroke on the sounding board of the guitar

Strum every compas in the same manner

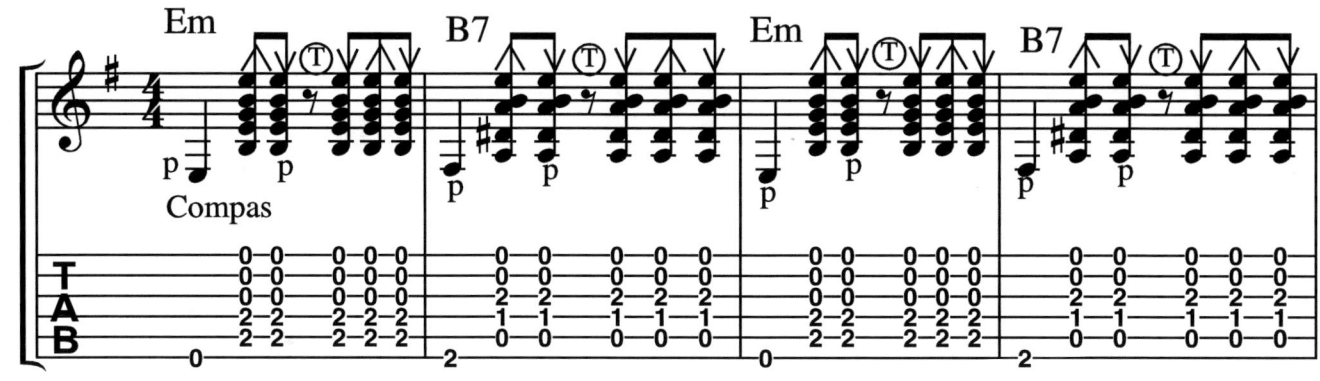

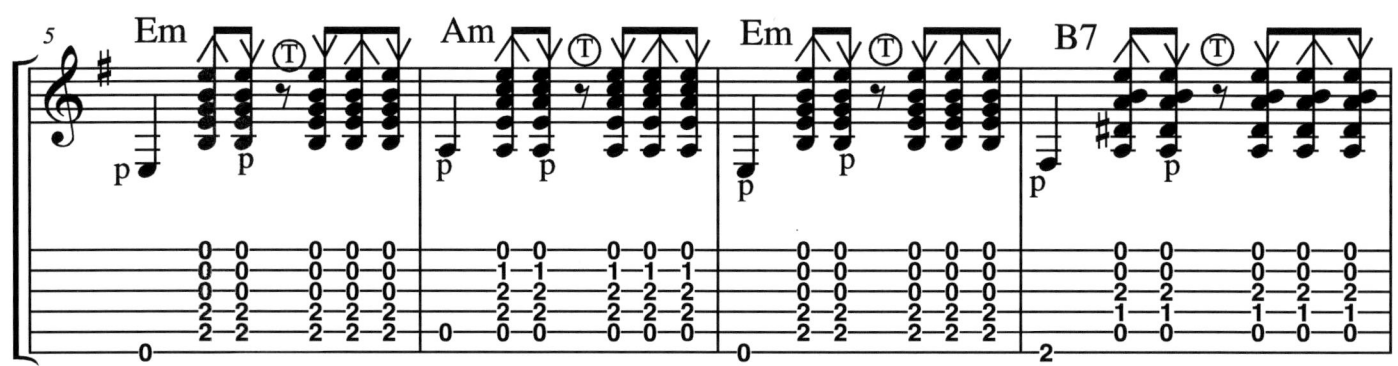

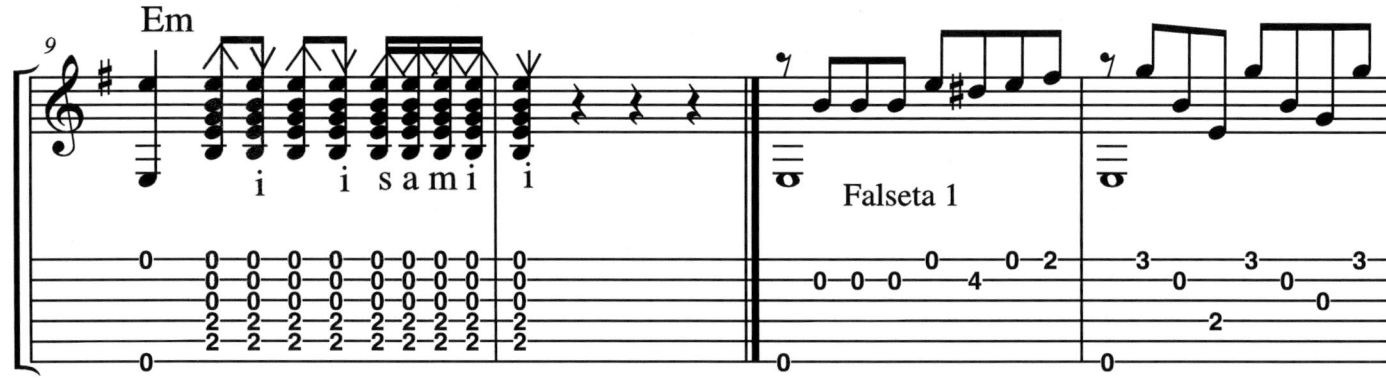

Falseta 1

RUMBA

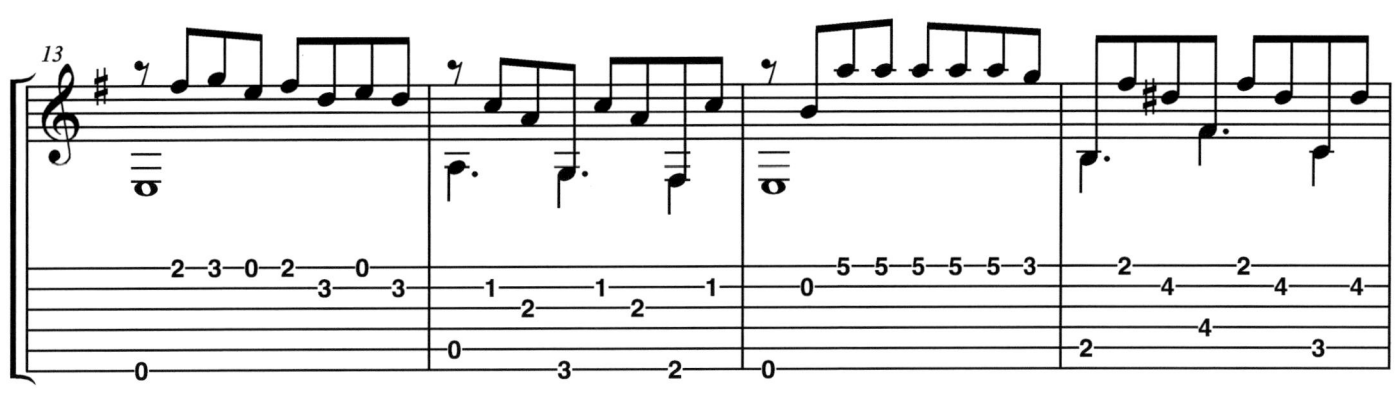
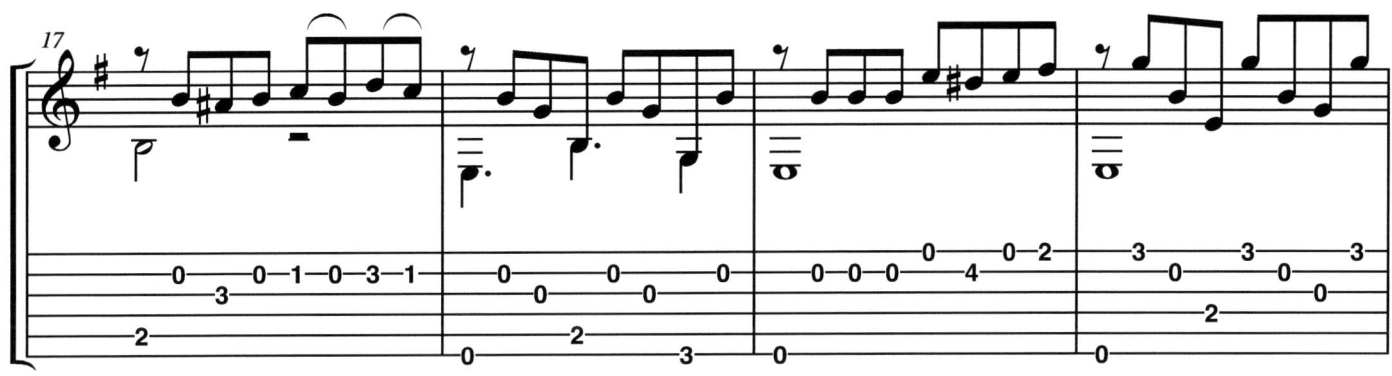
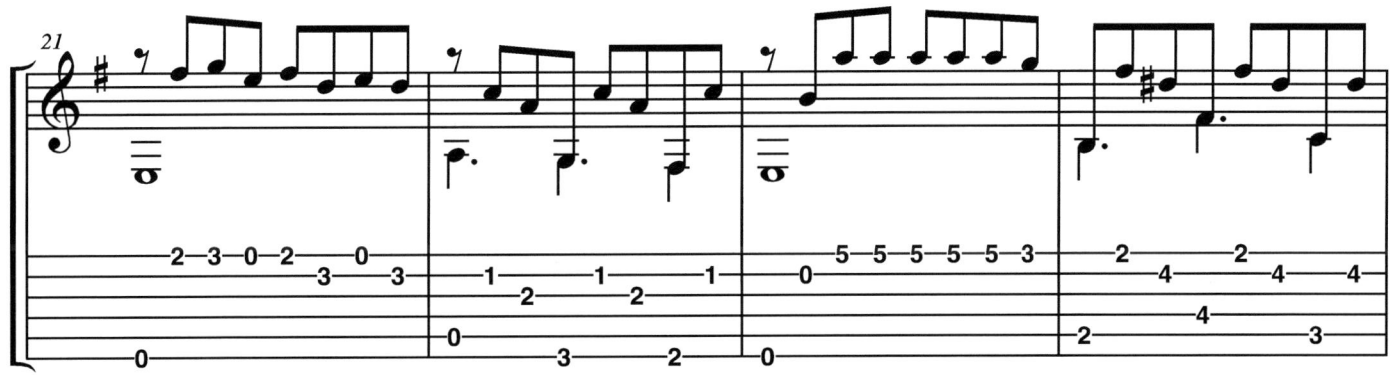
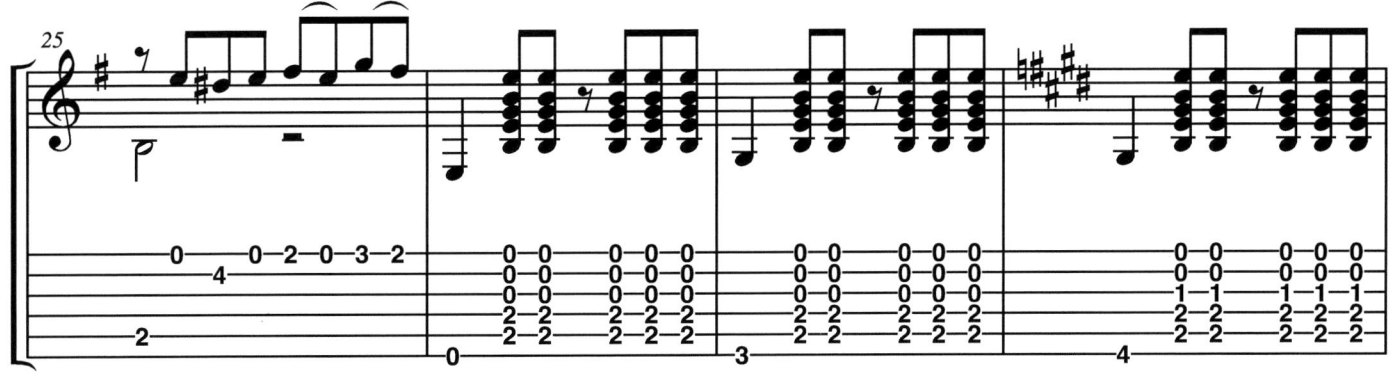

RUMBA

RUMBA

125

RUMBA

RUMBA

Falseta 2

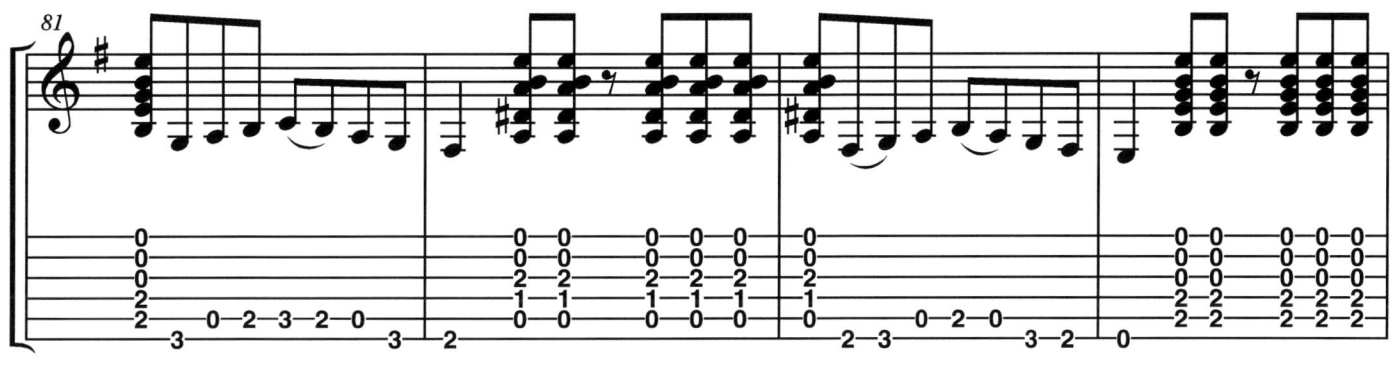

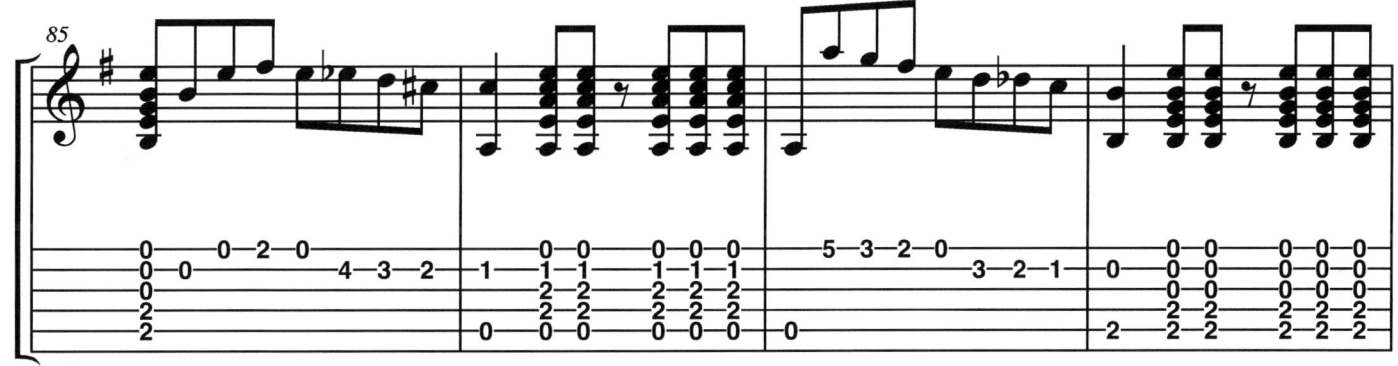

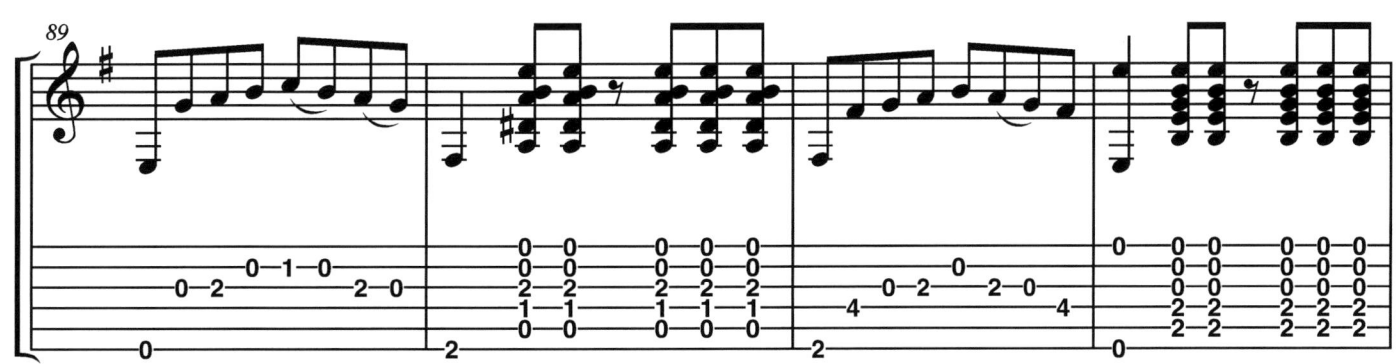

RUMBA

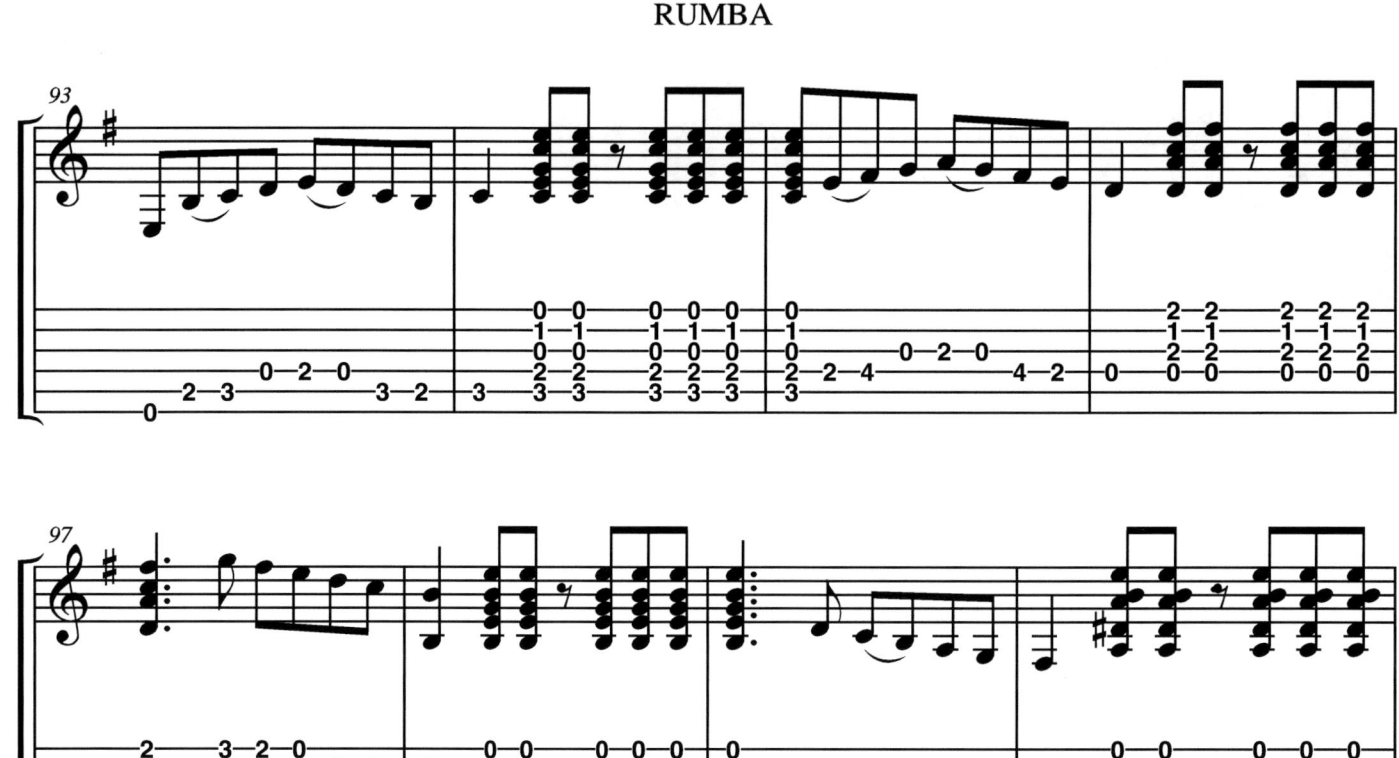
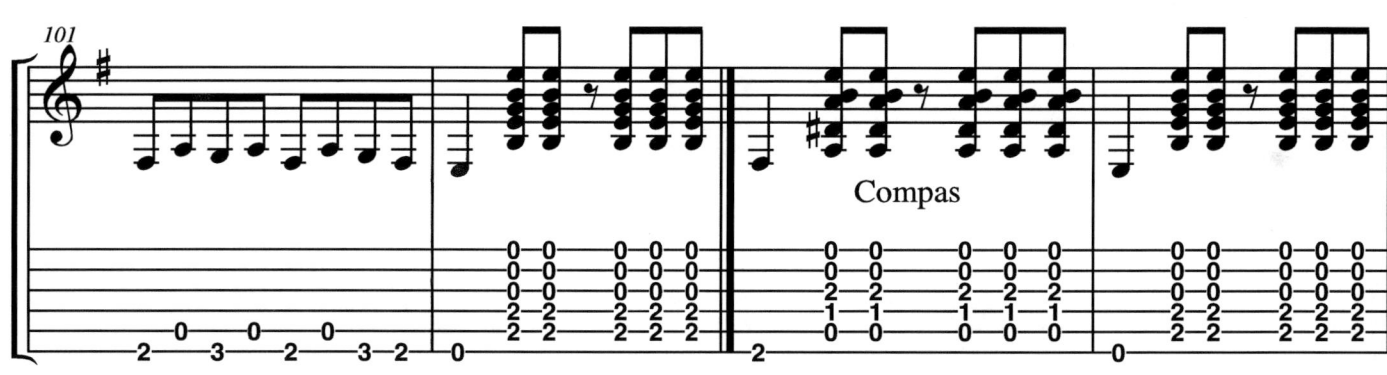
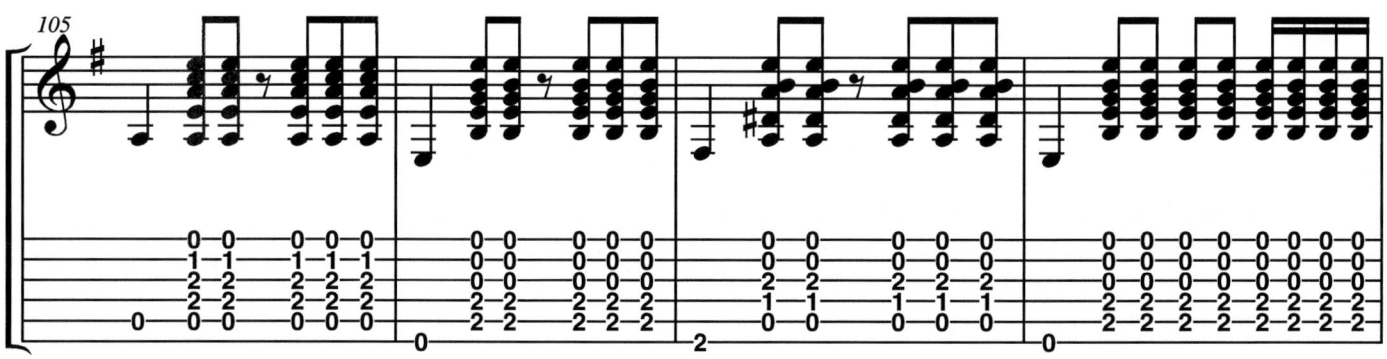

RUMBA

Falseta 3

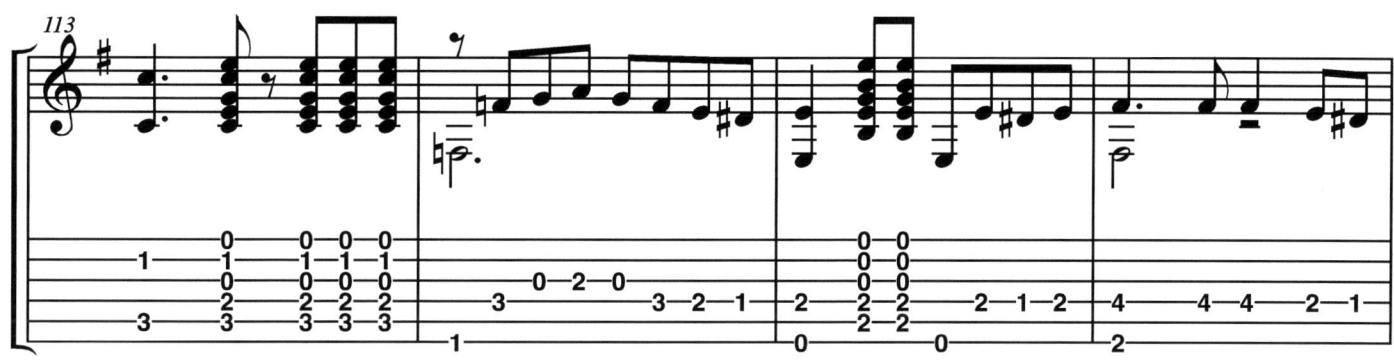

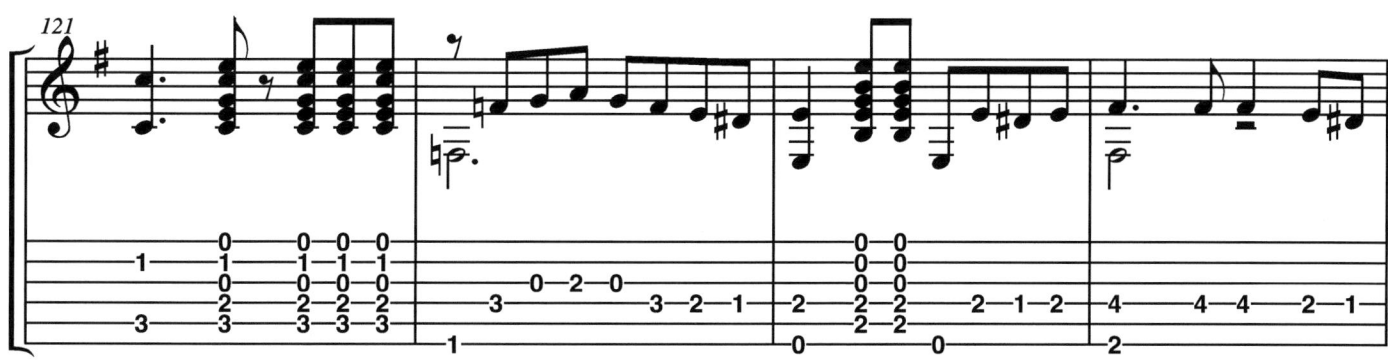

RUMBA

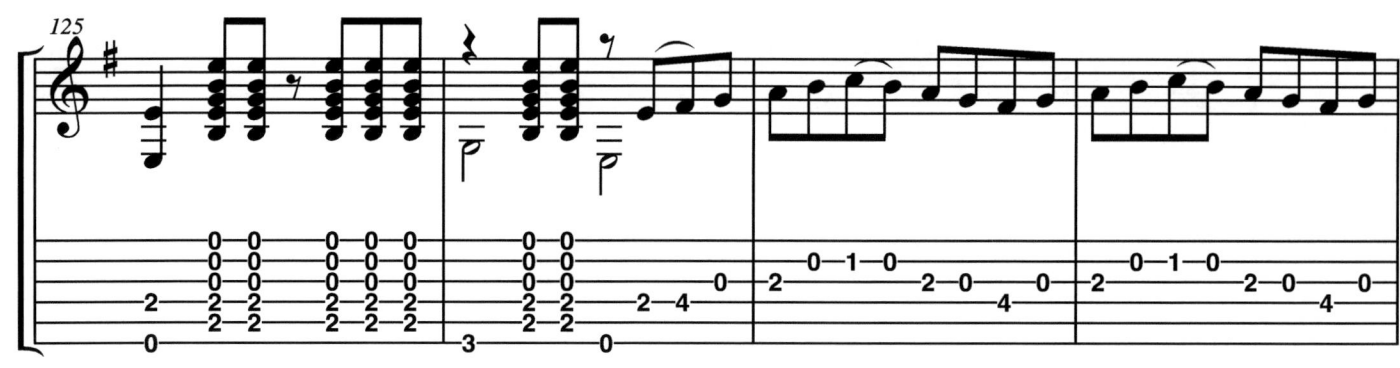
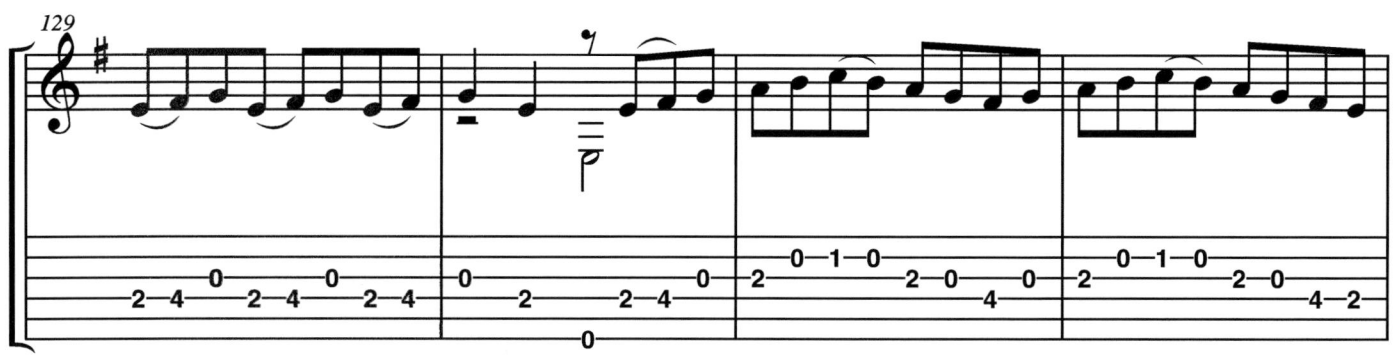

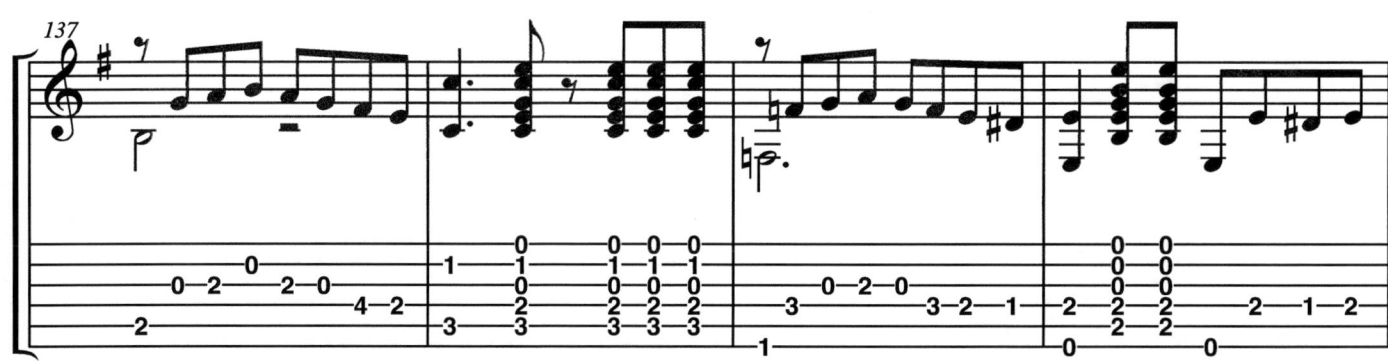

RUMBA

RUMBA

RUMBA

RUMBA

Falseta 5

RUMBA

Compas

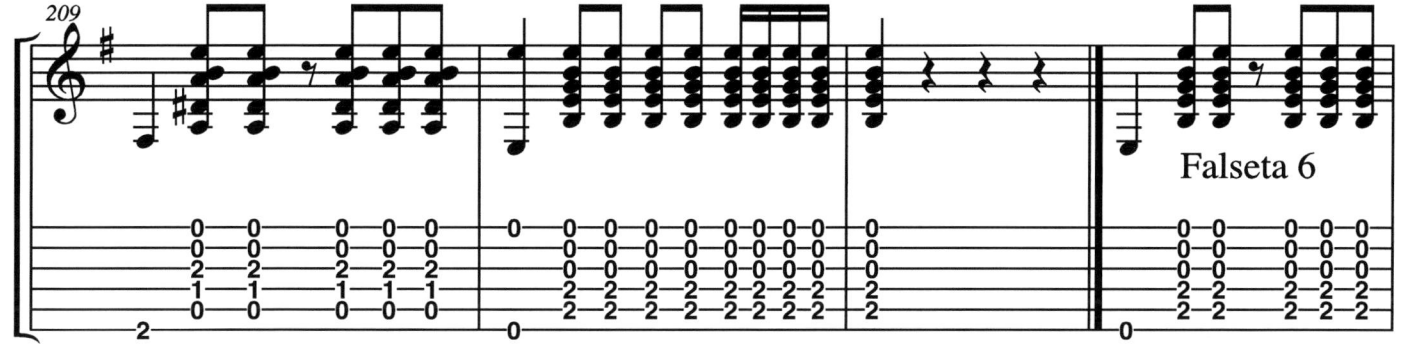
Falseta 6

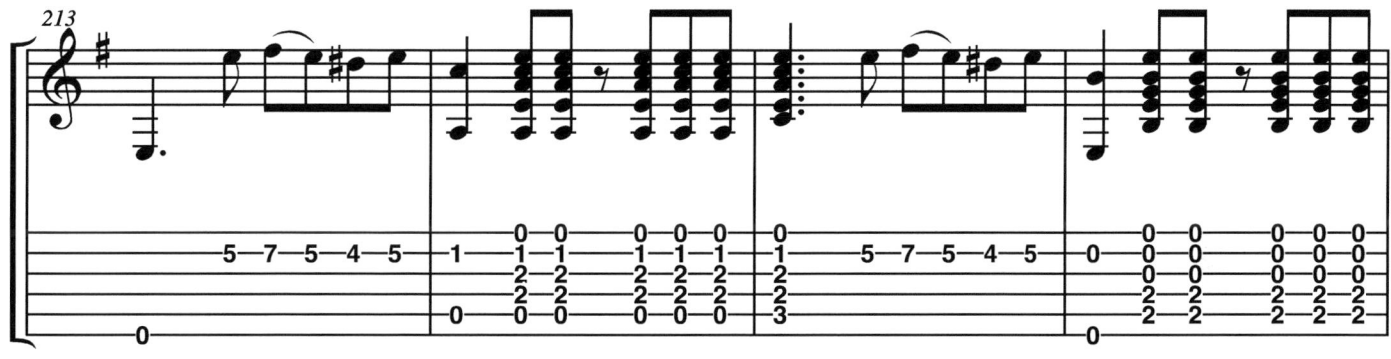

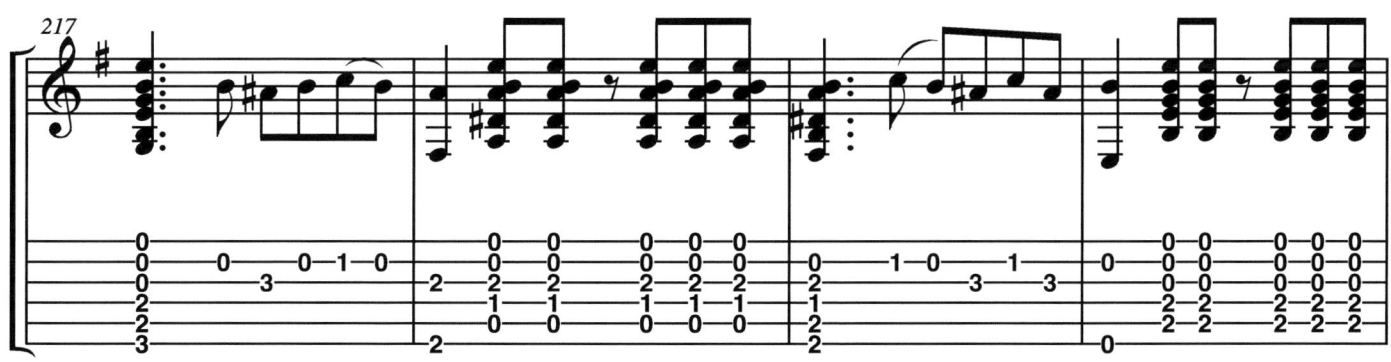

RUMBA

RUMBA

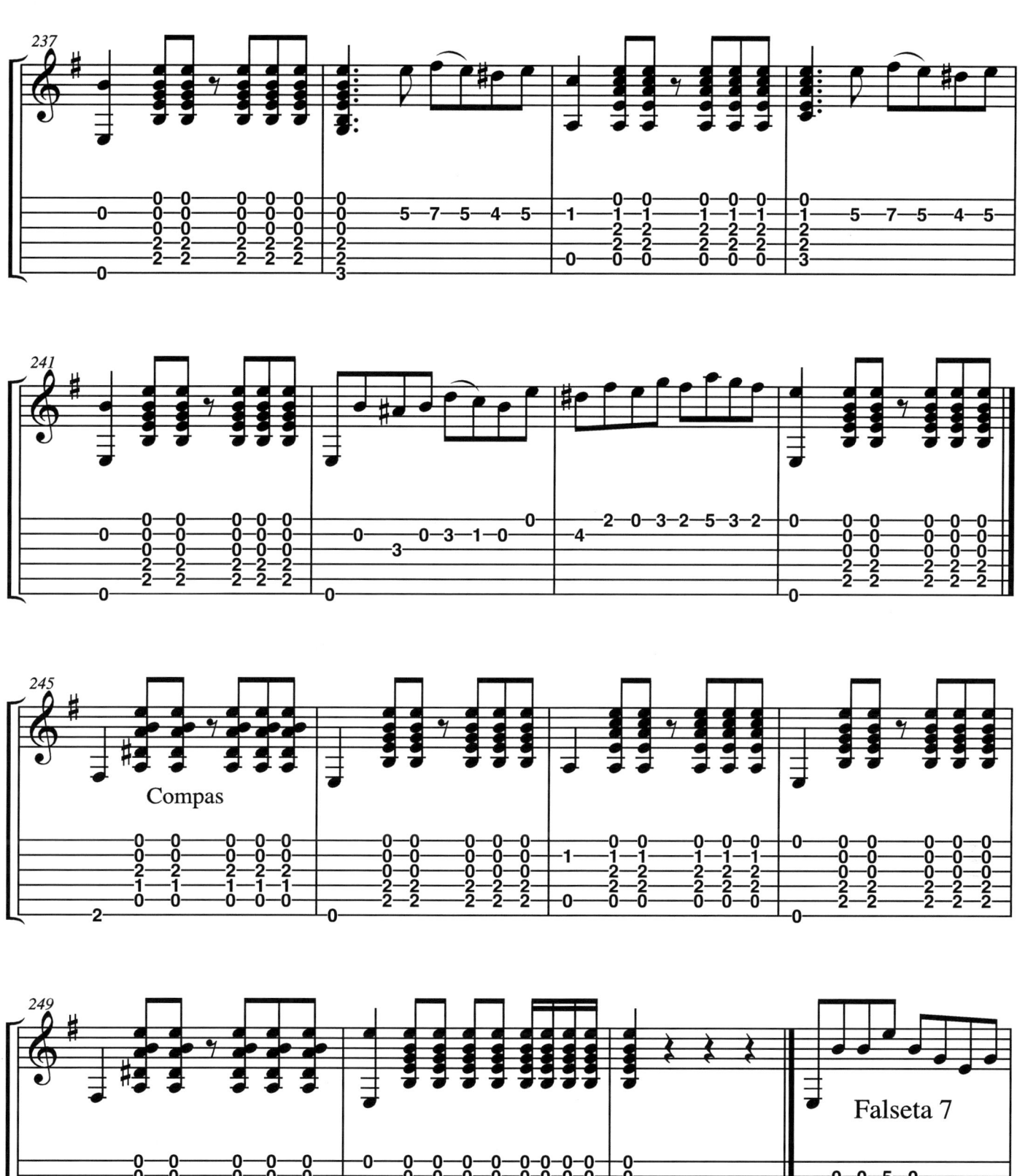

RUMBA

RUMBA

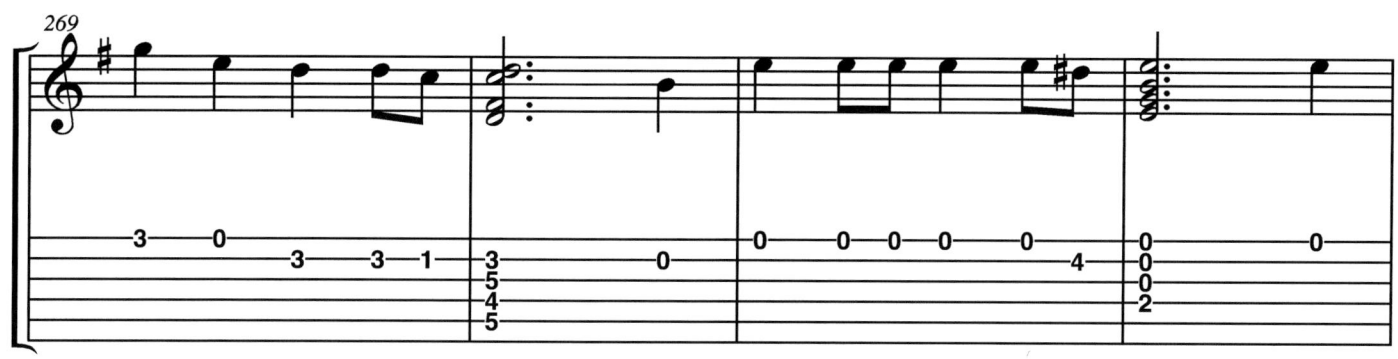
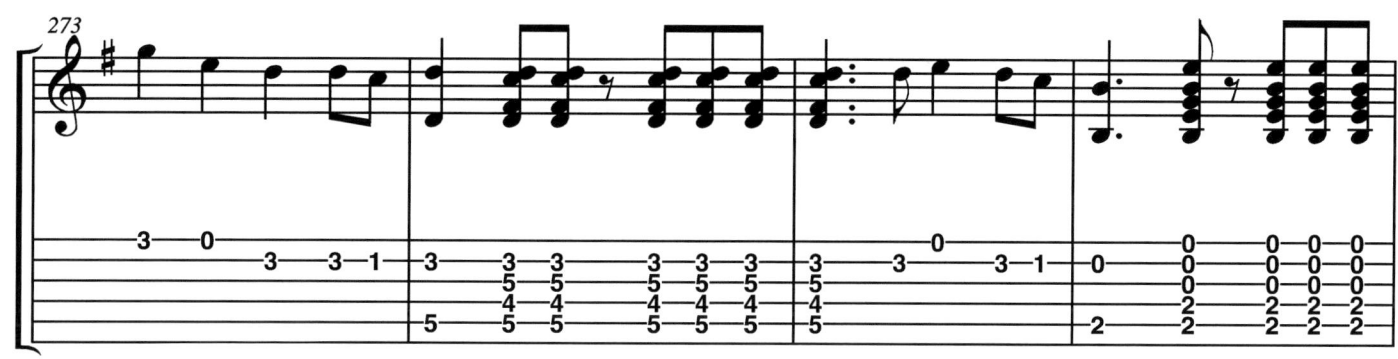
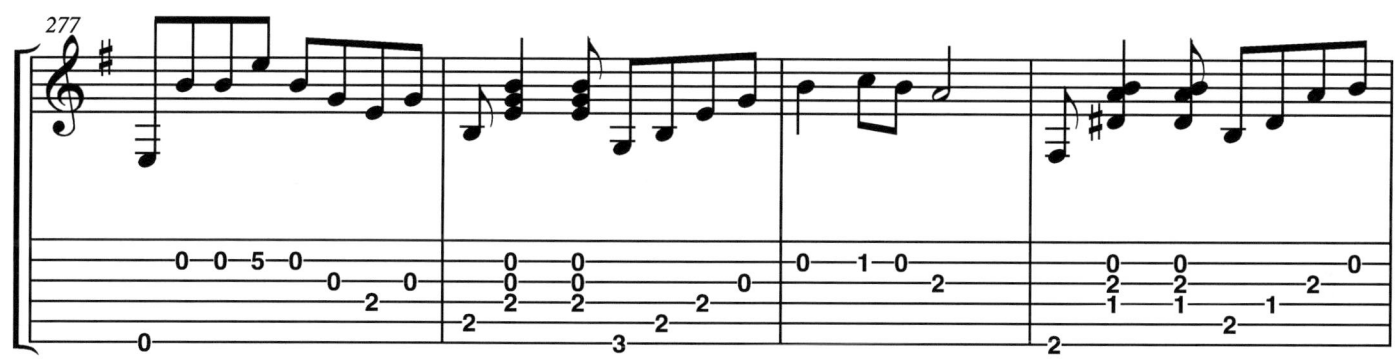
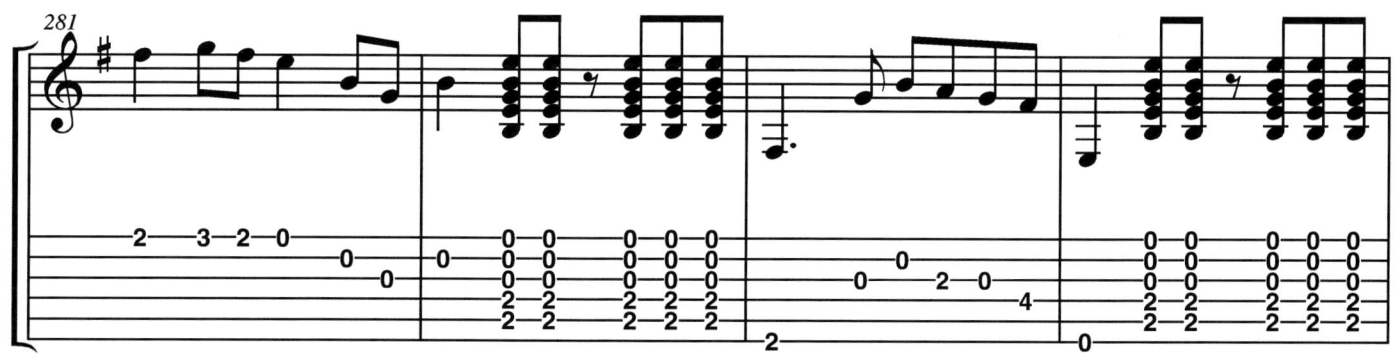

RUMBA

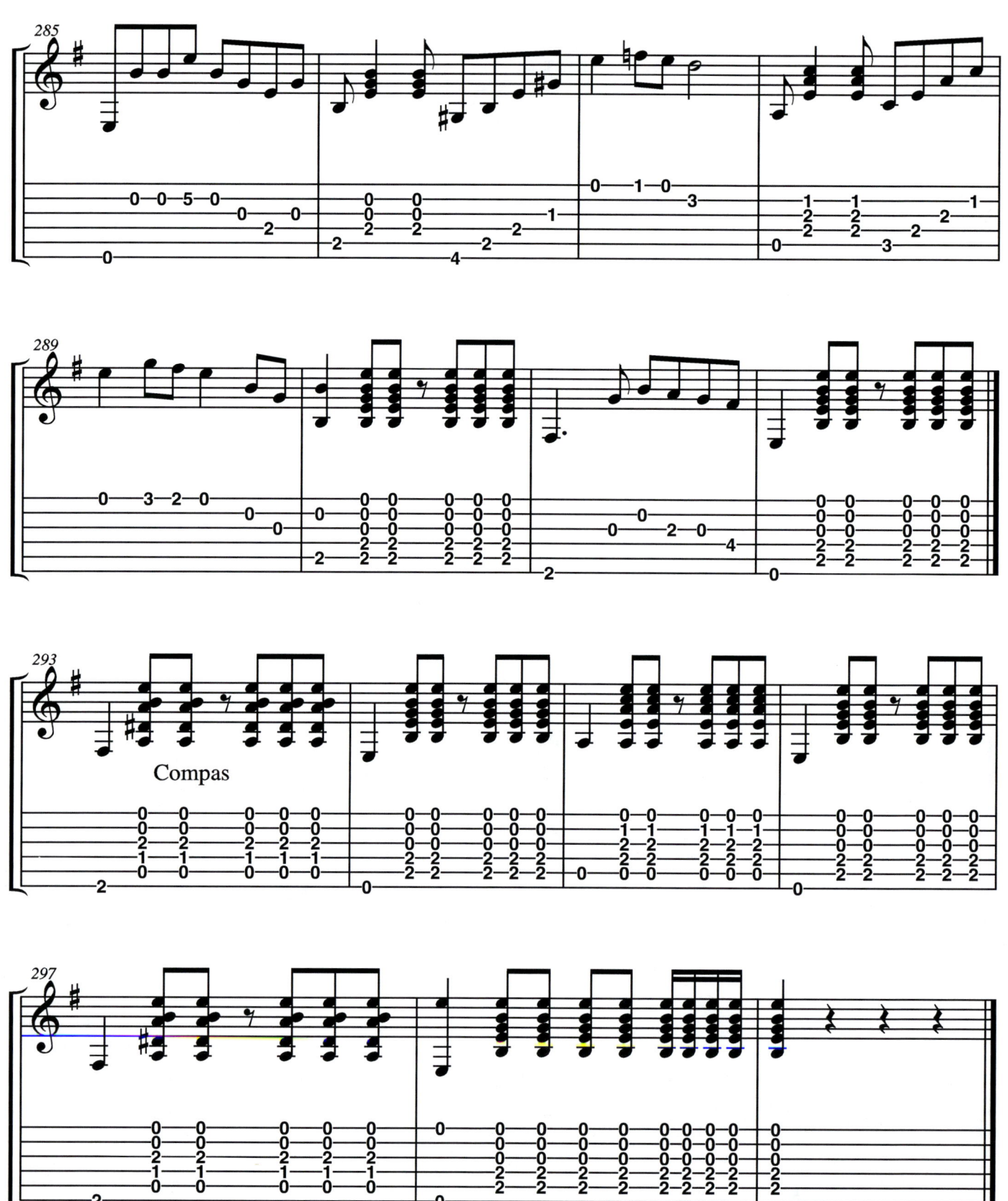

RUMBA

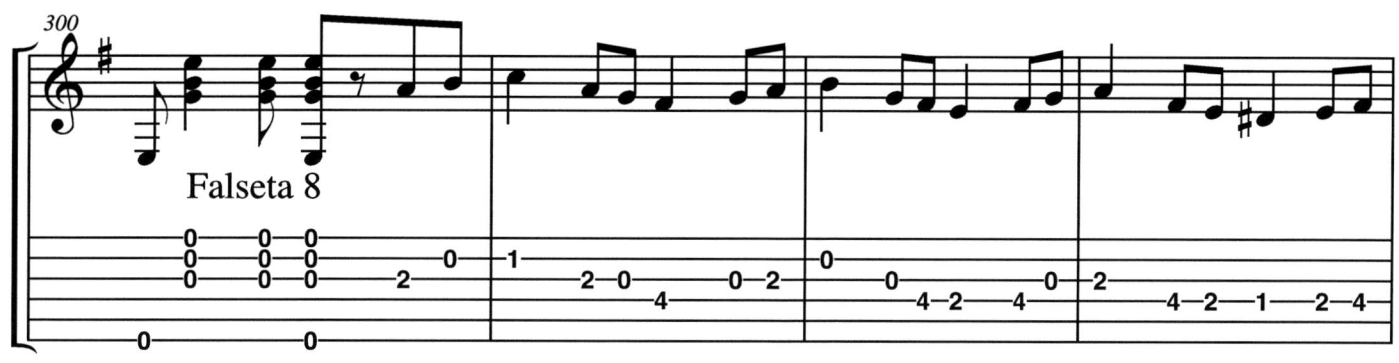

Falseta 8

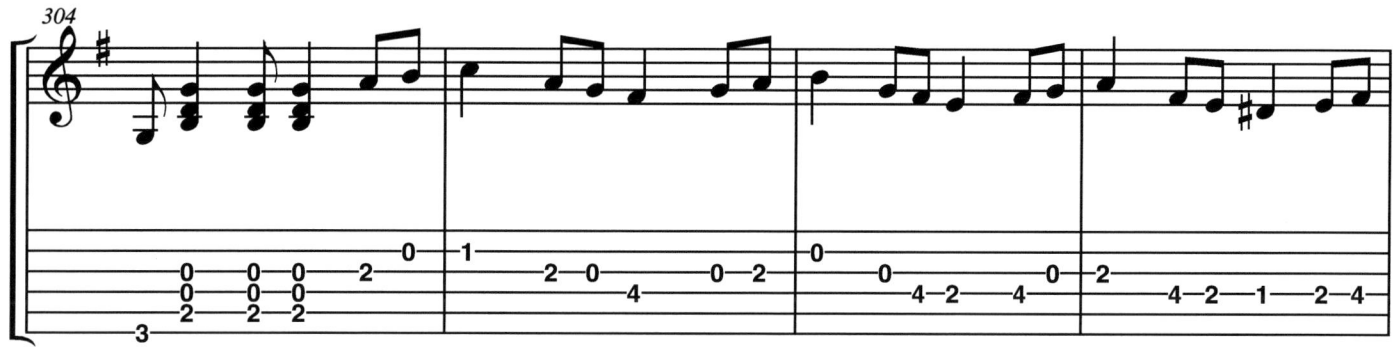

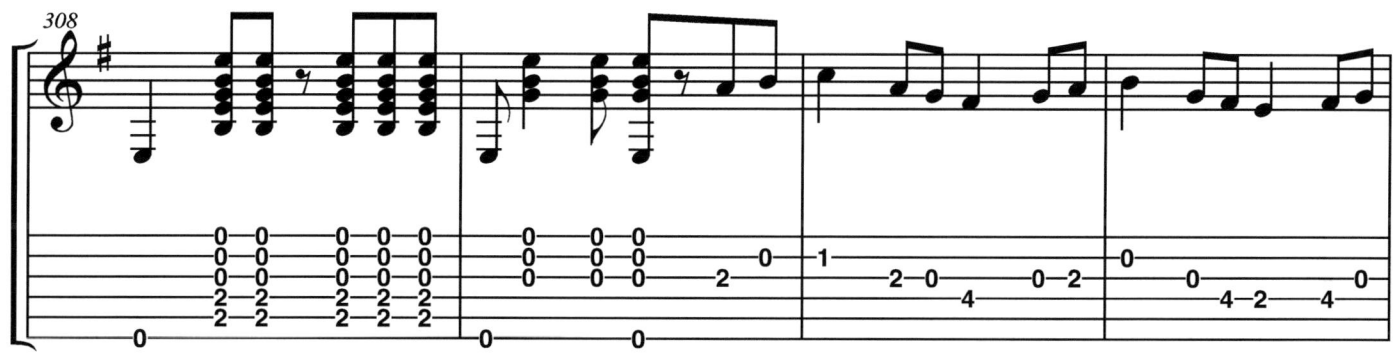

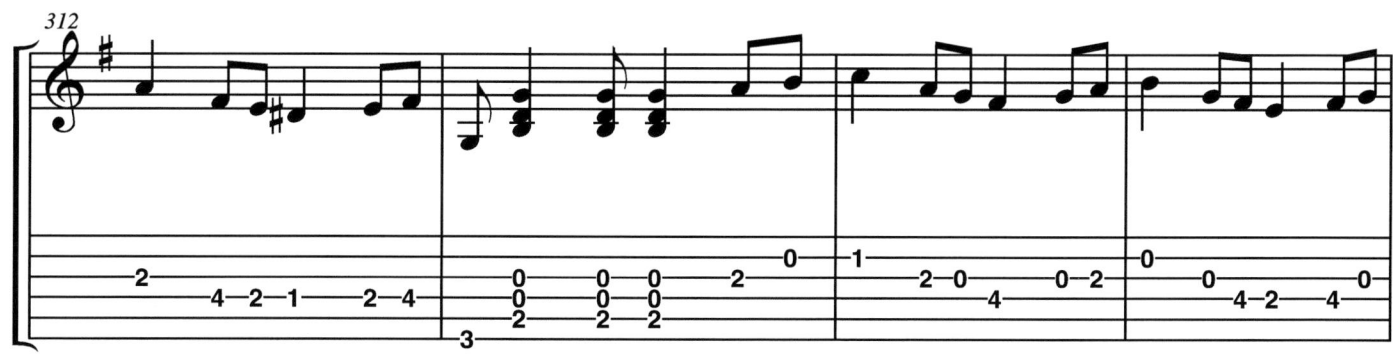

RUMBA

RUMBA

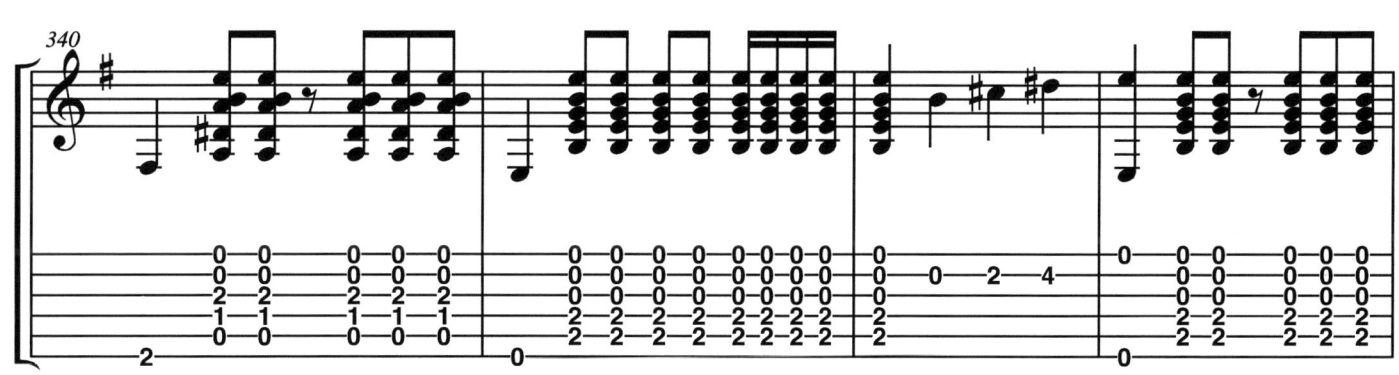
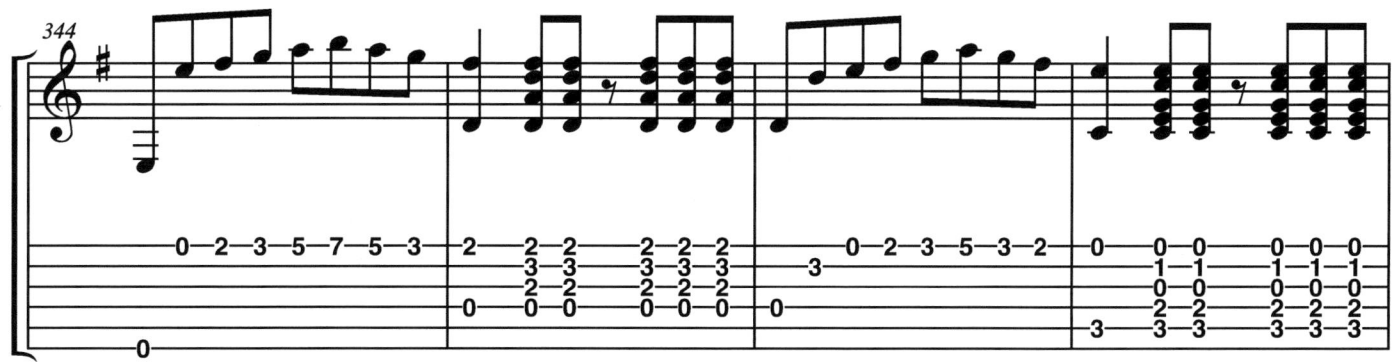

RUMBA

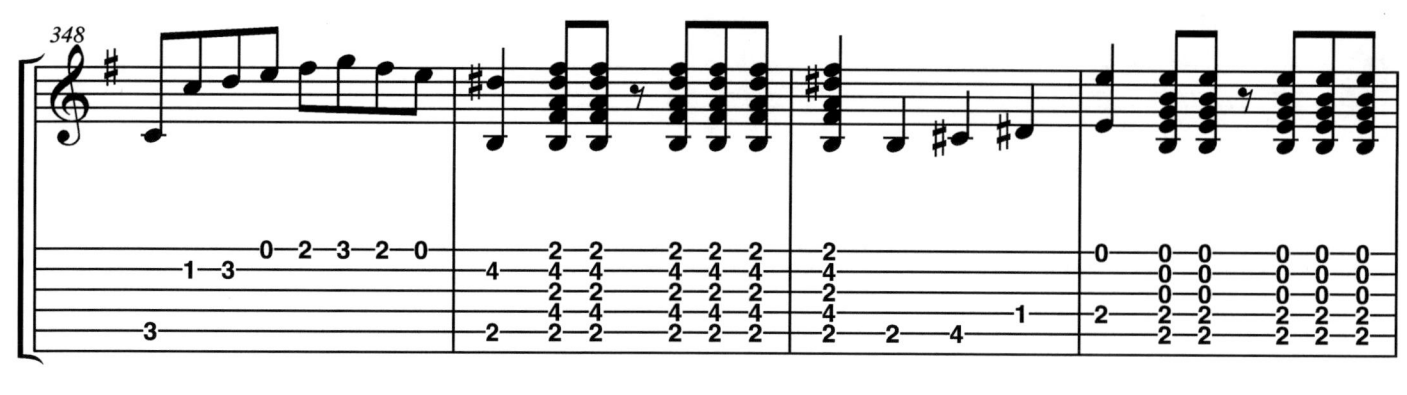
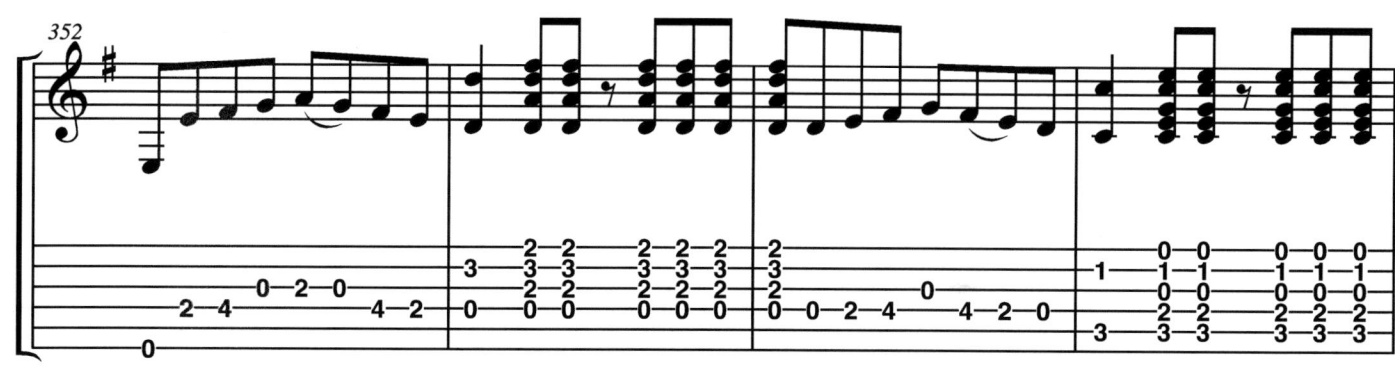
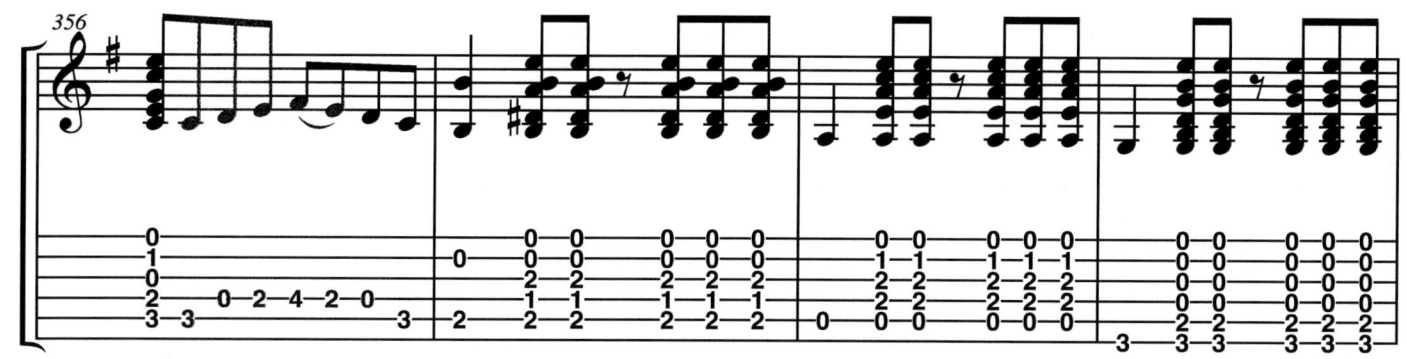

RUMBA

SEVILLANAS

1

Strum every compas in the same manner

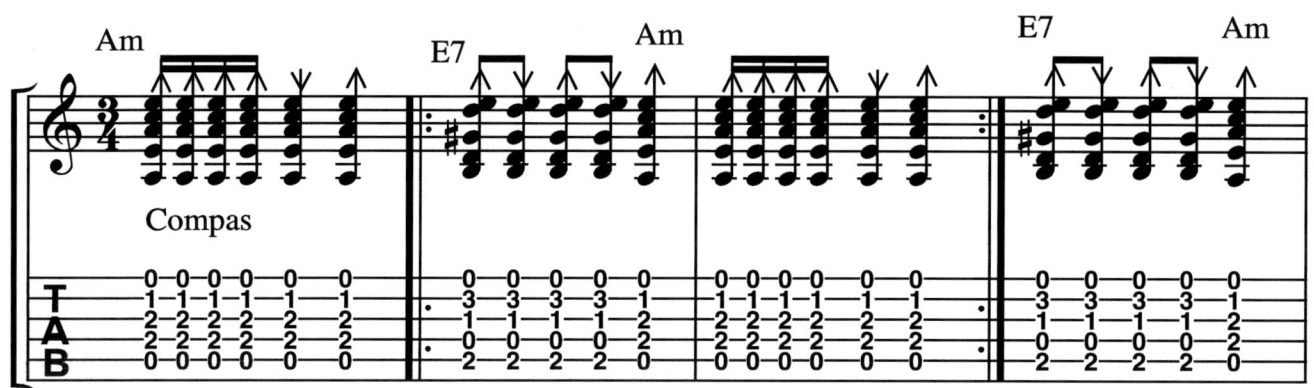

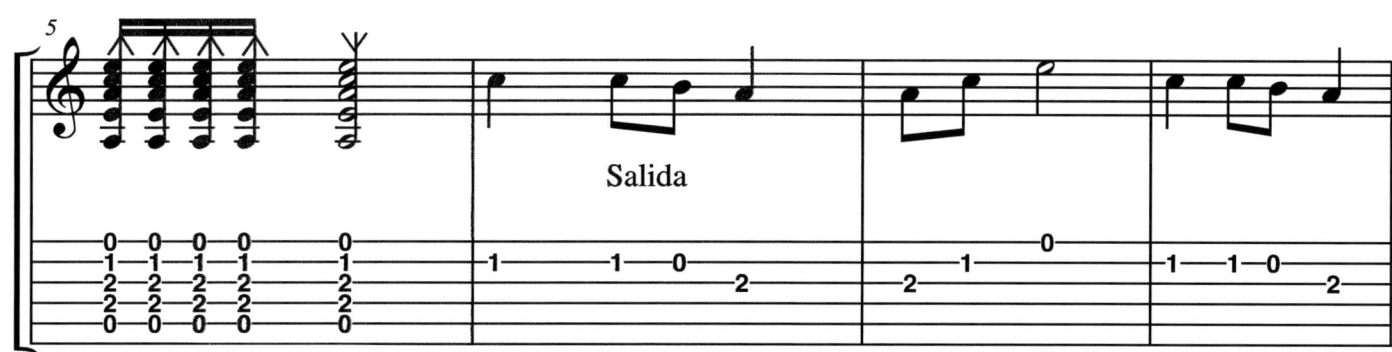

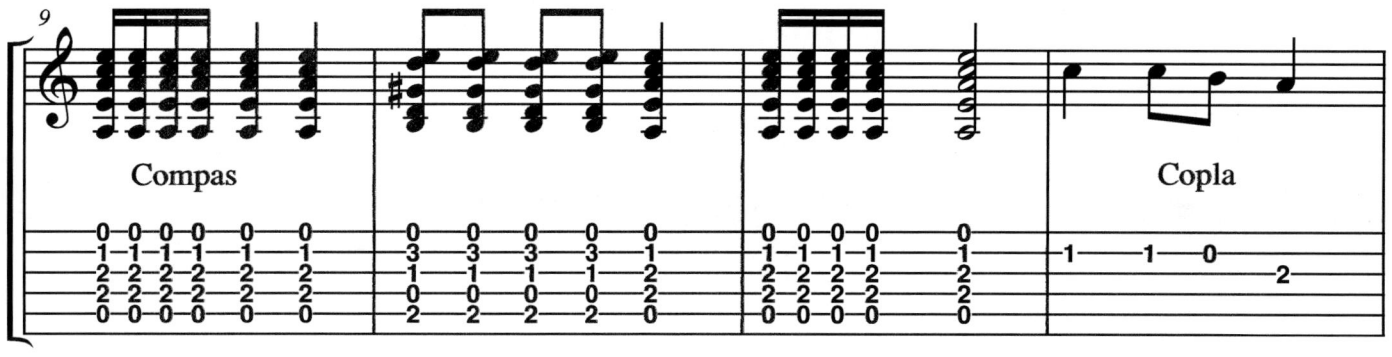

SEVILLANAS

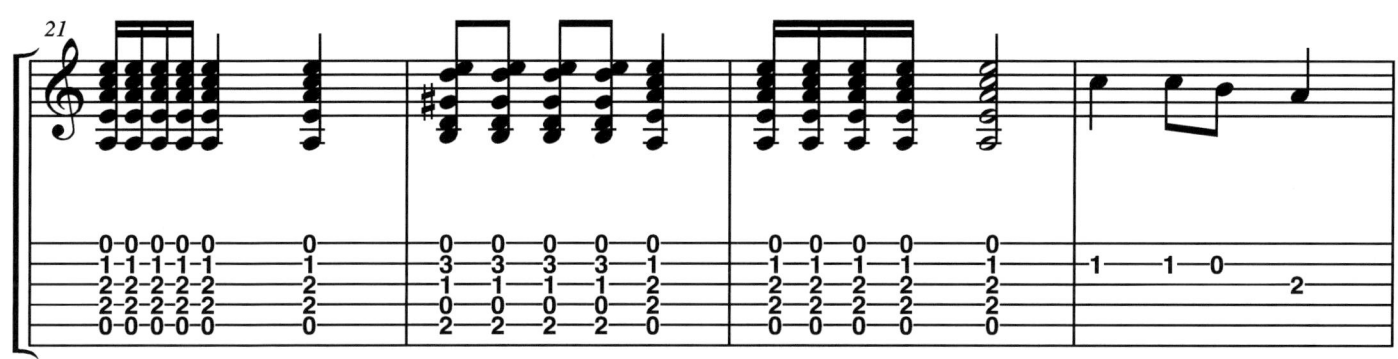
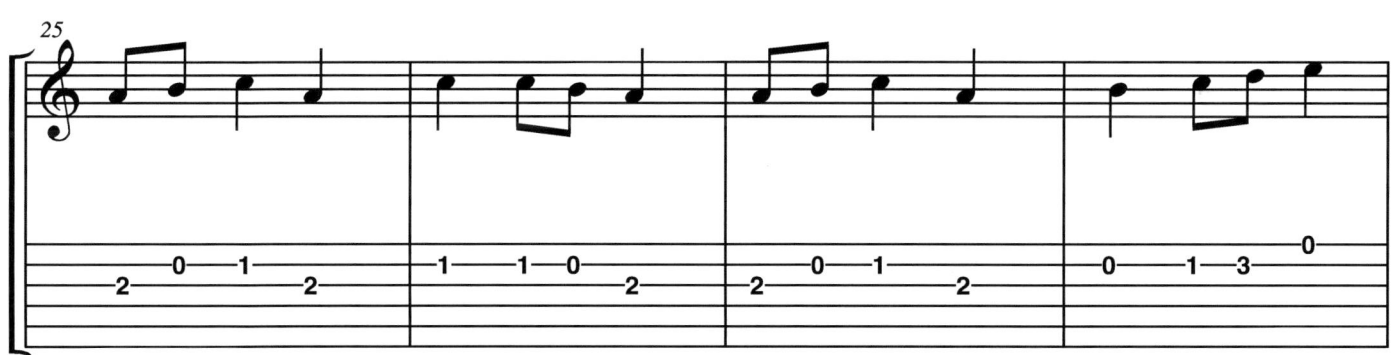
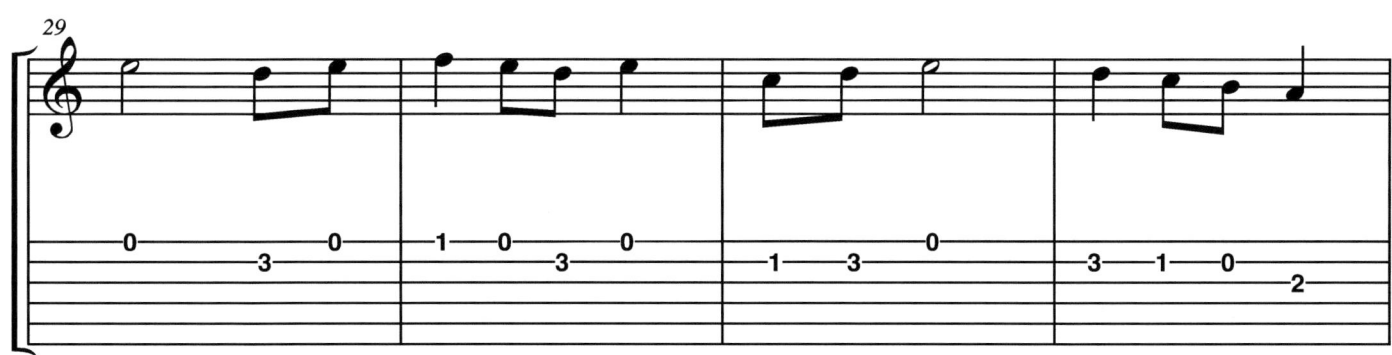

SEVILLANAS

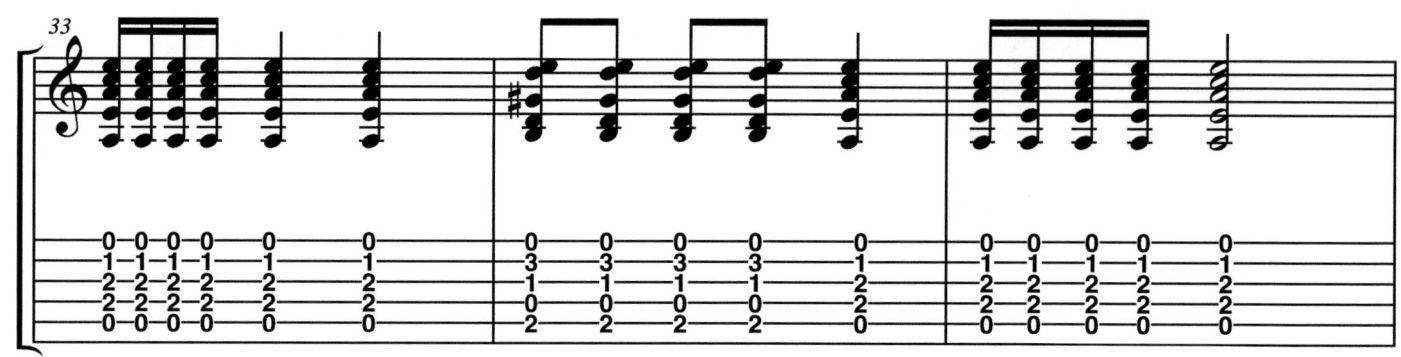
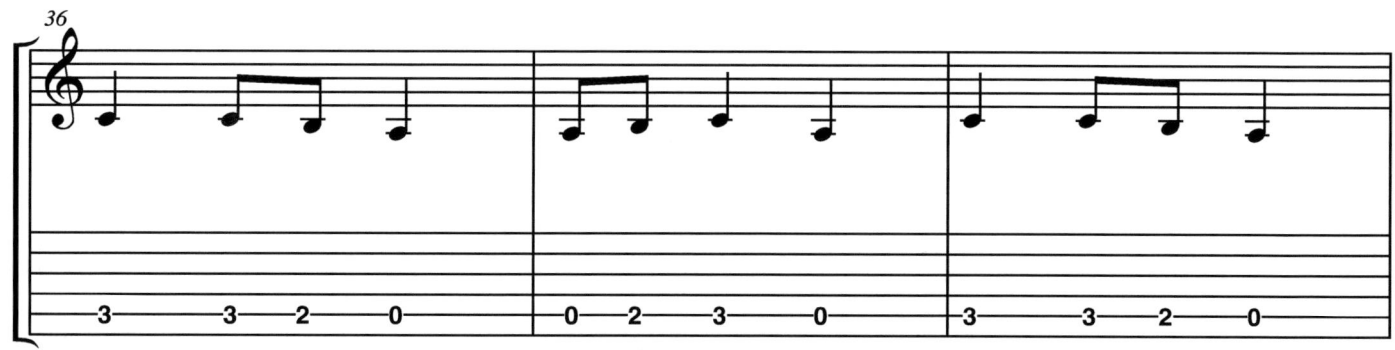

SEVILLANAS
2

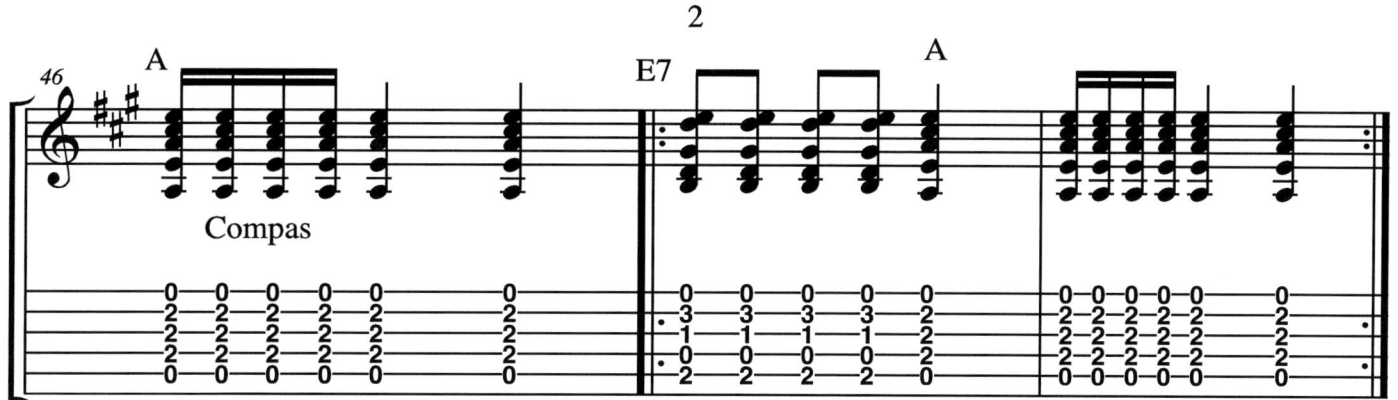
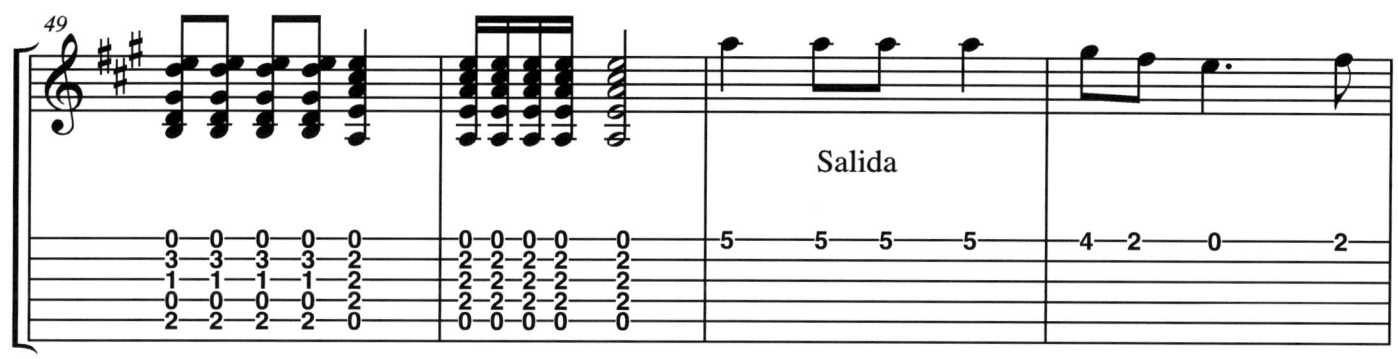
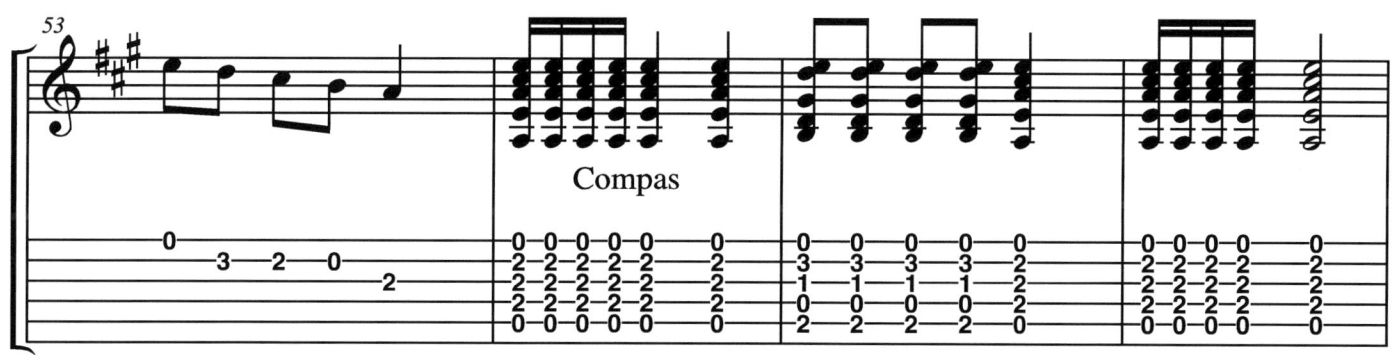
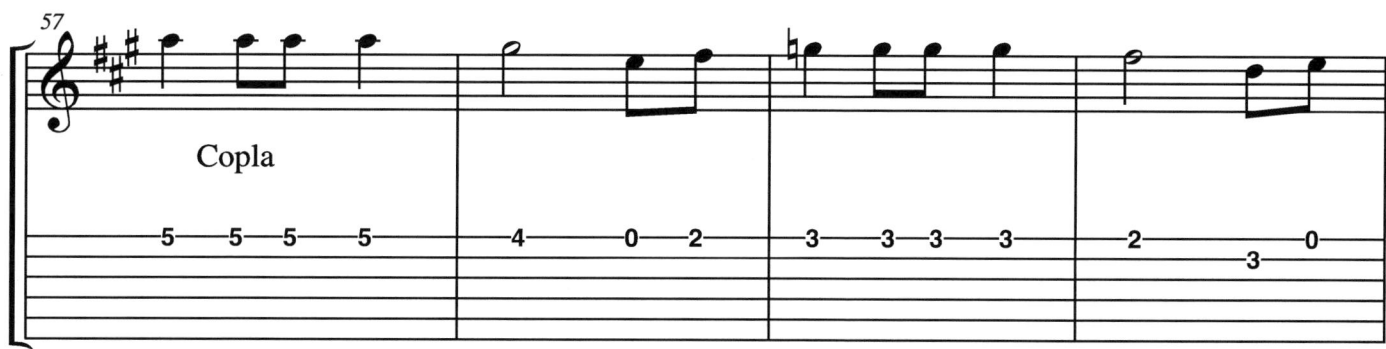

SEVILLANAS

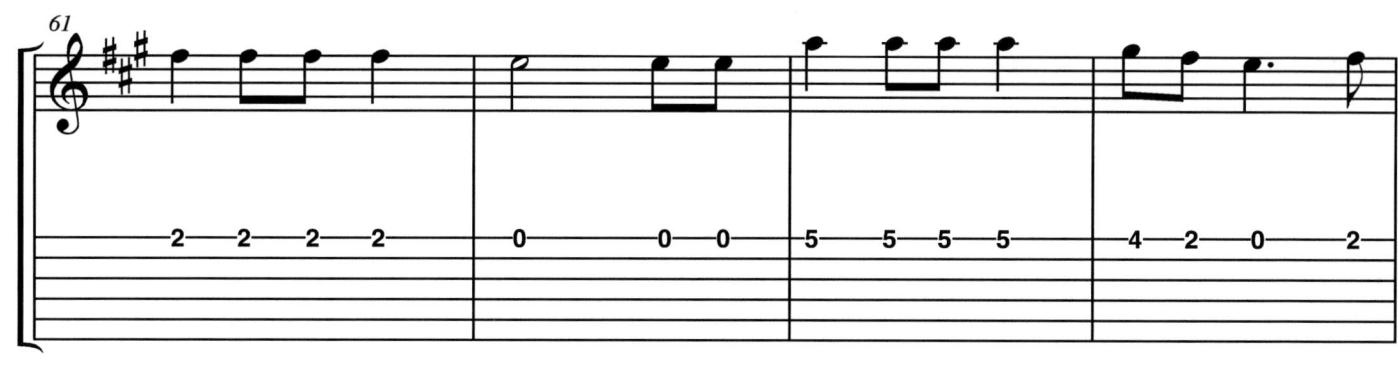
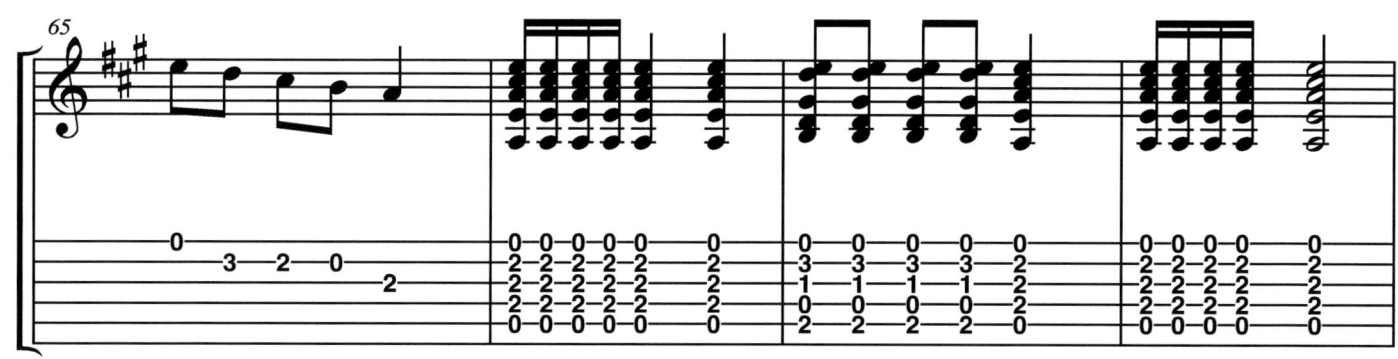
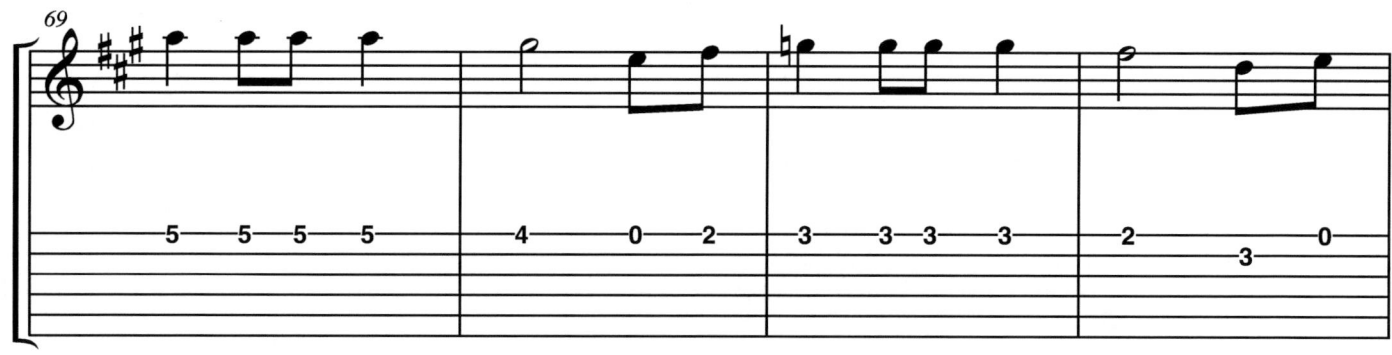
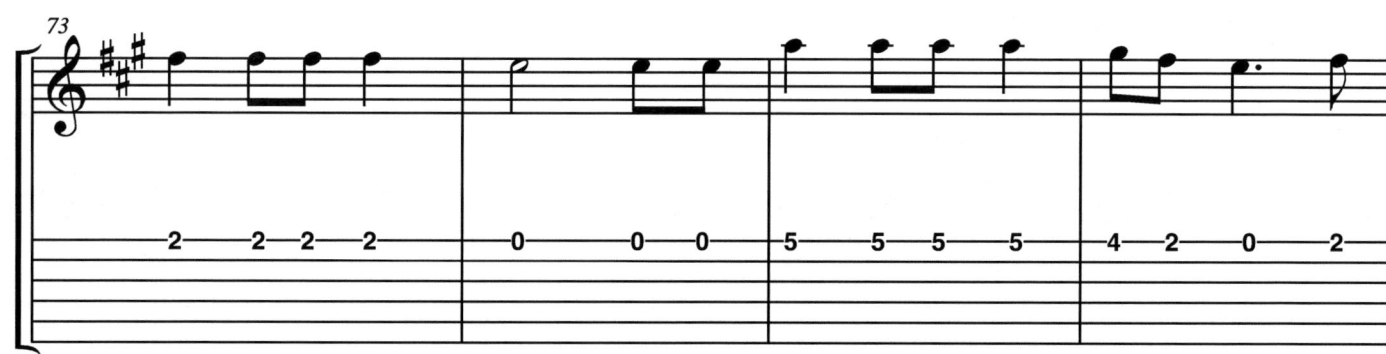

SEVILLANAS

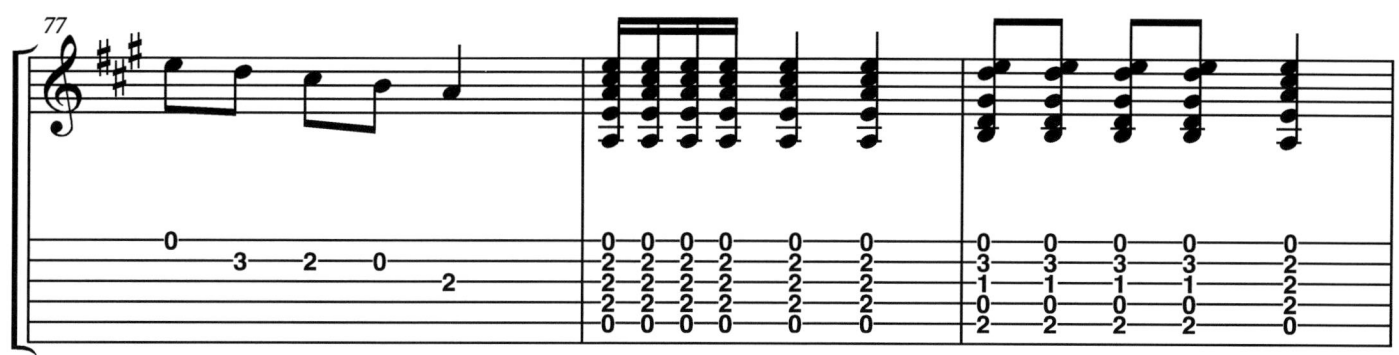
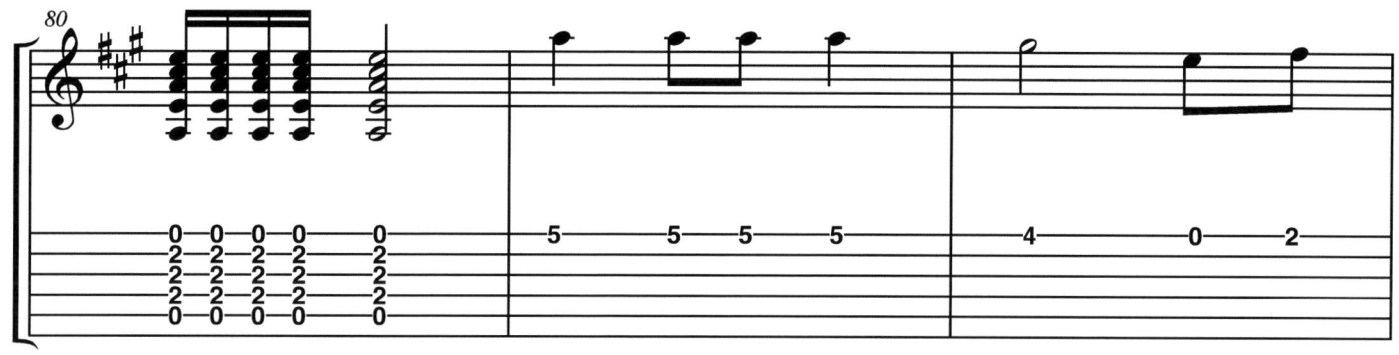

SEVILLANAS

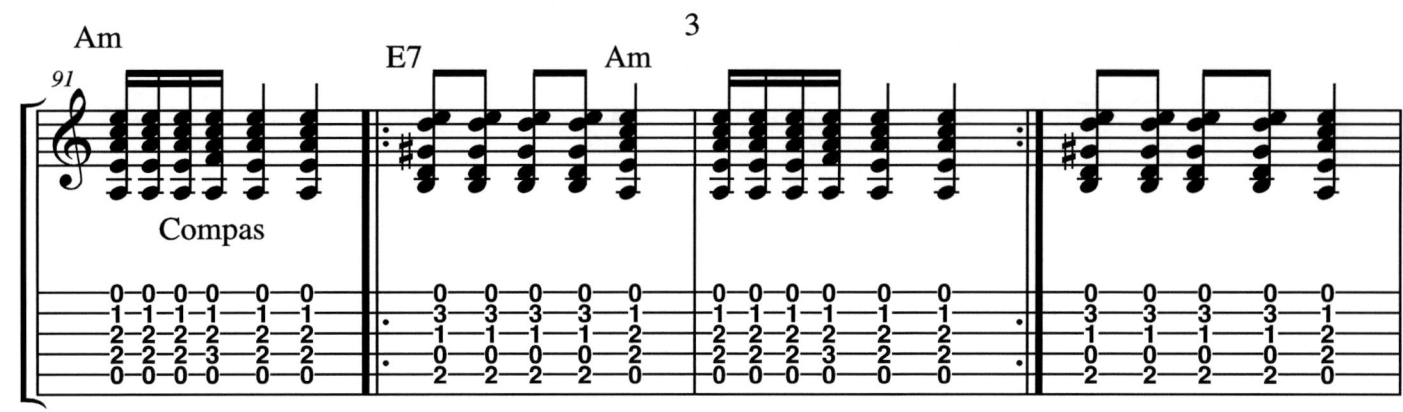

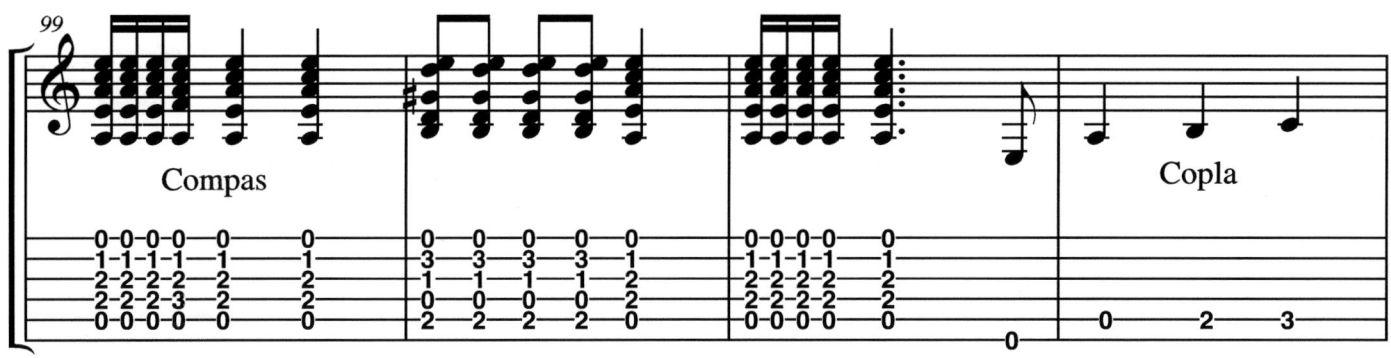
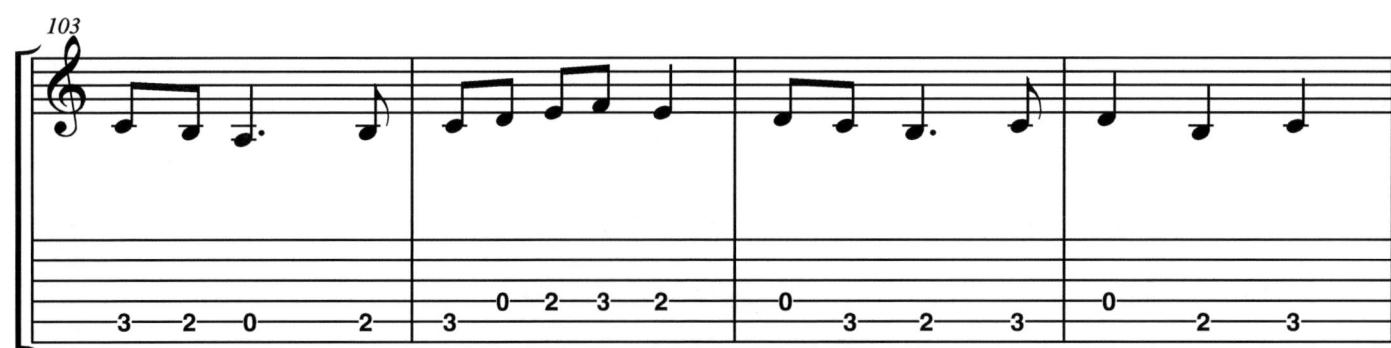

SEVILLANAS

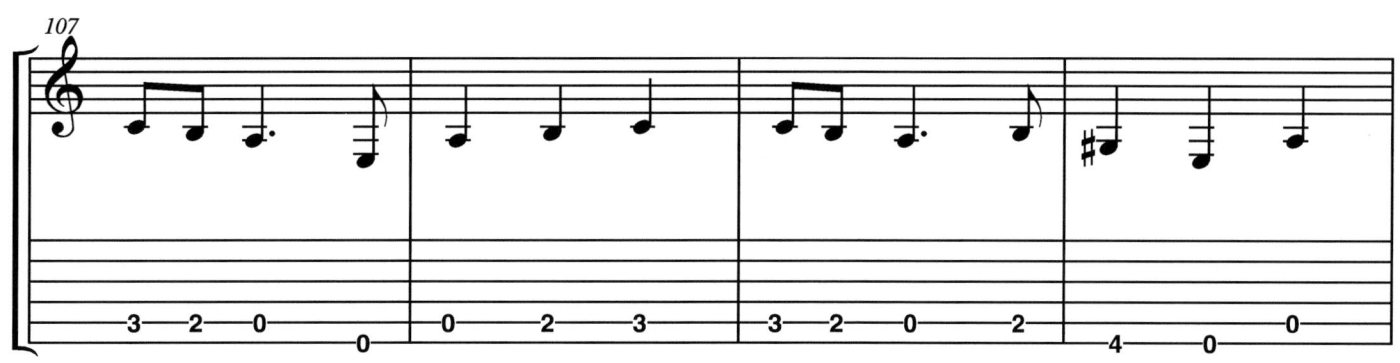
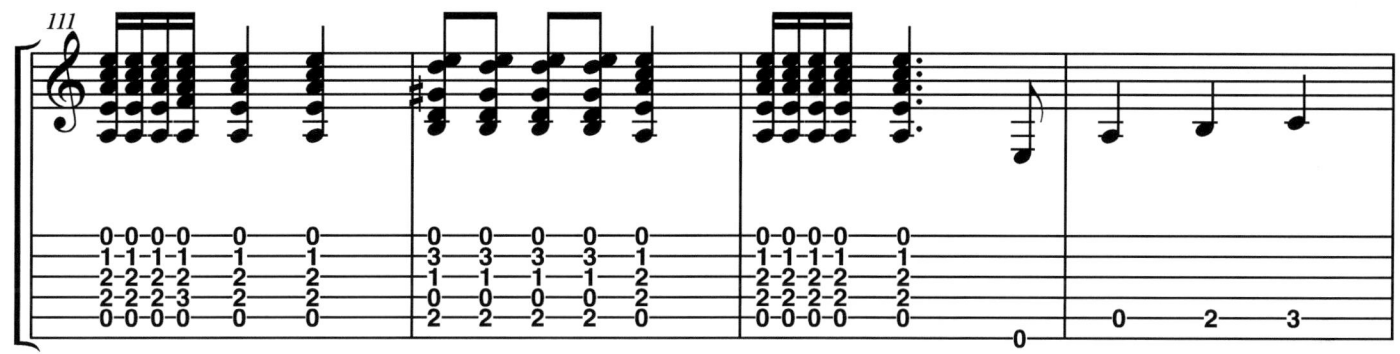

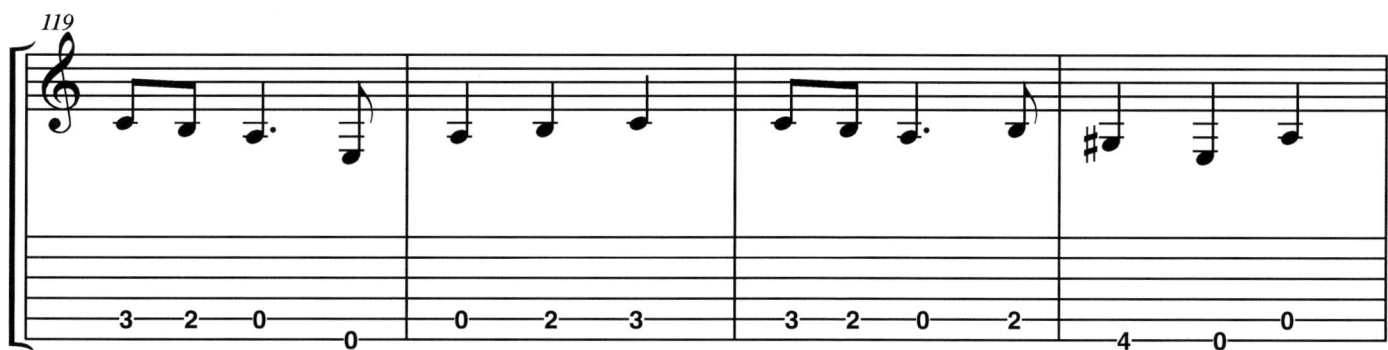

SEVILLANAS

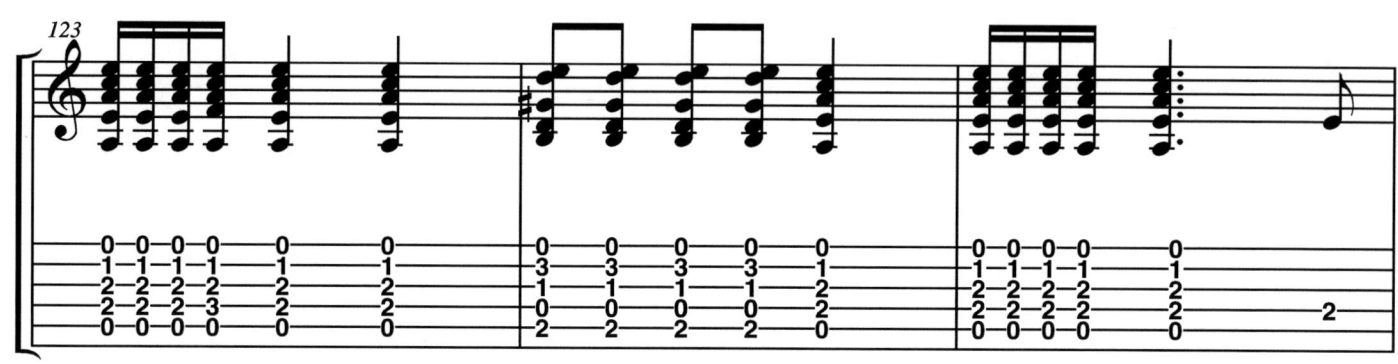
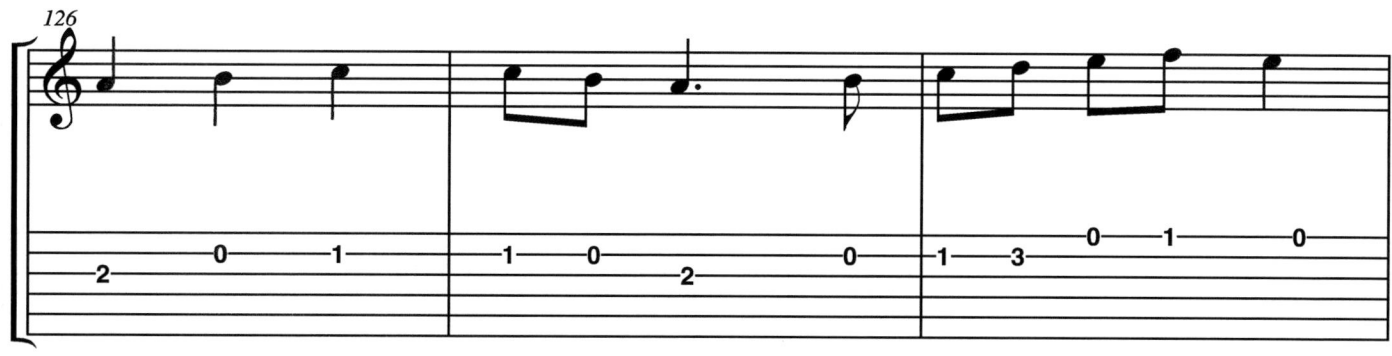

SEVILLANAS
4

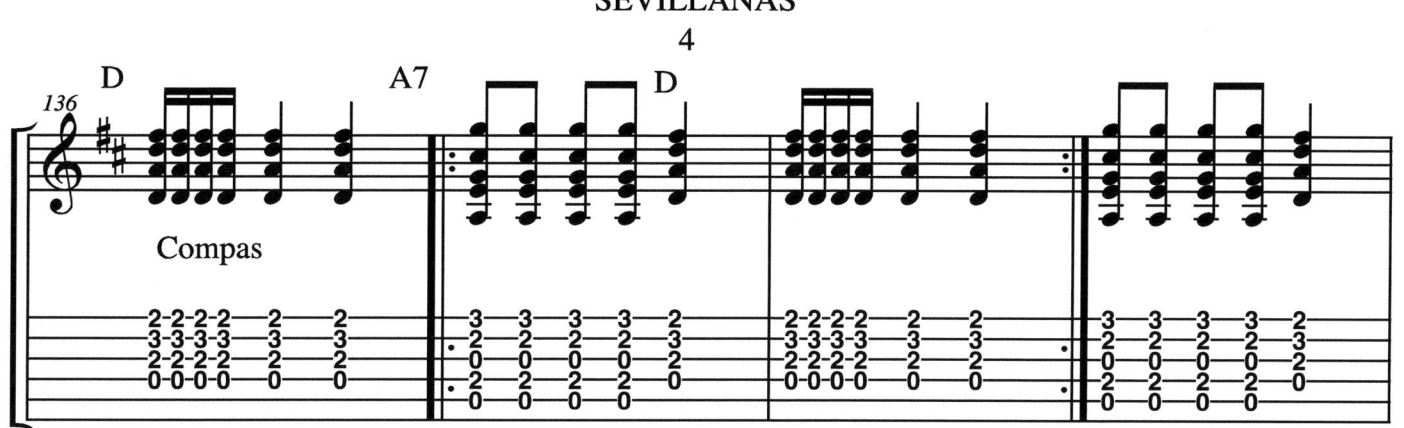

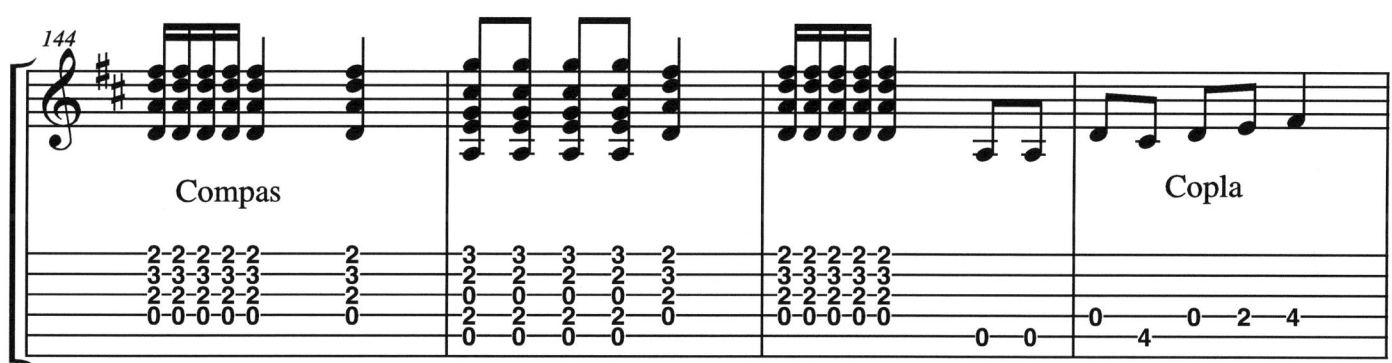

SEVILLANAS

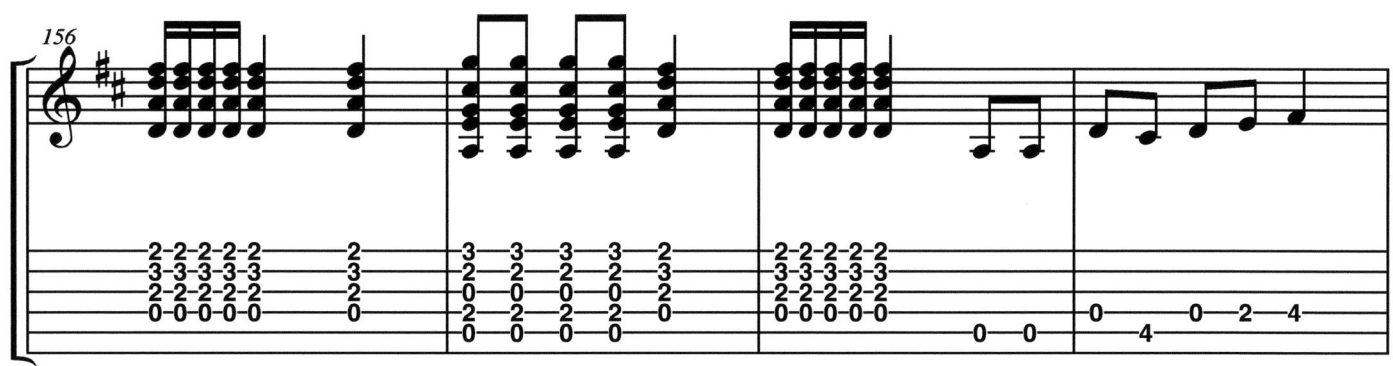
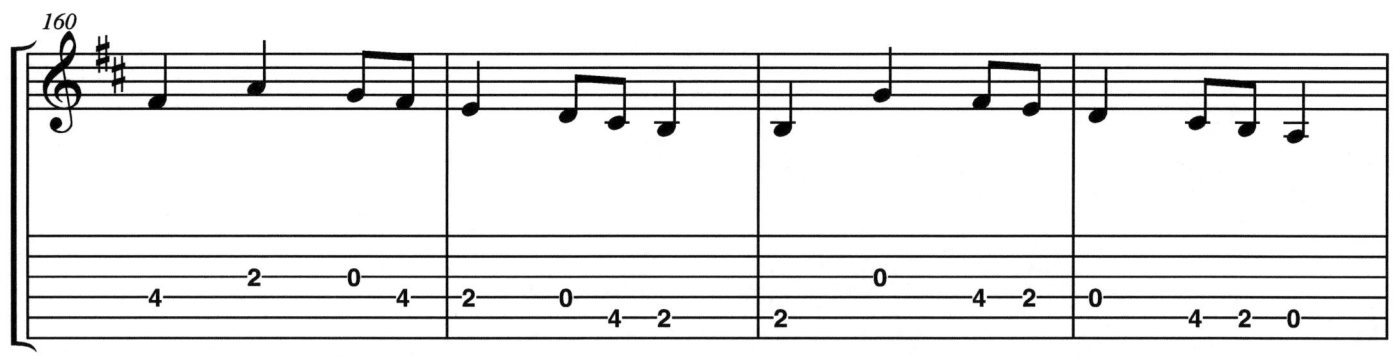

SEVILLANAS

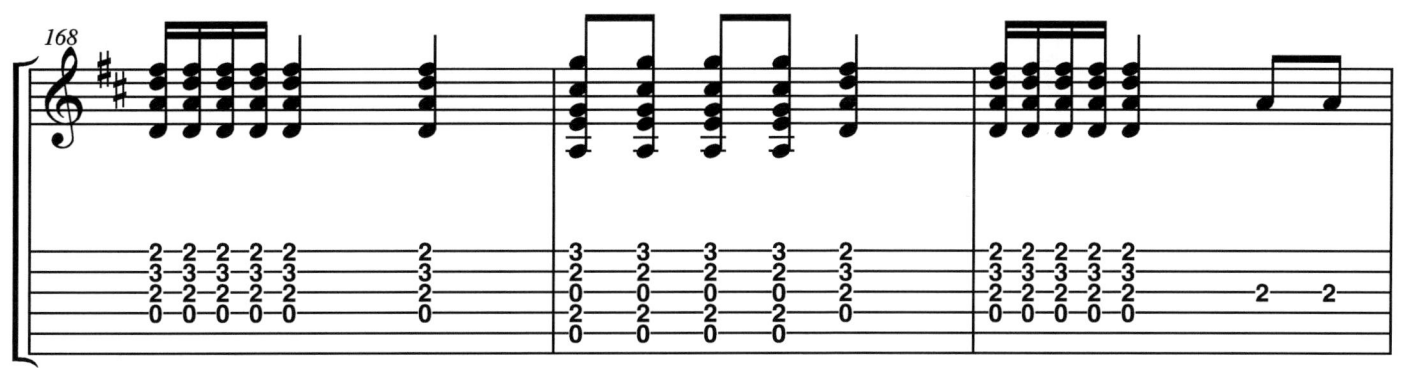
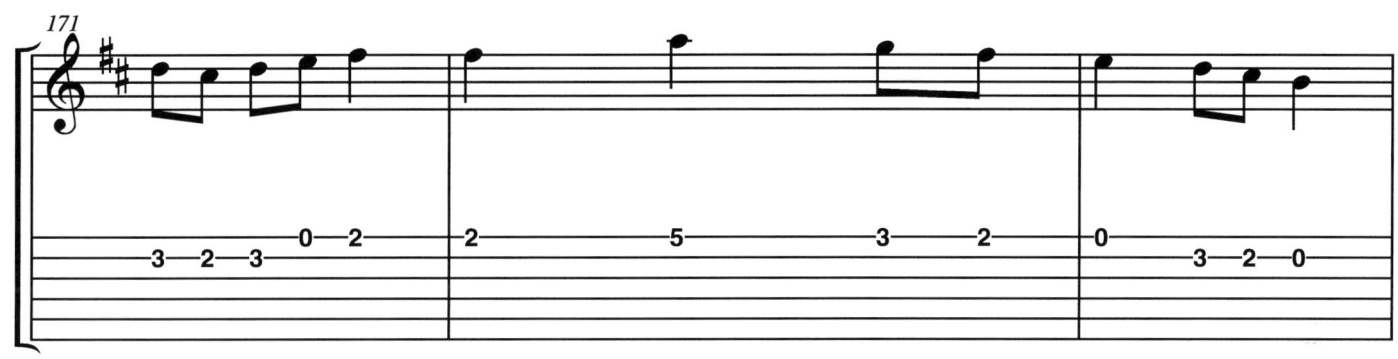
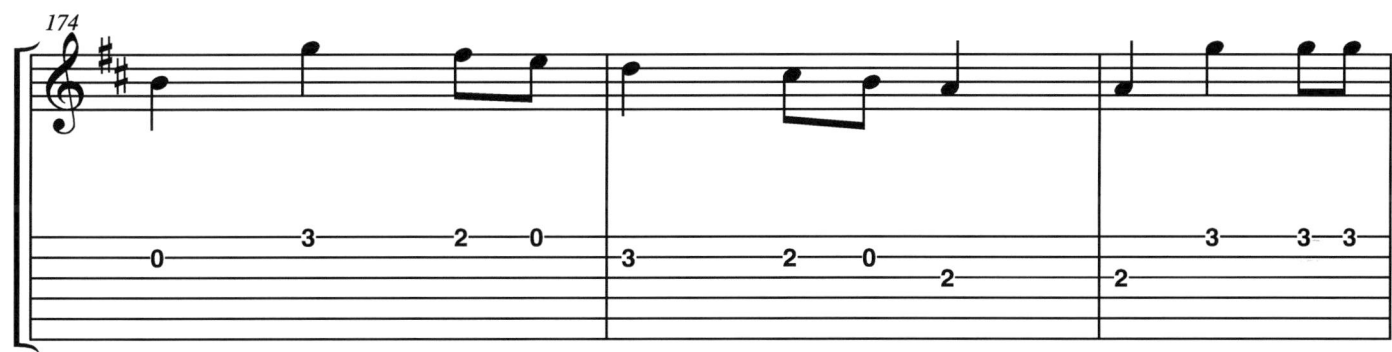
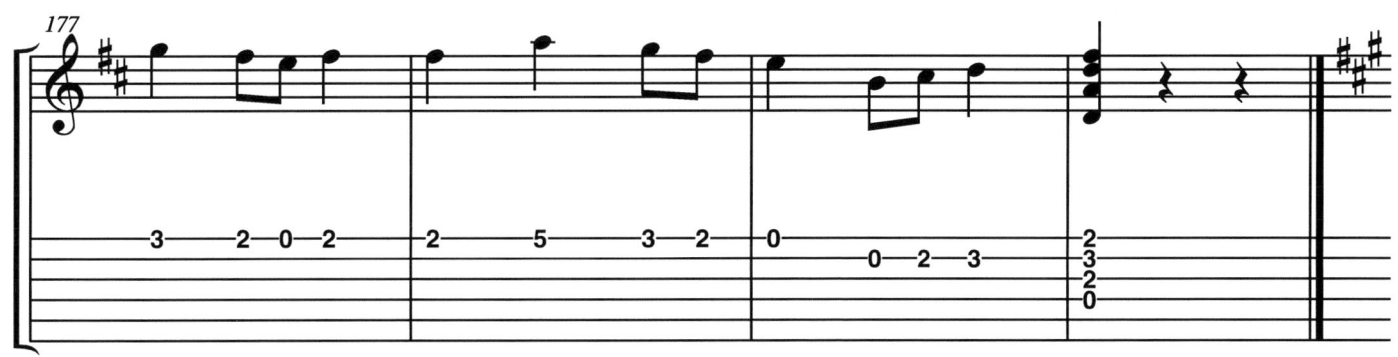

SEVILLANAS
5

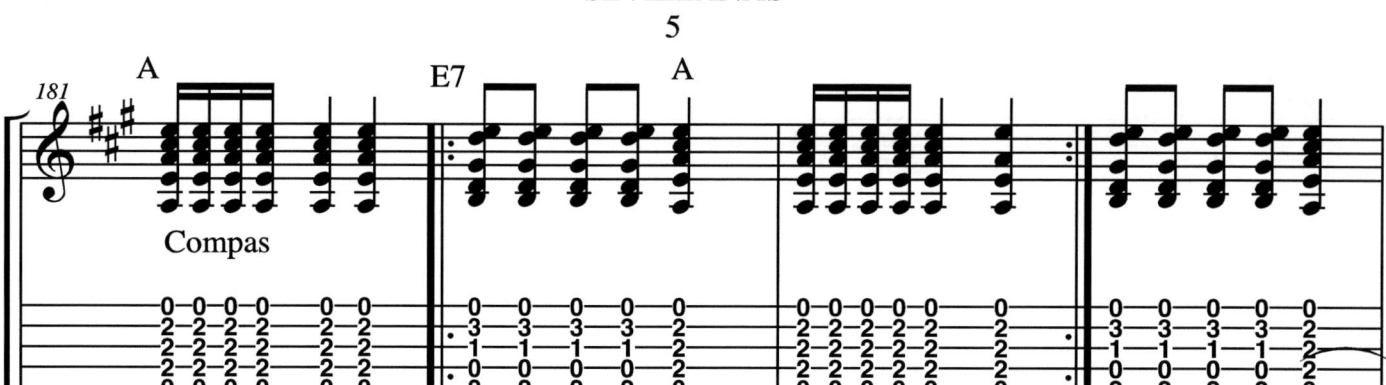

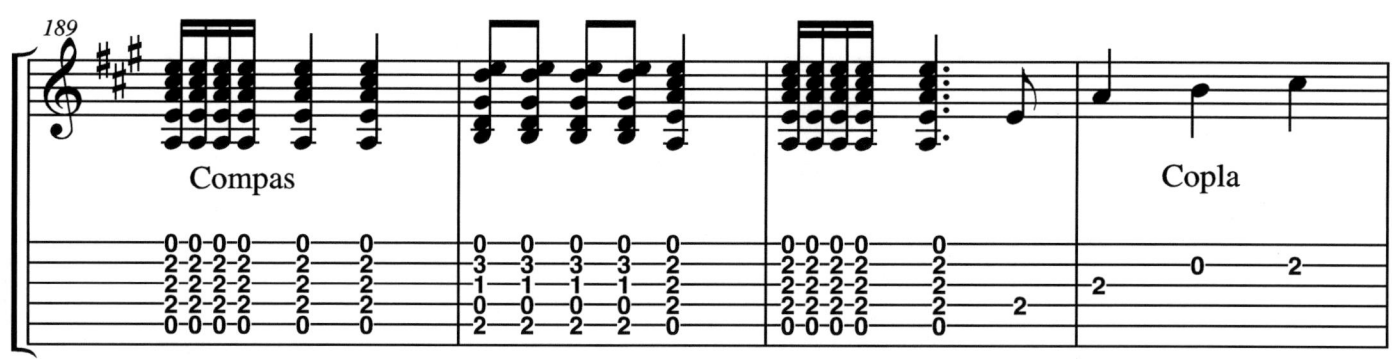
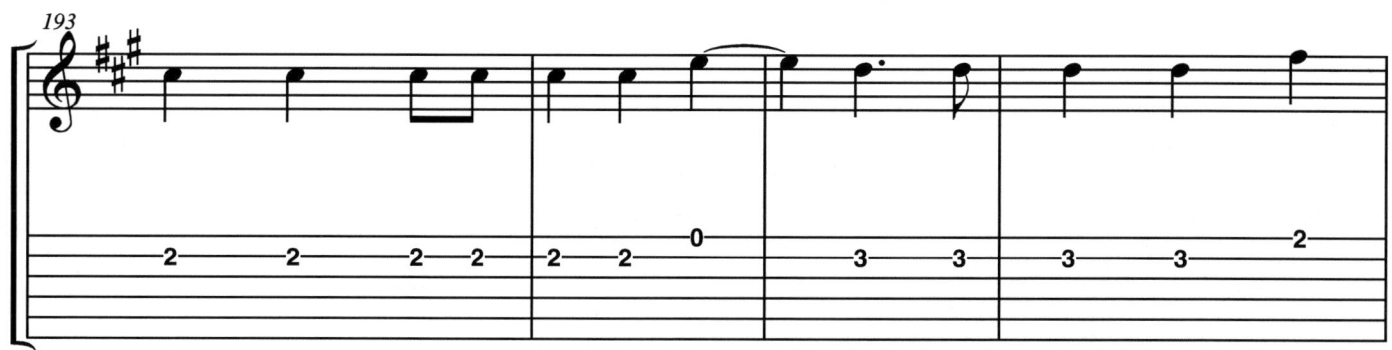

SEVILLANAS

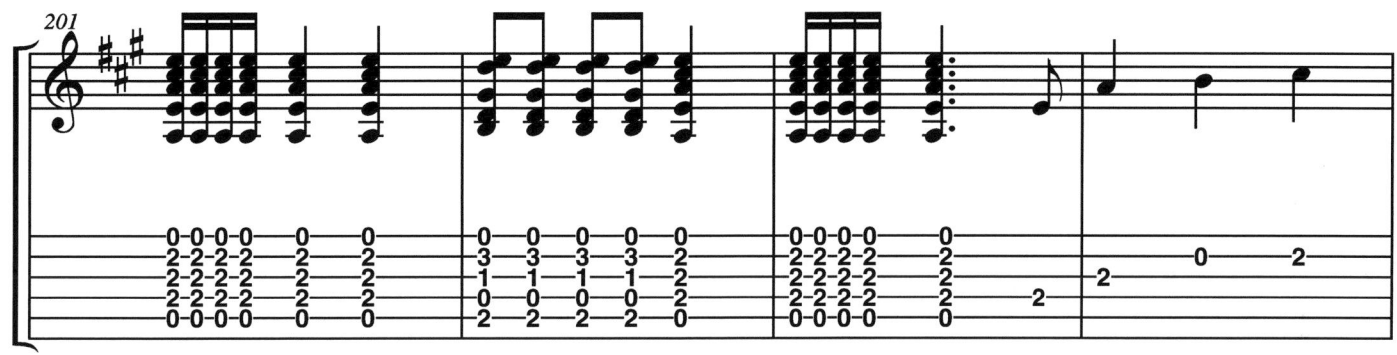
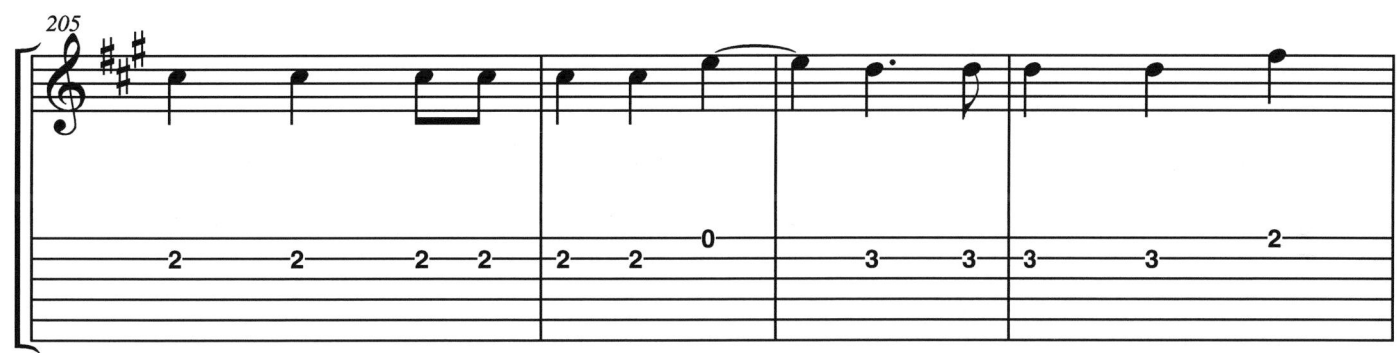
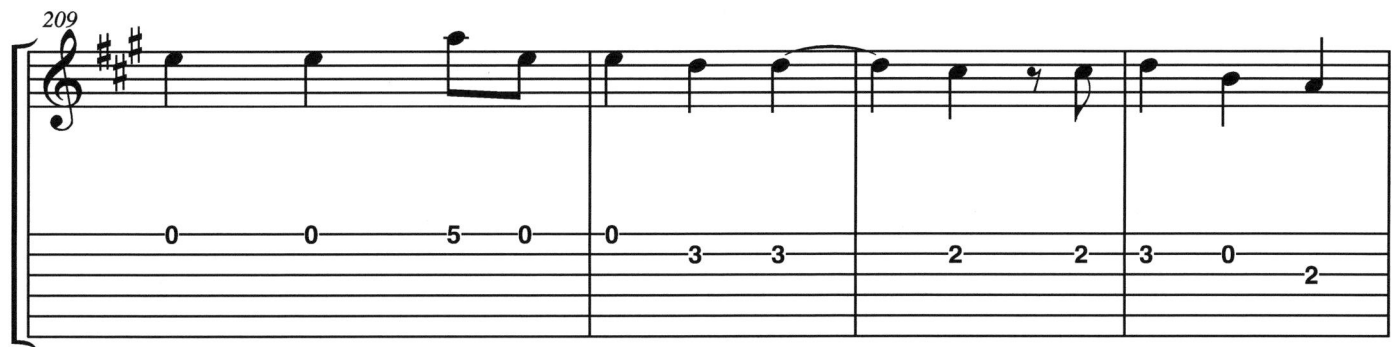

SEVILLANAS

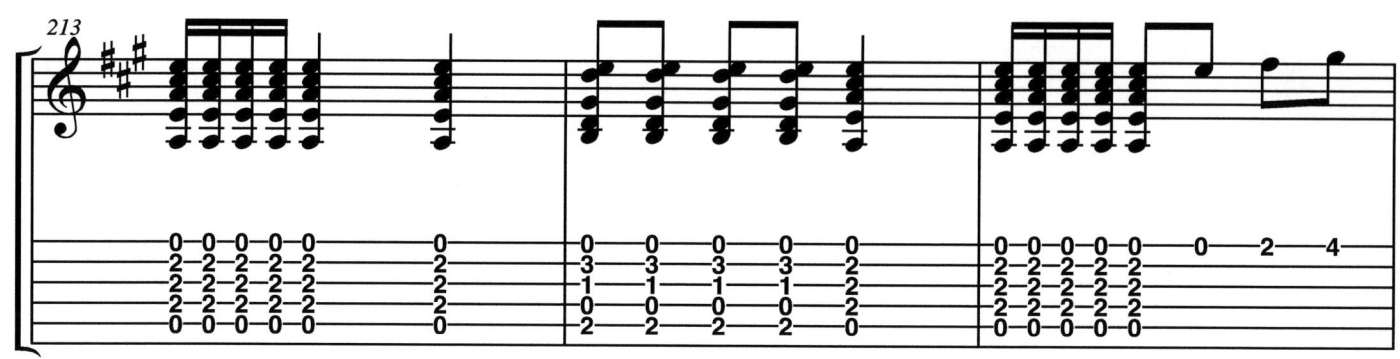
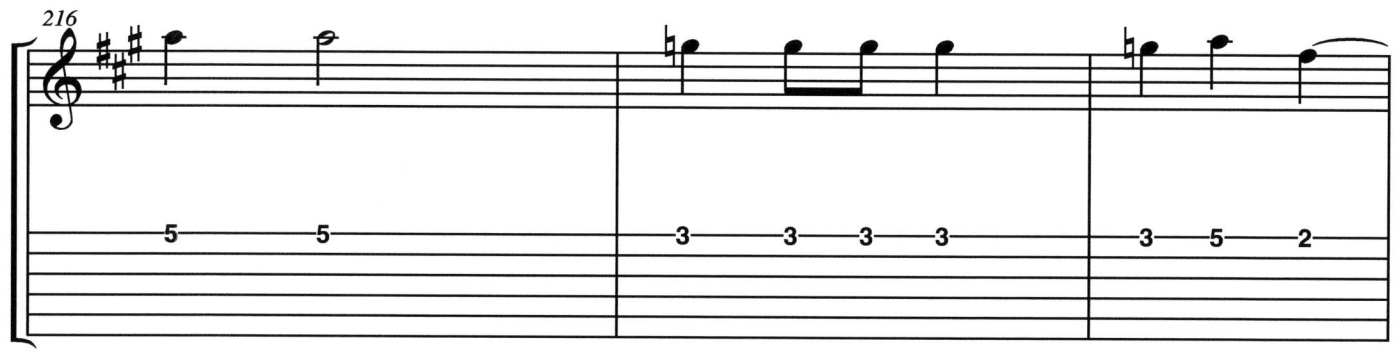
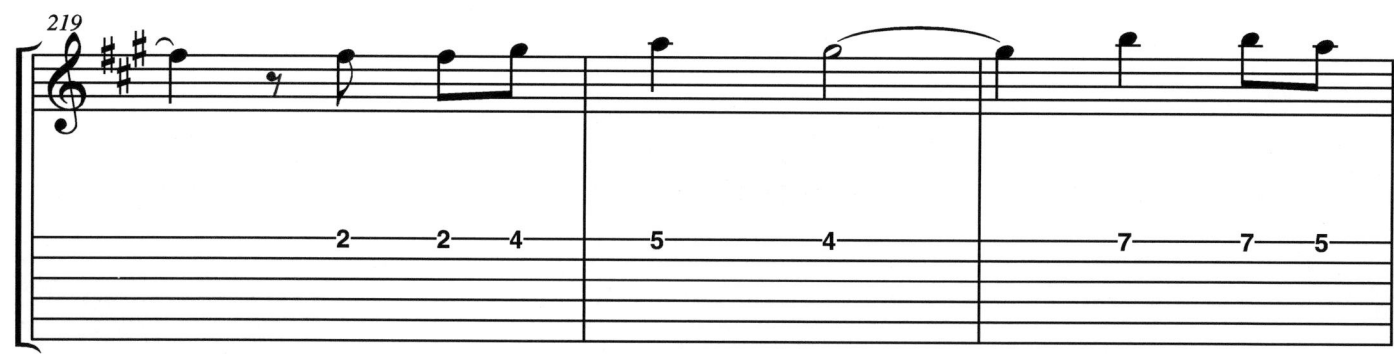
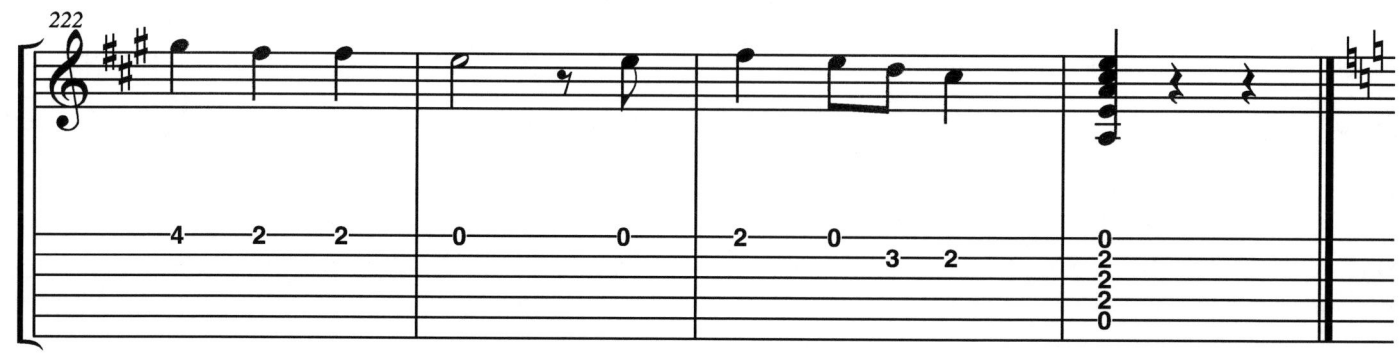

SEVILLANAS
6

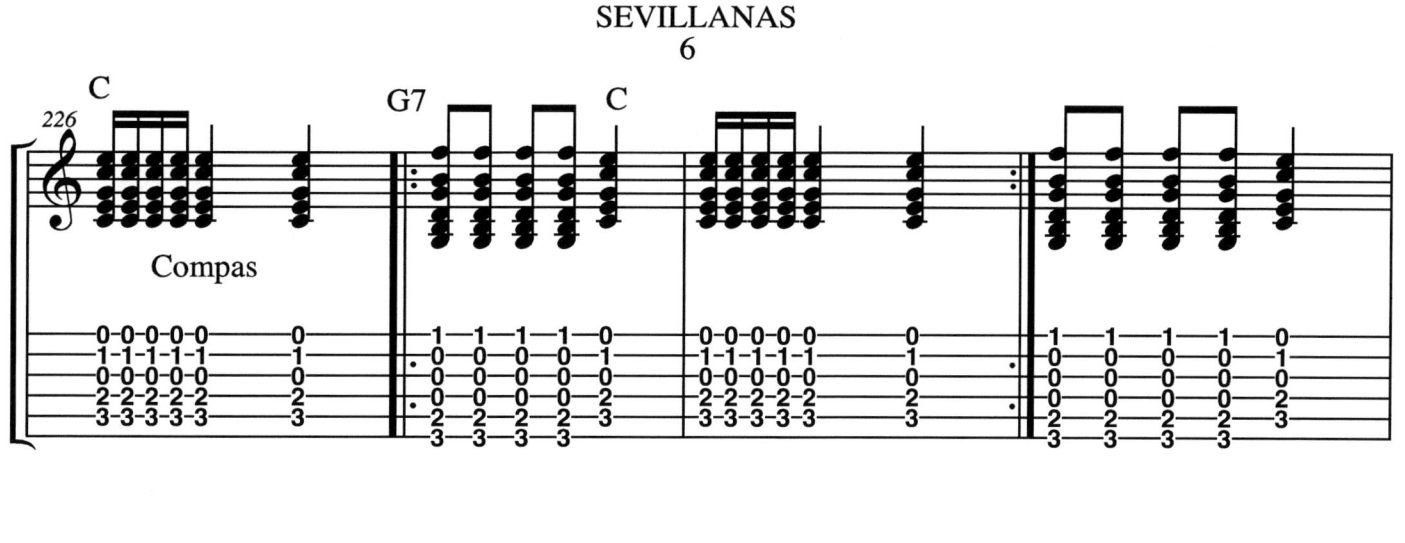
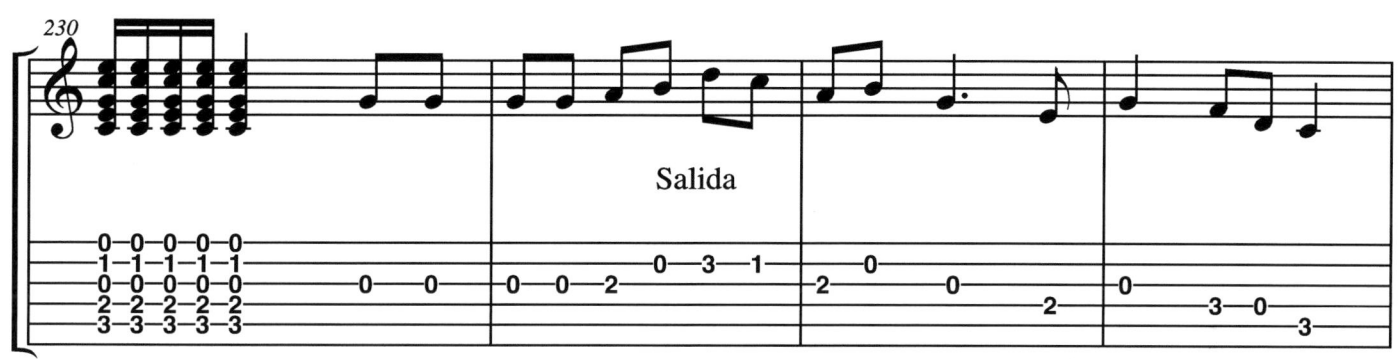
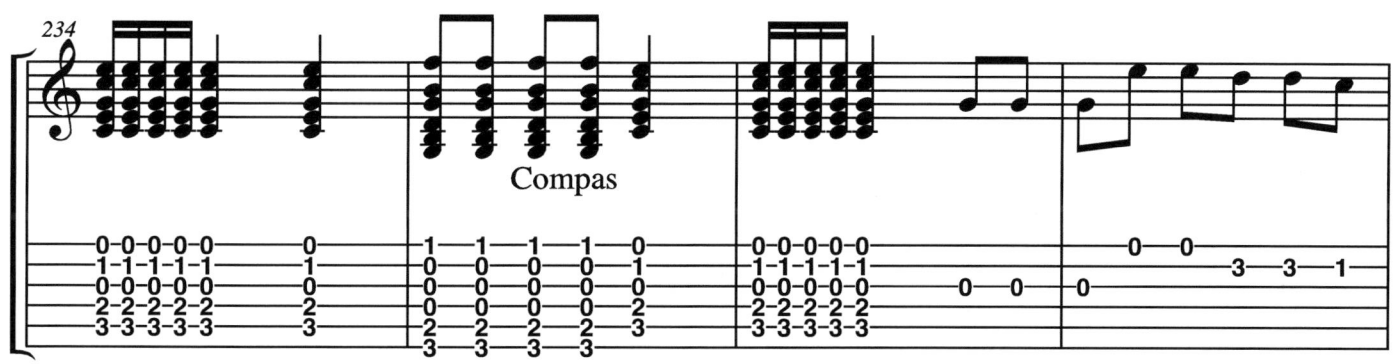

SEVILLANAS

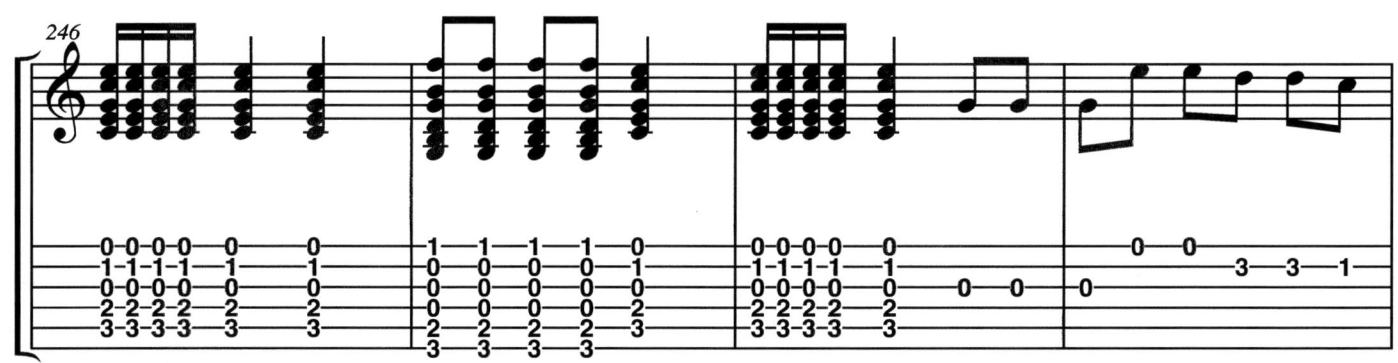

SEVILLANAS

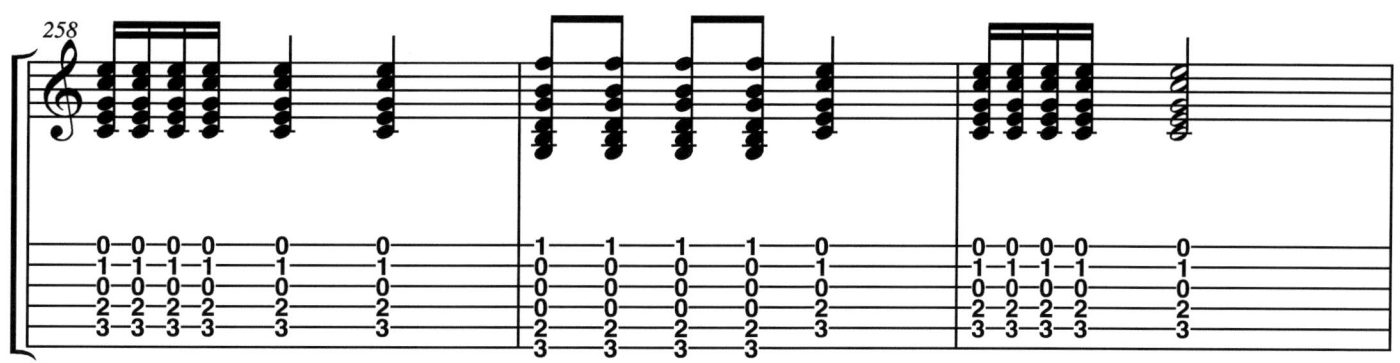

SEVILLANAS
7

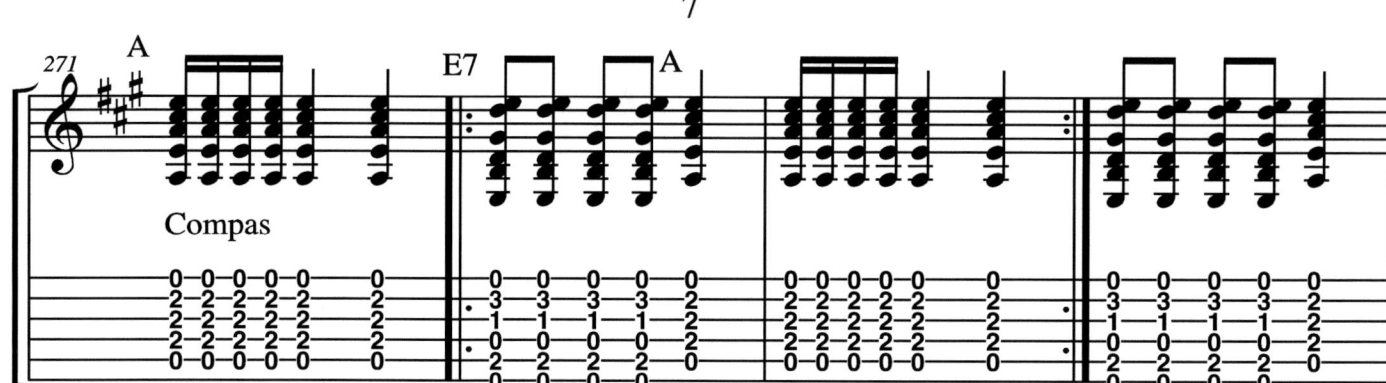

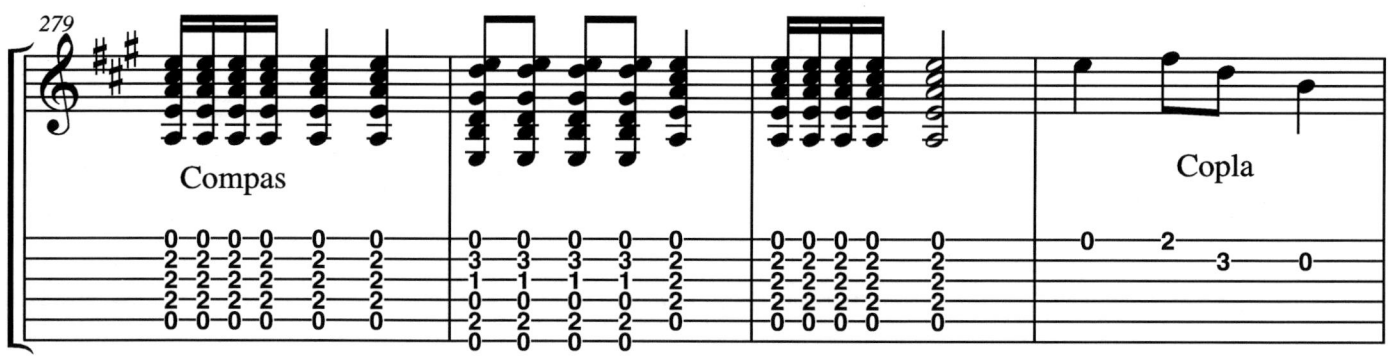

SEVILLANAS

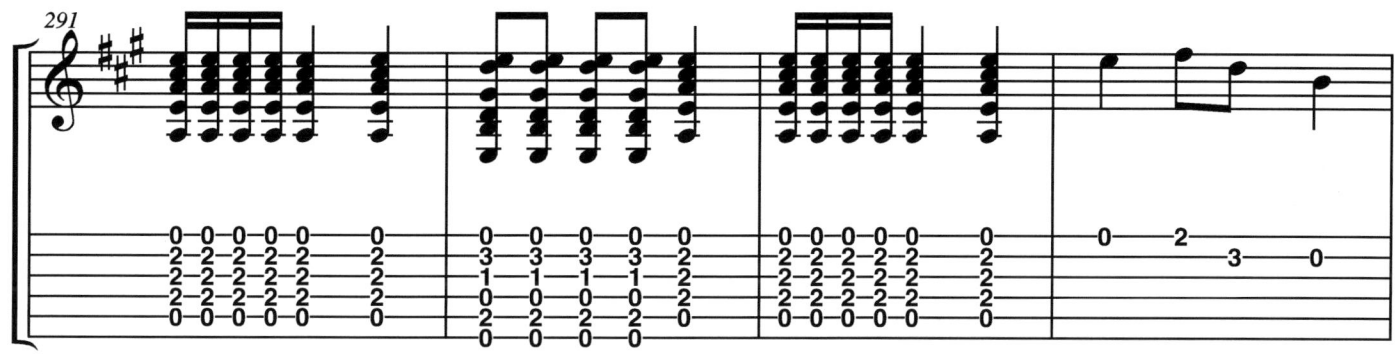

SEVILLANAS

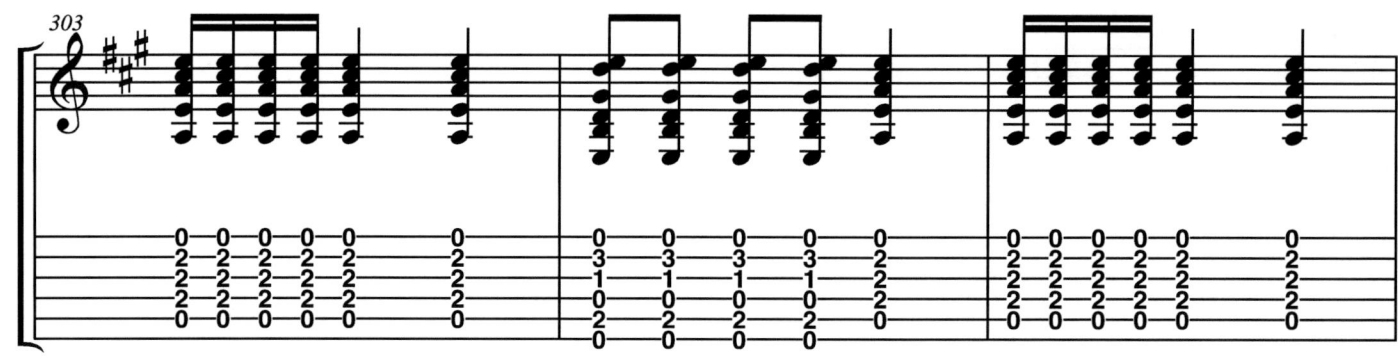
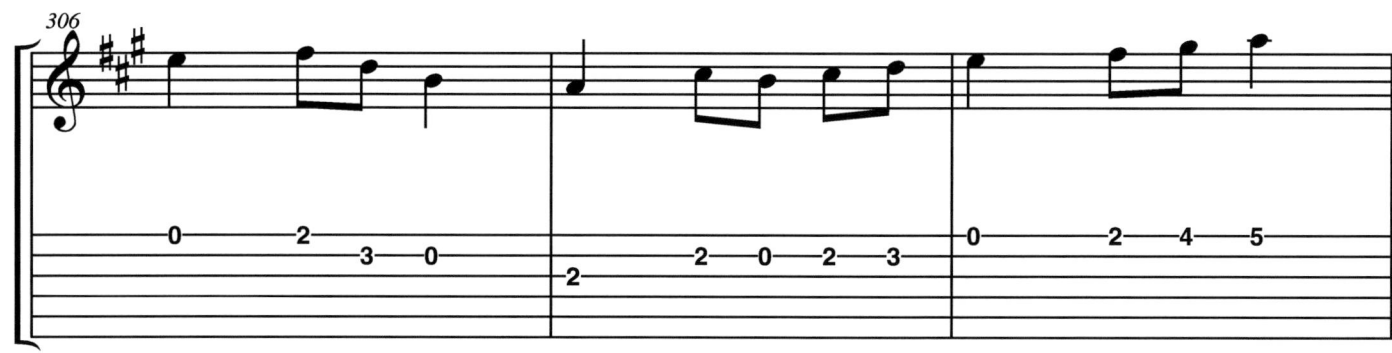
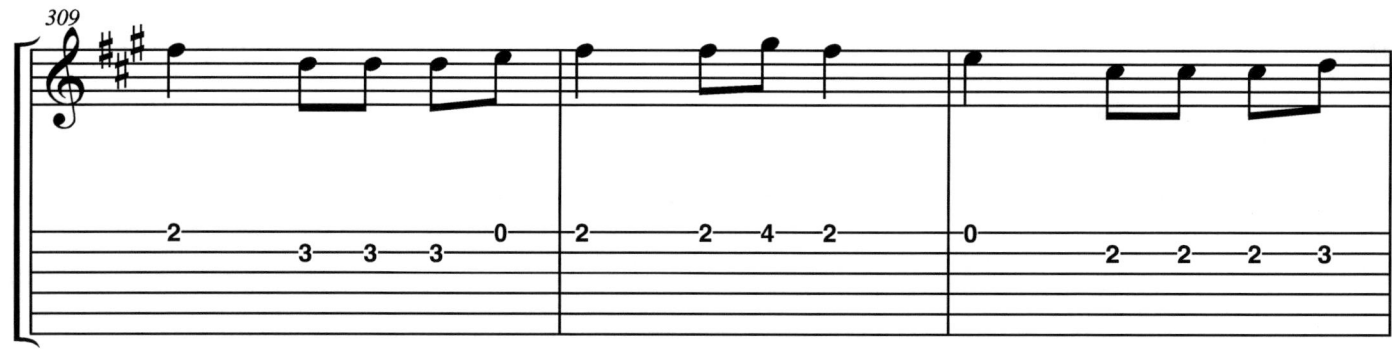

SEVILLANAS
8

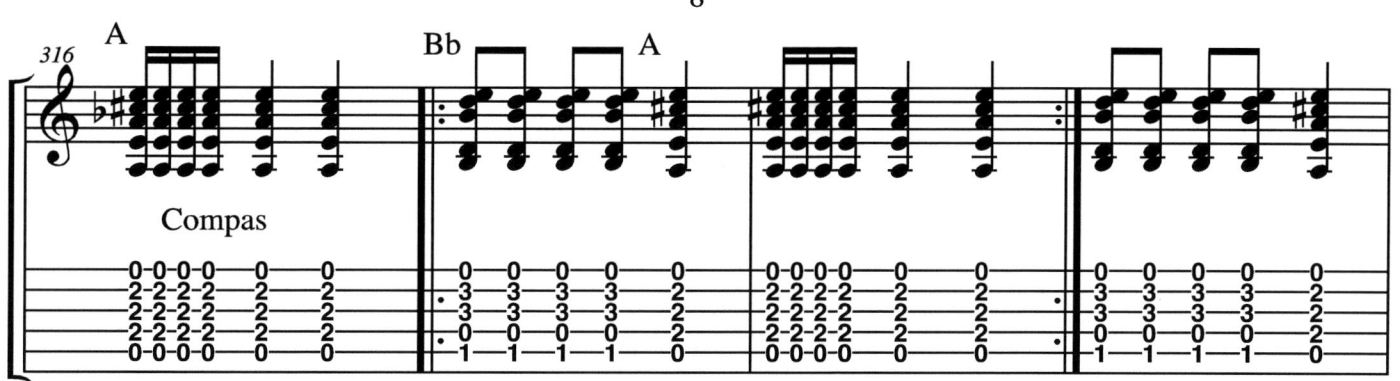

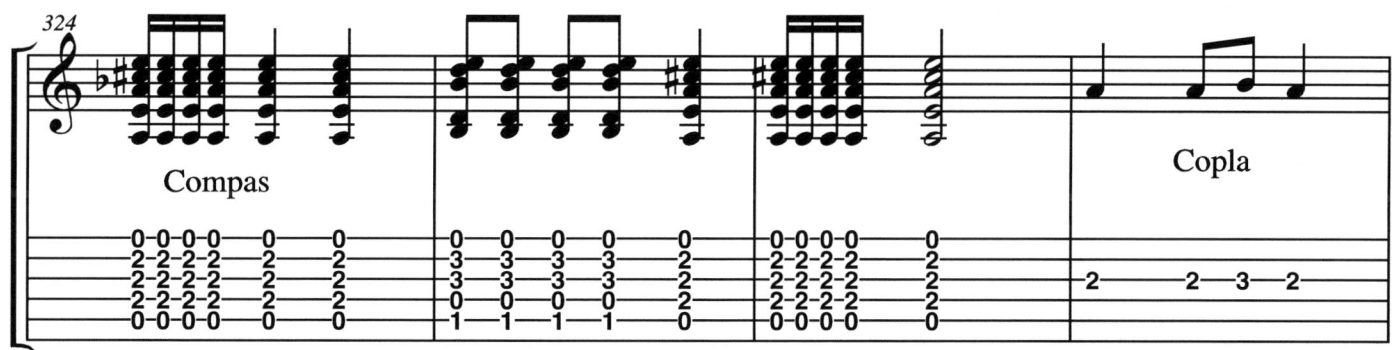
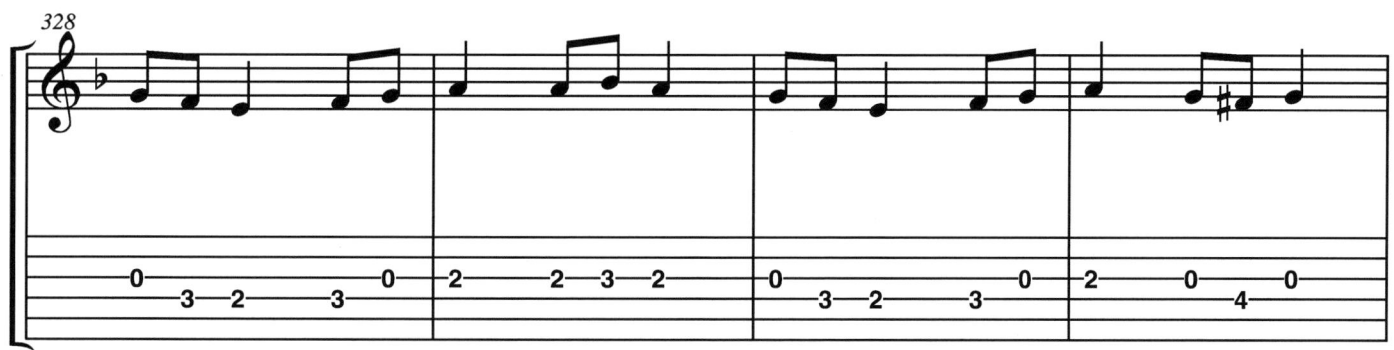

SEVILLANAS

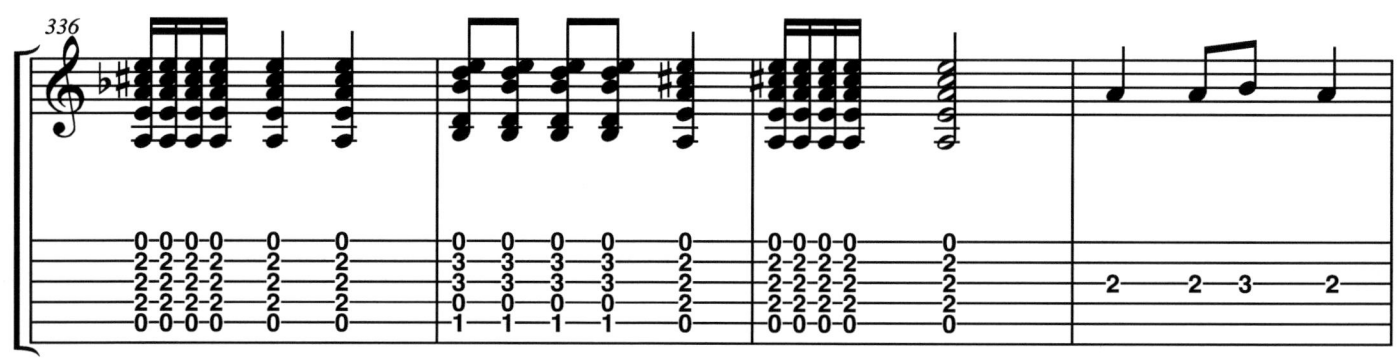

SEVILLANAS

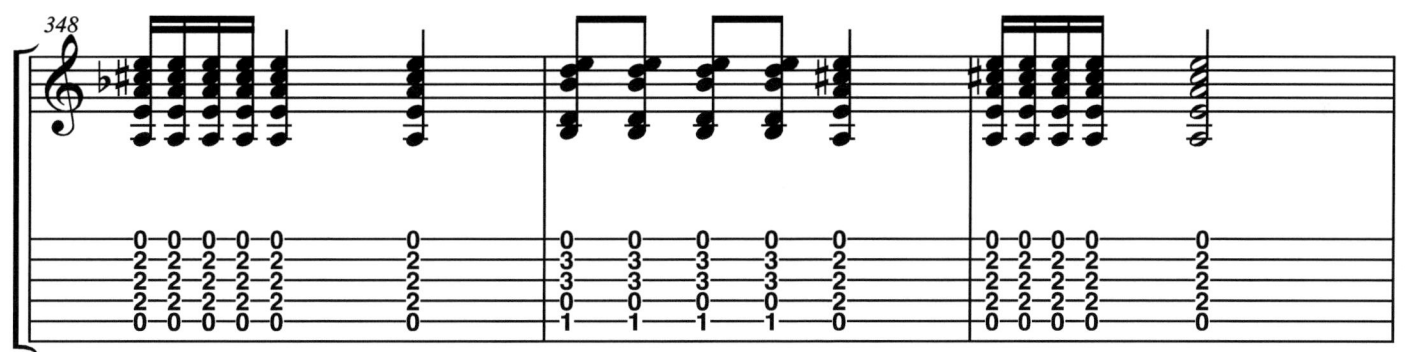
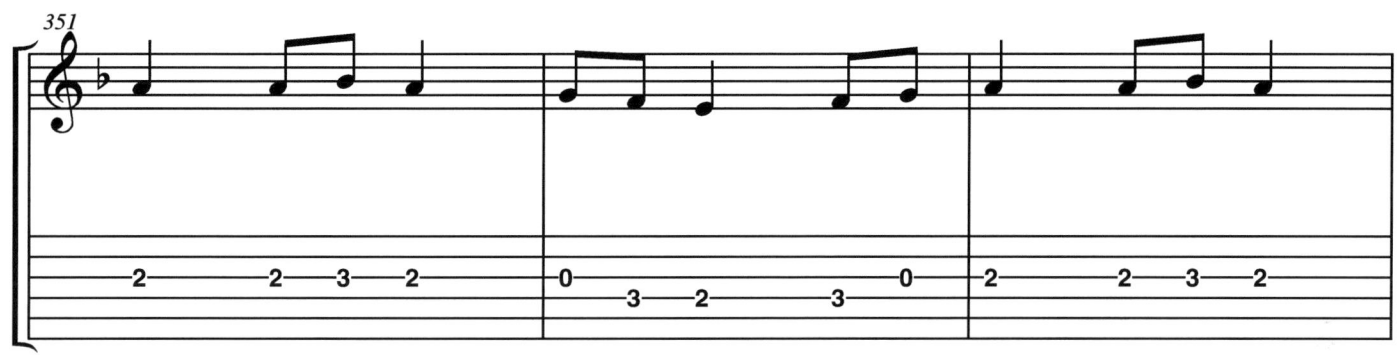

SEVILLANAS
9

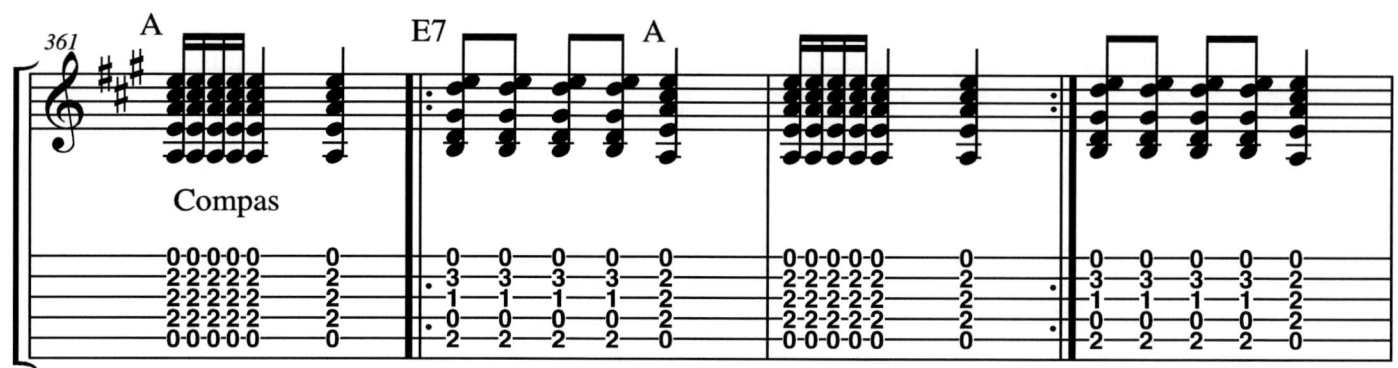
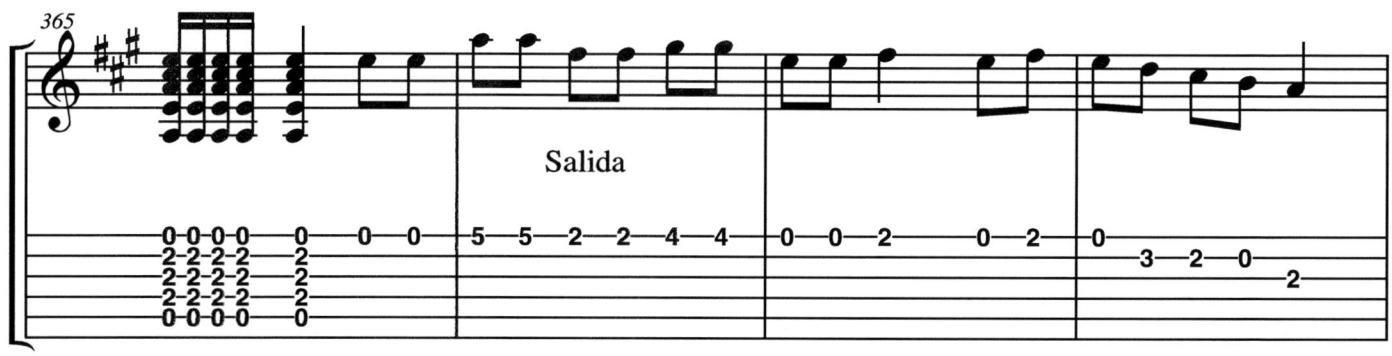
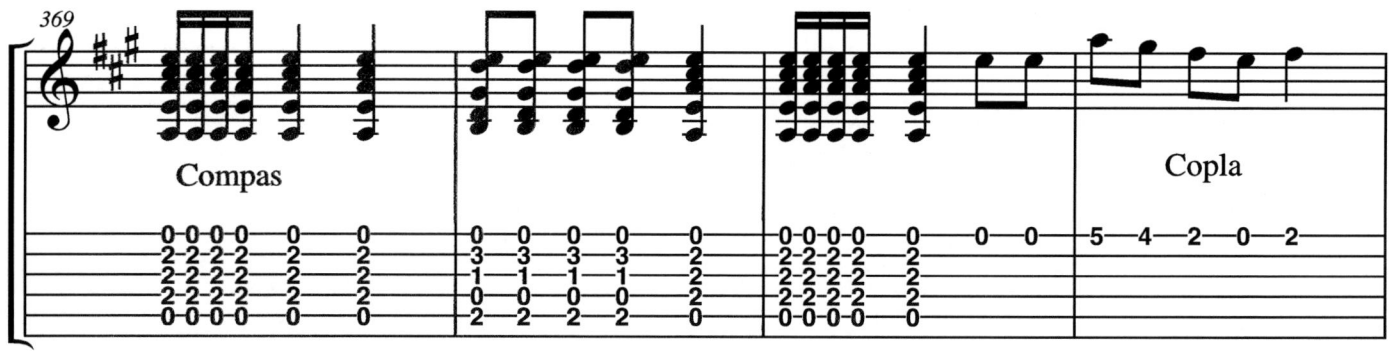

SEVILLANAS

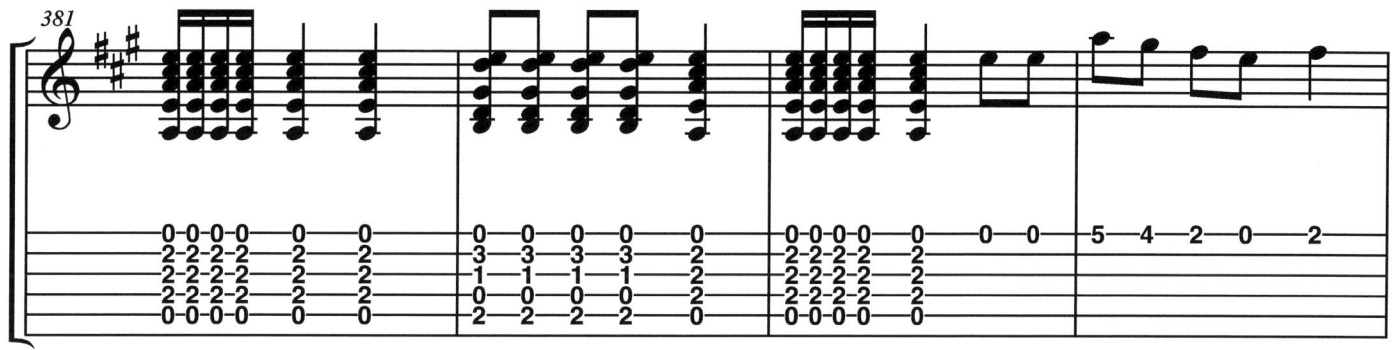

SEVILLANAS

9

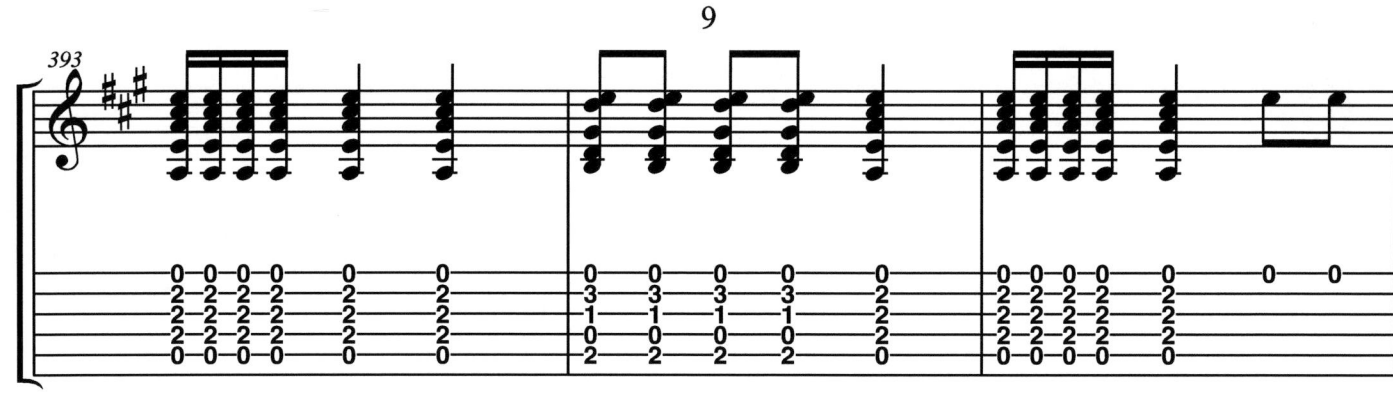
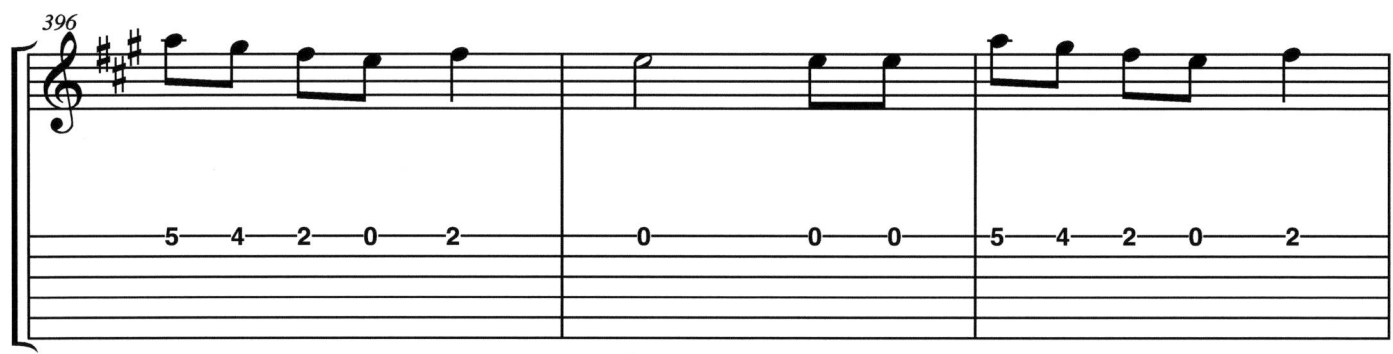
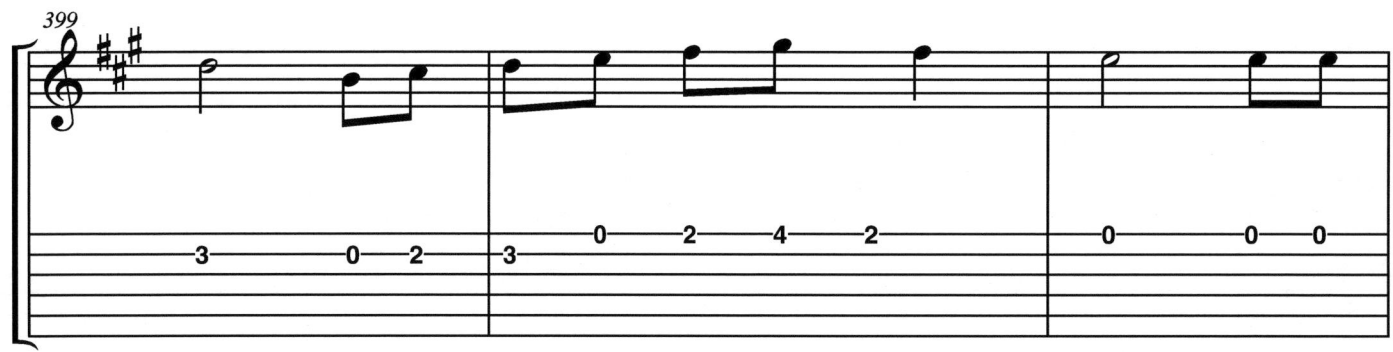
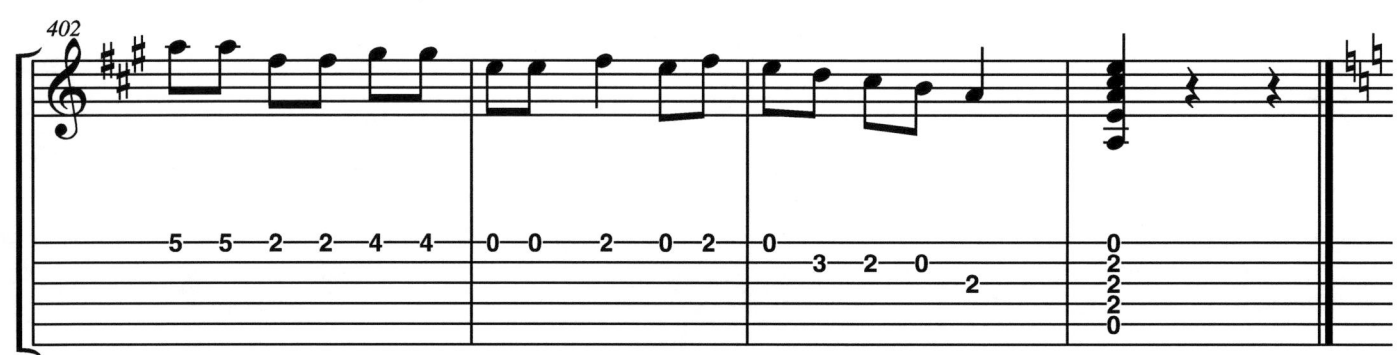

SEVILLANAS
10

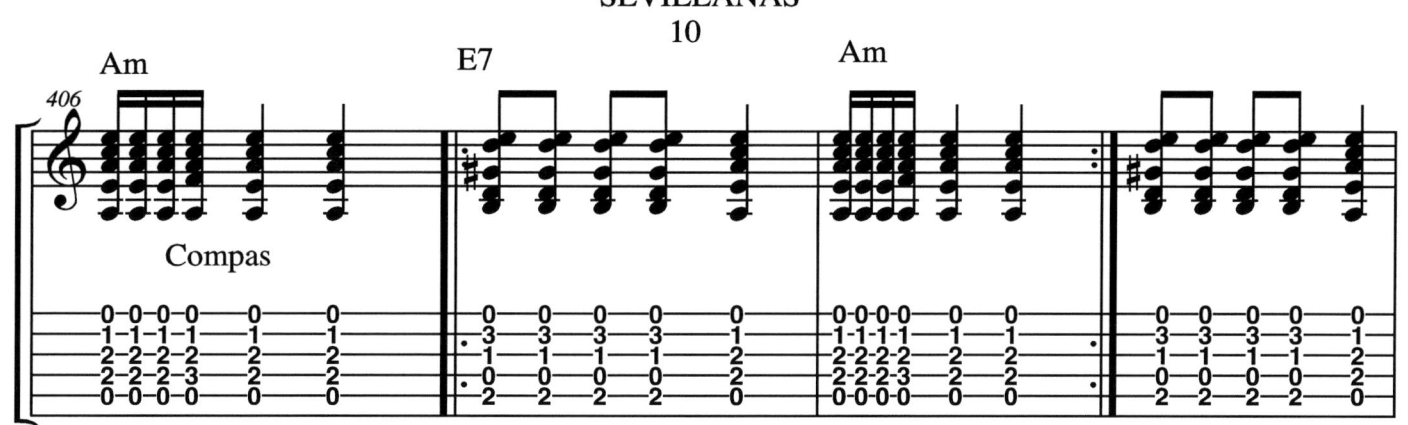

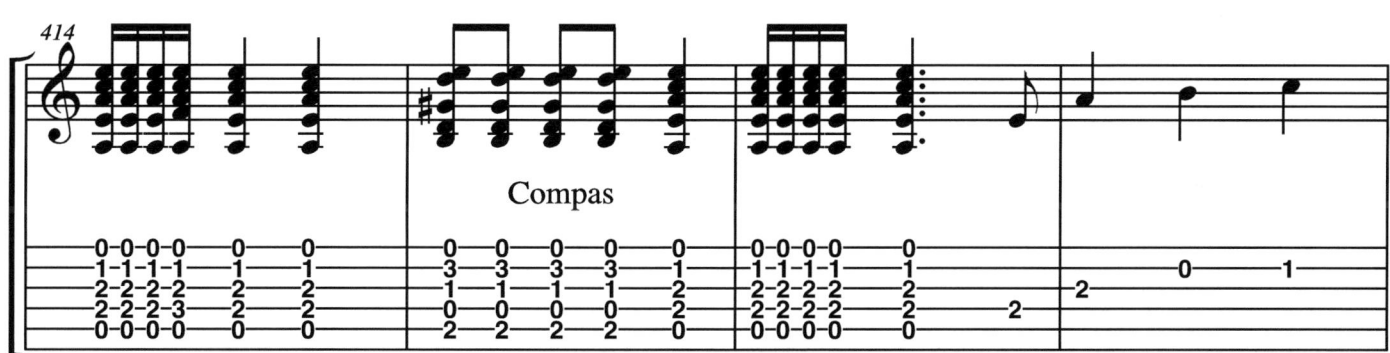

SEVILLANAS

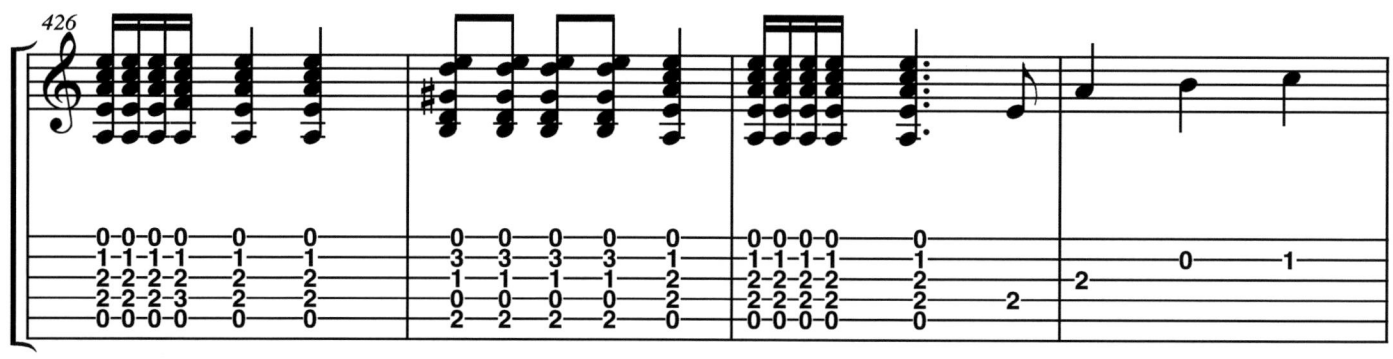

SEVILLANAS

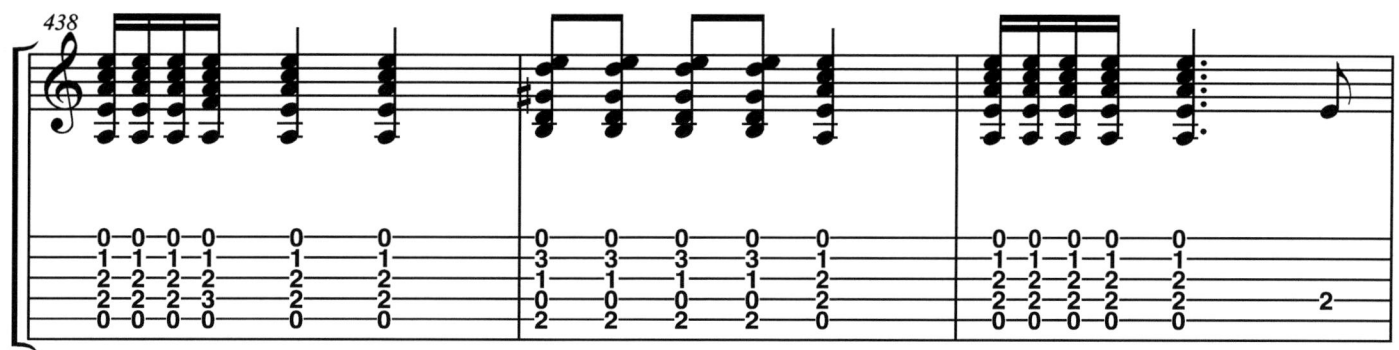

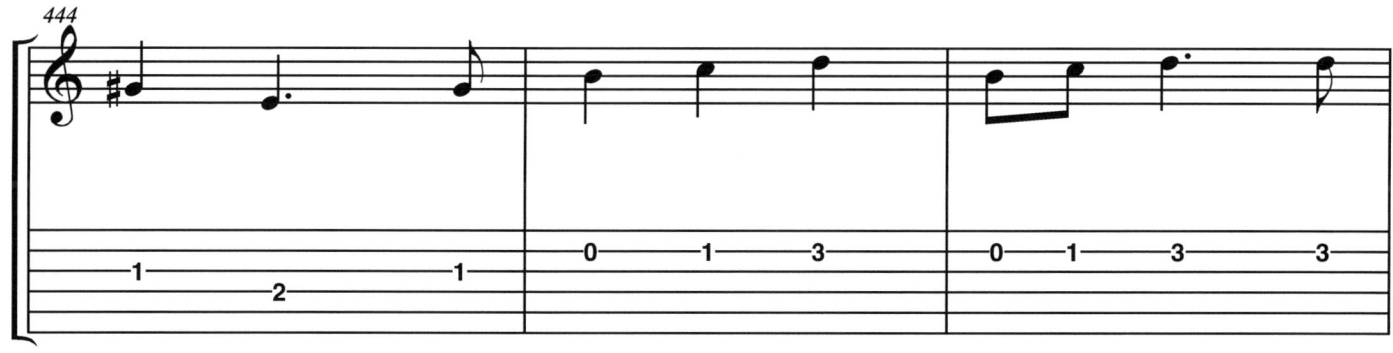

SIGUIRIYAS

Strum every compas in the same manner

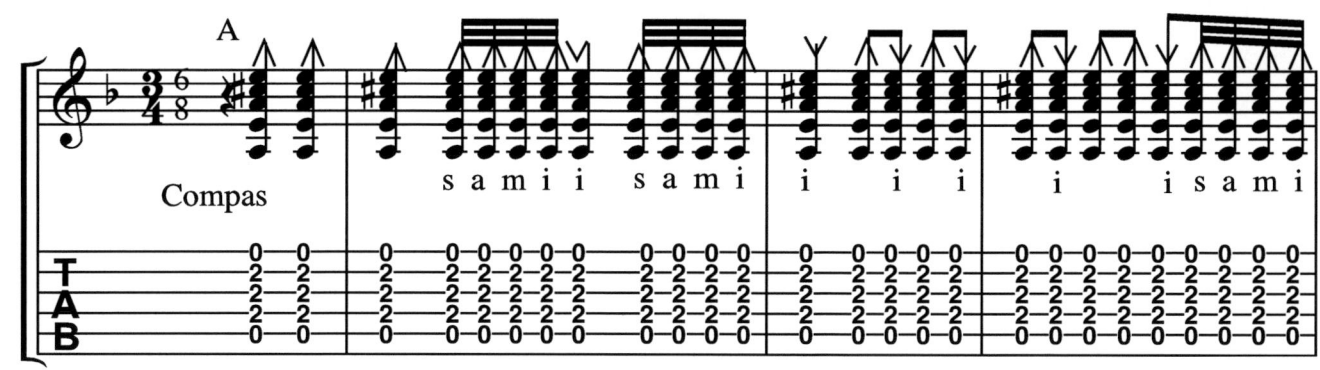
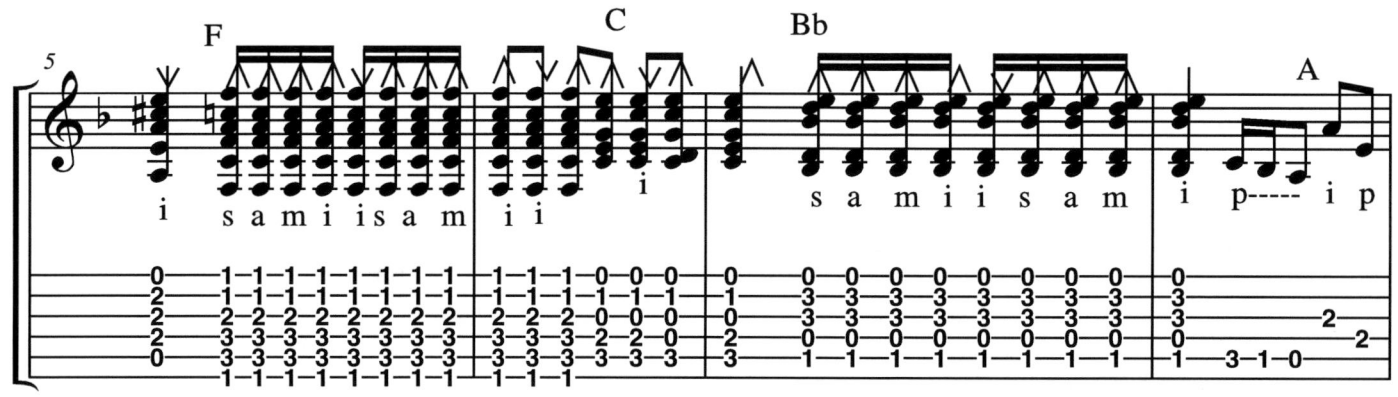
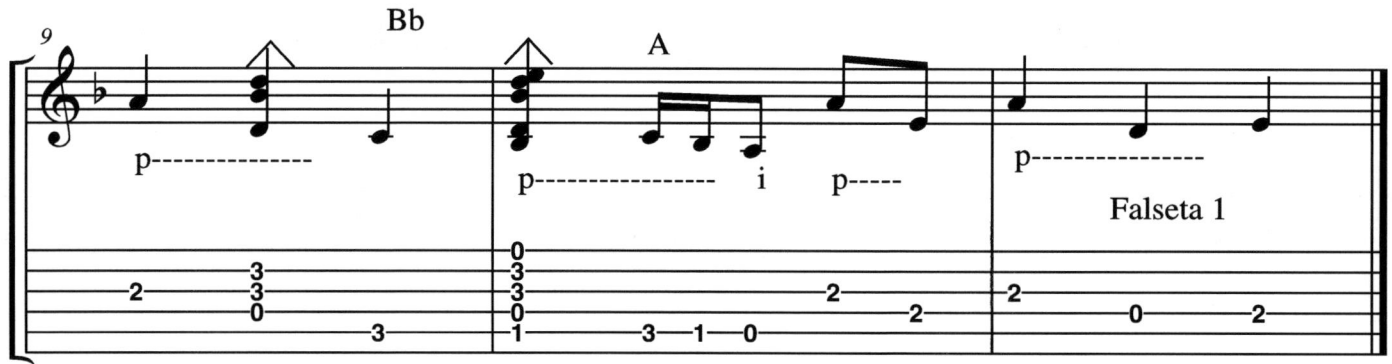

Falseta 1

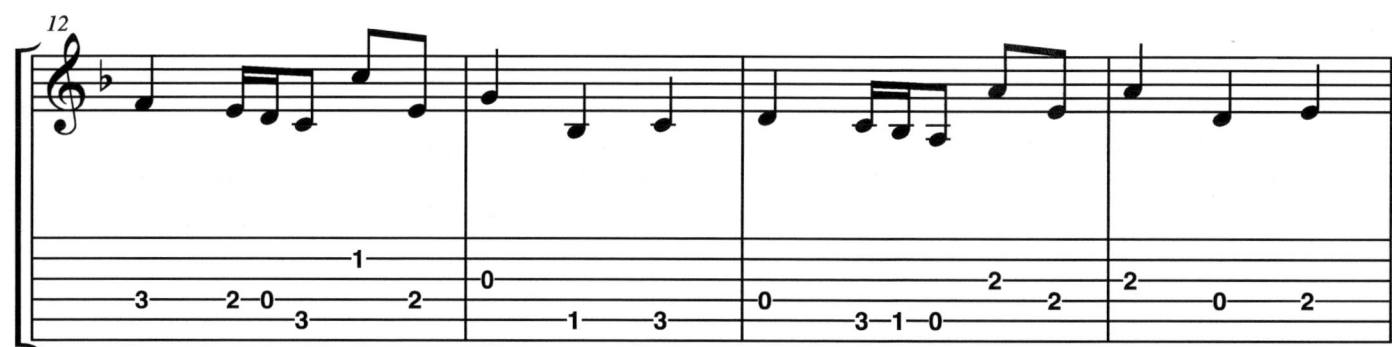

SIGUIRIYAS

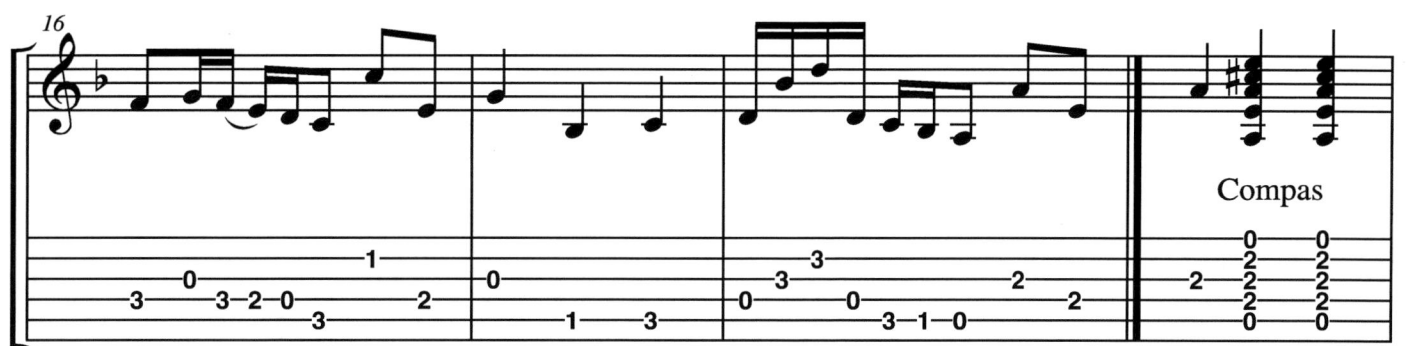

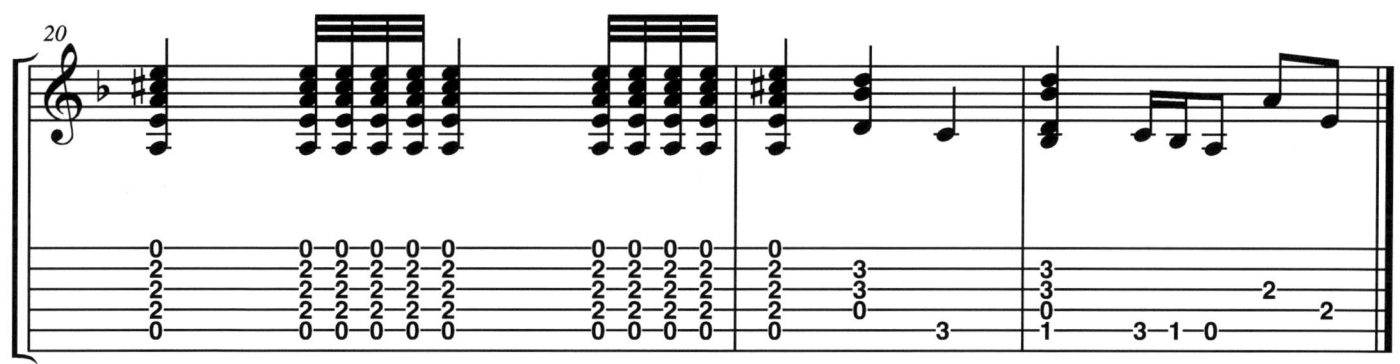

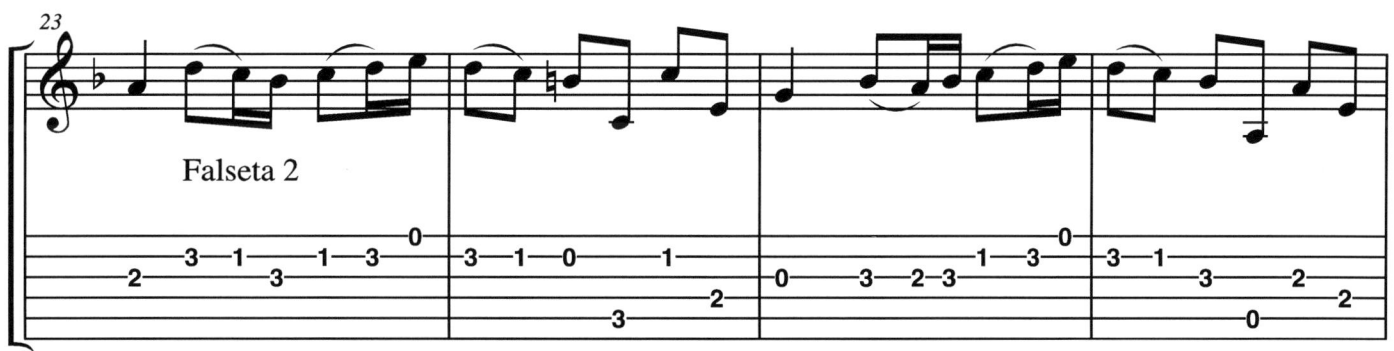

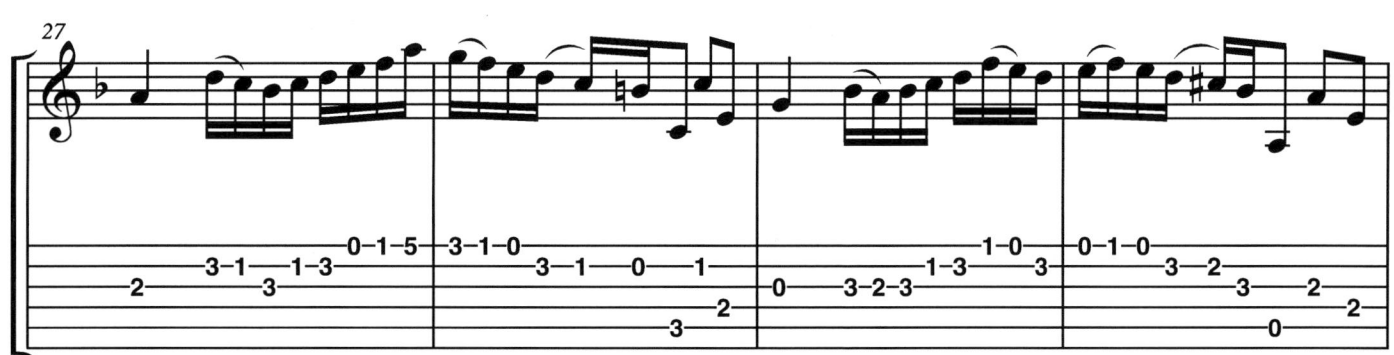

SIGUIRIYAS

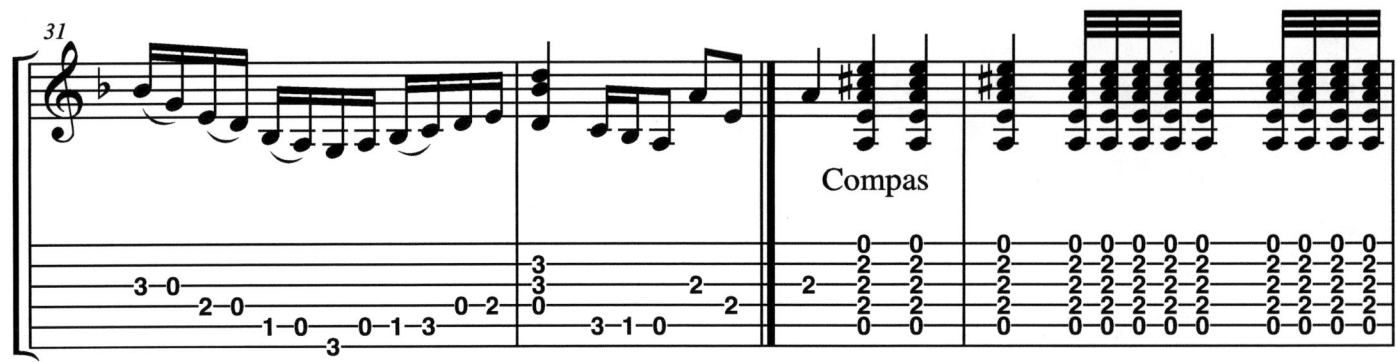

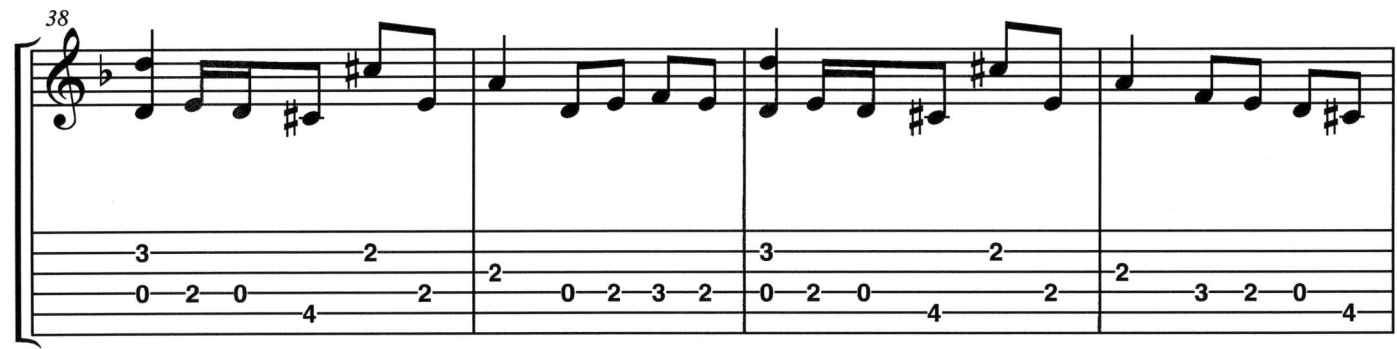

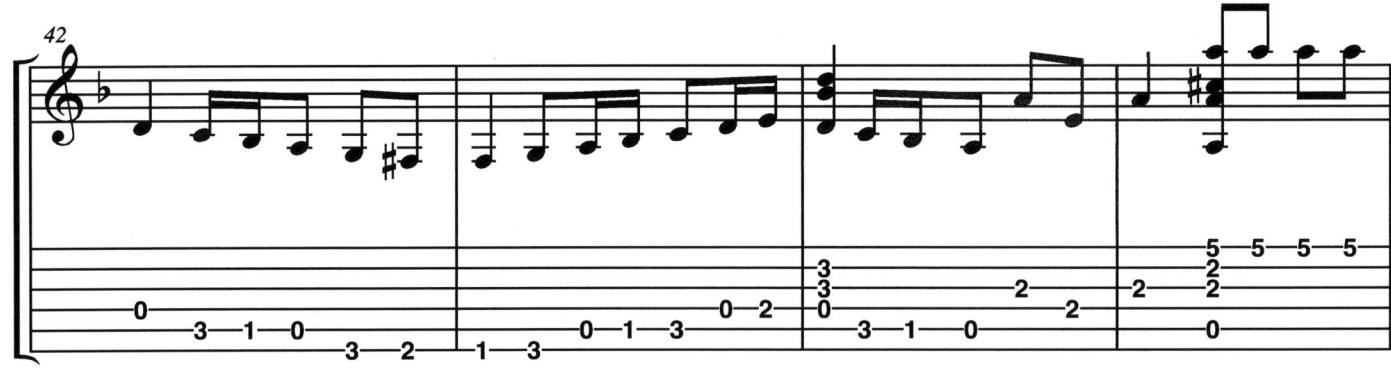

SIGUIRIYAS

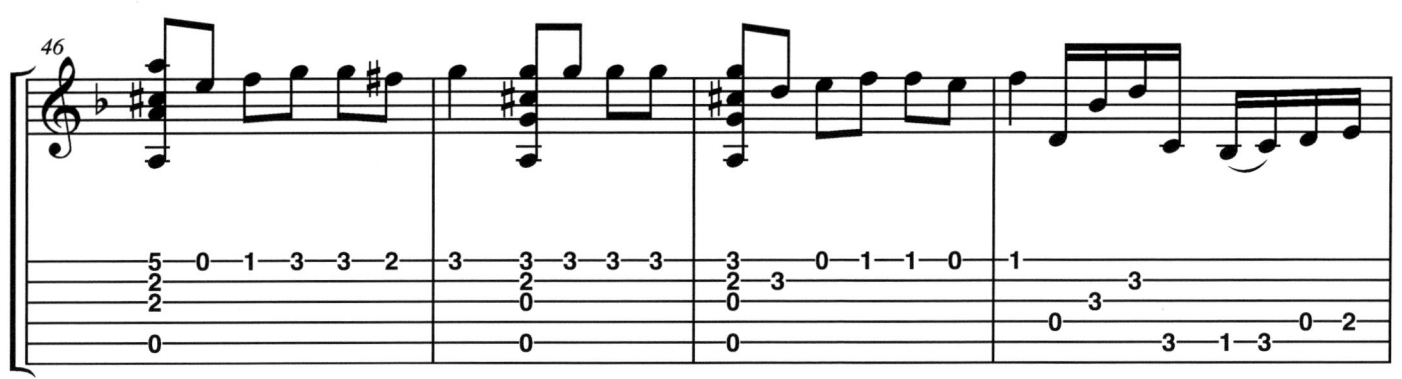

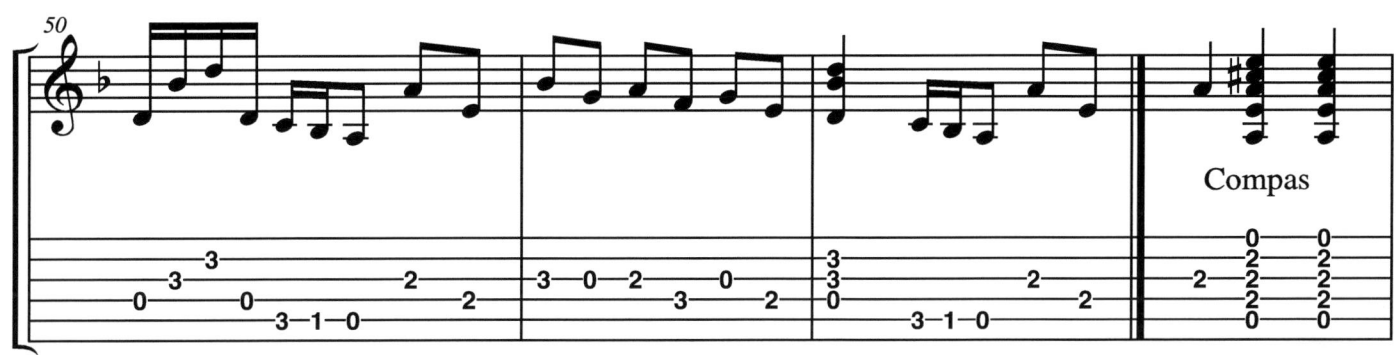

Compas

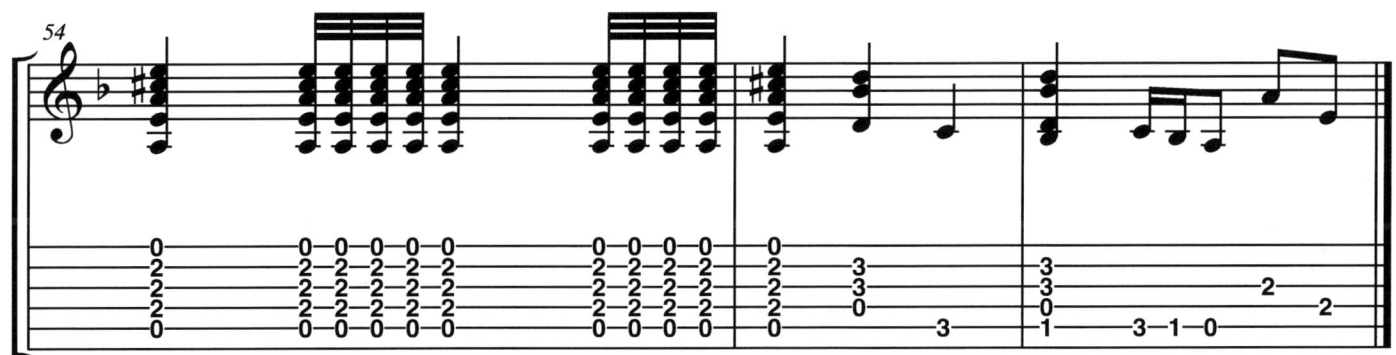

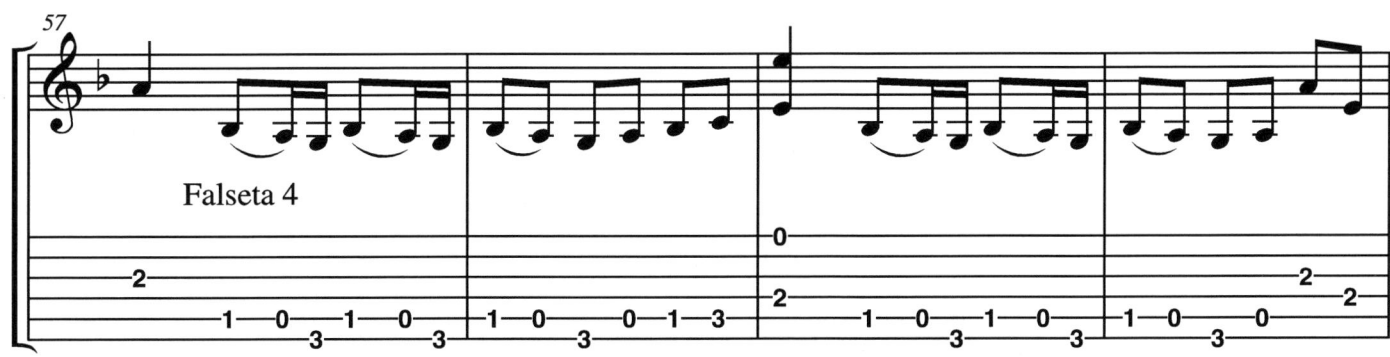

Falseta 4

SIGUIRIYAS

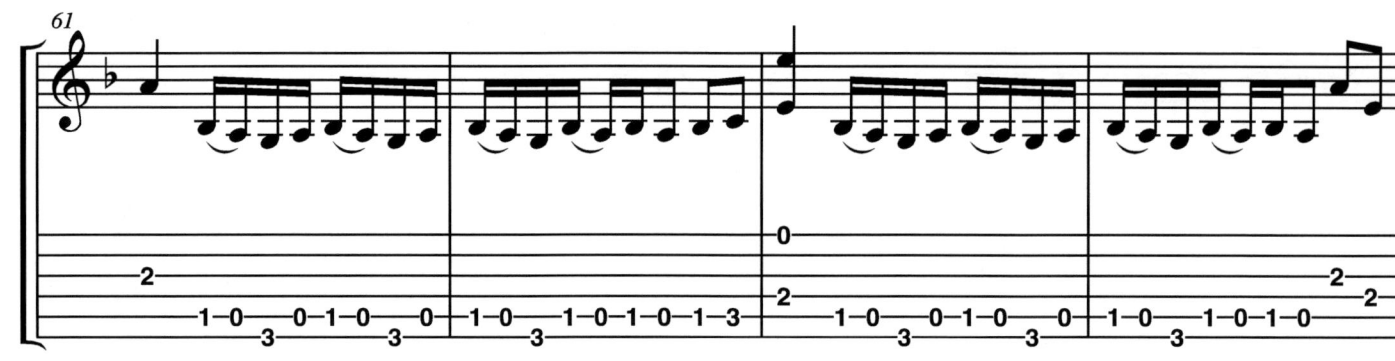
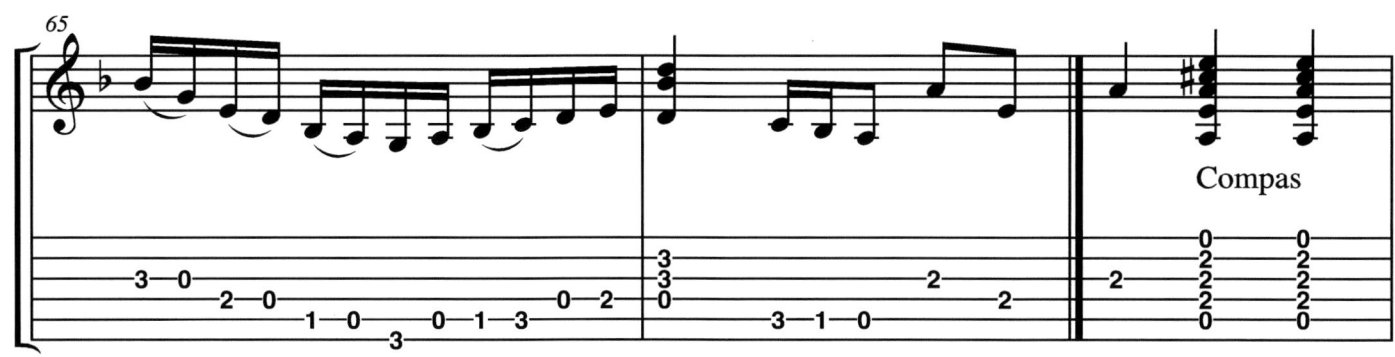
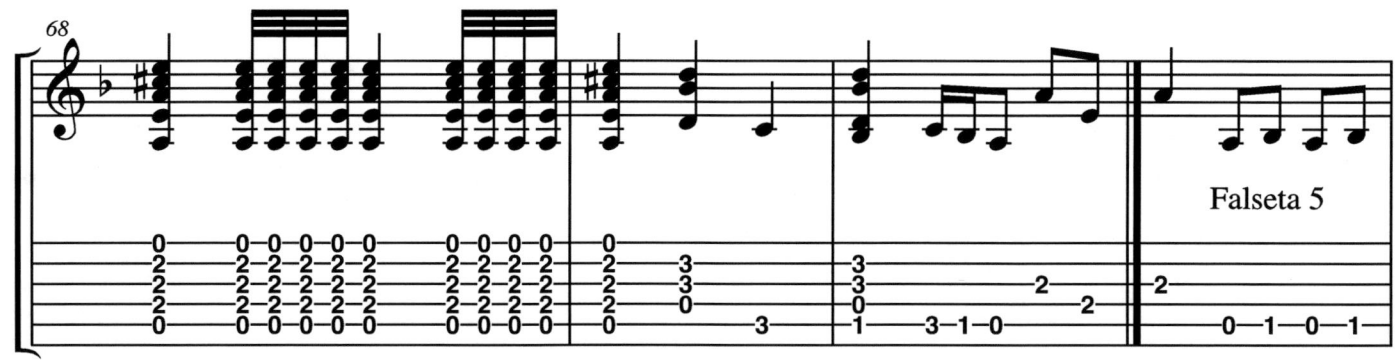
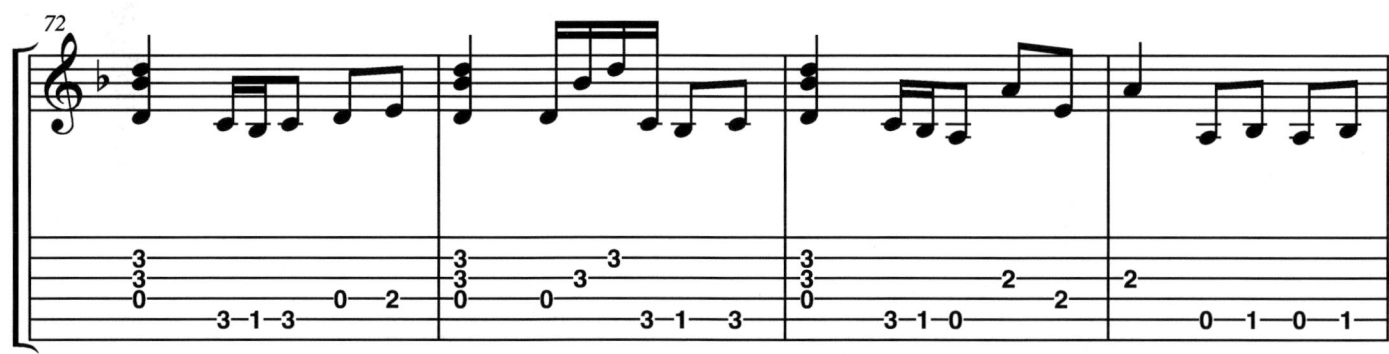

SIGUIRIYAS

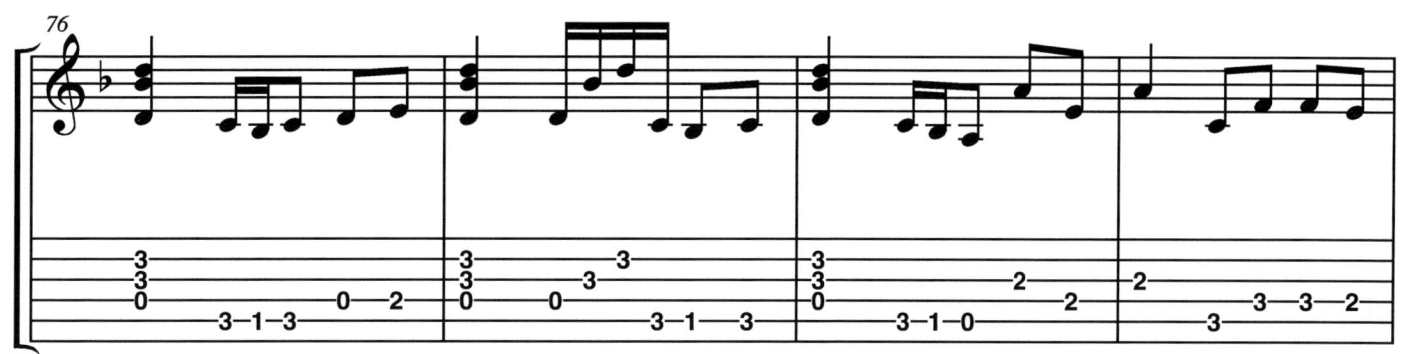
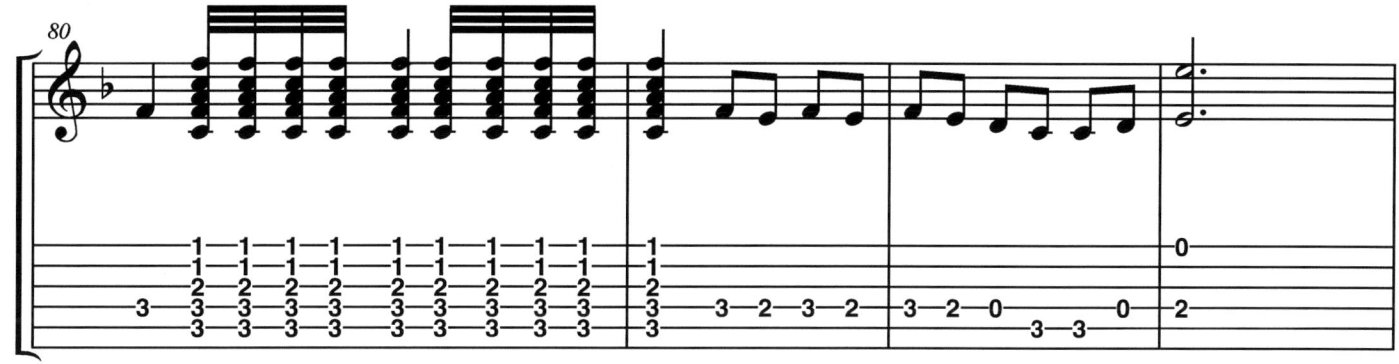
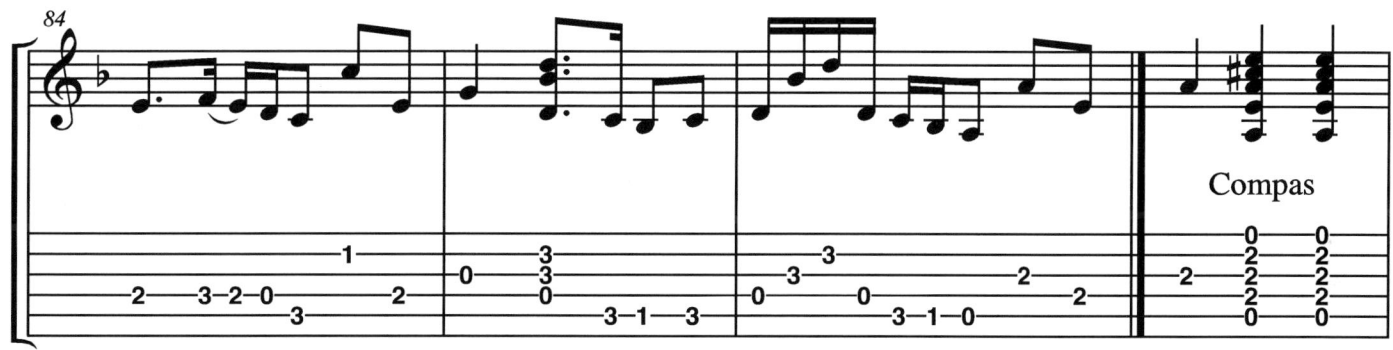
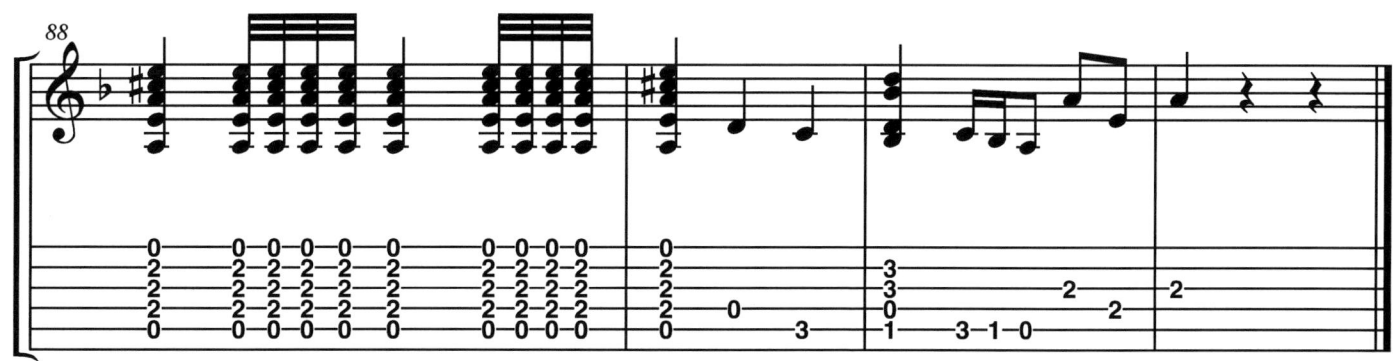

SIGUIRIYAS

Falseta 6

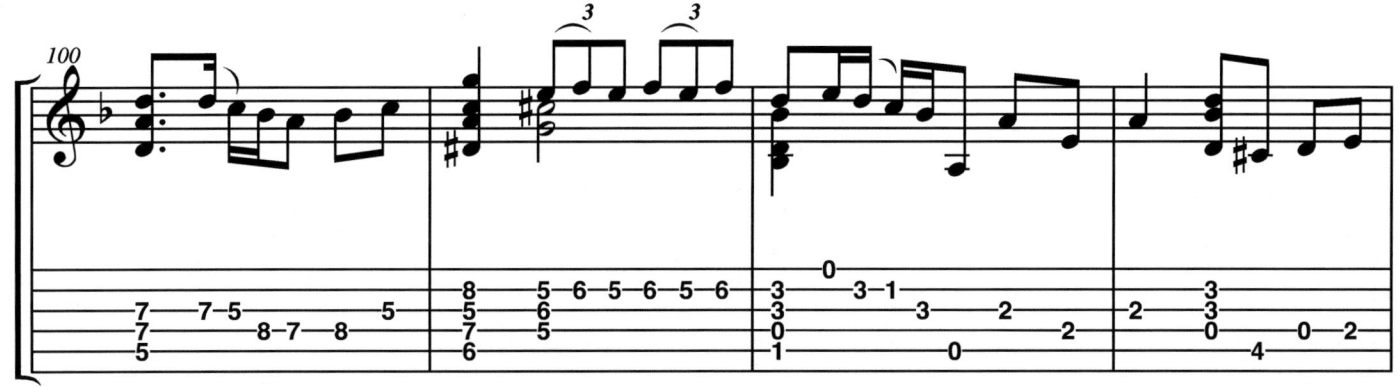

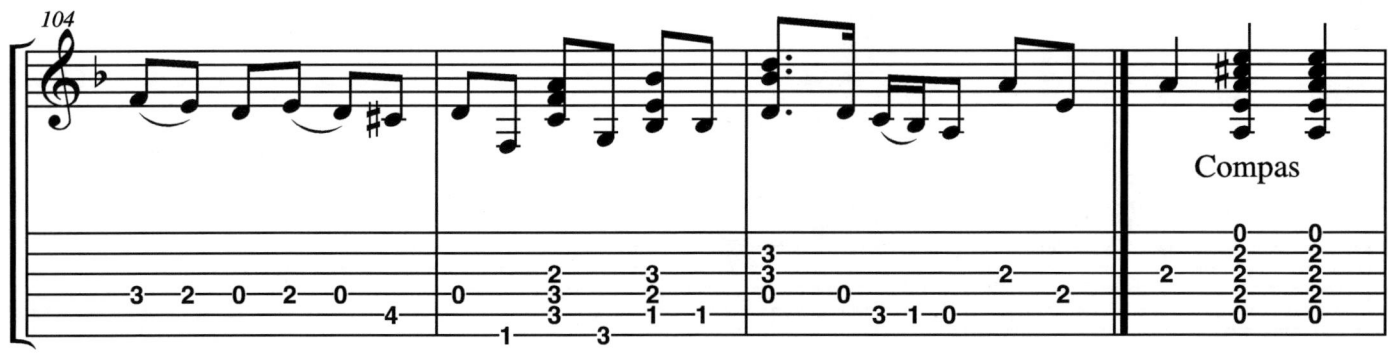

Compas

SIGUIRIYAS

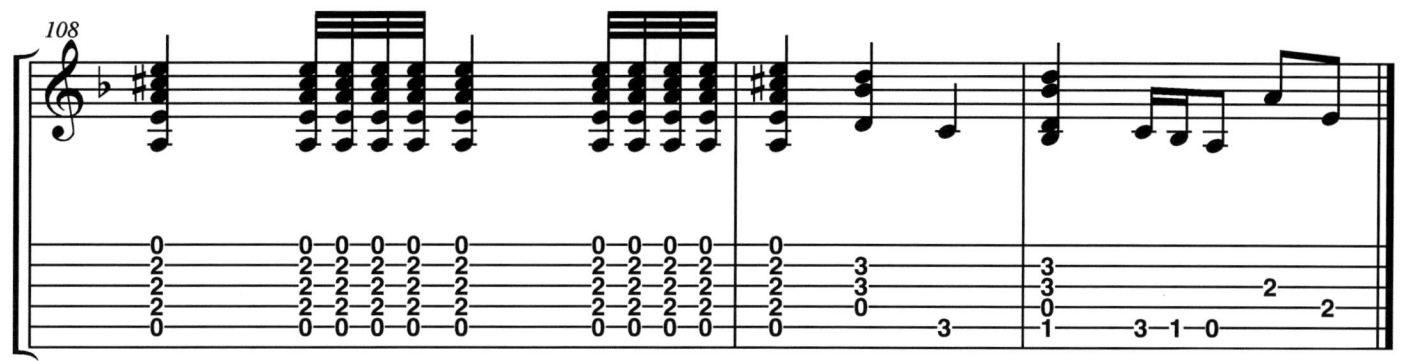

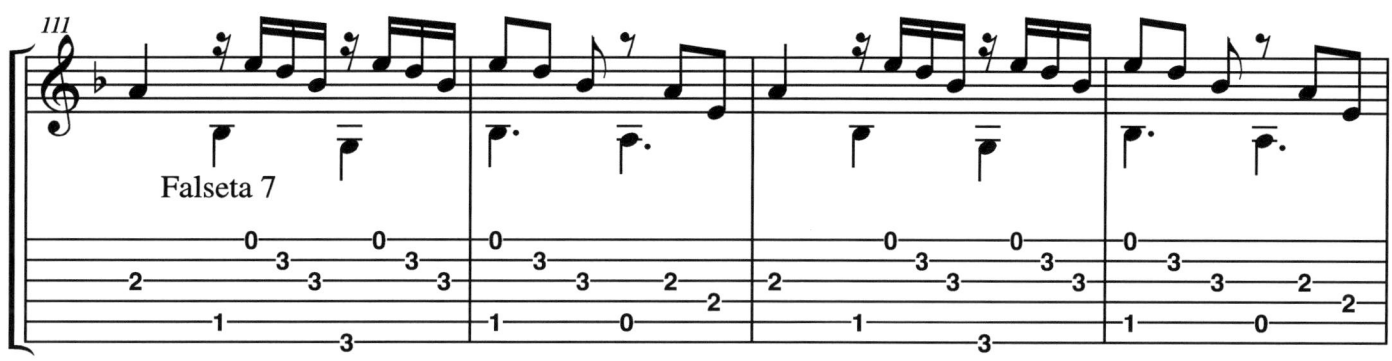

Falseta 7

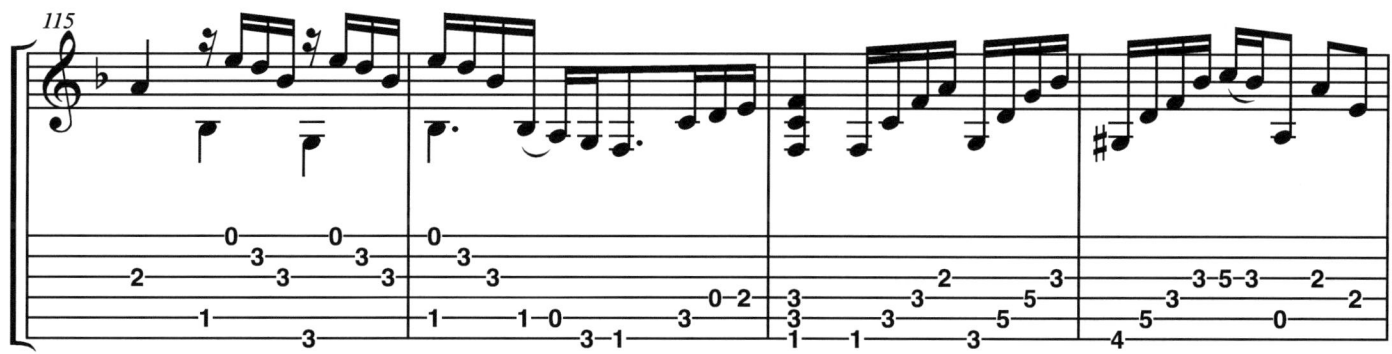

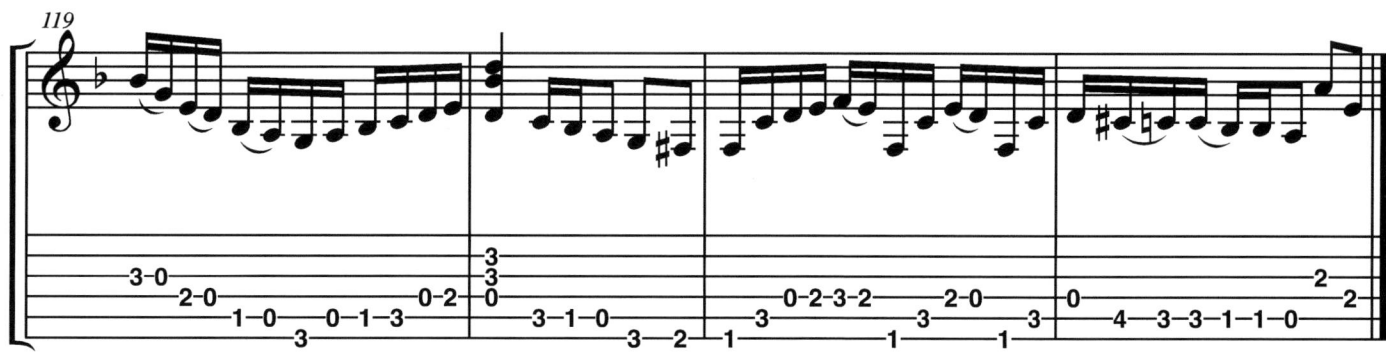

SIGUIRIYAS

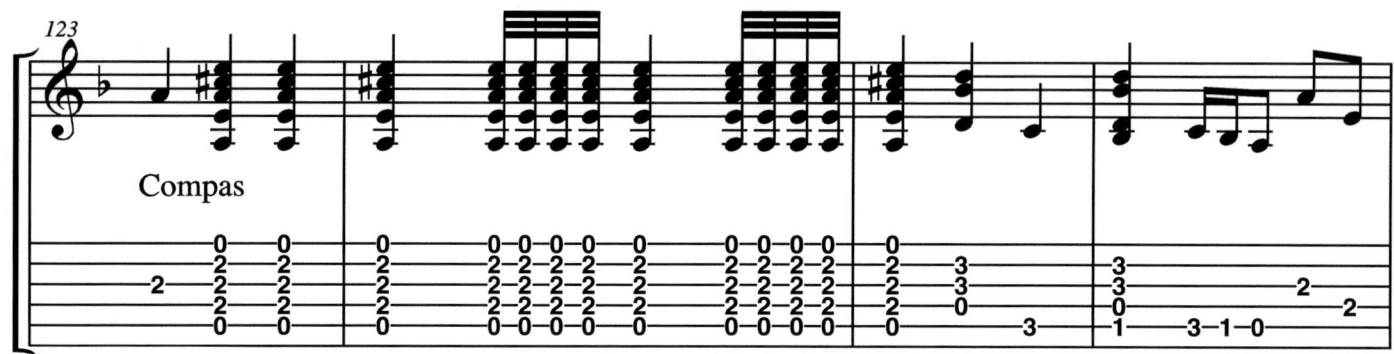

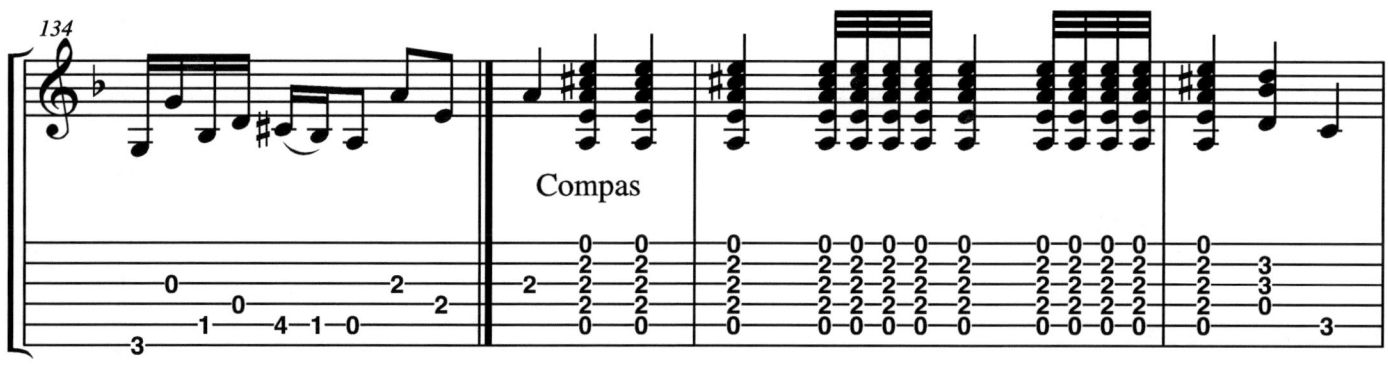

SIGUIRIYAS

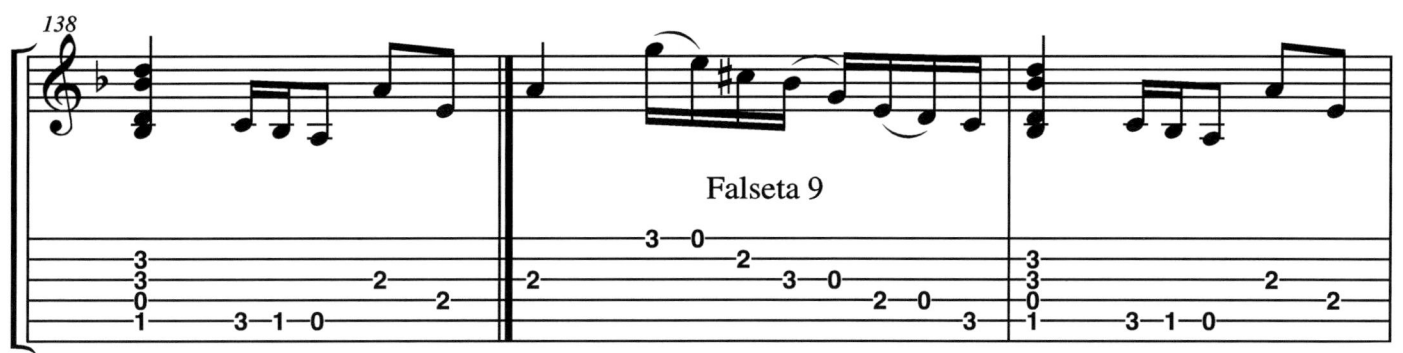
Falseta 9

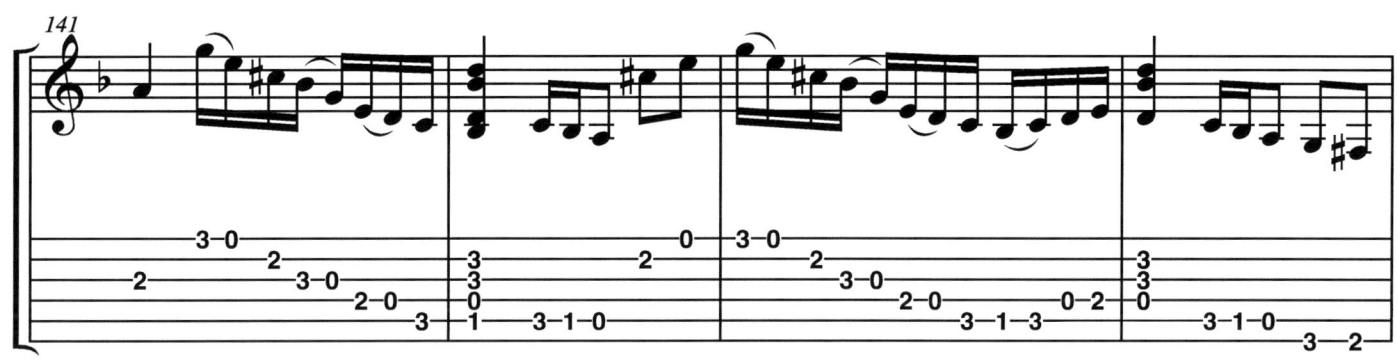

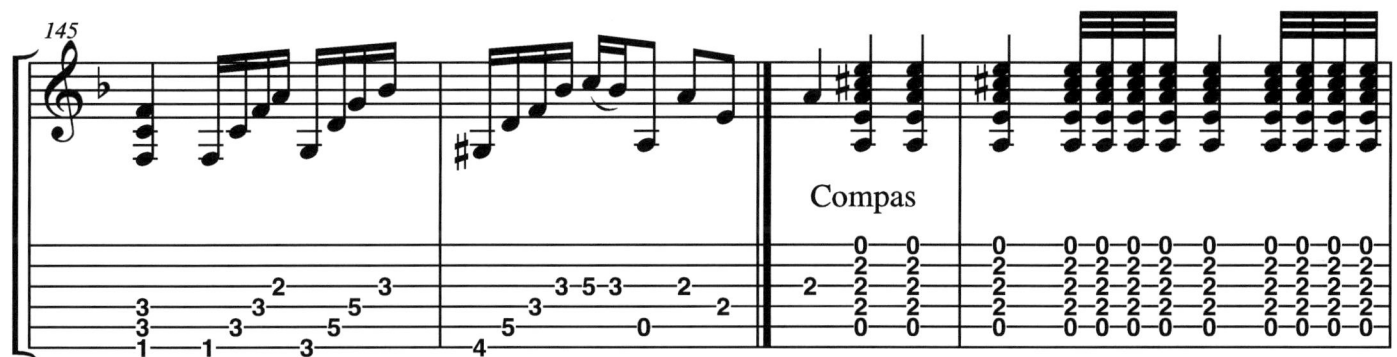
Compas

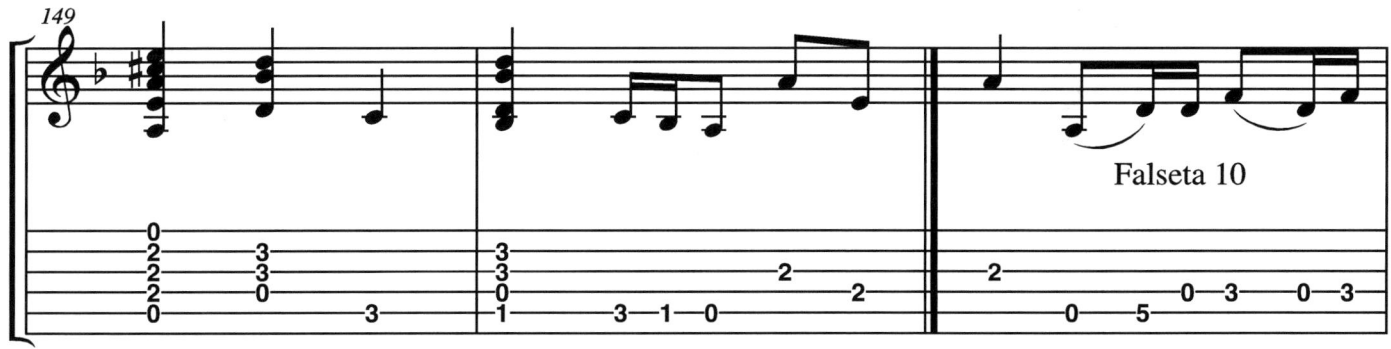
Falseta 10

SIGUIRIYAS

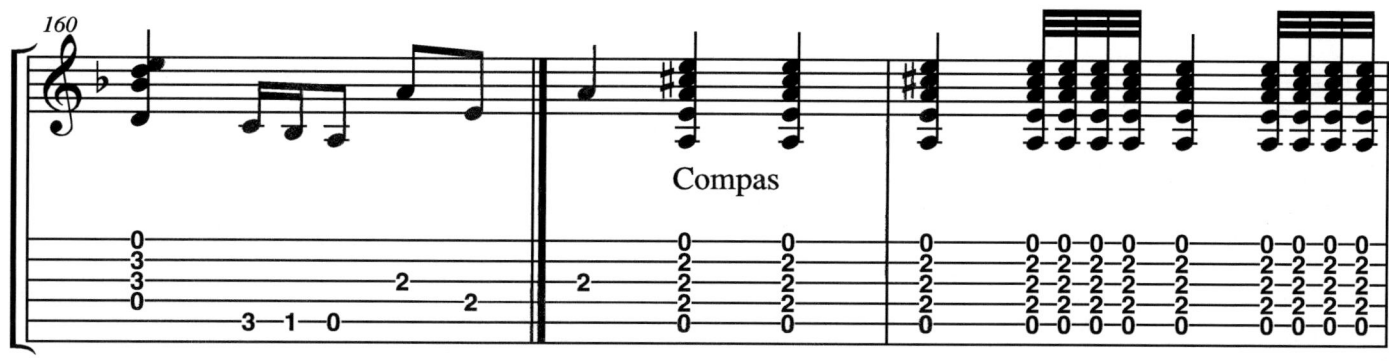
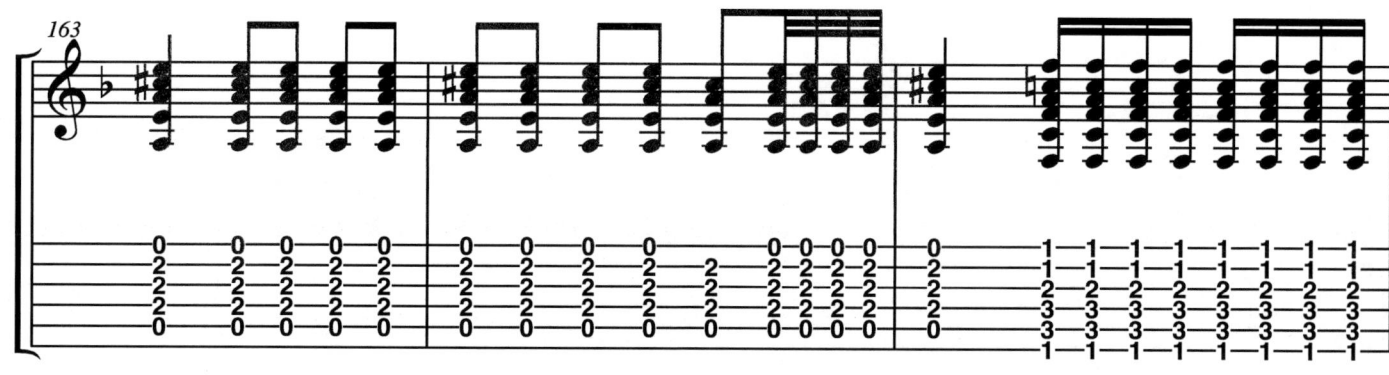

SIGUIRIYAS

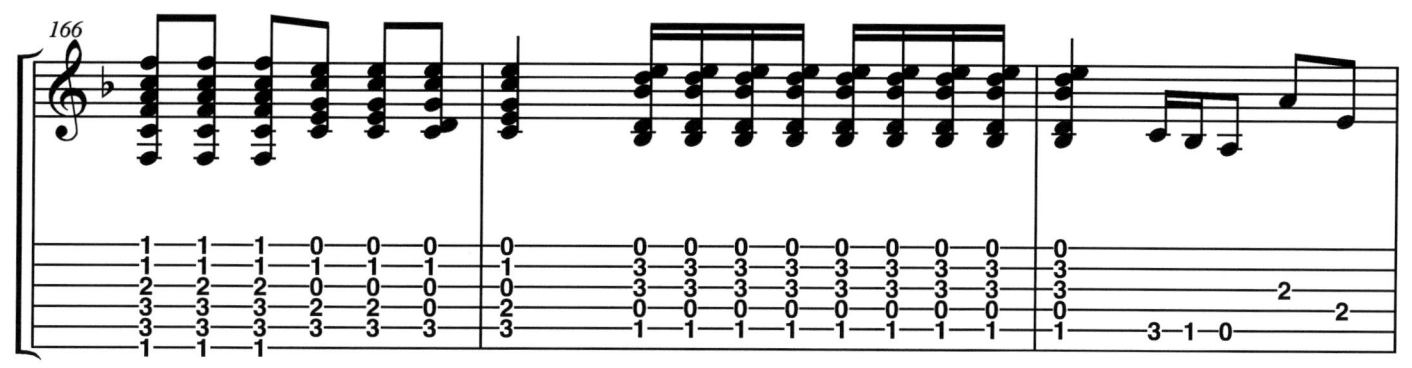
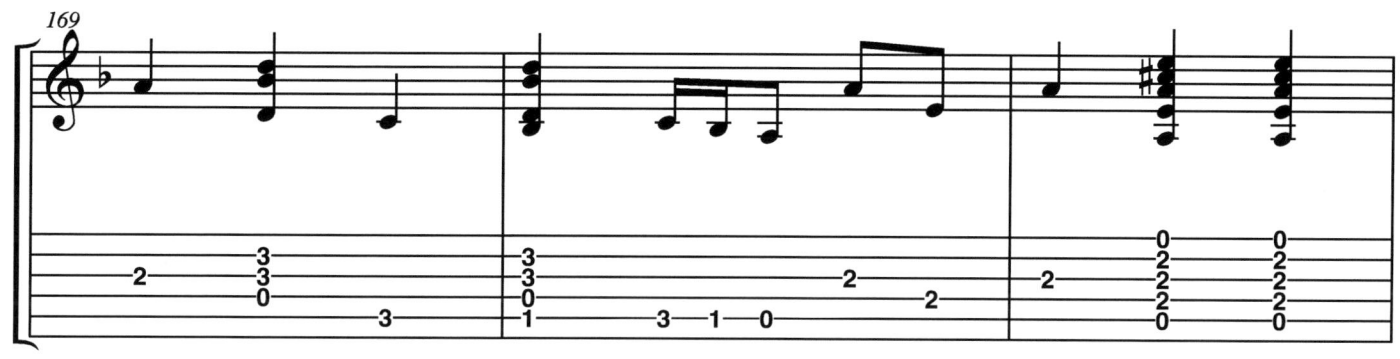
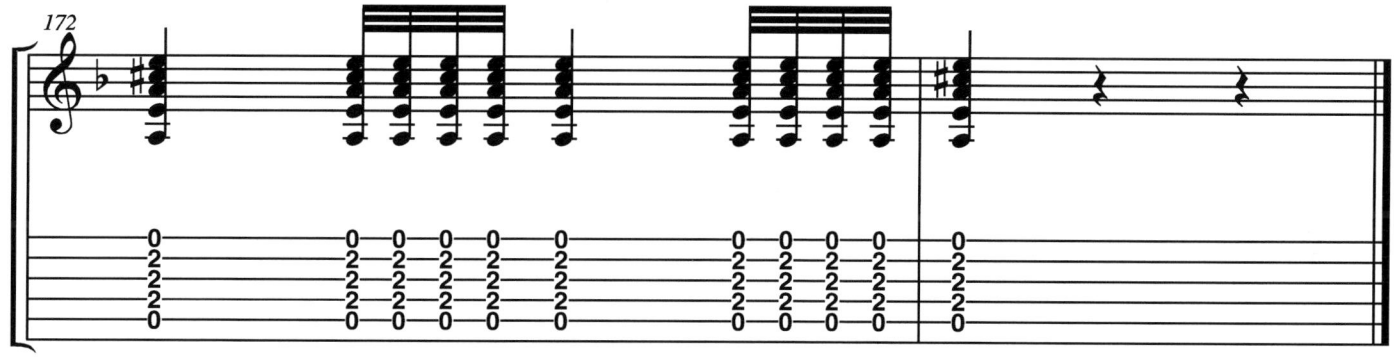

SOLEARES

Strum every compas in the same manner

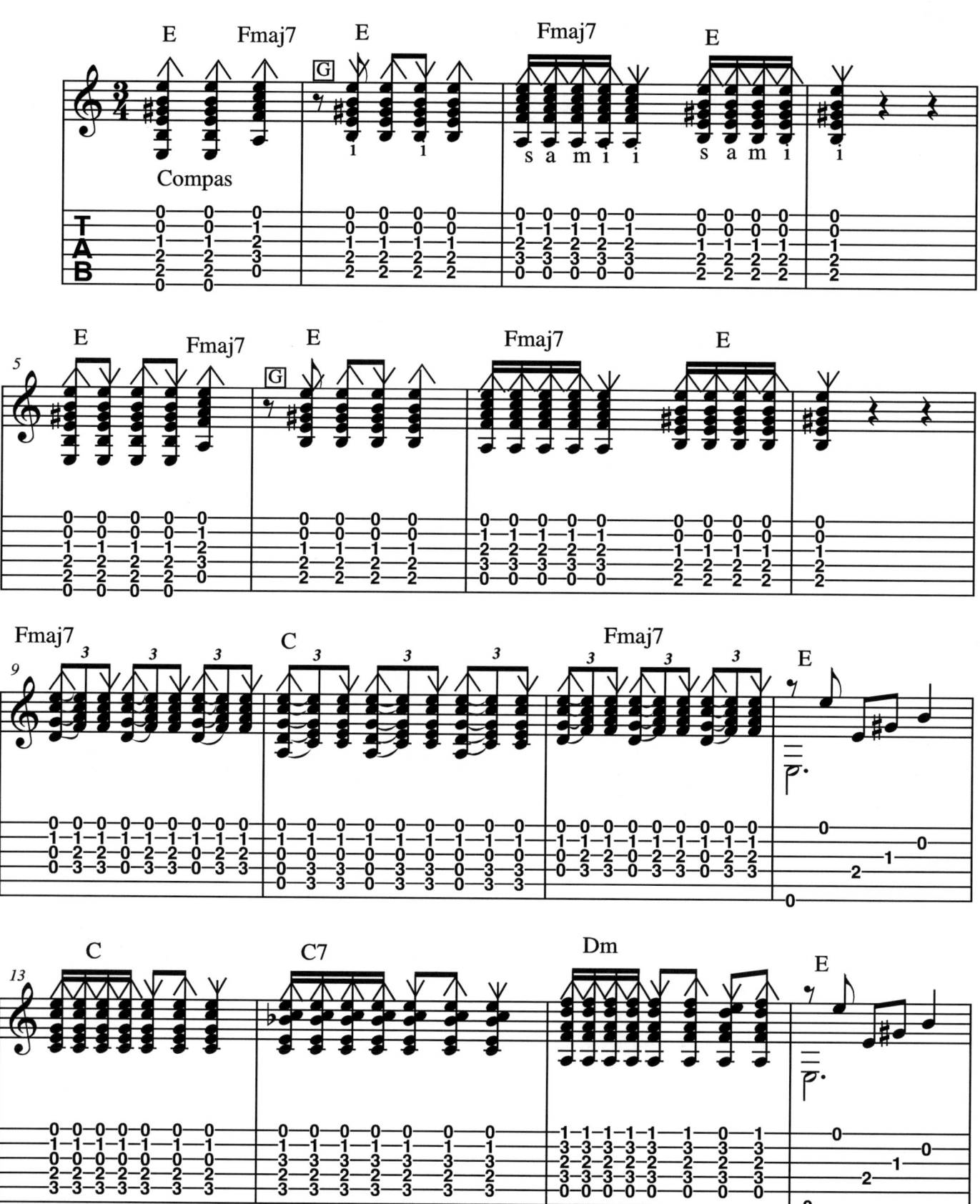

SOLEARES

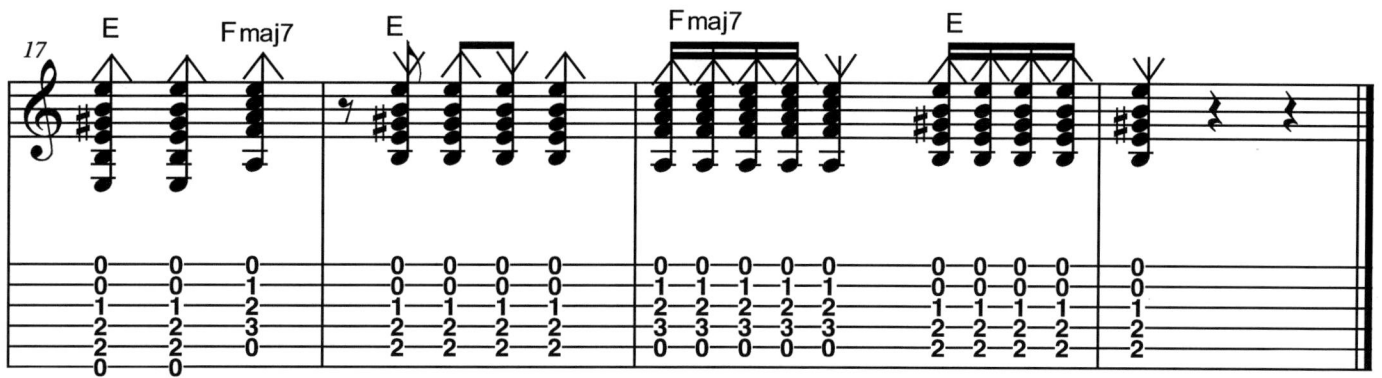
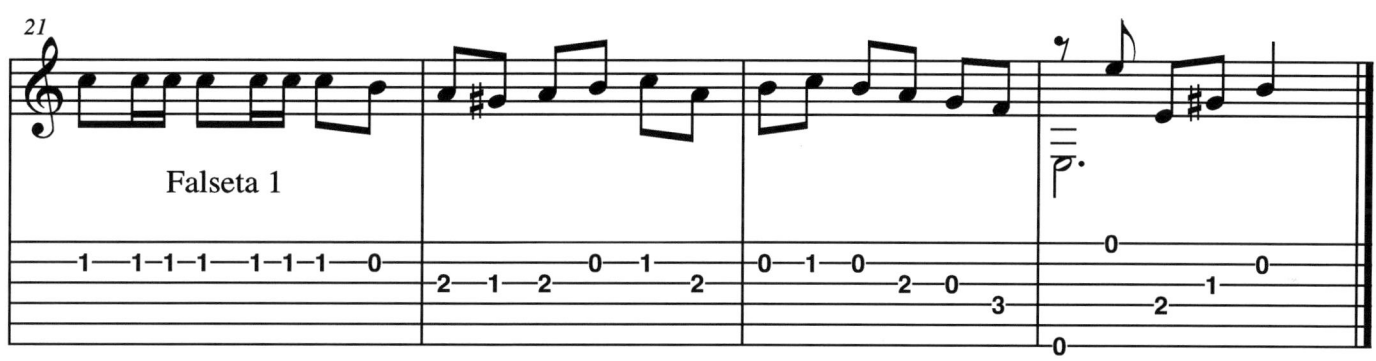

Falseta 1

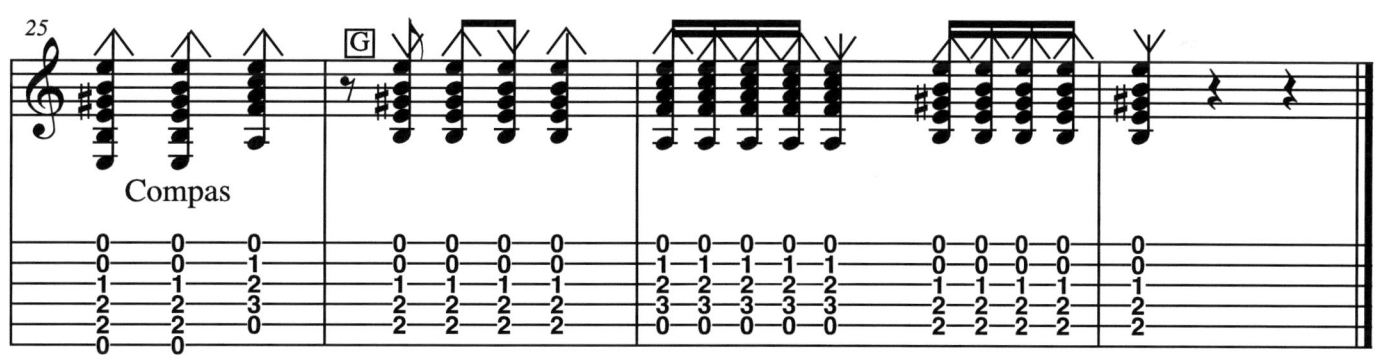

Compas

Falseta 2

SOLEARES

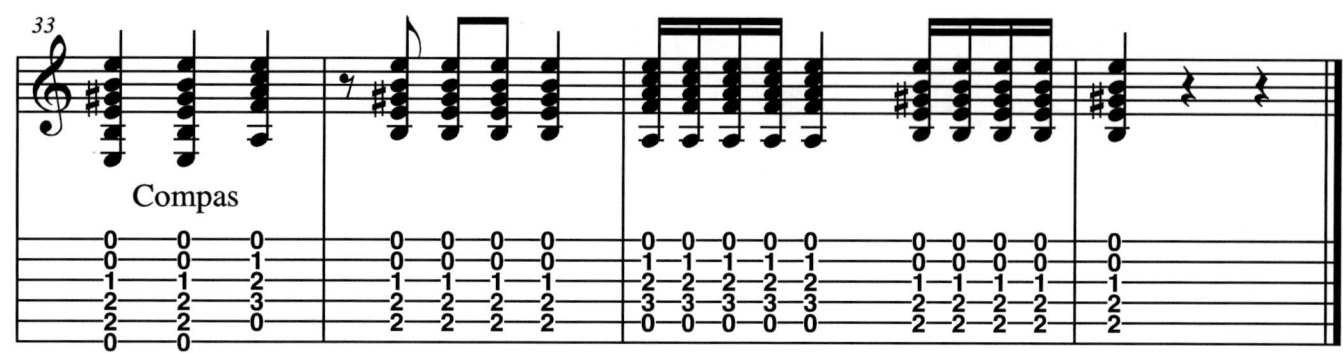

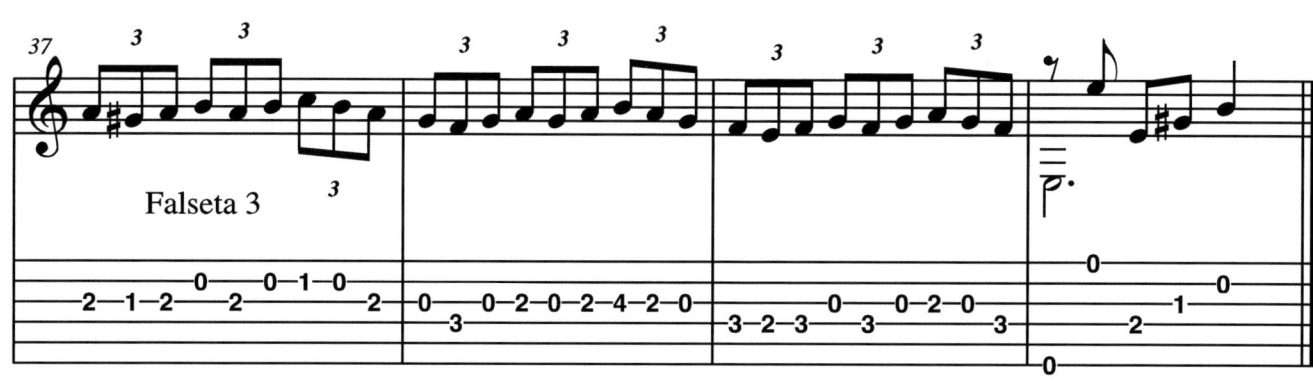

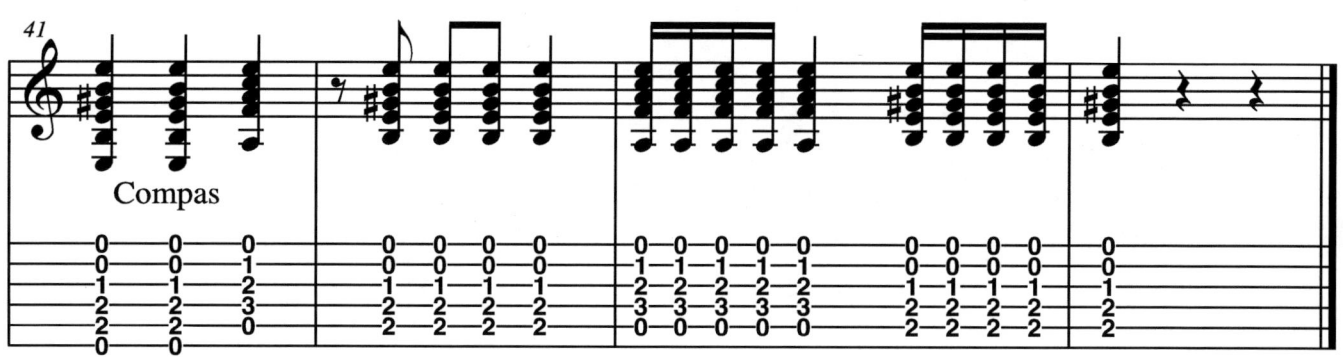

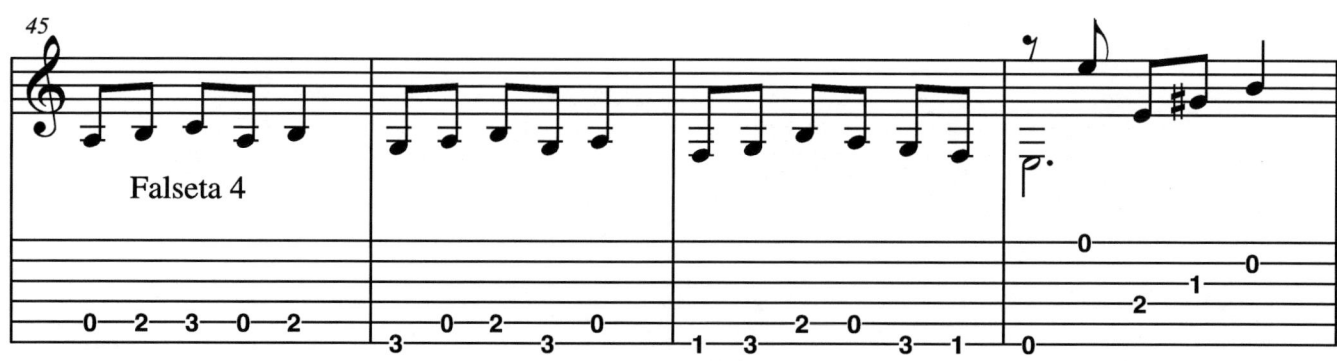

SOLEARES

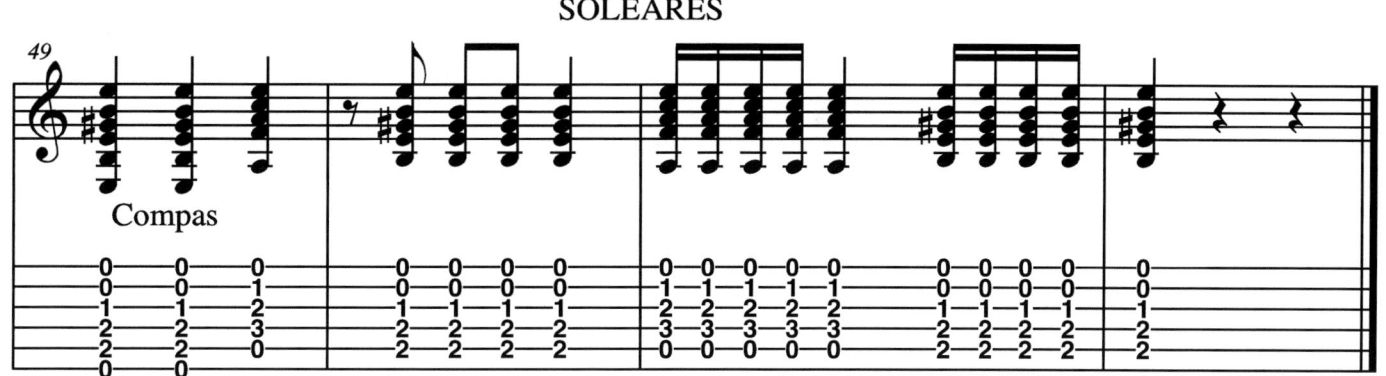

Compas

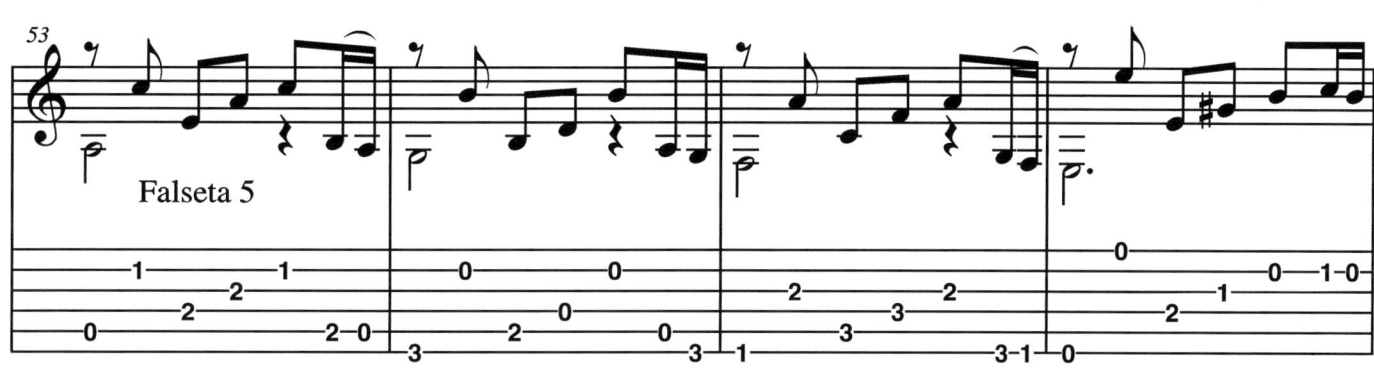

Falseta 5

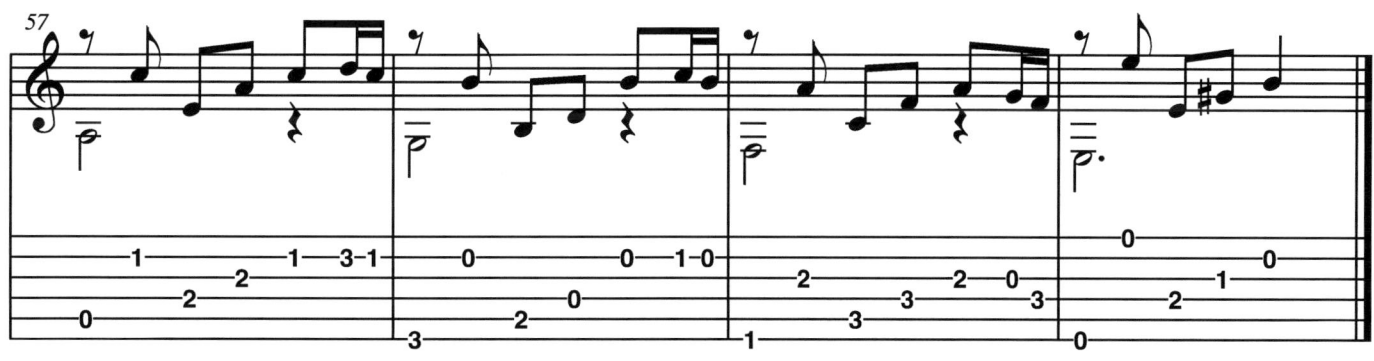

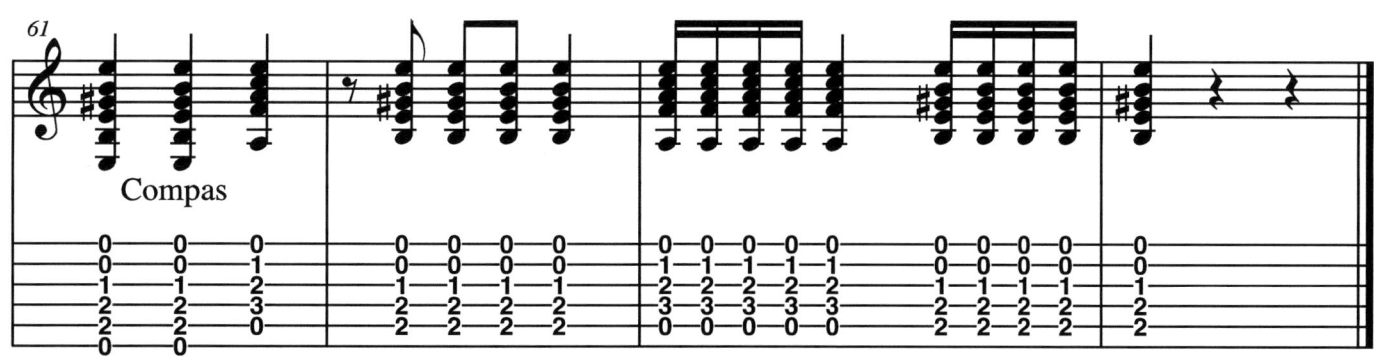

Compas

SOLEARES

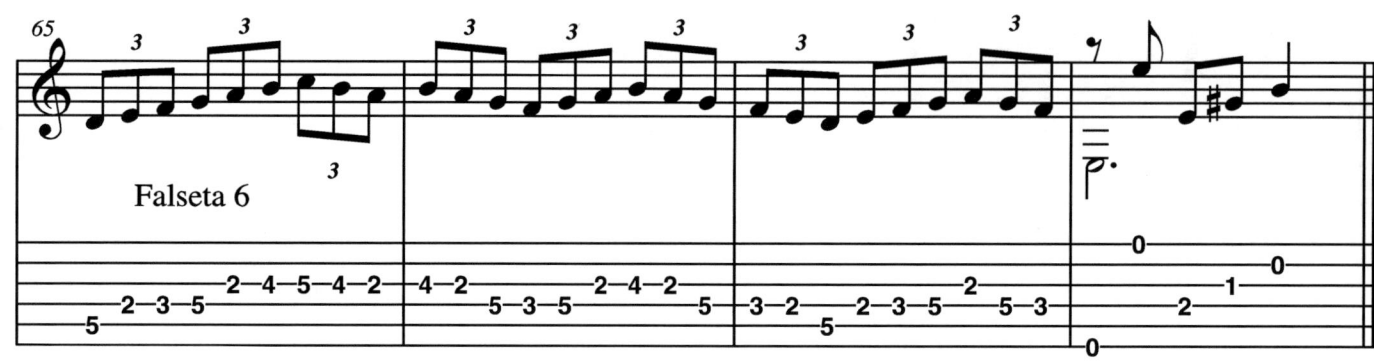
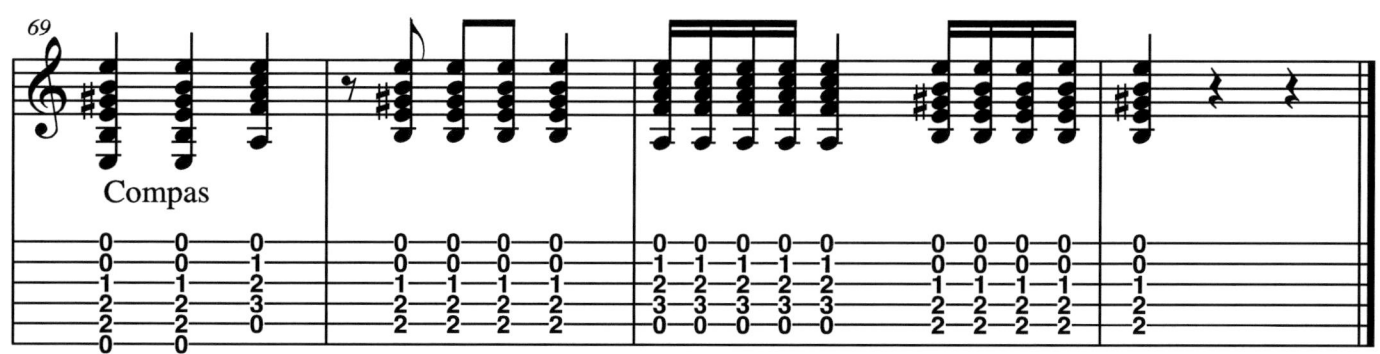

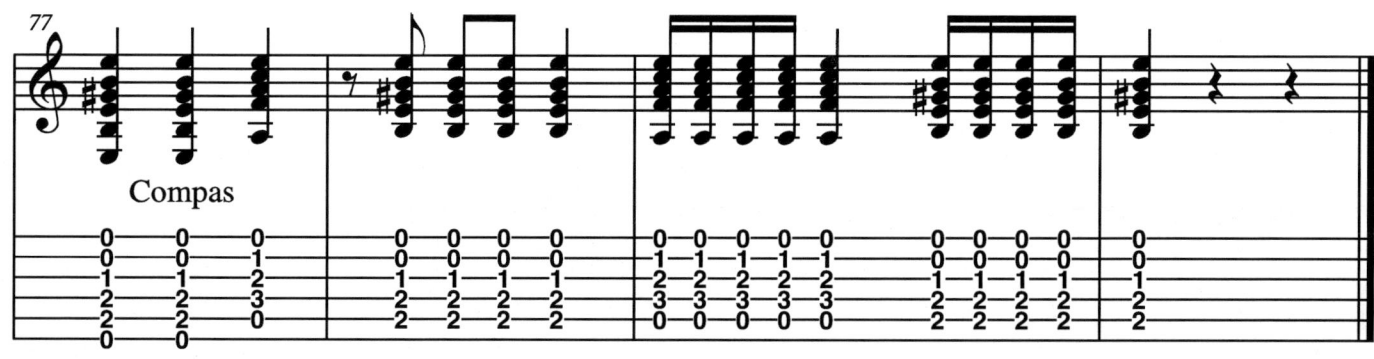

SOLEARES

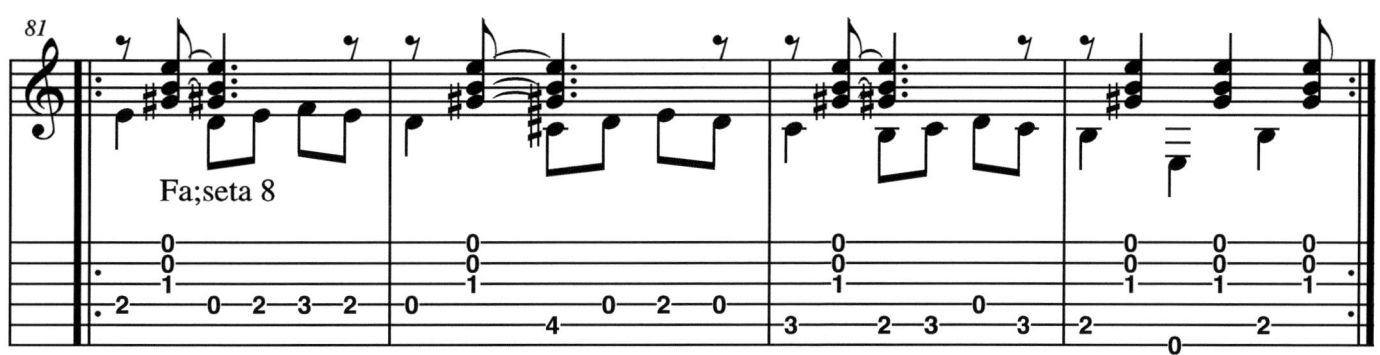
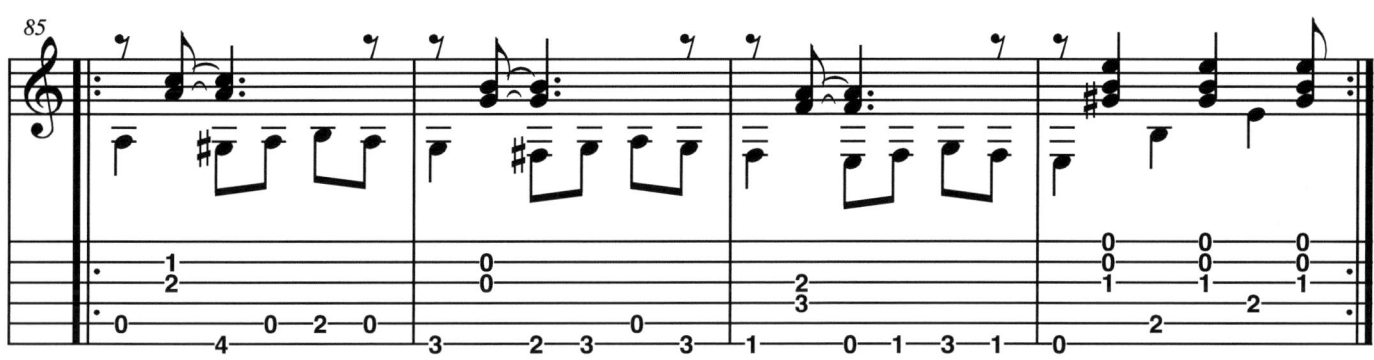

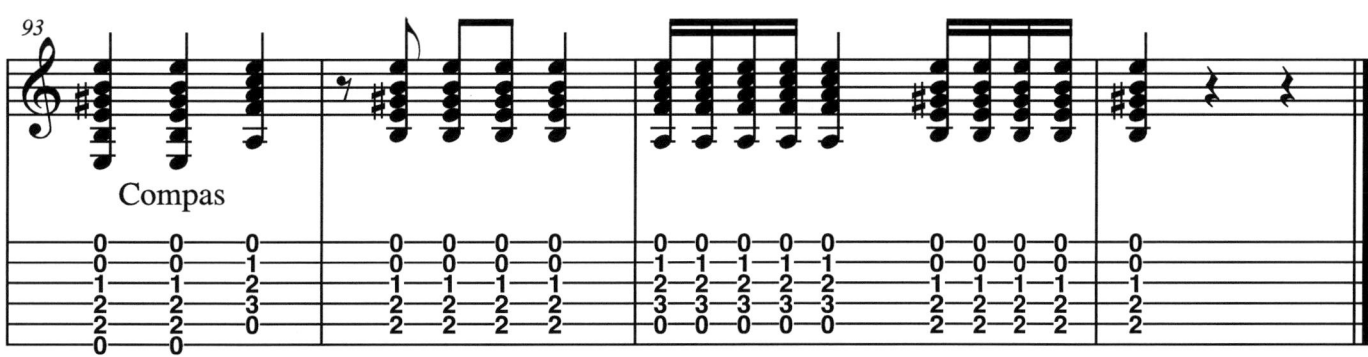

SOLEARES

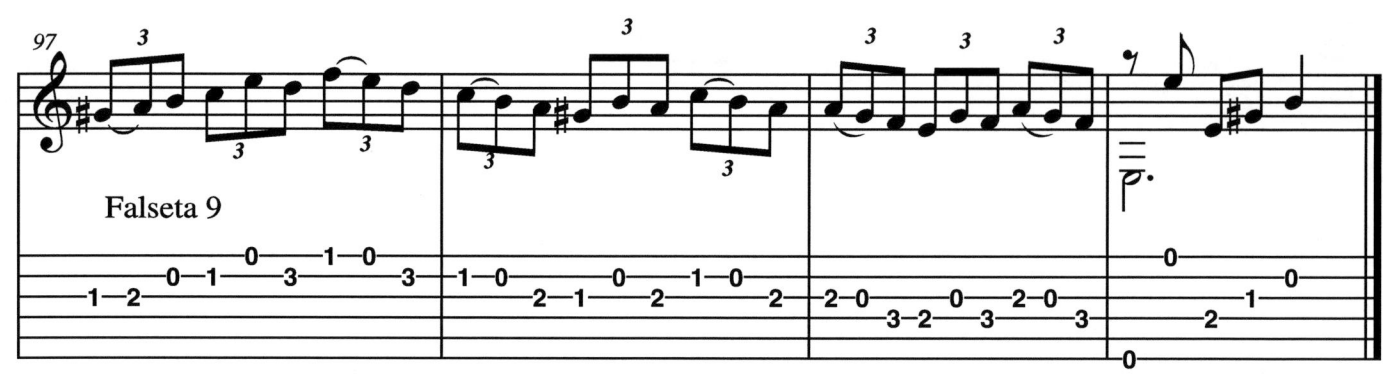
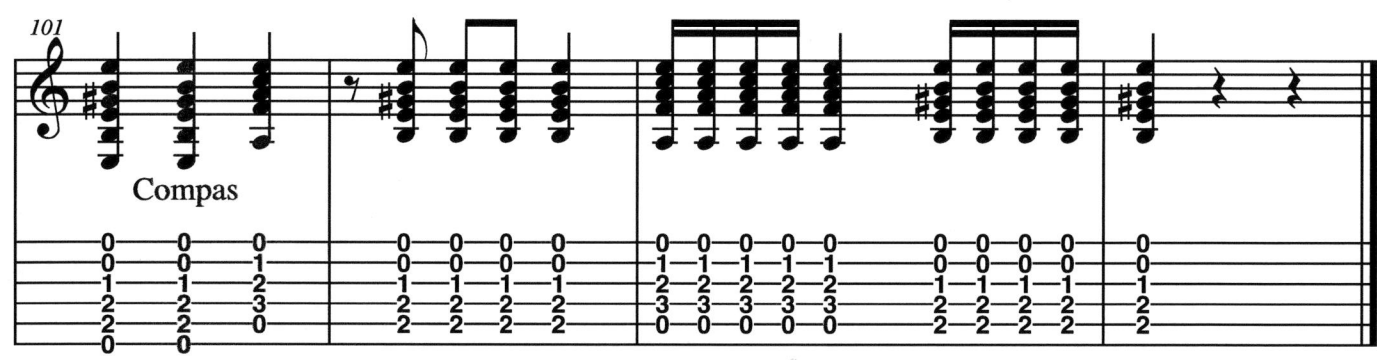
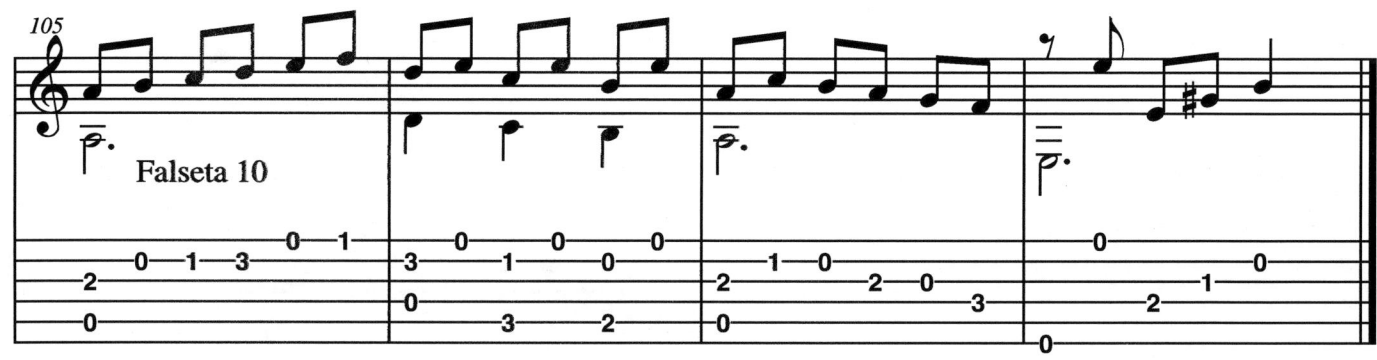
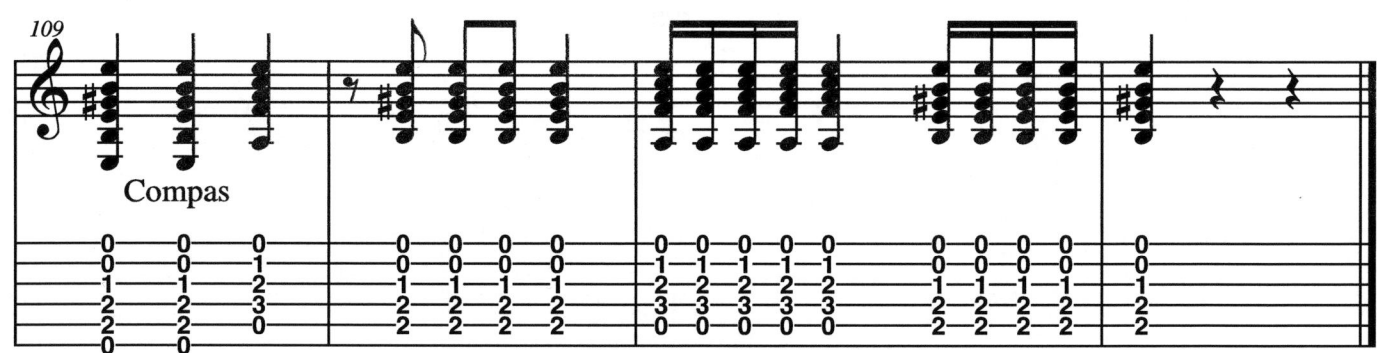

SOLEARES

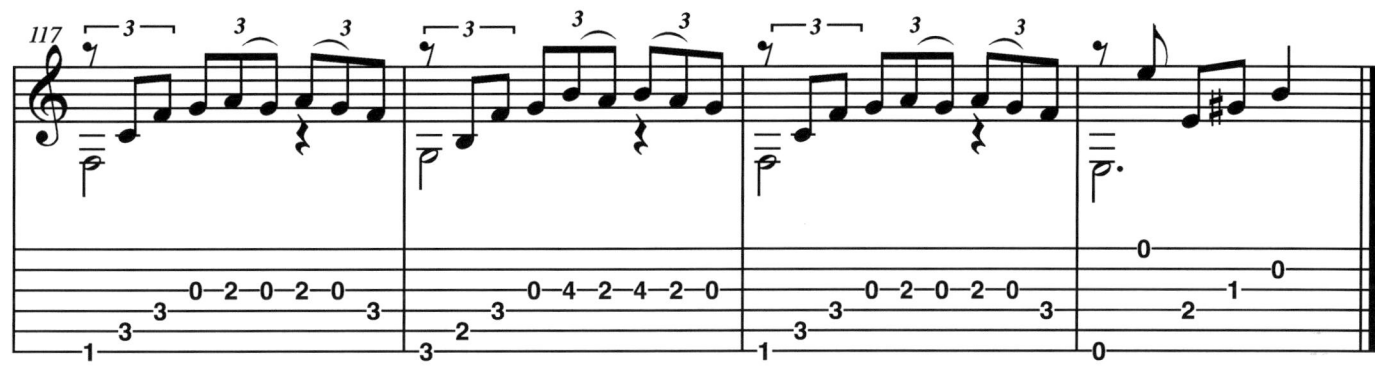

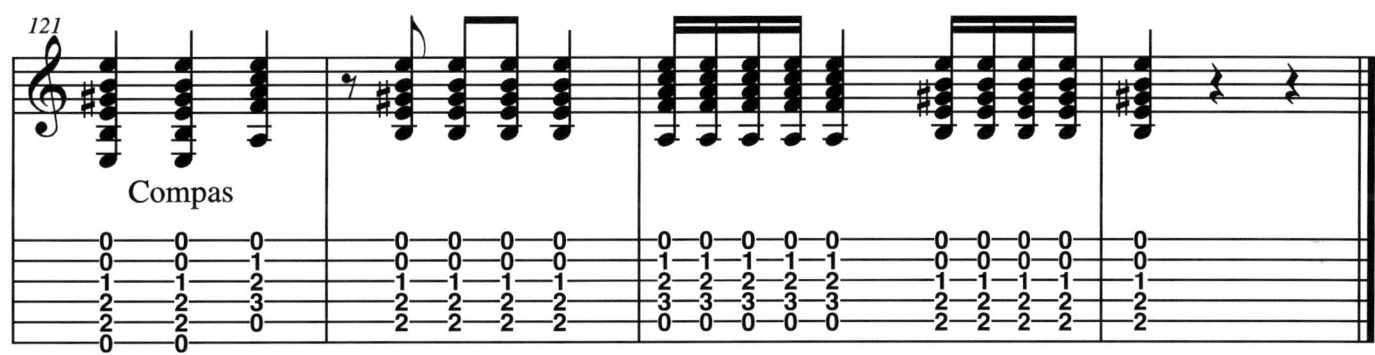

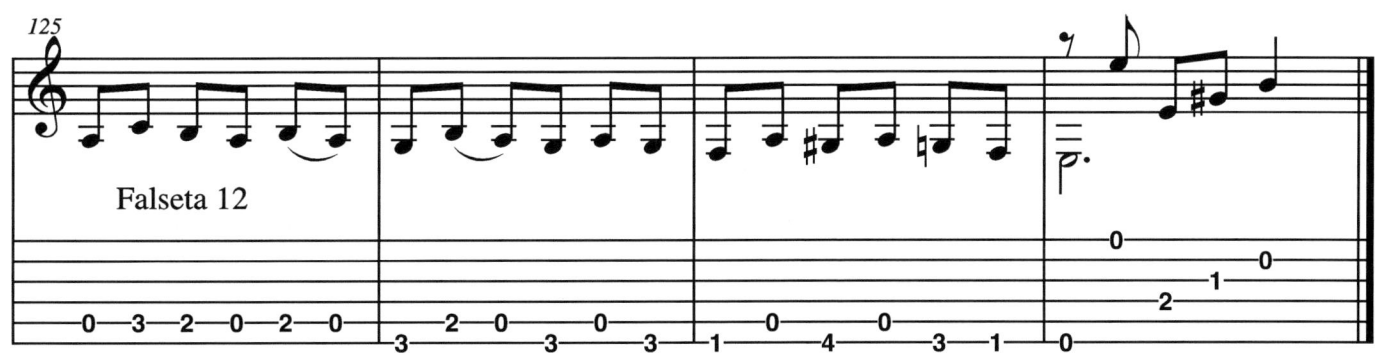

SOLEARES

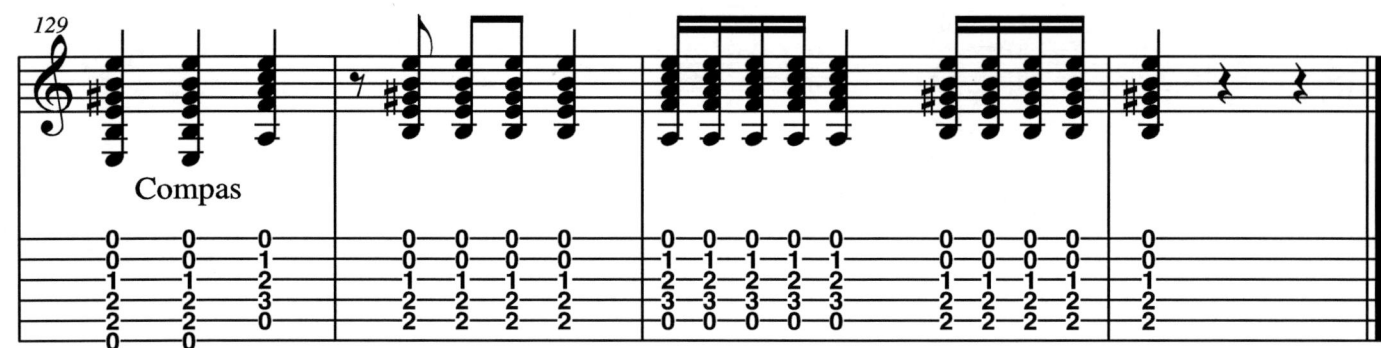

Compas

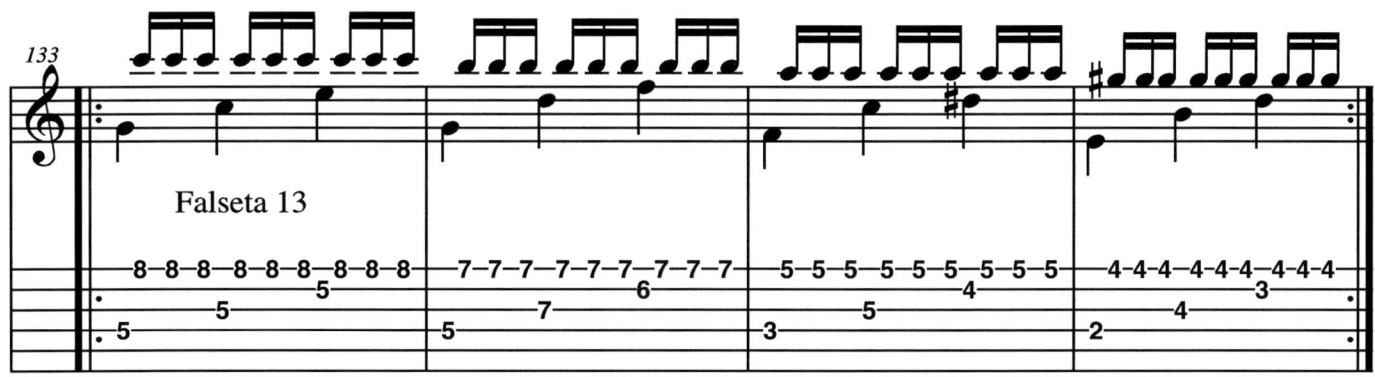

Falseta 13

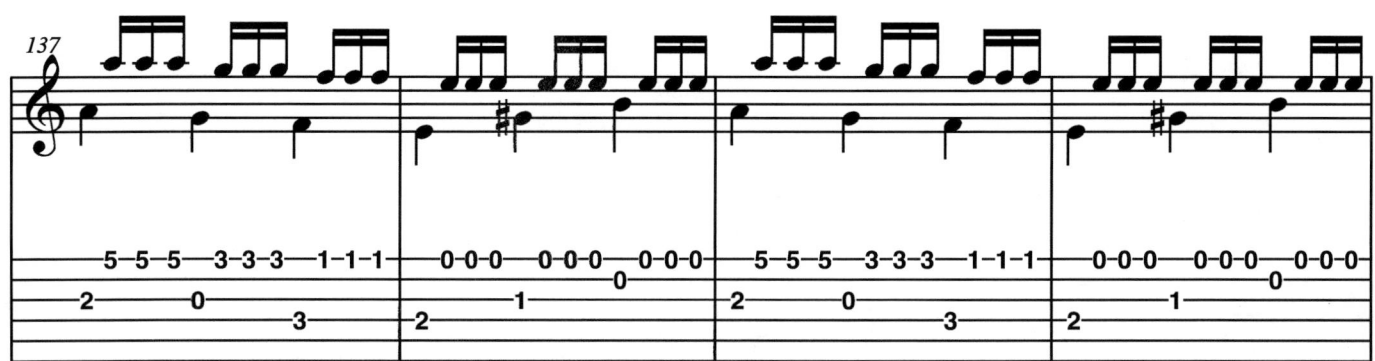

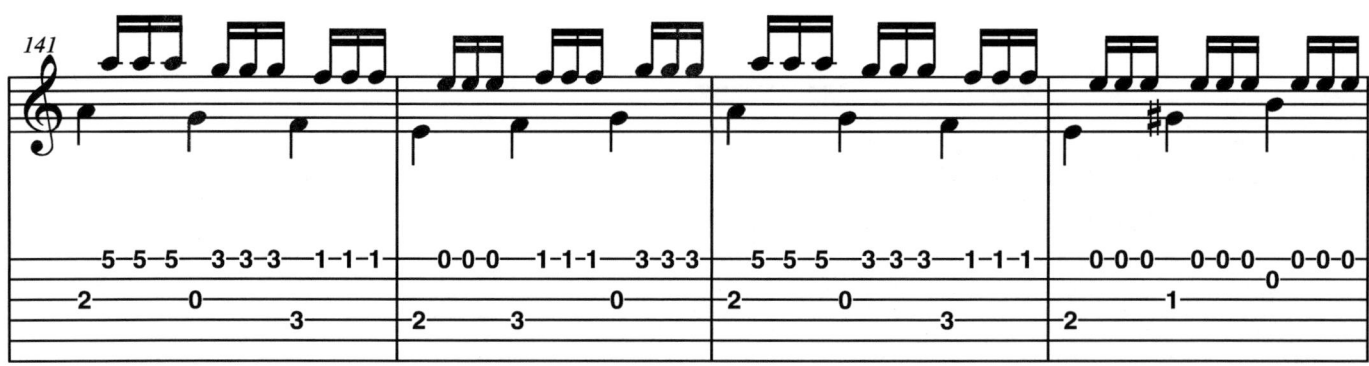

SOLEARES

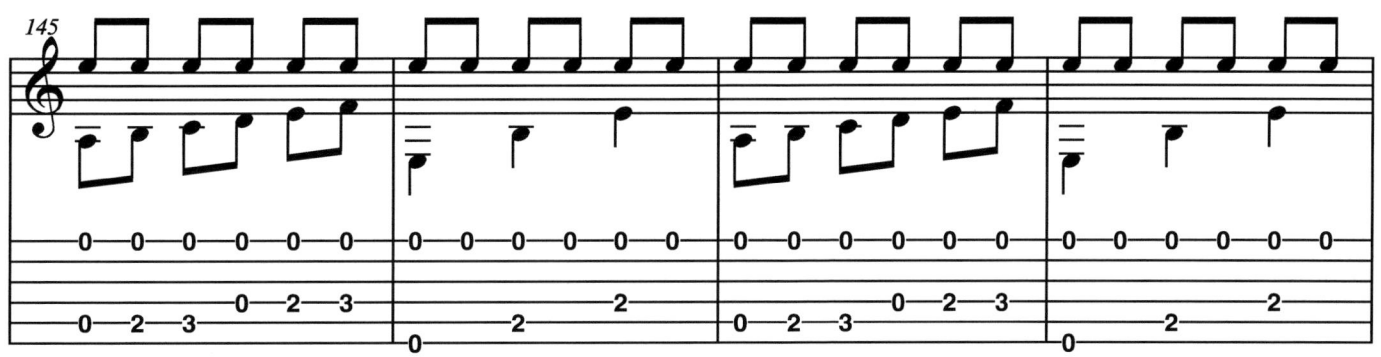

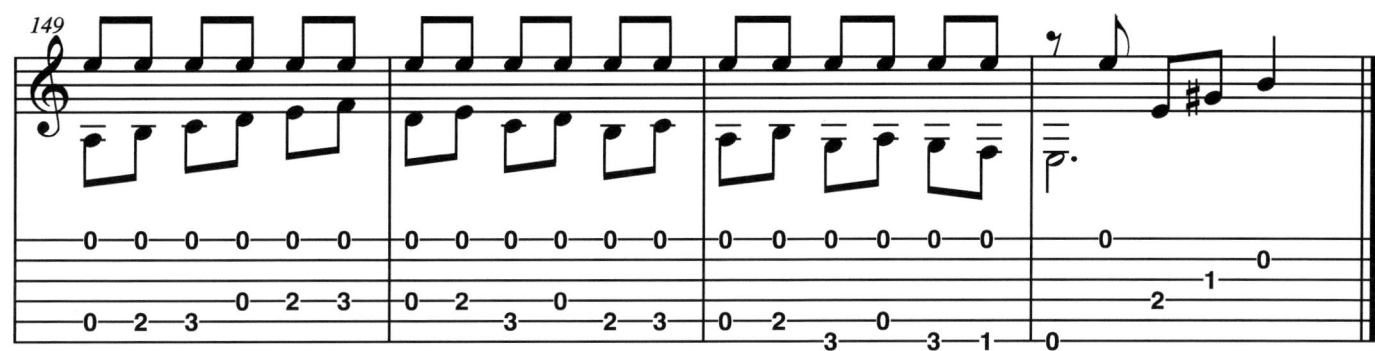

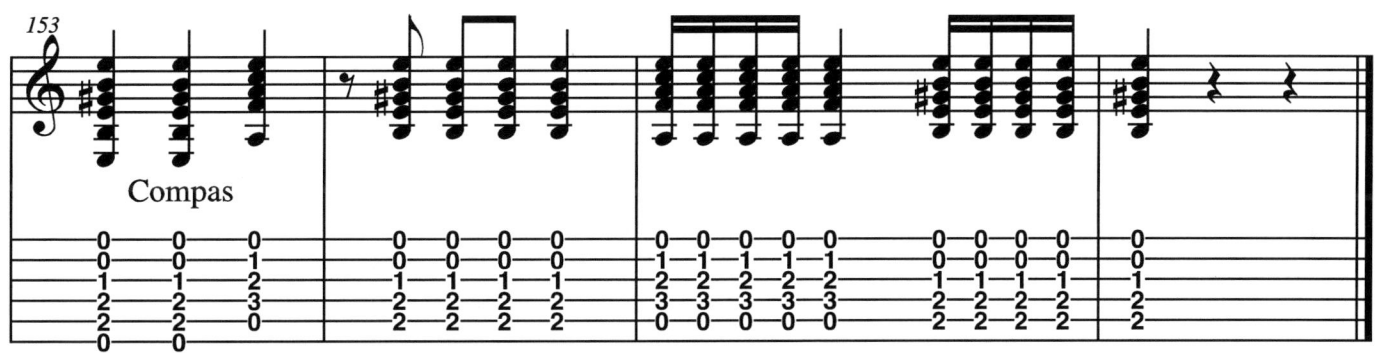

Compas

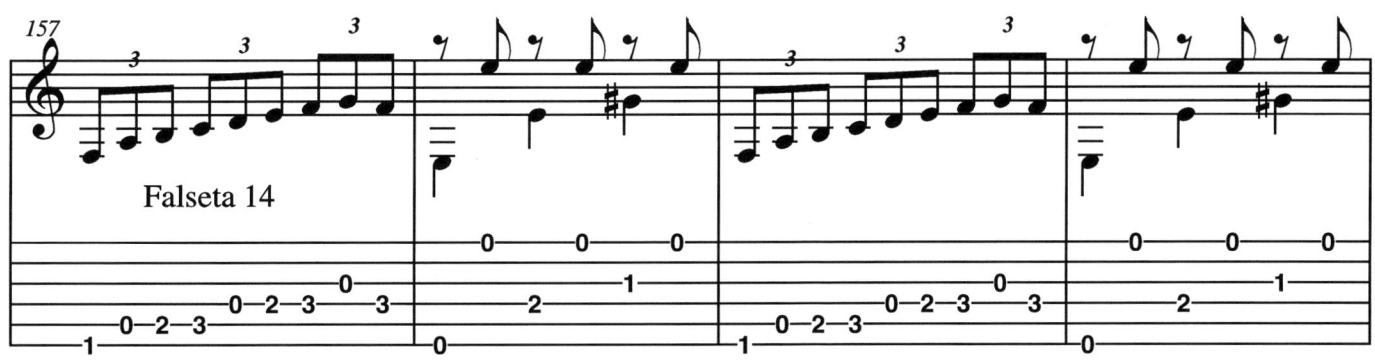

Falseta 14

SOLEARES

SOLEARES

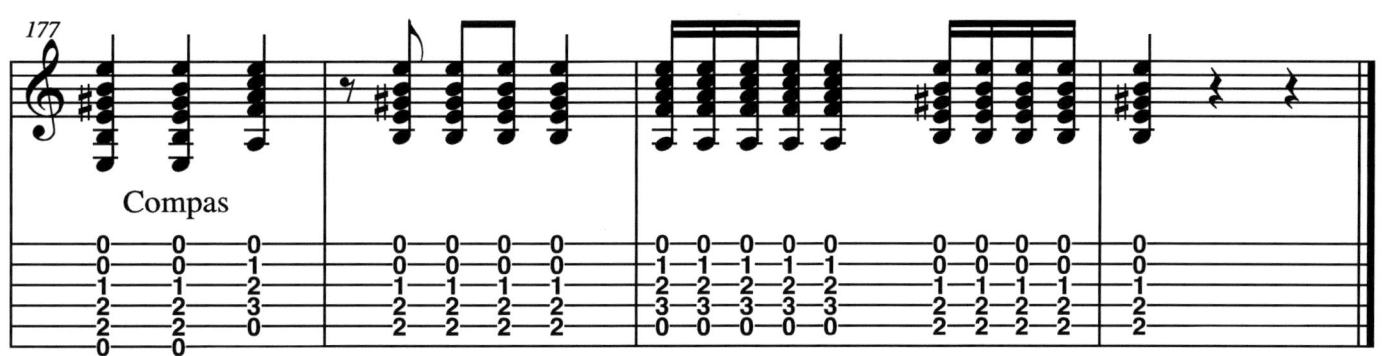

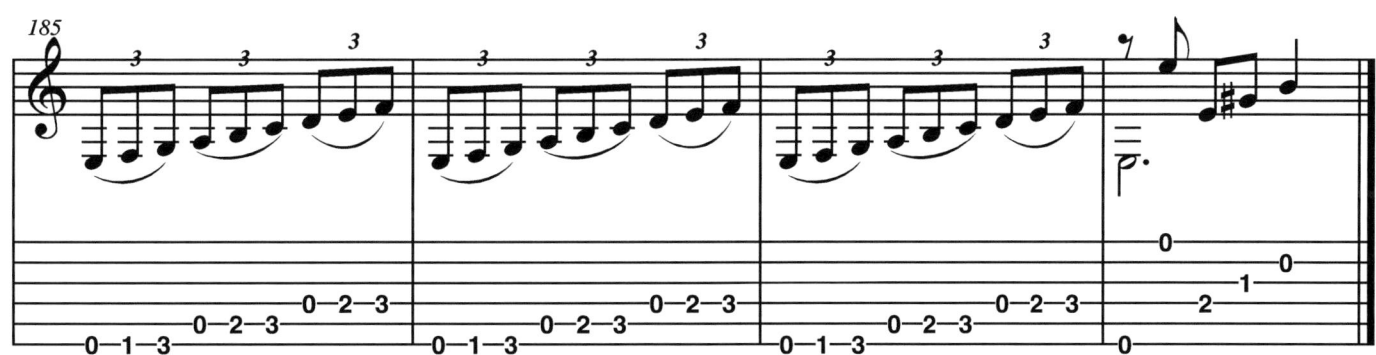

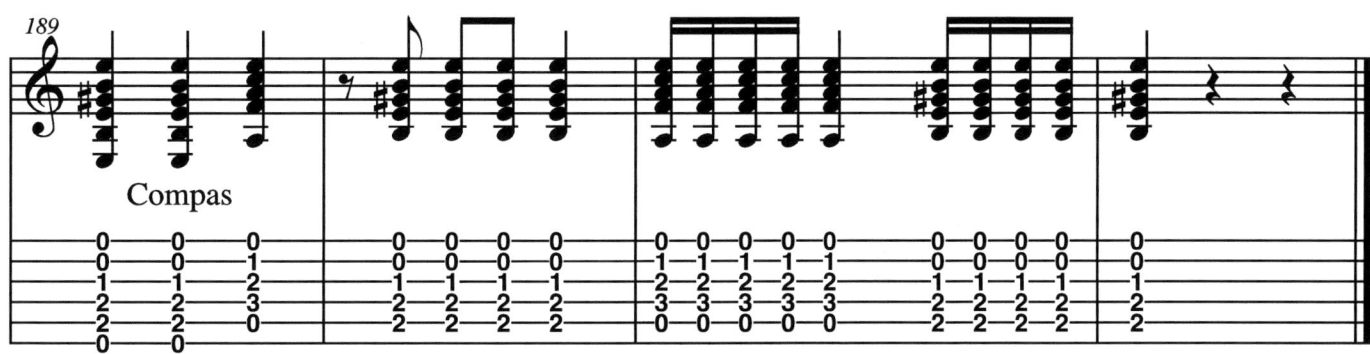

SOLEARES

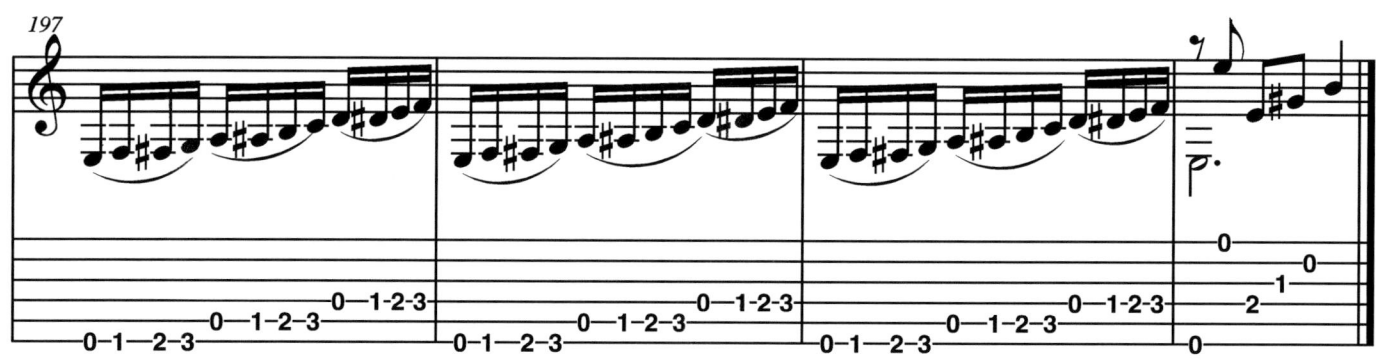

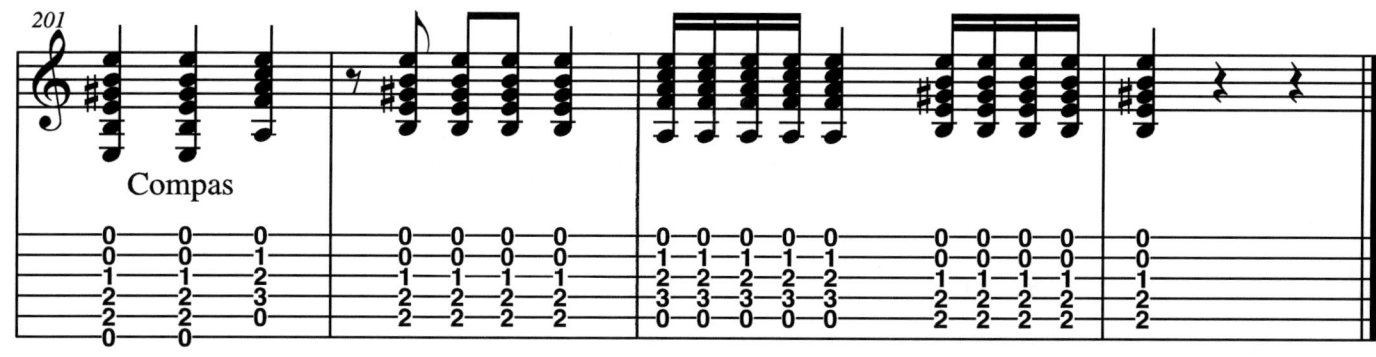

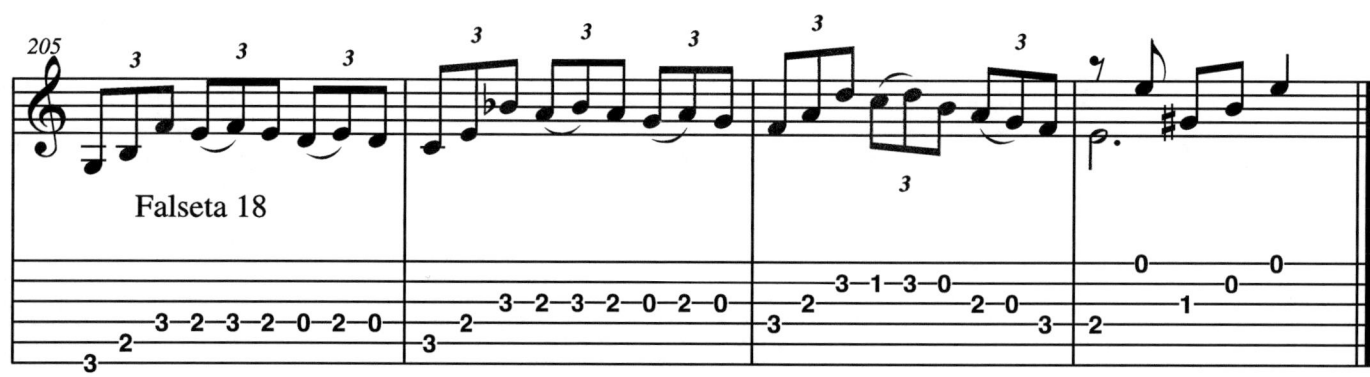

SOLEARES

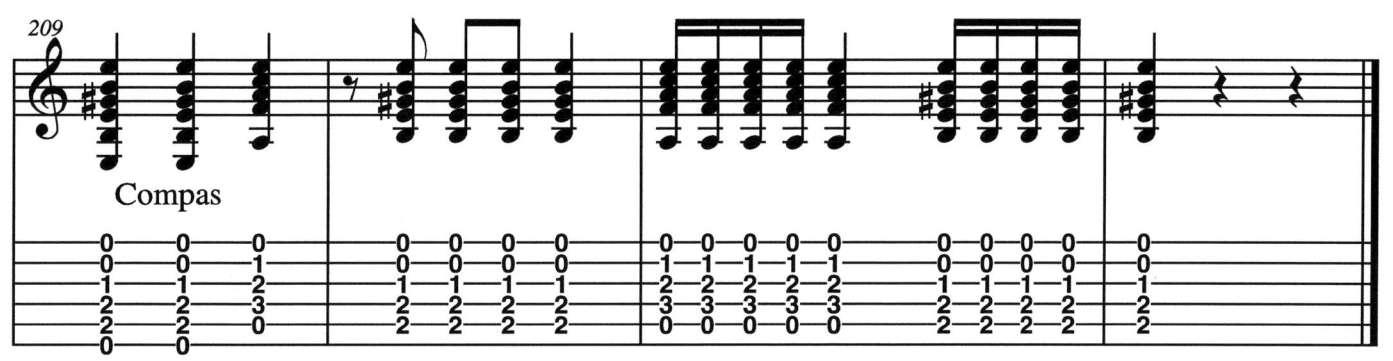

Compas

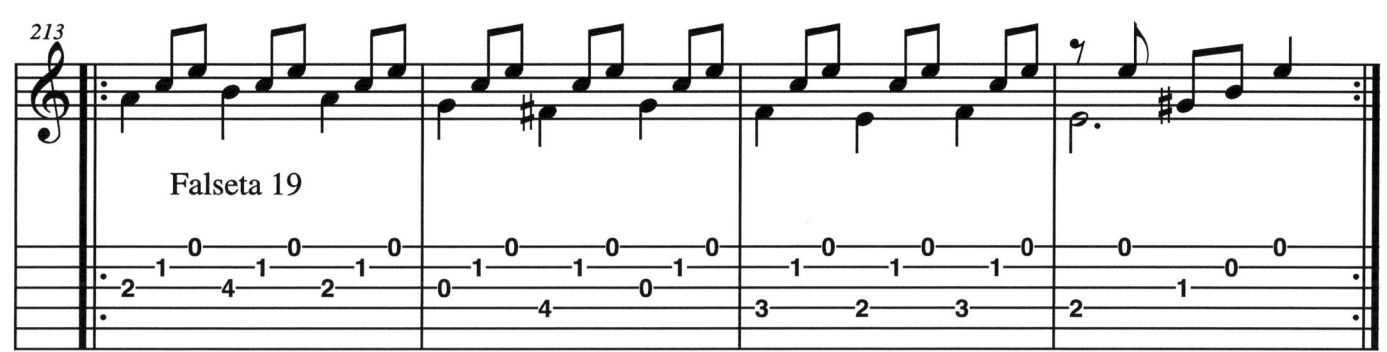

Falseta 19

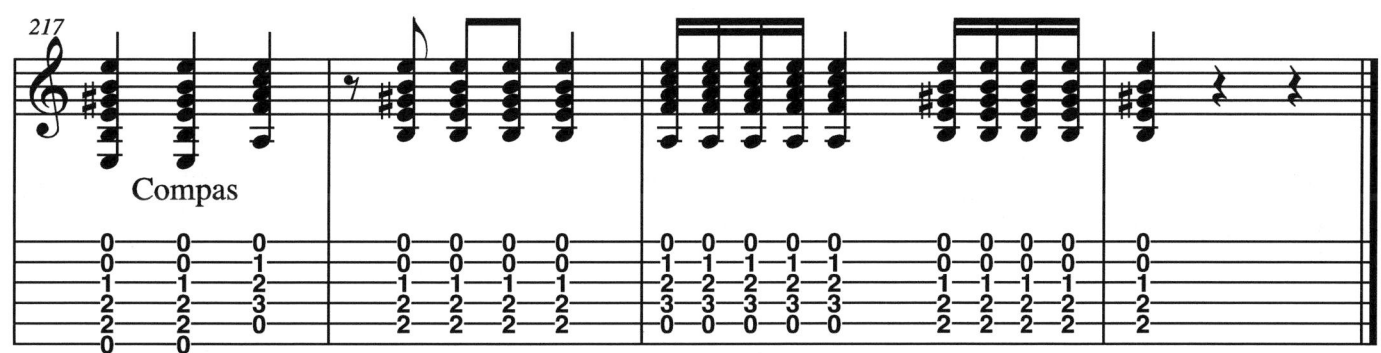

Compas

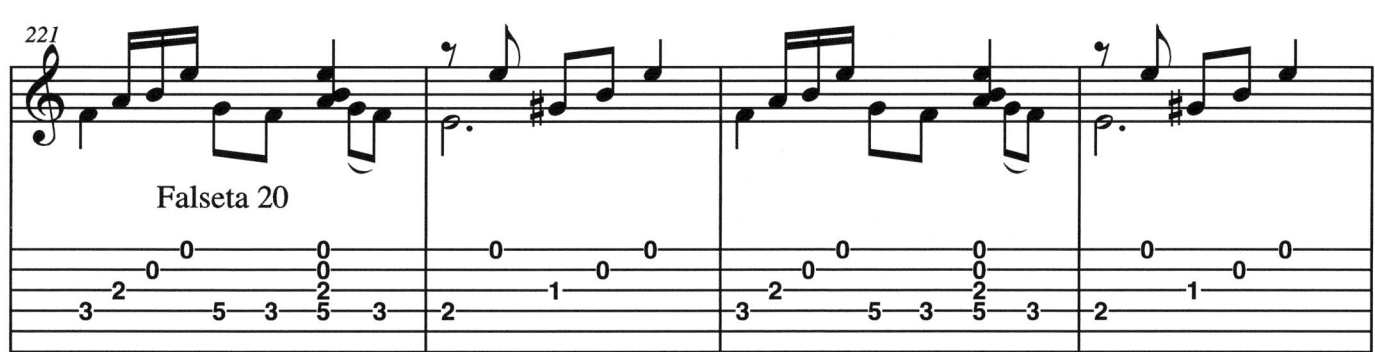

Falseta 20

SOLEARES

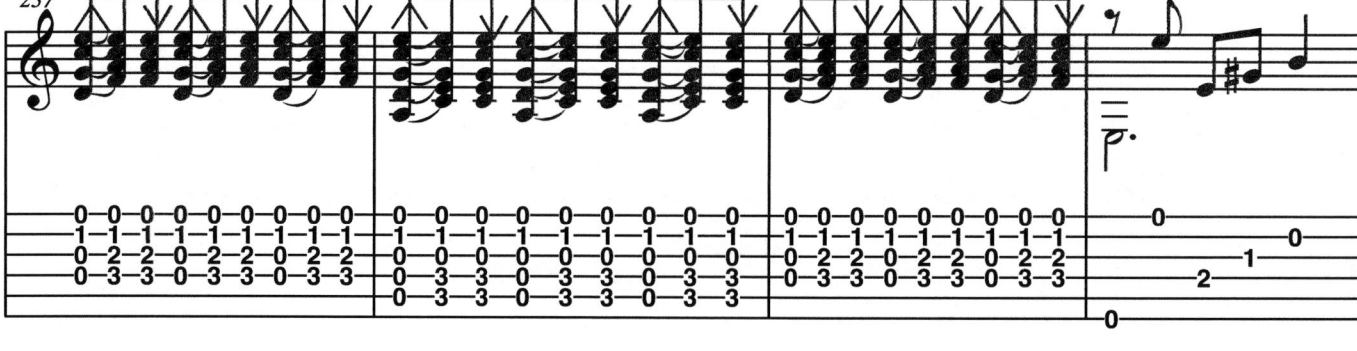

SOLEARES

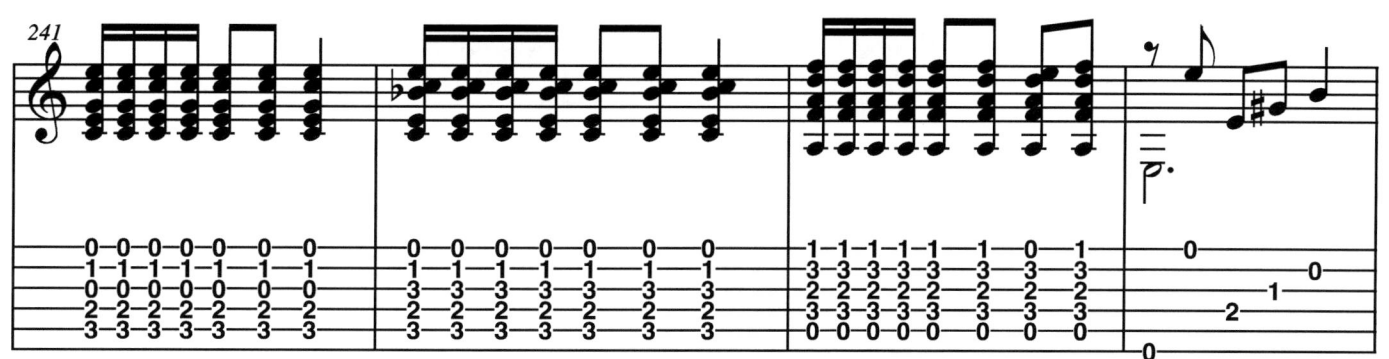
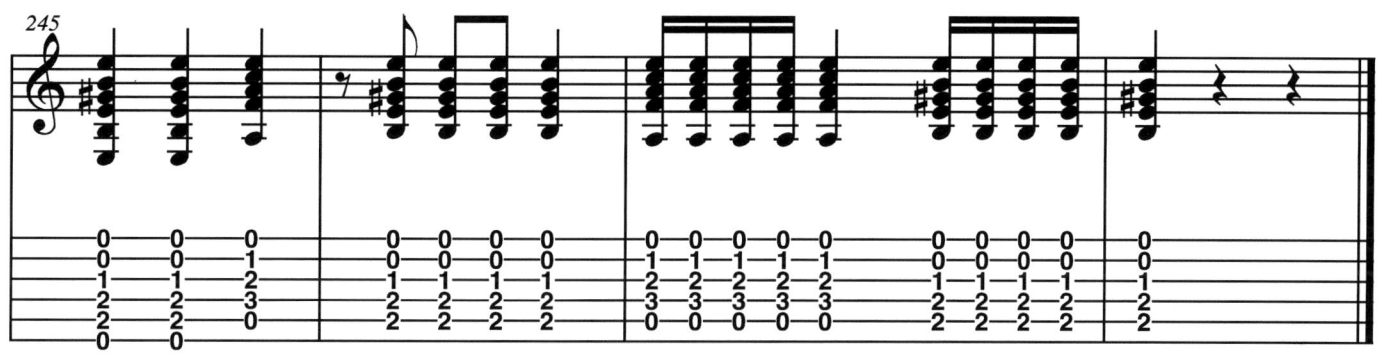

TARANTO

Strum every compas in the same manner

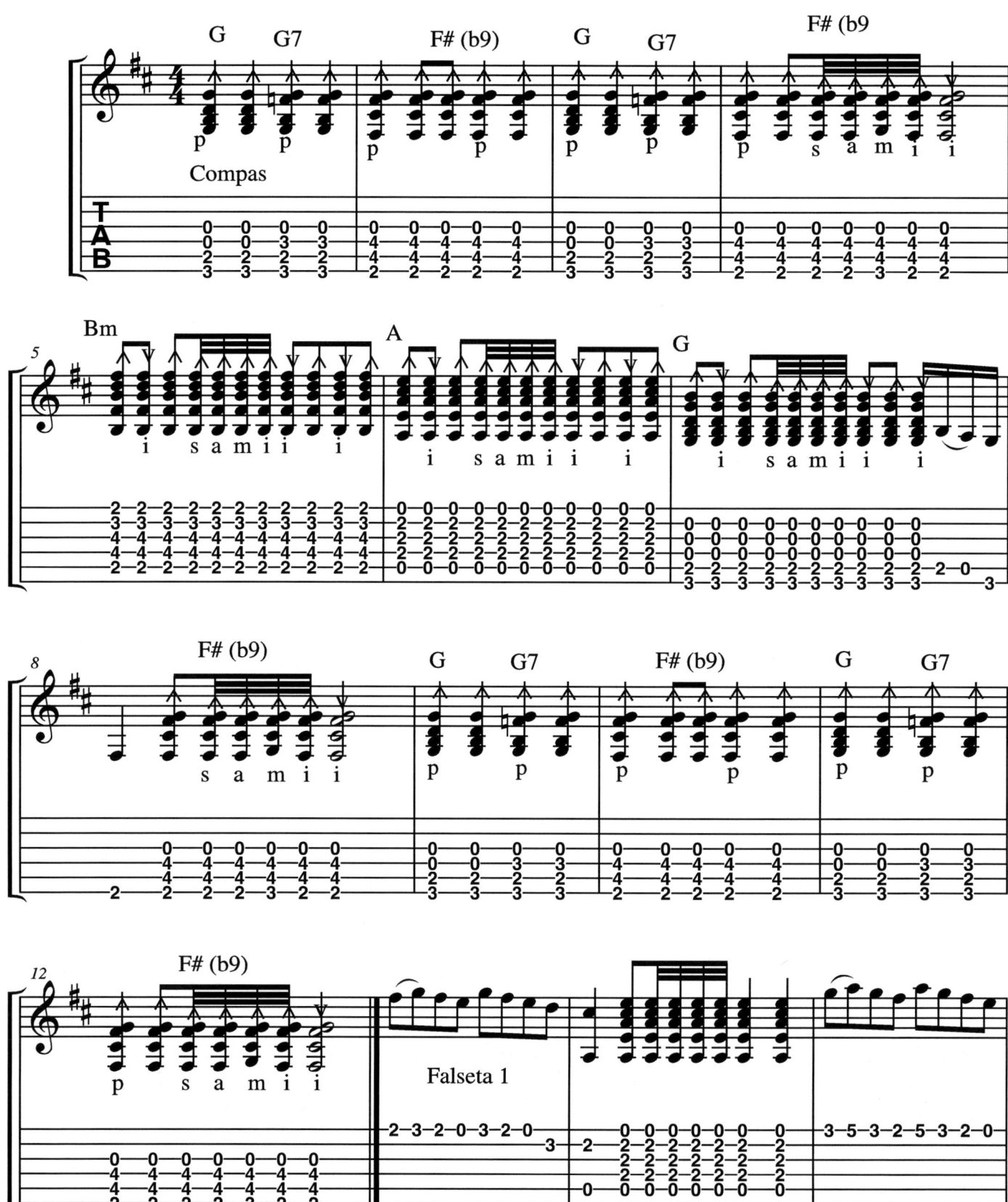

TARANTO

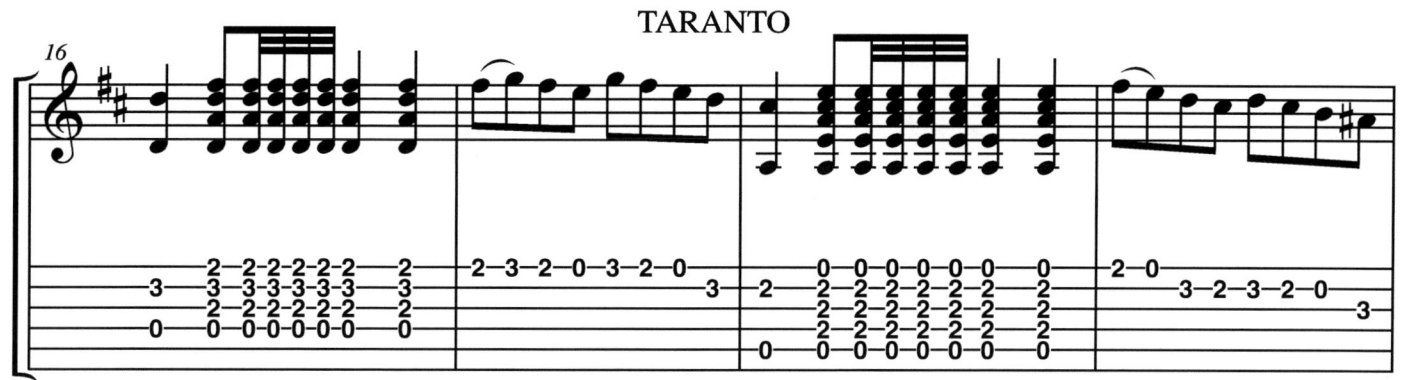
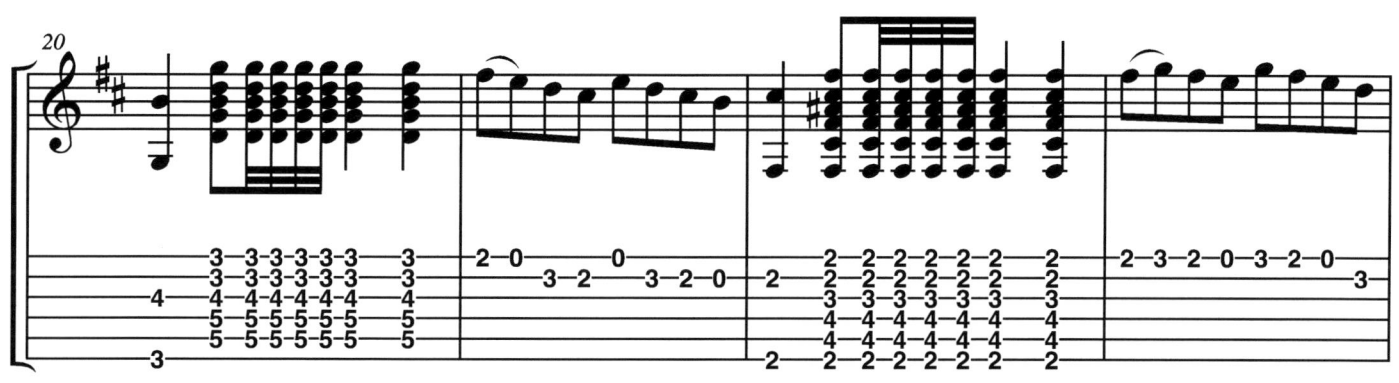
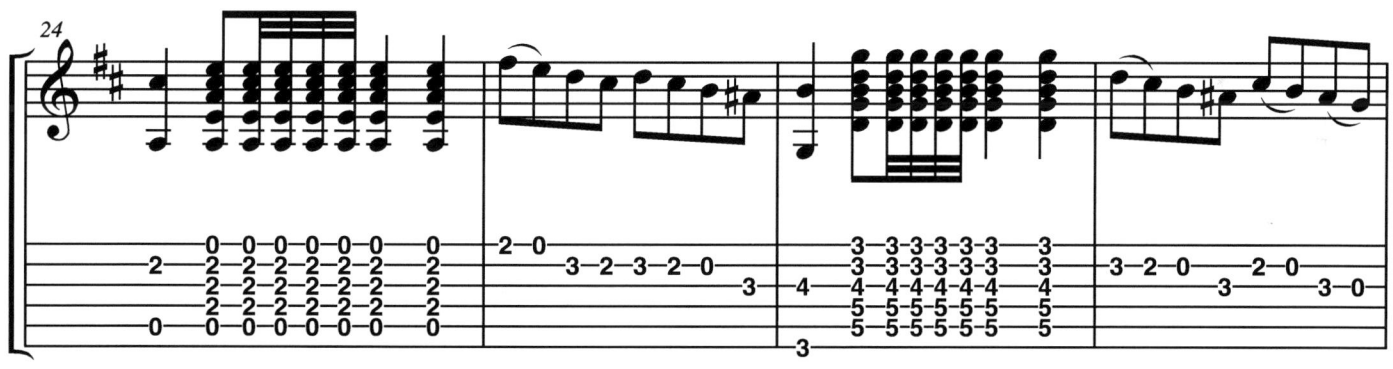
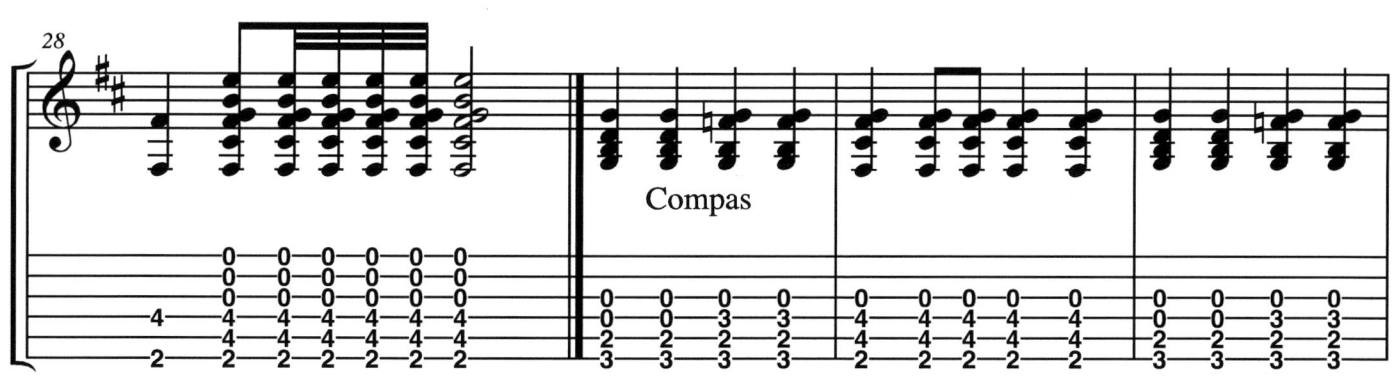

Compas

TARANTO

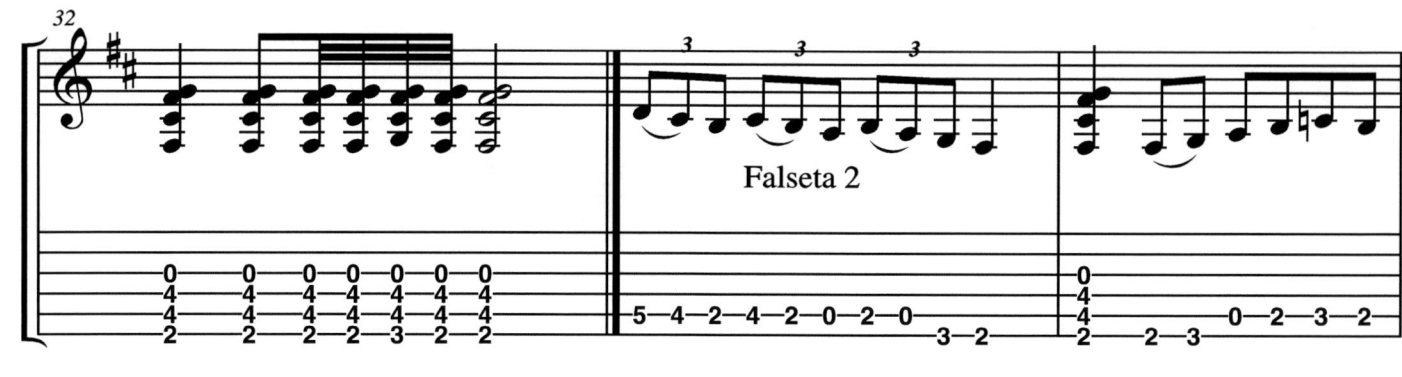

Falseta 2

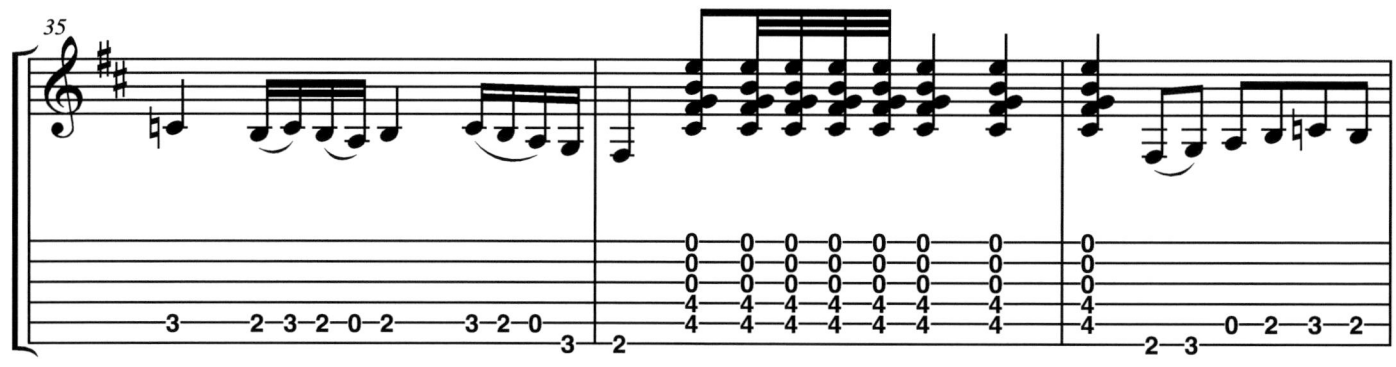

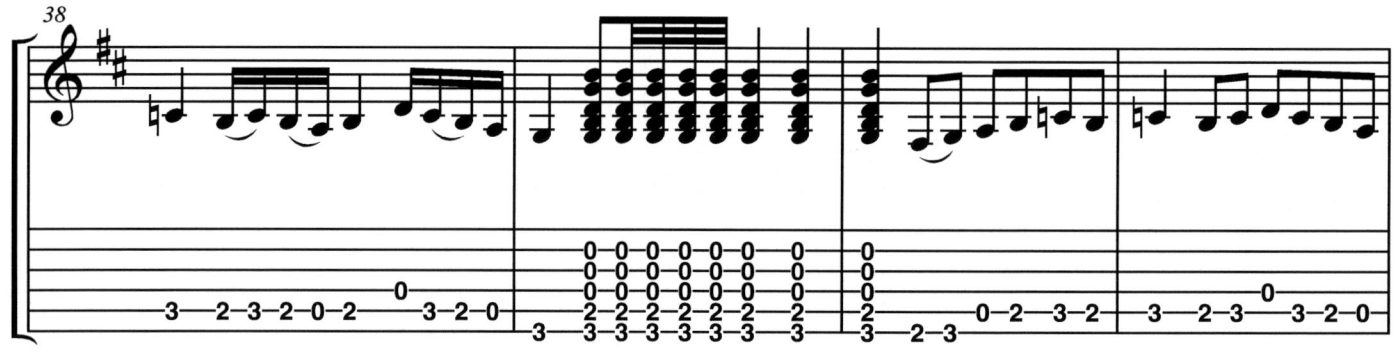

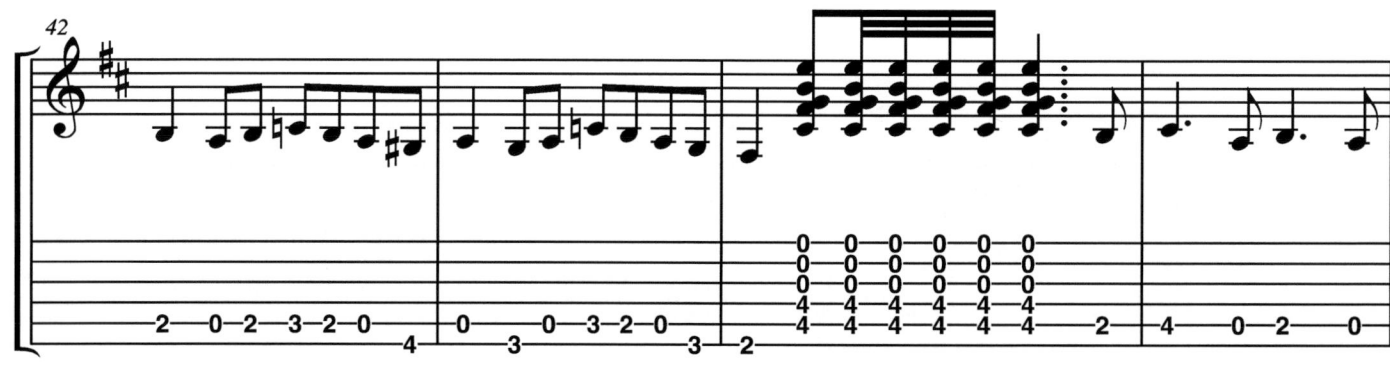

TARANTO

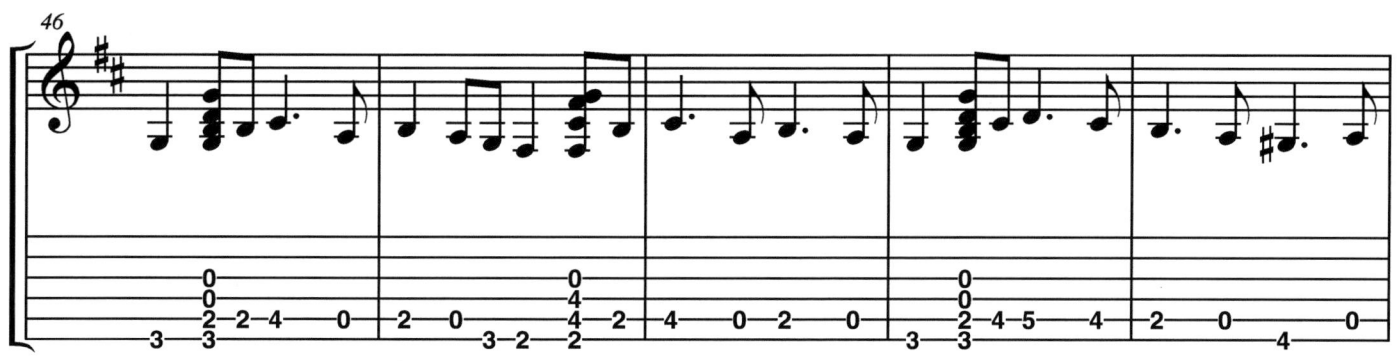
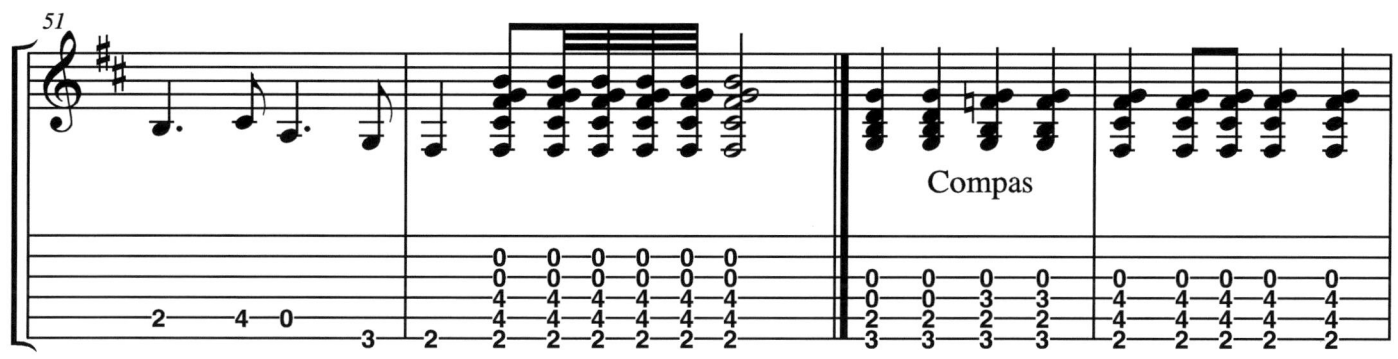
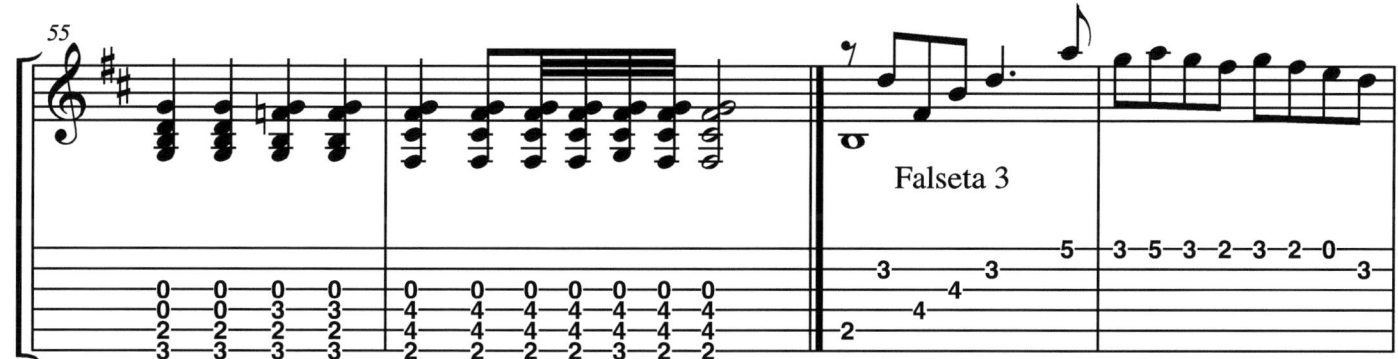
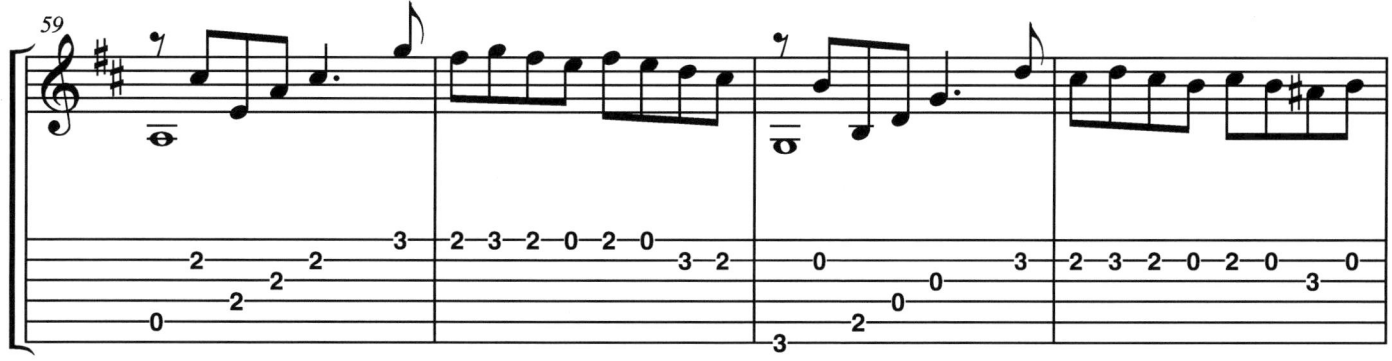

TARANTO

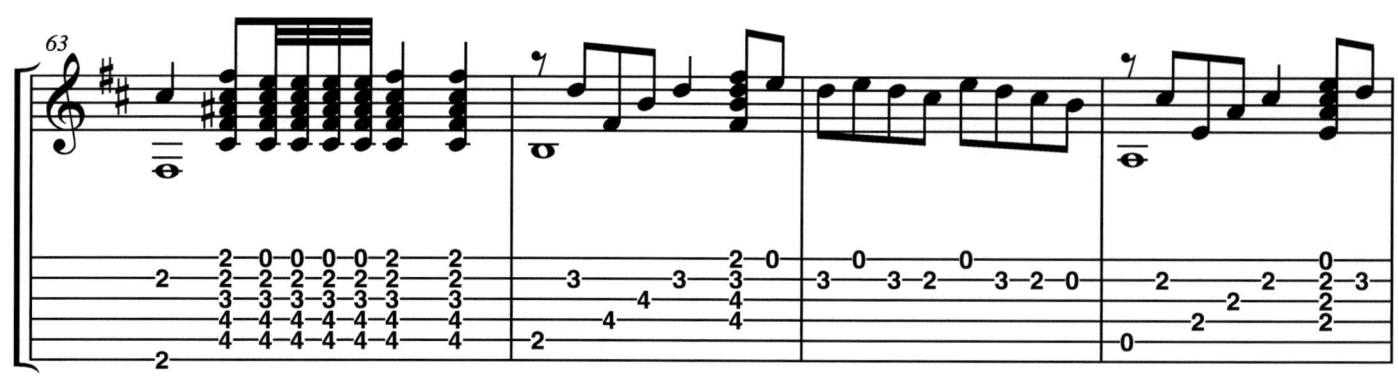

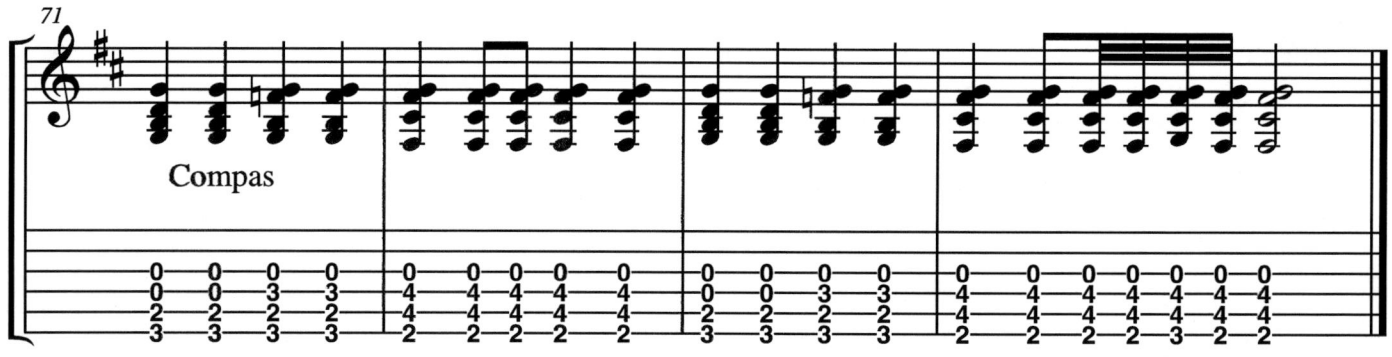

Compas

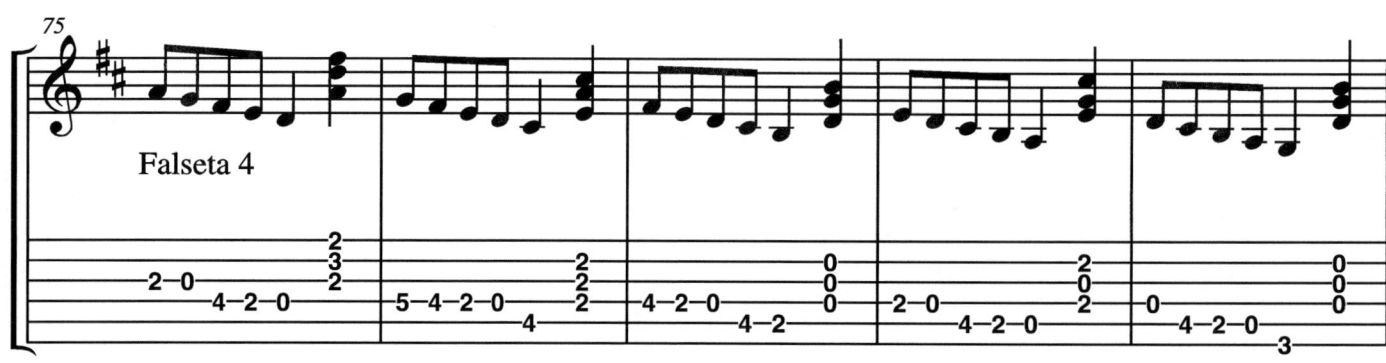

Falseta 4

TARANTO

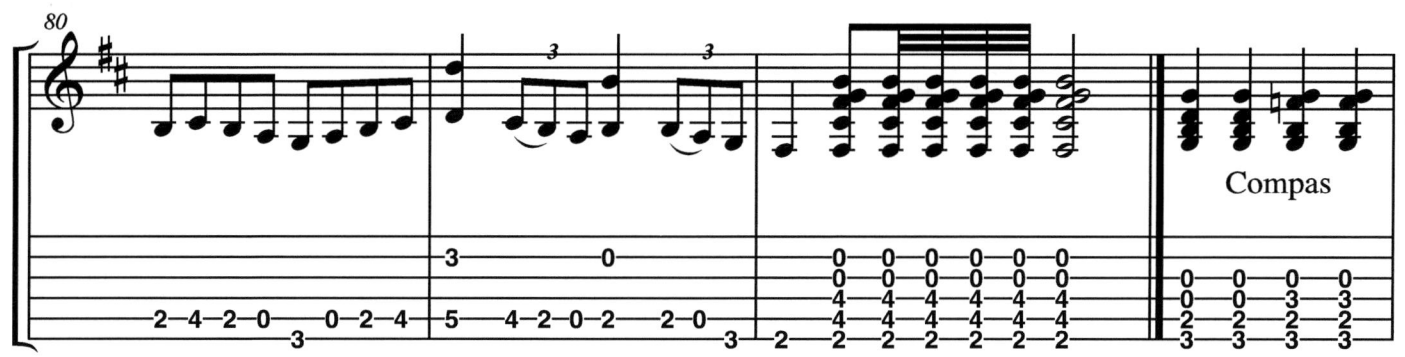

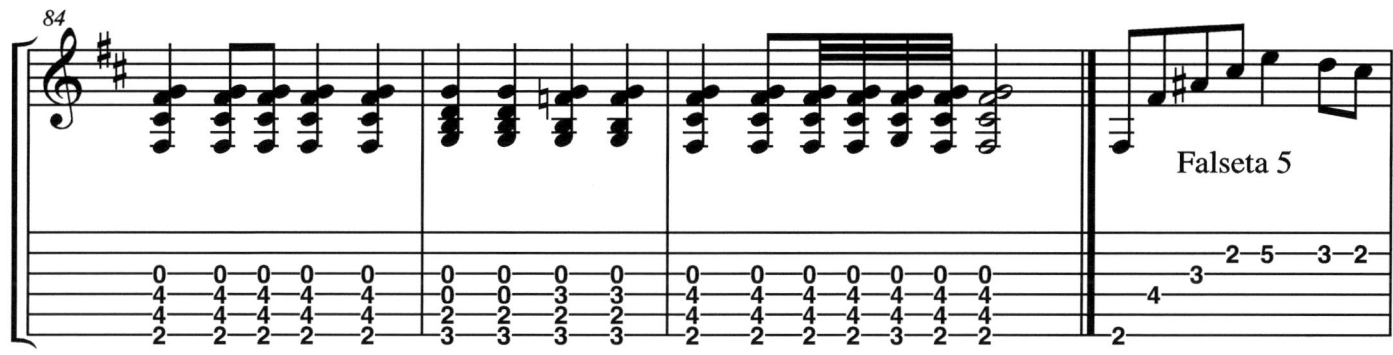

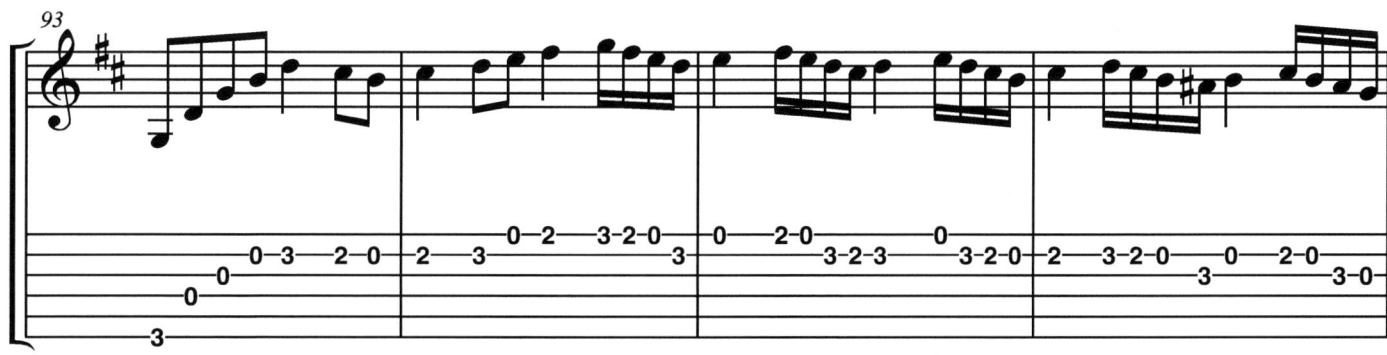

TARANTO

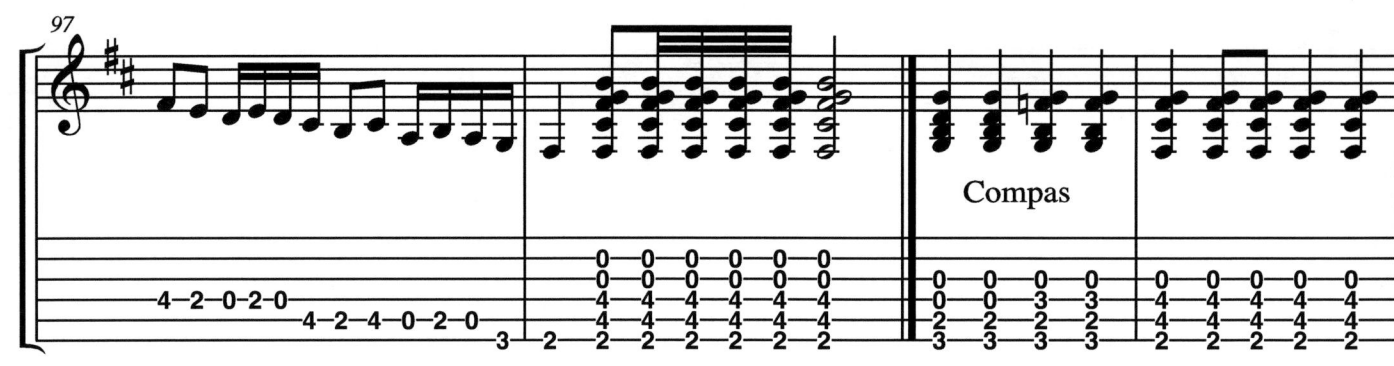
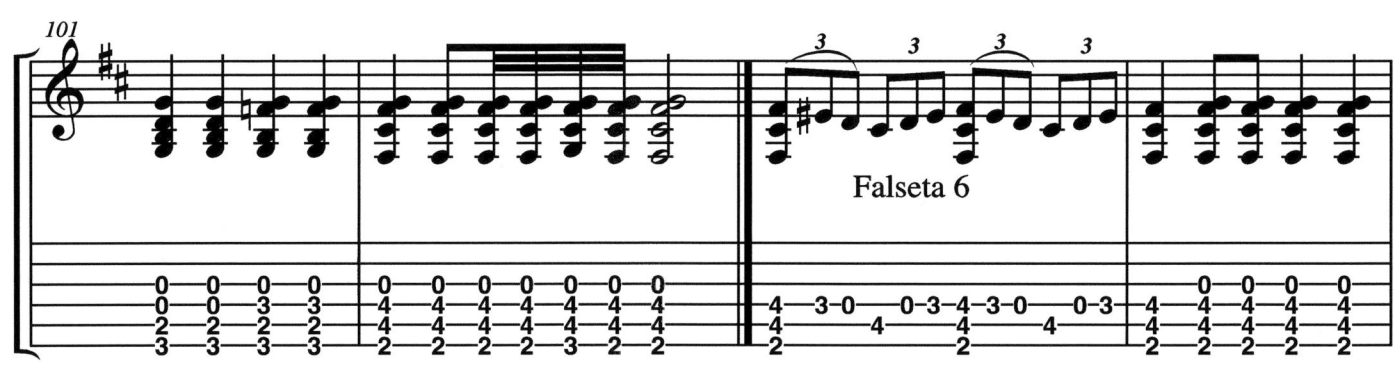
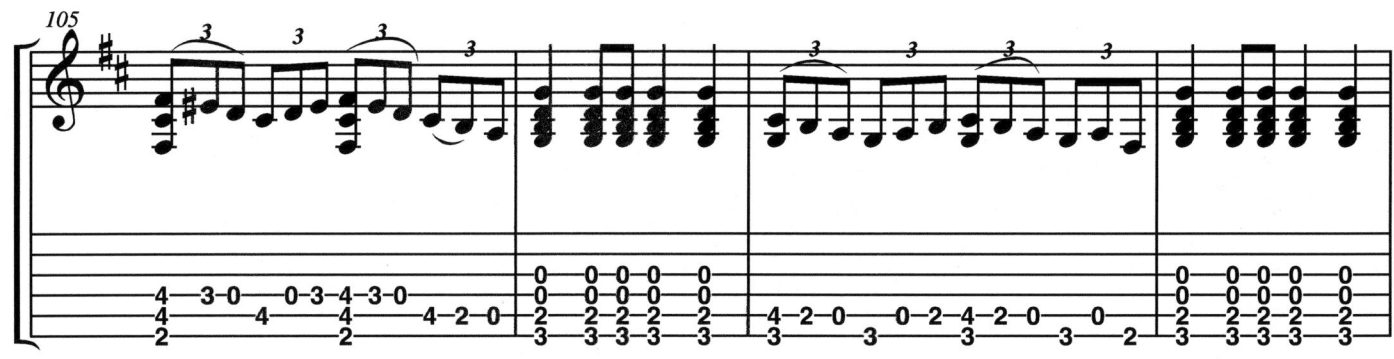
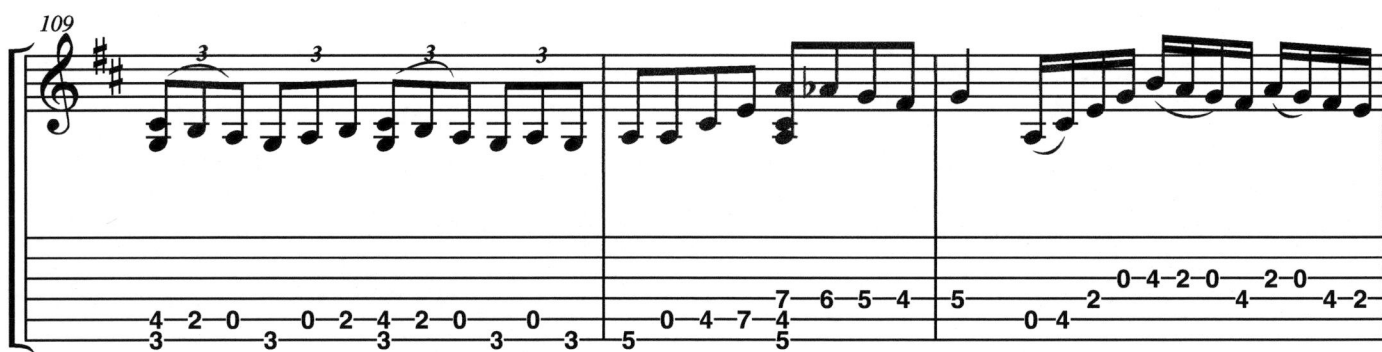

TARANTO

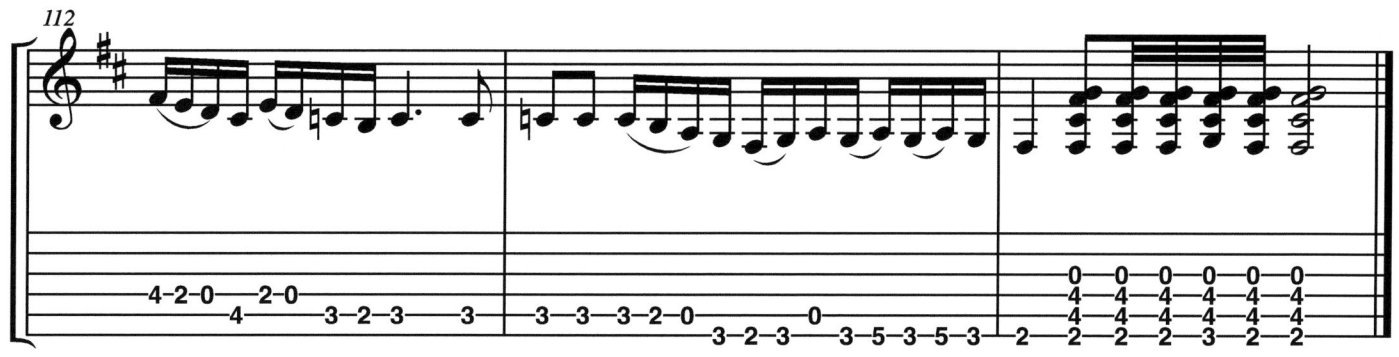

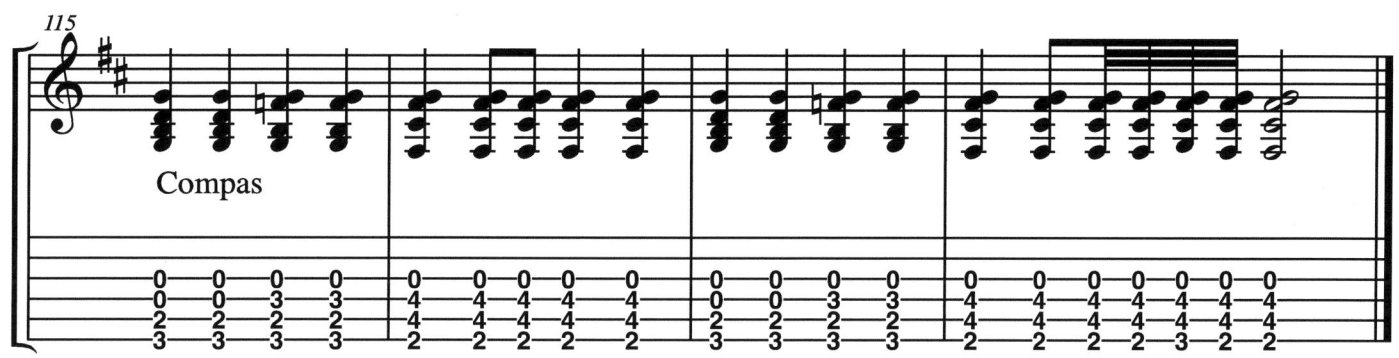

Compas

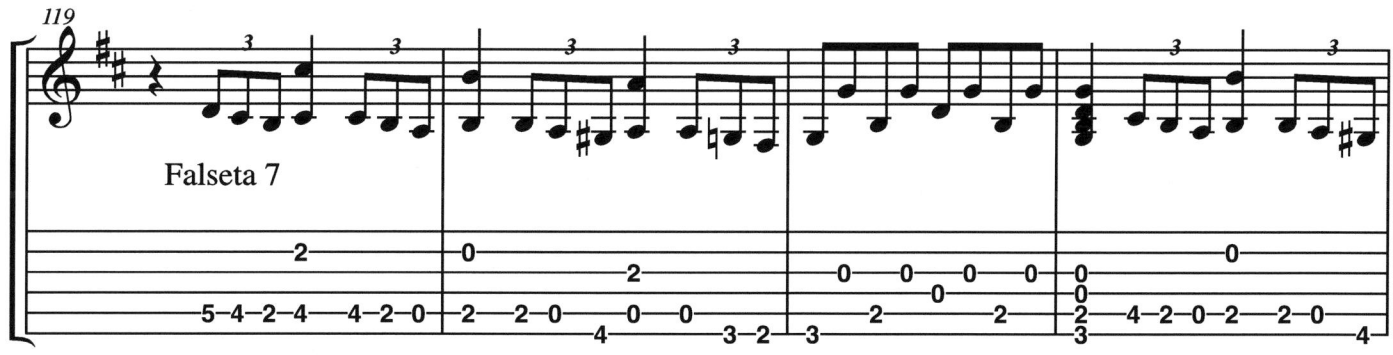

Falseta 7

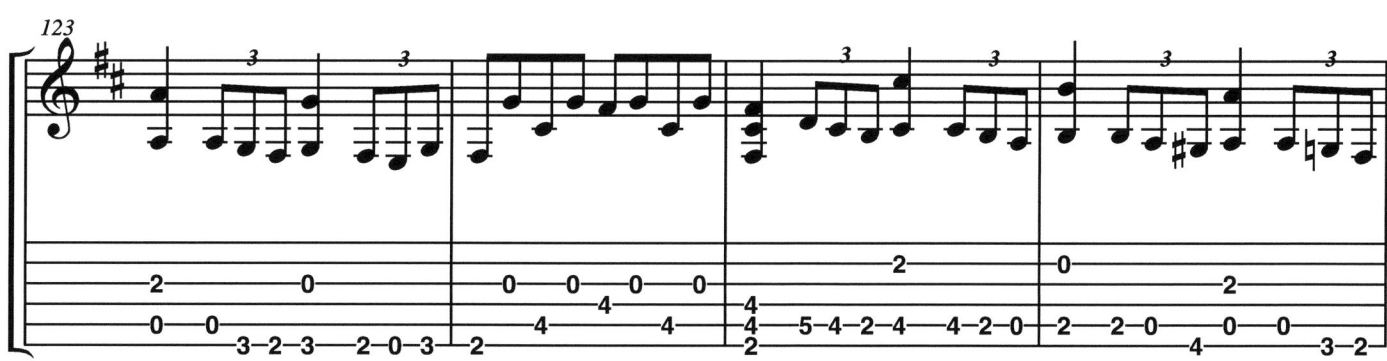

TARANTO

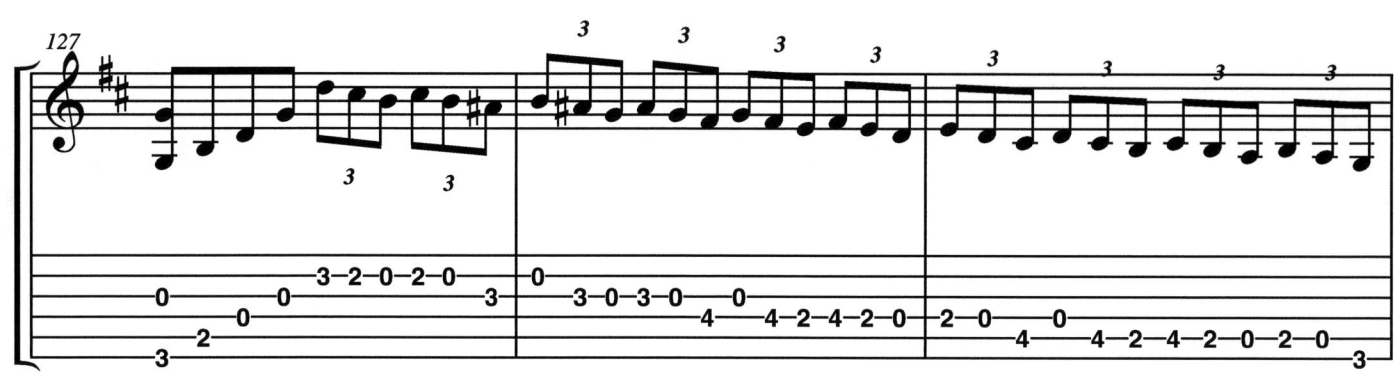
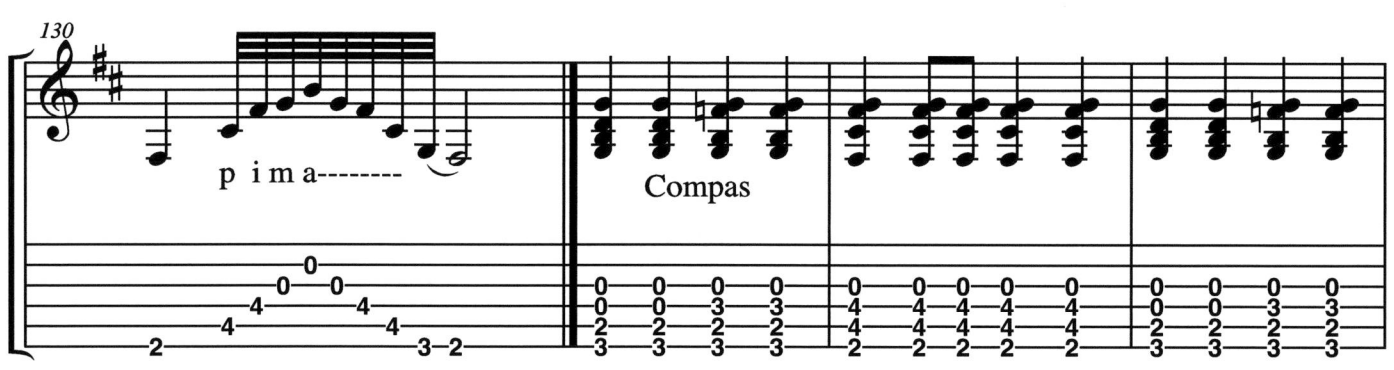
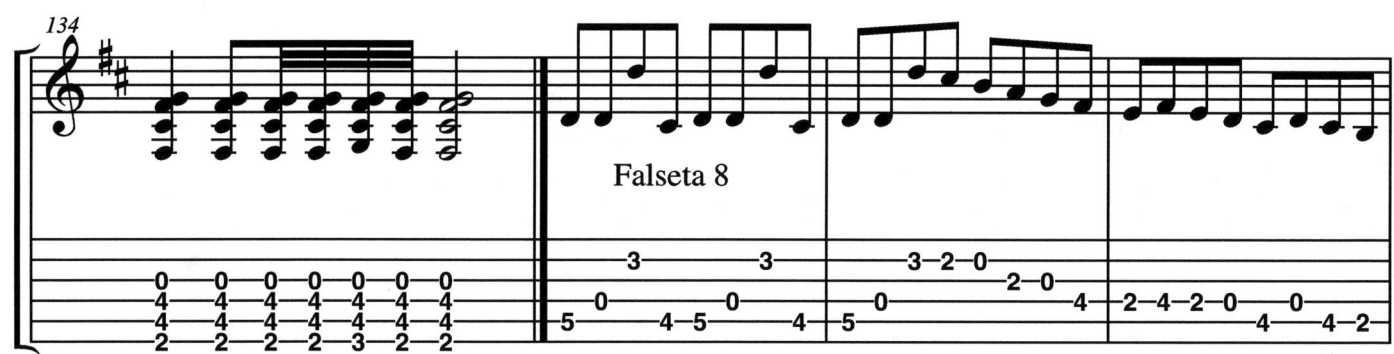
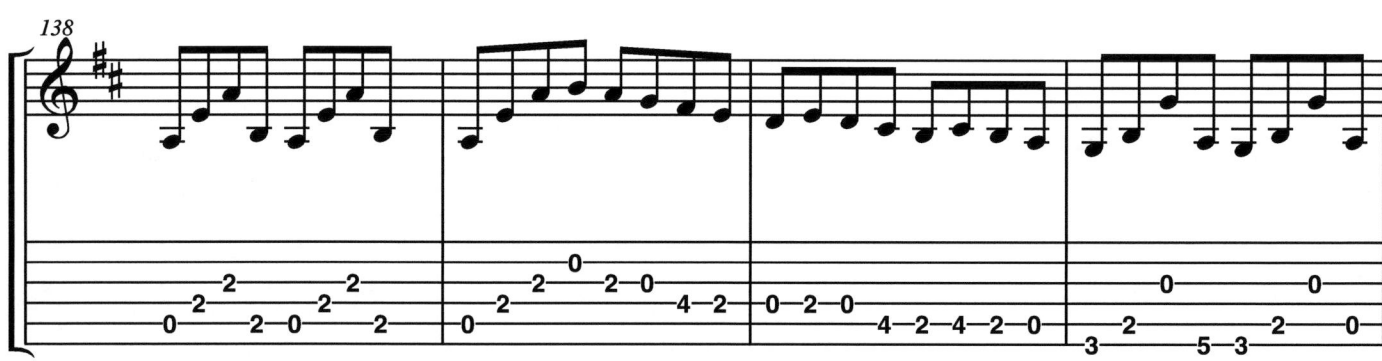

TARANTO

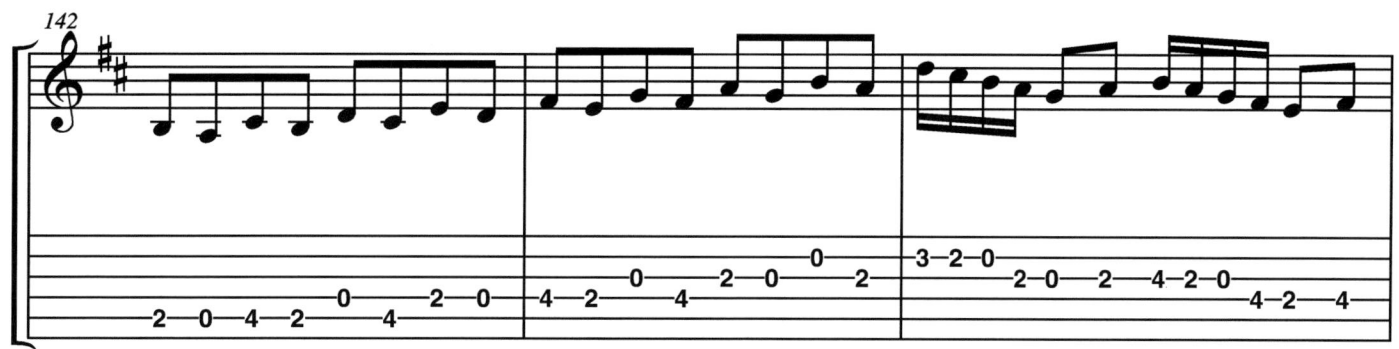
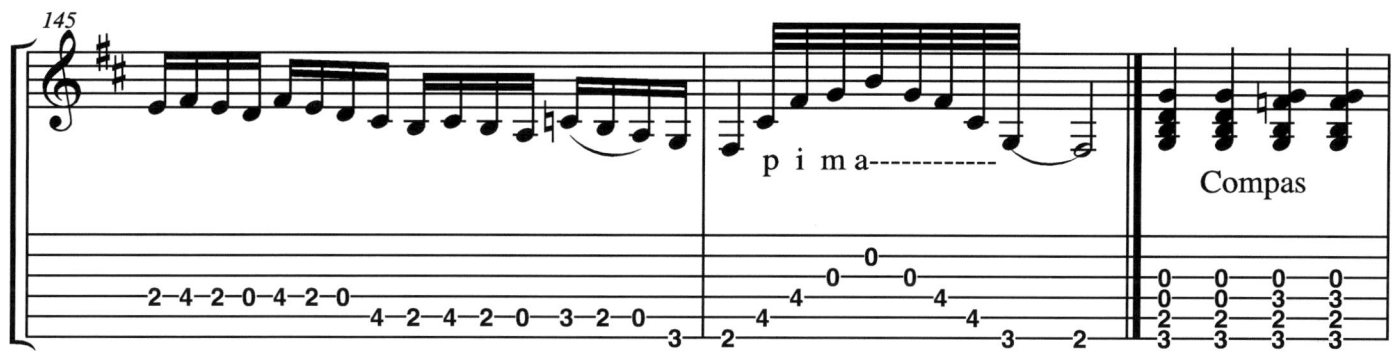
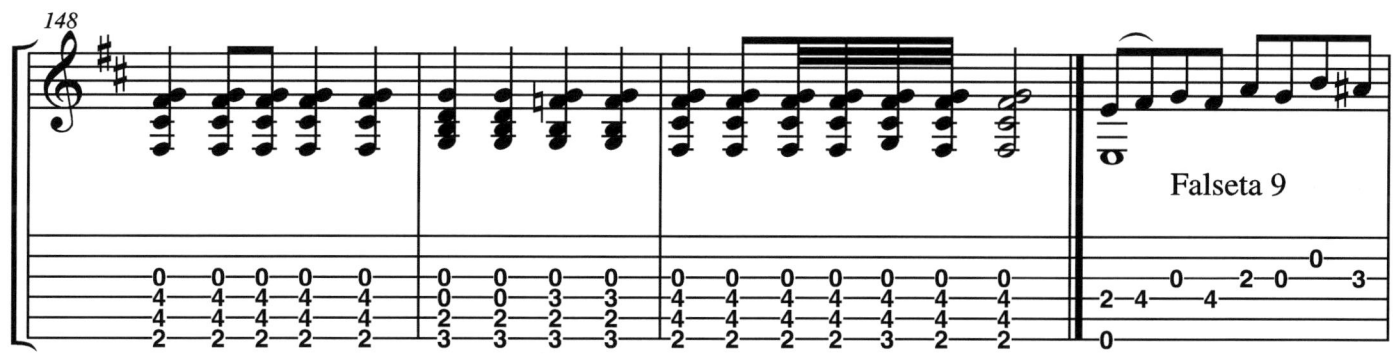
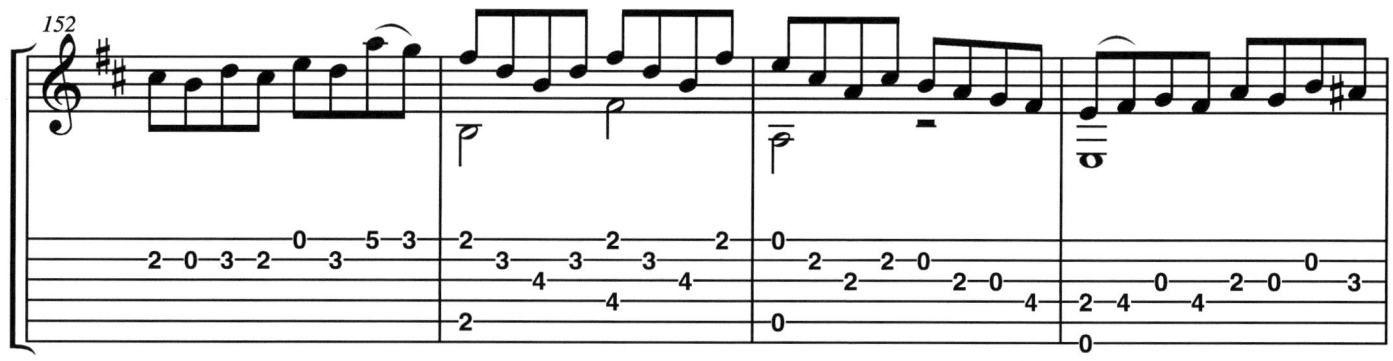

TARANTO

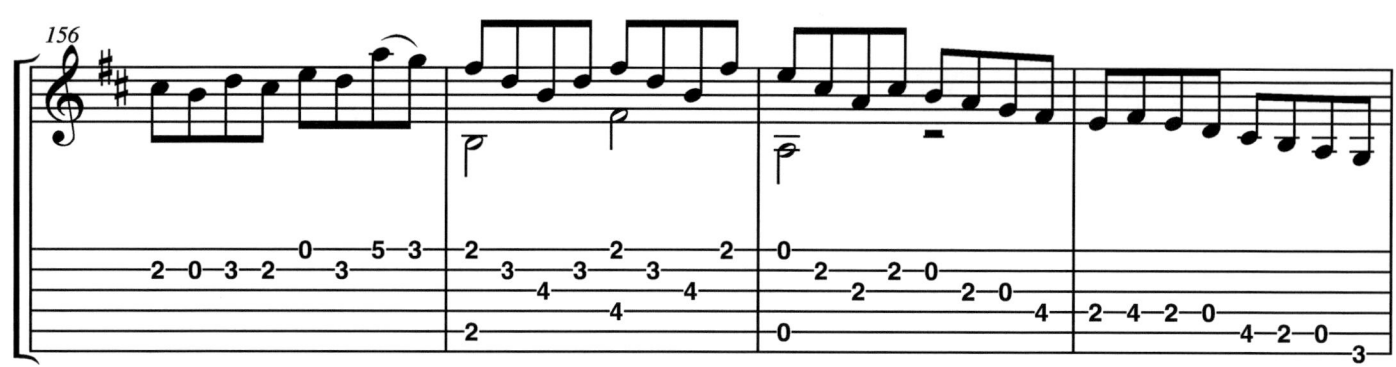
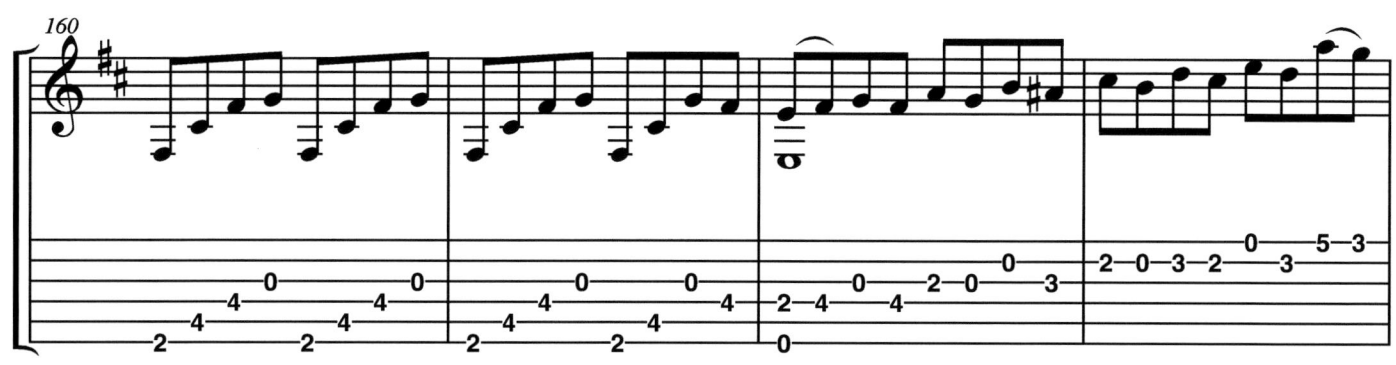
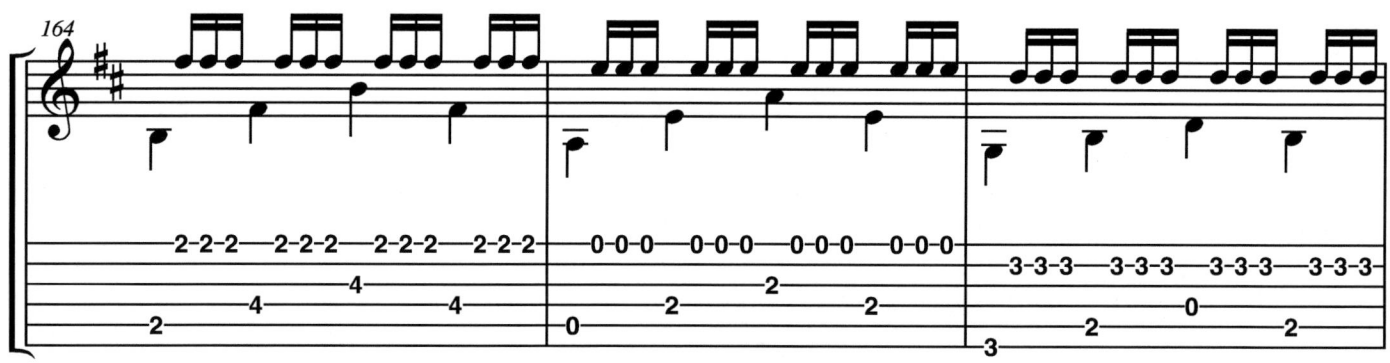
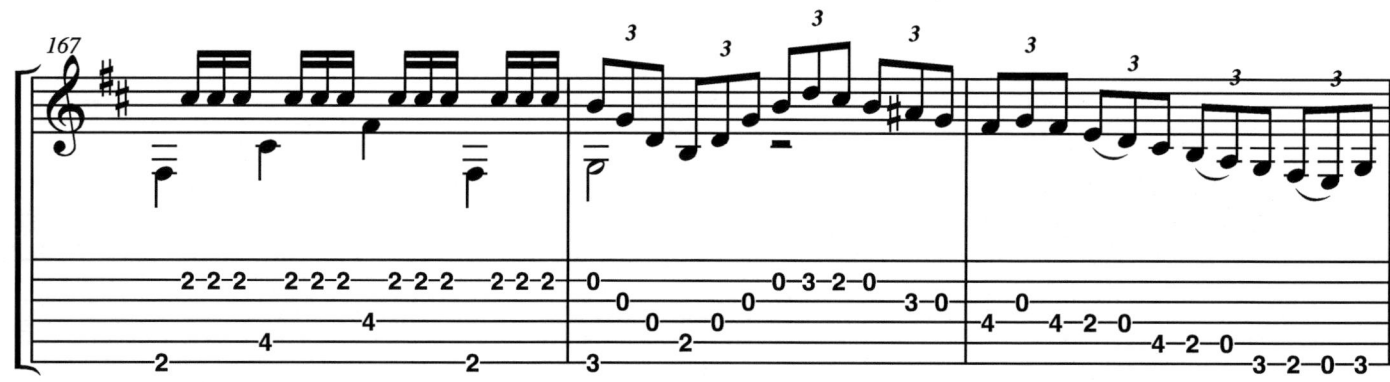

TARANTO

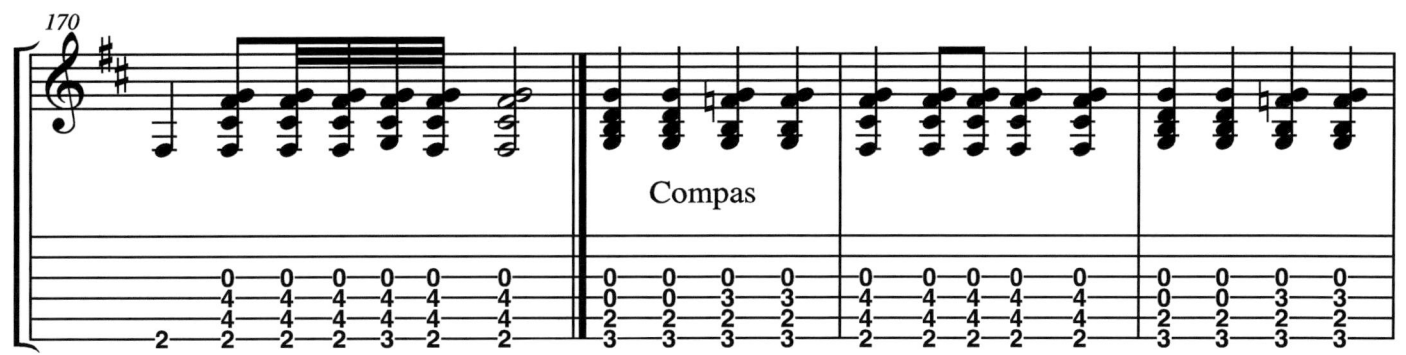

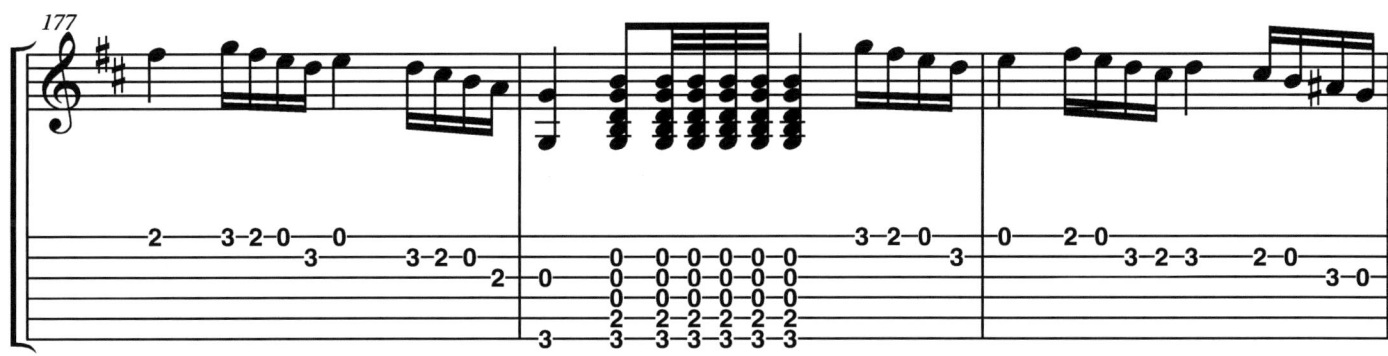
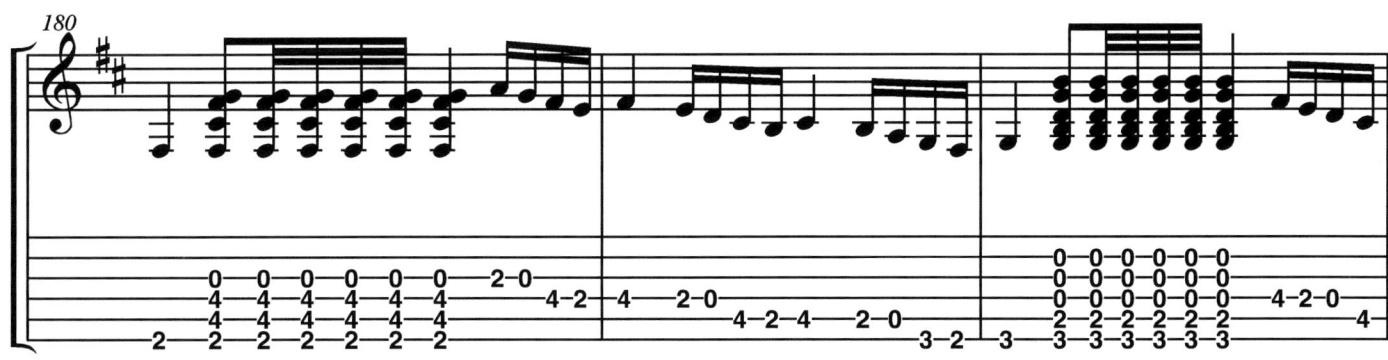

TARANTO

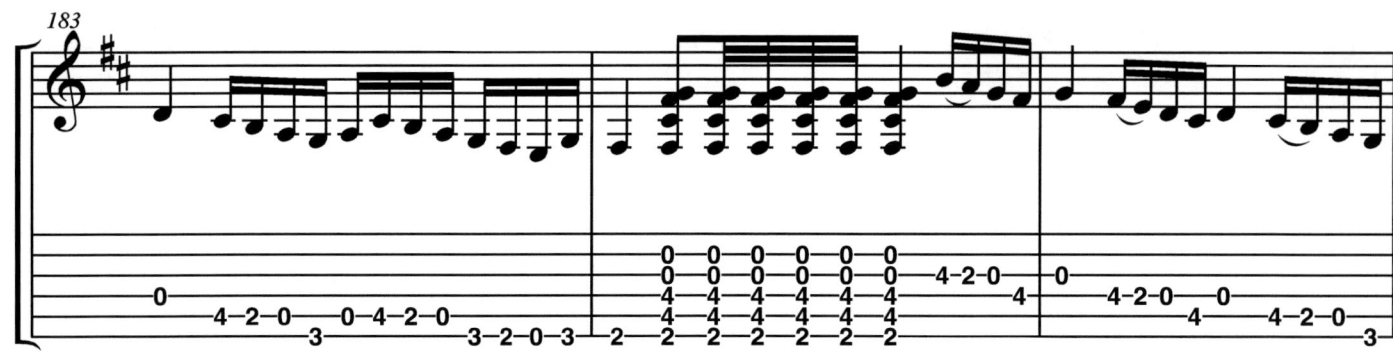
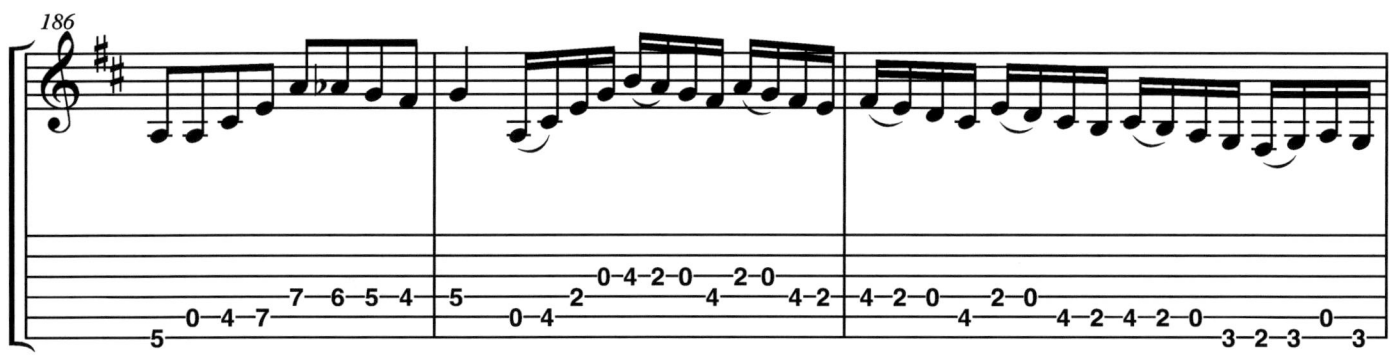
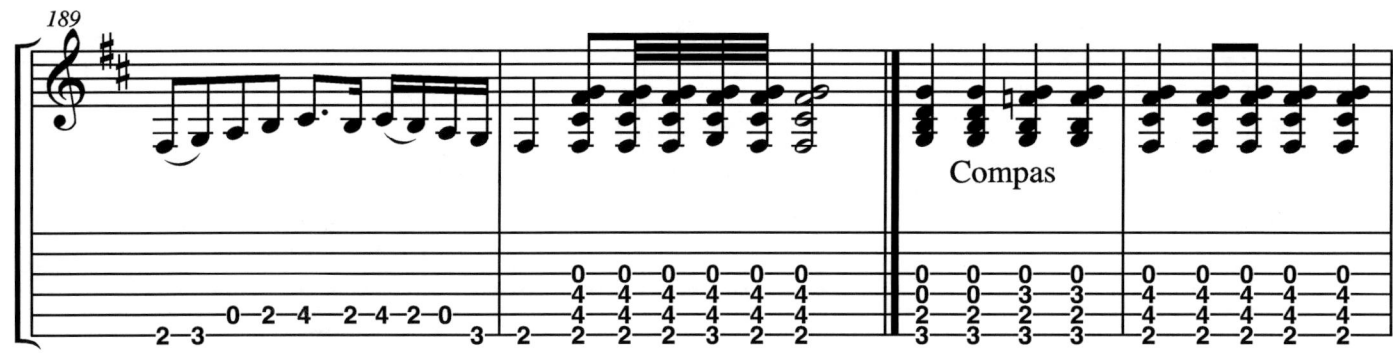

Falseta 11

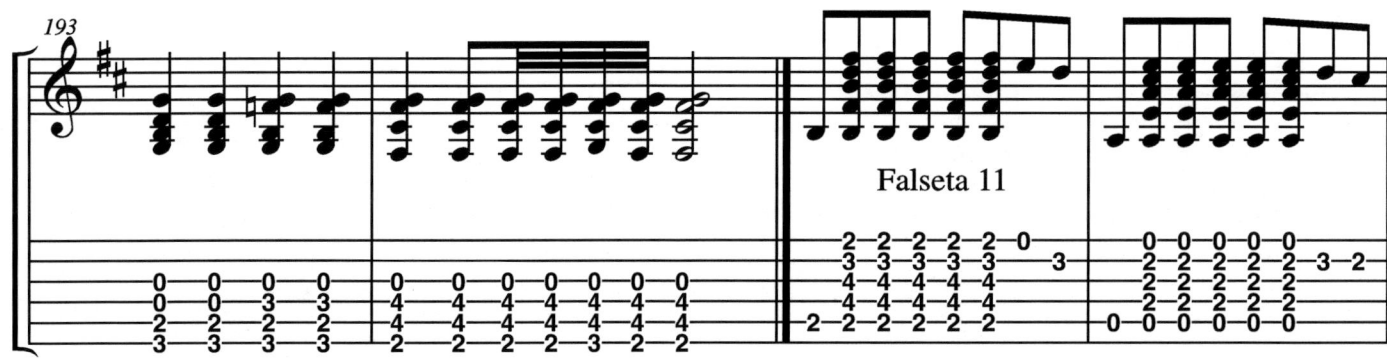

TARANTO

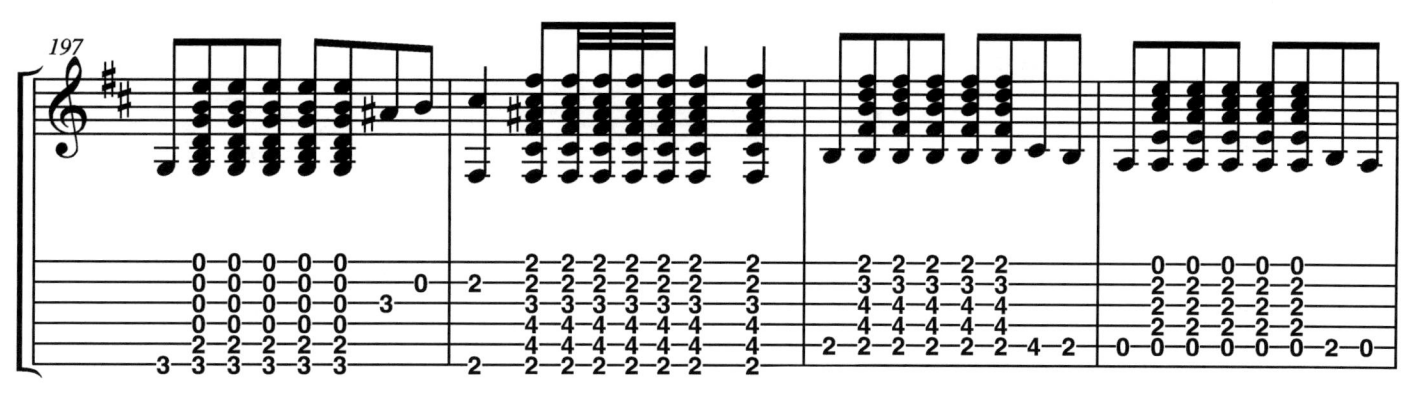
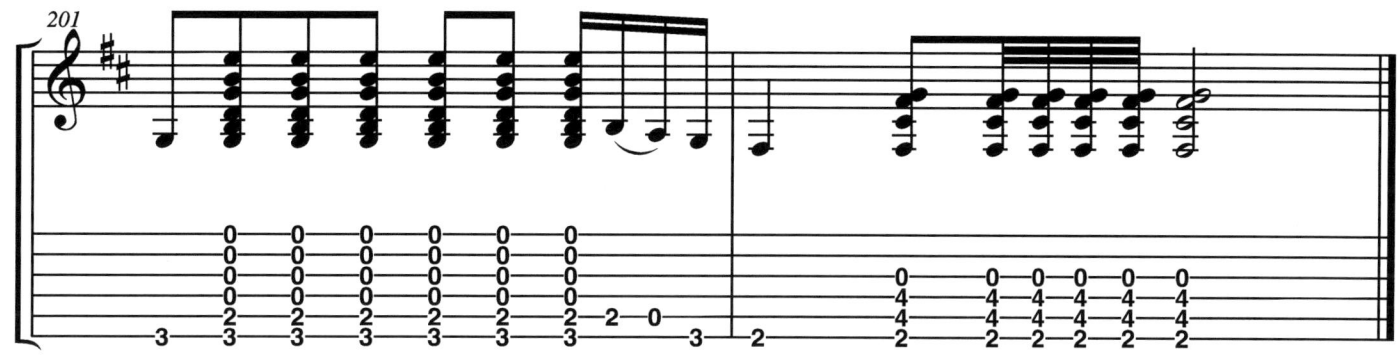

Compas

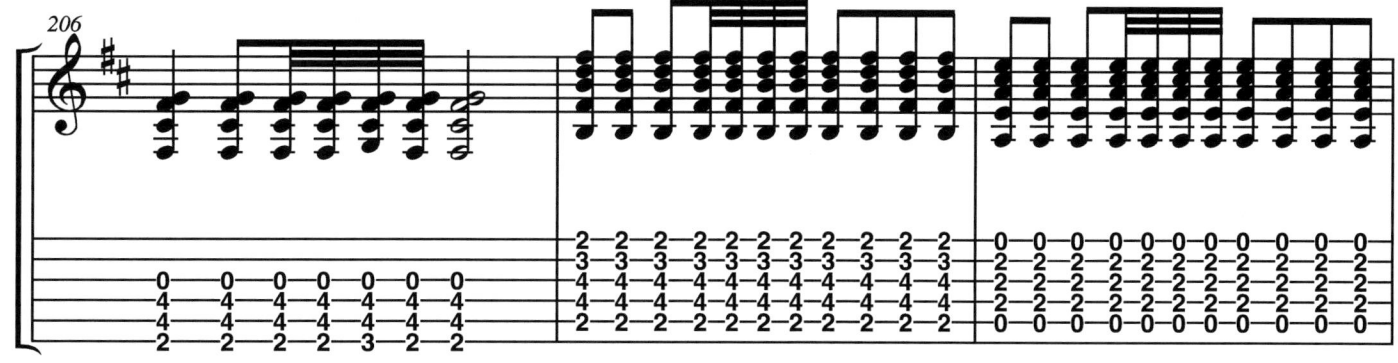

TARANTO

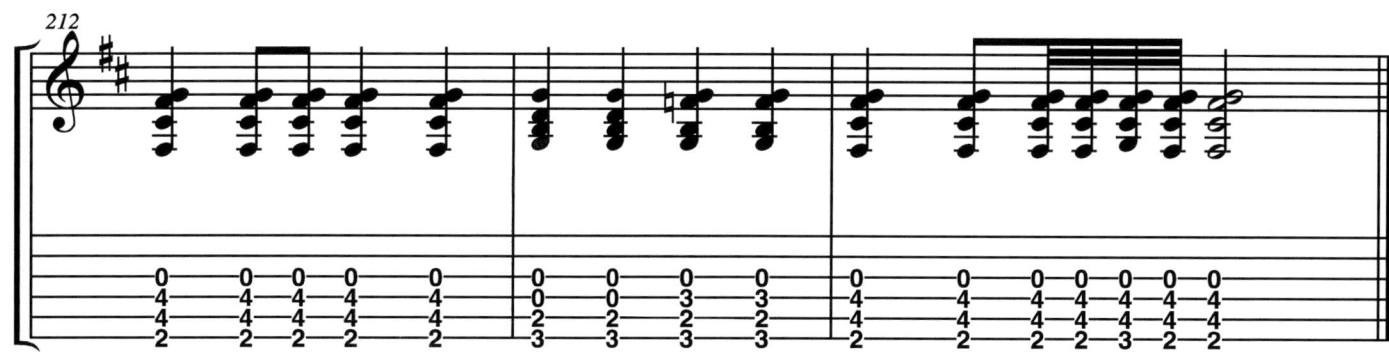

This page has been left black to avoid awkward page turns.

TIENTOS

Strum every compas in the same manner

TIENTOS

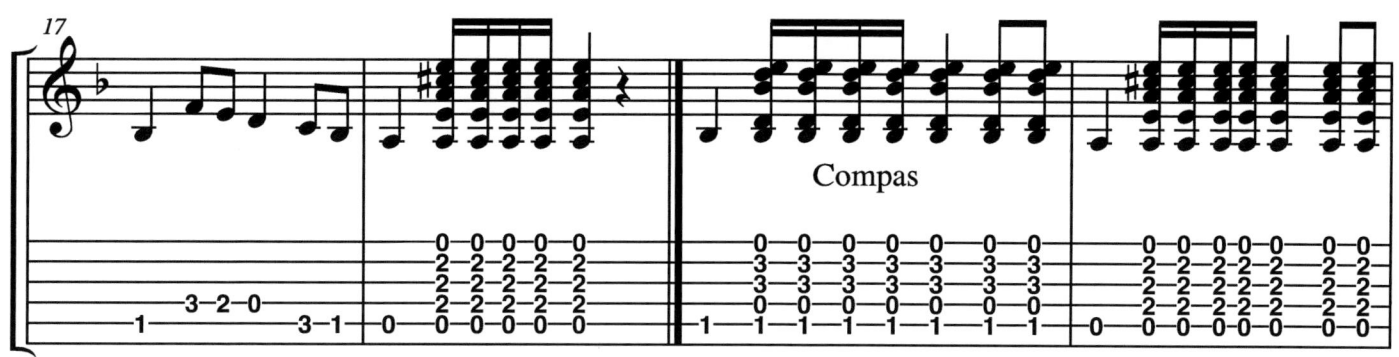

Compas

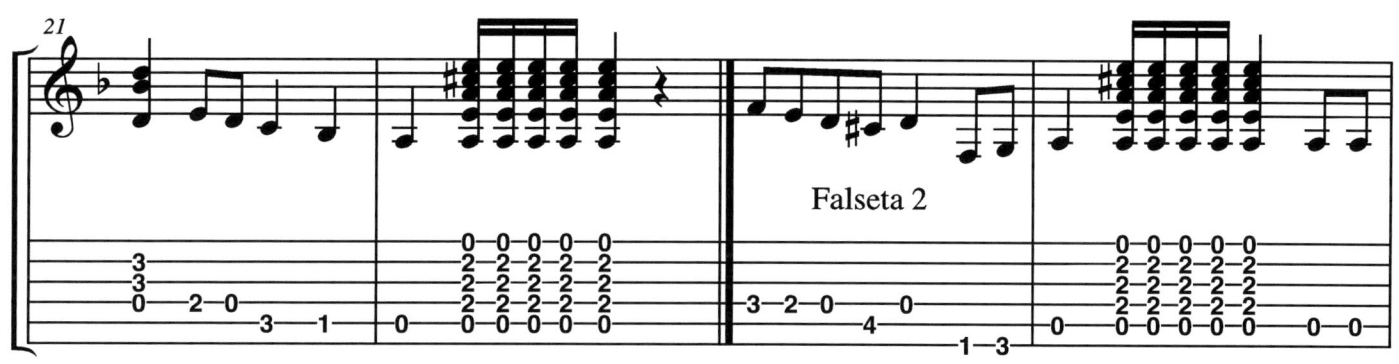

Falseta 2

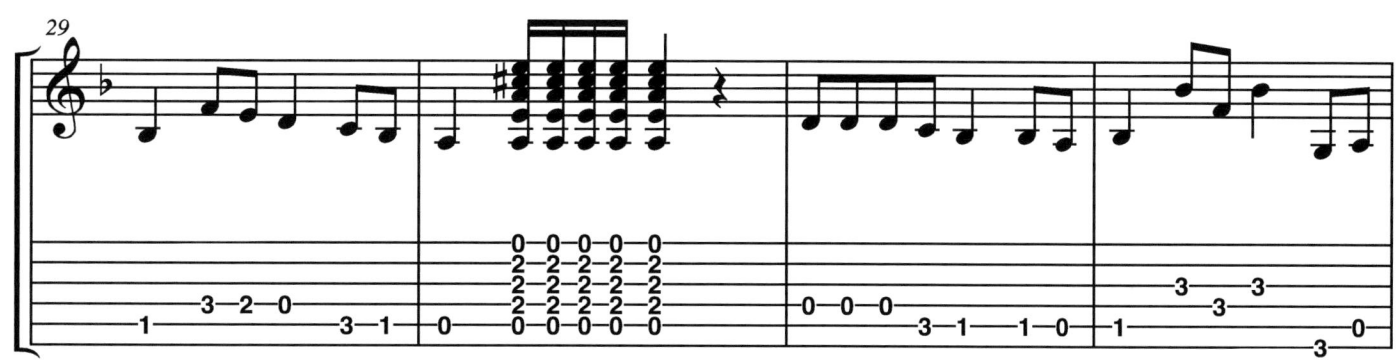

TIENTOS

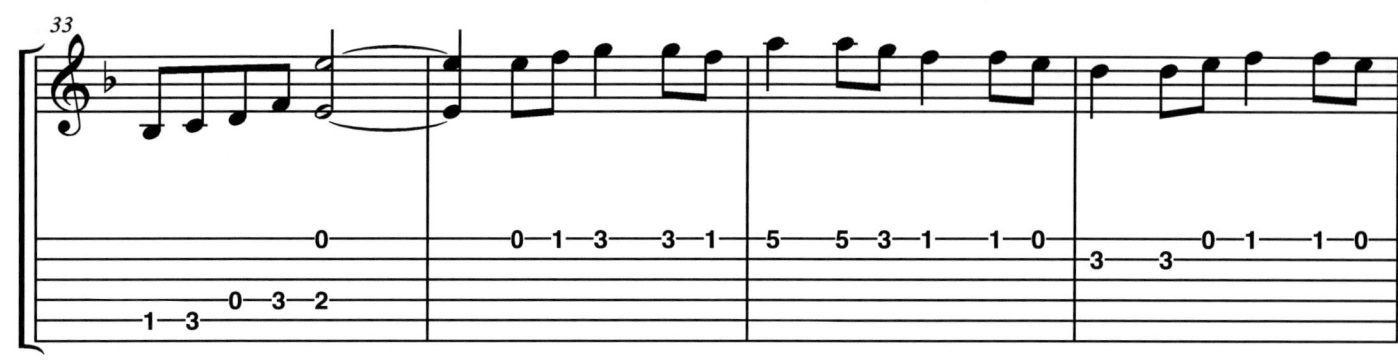
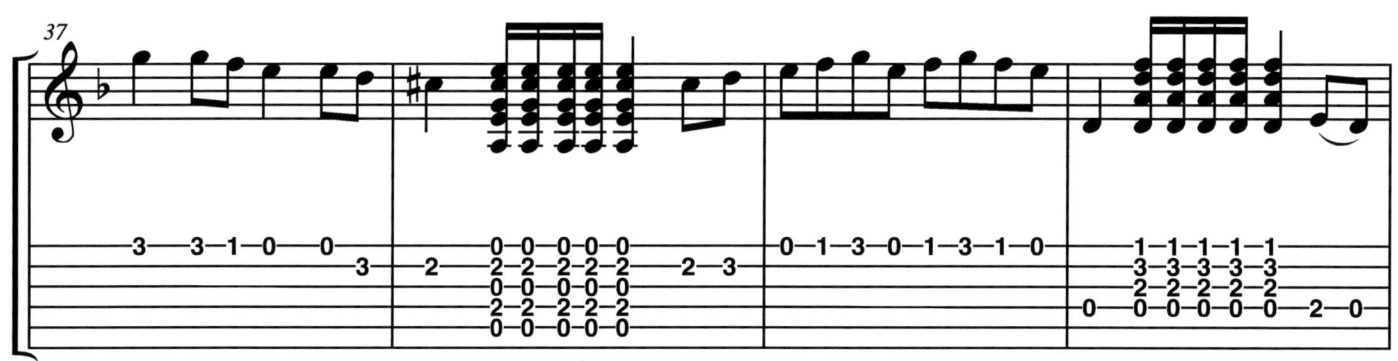
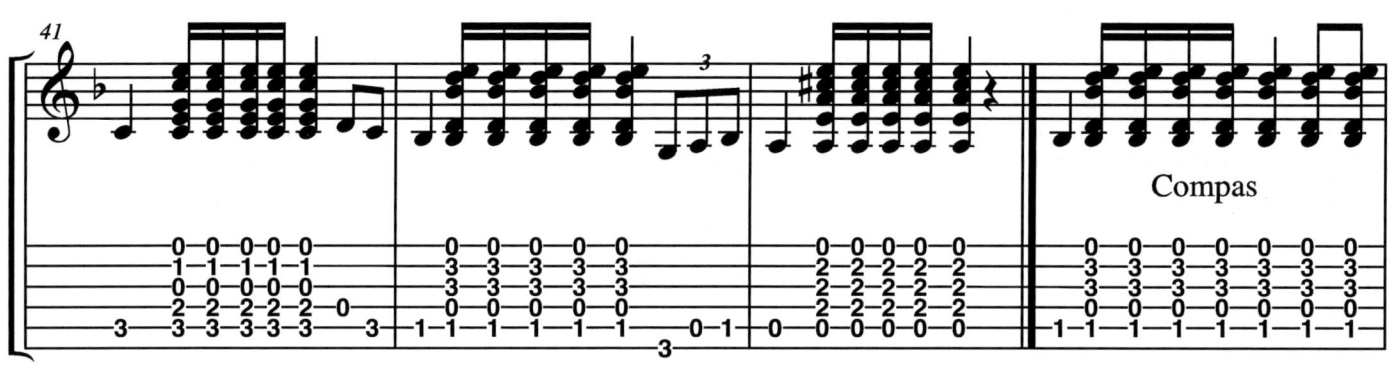
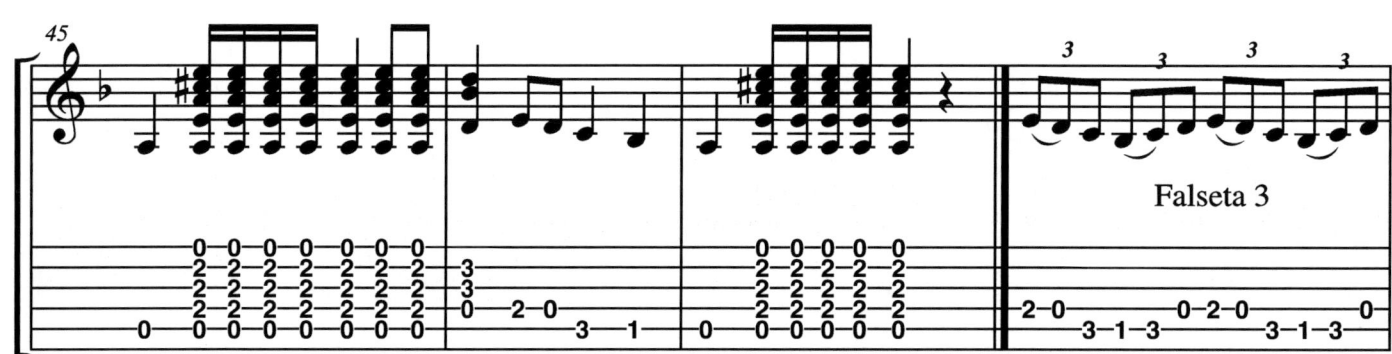

TIENTOS

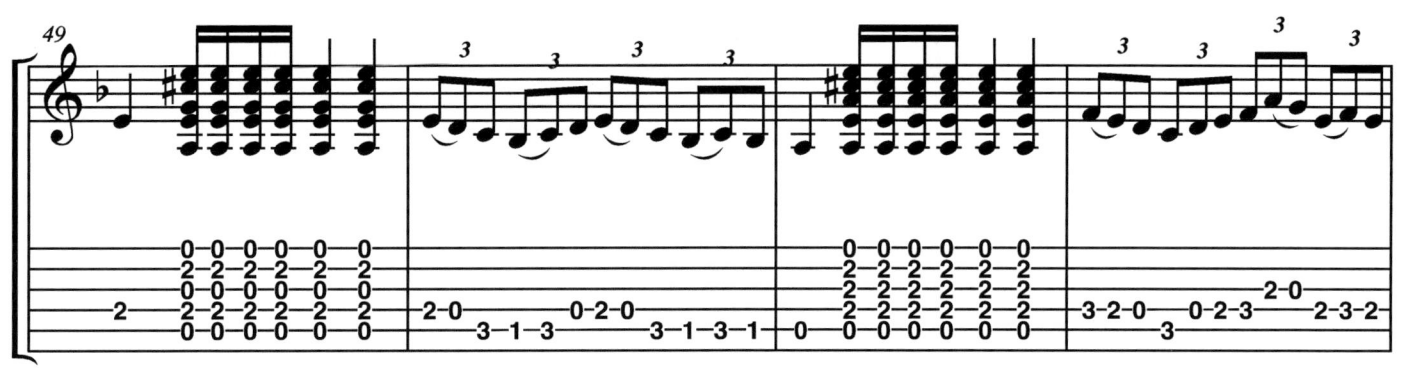

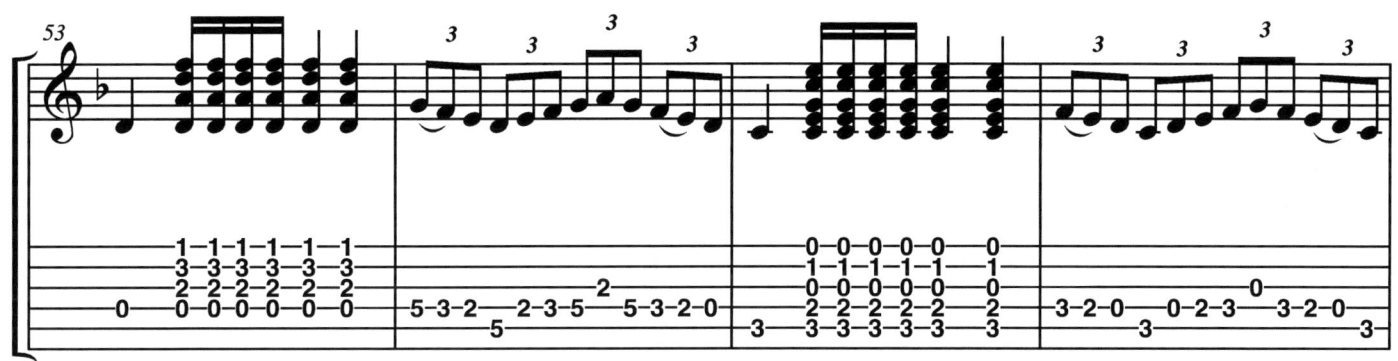

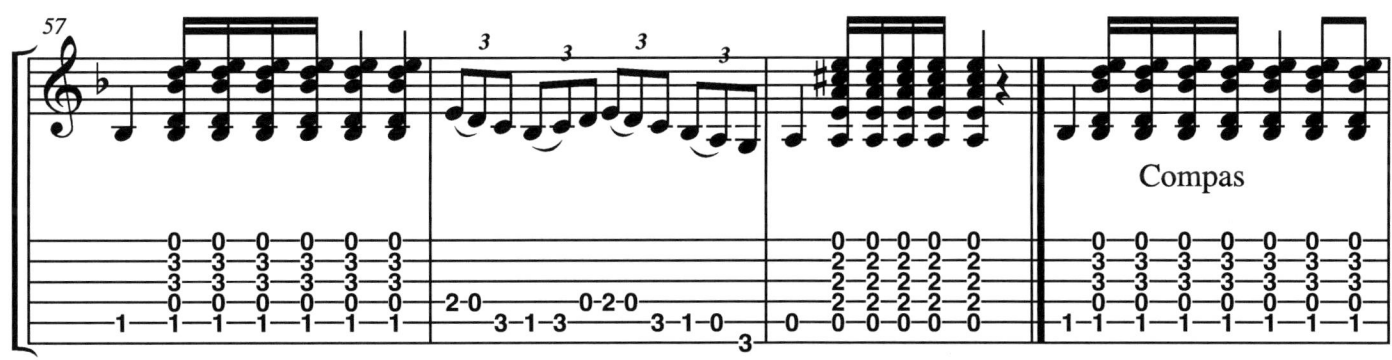

Compas

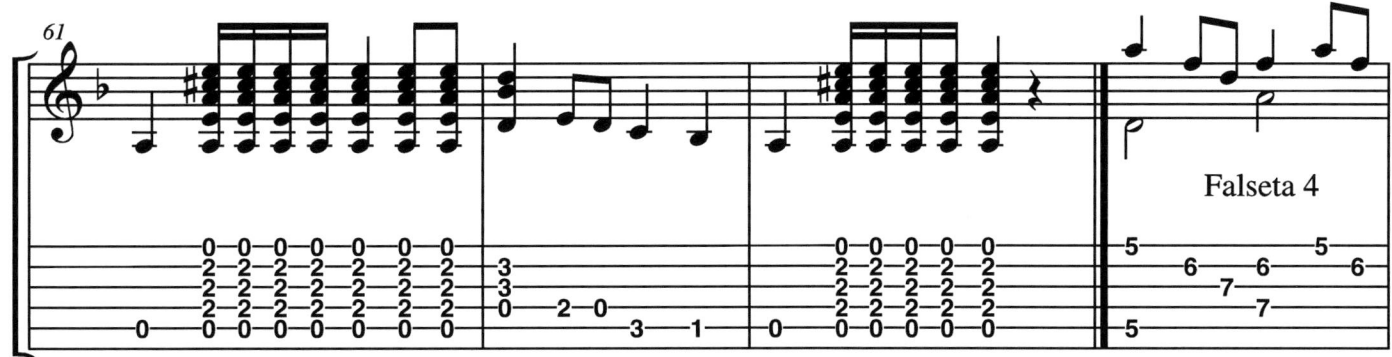

Falseta 4

TIENTOS

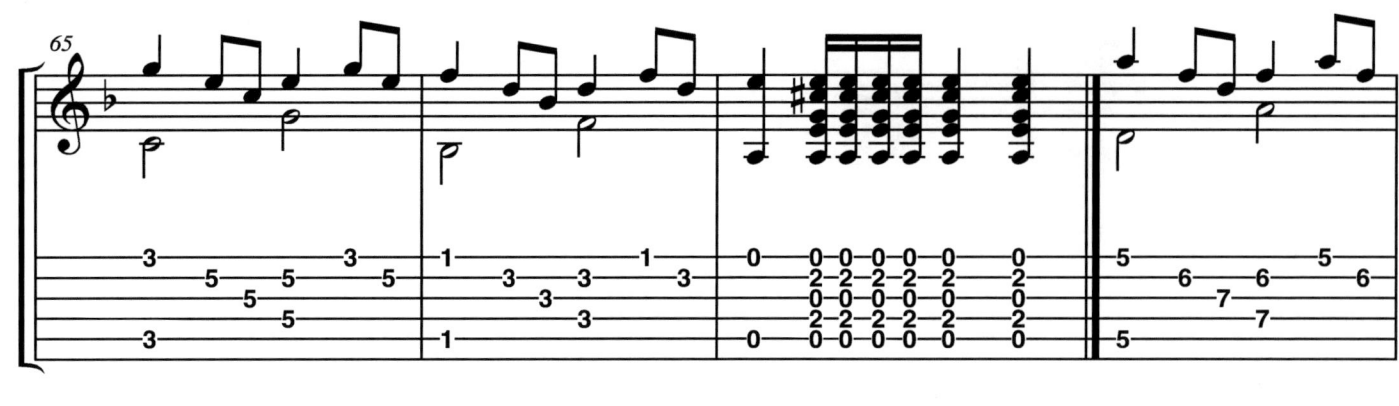
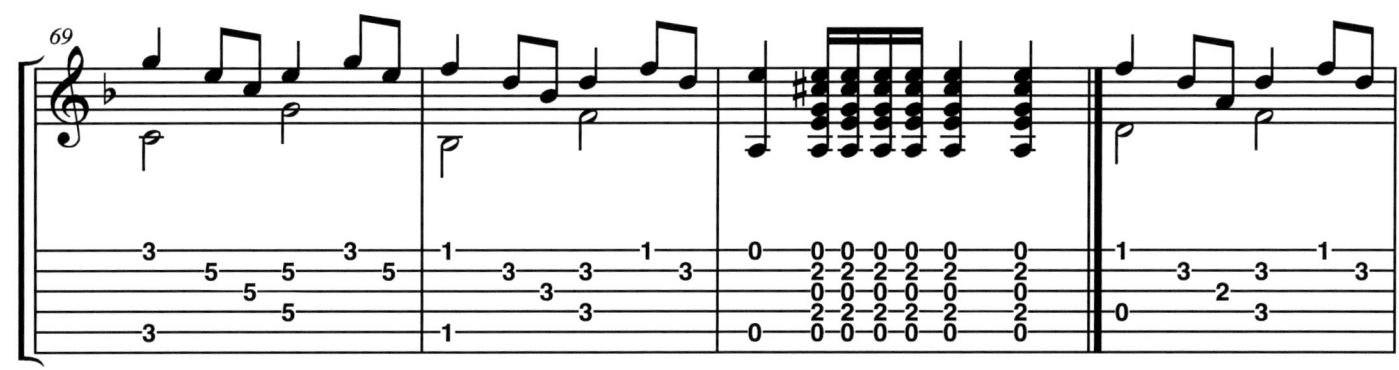
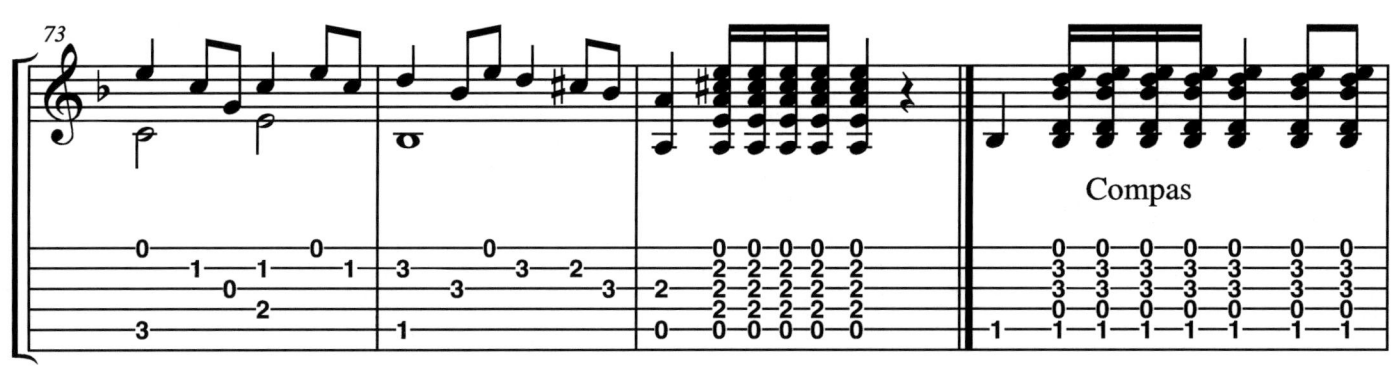

Compas

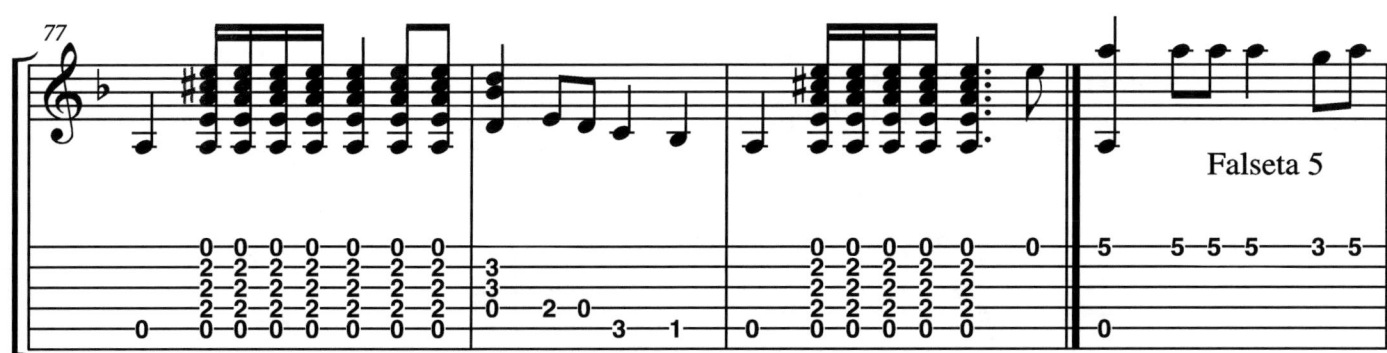

Falseta 5

TIENTOS

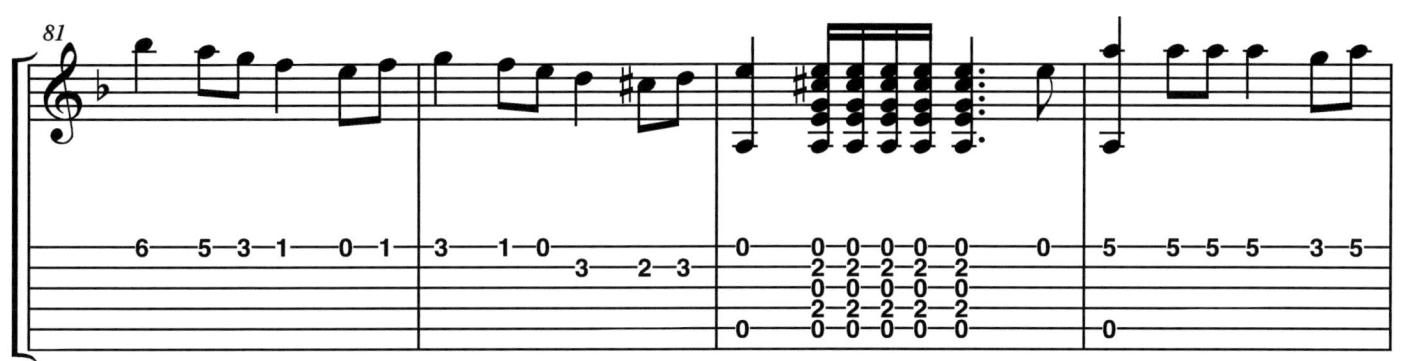
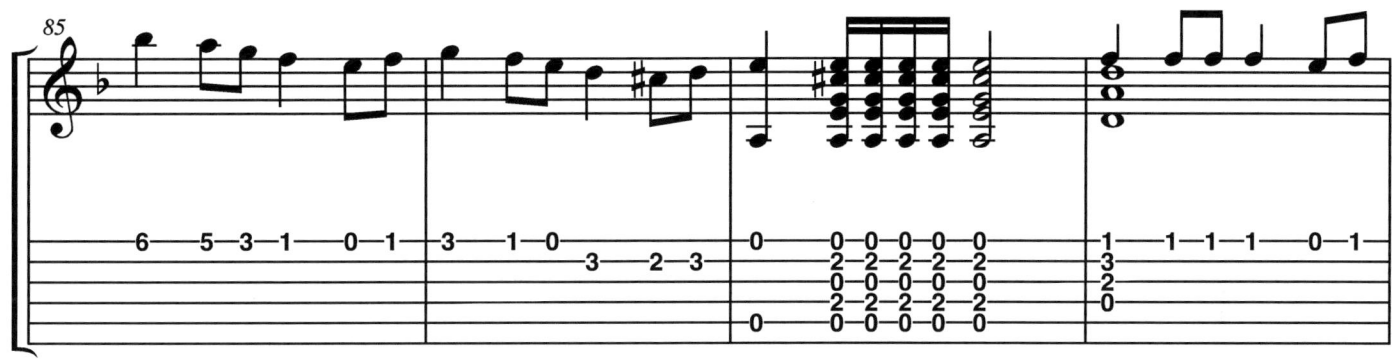
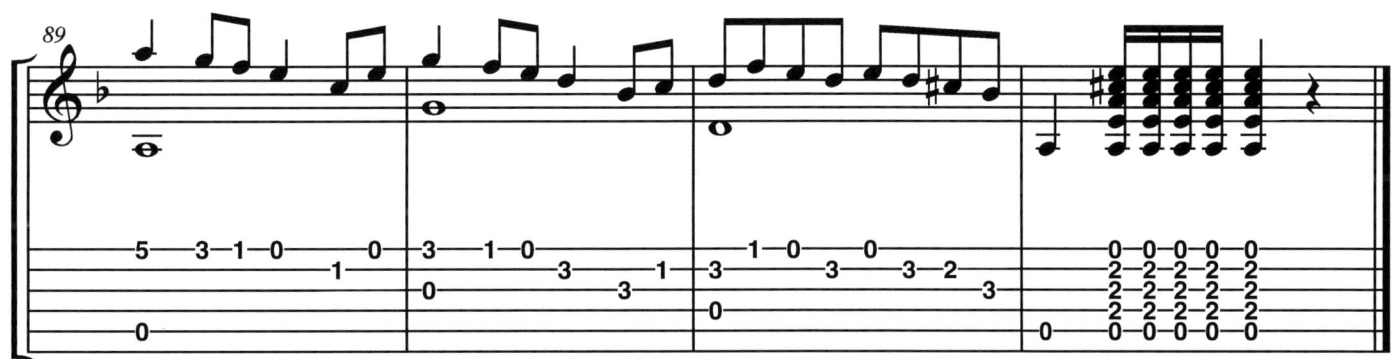
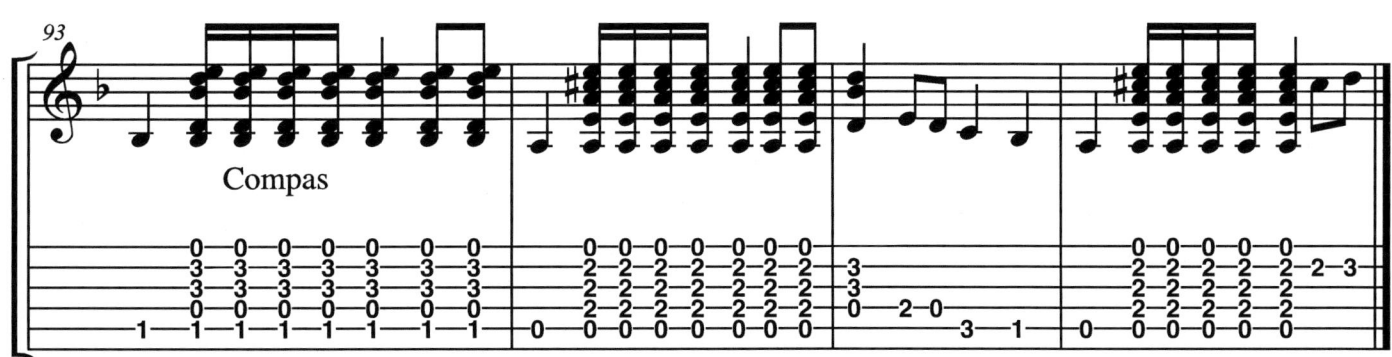

TIENTOS

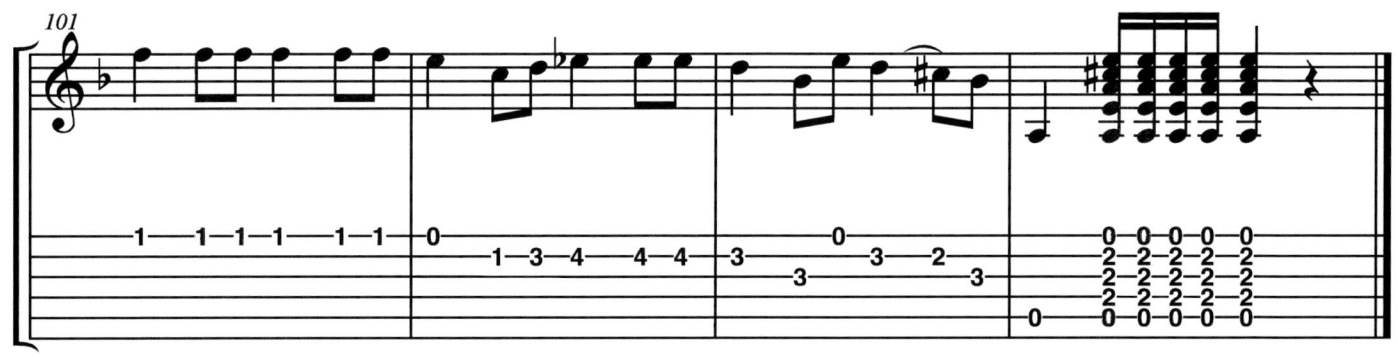

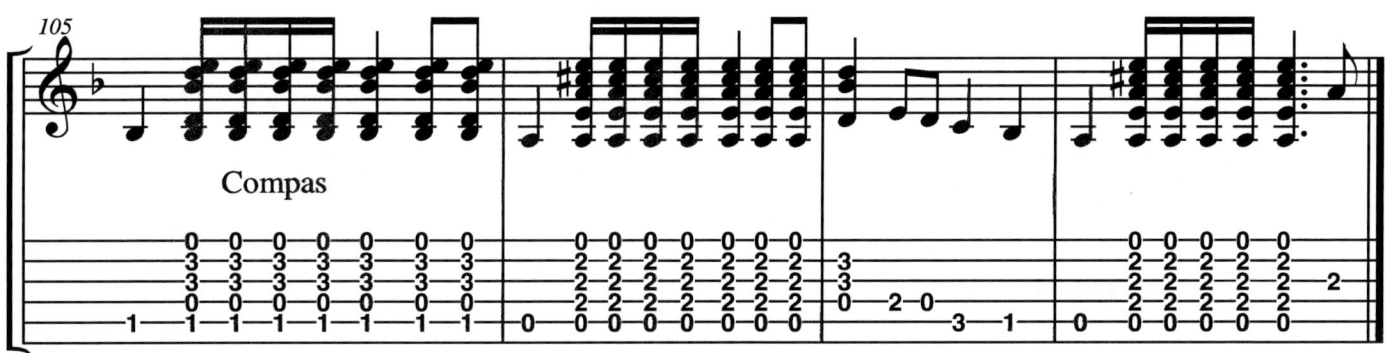

TIENTOS

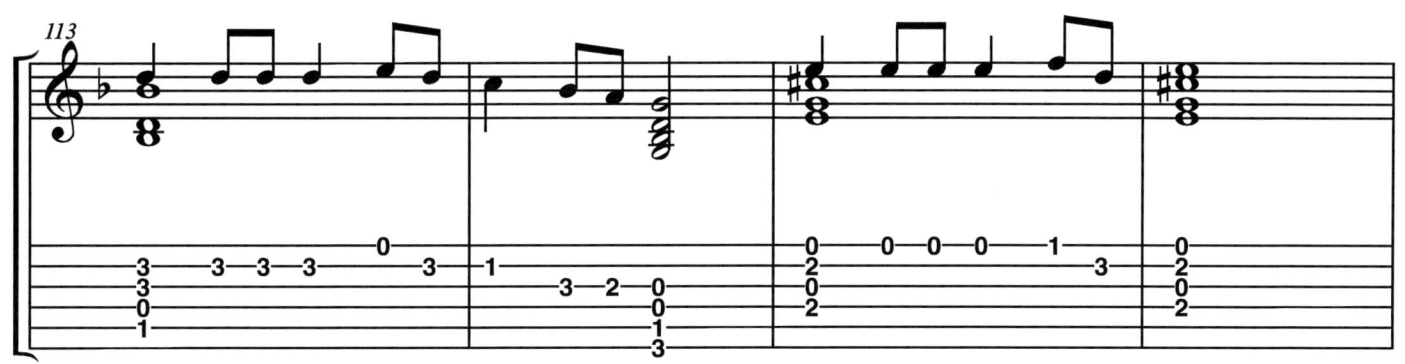

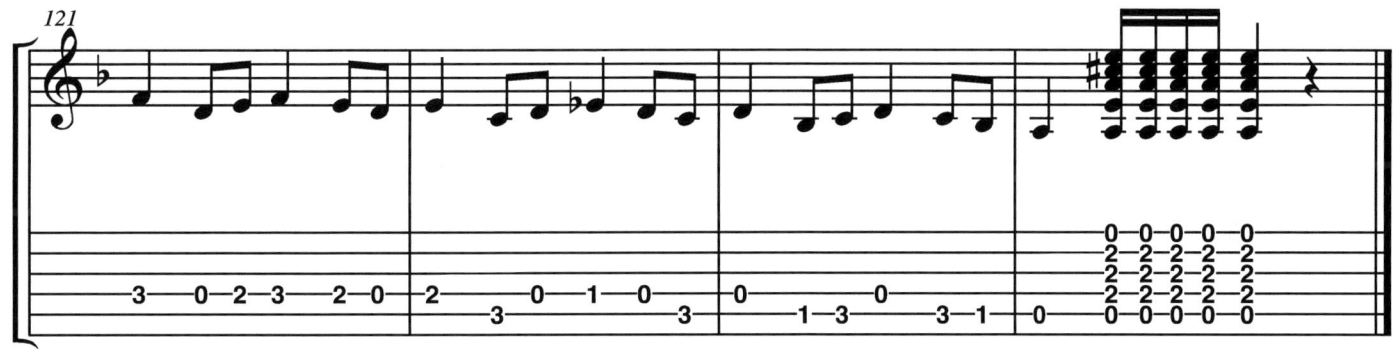
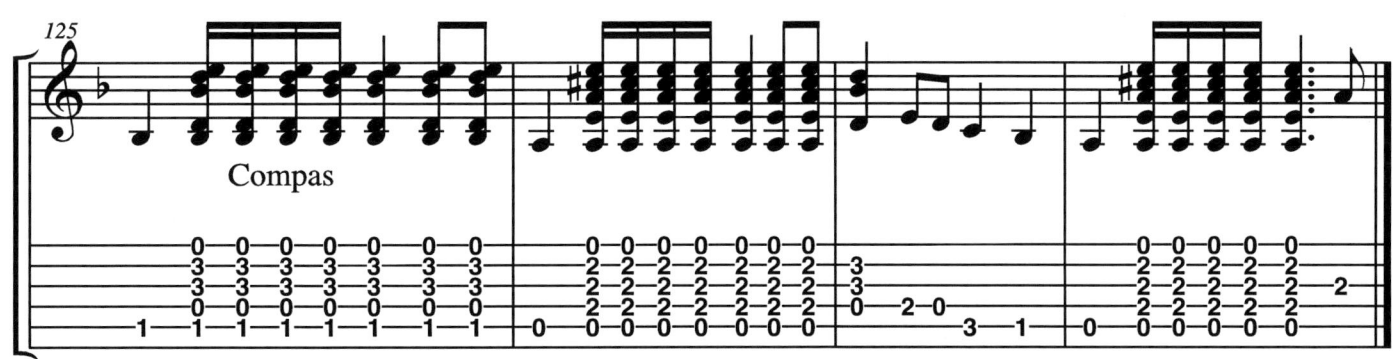

Compas

TIENTOS

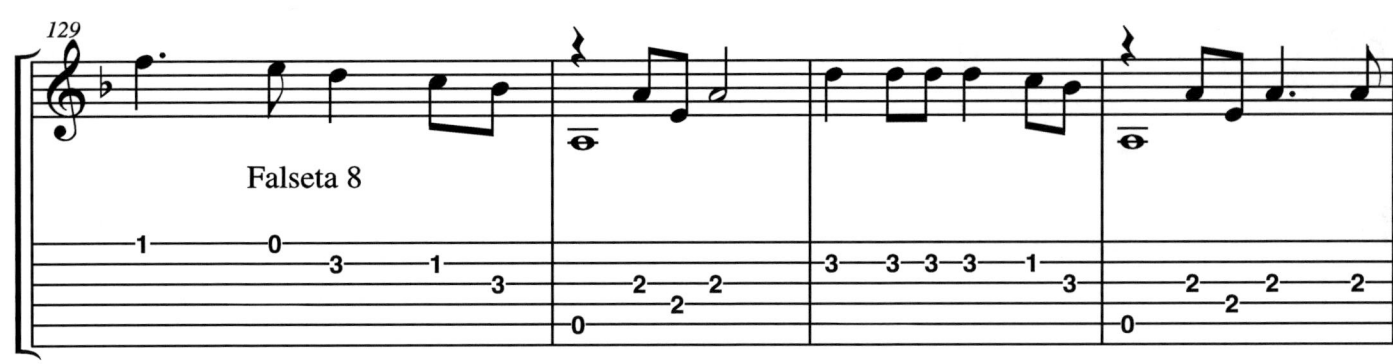

Falseta 8

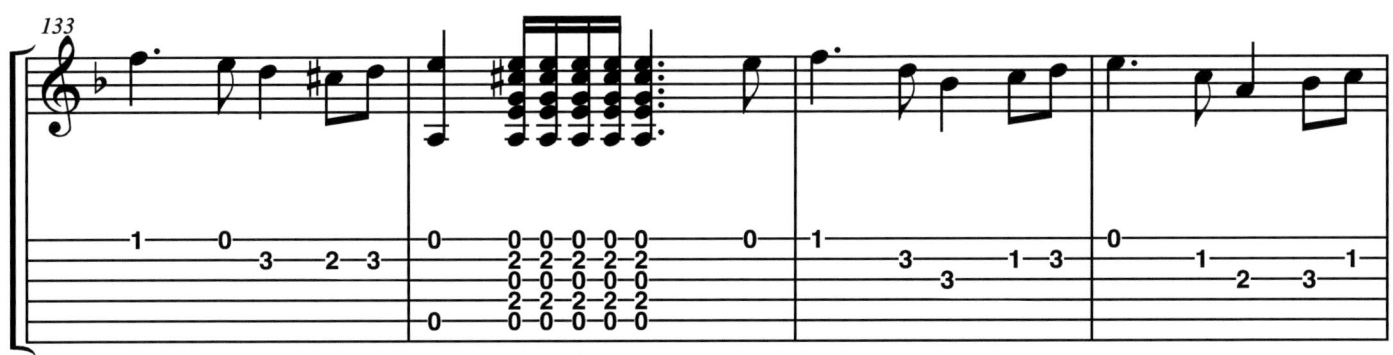

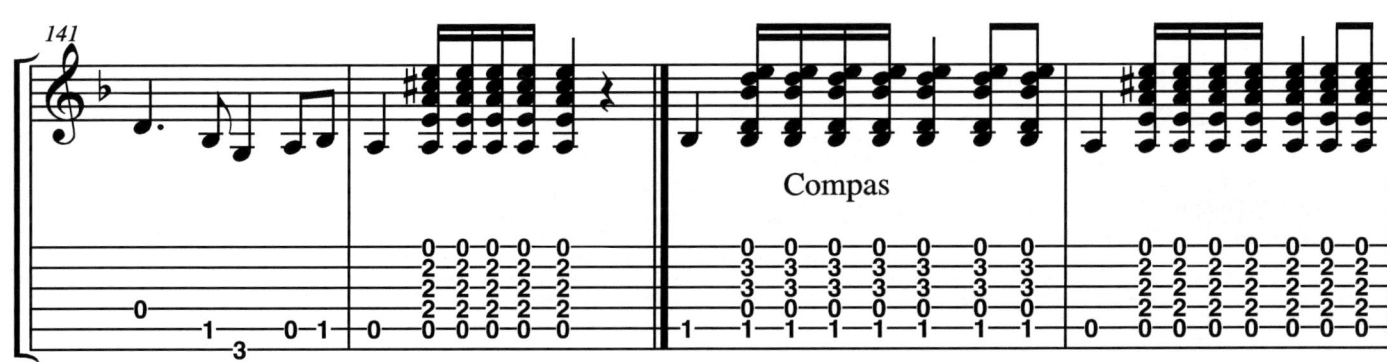

Compas

TIENTOS

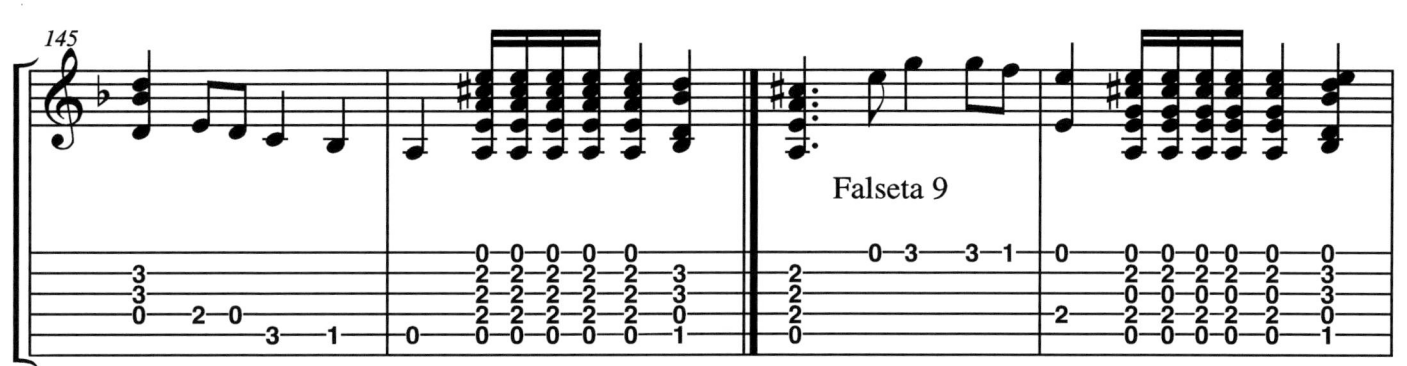

Falseta 9

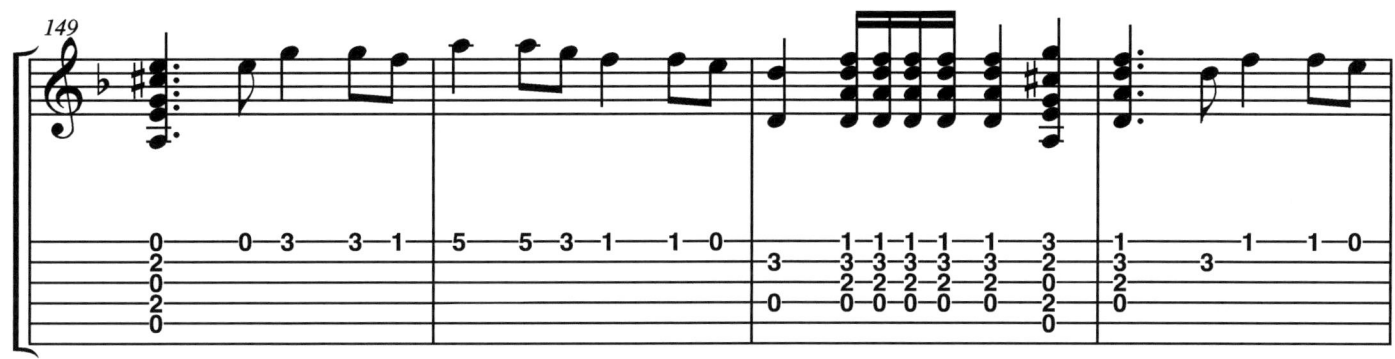

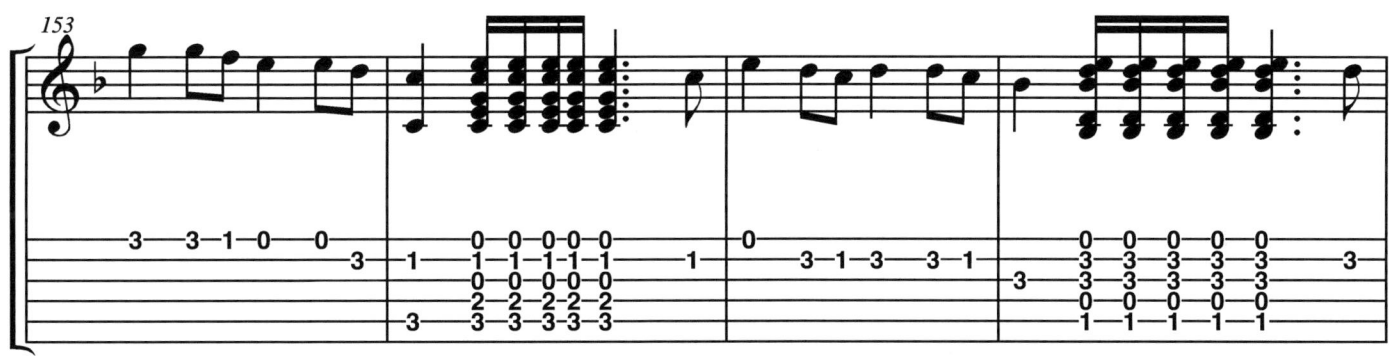

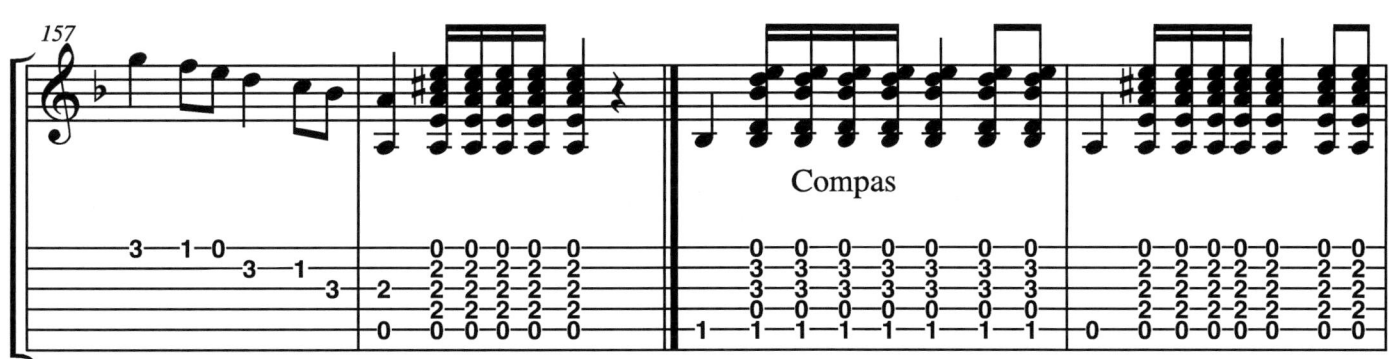

Compas

TIENTOS

Falseta 10

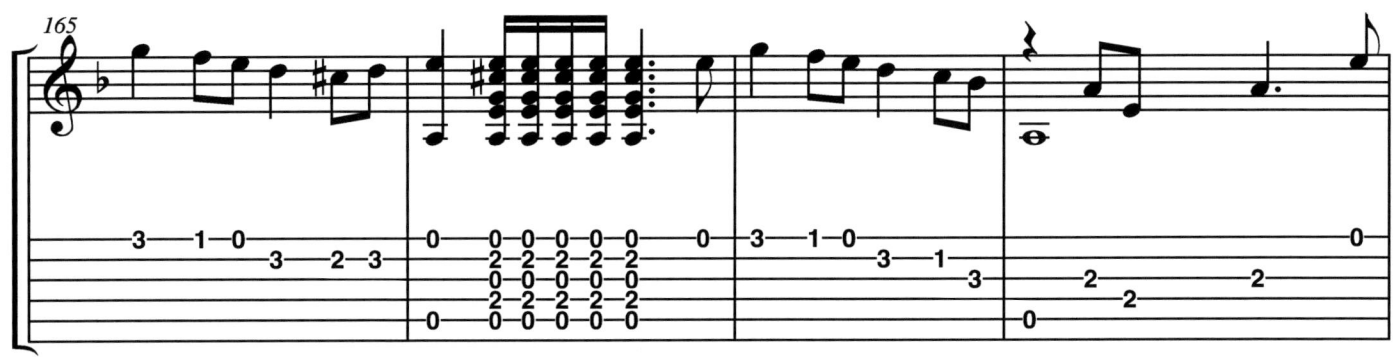

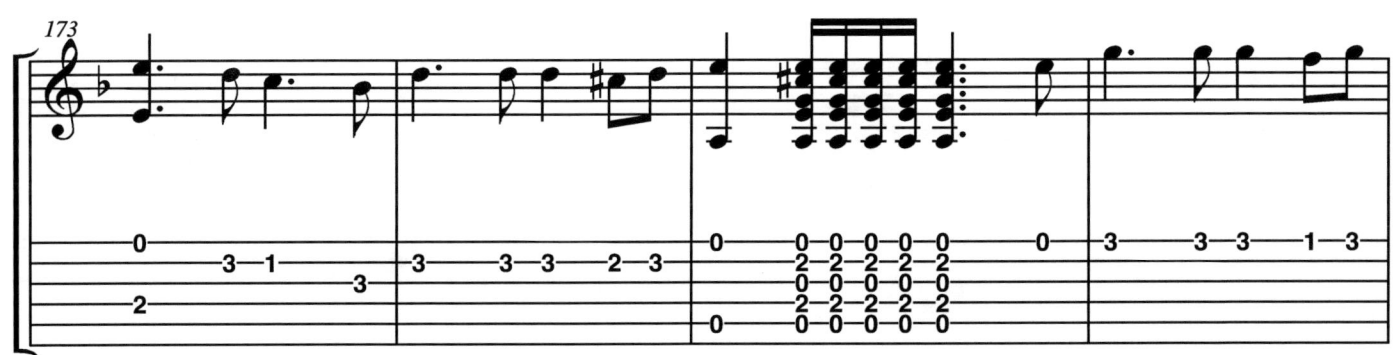

TIENTOS

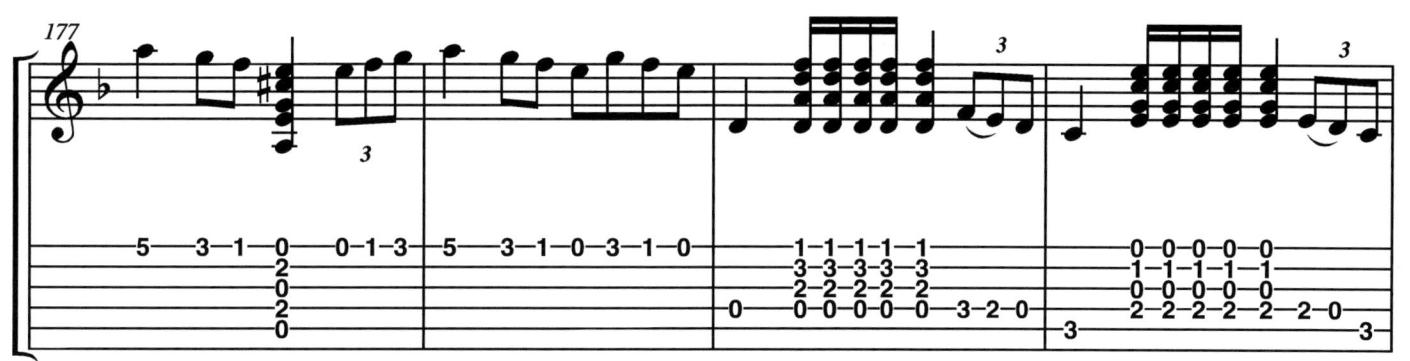
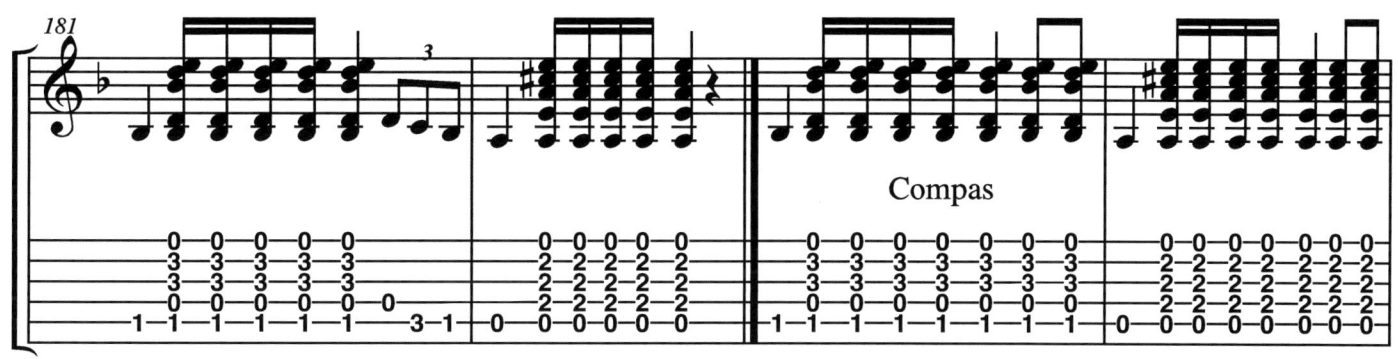
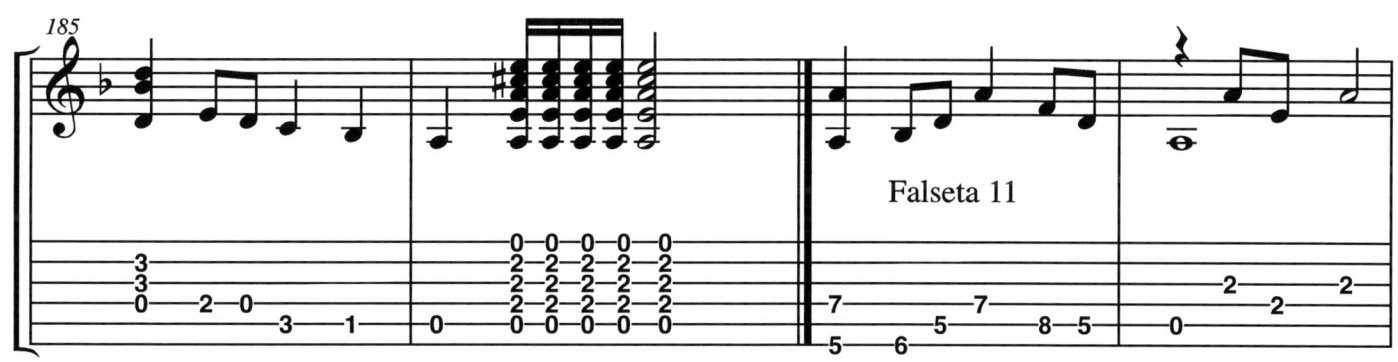

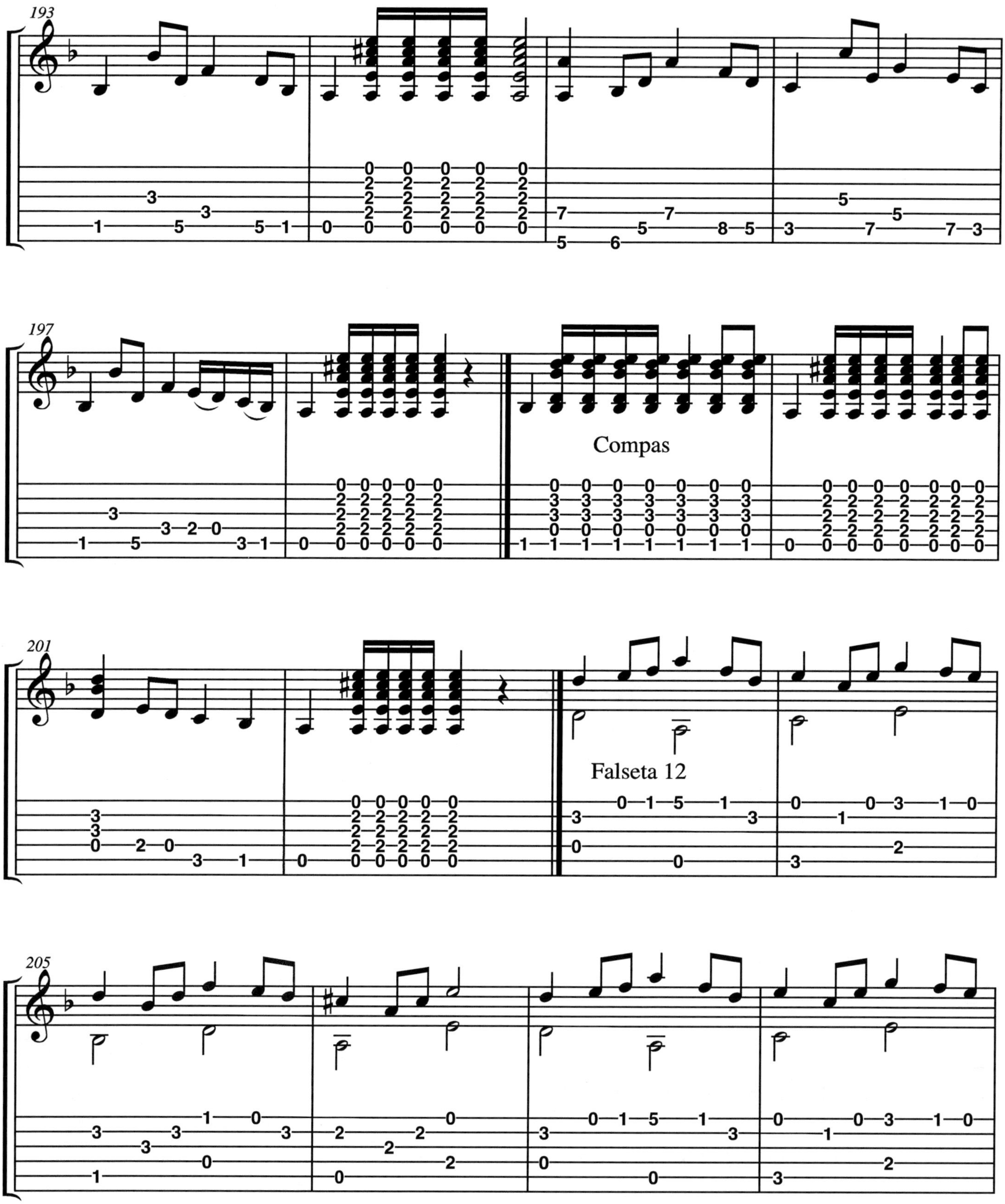
193
197
Compas
201
Falseta 12
205

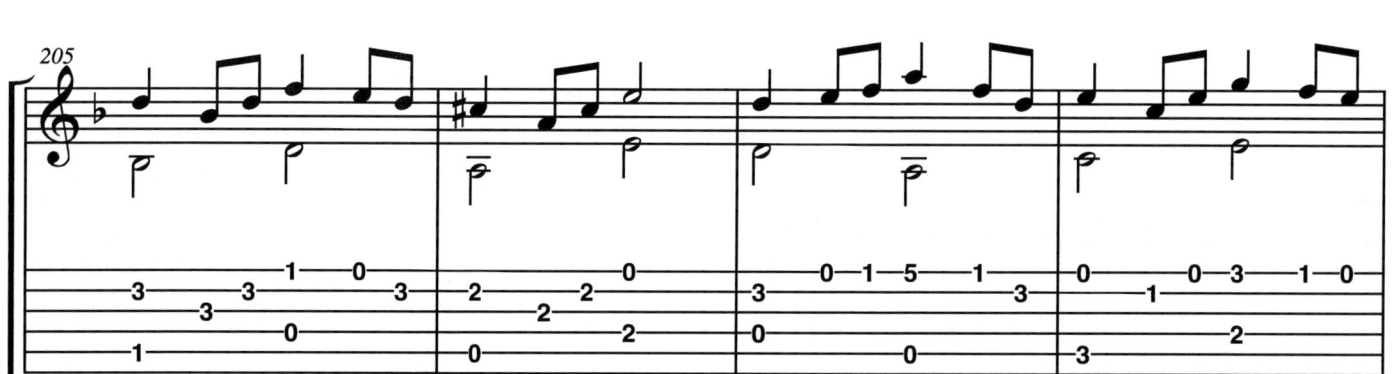

TIENTOS

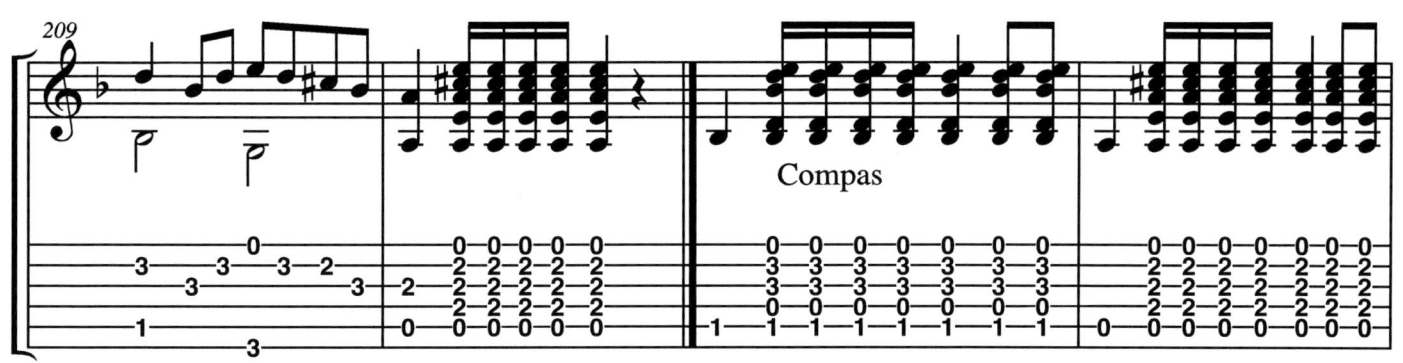
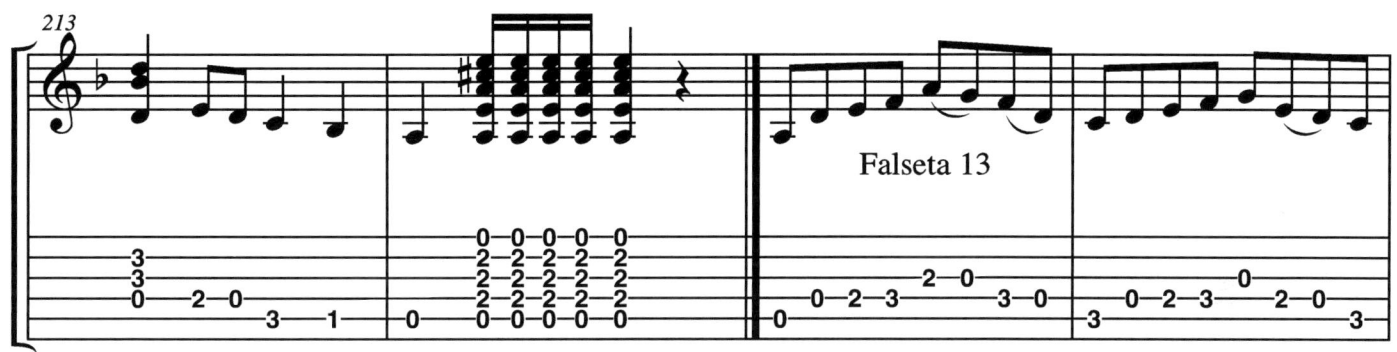
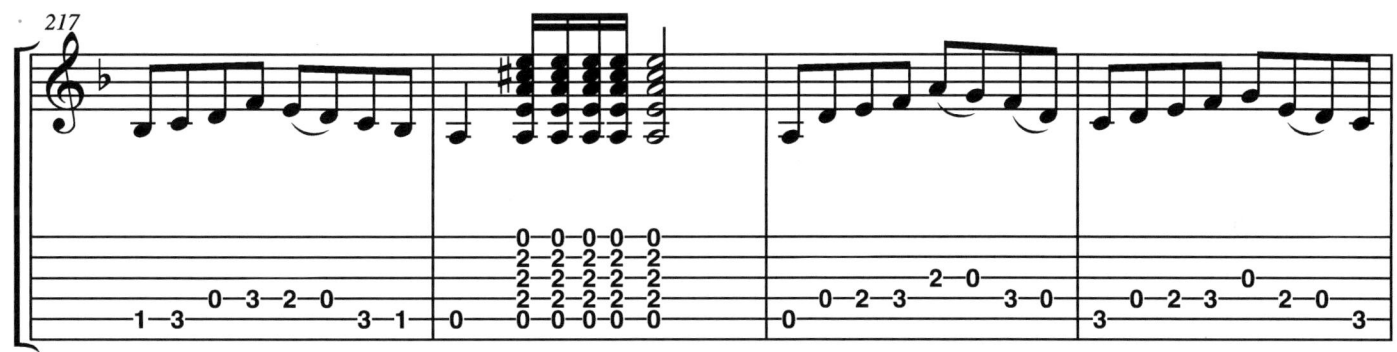
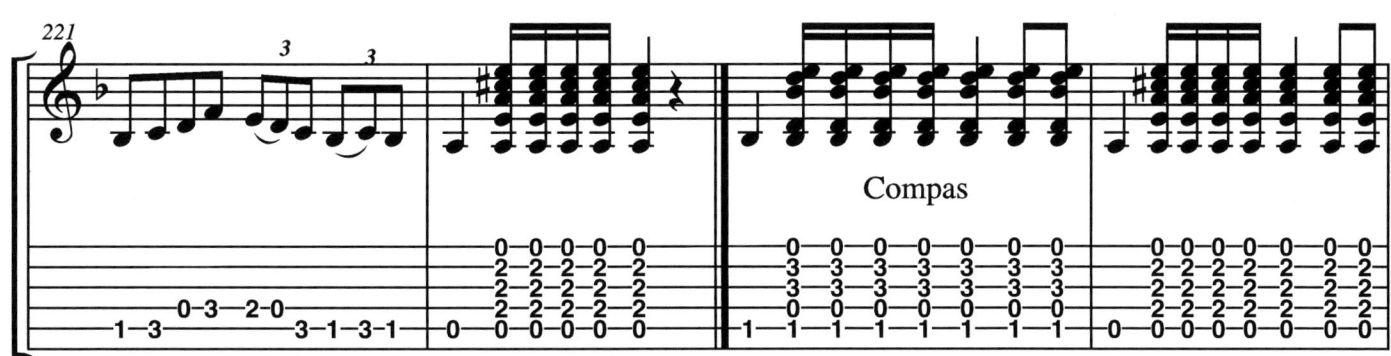

TIENTOS

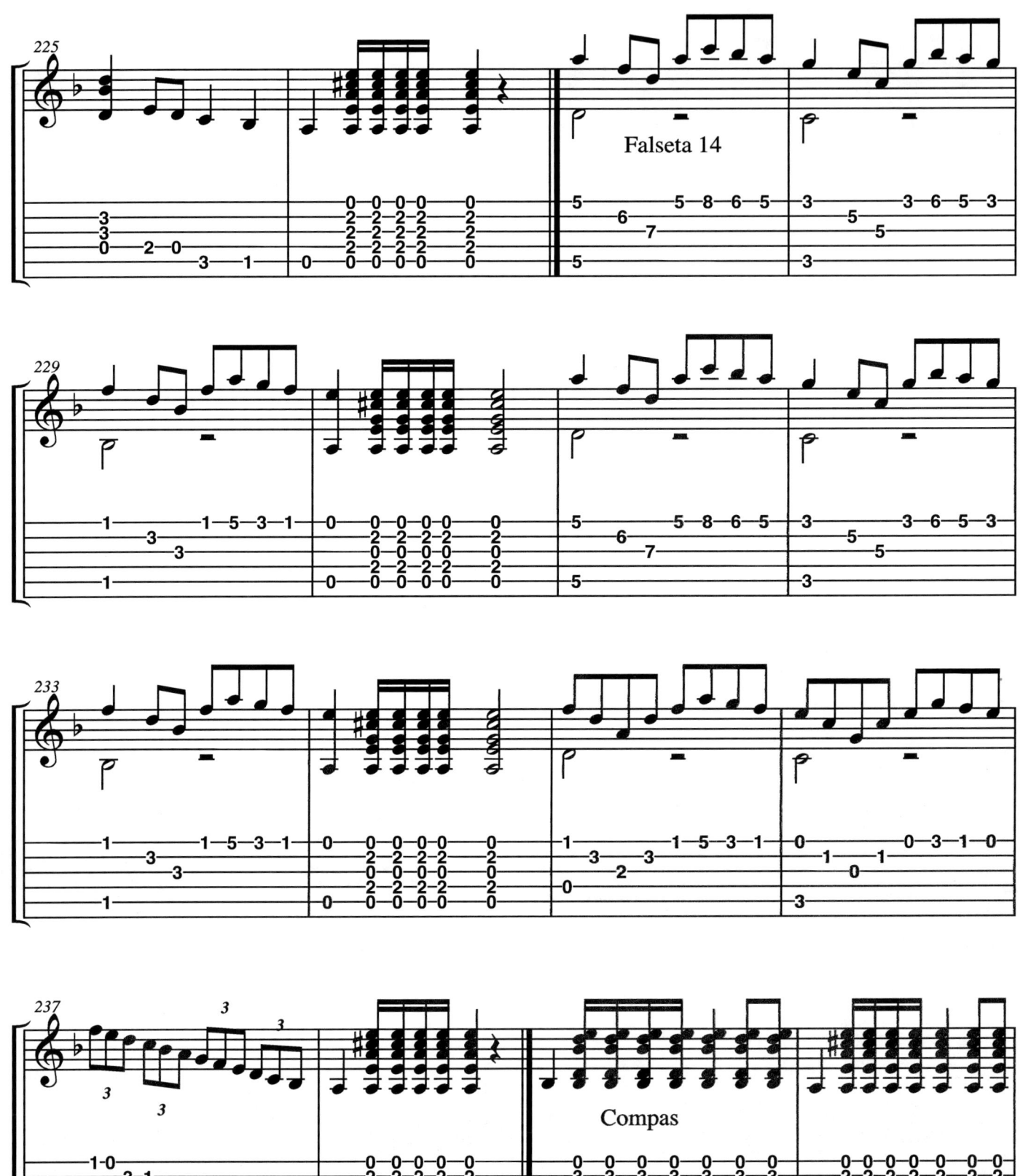

TIENTOS

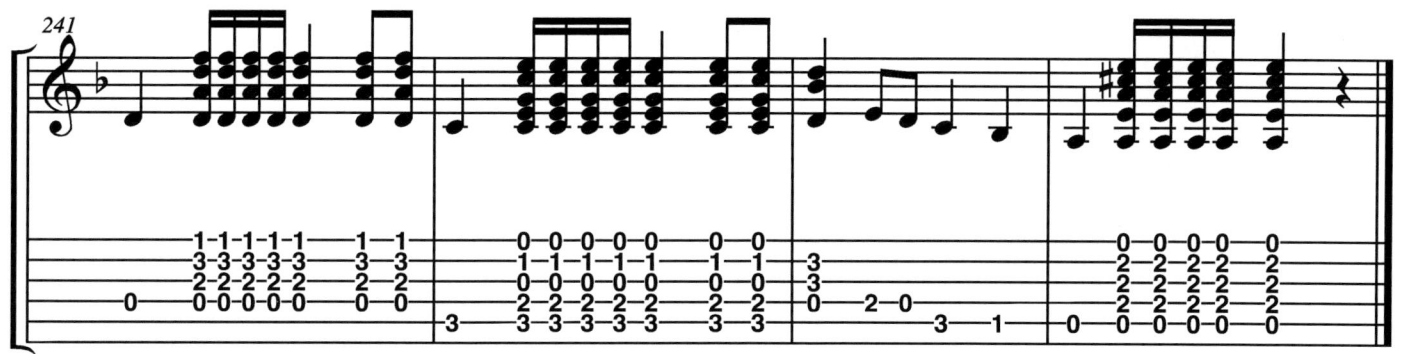

VERDIALES

Strum every compas in the same manner

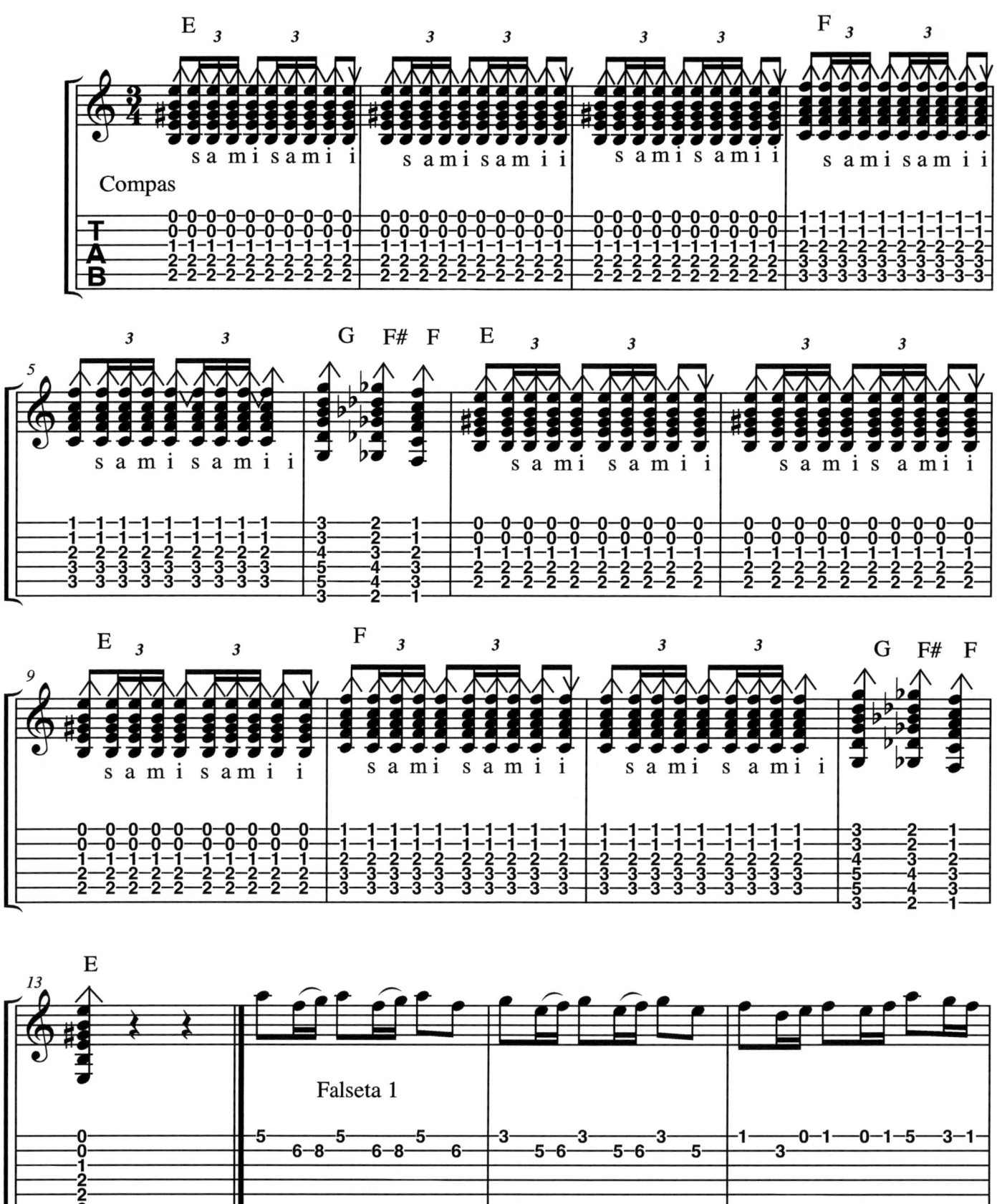

VERDIALES

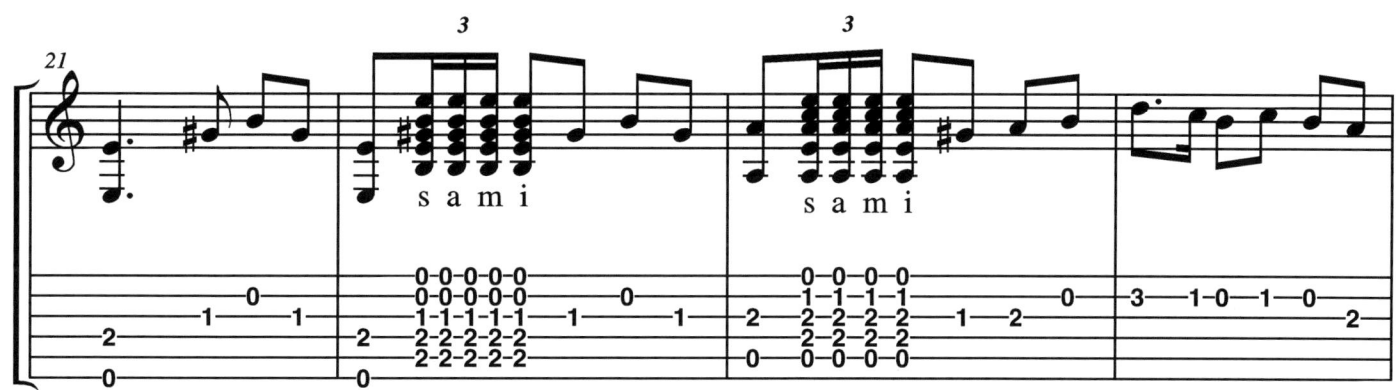
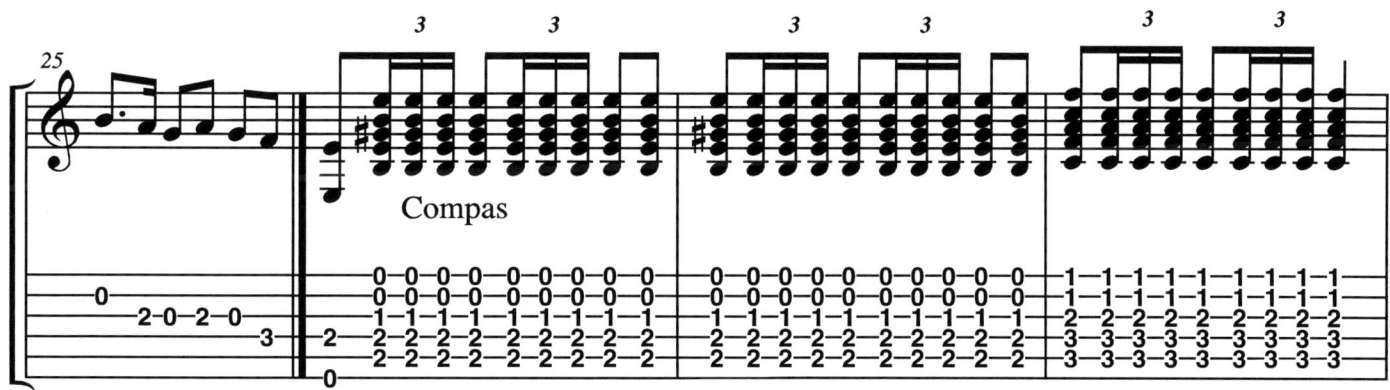

VERDIALES

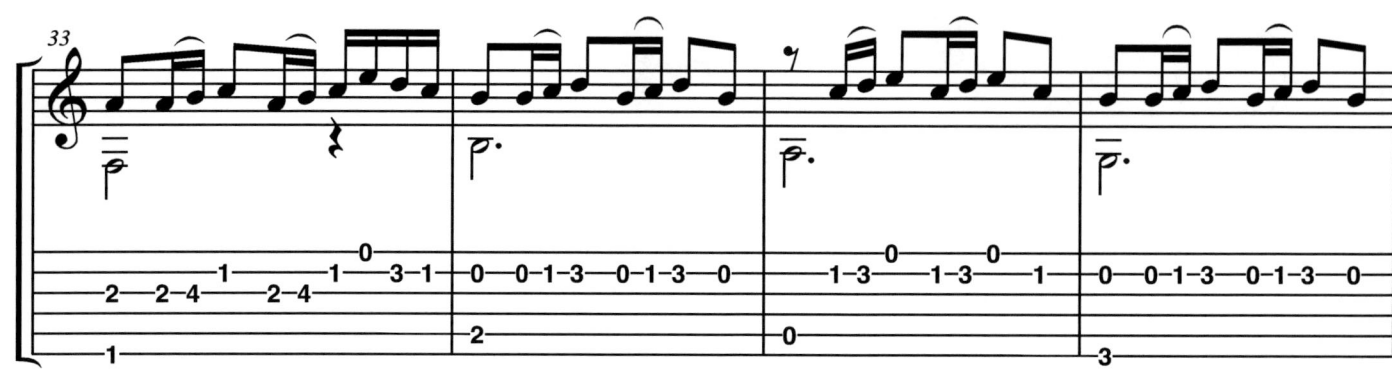
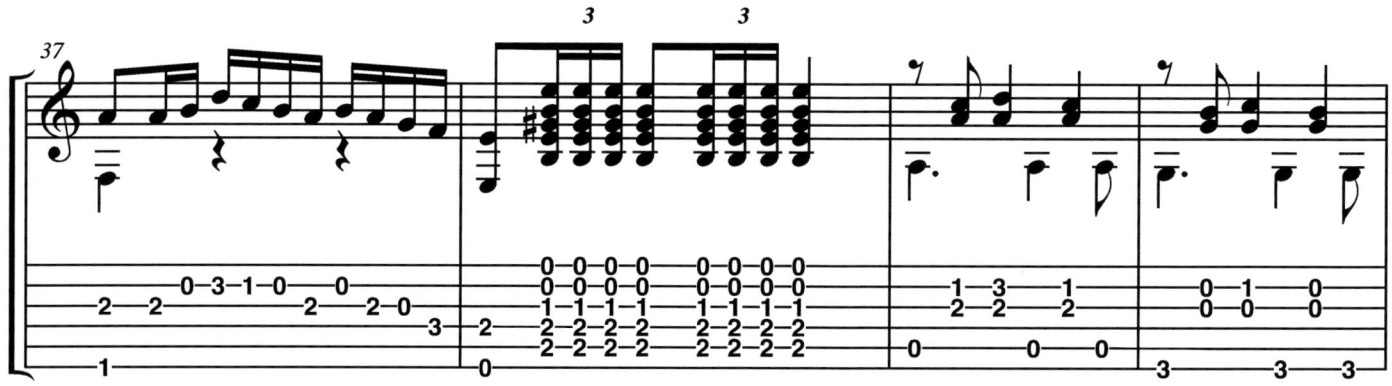

VERDIALES

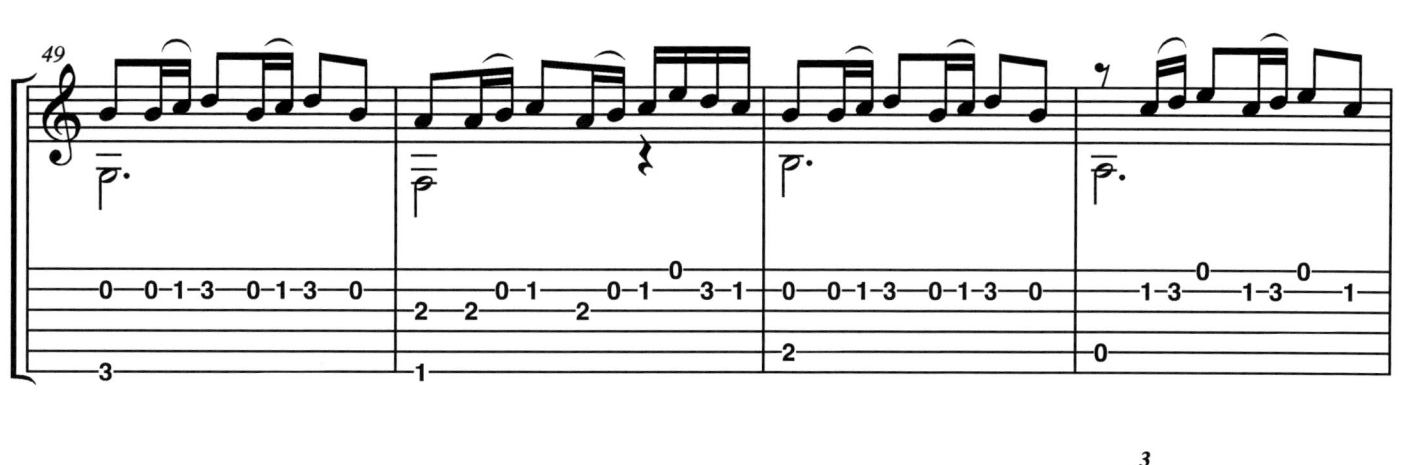
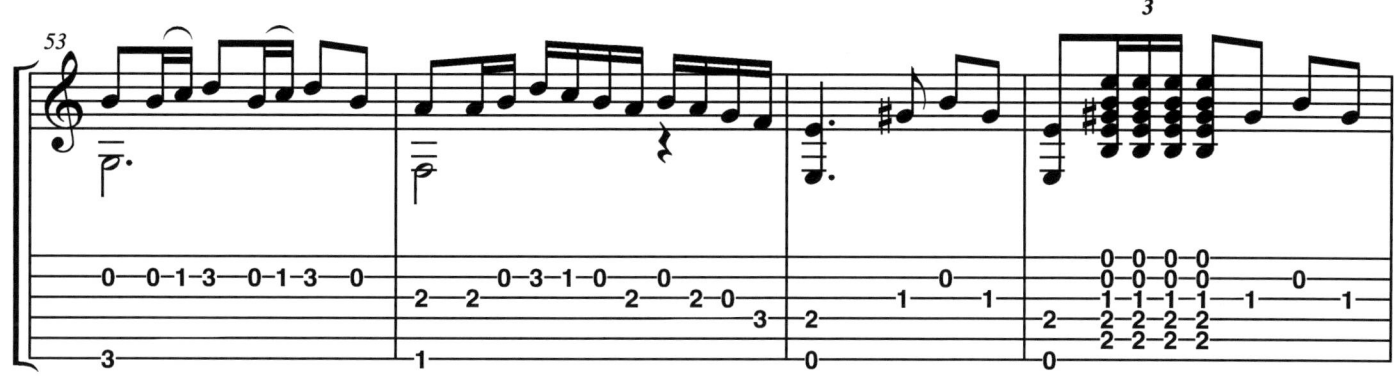

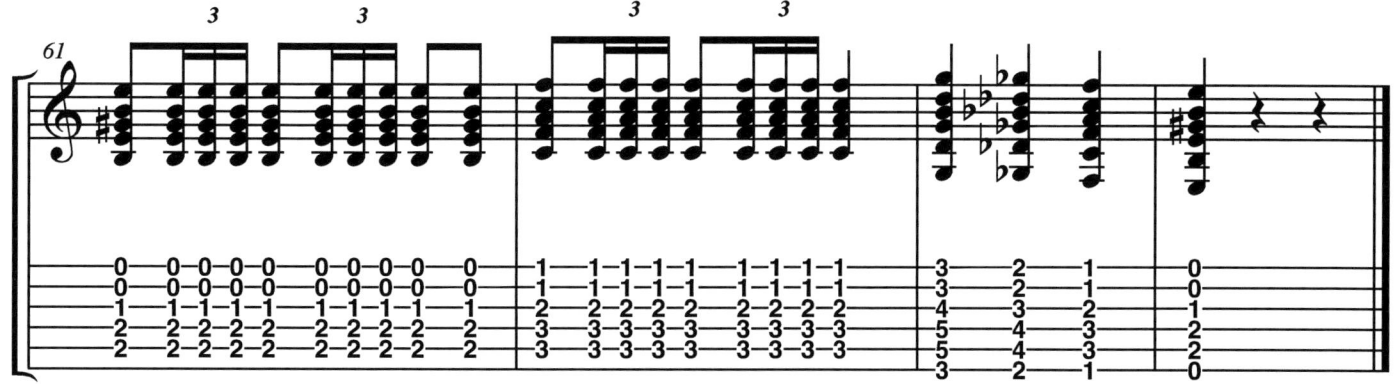

VERDIALES

Falseta 3

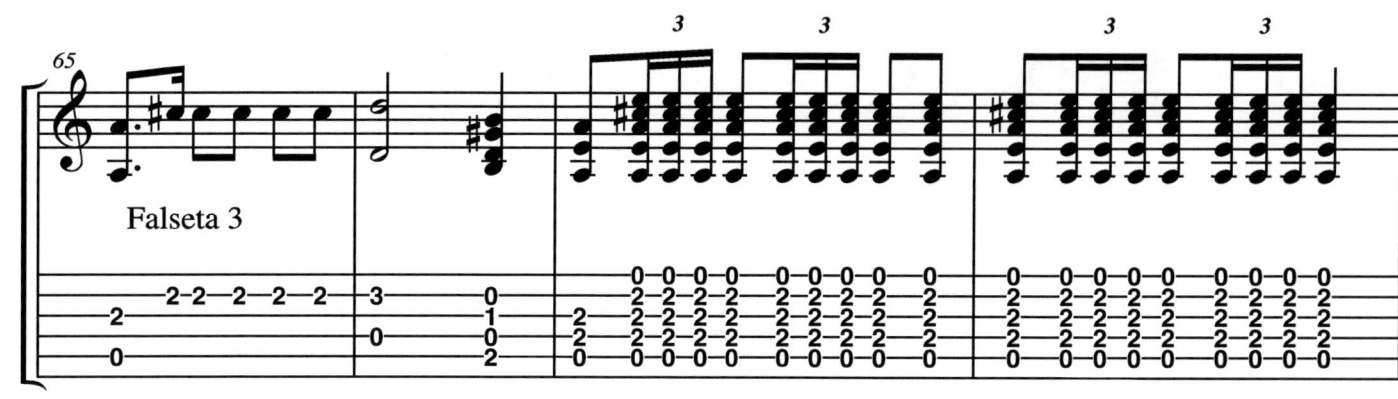

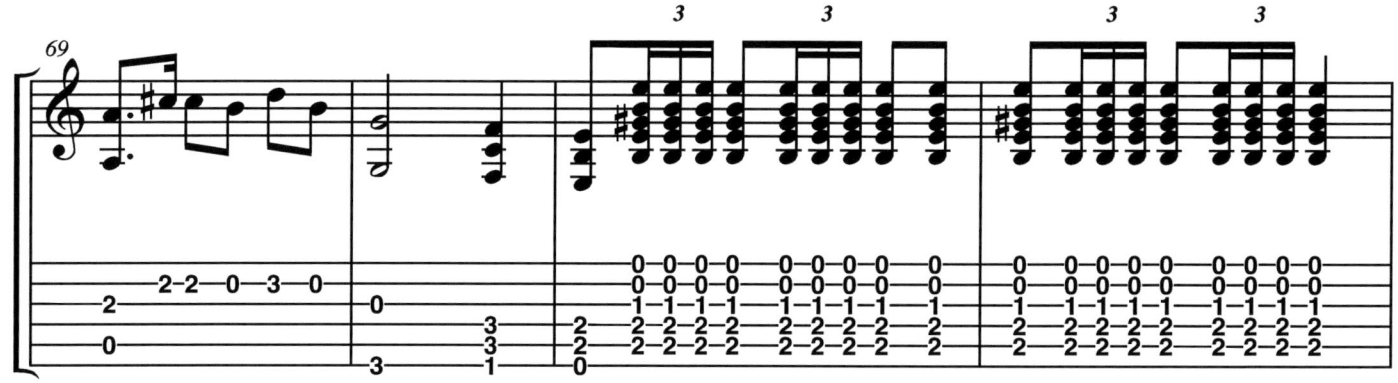

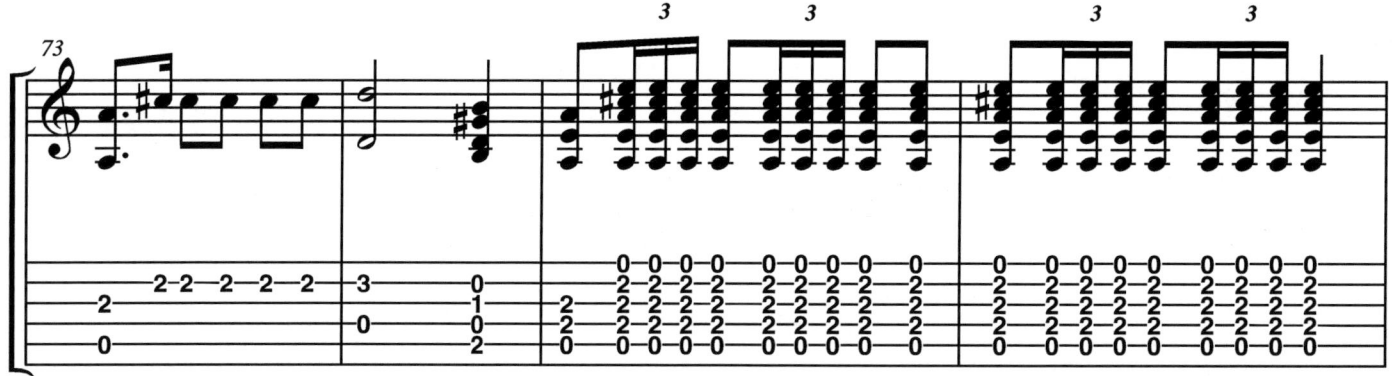

VERDIALES

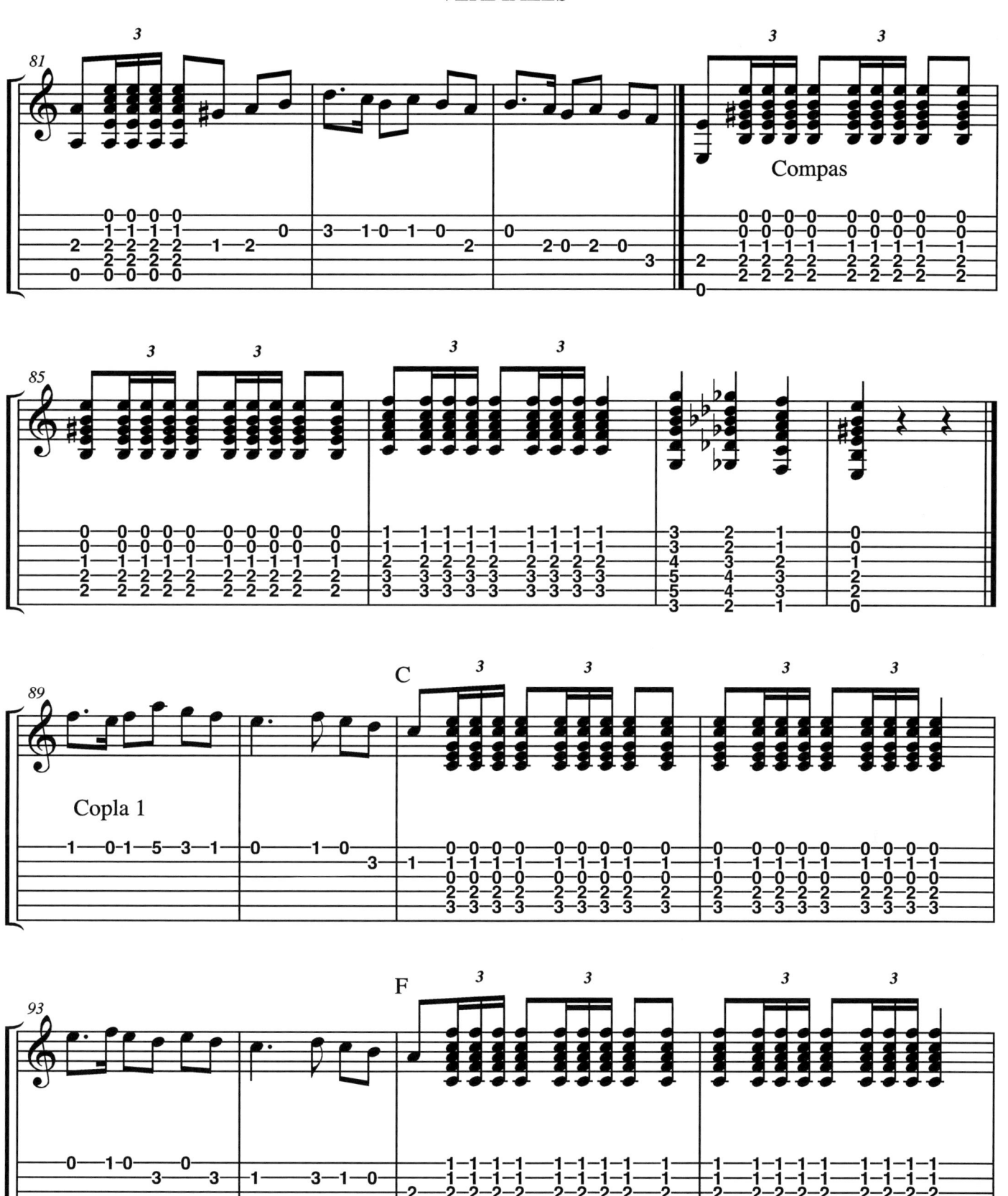

VERDIALES

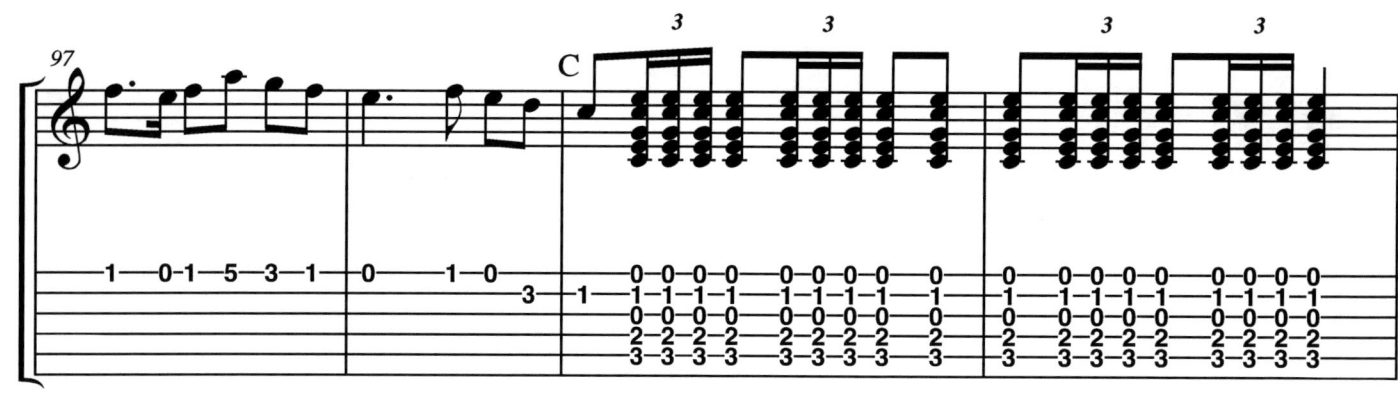
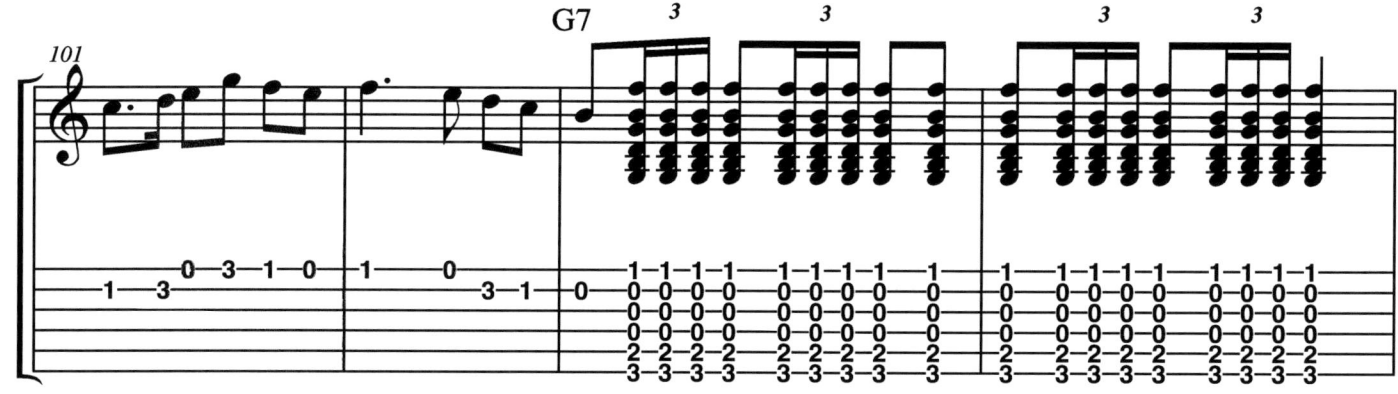
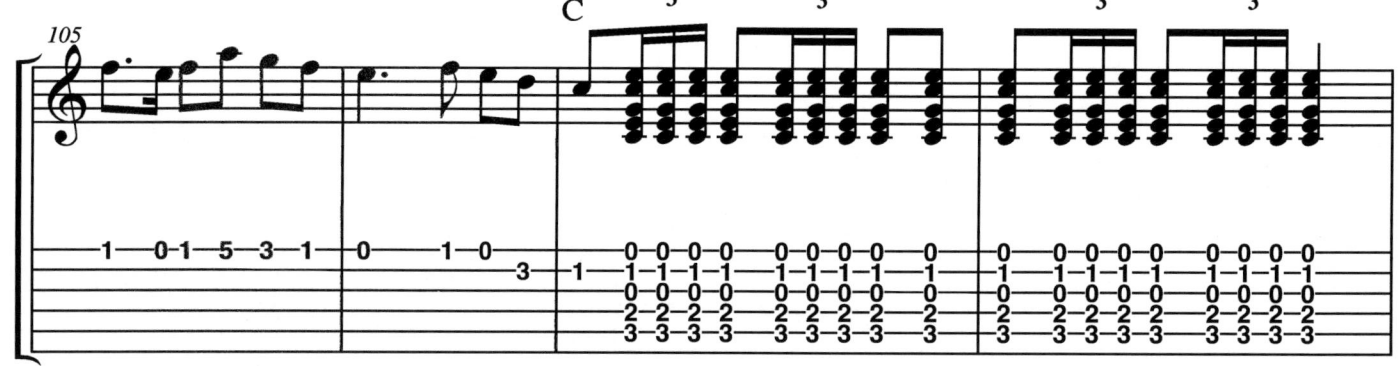

VERDIALES

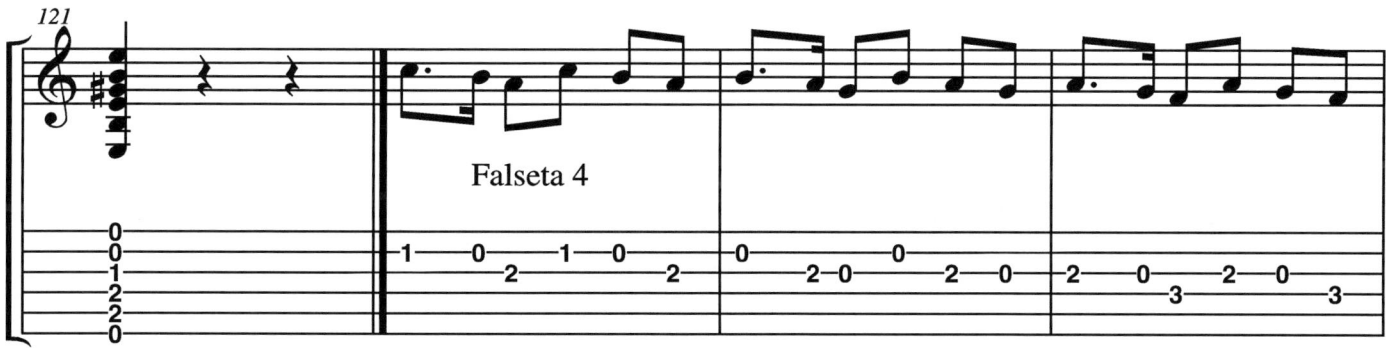

VERDIALES

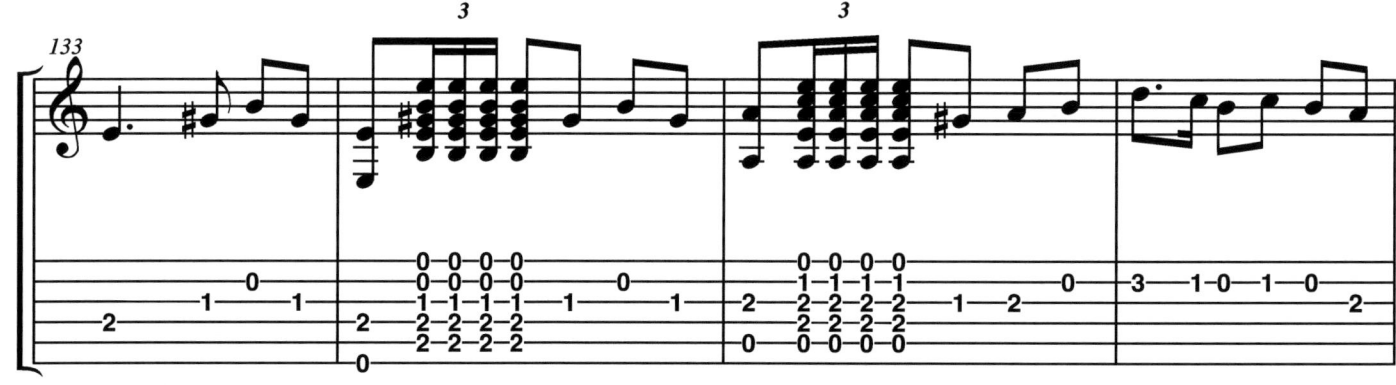
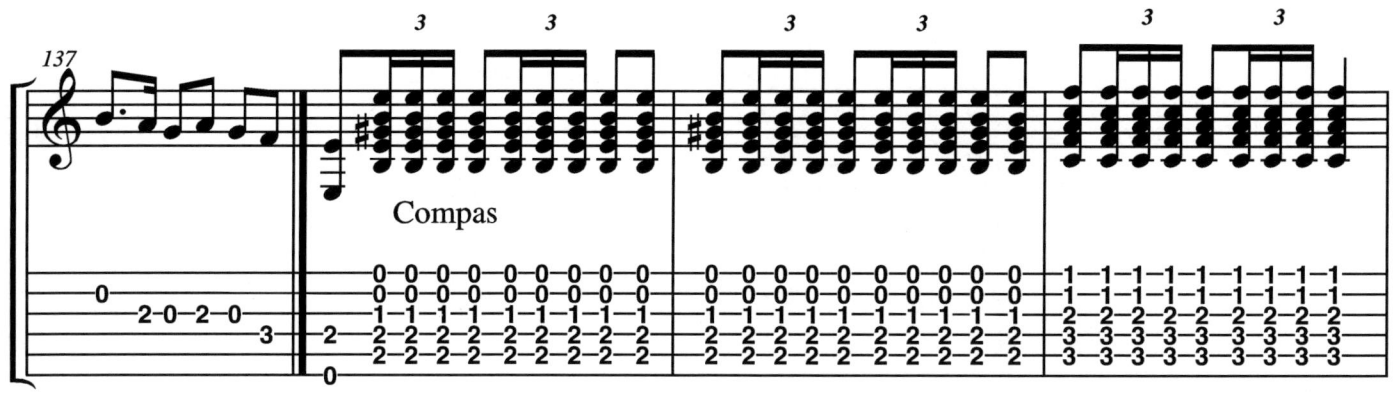
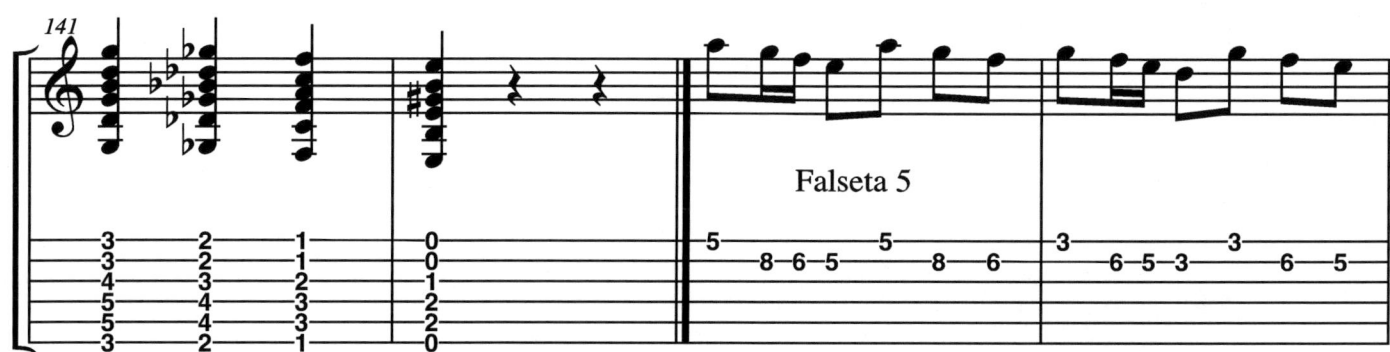

VERDIALES

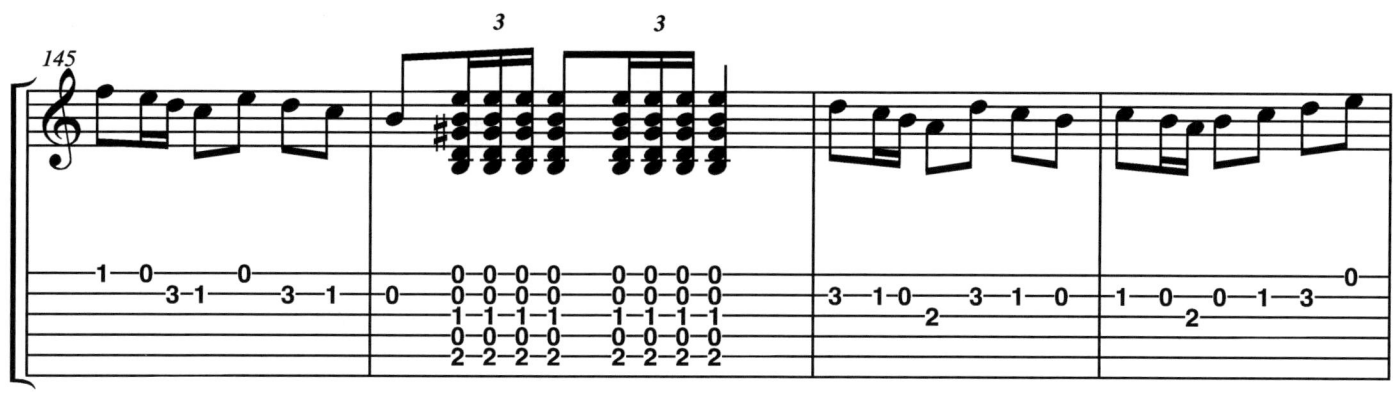
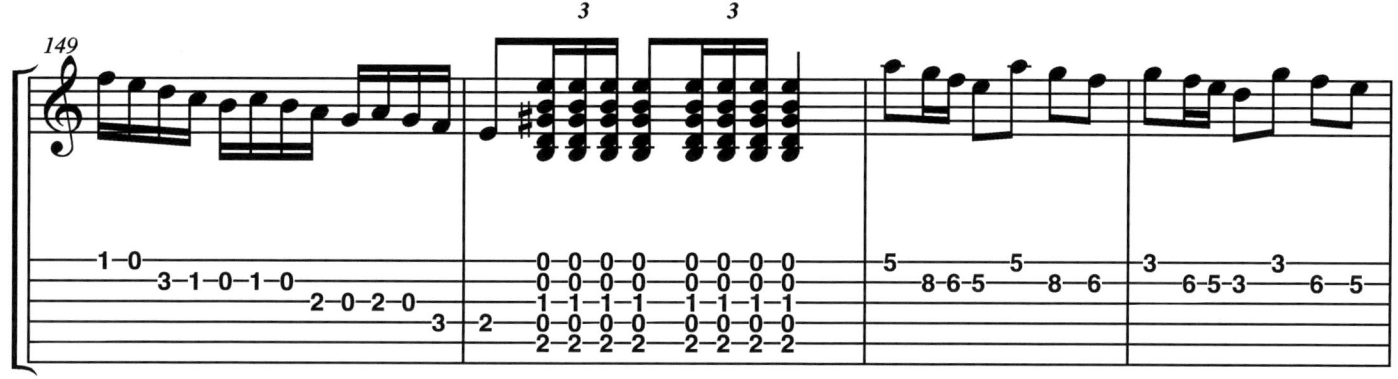
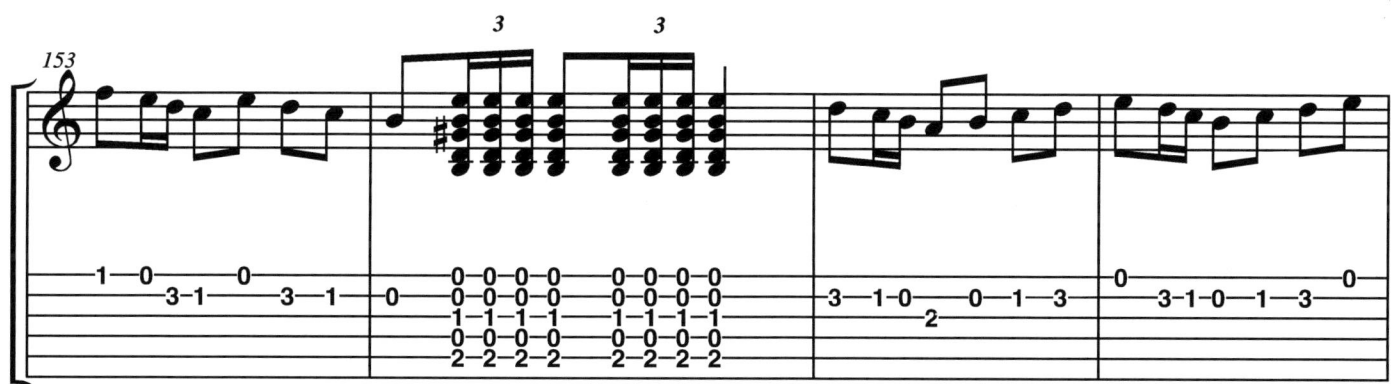
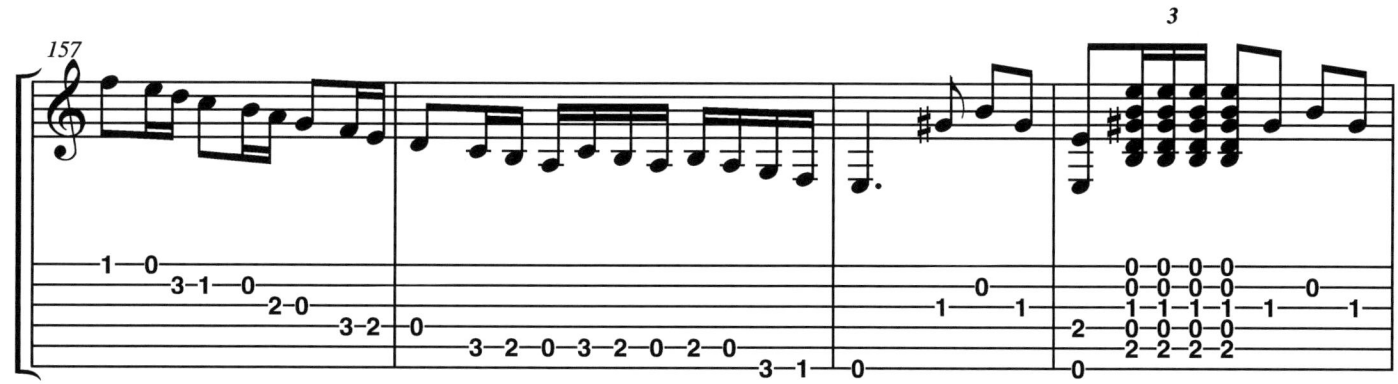

VERDIALES

VERDIALES

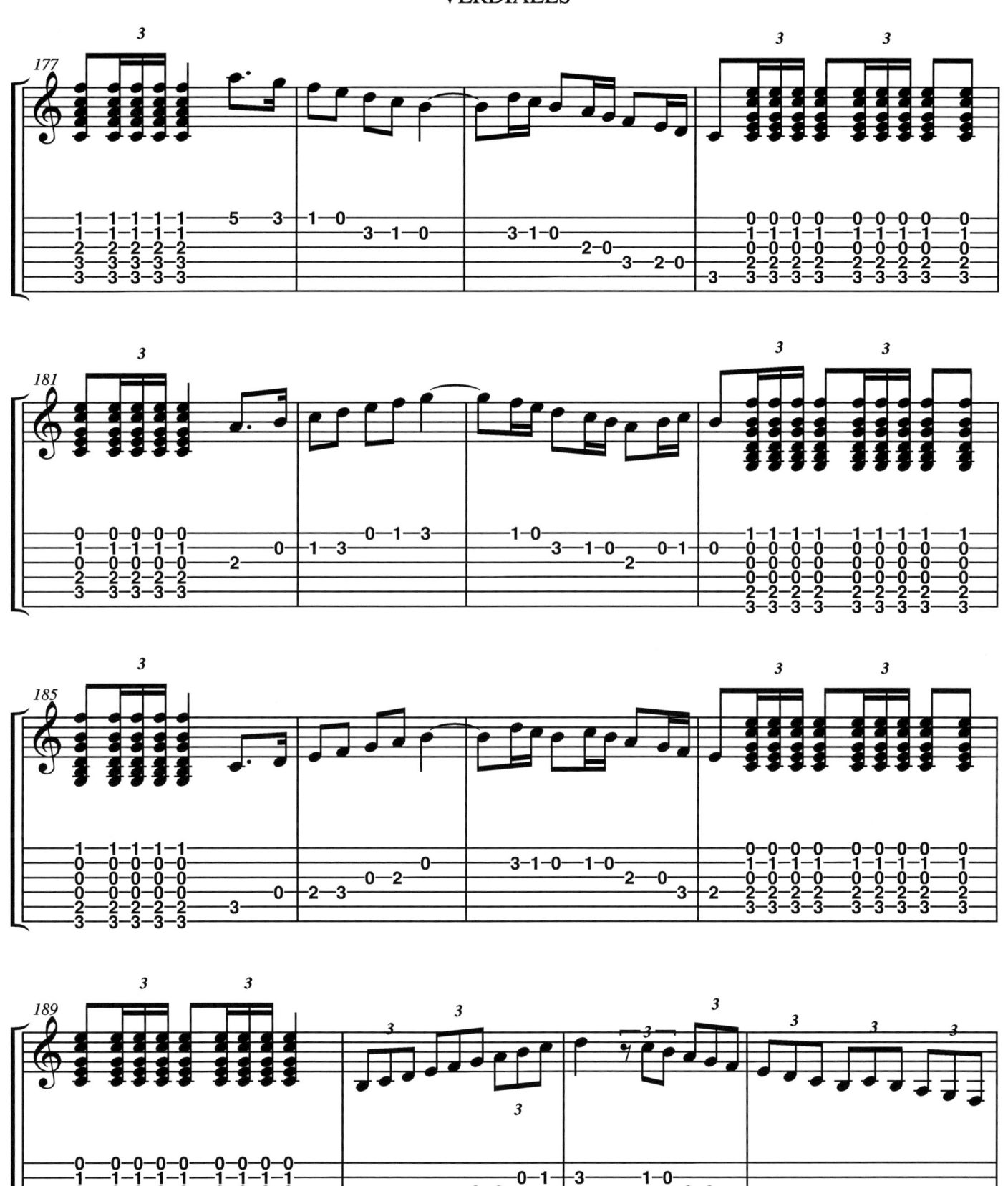

VERDIALES

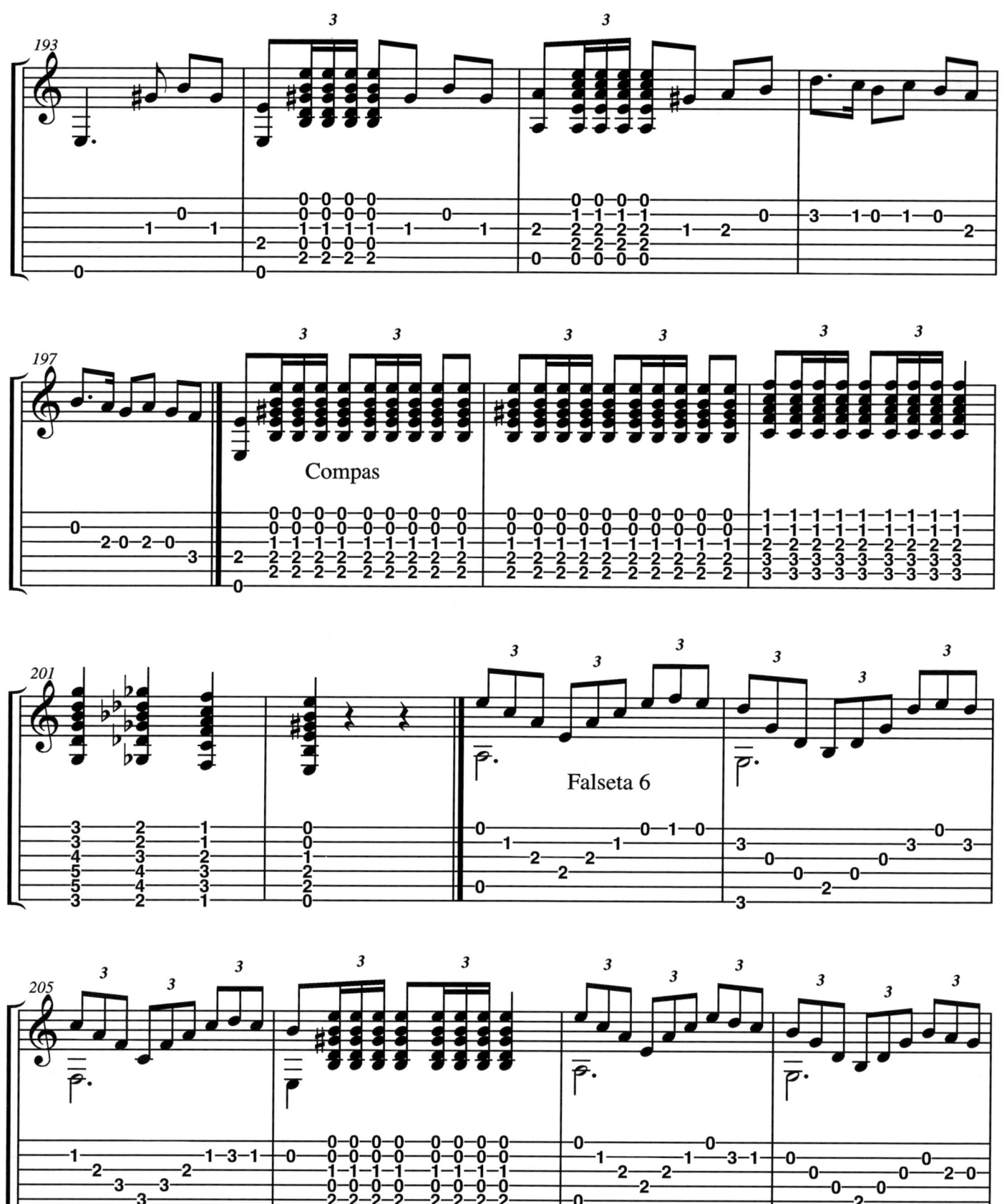

VERDIALES

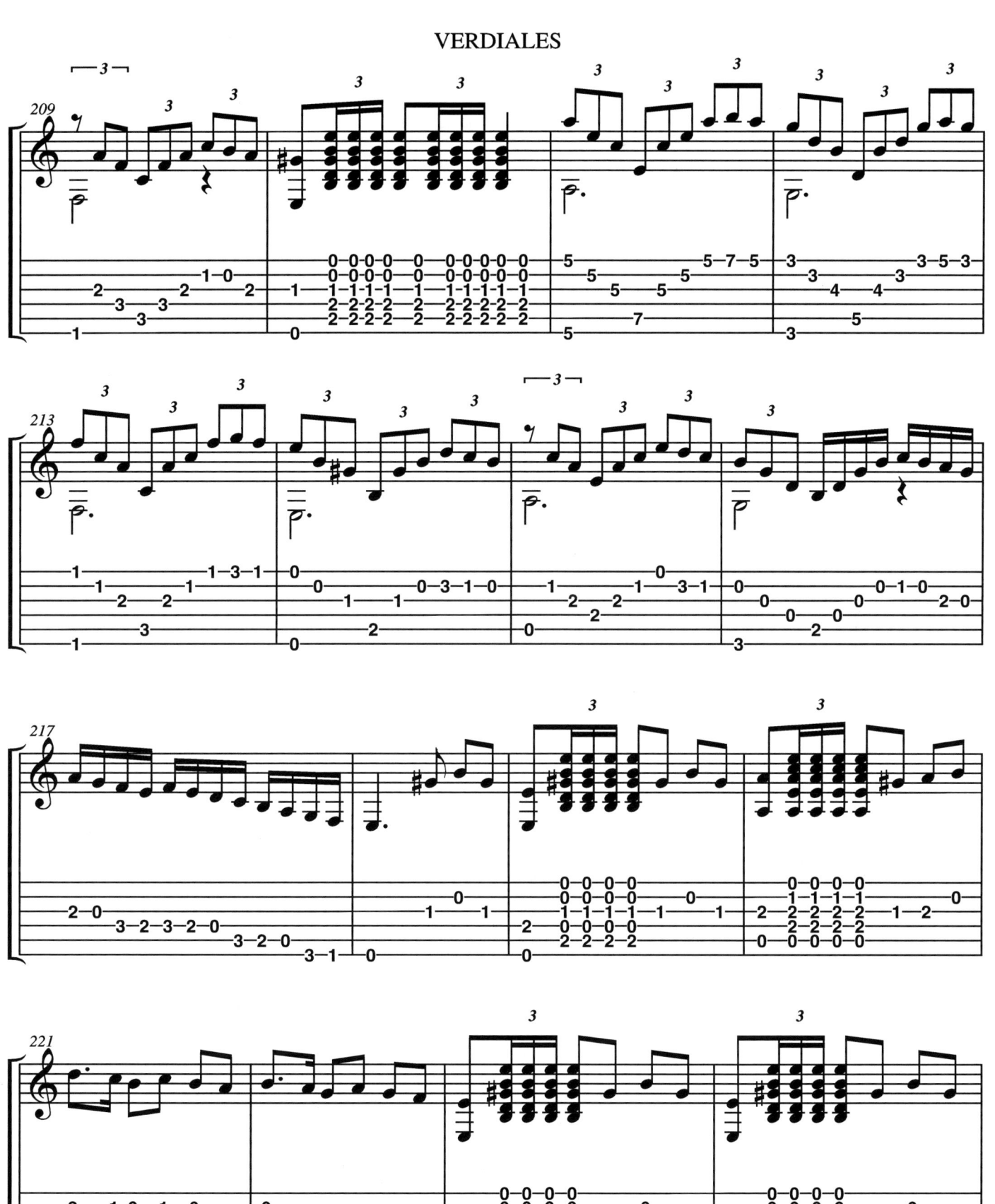

VERDIALES

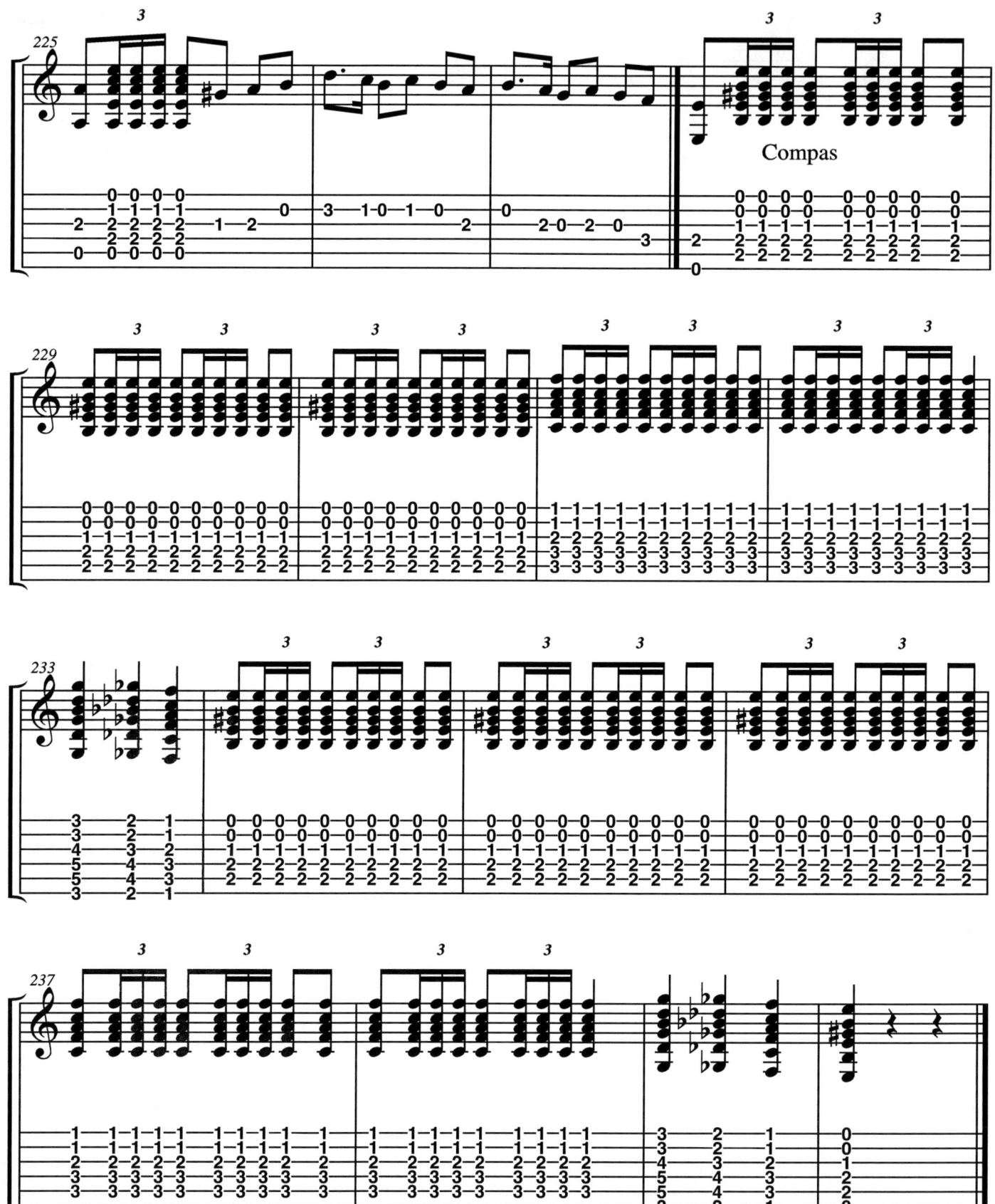

250

ZAPATEADO

Strum every compas in the same manner

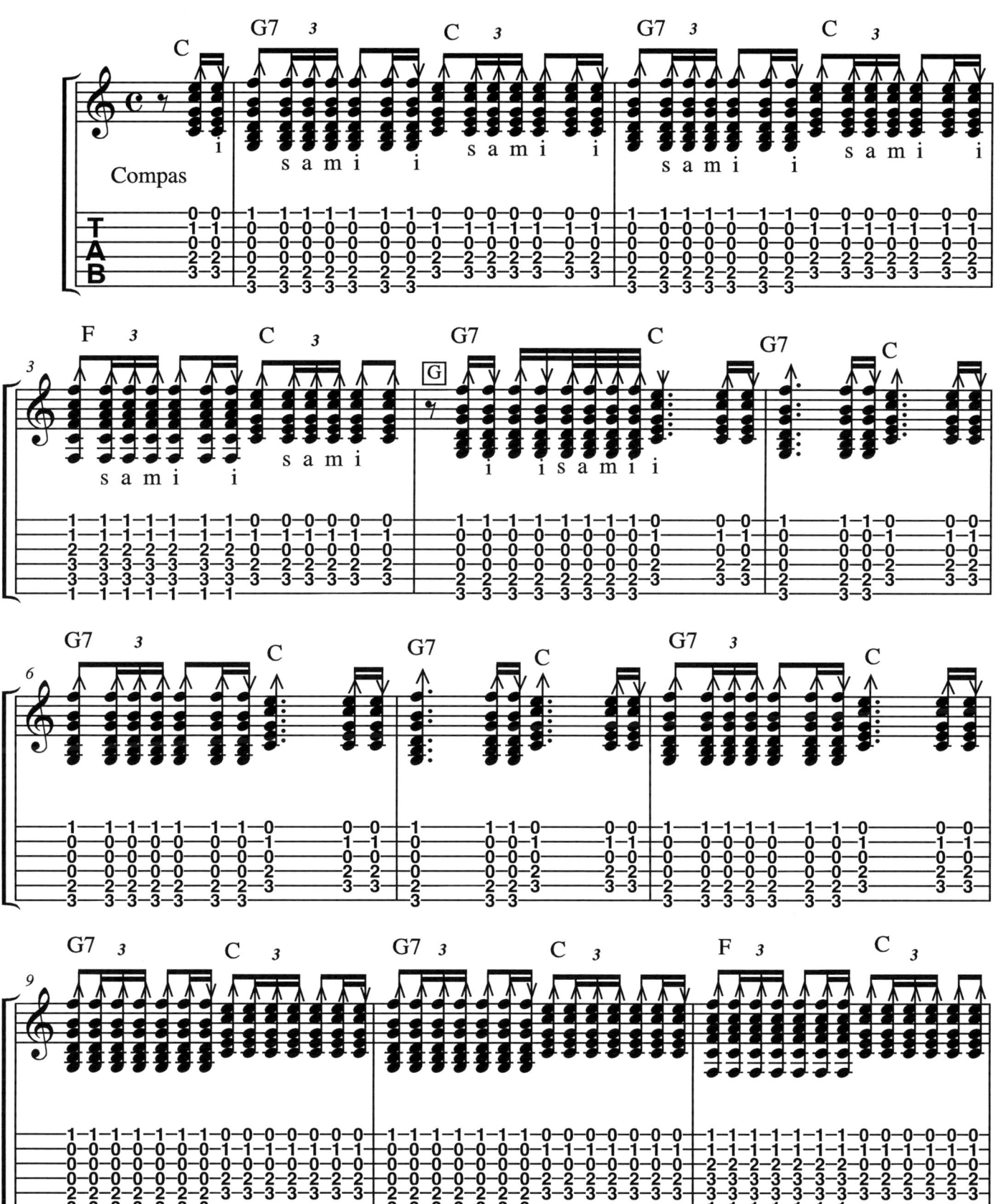

ZAPATEADO

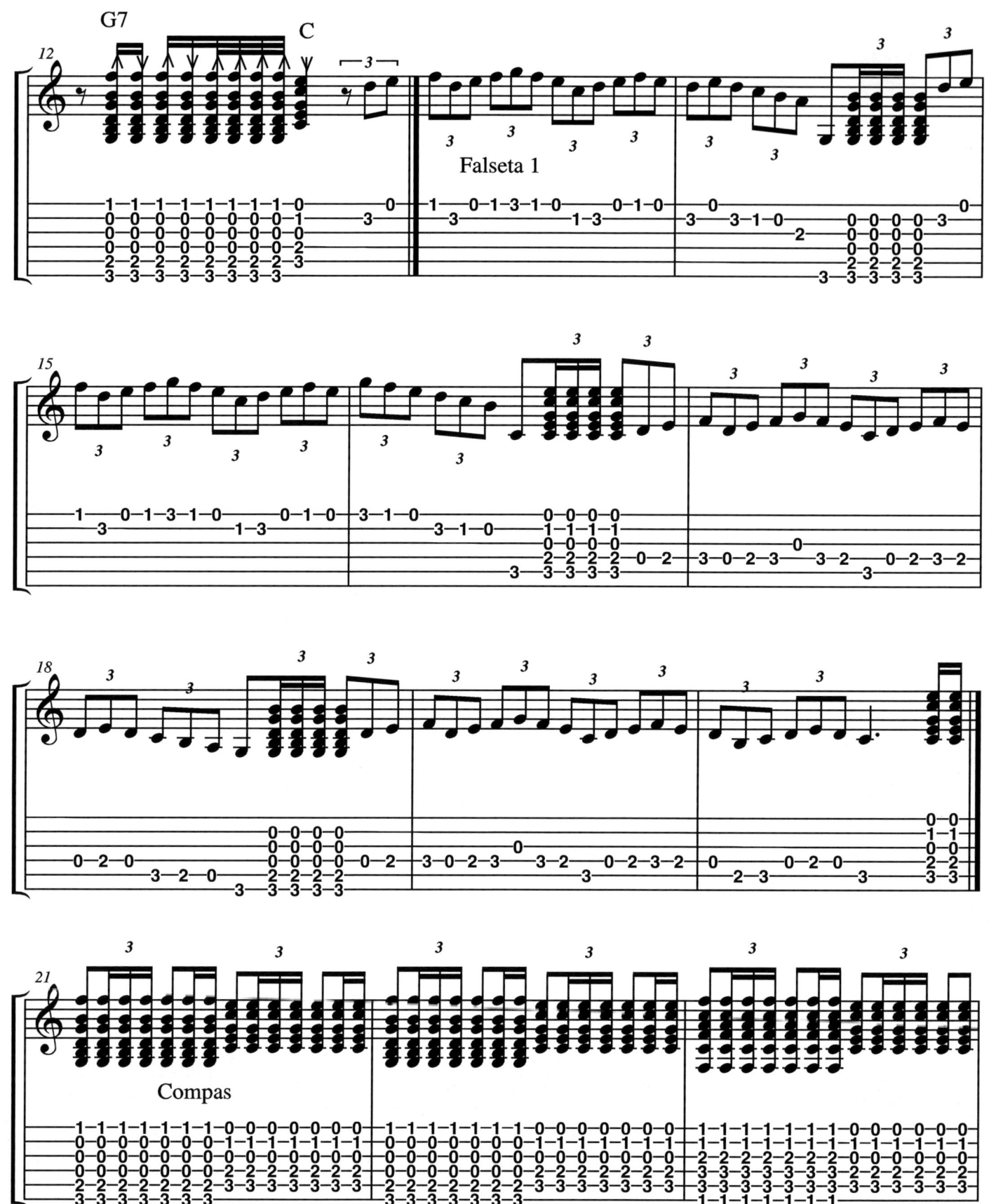

ZAPATEADO

Falseta 2

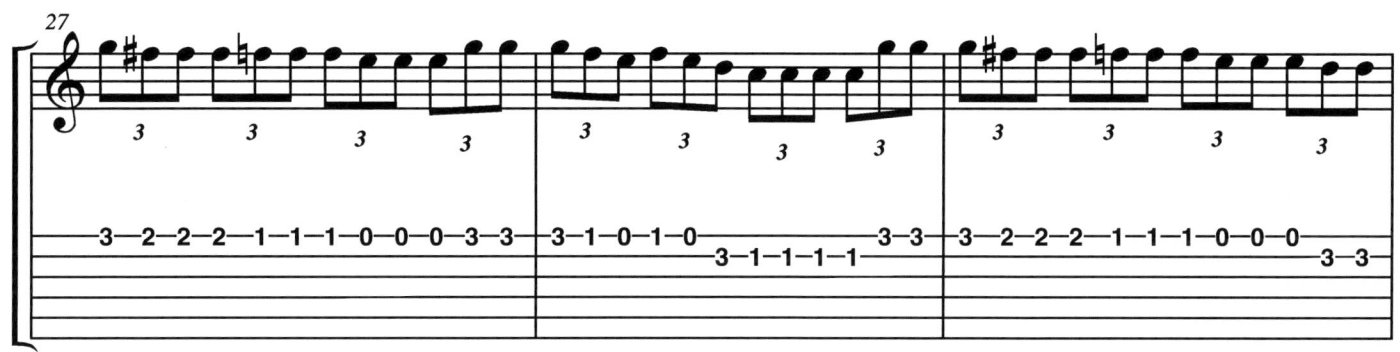

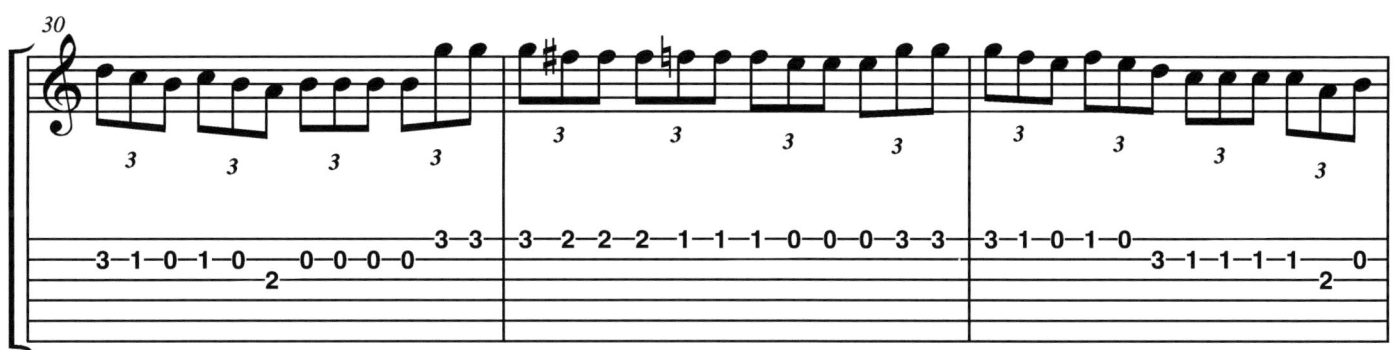

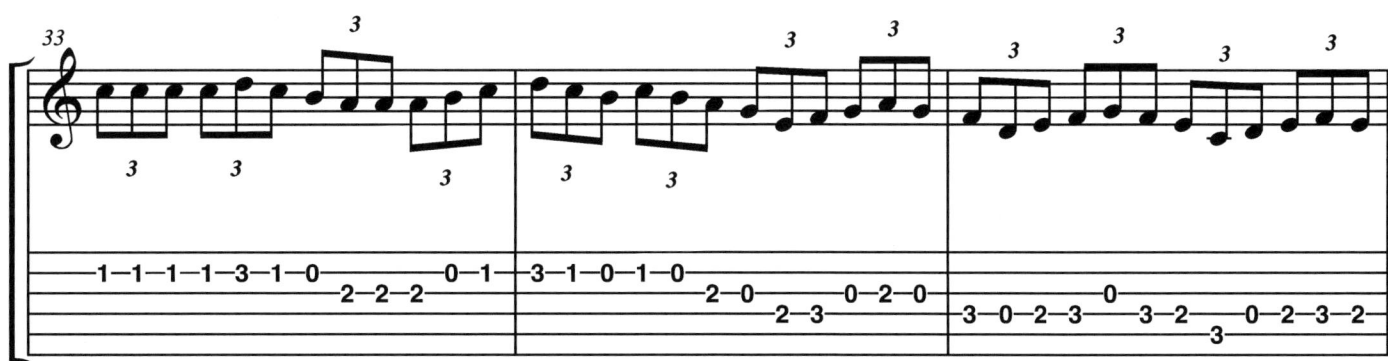

ZAPATEADO

ZAPATEADO

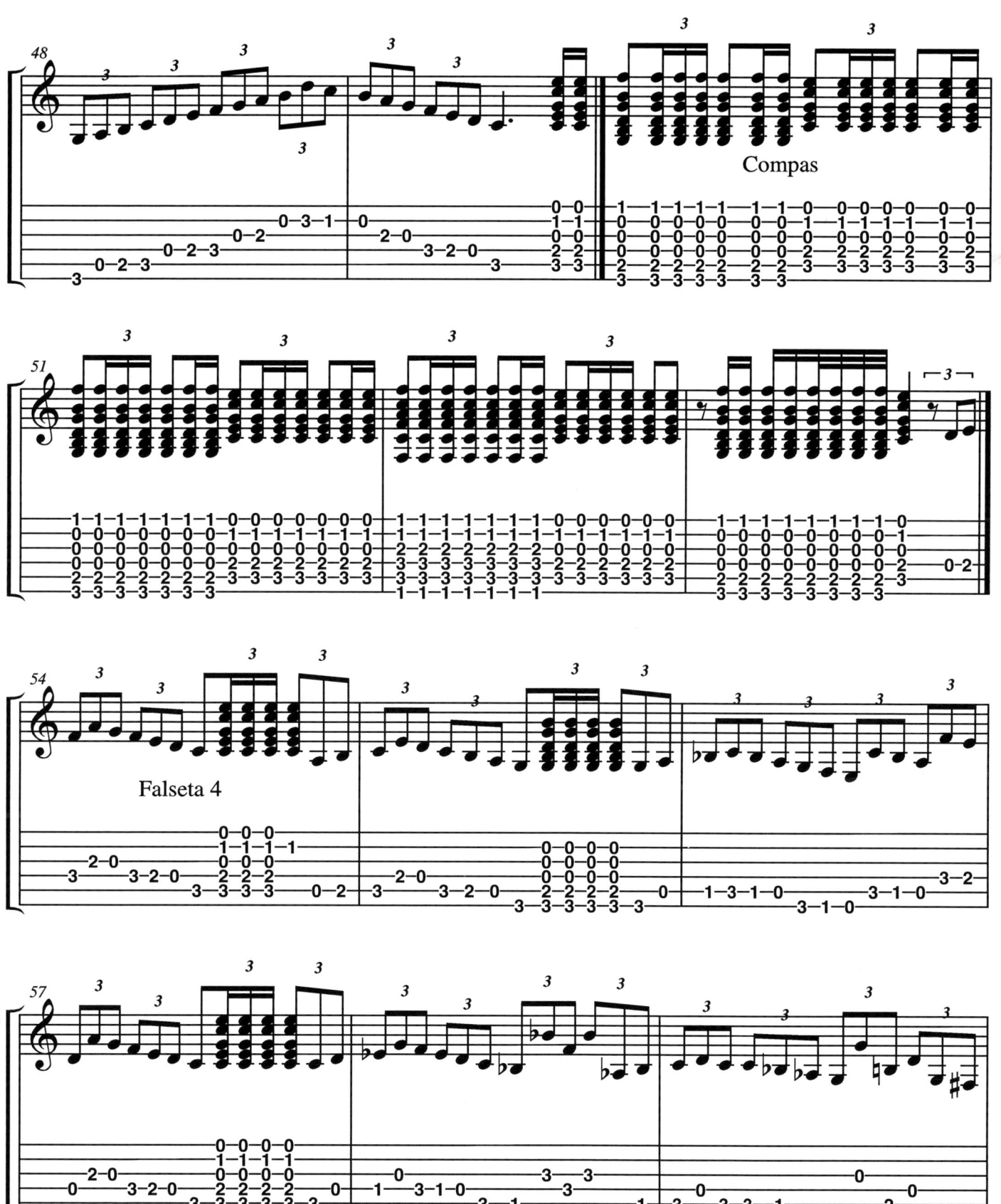

ZAPATEADO

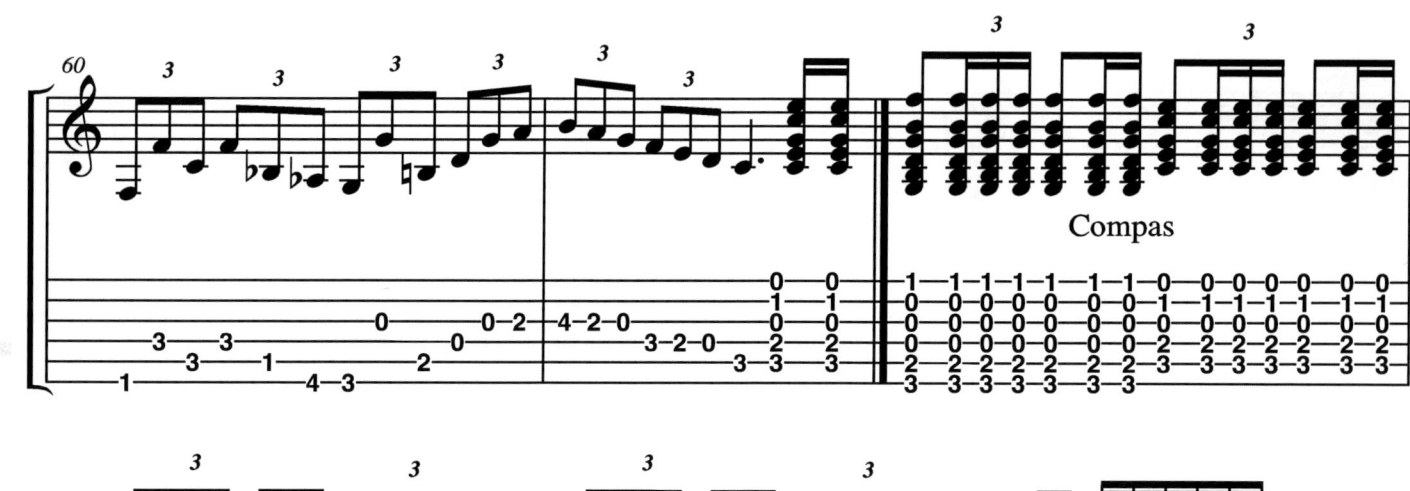

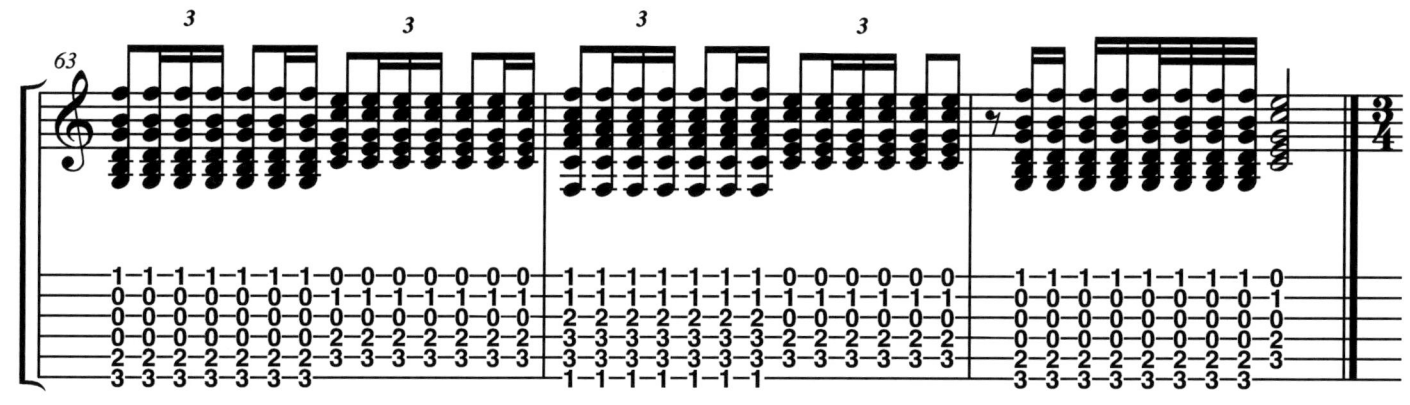

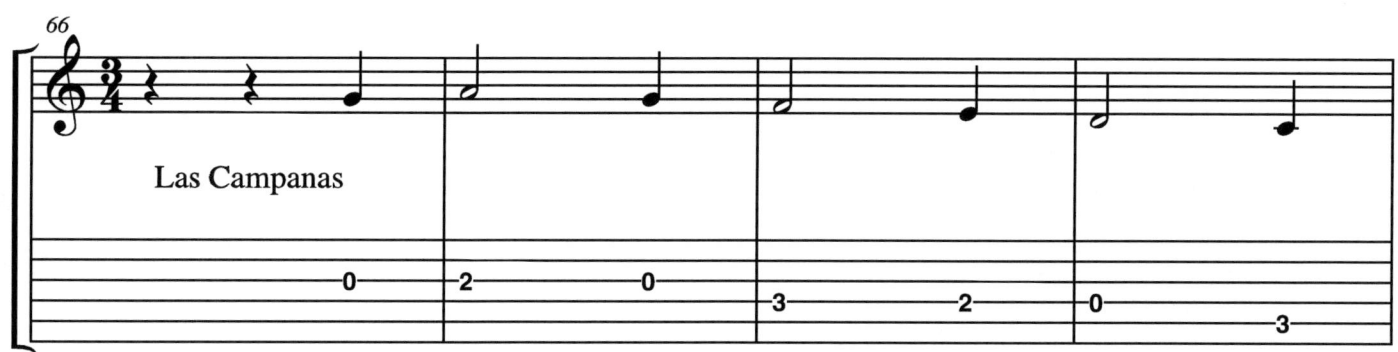

Las Campanas

ZAPATEADO

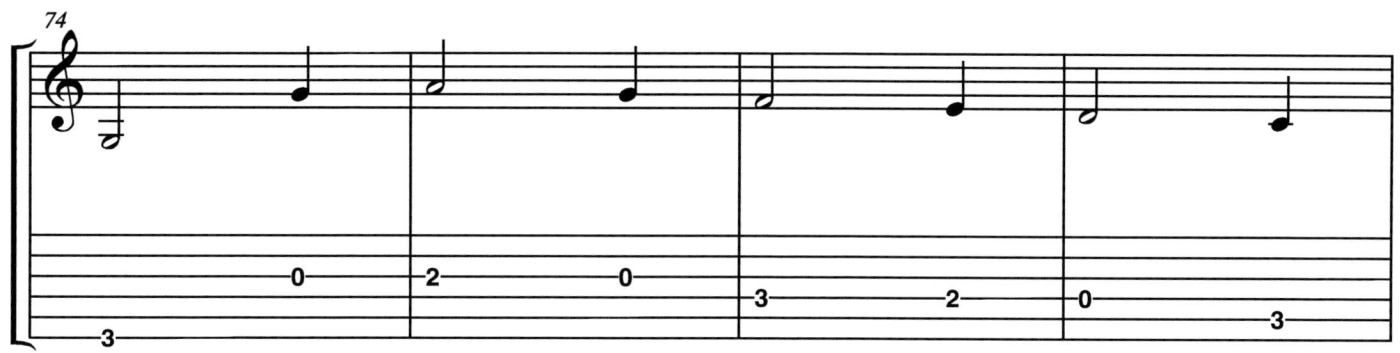
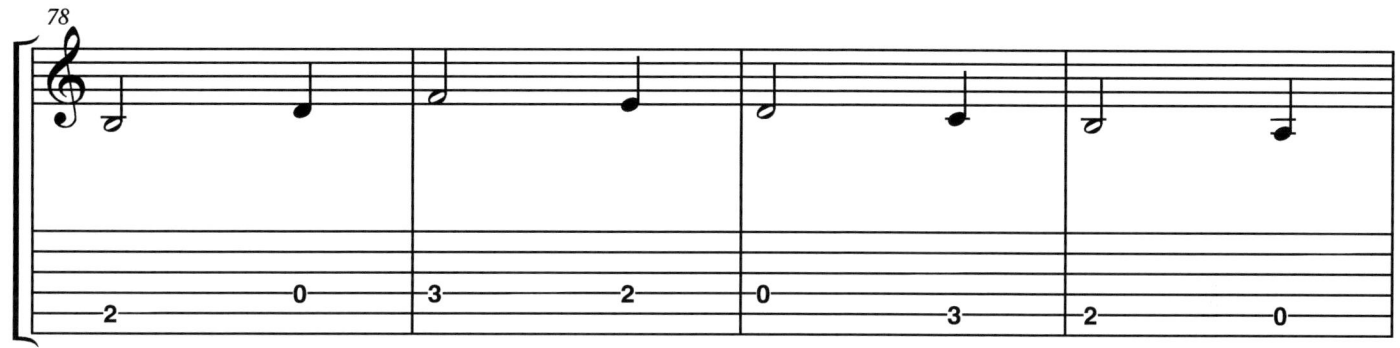
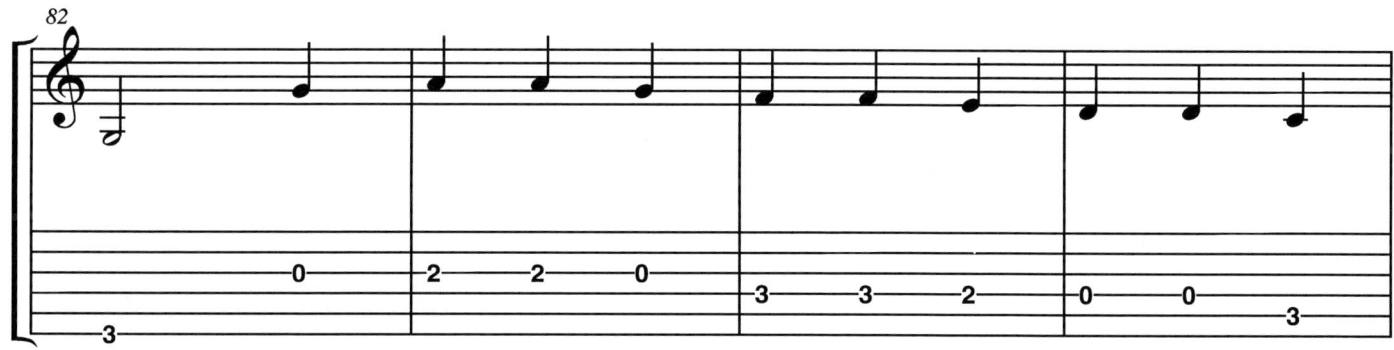
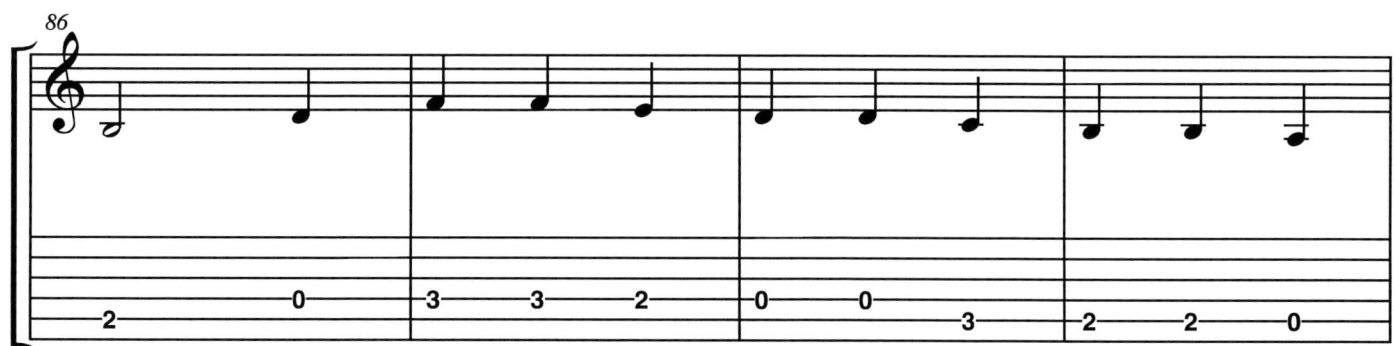

ZAPATEADO

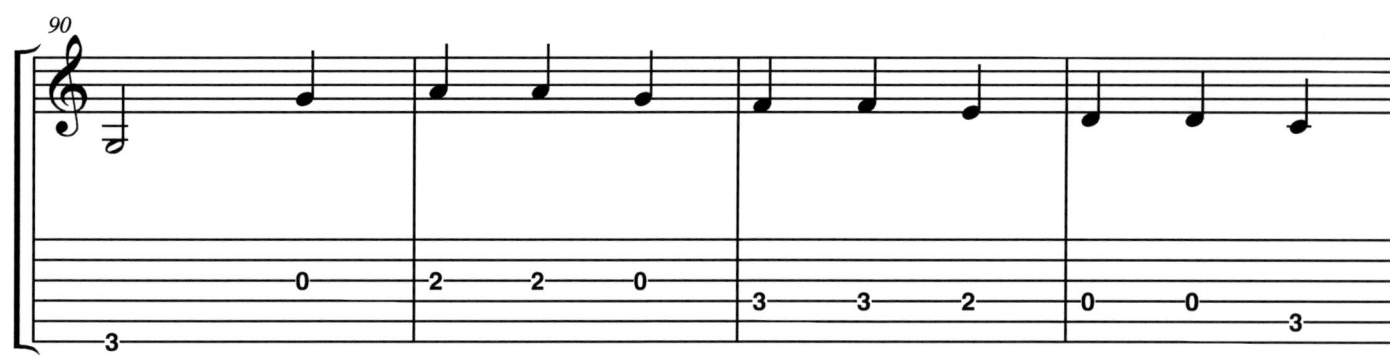
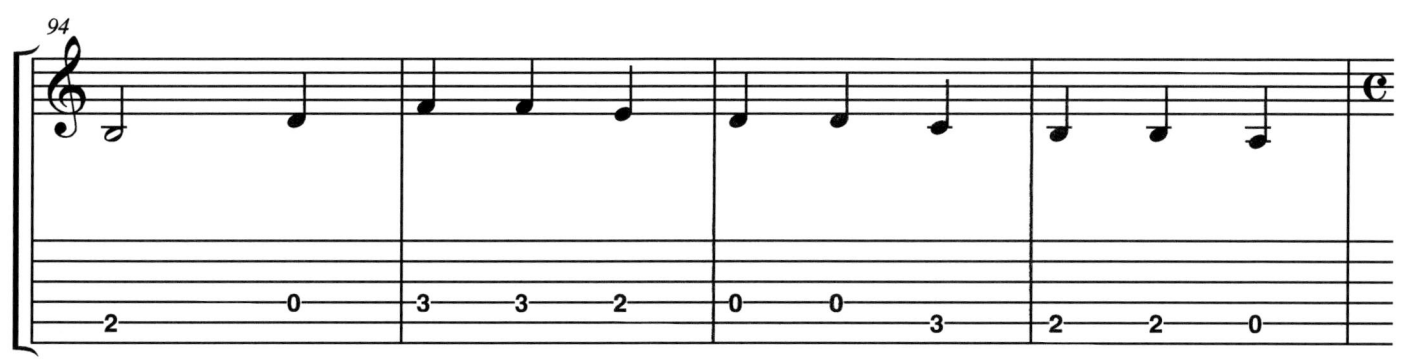
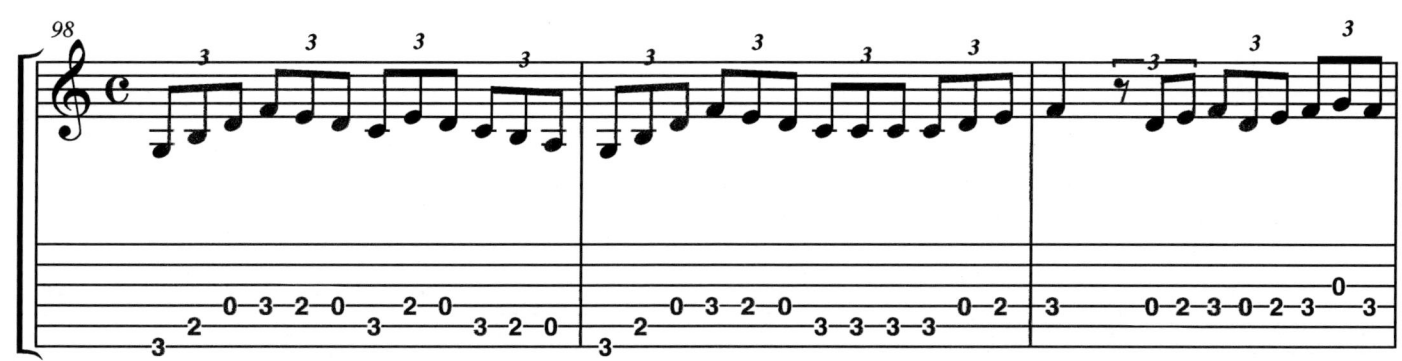

ZAPATEADO

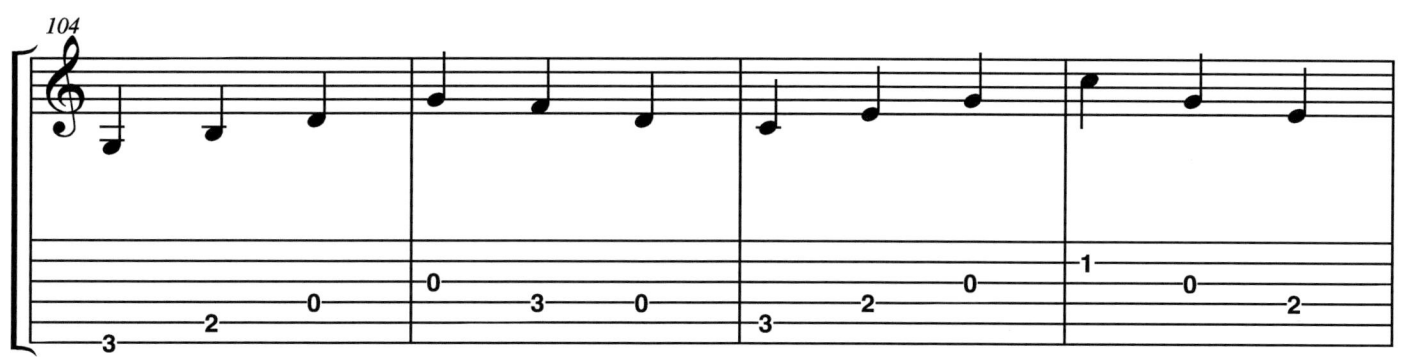
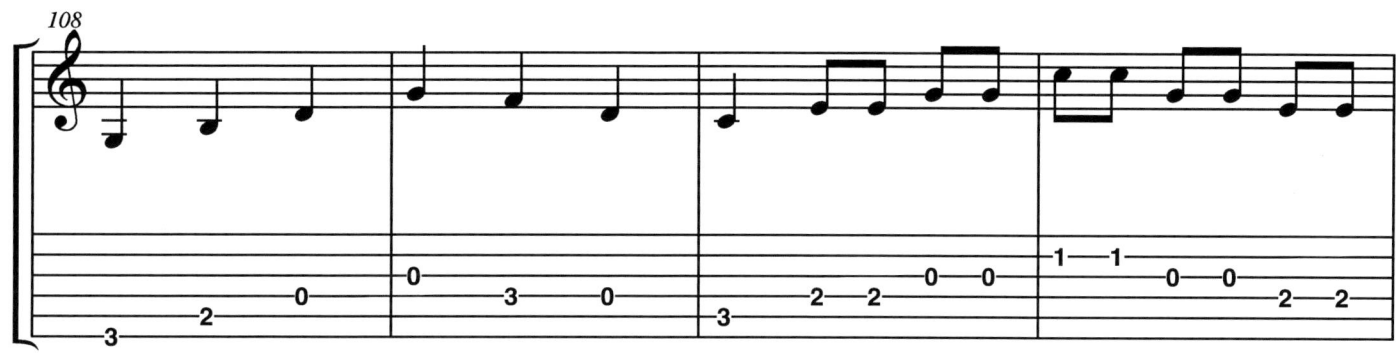
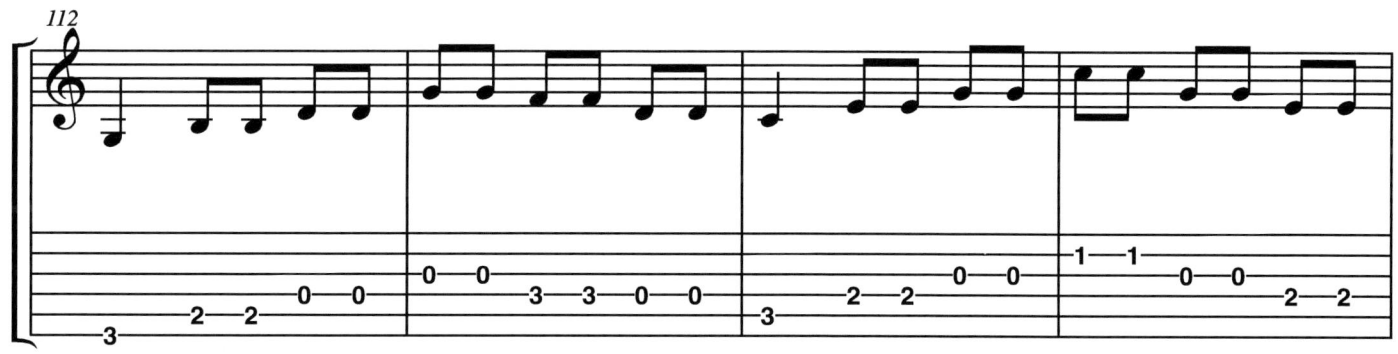
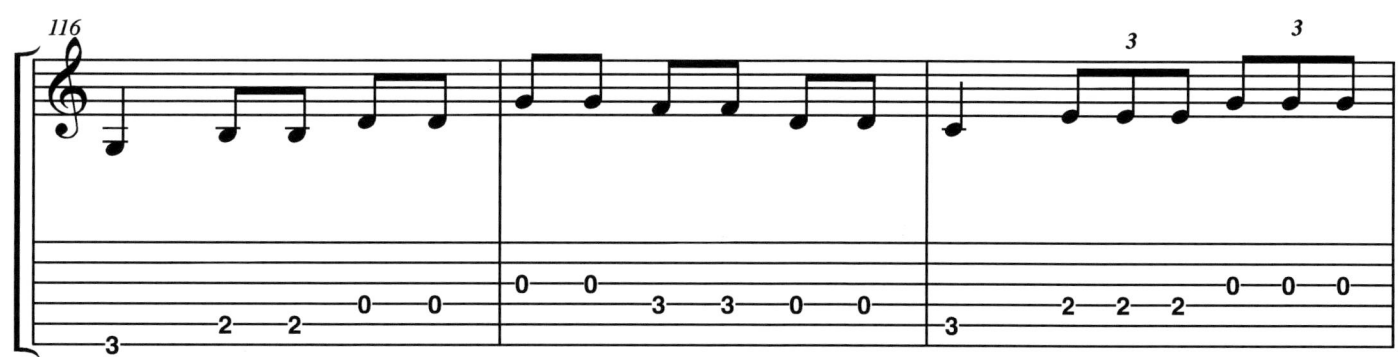

ZAPATEADO

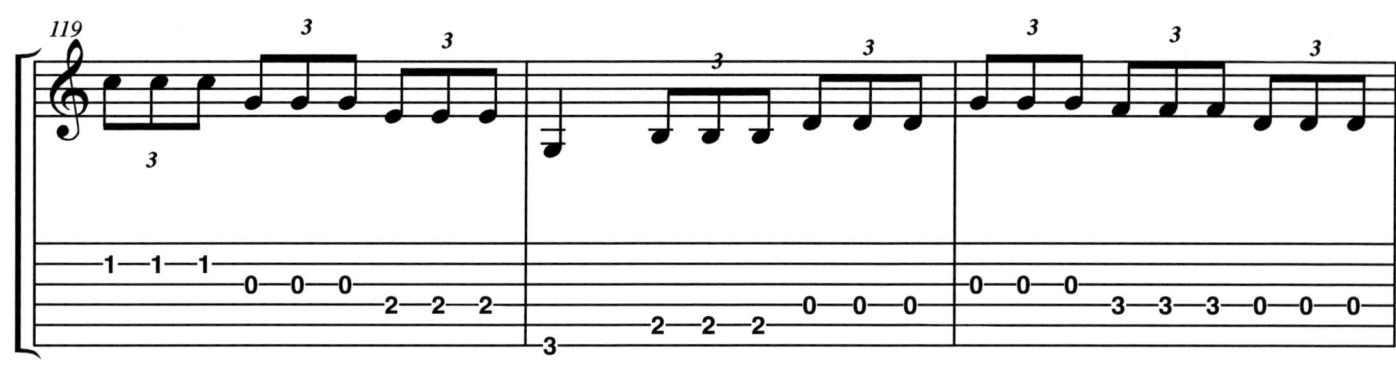
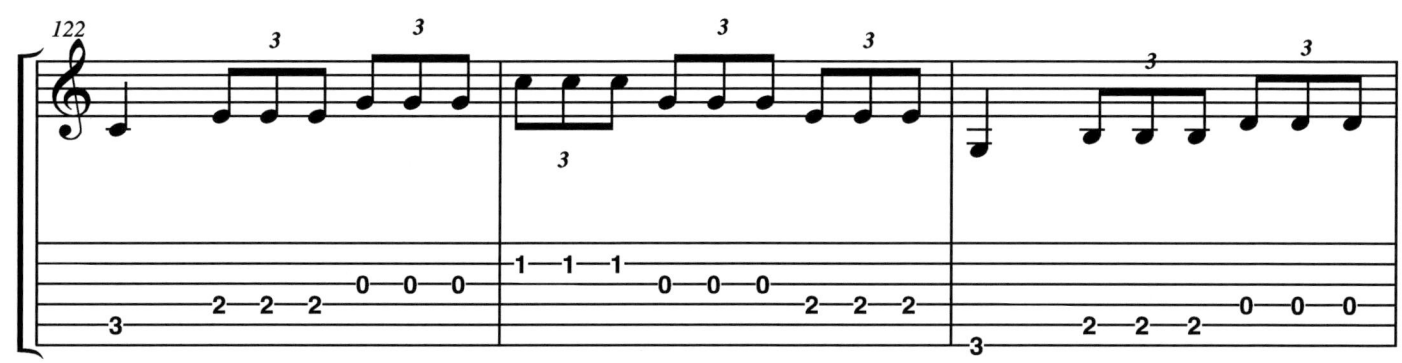
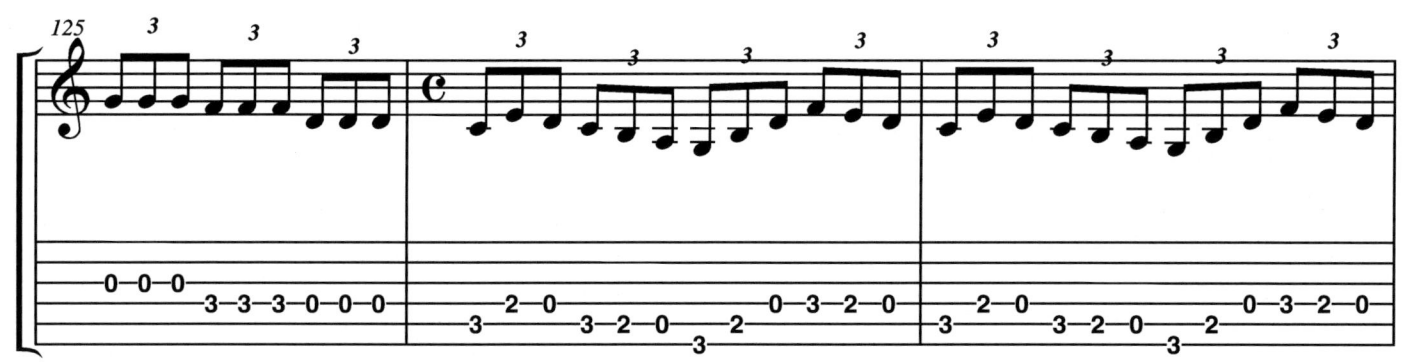
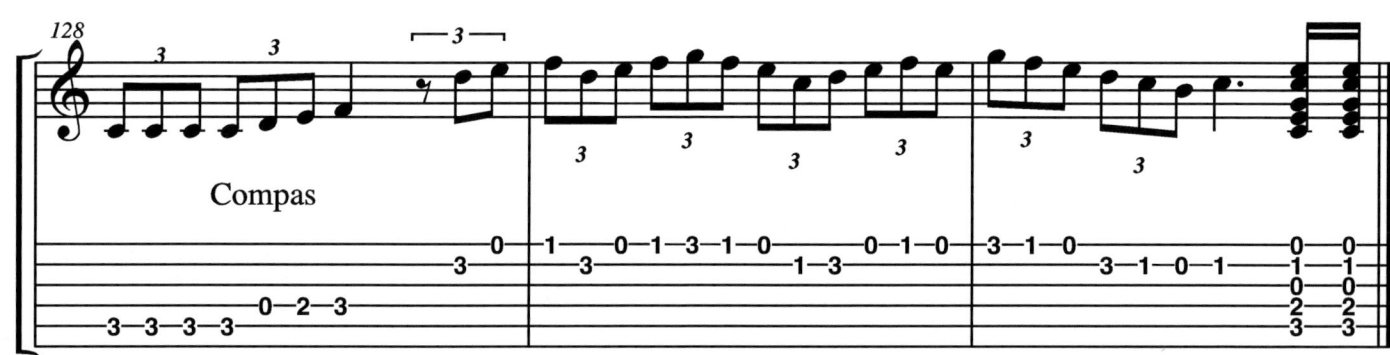

ZAPATEADO

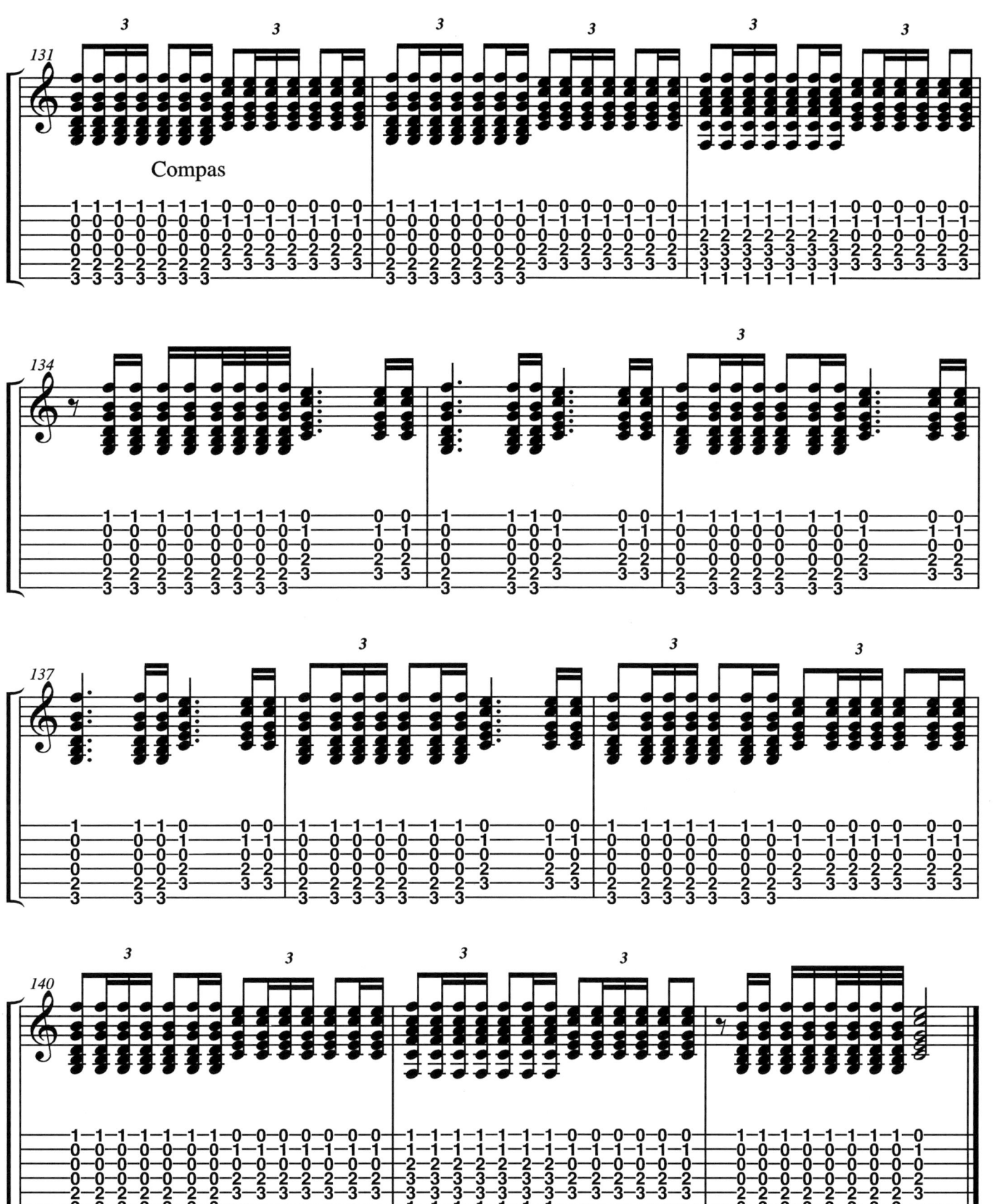